PALACES AND POWER IN THE AMERICAS

Palaces and Power in the Americas

FROM PERU TO THE NORTHWEST COAST

Edited by Jessica Joyce Christie and Patricia Joan Sarro

UNIVERSITY OF TEXAS PRESS, AUSTIN

Requests for permission to reproduce material from this work should be sent to:
    Permissions
    University of Texas Press
    P.O. Box 7819
    Austin, TX 78713-7819
    www.utexas.edu/utpress/about/bpermission.html

⊗ The paper used in this book meets the minimum requirements of ANSI/NISO
Z39.48-1992 (R1997) (Permanence of Paper).

LIBRARY OF CONGRESS CATALOGING-IN-PUBLICATION DATA

Palaces and power in the Americas : from Peru to the northwest coast / edited by
Jessica Joyce Christie and Patricia Joan Sarro.— 1st ed.
        p.   cm.
Based on a symposium held at the 2000 Conference of the Society for American
Archaeology in Philadelphia.
Includes bibliographical references and index.
ISBN 978-0-292-72599-7
    1. Indian architecture—Congresses.   2. Indians—Politics and government—
Congresses.   3. Indians—Kings and rulers—Congresses.   4. Chiefdoms—America—
Congresses.   5. Power (Social sciences)—Congresses.   6. Elite (Social sciences)—
Congresses.   I. Christie, Jessica Joyce, 1956–   II. Sarro, Patricia Joan.   III. Society
for American Archaeology. Meeting (2000 : Philadelphia, Pa.)
E59.A67P35   2006
725′.17′0970902—dc22
2005022928

We dedicate this volume to

OUR PARENTS

and to two women who have profoundly inspired us,
motivated our careers,
and driven the field of Mesoamerican Studies:

LINDA SCHELE
(1943–1998)
John D. Murchison Regents Professor of Art,
University of Texas at Austin,

and

DORIS HEYDEN
(1915–2005)
Senior Researcher in Mexican History and Religion,
Instituto Nacional de Antropología e Historia, and
Professor of Prehispanic Art,
Universidad Nacional Autónoma de México

CONTENTS

This volume grew out of a symposium Patricia Sarro and I organized for the 2000 Conference of the Society for American Archaeology (SAA) held in Philadelphia.

Both of us had been interested in Mesoamerican palaces for some time. After I completed my dissertation on Classic Maya period-ending ceremonies with Linda Schele in 1995, I began to look more closely at the architectural spaces in which such rituals took place and turned to the broader question of how we can find out what happened in specific Maya architectural settings. I quickly became fascinated with palaces—a passion I largely owe to Linda Schele's enthusiastic lectures and her latest and last co-authored book, *The Code of Kings* (1998). I read as much as I could about Maya palaces in different cities and organized my first symposium on Maya palaces and elite residences at the SAA Meetings in 1998. The volume based on this session was published in 2003. During the long publication process, I felt increasingly dissatisfied with the scope and goal of this work because it was limited to identifying palaces in archaeological, art historical, iconographic, and ethnographic contexts. I thought it must be possible to learn more about palaces, including their ritual and political contexts, and that it would be insightful to compare and contrast palaces in their cultural settings from different areas in the Americas. In my search for participants in a new symposium, I ran into my colleague and fellow student Rex Koontz, a leading expert on El Tajín. He referred me to Patricia Sarro as "the woman who knows everything about El Tajín palaces." I met Patricia at the 1998 Dumbarton Oaks conference in Washington, DC, which was about New World elite residences. We talked and decided to become a team and have remained a team as well as friends ever since.

Patricia's interest in palaces grew from her more general fascination with ritual space in Mesoamerica. In her studies at Teotihuacan and at El Tajín, she has focused on the role of elite structures in the creation of sacred space and in determining the passage of ritual procession.

We would like to thank, first of all, our participants. All were speakers at the original SAA session. We thank them for their timely submissions and for abiding by our deadlines. I had the opportunity to walk among the foundations of the Murciélagos Palace at Dos Pilas and visit the work at Farfán, and I would love to expand this collaboration by seeing firsthand all the sites that are analyzed in this volume.

Next we would like to thank University of Texas Press and Assistant Director and Editor-in-Chief Theresa May for accepting our manuscript and then working with me on an expedited schedule. We have appreciated the quick responses to our questions from all the staff working with Theresa.

We also thank our families for understanding that time dedicated to this volume is important and not a gesture of neglect toward them. I thank my son, Brian Christie Garrett, for putting off some playtime and for accompanying me to the SAA Conferences and on field trips to many palace sites. Patricia would like to thank her husband, Steven Nicoletos, for his support in spite of extended absences and long nights at the computer.

JESSICA JOYCE CHRISTIE

Correct orthography or the spelling of terms in native languages is a complex issue in the study of indigenous cultures in the Americas. Recently, many scholars, and in particular Mayanists, inspired by advances in linguistics, have attempted to use spellings that come as close as we can currently determine to the way ancient people may have pronounced and used certain names and words. But the body of linguistic knowledge we have varies from culture to culture, and it continues to change with new linguistic discoveries. Other authors prefer to use spellings that are most established in the existing literature. In Andean Studies, there is no shared consensus on what the correct spellings of native terms should be. Therefore, we, as the editors, decided to let each contributing author choose the spellings he or she is accustomed to. We did standardize "Inca" to "Inka," but otherwise the reader will find differing orthography between chapters in this volume.

PALACES AND POWER IN THE AMERICAS

Introduction

Jessica Joyce Christie

One of the most spectacular examples of a residence with political functions is without any doubt the palace of Versailles, built in France in the seventeenth century. Commissioned by Louis XIV as a royal residence as well as the seat of government, Versailles materialized Louis XIV's conception of kingship in its architectural layout and luxurious decoration. Building on the new scientific discoveries by Galileo Galilei that indeed the sun and not the earth was the center of the universe, Louis XIV claimed to be the human personification of the sun, the central celestial body. This notion entered into the architectural design of Versailles in that the royal bedroom was the central room of the large palace complex. Other official rooms were associated with the known planets and were arranged around Louis XIV's bedroom, approaching a circular formation that imitated the planets' rotation around the sun. Louis XIV's identification with the sun also entered into court ritual. All members of the royal court were required to gather in the bedroom to watch the daily *lever* (rising) and *coucher* (going to bed) rituals of their Sun King, and the whole court could only be active after Louis XIV had risen in the morning and until he had fully withdrawn for the night.

Several other examples of the identification of the ruler and his power with the palace exist outside the Western tradition. The Royal Palace of Benin, for example, expressed through its scale, exclusivity of access, and ornamentation the power of the Oba. The Forbidden City of China displayed royal power through these means and through its cosmic imaging and associations.

The examples from the Americas are different in many ways. The goal of this volume is to present cases of ancient American residential architecture for which there is evidence of a specific political context or propaganda strategy. We selected case studies from North America, Mesoamerica, and South America and from early to close-to-contact chronological periods to show that the relation between political power and architecture is a pervasive theme in the Americas. Nevertheless, the chapters presented should not be considered a complete whole that exhausts the topic. Some areas are noticeably missing, for example, the Mississippian culture in the southeastern United States or the Sican culture on the north coast of Peru. Rather, we hope that this volume will inspire palace studies in these missing areas as well as others outside the Americas and that scholars will be able to compare and contrast their data with the findings presented here. The volume would further be of interest to architectural historians seeking to understand the form of palaces in the Americas.

Most of the existing literature on the subject has been concerned with identifying and classifying residences. Indeed, as noted below, this is the subject of a number of the articles in the present volume. In the Maya area, the scholarly debate focused on the differentiation between temples and palaces in the early twentieth century (Spinden 1913; Tozzer 1911). Temples were understood as tall flat-topped pyramidal platforms supporting single-room structures, whereas palaces were longer multiroom structures standing on low platforms. As the data and number of known examples increased, researchers began to recognize hierarchies among residences (Christie 2003; Willey and Leventhal 1979; Willey et al. 1978). Palaces came to be understood as the royal residences as well as the seats of government and administration, and they were set apart from elite residences and the houses of commoners, which had only domestic functions. The distinguishing criteria were primarily size, quality of construction materials, sculptural decoration, and location with respect to proximity to the ceremonial center.

Similar issues have been discussed in southwestern and Moche archaeology. In Anasazi sites, a clear distinction can be drawn between religious structures or kivas and houses, as the latter are relatively small and simple rectangular rooms. It has not been possible to establish a hierarchy among rooms but perhaps among sites (Lekson, this volume).

The well-known Moche structures of Huaca del Sol and Huaca de la Luna have been variously interpreted as temples or palaces (Benson 1992:303–315; Moseley 1993:166–178). This discussion is particularly complicated by the fact that Huaca del Sol has never been professionally excavated. Claude Chapdelaine (this volume) presents evidence supporting some palace functions at Huaca de la Luna.

Other studies have attempted to reconstruct ancient social organization and political power structures partly from architectural data. The numerous settlement surveys conducted in Mexico and Central America in the second half of the twentieth century fall into this category (Blanton 1978; Kowalewski et al. 1989; Millon 1973; Puleston 1983; Willey and Leventhal 1979; Willey et al. 1978). This kind of research focuses on the density or scarcity of populations and aims to draw conclusions about social organization from these patterns. What emerged from the settlement-pattern data was the realization that most ancient American societies were not simply divided into the rulers and ruled but were a lot more complex. Arlen and Diane Chase discuss these complexities in their edited volume *Mesoamerican Elites* (1992). They and various contributors analyze what the archaeological evidence reveals about social and political organization in various Mesoamerican societies. Some authors address the question of whether the Maya were organized according to a segmentary or a unitary structure.

The present volume, *Palaces and Power in the Americas: From Peru to the Northwest Coast*, focuses on specific examples of architecture from various parts of the Americas and how they express aspects of political power. In this manner, it goes beyond two other recent volumes that cover only the Maya: *Maya Palaces and Elite Residences: An Interdisciplinary Approach* (2003), edited by Jessica Christie, is primarily concerned with identifying palaces and elite residences; *Royal Courts of the Ancient Maya* (2001), edited by Takeshi Inomata and Stephen Houston, attempts to reconstruct the structure of and life at royal courts in Maya cities, including some comparisons with other types of ancient courts in the Americas. The present volume is also different from the Dumbarton Oaks volume entitled *Palaces of the Ancient New World* (2004) and edited by Susan Evans and Joanne Pillsbury. Our volume concentrates more specifically on the context and issues of political power and, unlike any of the others mentioned, includes case studies from North America. Although the list of ancient American cultures represented does not in any way pretend to be complete, the goal is that the reader will develop an understanding of how ancient American societies at different times and with different levels of social organization used residential architecture for political purposes. In this light, the value of the volume is twofold: first, it publishes information and often very recent data (Isbell, Demarest) about specific cultures, and second, it compares the different architectural approaches societies take, thereby potentially contributing to architectural theory and history.

Given the variety of cultures represented in this volume, their different time periods, and the different aspects emphasized by the authors within the larger theme of political power, we have grouped the articles into four parts according to the authors' approaches.

Part 1. Identification of Palaces

The first section comprises studies that identify palaces in cultures in which palaces have not been identified before. All authors understand a palace as the residence of the highest-ranking member or institution of a polity and as the seat of governmental activities. Hence palaces can be considered an essential trait of complex stratified societies. In the archaeological data of a palace, one would expect to find evidence of domestic life, such as food production and eating, as well as official rooms, perhaps council rooms, audience halls, and state storage rooms for surplus products. Furthermore, palaces often include open spaces for the public display of the ruler. Elite residences, on the other hand, reveal evidence solely of domestic activities. They distinguish themselves from the simpler houses of commoners by means of size, construction materials, quality of construction, and often decoration, but they were usually not locations where political actions were taken (see Barber and Joyce, this volume, for a thorough discussion of the differences between a palace and an elite residence). The examples in which an argument can be made for a political context have to be specially noted, and these constitute the focus of this volume. It follows that palaces are more than just residences of the highest-ranking nobles. What distinguishes palaces from elite residences is the symbolic function of palaces as political statements within their respective societies. Palace architecture, including the layout, position, and decoration of palaces as well as their public (or sometimes exclusive) nature, reflects the structure of the political system in which the palaces exist. Palaces not only respond to the necessities of a society and its highest-ranking institutions to represent status and hierarchy, but they can actually shape the understanding of institutions and take an active role in their respective societies.

Claude Chapdelaine takes up the issue of identifying palaces and distinguishing them from elite residences for the Huacas of Moche Site. Many conjectures have been made and interpretations given in the literature with regard to the nature and function of Huaca del Sol and Huaca de la Luna (see Benson 1992; Moseley 1993). Chapdelaine devises a list of seven criteria that might identify a palace and discusses how they apply to Huaca de la Luna. His discussion includes new data obtained by a long-term Peruvian project codirected by Santiago Uceda and Ricardo Morales of the Universidad de Trujillo, but it does not provide a black-and-white answer. He concludes that Huaca de la Luna was a multifunctional building that included aspects of a palace and of a temple. He stresses the importance of the large northern plaza overlooked by many scholars prior to the Peruvian excavation of 1999. This plaza provides space for a large segment of the population to gather and to participate in religious and/or government rituals and thus supports the palace function of Huaca de la Luna. On the other hand, Chapdelaine admits that "no section has yet been identified as a residential section" and suggests that Complex 8, located immediately to the southwest of Huaca de la Luna, could possibly have been the residence of high priests or even of the ruler.

Of particular importance is Chapdelaine's presentation of new data from the urban sector between Huaca de la Luna and Huaca del Sol. He correlates architectural changes in Compound 9 with the integration of nuclear family households into a single large household unit. This emerging leader of Compound 9 enjoyed the power to modify the urban layout by placing a new street between his household and those of his neighbors, which may demonstrate his high position within the Moche social hierarchy. Compound 5 is of interest because during periods of its occupation it did not have a kitchen. Absence of food-production and cooking facilities may indicate that this compound was, at least during certain times, not an elite residence but a public building. Thus Chapdelaine's data establish evidence that the power of the ruler(s) of Huaca de la Luna and Huaca del Sol was to some degree decentralized.

William Isbell also uses a set of formal characteristics to identify Andean and, in his study, Wari palaces. Since very few data about Wari architecture are so far available, Isbell devises a list of diagnostic architectural features of Inka palaces and of those at the religious center of Pachacamac. Since the Inka succeeded the Wari chronologically, a fair amount of data about Inka architecture exists from Spanish descriptions and archaeological excavations. Isbell tests the presence or absence of such features on the Vegachayoq Moqo Palace at Huari and on the recently excavated Conchopata Palace. His analysis shows that especially the early architectural forms at Vegachayoq Moqo resemble Inka and Pachacamac palaces and that the possible palace at Conchopata shares more of the Inka characteristics.

Isbell then expands his discussion of Wari palaces to the rural hinterland. He examines several small settlements based on architectural form and distinguishes between cumulative residential buildings, which are complexes of small rooms constructed one after another, and planned orthogonal architecture, which consists of a rigidly rectangular compound with a large patio in one sector and orderly room complexes in another. His argument is that the presence of planned orthogonal architecture indicates the concentration of some form of political power, and he suggests that some of these settlements, such as Jargampata and Azángaro, were probably rural estates of a Wari king or nobleman. In addition, Isbell comments on the role of the provincial sites of Pikillacta and Viracochapampa, which exhibit a very rigid version of planned orthogonal architecture that he names the "orthogonal cellular horizon." Here the buildings are characterized by orthogonal enclosures, subdivided into smaller rectangular or square compounds that follow a limited number of standard patterns and create a cellular structure of repeating modular units. Isbell concludes that Pikillacta and Viracochapampa were important Wari administrative centers and that they housed the palaces of powerful governors. On the other hand, Pikillacta and Viracochapampa, as well as Conchopata, seem to lack rural estates, which Isbell understands as significant political power bases. This reasoning leads to the conclusion that Huari was indeed some kind of capital city, because it was the only large settlement ringed by hinterland estates, forming what Isbell calls a "regal landscape."

Stephen Lekson takes a rather different approach. He critically examines archaeological attitudes toward palaces in the context of Southwest archaeology and with specific reference to Chaco Canyon. His focus is not so much on the material evidence itself but on the politics of interpretation. The same archaeological evidence may be used for interpreting an ancient society as having a simple unified social organization or a complex stratified one. Southwestern and North American archaeologists have historically chosen the former interpretation and understand Native North American cultures as heterarchies of gentle people working in collectives mostly for ritual purposes. Lekson, on the other hand, prefers the latter and presents the argument that the Great Houses in Chaco Canyon were palaces that included wings of storage rooms, ritual architecture, and public assembly areas. He further argues that Chaco was the ceremonial, political, and economic center in the Southwest from about A.D. 900 to A.D. 1125 and was succeeded by two subsequent capitals—Aztec Ruins and Paquimé—each of which legitimized itself by conscious reference back to Chaco. Future research is needed to confirm Lekson's reasoning, but his ideas certainly "blow a fresh and new wind" into southwestern archaeology and provide "rich food for thought."

Part 2. Palaces as Active Stage Sets of Political Ideology

The second part of the volume includes articles that discuss palaces as "stage sets" for various types of activities that consolidate and express power. In this group fall studies that associate certain pre-Columbian societies with the so-called theater state. A "theater state" was first defined in the traditional society of Bali, Southeast Asia, by Clifford Geertz (1980). In a theater state, cosmic rituals of kingship are performed in such a manner that they do not just mirror reality but actually become it and thus open the potential to construct kingship in the way desired by those who hold it. Stanley Tambiah (1985) criticized Geertz's definition for leaving a disjunction between ideology and practice and proposed an expanded model to bring these two poles closer together. Tambiah (1985:252–259) has coined the label "galactic polity" to conceptualize an arrangement of a center and its surrounding satellites, which may be employed in spatial, social, and political contexts. He emphasizes (1985:324–326) that the center had to continually reaffirm its ideology of control in response to volatile factional struggles mounted by the periphery against the center and that galactic polities were by definition unstable. It follows that in theater states and galactic polities, political power is based on ideology, and architecture is thus designed and cities are laid out to make this ideology visible and public. Such a materialization of political ideology may include, but is not limited to, large open plazas for public assembly, cosmological orientation of buildings, and local cosmograms. In these cases, architecture takes an active role in the reaffirmation of rulership.

Arthur Demarest has elsewhere (1992, 2003) described the Classic Maya as a theater state. In this volume, he distances himself somewhat from the theater-state model and presents a compelling comparison of how architecture was used for differing political purposes by the ancient Maya. The Murciélagos Palace at Dos Pilas exemplifies how architecture would have been designed in a theater state. First, this palace was placed atop a cave system that passes beneath the eastern El Duende complex of Murciélagos and the West Plaza group of Dos Pilas, with the cave emerging in springs at each architectural complex. Thus the location of surface architecture was made sacred through the supernaturally charged underground caves. Second, the Murciélagos Palace was crossed by the east-west processional axis of Dos Pilas between El Duende and the West Plaza group. And third, a shrine in the northern residential compound of the palace did not contain the expected human burial, but instead it entombed the east-west cave system. Thus the symbolic connection between the ruler and his family and the Maya cosmogram was made very explicit: they resided and took political actions upon the sacred mountain above caves and their springs, where the axis mundi was localized by the family shrine. The east-west direction of the cave system was repeated in the public path of processions as well as in the movements of the Sun and Venus, which would have placed the royal family in the Murciélagos Palace quite literally in the center of the world.

One of the smaller elite compounds has been identified as the residence of the "Lady of Cancuén," a principal wife of Dos Pilas Ruler 3, and its primary political function was to proclaim Dos Pilas's alliance with Cancuén. It did so by displaying an architectural style derived from Cancuén and through its carved monuments, one of which shows a scene of bloodletting conducted by a young boy and observed by the Lady of Cancuén and Ruler 3.

By contrast, the Aguateca Palace, which was another seat of the Dos Pilas dynasty, had restricted access and was well defensible. Court artisans who manufactured elite goods also lived in this palace, and it may have been a locale for feasting.

The Cancuén Palace, which has been the focus of Vanderbilt University projects in the western Petén since 1998, presents yet another case. Cancuén is located on the upper Pasión River at a natural bay portage from where the Cancuén dynasty seems to have controlled the river trade between the lowlands and the highlands. The site of Cancuén lacks temples or any large plazas for the performance of public rites, which would have been essential to a theater state. The palace itself consists of a series of restricted courtyards that would have offered an ideal setting for feasting and impressing visiting elites. Workshops of lithic artifacts have been identified nearby. Thus the Cancuén Palace seems to have had primarily economic and political functions.

The conclusion of Demarest's comparison is a warning against quick labeling and an observation that the power of Classic Maya kings was not based on one single element, such as agricultural management, control of long-distance trade, or theater-state performance. Instead, elites in different regions and in different circumstances relied to varying degrees on alternate sources of power, which are reflected in the location and layout of palace architecture.

Colin Grier's work on Coast Salish households is included in this part of the volume even though Northwest Coast cultures have never been described as theater states. As indicated in the discussion of Lekson's article above, Northwest Coast cultures are widely understood as non-state-level societies.

Grier discusses the class system of household chief, nobility, commoners, and slaves and how individuals of these classes interacted and related within the social unit of the household itself. He then analyzes the wooden plank-house as the material expression of such power relations. His particular example comes from the precontact Coast Salish Dionisio Point village site located on one of the Gulf Islands of southern British Columbia, Canada. Although no standing architecture remains, the types and distribution of artifacts in House 2 provide insights into the power relations of its residents. In general, the typical Coast Salish dwelling was the shed-roof house consisting of a series of compartments, each of which provided a domestic family space with a small hearth. This type of building structure suggests egalitarian relations between families and provides little opportunity for social differentiation. However, in Dionisio Point House 2, status-indicating artifacts, such as carved stone bowls, labrets, and beads, were all found associated with the center of the house. Furthermore, the central hearth exhibited burning patterns pointing to ceremonial rather than cooking functions. Grier concludes that the economic, social, and ritual-symbolic sources of power were concentrated in the center of House 2 and were probably in the hands of the elite family residing in the nearest compartment. In this manner, the center of the house acted as a "stage set" within the context of the household and certainly on a very small scale when contrasted with other cultures, such as the Maya. The types of performances acted out in the center of House 2 were likely dances owned by the chief and elites as well as meetings and the reception of elite visitors from other households. Grier's study is the only example in the volume in which power relations are reconstructed within one residence.

In her study of Tajín Chico, the elite residential zone of El Tajín, Patricia Sarro argues that this elevated grouping of buildings, plazas, and ritual structures functioned as a palace, much like those of the lowland Maya. Within it were buildings in which the various rituals of rulership were carried out. In some, benches and a possible throne imply places of privileged gathering of noble counsels. Others appear to have been residences, but even these have open porticoes that overlook the areas with multiple courtyards and plazas. Sarro focuses on Building A, whose unique design constitutes a cosmogram in which the earthly zone takes the form of miniature ballcourts. Whatever this building's other functions—and these may include residence—Sarro believes that it served as the stage for rituals that connected the ruling elite with the power of the game.

Part 3. Correspondences between Material Aspects of Elite Residences and Social Status

The third part of the volume presents cases in which differences in elite residential architecture imply differences in the form of rulership or social status. The material differences may lie in the form of residences or in their size, location, or associated artifacts.

Michael Blake, Richard G. Lesure, Warren D. Hill, Luis Barba, and John E. Clark take the reader to the Early Formative village site of Paso de la Amada in Chiapas, Mexico. Paso de la Amada was founded around 1500 B.C., grew to its largest size in the Locona phase (1400–1250 B.C.), and began to lose population after 1000 B.C. Blake et al. present archaeological data from Mounds 6 and 12, which were obtained during major excavations carried out at the site between 1985 and 1995. Their data focus specifically on mound platform volumes; building structures, shapes, alignments, and superpositioning; features such as floors, hearths, pits, and burials; distribution of micro-artifacts on the floors, including obsidian, ceramics, charcoal, and bone; and chemical traces on structure floors, such as pH levels, phosphates, fatty acids, and albumen.

A comparison of these elements for both Mounds 6 and 12 shows that the differences were primarily architectural. For example, in Mound 6, before a new building was constructed, a layer of earthen fill was laid down to cover and ultimately protect the old floor and features. This practice resulted in the gradual raising and extending of the platform on which the buildings stood over a period of 200 to 250 years. In Mound 12, on the other hand, there was no platform construction until about 1100 B.C. As a consequence, the earlier floors were not protected by fill and are poorly preserved. But the analysis of the features, distribution of micro-artifacts, and chemical patterns shows no significant differences or changes in the floor sequence of Mound 6 or between Mound 6 and Mound 12. This would indicate that similar activities that left micro-artifactual or chemical traces were carried out over time and in both mounds.

Blake et al. use the results of their comparison to support the notion that the people of Paso de la Amada were organized in a transegalitarian society. In egalitarian societies, corporate groups may construct large public buildings, but transegalitarian societies exhibit not only public facilities but also the residences of emerging leaders, which distinguish them from the commoners. Blake interprets the platform construction in Mound 6 as just this kind of residential elaboration that sets the inhabitants of Mound 6 apart from the commoners in Mound 12. The observation that the activities carried out in both mounds were largely similar shows that this emerging elite continued to perform domestic tasks.

Sarah Barber and Arthur Joyce present a detailed overview of elite residential architecture in the Valley of Oaxaca from the Early Formative (1800–850 B.C.) to the Postclassic (A.D. 1200–1522) period. They evaluate what the architectural data reveal about forms of government and changes over time. The earliest differentiation in houses and evidence for economic inequality have been noted in the San José (1150–850 B.C.) and Guadalupe (850–700 B.C.) phases. At this time, some residences at San José Mogote, Tomaltepec, and Fábrica San José exhibited walls with whitewash, larger posts, drains, stone foundations, more participation in craft activities, and greater access to exotic items. In the Rosario phase (700–500 B.C.), some household units at Tomaltepec and San José Mogote were built in close physical proximity to public buildings or temples. Barber and Joyce interpret these and other data as efforts by an elite to define their identity as fundamentally separate from that of commoners.

Monte Albán was founded as a new settlement about 500 B.C. and grew rapidly in the Late Formative (Monte Albán I, 500–100 B.C.) and Terminal Formative (Monte Albán II, 100 B.C.–A.D. 200). Iconographic references indicate that the layout of Monte Albán reflected the cosmos, and high-status residences were part of this cosmogram. The latter were concentrated around the northern end of the Main Plaza, implying a connection between nobles, the celestial realm, and noble ancestors whose tombs often contained effigy vessels depicting the Zapotec lightning or sky deity. More high-status residences were found at other sites in the Valley of Oaxaca as well as in some of Monte Albán's barrios beyond the Main Plaza. This increase in numbers of elite residences is seen as the spread of a separate noble identity and as the development of a more decentralized administrative organization.

During Monte Albán IIIa (A.D. 200–500), elite residences continued to be built close to the North Platform. Three residential "types" may be distinguished, mostly by size, since all consist of enclosed patio groups. Elite status was primarily expressed through the ornamentation of tombs with elaborate polychrome murals. From a political point of view, tombs can only be viewed by small audiences and never provide a public forum for the expression of power.

The spatial layout and the architectural elaboration of elite residences in Periods IIIb–IV (A.D. 500–1200) follow the Period IIIa examples, at least in Monte Albán itself, which loses its position as the major center in the Valley of Oaxaca by about A.D. 800. Other sites on the valley floor develop new ways of displaying power. For example, in Lambityeco Structure 195, stucco panels depict named individuals holding human femurs on the walls of a semipublic patio.

By Monte Albán V, or the Late Postclassic (A.D. 1200–1521), the distinction between private and public spaces had become blurred, and monumental architecture clearly combined residential and public functions, as, for example, in the Palace of the Six Patios at Yagul or the Group of Columns at Mitla.

Barber and Joyce's chronological discussion emphasizes that although elites began to separate themselves from commoners as early as 1150 B.C., Zapotec elite residences did not organize space in a way that allowed for the public expression of individual power until after the collapse of Monte Albán in about A.D. 800, as in Lambityeco Structure 195. Only the Late Postclassic examples from Yagul and Mitla were palaces in the sense that they not only combined but fully merged open and public spaces with residential spaces. It follows that in the Valley of Oaxaca, architecture expressed political power in ways that sharply contrast with the theater-state examples of the Maya or El Tajín. Thus Barber and Joyce offer an important alternative perspective.

William T. Sanders and Susan Toby Evans trace the development of Teotihuacan rulership through different stages of palace architecture. They postulate that the earliest palace was possibly the Xalla compound, located between the Pyramids of the Sun and Moon in the northeastern sector of the city. In the third century A.D., it was replaced by the Ciudadela as the political administrative center. Sanders and Evans suggest that the Ciudadela functioned as the possible residence and seat of government of one or two powerful rulers whose lineages were associated with the Feathered Serpent and with the Fire Serpent, as depicted on the Temple-Pyramid of the Feathered Serpent. Around 300 A.D., a reaction against the political dynasts set in, and this Temple-Pyramid was concealed by the Adosado. At approximately the same time, many of the city's apartment compounds were constructed, including the Street of the Dead Complex that straddles the Street of the Dead between the Pyramid of the Sun and the Ciudadela. According to Sanders and Evans, the Street of the Dead Complex was the palace of a new type of government that consisted of a hierarchy of relatively depersonalized bureaucrats whose identity as individual power holders was not emphasized in the visual arts.

Sanders and Evans continue to discuss the power and influence Teotihuacan had exerted abroad, and they relate the changes in government to the contemporary developments at Tikal. They show that the much-debated Early Classic Teotihuacan presence at Tikal occurred in the late fourth century, based on hieroglyphic as well as archaeological evidence that corresponds to the proposed change in Teotihuacan government from the powerful dynast(s) to less individualized bureaucrats. Sanders and Evans pose the question of whether a ruling Teotihuacan dynasty associated with the cult of the Feathered Serpent traveled to the Maya region, possibly into exile, which led to the outlined changes at home. They further ask whether Teotihuacan's political advance into the Maya area may have been an Early Classic actualization of the Early Postclassic story of Quetzalcoatl. Quetzalcoatl, or the Feathered Serpent, was said to have been exiled from Tula and subsequently became an influential figure among the Maya in Yucatán. These ideas will contribute to the current scholarly debate about the relationship between Central Mexico and the Maya.

In a separate article, Susan Toby Evans brings to life the Aztec palace and then goes on to compare its form to what is known about Teotihuacan's and Tula's palaces and to deliberate what the observed similarities and differences might suggest about state administration. The Aztec palace, called a *tecpan* in the Nahuatl language, is well known from several Spanish eyewitness accounts. They all agree that the *tecpan* had three identifying elements: (1) a dais room reserved for the ruler and located on the short side of (2) a courtyard in which probably the noble class gathered. This courtyard, in turn, faced (3) a main plaza in which the common people assembled. The archaeological evidence of *tecpans* is scarce because very few examples have been fully excavated, but Evans illustrates a city-state *tecpan* and a village *tecpan* that seem to share the layout described in the ethnohistorical sources.

She then poses the question of whether the *tecpan* had antecedents in earlier cultures of Central Mexico, such as Teotihuacan and Tula. As Evans and William T. Sanders outline in their chapter on Teotihuacan (this volume), there may have been a chronological sequence of three palaces, all located adjacent to the Street of the Dead: the earliest was possibly the Xalla compound in the northeastern sector; the second was the Ciudadela; and finally, Teotihuacan's rulers may have occupied the Street of the Dead Compound in the center of the city. A comparison of the plans of these Teotihuacan palaces with that of the Aztec *tecpan* shows that they do not clearly contain the package of dais/entry courtyard/plaza. Therefore, Evans concludes, Teotihuacan's government system must have been unlike that of the Aztec.

At the site of Tula, many large buildings have been called palaces since the nineteenth century. Evans observes that the Palacio Tolteca was most similar to the Aztec *tecpan* because it includes the characteristic package: it is next to the main plaza, it has a huge main courtyard, and the entryway faces a raised dais room. She argues that the Aztec copied and appropriated elements of Toltec elite architecture as well as economic and spiritual power and that the function of the *tecpan* and its Toltec predecessor was largely secular and administrative.

Part 4. Comparison of Palaces across Cultures

The fourth part of the volume consists of two articles that compare the architectural strategies of two cultures and how their leaders made political statements in the design of buildings. In this approach, it is significant whether the social organization of the cultures under consideration is similar—as it is in Carol Mackey's study, which compares two centralized militaristic states, the Chimú and the Inka—or different—as in Jessica Christie's report, which mostly contrasts the Inka with the Maya, who, unlike the Chimú and the Inka, were organized in independent city-states and were less expansionistic.

Carol Mackey's essay is a comparison of the elite architecture at Farfán, a provincial center on the north coast of Peru, during the occupation of two empires—the Chimú and the Inka. As the Chimú expanded their territory from their capital, Chan Chan, to the north, they confronted polities affiliated with the Lambayeque culture. The political and ceremonial center in the Jequetepeque Valley was Pacatnamu. The Chimú subdued Pacatnamu and built Farfán as an intrusive center in the middle of this valley that functioned as the northern frontier of their empire from about A.D. 1200 to A.D. 1350. Intrusive centers typically use an imperial architectural style, which Mackey demonstrates in her analysis of Farfán Compounds II and VI. Both compounds contain U-shaped *audiencias*, storage rooms, enclosed plazas, and a burial platform, all of which are "loan" elements from Chan Chan. Mackey emphasizes that throughout the history of Farfán, an imperial style was used in architecture as well as in ceramics. These stylistic findings may be an indicator that it was not important for the Chimú to incorporate indigenous lords into the highest echelons of their political system. Instead, the integration of local lords seems to have occurred at lower-ranked sites, many of which have been identified throughout the valley. Given Farfán's size and importance as the seat of the provincial government and the residence of the regional governor, it is striking that it appears to have been staffed by only a small number of high-ranking elites at any given time.

The Inka conquered the Chimú Empire in approximately the 1470s and established their presence as well at Farfán. However, the Inka chose to coopt Farfán as their settlement. Mackey describes how they changed and altered Compound VI to their interests and liking; for example, they allocated more space for storage, increased security by further restricting access to stored goods, and added a large area of well-planned *tapia* structures outside and to the west of Compound VI. Altogether, Compound VI and the *tapia* units housed a larger number of Inka officials than they had of the previous Chimú elite. Mackey stresses that it was not always Inka policy to co-opt existing settlements as their own regional centers, noting that they built intrusive centers on the southern coast. On the north coast, however, the Inka co-opted centers, probably because Chimú sites such as Farfán, Manchan, and Tucume already existed, and it became a matter of convenience to reuse them.

Mackey's comparison clearly illustrates that though the Chimú and Inka were both hierarchically organized, expansionistic states, their methods of establishing control in conquered areas differed, as did some of their political priorities. One could also conclude that there was more than one successful way of administering political control in the Jequetepeque Valley from a faraway capital.

Jessica Christie discusses ways political strategies of the Maya and Inka were expressed in residential architecture. The formal comparison shows that the general layout of houses around courtyards was similar, but that the similarities ended there. Each Inka emperor had to construct his own palace, whereas Maya rulers continued to occupy the palace complexes of their predecessors. From this perspective, the Inka palace may be understood as a monument to a particular ruler, whereas Maya palaces functioned as lineage compounds.

Christie continues to address the ranking of residential architecture in both societies. In Maya studies, various models have been developed that attempt to classify and group houses and sites in a hierarchical order with regard to the social status of their inhabitants (for example, Gordon Willey's model for Barton Ramie and Copán). Other attempts have been made to reconstruct ancient Maya social organization based on the number of high-status residences and their location and distribution. The debate targets the issue of whether the Maya had a segmentary or a unitary state.

The database of Inka residences remains small when compared to that of the Maya. Yet the urban design of many Inka sites, house compounds, masonry, and rock art displays a style that favors geometric elements. Christie discusses numerous examples and concludes that this geometric style often functioned like a signature of the Inka state. Although its origins predate the Inka, they elaborated it into an aesthetic system derived from geometry, which seems to have been employed as a symbol of control and political power over the landscape and subjected peoples.

Christie applies a model developed by Olivier de Montmollin that analyzes the degrees of a segmentary or a unitary organization within a given society but does not endeavor to classify an entire culture in terms of absolute typologies. The comparison of the architectural data suggests that Maya political organization had more elements of a segmentary structure, whereas the Inka system was more unitary.

Thus our volume presents a great variety and complexity of palace structures and cultural scenarios, as well as differing levels of our knowledge and understanding of these cultures. I would conclude that three important variables should be analyzed when studying palaces and power in the Americas: (1) form, (2) a thorough comparison with elite residences, and (3) the culture- and case-specific sources of power.

Form

Form is certainly the starting point for any investigation of palaces. Such a formal analysis involves the tracing of existing walls, determining their relationship to open spaces, and a reconstruction of original walls and possible earlier substructures. In my previous volume (Christie 2003:316–322), I defined four different Maya palace types. In this volume, Chapdelaine (Chapter 1) offers a list of formal elements that might characterize a Moche palace, and Isbell (Chapter 2) presents related but not identical lists of features that would be present in Inka and Pachacamac palaces. He further examines Wari sites with planned orthogonal architecture that consists of rigidly rectangular compounds often resulting in a cellular structure of repeating modular units. Isbell interprets this form of architecture as an indicator of political power at, for example, Pikillacta. A version of planned orthogonal architecture is present at selected Inka sites, such as at Ollantaytambo or Raqchi. However, I think the Inka examples exhibit less formal rigidity and that other factors influenced the design of elite architecture as well. Indeed the Inka generally sought a harmony with nature when they laid out their settlements and designed their buildings. Therefore, planned orthogonal examples are all the more significant. The arguments by Sanders and Evans (Chapter 9) about changes in the government structure of Teotihuacan and Evans's discussion of the Aztec *tecpan* (Chapter 10) are heavily based on form. Evans investigates whether the basic structure of the *tecpan*—plaza, courtyard, dais room—occurs in the architecture of earlier cultures in Central Mexico (Tula and Teotihuacan), and based on this comparison, she discusses whether their government systems were similar to that of the Aztec.

All the palaces discussed in this volume seem to have one formal element in common: at least one open plaza space—with one exception. The foregrounded space at Dionisio Point lies within the shed-roof house; it is a central area where status items were found concentrated and where larger, perhaps ceremonial fires were lit (Grier, Chapter 5). The confinement of activities to the interior of communal houses is due to the climatic conditions on the Northwest Coast. Winter was the traditional ceremonial season because temperatures were low and rainfall was high. Thus climate should be considered another palace variable!

The form of the Inka palace remains somewhat elusive to researchers. Some of the chroniclers have described and even drawn examples of their vision of what these palaces may have looked like, and Isbell (Chapter 2) offers a list of features that help define an Inka palace. The problem is that very few cases are fully known archaeologically. A general consensus is that the Inka palace was a large, expanded, and extravagant version of a *kancha*—which is a courtyard surrounded by four single-room structures and often enclosed by walls—and that elites and commoners lived in more modest versions of the *kancha*.

Comparisons between Palaces and Elite Residences

Any palace has to be understood in relation to the form and numbers of elite residences. Chapdelaine (Chapter 1) distinguishes between Huaca de la Luna, which clearly exhibits aspects of a palace, and the elite residential compounds located between Huaca de la Luna and Huaca del Sol. In Maya architecture, the formal differences between palaces and elite residences are minor, and one has to focus on size, ornamentation, and location—the latter because palaces typically sit in the ceremonial core of Maya cities (for an in-depth discussion, see Christie 2003). In Chaco Canyon, the roads connecting the Great Houses to the smaller outliers are fundamental to conceptualizing the power of the former. Yet at the same time, it would be too speculative to call the outliers "elite residences," since we know little about social stratification in Anasazi societies (Lekson, Chapter 3; Lekson 1999). Barber and Joyce (Chapter 8) carefully trace the development of elite residences in the Valley of Oaxaca from the Early Formative to the Late Postclassic period. They clearly separate high-status houses from the dwellings of commoners, but they are unable to pinpoint palaces that would incorporate larger open public spaces until the Postclassic. In their view, some of the first and few examples of fully developed Zapotec palaces are the Postclassic Palace of the Six Patios at Yagul and the Group of Columns at Mitla because they clearly combine residential functions and public spaces. Thus the Zapotec scenario paints a picture of power relations quite unlike that of the Maya, who elevated one-man rulership in each city. The Maya system of kingship is mirrored in the identification of one dominant palace in most cities.

Teotihuacan had many higher and lower elite residences, represented by the large number of apartment compounds,[1] but palaces are harder to identify. Sanders and Evans (Chapter 9) propose that the Xalla compound, the Ciudadela, and the Street of the Dead Complex were successive palaces. One important aspect that sets these palaces apart from the elite residences is location: they line or straddle the Street of the Dead, whereas most apartment compounds are located farther away from the city's axis. Based on the form and layout of the palace complexes, Sanders and Evans argue for changes in the government structure over time.

Chimú palaces can be securely identified by the *ciudadelas* at Chan Chan. Mackey (Chapter 11) reports on two compounds that are formally very similar to the Chan Chan examples at Farfán, an intrusive center the Chimú established in the Jequetepeque Valley at the northern border of their empire. At Chan Chan, elite residences accumulated outside the *ciudadela* walls. Mackey investigates how the Inka reused Compound VI and shows that they added an immense area of *tapia* (battered mud wall) structures to the west of this compound. These *tapia* architectural units constituted elite residences, which in this case are neatly separated — spatially and formally — from the palace.

Palaces should be compared to elite residences not only with regard to form but also with regard to numbers. The ratio between the numbers of palaces and elite residences is an indicator of social organization. Thus, in most Maya cities, the number of elite residences increased dramatically during the Late Classic, showing that the absolute power of the ruler declined and that elites probably played an expanding role in the political decision-making process. Barber and Joyce (Chapter 8) report similar data from Monte Albán: during Monte Albán II (100 B.C.–A.D. 200), large numbers of high-status residences were built, which they interpret as the emergence of a decentralized administrative structure.

Finally, the very important issue must be raised that elite residences cannot be lumped into one general category. Already in 1992, Diane and Arlen Chase (1992:7–11) questioned the traditional two-tiered model of grouping Mesoamerican societies into rulers and the ruled or elites and commoners. In their edited volume, they present case studies from throughout Mesoamerica as well as theoretical discussions emphasizing that there was a third intermediate group, or middlemen, and that Mesoamerican political and social organization was a lot more complex than previously assumed. Their findings are relevant to this volume as well and probably also apply to South American and North American societies. The problem is that the data needed to fine-tune elite residences are often lacking and may appear lumped together in scholarly texts. The reader should keep in mind that elites were stratified probably in all precontact and postcontact American cultures.

Sources of Power

Demarest (Chapter 4) emphasizes the important point that Maya rulers relied on various sources of power, which are reflected in the location and the layout of palace architecture. Depending on the site-specific circumstances of different Maya cities, individual rulers might base their power on economic aspects such as agricultural management or long-distance trade, on military planning, or primarily on ideology and theater-state performance. His examples from Dos Pilas, Aguateca, and Cancuén clearly illustrate differing settings of power.

Thus the concept of power should be further analyzed and defined as to what it meant in particular political systems. In the Inka state, one fundamental source of power for individual emperors was private property. Land belonged to the *panaca* (royal lineage) of an emperor, and each new, succeeding ruler had to acquire his own properties. These private properties were often graced with royal estates to which the ruler would withdraw to relax as well as to carry out more private administrative and political functions (see Niles 1999). The study of such estates and how they articulate power poses an ongoing and fascinating challenge (Burger and Salazar 2004; Christie in preparation). Isbell (Chapter 2) argues that the city of Huari was surrounded by similar rural estates that formed significant political power bases with regard to agricultural wealth produced and the large group of loyal retainers who maintained them. These estates may rank the city of Huari as a type of capital over the administrative centers of Pikillacta and Viracochapampa, which lacked rural estates. Most Inka private properties were located in the Urubamba Valley and stood in a similar relationship to Cusco as the rural estates did to Huari in that example.

Alternate sources of power could be a road system between the center and the periphery (as in the Inka and Chaco Canyon cases) or a deliberate referral back to ancestral models on the part of rulers or elites. Lekson (Chapter 3) presents such a case in which the elites of Aztec Ruins and Paquimé consciously recalled Chaco. Sarro (Chapter 6) shows that one source of power for the elite ruling El Tajín was a connection with the ballgame of their ancestors.

An additional source of power is undoubtedly military might and conquest. Mackey (Chapter 11) demonstrates how two conquest states established different kinds of settlements at Farfán: The Chimú built Farfán as an intrusive center, but the Inka co-opted the existing Chimú settlement. The data highlight opposing strategies employed by two conquest states to establish their presence in newly conquered territories. The case of Farfán speaks to the shortcomings of models and the pitfalls of quick labeling. It shows that conquest states act in individual ways and cannot be lumped into one generic category. For example, Mackey points out that the Inka erected intrusive centers on the south coast, but on the north coast, it was probably more convenient for them to reuse existing Chimú settlements.

To conclude, this brief introduction has made it clear that "palaces and power in the Americas" is still a gigantic mosaic puzzle. Though pieces of data are constantly being added, many empty sections remain, and the picture is far from complete. Lack of information limits the validity of comparisons between many palaces, cultures, and regions. It is also imperative to include variables outside strict architectural parameters, such as sources of power, burials, and others. Gair Tourtellot, Jeremy Sabloff, and Kelli Carmean (1992) reinforce this issue in their analysis of elite architecture at the Maya cities of Sayil and Seibal. They conclude that architectural construction per se is not always a conclusive indicator of status and that archaeologists must search for "still finer discriminations within construction types at similar levels of apparent expenditure" (98). I think the excitement of future research is in doing just that and in filling in diverse pieces of the puzzle and watching a more complete picture of palaces and elite residences emerge.

Note

1. Relatively little work has been done to further identify the compounds—many of which display brilliant mural programs—as elite residences; see Hall 1962; Taube 2003.

References Cited

Benson, Elizabeth P.
1992 The World of Moche. In *The Ancient Americas: Art from Sacred Landscapes*, edited by Richard F. Townsend, pp. 303–315. The Art Institute of Chicago and Prestel.
Blanton, Richard E.
1978 *Monte Alban: Settlement Patterns at the Ancient Zapotec Capital.* Academic Press, New York.
Burger, Richard L., and Lucy C. Salazar (editors)
2004 *Machu Picchu: Unveiling the Mystery of the Incas.* Yale University Press, New Haven and London.
Chase, Diane Z., and Arlen F. Chase (editors)
1992 *Mesoamerican Elites: An Archaeological Assessment.* University of Oklahoma Press, Norman.

Christie, Jessica Joyce
In preparation   The Sculpted Outcrops of the Inka.
Christie, Jessica Joyce (editor)
2003 *Maya Palaces and Elite Residences: An Interdisciplinary Approach.*
University of Texas Press, Austin.
Demarest, Arthur
1992 Ideology in Ancient Maya Cultural Evolution: The Dynamics of
Galactic Polities. In *Ideology and Pre-Columbian Civilizations,*
edited by Arthur Demarest and G. Conrad, pp. 137–157. University of
New Mexico Press, Albuquerque.
2003 The Political Acquisition of Sacred Geography: The Murciélagos
Complex at Dos Pilas. In *Maya Palaces and Elite Residences: An
Interdisciplinary Approach,* edited by Jessica Joyce Christie, pp.
120–153. University of Texas Press, Austin.
Evans, Susan, and Joanne Pillsbury (editors)
2004 *Palaces of the Ancient New World.* Dumbarton Oaks Research
Library and Collection, Washington, DC.
Geertz, Clifford
1980 *Negara: The Theater State in Nineteenth-Century Bali.* Princeton
University Press, Princeton.
Hall, Clara (Millon, Clara)
1962 A Chronological Study of the Mural Art of Teotihuacan. Unpublished Ph.D. dissertation, Department of Anthropology, University of
California at Berkeley.
Inomata, Takeshi, and Stephen Houston (editors)
2001 *Royal Courts of the Ancient Maya.* 2 vols. Westview Press, Boulder,
Colorado.
Kowalewski, Stephen A., Gary M. Feinman, L. Finsten, Richard E. Blanton,
and L. M. Nicholas
1989 *Monte Alban's Hinterland, Part II: Prehispanic Settlement Patterns
in Tlacolula, Etla, and Ocotlan, the Valley of Oaxaca, Mexico.* Memoirs of the Museum of Anthropology 23. University of Michigan, Ann
Arbor.
Lekson, Stephen
1999 *The Chaco Meridian.* Altamira Press, Walnut Creek, California.
Millon, René (editor)
1973 *Urbanization at Teotihuacan, Mexico,* vol. 1. University of Texas
Press, Austin.
Moseley, Michael E.
1993 *The Incas and Their Ancestors.* Thames & Hudson, New York.
Niles, Susan
1999 *The Shape of Inca History.* University of Iowa Press, Iowa City.
Puleston, Dennis E.
1983 *The Settlement Survey of Tikal.* Tikal Report No. 13, University
Museum Monograph 48. The University Museum, University of
Pennsylvania.
Schele, Linda, and Peter Mathews
1998 *The Code of Kings.* Scribner, New York.

Spinden, Herbert J.

1913   *A Study of Maya Art, Its Subject Matter and Historical Development*. Memoirs of the Peabody Museum of American Archaeology
and Ethnology Vol. VI. Harvard University, Cambridge.

Tambiah, Stanley J.

1985   *Culture, Thought, and Action: An Anthropological Perspective*.
Harvard University Press, Cambridge and London.

Taube, Karl

2003   Tetitla and the Maya Presence at Teotihuacan. In *The Maya and
Teotihuacan*, edited by Geoffrey Braswell, pp. 273–314. University of
Texas Press, Austin.

Tourtellot, Gair, Jeremy Sabloff, and Kelli Carmean

1992   "Will the Real Elites Please Stand Up?": An Archaeological Assessment of Maya Elite Behavior in the Terminal Classic Period. In
Mesoamerican Elites, edited by Diane Chase and Arlen Chase, pp.
80–98. University of Oklahoma Press, Norman and London.

Tozzer, Alfred M.

1911   *A Preliminary Study of the Prehistoric Ruins of Tikal, Guatemala*.
Memoirs of the Peabody Museum of American Archaeology and
Ethnology, vol. 5, no. 2. Harvard University, Cambridge.

Willey, Gordon R., and Richard M. Leventhal

1979   Settlement at Copan. In *Maya Archaeology and Ethnohistory*, edited
by N. Hammond and G. R. Willey, pp. 75–102. University of Texas
Press, Austin.

Willey, Gordon R., Richard M. Leventhal, and William Fash

1978   Maya Settlement in the Copan Valley. *Archaeology* 31:32–43.

PART I

Identification of Palaces

CHAPTER I

Looking for Moche Palaces in the Elite Residences of the Huacas of Moche Site

Claude Chapdelaine

Introduction

The Moche civilization is considered a class-structured society and an Archaic State. It is difficult, however, to establish its pristine nature because the North Coast of Peru is known for an early development of public architecture, dating back to the end of the Preceramic period around 2000 B.C. (Moseley 1992; Pozorski and Pozorski 1992). While the Moche civilization inherited the achievements of several preceding complex societies, the Huacas of Moche Site stands out as the first capital city of a multivalley state (Chapdelaine 2000, 2001, 2002, 2003; Shimada 1994; Topic 1982; Wilson 1988, 1999). Within this perspective of a Moche territorial state with a centralized urban center (Figure 1.1), this chapter is an investigation of possible palace locales in and near the monumental building called Huaca de la Luna.

Kent Flannery (1998) has designed a ground-plan approach to study the Archaic States. Several criteria are considered, among them the existence of a palace for the king, which represents an interesting difference between chiefdoms and states (Sanders 1974, cited in Flannery 1998:21). The palace, monumental in nature, is the king's residence, and it should express the power base of the supreme ruler. What was the power base of the Moche ruler? Was this power strong enough to have a palace built, and therefore this monumental residence is a characteristic of the Moche State? It might also be appropriate to verify the existence of a noble class and its elite residences by looking at domestic architecture recently excavated in the urban sector of the Huacas of Moche Site.

Moche Palaces

In a major conference held at Dumbarton Oaks in October 1998, "Ancient Palaces of the New World: Form, Function, and Meaning," the Moche civilization was not addressed directly. It would therefore appear that there is no such thing as a Moche palace. Furthermore, although Andeanists believe that the first pristine state for their region was Moche, they do not yet have the ground plans of palaces for Moche kings (Flannery 1998:47). Another scholar in the same book shares this statement: "We know something of their pyramids (huacas) and flamboyant tombs but lack data on whether or not its rulers had palaces" (Marcus 1998:75).

In this research, it is relevant to ask ourselves what we are looking for that could be considered a Moche palace. It should, of course, be the residence of the supreme ruler. In addition, and at a very hypothetical level, using a list of components based on cross-cultural comparisons (Flannery 1998; Viollet-Le-Duc 1996), the palace of the Moche ruler could be composed of:

1. A large monumental structure with high-quality construction and embellishment
2. A residential section with distinctive decoration
3. A large audience room (with an elevated platform or bench for the ruler) to conduct religious, civic, and political duties
4. Several storage rooms to accumulate wealth
5. Rooms for the administration
6. A large enclosure or plaza to permit the gathering of a large segment of the population (this assembly could be done inside or outside the palace grounds)
7. A defensive wall or some defensive features (such as location on top of a hill)

Several elements could be added to this list or removed from it. For example, the defensive feature might be replaced by a central location with limited and controlled access to the palace grounds. A religious temple within the palace might be an added feature as well as a burial chamber for the ruler and his family. It should be mentioned that the Moche State could have been a theocracy, in which case religious and military power could have been in the same hands. If this were so, the temple and the palace may have been established together in the same government building. It is also possible to imagine that the palace as a public building could have been the seat of the polity but not the residence of the ruler. However, our basic idea is to consider the Moche palace as a multifunctional building from which the ruling elite was governing a large territorial state (see Wilson 1997 for a critique of the city-state concept applied to the Moche polity).

Since we are looking for the palace of the supreme ruler, it is at the Huacas of Moche Site, the state capital, that we should direct our attention. A regional palace for the Moche ruler in each valley could also be considered, but that is beyond the scope of this study. There are only two large public buildings at the Huacas of Moche Site (Figure 1.2), and both are huge platforms made of adobe bricks and constructed over a long period. In fact, they are composed of several buildings constructed over each other, each time getting bigger at the base and higher at the top.

FIGURE 1.1 General location of the Huacas of Moche Site

We know very little about the largest of these two structures, Huaca del Sol, but it is believed that it was the seat of economic power because of food remains discovered on the western terrace that might indicate that some sort of feasts took place there (Pozorski 1979; Uceda and Paredes 1994). Its economic function is only an educated guess at this time; we must wait for a new research program on this massive building before attributing to it a precise scenario.

Huaca de la Luna is the other large public building. Located at the foot of a small but prominent hill, Cerro Blanco, it is an architectural complex made of different sections, including a principal platform (Platform 1) with several rooms, a large interior patio, and many specialized rooms. This principal platform is flanked by two smaller platforms linked by terraces, outdoor patios, ramps, and a very large northern plaza (Figure 1.3). This architectural complex has been the object of a long-term Peruvian research and

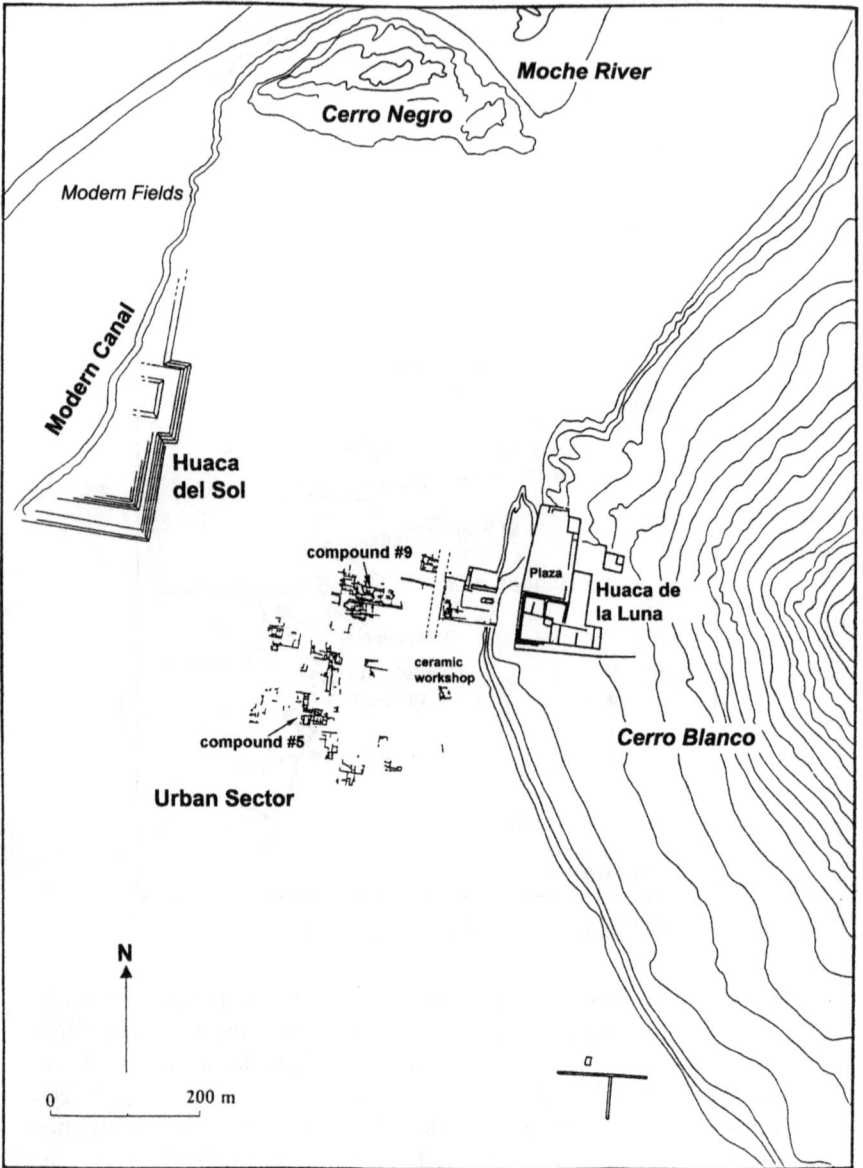

FIGURE I.2 Plan of the Huacas of Moche Site

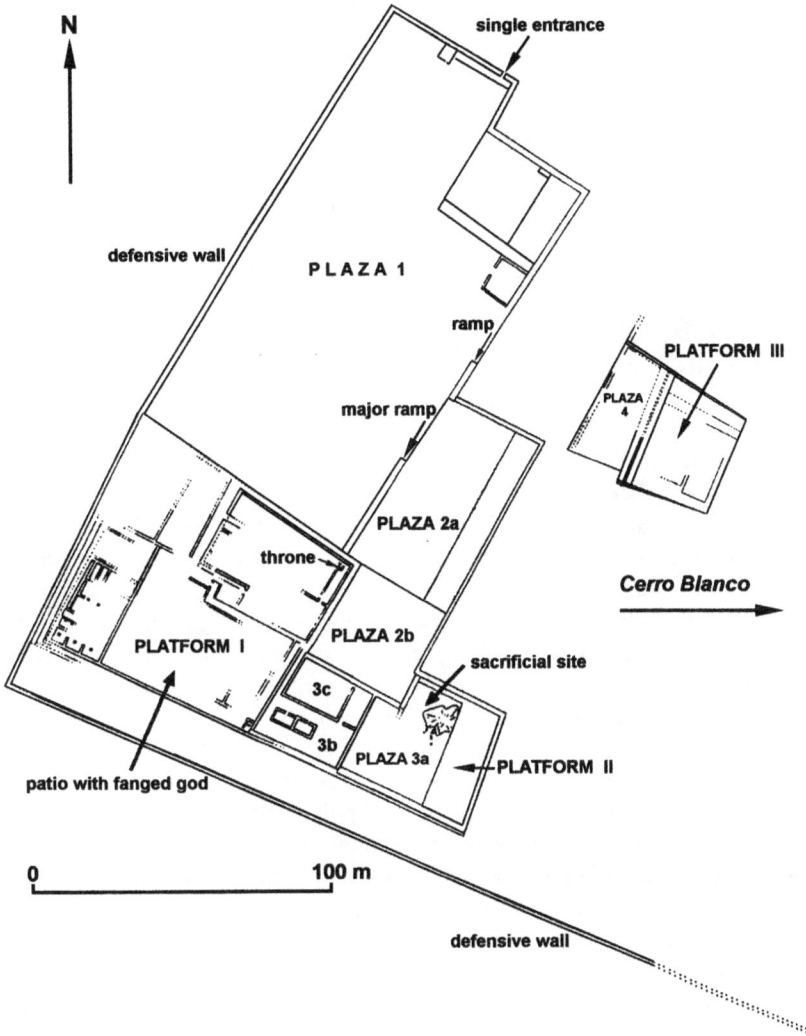

FIGURE 1.3 Plan of Huaca de la Luna. Modified from Uceda et al. 2000:18.

excavation project codirected by Santiago Uceda and Ricardo Morales of the Universidad de Trujillo (Uceda 2001; Uceda and Chapdelaine 1998; Uceda and Mujica 1994; Uceda and Tufinio 2003; Uceda et al. 1997, 1998, 2000).

Huaca de la Luna as the Moche Palace of the Supreme Ruler?

Every year the results of this Peruvian project give us a new vision of the Huaca de la Luna complex, both synchronically and diachronically. The on-going project is directed toward the understanding of the principal platform as well as the area surrounding it, in particular the large plaza located north of the main building (Uceda and Tufinio 2003). Considering all the discoveries made so far at this impressive monumental building, can it be classified as a Moche palace? Of course there is no definitive answer, but let us look at the criteria previously mentioned.

1. Huaca de la Luna is definitely a large monumental structure with high-quality construction. Some interior walls as well as exterior walls are embellished with polychrome decoration. The layout is complex and it seems to be unique, but there is no clear indication of a ground plan for a temple or a palace.

2. The last best-preserved monument of Huaca de la Luna, dated to Phase IV (A.D. 400–700), has been cleaned and then filled to establish the foundation of a new monument (Uceda and Canziani 1998). In these conditions, no section has yet been identified as a residential area with distinctive features such as a kitchen, serving dishes, sleeping rooms with benches along the walls, or other characteristics.

3. Huaca de la Luna has a large room known as the central interior patio or ceremonial plaza, whose interior walls are decorated with the relief effigy of a "fanged god" known as the Degollador, a supernatural being very often represented in the iconography with a ceremonial knife in one hand and a trophy head in the other. Although this central room has never been completely excavated due to its size (60 m × 40 m), it may have been used as an audience room. In the northeast corner of the principal platform (Platform 1), where a late construction brought this corner to a higher level than the rest of the platform, an elevated platform or bench for the ruler has been found with steps decorated with a typical polychrome Moche motif mixing zoomorphic and marine themes (Uceda and Tufinio 2003:198, 209–210).

4. Huaca de la Luna has several large rooms that might have been used to accumulate wealth. They are not standardized in shape, but since the access to this building was very limited, the available space would not pose a problem for the ruler to store goods. No direct evidence of storage has been found so far, and the near absence of large storage vessels argues for another type of storage device.

5. Huaca de la Luna has several rooms, but it is very difficult to identify their function and therefore to suggest that they were used for administration. However, it can be said that there were several rooms within this architectural compound that could have accommodated state officials.

6. Huaca de la Luna has always been associated with religious beliefs because of its polychrome murals, and many scholars over the years have overlooked one of its main architectural features. This feature is Plaza 1, a large walled enclosure that would have permitted the gathering of a large segment of the population. This huge plaza is a key to understanding the whole architectural complex for several reasons: First, it has a single narrow northern entrance, 1.90 m wide, which is the only access to the whole complex; sec-

ond, it is from this central plaza that one can access the long ramp to get to the principal platform; third, it is also from this central plaza that one can access a second, shorter ramp to go to a second plaza or architectural space between the principal platform and the third platform, located higher along the Cerro Blanco flanks; fourth, its internal complexity—with several rooms located along its eastern wall and a monumental wall to delimit its western and northern boundaries—is another indication that this underestimated architectural feature, poorly known prior to the Peruvian excavation, may have had a complex function (Haro and Regalado 2000; Uceda and Tufinio 2003). There is room to gather people outside Huaca de la Luna, but this large plaza indicates the capacity of the Huaca de la Luna governing body to assemble, inside its walls, a large segment of the population to participate in several types of ceremonies. These relatively private festivities might have permitted several hundred of Moche's urban dwellers to celebrate without being seen from the outside. This aspect is different from the spatial organization of Huaca del Sol, where the public gatherings were held at the foot of this massive building. The organization of private ceremonies in temples or rooms on top of Huaca del Sol would have been possible, but they would not have been on the same scale as the ones suggested at Huaca de la Luna.

7. Huaca de la Luna has a defensive wall running along its southern limit, and of course the massive wall of the northern plaza defends the only known single entrance to the whole complex. The wall of the plaza is rather impressive, being more than 5 m wide at its base and about 8 m high, with a ledge running parallel to it to allow people to walk along the wall or to have a seat during ceremonies. It is like a fortress wall, and the reason for this investment may have been to illustrate the power of the governing body. The location of Huaca de la Luna at the foot of Cerro Blanco might also be associated with some defensive features. The remains of a massive wall running parallel to its southern façade are still visible, and the wall continues until it reaches the rocky flanks of the hill. These massive walls, if they are not defensive, could also be related to the rulers' wish to distance themselves from their subjects.

In conclusion, it is increasingly evident that our understanding of Huaca de la Luna should take into account various lines of evidence and that it is problematic to consider that this architectural complex was dedicated only to the religious sphere. The sacrificial site excavated on the west side of the second platform in Plaza 3a (Bourget 1998, 2001), combined with similar evidence found in Plaza 3c of the same complex, supports the importance of religious activities within the walls of Huaca de la Luna. This activity of human sacrifice is now getting much attention, but it should be remembered that the whole complex was not designed for this single purpose. It could be argued that these punctual events are highly circumstantial and may have been related to exceptional events such as El Niño–caused catastrophic events (Bourget 1998).

Though we should accept the religious function of some sectors within the Huaca de la Luna complex, the idea of the king having his funerary chamber within the palace cannot be ruled out. No burial of a king has yet been recorded within Huaca de la Luna, but most of the principal platform has been damaged by a large, deep looters' pit made by the Spaniards during the sixteenth century, presumably to find gold. Historical data confirm the success of the colonial looters. And the burials recently discovered, while giving us some indications of the wealth of the buried priest or state officials, are not associated with the supreme elite (Uceda et al. 1994).

A funerary platform known as Uhle's Platform, situated at the foot of the western façade of Huaca de la Luna (Uhle 1913), might have been dedicated to the ruling family, but no burial can be attributed to a king (Chauchat 2000; Pimentel and Alvarez 2000).

The residential character and the administrative function of Huaca de la Luna are not yet well established, and there is always the possibility that the ruler did not inhabit the state building center. In this case, it is worth mentioning an architectural compound (abbreviated as A.C. hereafter and in Figure 1.4) located immediately to the southwest that might have been the residence of a high-status elite. A.C. 8 is of good construction quality and has an interior patio with benches forming a U-shaped structure with niches; two trophy heads were put in one of the niches (Figure 1.4; Verano et al. 1999). This compound has been considered more religious in nature. Its occupants were located at a prestige spot in the immediate shadow of Huaca de la Luna and beside the upper-class Uhle funerary platform. The priests in charge of conducting the human sacrifices inside Huaca de la Luna might have occupied A.C. 8 (Bourget 1998; Bourget and Newman 1998). Could it also be the residence of the supreme ruler? We don't know, but this compound is definitely part of a larger architectural unit associated with Huaca de la Luna and separated from the rest of the urban sector by a rather large street running north–south.

The hypothesis that Huaca de la Luna is the major Moche religious temple is still the most popular among Peruvian scholars (Campana and Morales 1997). Nevertheless, it seems that it was a multifunctional building where the governing body was also running state affairs. It might not be a typical palace, but it is certainly not a typical Moche temple either.

Elite Residences in the Urban Sector

The urban sector between the two monumental buildings has been our focus of attention since 1995 (Figure 1.4). After five years of horizontal open-area excavation, exposing large sections of domestic compounds, the central sector is recognized as an urban nucleus for an emerging urban class composed of the middle and upper strata of Moche society (Chapdelaine 2000, 2001, 2002, 2003). Most of these excavated residential compounds are considered

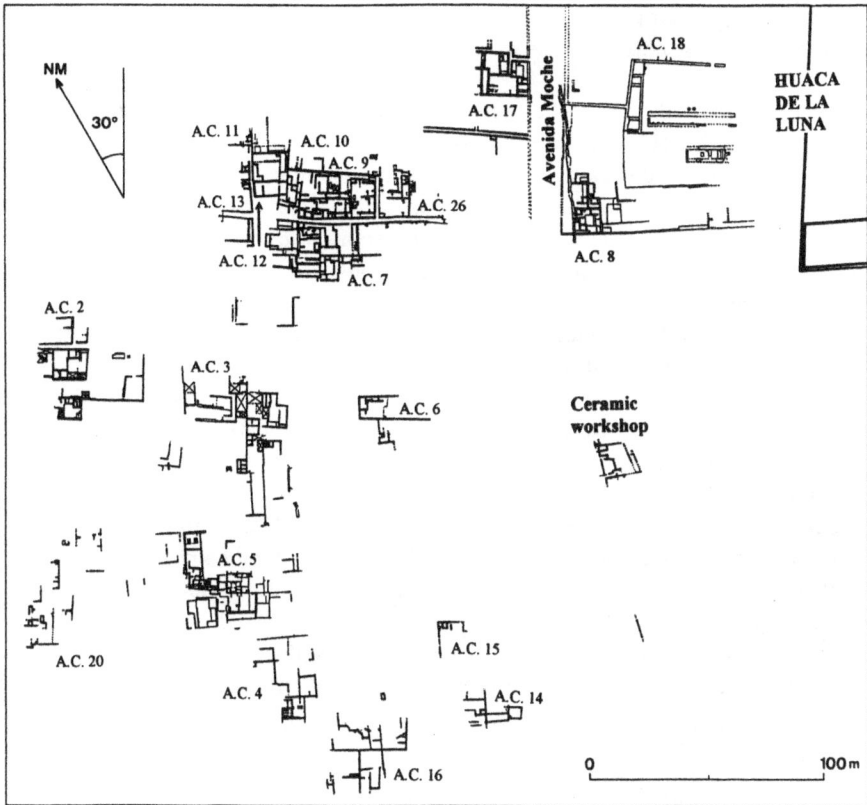

FIGURE 1.4 Plan of the south-central sector of the Huacas of Moche Site

elite residences. Several criteria can be put forward to support this state-ment, and we have argued elsewhere that the leaders of these compounds were accumulating wealth (Chapdelaine 2001, 2002). Within the large vari-ability of domestic layouts, it is still impossible to recognize a type of palace for the supreme ruler, but some compounds are wealthier and can be asso-ciated with a distinct class of nobility. At this point, it is best not to use the concept of palace to designate the residences of the Moche nobility or its leaders. The term *elite residence* is more appropriate, and I will concentrate on these elite residences to show that the upper class at the Moche Site was constantly growing and that the power was shared among several leaders.

A network of narrow streets delimiting large compounds and small plazas characterizes the urban sector. The access to these types of spatial organiza-tion is limited to a single entrance. Storage is a major aspect in these large and private compounds that average 30 × 15 m in size. It can be argued that the space available for storage well exceeds the needs of a single nuclear family. A large room with benches along the walls, usually located in the center of the compound, acted as the leader's quarters. Several criteria can be used to assess the leader's wealth within each compound:

1. The burials found (the richest tomb is considered the chief burial)
2. The quantity and quality of the funerary offerings, along with their prestige and their symbolic authority and power
3. The space available to store goods or to produce goods
4. The nature of these goods and their economic importance
5. The number of people living in the household
6. The wealth of the entire household
7. The specific artifacts or architectural features that can be associated with prestige and power

With respect to criterion seven, the quality of construction, the size of rooms, and the material culture associated with them (with an emphasis on nonutilitarian items such as decorated ceramics, pendants, figurines, and some metal objects) are often used to classify compounds and to segregate the rich from the poor or to determine the high, moderate, and low status of their inhabitants (see Donnan 1995 for funerary practices; also Donnan and Mackey 1978).

Of the 14 compounds that have been excavated during our project, only 2 have been exposed completely. Our criteria should only be applied, therefore, to A.C. 9 and to a lesser extent to A.C. 5 (Figure 1.4).

Architectural Compound 9

The layout of A.C. 9 is roughly rectangular (Figures 1.5 and 1.6). The whole compound, located downtown, has known many changes over several generations. It was probably occupied at one time by a minimum of three related nuclear families, but one group apparently managed to take control over most of the compound. In fact, the leader of the north-central subunit became the most powerful leader of the compound. Unfortunately, his presumed burial chamber has been looted, but a few pieces of carved bones and copper objects, as well as numerous fragments of funerary vessels found in this centrally located funerary platform, show his wealth (Figure 1.5, Room 33 [r-33 on Figure 1.5]).

The occupational sequence of A.C. 9 illustrates the growth of power of a multinuclear household leader who came to control most of the original compound. The evolution of A.C. 9 from four subunits to a single large unit or household could be an example of nuclear family households being integrated into a multinuclear family household. This happened probably when the leader of the north-central subunit unified the whole compound under his authority by being able to build a funerary platform in its central place, Room 33, and by forcing members of the south-central unit to abandon their

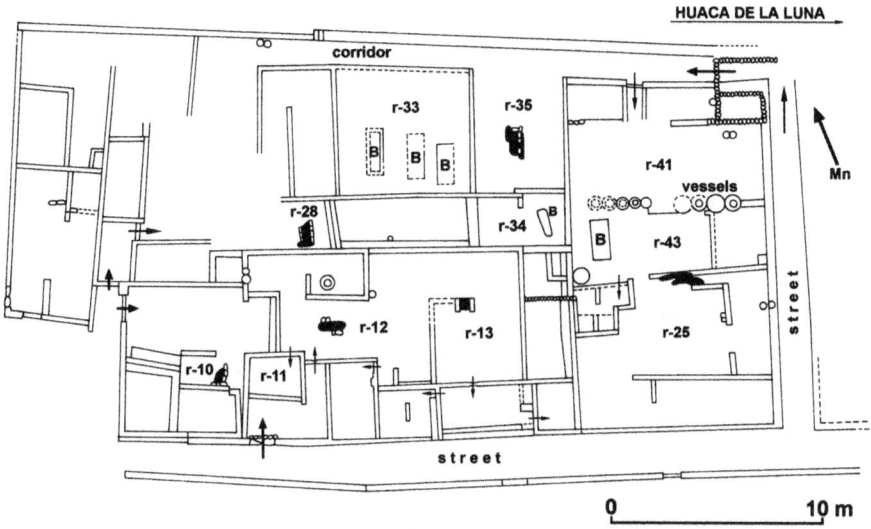

FIGURE 1.5 Plan of A.C. 9 of the Huacas of Moche Site

FIGURE 1.6 General view of A.C. 9. Photo by Claude Chapdelaine.

TABLE 1.1. Distribution of utilitarian and nonutilitarian goods found in the richest rooms of Architectural Compound 9, Huacas of Moche Site

Room	Utilitarian Frequency	%	Nonutilitarian Frequency	%	TOTAL
9-13	185	60.6	77	39.4	262
9-33	133	50.4	134	50.6	267
9-41	71	39.3	110	60.7	181
9-35	73	43.5	95	56.5	168
9-34	91	53.2	80	46.8	171*
9-25	62	45.6	74	54.4	136

*Excluded from this total is a necklace composed of 434 beads that was found in a burial.

central room, Room 13 (r-13), so it could be used as an area for dumping trash! When expanding his compound eastward to construct an area to produce and store goods (eastern subunit), the leader of the north-central subunit had to deal with his neighbors, so he designed a narrow street between them. The ruler of A.C. 9 had the power to modify the urban layout, placing a new street between his household and his neighbors to the east and planning a new entrance connected to that new street. The leader was also certainly involved in the activities carried out in the nearby plazas associated with these streets.

A.C. 9 presents the highest artifact density, and the percentage of nonutilitarian goods is also very suggestive. Numbers are high compared to other partially excavated compounds. This is related probably to the length and intensity of the last occupations. We recovered from this large compound of 40-plus rooms more than 3,000 artifacts. Included in this total were 440 painted ceramic vessels and fragments, with the dominant type (32%) being the flaring bowl, or *florero;* close to 800 domestic ceramic vessels (dominated by medium-size jars and 100 large storage jars, plus a few small bowls); 125 spindle whorls; approximately 50 copper items; 726 pendants and beads (Bernier 1999); 202 figurines; 128 musical instruments; and 64 spoons (Chapdelaine and Armas 1999). A fair number of manos and metates were also recorded, but few bone tools, lithic flakes, chipped tools, and other organic tools have been identified.

The distribution of these artifacts indicates a strong concentration in several rooms. If we consider domestic vessels, spindle whorls, and spoons as utilitarian and all the other categories as nonutilitarian, A.C. 9 had about 1,546 nonutilitarian objects, or 52 percent of the total. Calculating the ratio of utilitarian/nonutilitarian objects for each of the richest rooms, we arrived at the results shown in Table 1.1.

The implications of this distribution are not yet well understood, but with the exception of Room 34, the other five rooms are among the largest of the compound, and Rooms 13 and 35 were at one point used to prepare food, since a hearth and refuse were found.

The types of goods found in A.C. 9 (and in other compounds throughout the urban sector) are the same as the ones found inside the Huacas (Huaca de la Luna and Huaca del Sol), with the exception of highly precious and rare items such as massive gold and silver objects and specimens made of *Spondylus* shell that is obtained from long-distance trade with Ecuador. The high density of spindle whorls (125 of the 400 recorded for the whole site), the recovery of cotton seeds, and the number of storage rooms are used to hypothesize the importance of textile production in this compound, and that the leader may have been a powerful official of the state. The limited access to its quarters is a good indication that the leader of this compound was able to accumulate goods and that he may have been a member of a nobility class that was evolving behind adobe walls right in the middle of the capital city.

Architectural Compound 5

A.C. 5 is an architectural complex located in the southern part of the urban sector, about 275 m southwest of Huaca de la Luna. This well-preserved compound is different from A.C. 9 in several ways. The first distinction is its single entrance in the northwest corner (Figure 1.7). This compound is probably the southern portion of a larger building of independent but related complexes sharing common walls. A.C. 5 is not connected to a street or a plaza, but limited excavation in its periphery might be the explanation (Figure 1.8).

Besides the high quality of the construction, in particular the plastered walls and the two large patios with multiple benches—the smaller one having a little ramp to access the bench—the most intriguing feature of A.C. 5 is the absence of a kitchen with a hearth within its interior limits. At one point in time, a door was cut in the northern wall of the northeastern patio with the small ramp, and it led to an area dedicated to the production of food, as evidenced by its embedded mortars and big central hearth. That door was later sealed, indicating that, similar to A.C. 9, the inhabitants of this complex were very dynamic and that a long history lies beneath the sand. It is thus possible to suggest that at an earlier period this complex was not a typical residence but rather an administrative center for the southern portion of the Moche Site urban center. It was not an elite residence, and it may be our first example of a public building that gives us insights into the power decentralization of the Huacas' ruling elite, allowing the urban class to play an active role within the limits of the city.

Conclusion

The two Huacas at the Moche Site probably served religious purposes as well as providing sites for social or political events. They are the expression of a

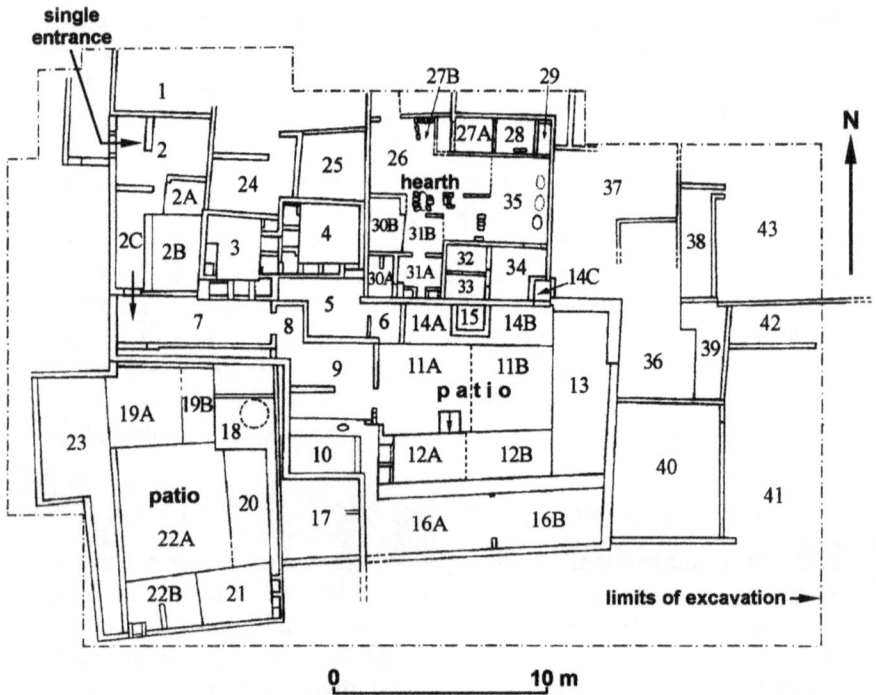

FIGURE 1.7 Plan of A.C. 5 of the Huacas of Moche Site

centralized power, but the relation between them is unknown. It is tempting to consider the Mesopotamian duality of temple and palace, but this is not an easy task (Manzanilla 1987). Elsewhere I have argued that the Huacas of Moche Site was in fact a true city with a diversity of functions related to religious, administrative, and craft-production activities (Chapdelaine 2002, 2003). If the idea of a single expansionist Moche State was, until recently, well accepted (Haas et al. 1987; Moseley 1992; Shimada 1994; Topic 1977, 1982; Wilson 1988), it is now challenged by the hypothesis of several states centered in different valleys and having different types of relations between them and the ruling elite at the Moche Site (Bawden 1996; Castillo and Donnan 1995; Quilter 2002). More data are needed to resolve this issue of a single Moche State or of several North Coast States all linked in a broadly defined culture called Moche and to address the dilemma of political unity versus political fragmentation.

At other Early Intermediate period centers, very little can be said about the existence of palaces. For example, at Sipan, we now have the burials of several great leaders or kings (Alva and Donnan 1993), but prior to these discoveries the site was considered a secondary center. And there is no palace for the Sipan king! At the El Brujo Site in the Chicama Valley, the Huaca Cao

Viejo, which is also a platform with multiple rooms built on top and with a great plaza, might represent the seat of power of the Moche domination of the lower valley (Franco et al. 1994, 2003). At the Huancaco Site in the Virú Valley, the excavations directed by Steve Bourget led him to consider a section of the monumental structure as a banquet hall and that the ruler resided in a palace (Bourget 2003). This palace seems to have been occupied by a local elite quite distinctive from the Moche, and thus it could not be considered a Moche palace, although it is contemporaneous with the major occupation at Huaca de la Luna. At the Guadalupito Site in the lower Santa Valley, high walls surround large platform mounds, and elite residences are visible at the foot of a low hill, which was densely occupied during the Moche period. Excavations carried out at this site in 2002 by the author revealed elite residences attributed to the governing body (Chapdelaine et al. 2003).

In the meantime, the Huacas of Moche Site is still considered the center of the Moche realm that may have served as an advanced urban center and the capital of an unknown number of valleys. Huaca de la Luna was probably the seat of the governing body and was most likely used to carry out several functions that are generally associated with the palace in other Archaic States (Manzanilla 1987). At the same time, it can still be considered a temple and a major building from which to conduct various religious ceremonies,

FIGURE 1.8 General view of A.C. 5. Photo by Claude Chapdelaine.

some quite clearly related to the legitimization of the rulers. It would seem, however, that for the Moche rulers, the palatial residence was not the primary means to express and legitimize their political power. Funerary programs with excessive wealth concentration seem to be the privileged way to express their political power. It should be pointed out that the massive public monuments, which may have served multiple purposes, were used as the burial place of the Moche kings, a practice comparable to that of other civilizations.

The recognition of the compounds excavated so far as elite residences (Chapdelaine 2001, 2002, 2003) is based on the high density of nonutilitarian artifacts, the quality of construction, the size of the compounds, and their controlled access, combined with the variability encountered in the burial patterns. In this hierarchical society, a minimum of three classes can be proposed: the high class might be associated with the royal family or with the lineage of the supreme ruler; the middle class could be composed of a wide variety of interest groups such as weavers, potters, metallurgists, and other specialists such as priests, state officials, and warriors. These groups all have a home in the nucleus of the urban center, whereas the lower class seems to be absent from the Moche Site, or it has not been found yet. It is possible that this lower class, corresponding to the working class that included makers of adobes, farmers, fishermen, and servants, were living at the periphery of the site or in nearby villages located on the valley floor but within walking distance of the Huacas of Moche Site.

Within the urban sector, diversity of material manifestations supports the idea of an important urban class, including several leaders, that may have had a special link with the lineage in power. This nobility class inhabited the area between the two Huacas, surrounded by a middle class. The urban centralization was possible only with an efficient agrarian organization to provide food and surplus to the state. The scarcity of large secondary centers in the Moche Valley indicates clearly the centralization achieved by the Huacas of Moche rulers (Billman 1996). The leaders inhabiting the Huacas and the urban sector thus shared the centralized power in some ways. Their power was unchallenged within the Moche Valley, and it was possible to see it and feel it by looking at the two monumental buildings, Huaca del Sol and Huaca de la Luna. The theocratic ruler was certainly at home in these monuments where he could preside over various ceremonies, including state affairs, with the support of a privileged urban class. This theocratic power was maintained for several centuries, and a Moche dynasty ruled a territorial state that included several coastal valleys and influenced an area encompassing over 600 km of the Peruvian North Coast.

Acknowledgments

This long-term project on the urban zone of the Huacas of Moche Site would not have been possible without the financial support of the Social Sciences and Humanities Research Council of Canada, and I would like to acknowledge it. I would also like to express my deep gratitude to Dr. Santiago Uceda, who has provided us with unpublished data and a scientific atmosphere that facilitated our fieldwork. I would like to thank all the Peruvian archaeologists and workers of the Huaca de la Luna archaeological project and all the graduate and undergraduate students from the Université de Montréal, who have contributed to the success of this project. My thanks go to Dr. Steve Bourget for his generous comments on an earlier draft of this chapter and to Adrian Burke for making many editing suggestions to enhance it.

References Cited

Alva, Walter, and Christopher B. Donnan
1993 *Royal Tombs of Sipan.* Fowler Museum of Cultural History, UCLA.
Bawden, G.
1996 *The Moche.* Blackwell, London.
Bernier, H.
1999 Cuentas geométricas, características morfológicas y tecnológicas en el sitio Moche. *Sian,* pp. 24–27.
Billman, Brian R.
1996 Prehistoric Political Organization in the Moche Valley, Peru. Unpublished Ph.D. dissertation, Department of Anthropology, University of California at Santa Barbara.
Bourget, Steve
1998 Pratiques sacrificielles et funéraires au site Moche de la Huaca de la Luna, côte nord du Pérou. *Bulletin de l'Institut Français d'Études Andines* 27(1):41–74.
2000 Daily Life in a Palace: Recent Archaeological Investigations at Huancaco, Virú Valley. Paper presented at the Annual Andean Conference at Berkeley, January.
2001 Rituals of Sacrifice: Its Practice at Huaca de la Luna and Its Representation in Moche Iconography. In *Moche: Art and Political Representation in Ancient Peru,* edited by Joanne Pillsbury, pp. 89–109. National Gallery of Art, Washington, DC.
2003 Somos diferentes: Dinámica ocupacional del sitio Castillo de Huancaco, valle de Virú. In *Moche: Hacia el final del milenio: Actas del Segundo Colloquio sobre la Cultura Moche,* edited by Santiago Uceda and Elias Mujica, 1:245–267. Universidad Nacional de Trujillo and Pontificia Universidad Católica del Perú, Lima.
Bourget, Steve, and M. Newman
1998 A Toast to the Ancestors: Ritual Warfare and Sacrificial Blood in Moche Culture. *Baessler-Archiv* 46:85–106.
Campana, C., and Ricardo Morales
1997 *Historia de una deidad mochica.* Editorial A & B, Lima, Peru.
Castillo, L. J., and Christopher B. Donnan
1995 Los Mochica del Norte y los Mochica del Sur. In *Vicus,* edited by Krzystof Makowski et al., pp. 143–176. Banco de Crédito del Perú, Lima.

Chapdelaine, Claude
1998 Excavaciones en la zona urbana Moche durante 1996. In *Investigaciones Huaca de la Luna 1996*, edited by Santiago Uceda, Elias Mujica, and Ricardo Morales, pp. 85–115. Facultad de Ciencias Sociales, Universidad Nacional de Trujillo, Peru.
2000 Struggling for Survival, the Urban Class of the Moche Site, North Coast of Peru. In *Environmental Disaster and the Archaeology of Human Response*, edited by G. Bawden and R. Reycraft, pp. 121–142. Maxwell Museum of Anthropology, Anthropological Papers No. 7. Albuquerque, New Mexico.
2001 The Growing Power of a Moche Urban Class. In *Moche: Art and Political Representation in Ancient Peru*, edited by Joanne Pillsbury, pp. 69–87. National Gallery of Art, Washington, DC.
2002 Out in the Streets of Moche: Urbanism and Socio-political Organization at a Moche IV Urban Center. In *Advances in Andean Archaeology and Ethnohistory*, edited by William Isbell and H. Silverman, pp. 53–88. Plenum Press, New York.
2003 Ciudad Moche: Urbanismo y estado. In *Moche: Hacia el final del milenio: Actas del Segundo Colloquio sobre la Cultura Moche*, edited by Santiago Uceda and Elias Mujica, 2:247–285. Universidad Nacional de Trujillo y Pontificia Universidad Católica del Perú, Lima.
Chapdelaine, Claude, and J. Armas
1999 Cucharas Moche, descripción y función. *Sian*, pp. 18–23.
Chapdelaine, Claude, et al.
1997 El sector urbano. In *Investigaciones Huaca de la Luna 1995*, edited by Santiago Uceda, Elias Mujica, and Ricardo Morales, pp. 109–123. Facultad de Ciencias Sociales, Universidad Nacional de Trujillo, Peru.
Chapdelaine, Claude, V. Pimentel, and H. Bernier
2003 Informe del Proyecto Arqueológico PSUM (Proyecto Santa de la Universidad de Montreal) 2002—La presencia Moche en el valle del Santa, Costa Norte del Perú. Lima: Unpublished report submitted to the Instituto Nacional de la Cultura, Perú. 463 pp. (www.mapageweb.umontreal.ca/chapdelc)
Chauchat, C.
2000 Découverte dans la mystérieuse grande cité de Moche. *Archéologia* 368:32–41.
Donnan, Christopher B.
1995 Moche Mortuary Practice. In *Tombs for the Living: Andean Mortuary Practices*, edited by Tom Dillehay, pp. 111–159. Dumbarton Oaks Research Library and Collection, Washington, DC.
Donnan, Christopher B., and Carol J. Mackey
1978 *Ancient Burial Patterns of the Moche Valley, Peru*. University of Texas Press, Austin.
Flannery, Kent V.
1998 The Ground Plans of Archaic States. In *Archaic States*, edited by G. M. Feinman and Joyce Marcus, pp. 15–57. School of American Research Press, Santa Fe, New Mexico.

Franco, R., C. Gálvez, and S. Vásquez
1994 Arquitectura y decoración mochica en la Huaca Cao Viejo, Complejo El Brujo: Resultados preliminares. In *Moche: Propuestas y perspectivas*, edited by Santiago Uceda and Elias Mujica, pp. 147–180. Actas del Primer Coloquio sobre la Cultura Moche. Travaux de l'Institut Français d'Études Andines 79, Lima, Peru.
2003 Modelos, función y cronología de la Huaca Cao Viejo, Complejo El Brujo. In *Moche: Hacia el final del milenio: Actas del Segundo Coloquio sobre la Cultura Moche*, edited by Santiago Uceda and Elias Mujica, 2:125–177. Universidad Nacional de Trujillo and Pontificia Universidad Católica del Perú, Lima.
Haas, Jonathan, Shelia Pozorski, and Thomas Pozorski (editors)
1987 *The Origins and Development of the Andean State*. Cambridge University Press, Cambridge.
Haro, O., and D. Regalado
2000 Plaza 1 de Huaca de la Luna. *Sian* 9:25–32.
Manzanilla, Linda
1987 The Beginnings of Urban Society and the Formation of the State: Temple and Palace as Basic Indicators. In *Studies in the Neolithic and Urban Revolutions: The V. Gordon Childe Colloquium*, edited by L. Manzanilla, pp. 271–286. BAR S349. British Archaeological Reports, Oxford.
Marcus, Joyce
1998 The Peaks and Valleys of Ancient States: An Extension of the Dynamic Model. In *Archaic States*, edited by Gary M. Feinman and Joyce Marcus, pp. 59–94. School of American Research Press, Santa Fe, New Mexico.
Moseley, Michael E.
1992 *The Incas and Their Ancestors*. Thames and Hudson, New York.
Pimentel, V., and G. Alvarez
2000 Relieves policromos en la plataforma funeraria Uhle. In *Investigaciones en la Huaca de la Luna 1997*, edited by Santiago Uceda, Elias Mujica, and Ricardo Morales, pp. 181–203. Facultad de Ciencias Sociales, Universidad Nacional de Trujillo, Peru.
Pozorski, Shelia
1979 Prehistoric Diet and Subsistence of the Moche Valley, Peru. *World Archaeology* 11(2):163–184.
Pozorski, Shelia, and Thomas Pozorski
1992 Early Civilization in the Casma Valley, Peru. *Antiquity* 66:845–870.
Quilter, Jeffrey
2002 Moche Politics, Religion, and Warfare. *Journal of World Prehistory* 16(2):145–195.
Sanders, William T.
1974 Chiefdom to State: Political Evolution at Kaminaljuyu, Guatemala. In *Reconstructing Complex Societies: An Archaeological Colloquium*, edited by C. B. Moore, pp. 97–116. Supplement to the Bulletin of the American Schools of Oriental Research, 20. Cambridge, MA.

Shimada, Izumi
1994 *Pampa Grande and the Mochica Culture.* University of Texas Press,
      Austin.
Topic, Theresa
1977 Excavations at Moche. Unpublished Ph.D. dissertation, Harvard
      University, Cambridge.
1982 The Early Intermediate Period and Its Legacy. In *Chan Chan: Andean
      Desert City,* edited by Michael E. Moseley and Kent C. Day, pp.
      255–284. School of American Research Advanced Seminar Series.
      University of New Mexico Press, Albuquerque.
Uceda, Santiago
2001 Investigations at Huaca de la Luna, Moche Valley: An Example of
      Moche Religious Architecture. In *Moche: Art and Political Repre-
      sentation in Ancient Peru,* edited by Joanne Pillsbury, pp. 47–67.
      National Gallery of Art, Washington, DC.
Uceda, Santiago, and J. Canziani
1998 Análisis de la secuencia arquitectónica y nuevas perspectivas de in-
      vestigación en la Huaca de la Luna. In *Investigaciones en la Huaca
      de la Luna 1996,* edited by Santiago Uceda, Elias Mujica, and Ricardo
      Morales, pp. 139–158. Facultad de Ciencias Sociales, Universidad
      Nacional de Trujillo, Peru.
Uceda, Santiago, and Claude Chapdelaine
1998 El Centro Urbano de las Huacas del Sol y la Luna. *Arkinka* 33:94–
      103.
Uceda, Santiago, et al.
1994 Investigaciones sobre la arquitectura y relieves policromos en la
      Huaca de la Luna, valle de Moche. In *Moche: Propuestas y perspecti-
      vas,* edited by Santiago Uceda and Elias Mujica, pp. 251–303. Travaux
      de l'Institut Français d'Études Andines 79, Lima.
Uceda, Santiago, and Elias Mujica (editors)
1994 *Moche: Propuestas y perspectivas.* Actas del Primer Coloquio sobre
      la Cultura Moche (Trujillo, 12 al 16 de abril de 1993). Travaux de
      l'Institut Français d'Études Andines 79, Lima.
Uceda, Santiago, Elias Mujica, and Ricardo Morales (editors)
1997 *Investigaciones en la Huaca de la Luna 1995.* Facultad de Ciencias
      Sociales, Universidad Nacional de Trujillo, Peru.
1998 *Investigaciones en la Huaca de la Luna 1996.* Facultad de Ciencias
      Sociales, Universidad Nacional de Trujillo, Peru.
2000 *Investigaciones en la Huaca de la Luna 1997.* Facultad de Ciencias
      Sociales, Universidad Nacional de Trujillo, Peru.
Uceda, Santiago, and Arturo Paredes
1994 Arquitectura y función de la Huaca de la Luna. *Revista Cultural des
      Indes* 7:42–46.
Uceda, Santiago, and M. Tufinio
2003 El Complejo Arquitectónico religioso Moche de Huaca de la Luna:
      Una aproximación a su dinámica ocupacional. In *Moche: Hacia el
      final del milenio: Actas del Segundo Colloquio sobre la Cultura
      Moche,* edited by Santiago Uceda y Elias Mujica, 2:179–228. Univer-

sidad Nacional de Trujillo y Pontificia Universidad Católica del Perú, Lima.

Uhle, Max

1913 Die Ruinen von Moche. *Journal de la Société des Américanistes* (Paris), n.s. 10(1):95–117.

Verano, John W., Santiago Uceda, Claude Chapdelaine, R. Tello, M. I. Paredes, and V. Pimentel

1999 Modified Human Skulls from the Urban Sector of the Pyramids of Moche, Northern Peru. *Latin American Antiquity* 10(1):59–70.

Viollet-Le-Duc, E.

1996 *Encyclopédie Médiévale.* Bibliothèque de l'Image, Bayeux, France.

Wilson, D. L.

1988 *Prehispanic Settlement Patterns in the Lower Santa Valley, Peru: A Regional Perspective on the Origins and Development of Complex North Coast Society.* Smithsonian Institution Press, Washington, DC.

1997 Early State Formation on the North Coast of Peru: A Critique of the City-State Model. In *The Archaeology of City-States, Cross-Cultural Approaches,* edited by D. L. Nichols and T. H. Charlton, pp. 229–244. Smithsonian Institution Press, Washington, DC.

1999 *Indigenous South Americans of Past and Present: An Ecological Perspective.* Westview Press, Boulder, CO.

CHAPTER 2

Landscape of Power
A NETWORK OF PALACES
IN MIDDLE HORIZON PERU

William H. Isbell

Archaeologists know little about political power and kingship in pre-Inka Andean societies. In significant part this is because we have ignored the principal engine of regal power, the royal palace. In fact, many archaeologists avoid identifying palaces and kings in the Andean past, preferring to classify monumental buildings as temples and paramount individuals as priests.

I suspect that the reluctance to recognize royal palaces in the Andean archaeological record springs from a couple of prejudices. First, archaeologists tend to exaggerate the difference between secular and sacred domains. Kings are secular, and priests are sacred. Wherever the material record reveals significant evidence for ceremony, Andean archaeologists imagine priests. Of course, this is contradicted by descriptions of elaborate ceremonies that surrounded Inka rulers and other archaic kings. Second is a commitment to processual archaeology, the adaptive nature of culture, and cooperation theories of state origins. Economic relations, not power, are assumed to explain the past. Many Andean archaeologists assume that pre-Hispanic rulers were servants of the community; benevolent organizers of redistribution; philanthropic managers of land, water, and labor; and the first to die in military defense. "King" emphasizes power and politics, so "lord" or "warrior-priest" are preferred classifications. But surely, the "Lord of Sipán" (Alva 1988, 1990; Alva and Donnan 1993; Donnan 1988; Donnan and Castillo 1992), the principal individual buried in a spectacular tomb from Peru's pre-Inka Moche culture, should be recognized as a king who ruled from a royal palace. One of the "temple platforms" at monumental Sipán must have been capped by a royal palace, not a temple.

A royal palace is a tool for constructing regal power. Just as the nature, quality, and quantity of royal power differ from one kingdom to another, so do the nature, size, and distribution of royal palaces. In significant part, power to rule is produced by and in palaces. The palace of one polity may be a center for storage and redistribution, where a king promotes himself by managing the pooled wealth of the community, part of which he appropriates for personal aggrandizement (Thomas and Conant 1999:9–15). Another palace may be a cosmological model proclaiming the king and his court to be the center of the universe. In "theatre states," the palace community sponsors recurrent rituals that present an ideal model for the real world (Geertz 1980). Of course, all palaces must accommodate multiple strategies for producing power, and the palace was never the only tool of empowerment. Power is constructed in the spatial relations of people in their households and communities, in relations of production, and through the control of force. But palaces are dedicated engines of royal power, and their archaeological remains document the nature, quality, and extent of power a monarch could produce, at least under most conditions.

An example of a minimal palace is the residence of the Great Sun of the Natchez. He lived in a log house about 12 × 16 m (Neitzel 1965:19) that was similar to ordinary Natchez cabins except for being two or three times as large, and raised on an earthen mound about 4 m high. At the end of the seventeenth century, the Great Sun was a paramount who commanded some eight lesser chiefs along the lower Mississippi River (Brown 1990; Neitzel 1965; Swanton 1911). His polity totaled about 3,500 persons residing in about 400 cabins widely dispersed around a ceremonial center. The chief's palace was in the central settlement, preferentially located relative to a great plaza and its important temple areas.

Clifford Geertz (1980) developed a model of the Negara, or traditional Balinese state. As part of his analysis he presents a drawing of the palace of the Klungkung polity at the turn of the nineteenth century. At that moment the king of Klungkung was the paramount monarch of southern Bali, with perhaps as many as 1.5 million subjects. An illustration of the palace (Geertz 1980:Figure 11) was drawn from memory by an informant who lived there as a child, so its size is only approximate—a square about 150 m on each side. But the informant's drawing is replete with knowledge and experience of the royal residence. Ceremonial rooms, funerary spaces, compartments for sacred heirlooms, counsel chambers, stairways, and portals were placed to emphasize more- and less-public space, inside and outside, high and low, and other oppositions constructive of differences in rank and authority. The Negara palace was a tool that impacted the emotions of everyone who entered it, promoting a world order composed of social difference and superior power for the king and his family. Also salient in the informant's representation of the Negara palace are extensive residential facilities for a vast number of noble relatives who constituted the core of the king's court, including the king's deceased father, the his primary wife, his secondary wives, and his children of different statuses. Unfortunately, we know little about how the palace related to surrounding spaces, such as gardens, plazas, and hinterland mansions, that may also have fulfilled functions of state.

Perhaps the most spectacular palace ever constructed by an archaic potentate was the residence and mausoleum of Qin Shi Huang Di, the first emperor of China (Chang 1980, 1986; Fitzgerald 1978; Guisso et al. 1989;

Wheatley 1971; Zilin 1985). Emperor Qin united the warring states of Chou in 221 B.C., creating an empire that may have embraced 50 million people. He constructed himself a vast palace that included a great tomb full of terracotta armies, as well as 260 buildings, some of immense size, that sprawled over 56 km². Emperor Qin's palace-city included the court and all the first-order institutions of state within its walls.

In 1532 a small cohort of Spanish soldiers fell upon the Inka Empire, a polity of 6 to 10 million persons stretching across 1,835,000 km² (Wilson 1999:413). Several early invaders described the capital city, Cuzco, as composed of many spectacular palaces. According to some eyewitness accounts, each emperor—or at least each of the late rulers—constructed his own palace within the capital (Chávez 1970; Hemming 1970; Hemming and Ranney 1982; Rowe 1967).

Cuzco must have been a city full of palaces. One belonged to the ruling emperor, another to his deceased father, another to his father's father, and others to more distant royal ancestors. Palaces of deceased kings were occupied by the lineal descendents, who maintained themselves with the resources of his estate. Apparently, the capital city was constructed around palaces.

Cuzco's primary palace was the reigning king's residence and the focus of state activities. In addition, kings and high nobles owned palaces on royal estates located in the hinterlands surrounding the capital (Burger and Salazar 2004; Farrington 1995; Niles 1987, 1988, 1999; Protzen 1993), and they also maintained palaces in the administrative capitals of distant provinces (Guaman Poma [1615] 1980; Morris 2004). But the early accounts and documents are confusing and contradictory, in no small part because the invaders were translating Inka institutions and meanings into Spanish colonial culture even as they witnessed and described them.

Were multiple royal palaces the organizing principle behind Andean capital cities and their hinterlands? Of course, understanding Andean palaces and royal power requires a broader perspective than Cuzco at the moment of European contact. Michael Galaty and William Parkinson (1999a) show that Mycenaean palaces shared important features, but no single example characterizes a millennium of Aegean palaces. There was significant diversity in economic organization, architectural design, and mechanisms for constructing regal power. In this chapter I hope to expand our understanding of Andean palaces and royal power by examining Peru's pre-Inka highland ancestor, the Middle Horizon (A.D. 550–1000) Huari[1] Empire (Figure 2.1). How can we identify Wari palaces? What were they like? Did collections of Huari palaces constitute Huari's capital cities? What more can Wari palaces teach us about the development of royal power in the Andean past?

Based on the broad distribution of its material remains, Huari was probably the largest pre-Inka empire in the Andes (see Figure 2.1). It most likely embraced about one-quarter of the territory dominated by the Inka, or an

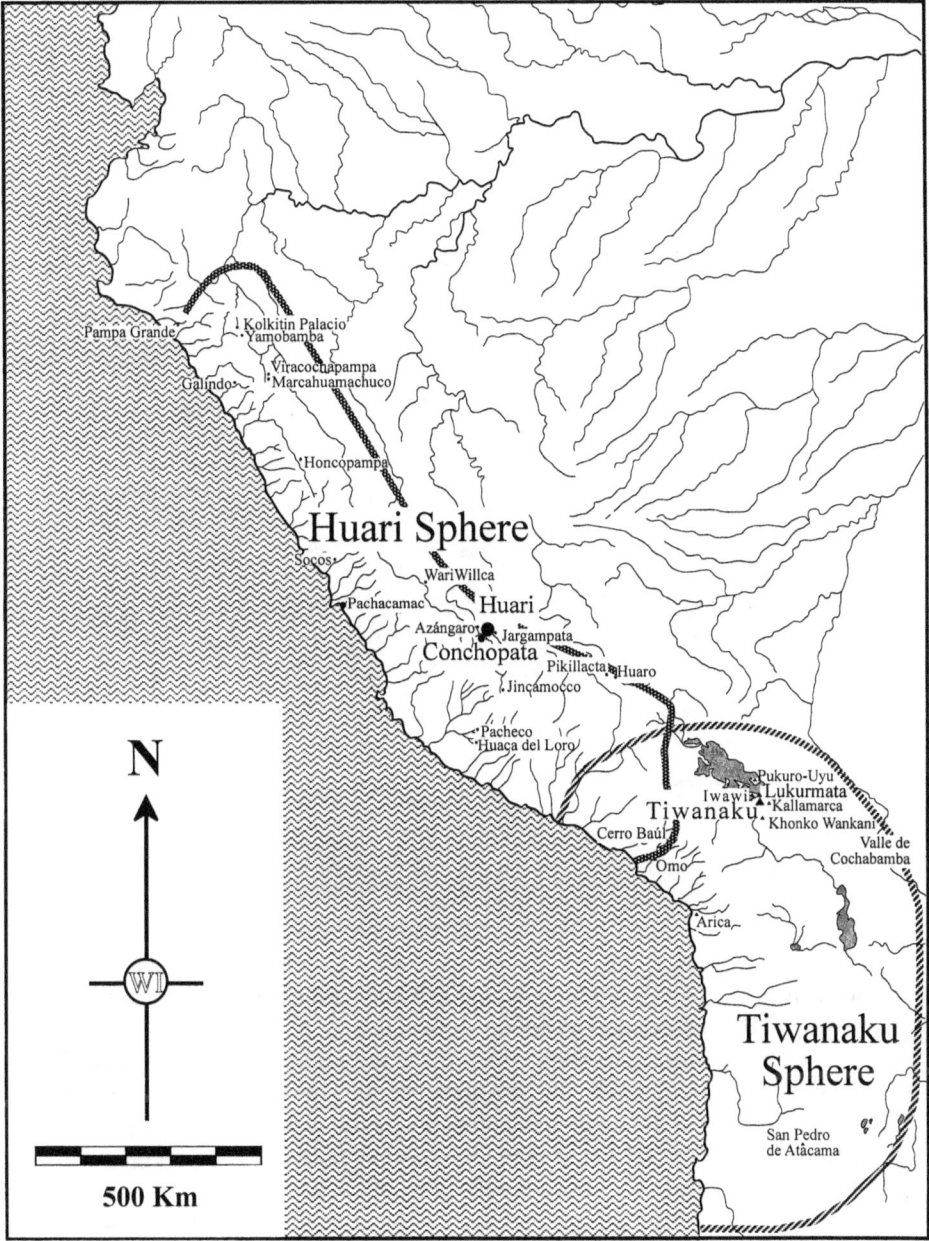

FIGURE 2.1 Huari and Tiwanaku spheres in the Central Andes locating Middle Horizon centers

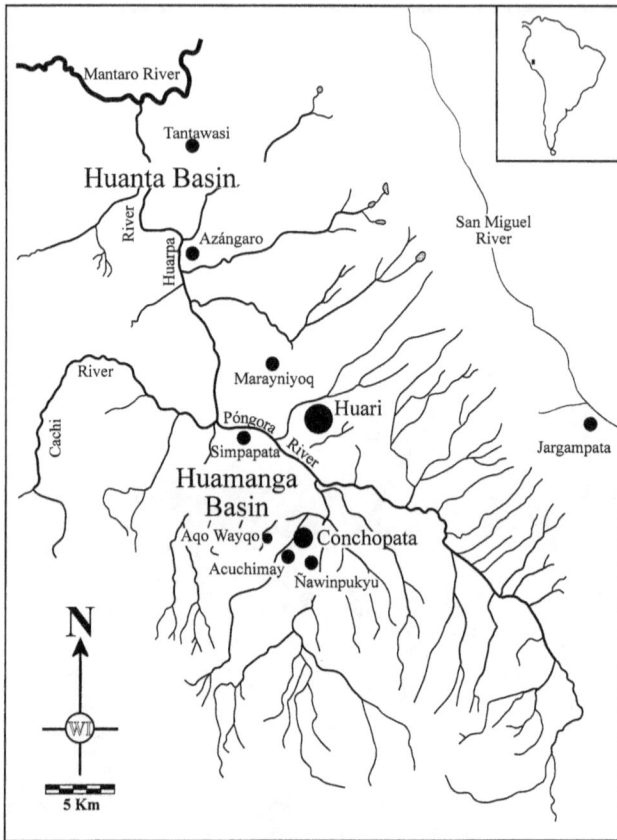

FIGURE 2.2 Ayacucho Valley with principal archaeological sites

empire of some 1 to 2 million persons. Did one capital city control all the territory? Were Wari kings lords who depended on religion and ideological consensus, or did they command force and rule with unbridled power? Such issues are best addressed by the study of palaces.

The Huari capital city, from which the empire takes its name, is located in Peru's central highlands in the Ayacucho Valley (Figure 2.2). The ancient city sprawls across hundreds of hectares, where the surface ruins reveal enormous rough-stone walls that appear to have constituted great rectangular enclosures (Figure 2.3). Unfortunately, none of the ancient buildings can be mapped completely on the basis of the standing remains, and only four compounds have been excavated extensively enough to reveal meaningful information about form and function (Isbell 1997b; Isbell et al. 1991; Pérez 1999).

In the past, none of Huari's buildings were identified as palaces. Furthermore, the absence of a tradition of Andean palace investigation leaves ar-

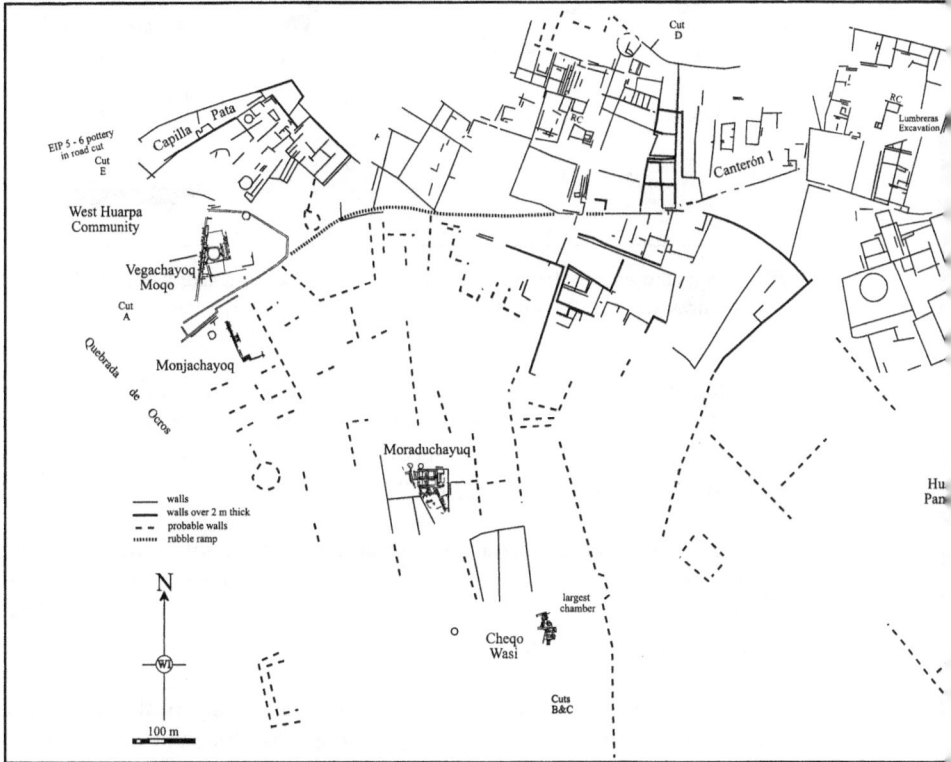

FIGURE 2.3 Huari architectural core

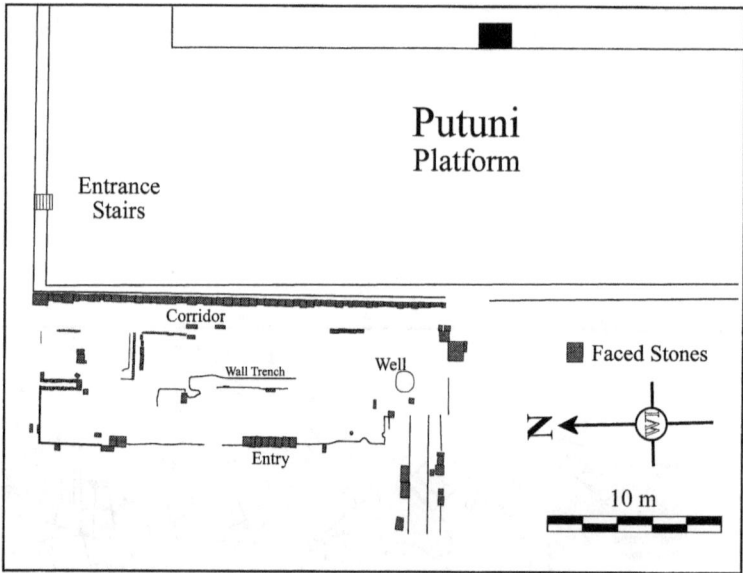

FIGURE 2.4 Tiwanaku's Palace of the Multicolored Rooms. Redrawn from Kolata 1993:Figures 5.36a and 5.36b.

chaeologists without meaningful criteria to use when searching for probable palaces among the ruins of Huari and contemporary settlements. Andean archaeologists need a set of formal criteria similar to those used by Aegean prehistorians to identify Mycenaean palaces:

> . . . a large ashlar construction centered on a megaron unit: a rectangular room with four columns surrounding a hearth, its long walls extending to form a porch and a vestibule. (Shelmerdine 1997:558, quoted by Galaty and Parkinson 1999a:5)

An exception to the avoidance of "palace" and "king" in the Andean past is Alan Kolata's (1993:149–162; Sampeck 1991) discussion of Tiwanaku—the capital of a southern polity broadly contemporary with Huari (see Figure 2.1). Does Kolata's identification of the Palace of the Multicolored Rooms (Figure 2.4) rely on material diagnostics that may help distinguish other Middle Horizon palaces? Unfortunately, the answer is no. The only material attribute Kolata lists is a stone architrave. His identification springs from an ideological conviction that the core of Tiwanaku was a sacred precinct isolated from the rest of the city by a water-filled moat—a precinct that he believed contained "not only the largest ceremonial structures, but also the elite and royal residences as well" (Kolata 1993:104). But close inspection shows that the water-filled moat, and consequently the isolated sacred precinct, could not have existed.[2] Furthermore, cross-cultural comparisons suggest that the Palace of the Multicolored Rooms was much too small to have been Tiwanaku's royal residence.[3]

To develop a list of formal diagnostics for Andean palaces we must depend on recent discussions of Inka palaces (Burger and Salazar 2004; Morris 2004) found in a few papers on royal residences of pre-Inka kings at late cities such as Chan Chan (Pillsbury and Leonard 2004) and Pachacamac (Eeckhout 1999a). Huari was probably the lineal ancestor of the Inka state (Hiltunen 1999; McEwan 1998b, 1999), and it contributed profoundly to the rise of central-coastal Pachacamac (Isbell 2004; Menzel 1964, 1968). Consequently, it is likely that Wari palaces had at least some influence on the form later palaces took in Inka Cuzco and in the religious center of Pachacamac. I turn to these palaces in my effort to define a set of formal characteristics for identifying Andean, and particularly Wari, palaces.

The chronicler Martín de Murúa ([1605] 1987) provided the best description of Inka palaces. It is remarkably consistent with major building complexes at the well-preserved Inka centers of Huánuco Pampa (see Morris and Thompson 1985 and Isbell 2004b) and Pumpu (Matos 1994). On this basis, I propose the following list of nine diagnostic architectural features for Inka palaces.

DIAGNOSTIC ARCHITECTURAL FEATURES OF THE INKA PALACE

1. Careful enclosure of the palace complex by strong walls
2. An outer plaza and an inner patio that decline in size as access became more restricted
3. Imposing and defensible gateways, portals, or passages controlling access to each courtyard
4. Various special-function buildings around the first plaza and the second patio, where noble captains awaited commissions from the king and administrative business could be conducted
5. A proliferation of elaborate and relatively private residential buildings associated with or beyond the second courtyard, probably including a water source and a bath
6. Large halls in front of, or as part of, the entrance to the palace. These buildings housed the palace guard and also furnished roofed space for public ceremonies during rainy weather (Inka halls of this type are frequently called *kallanka* or *carpawasi*).
7. Superior architecture as well as artifacts, especially among the relatively private residential rooms
8. Space for a garden and zoo beyond the area of private rooms, probably with its own water supply
9. Location for the mummified body of a king within the palace structure. After the death of a king his body was mummified and treated more or less as though it were still alive. It was kept within the

royal palace, and there is no indication that significant architectural modifications, such as construction of a royal tomb, were required.

At Pachacamac, a recurrent building type was called the "terrace house" by archaeologist Max Uhle (1991:37) and interpreted as elite residences or palaces for noble *curaca* (ruler, chief, or king). More recently this kind of building has been named the "pyramid with ramp" (Bueno 1974–1975, 1982, 1983a, 1983b; Franco 1993, 1996, 1998; Jiménez 1985; Jiménez and Bueno 1970; Paredes 1984, 1985, 1988; Paredes and Franco 1985, 1987, 1987/88; Patterson 1985; Rostworowski 1992; Shimada 1991; Uhle 1991). Currently, popular archaeological interpretation considers the pyramid with ramp to have been a religious embassy.[4] However, Peter Eeckhout (1997, 1998a, 1998b, 1999a, 1999b, 2000) and I (Isbell 2004b) independently reached the conclusion that Uhle was correct: Pyramids with ramps were the palatial residences of kings. In fact, one example, albeit slightly divergent in form, was the palace of the Inka governor Tauri Chumpi (Bueno 1983b:6–11). Another was expropriated by Francisco Pizarro as his personal residence when he moved from Cuzco to the coast, that is, until he founded Lima and built himself an Iberian-style palace.

Examining the Pachacamac information, and keeping in mind the diagnostics of Inka palaces, I propose a list of eight attributes that identify palaces of the central-coastal Pachacamac tradition (see Eeckhout 1999 and Isbell 2004b).

DIAGNOSTIC ARCHITECTURAL FEATURES OF THE PACHACAMAC PALACE
1. A massively constructed compound, securely walled, with a defensible entryway controlling access to the interior. However, parts or all of the palace complex can be elevated on artificial platforms, so freestanding enclosure walls may be dispensed with and gateways may be replaced by ramps. In some cases, gateways and ramps are combined in the same entrance. And in other examples, platforms and walls grade into one another as walls become so thick that they support roads, buildings, and courts.
2. A sizable courtyard with one end raised to produce a prominent stage overlooking a lower assembly area. The stage is connected to the assembly area by a ramp.
3. A complex of rooms or walls on the raised stage forming a U-shaped backdrop that might have been draped with textiles
4. A second and smaller patio in the interior of the building, lower in elevation than the stage
5. A proliferation of relatively private rooms, some quite grand and others quite modest, as well as kitchen and work areas associated with the second, smaller patio. The floors of these rooms are often at different levels of elevation.

6. No garden, zoo, or other space at the rear of the complex (as in Inka palaces)
7. Use of variation in elevation—above/below—as the favored opposition for spatially constructing difference in social rank
8. Deliberate closure and/or interment of all or some parts of the building, accompanied by high-status burials placed in unoccupied areas

We must anticipate variation and difference in the Middle Horizon, but these diagnostics should help identify Wari royal palaces if and where they existed. I will rely upon them in my search of the Huari capital city; Huari's largest neighboring city, Conchopata; Huari's surrounding hinterland; and Huari's provincial capitals (see Figures 2.1 and 2.3), which together exhaust the possible locations and contexts for Wari palaces that are known archaeologically.

Huari and the Vegachayoq Moqo Palace

Only four of Huari's compounds have been excavated sufficiently to provide information about their architectural configurations and functions. They are Cheqo Wasi, Moraduchayuq, Monjachayoq, and Vegachayoq Moqo (Figure 2.3).

Cheqo Wasi consists of numerous complexes of megalithic tombs. It includes an elongated room that served as an ossuary, as well as several rooms and small patios. Thick rough-stone walls divide and surround the complex, although a complete compound enclosure has never been defined (Benavides 1984, 1991). On the basis of what is excavated at Cheqo Wasi, I believe that it lacks key features of Andean palace architecture, such as courtyard assembly areas, stages or platforms, special-function administrative rooms, and elite residential buildings. Of course, I cannot reject the possibility that Cheqo Wasi was the mortuary sector of a larger palace or of several palace compounds that may have backed up to one another. However, at present it should not be identified as royal palace architecture.

Moraduchayuq was a residential complex composed of "patio groups," small rectangular courts surrounded by two or more stories of narrow lateral rooms that served domestic functions. These patio groups were built side by side to completely fill a walled compound (Isbell 1984, 1997b; Isbell et al. 1991). The Moraduchayuq "apartment house" might have been a section within a large complex, possibly even a royal palace, but based on what has been excavated, the remains do not have the specific diagnostics of Andean palace architecture. Furthermore, excavations indicate that the residents were of intermediate status—comfortable, but not wealthy (Isbell et al. 1991).

Monjachayoq is terribly damaged from looting. What remains on the surface are the foundations of several large buildings, one with a rounded corner (see Figure 2.8). Below ground is an extensive complex of subterranean halls and chambers (Pérez 1999). The underground masonry consists of large ash-lars combined with rough-stone construction, creating a truly monumental edifice. The largest and deepest gallery was violated by grave robbers long ago, and today it contains little more than fragments of human bones. How-ever, the majesty of the architecture leaves little doubt that Monjachayoq in-cluded a royal tomb (see Figure 2.9). Consequently, it seems to have belonged to a palace so completely destroyed that it will never be well known.

Vegachayoq Moqo (Bragayrac 1982, 1991; González and Bragayrac 1986; González et al. 1996; Solano and Guerrero 1981), the fourth complex, rep-resents the largest excavated area at Huari, although only a portion of the complex has been exposed (Figures 2.3 and 2.5–2.7). During its excavation, Vegachayoq Moqo was named El Templo Mayor. Classifying this building as a temple is probably not completely in error, for it does seem to have functioned as a mortuary monument during part of its history. However, the name fails to recognize the palatial functions, as well as the transformational nature, of this important architectural compound.

I believe that Vegachayoq Moqo (Figures 2.5–2.8) was first built to fulfill the functions of a royal palace. Subsequently, it appears to have become a mortuary monument. Eventually it became a popular cemetery, where buri-als of nonroyals took place, including secondary burials composed of de-fleshed bones. At each stage, Vegachayoq Moqo was significantly modified architecturally, and some parts of the building were retired by being covered with clean earth.

Vegachayoq Moqo is located in the oldest part of Huari (Isbell 1997b, 2004a; Isbell et al. 1991), implying that its initial construction was early in the history of the city. Confirming the early date is a partially looted burial with fragments of rope, basketry, textiles, and ceramics that was found in Vegachayoq Moqo's west wall. This interment should date late in the trans-formational history of Vegachayoq Moqo, when it functioned as a popu-lar cemetery. Organic fibers yielded two radiocarbon dates close enough in time to confirm one another. They indicate mid-seventh century in uncali-brated time[5] for the burial. Ceramics from the site include mid–Epoch 1B-style sherds (Knobloch 1991), although they may represent trash and offering pottery placed in the building after it was more or less abandoned. Conse-quently, urban chronology, ceramics, and radiocarbon dates all suggest that the initial construction of Vegachayoq Moqo took place early in Middle Hori-zon Epoch 1, by at least A.D. 600, uncalibrated. I conclude that Vegachayoq Moqo must have been the palace of one of Huari's early monarchs, who ruled when imperial expansion first began.

Vegachayoq Moqo appears to have begun as a walled precinct containing a courtyard or plaza (Figures 2.5, 2.6A, 2.7, and 2.8) that was enclosed by a platform pyramid[6] composed of three mounds forming a U around the east end of the courtyard. The largest of the three mounds was 70 to 80 m long on a north-south axis and rose 8 m in two terraces. It was probably about 40 m

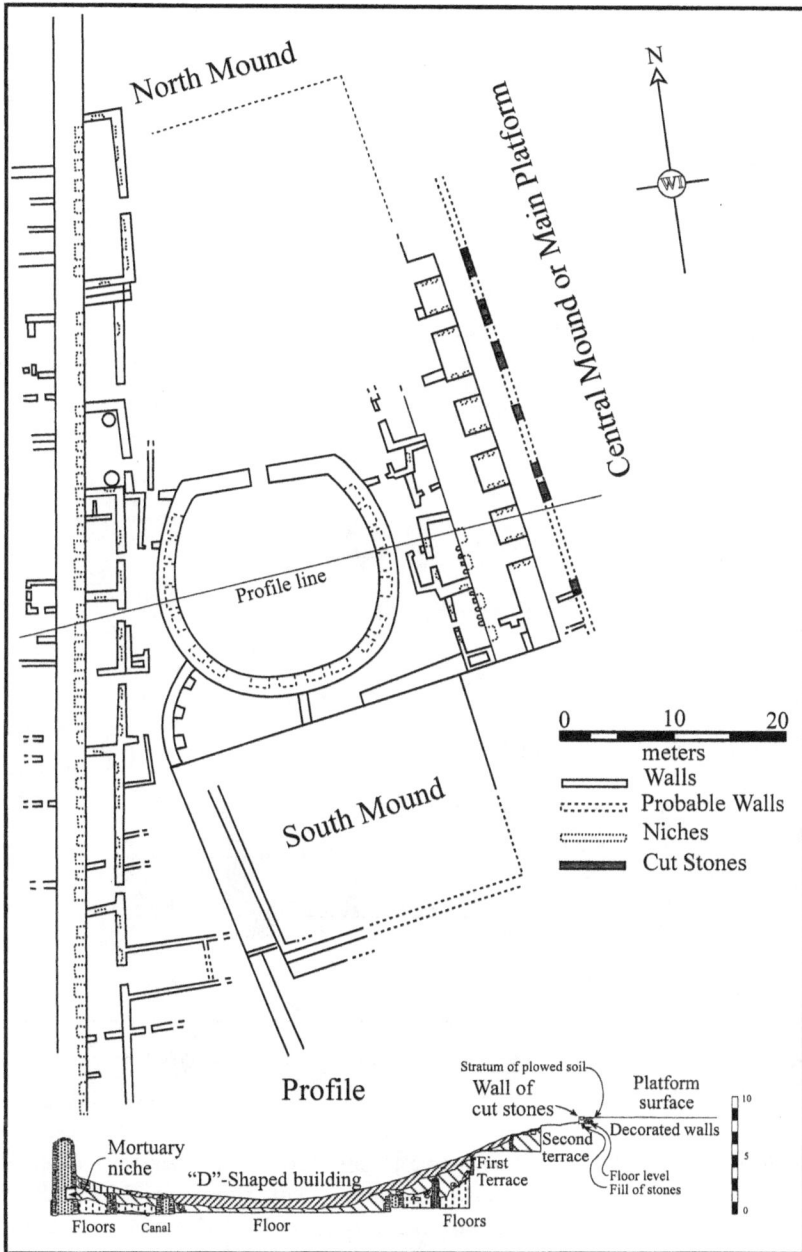

North Mound

Central Mound or Main Platform

N

Profile line

South Mound

0   10   20

meters

	Walls
	Probable Walls
	Niches
	Cut Stones

Profile

Stratum of plowed soil
Wall of
cut stones

Platform
surface

Decorated walls

Second
terrace

First
Terrace

Floor level
Fill of stones

Mortuary
niche

"D"-Shaped building

Floors   Canal   Floor   Floors

10

5

0

FIGURE 2.5 Vegachayoq Moqo palace complex, Huari

Third Phase: Popular Cemetery

Roof Mortuary
niche

"D"-shaped building

Room
floors

Floors

Palace Compound,
probably abandoned
and in ruins

C

Second Phase: Mortuary Monument

"D"-shaped building
Probably for royal mortuary activities

Courtyard

Palace Compound,
perhaps abandoned or
functionally transformed

B

First Phase: Royal Palace

Terrace wall may have created a closed hall
at some times in the history of the palace

Roof

Courtyard extended farther to the west

Earlier courtyard floor

Roof

Room,
possibly later

Megalithic wall

Elite residential
buildings with
polychrome walls

Elongated, multilevel hall
and palace complex
placed on pyramid

A

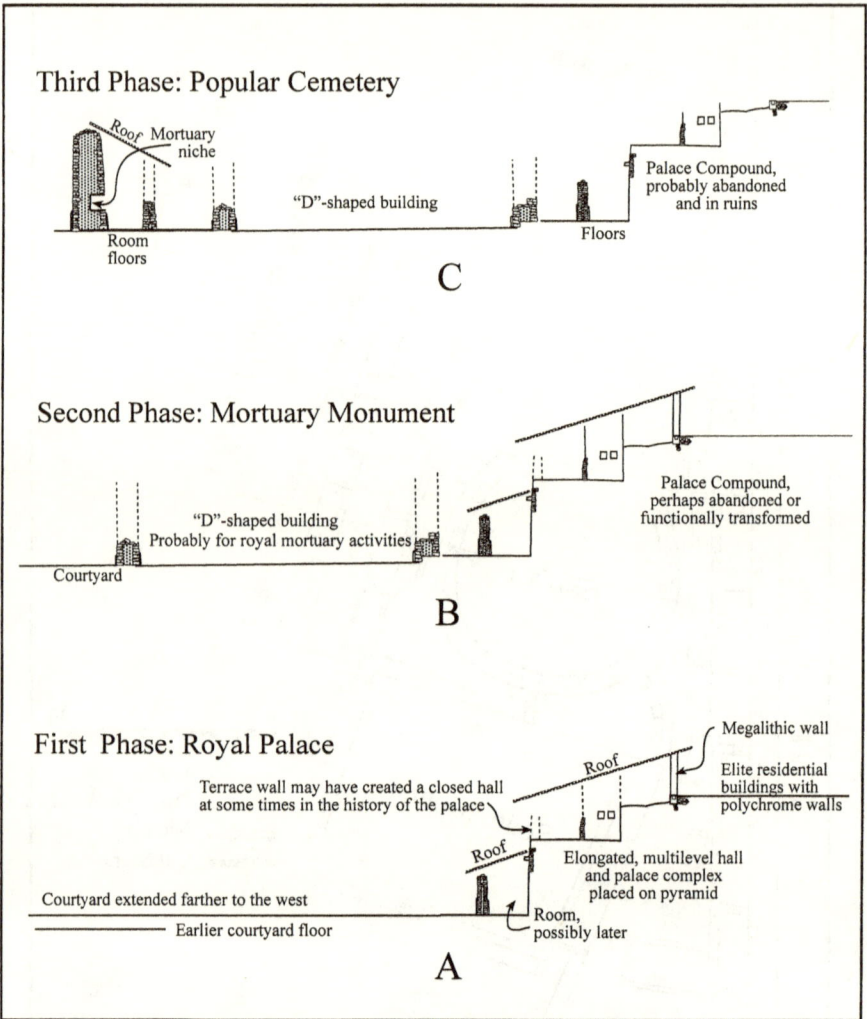

FIGURE 2.6 Formal and functional transformations of the Vegachayoq Moqo palace complex, Huari

wide and may have had a stairway or ascent on the rear, or eastern, side. At the south end, a smaller and lower mound projected some 30 m toward the west. In the north, where the least excavation has been conducted, it seems that another mound projected west to complete the three-lobed, U-shaped volume, but this northern mound was partially demolished to make way for the west wall in the final rebuilding episode.

Vegachayoq Moqo's courtyard was one of the earliest features of the building. Below its plastered floor was an older floor with pottery belonging to the

Huarpa style, which ended around A.D. 550 (Figure 2.6A). The triple mound is probably at least as old as the second courtyard floor. On the top, above the two terraces, was a megalithic stone wall of fine ashlars. Eventually, most of these stones were taken away for reuse elsewhere, but in the early phase, the wall probably stood tall, creating an elongated hall resembling an Inka *kallanka* (Figure 2.7).

The first terrace of the pyramid at Vegachayoq Moqo is about 5 m tall. Its surface was 6.1 m wide and originally more than 35 m long—perhaps as much as 60 m in length. It is surmounted by a second terrace, originally probably 2 m high, that reached the top of the mound. The surface of the lower terrace has huge masonry rectangles a little more than 2 m², with pairs of small niches in their sides, abutting the wall of the second terrace. These solid objects have been called altars, but they are too tall to have fulfilled that ceremonial function. More likely, they were pilasters that supported the long *kallanka*-like roof.

The elegant ashlars of the wall on top of the pyramid were removed long ago, leaving only foundations. Today this foundation consists of several groups of fine blocks, with rough-stone masonry filling spaces between the sets of expertly shaped stones. Some of the ashlars have holes cut in their top edge resembling mortises, which probably anchored the upper courses of blocks. I suspect that Vegachayoq Moqo's dressed stones were taken away

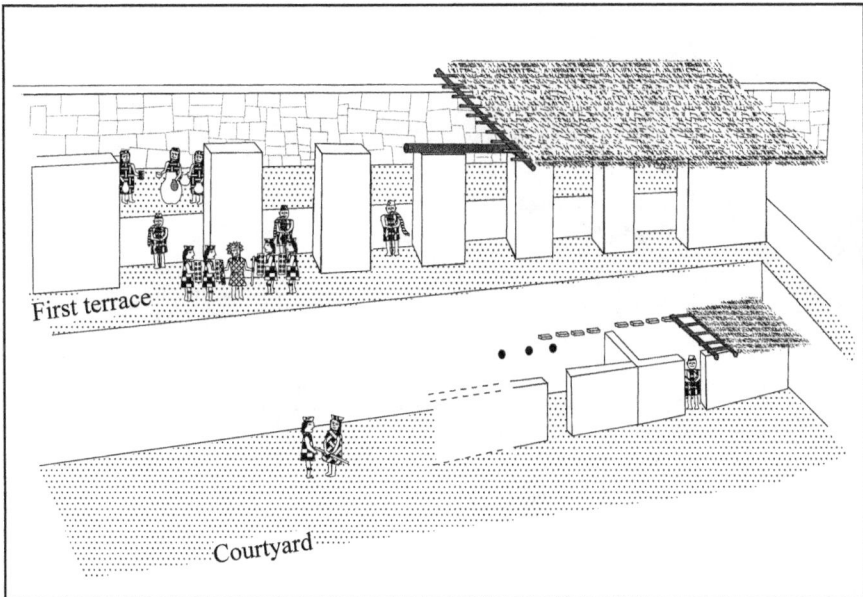

FIGURE 2.7 Vegachayoq Moqo palace plaza, hypothetical reconstruction

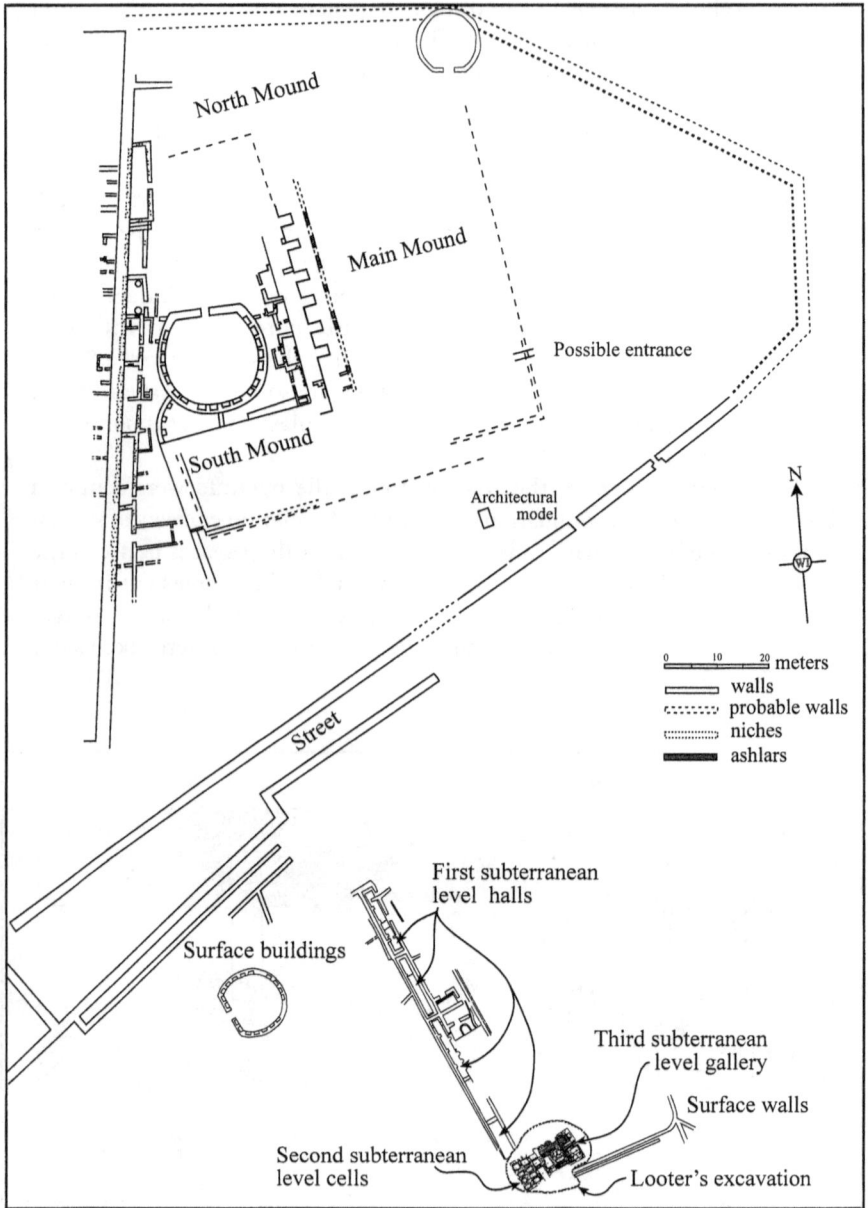

FIGURE 2.8 Vegachayoq Moqo palace and Monjachayoq royal tomb, Huari

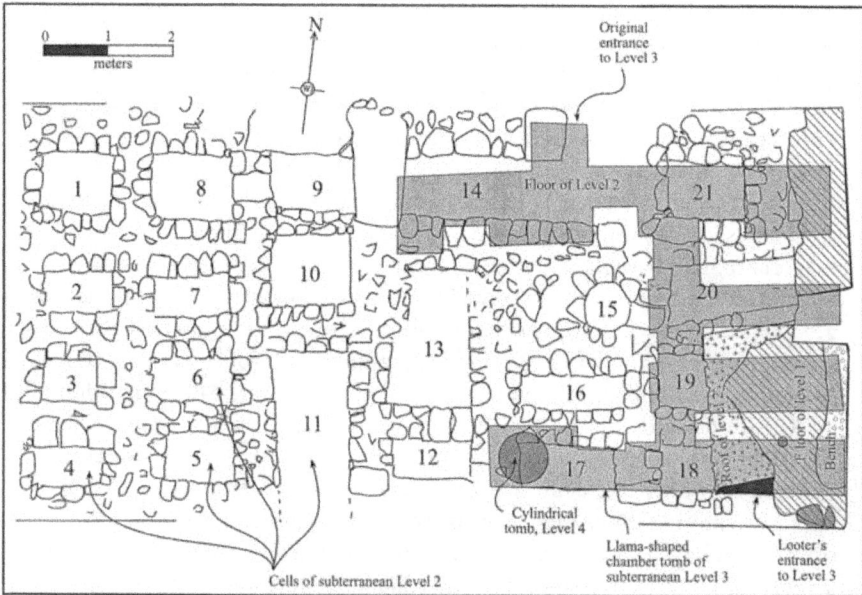

FIGURE 2.9 Monjachayoq, probable royal tomb, showing second and third subterranean-level cells and chamber tomb

during its transformational history, probably when it ceased to function as a palace. Indeed, many beautifully finished ashlars were reused in rough-stone walls here and there about Huari. Wendell Bennett (1953:24–25) observed this reuse of cut stones and argued that dressed-stone masonry preceded rough-stone construction at Huari, a conclusion with some merit, although it oversimplifies the situation.

I suspect that in Vegachayoq Moqo's first architectural era, one side of an expansive roof rested on the fine ashlar wall (Figure 2.7). This roof also rested on the pilasters discussed above, creating a fine covering over the long terraces that rose from the courtyard. This created an elongated building similar to a *kallanka*, open to a ceremonial courtyard, except that it consisted of an upper and a lower floor.

Fully roofed, Vegachayoq Moqo's terraces were an excellent assembly hall similar to the *kallanka* of Inka palaces. But if Vegachayoq Moqo was a palace, at least in its initial existence, where were its elite residences? Only two small excavations have been conducted behind the ashlar wall on top of the pyramidal mound. One, against the east side of the wall, revealed an ancient floor. The second excavation was located about 10 m east of the wall. It produced clay walls with decorations modeled and painted in red, green, and yellow (Figure 2.6A). The excavation was quickly filled to prevent the destruction of these decorations (González et al. 1996:35–37), and excavation has never been resumed. But there can be little doubt that such elaborate wall finishing indicates special buildings—and probably elite residences.

The early architectural forms at Vegachayoq Moqo (Figures 2.6A and 2.7) resemble Inka palaces and, even more, the "pyramid with ramp" palaces of Peru's central coast (Eeckhout 1997, 1998a, 1998b, 1999a, 1999b, 2000; Isbell 2004b). As in both of these palace traditions, Vegachayoq Moqo appears to have been securely walled, with one or two gateways. It had a large courtyard with a raised platform or stagelike complex at one end. There is no evidence for a ramp, but Vegachayoq Moqo's ramp may have been removed when a D-shaped building was constructed in front of the pyramid platform (Figures 2.5 and 2.6B). Alternatively, the prominent ramp of central-coast pyramid palaces may have come from T-shaped pyramid palaces of Peru's north coast, in which case ramps may never have been part of a Wari palace tradition.

A third feature of palaces at Vegachayoq Moqo is the platform pyramid that forms a U-shaped backdrop at one end of the courtyard. Architectural features crowning late central-coast palace pyramids also form a U-shaped enclosure around an exalted seat for the *curaca*, albeit smaller in size. Indeed, Vegachayoq Moqo's roofed terraces would have been an excellent assembly hall as well as a stage from which a king, surrounded by dignitaries, could represent himself as exalted over his subjects, who were gathered in the courtyard below (Figure 2.7).

At Vegachayoq Moqo, differences in vertical space were clearly employed to create social distinction, just as in Peruvian central-coast palaces. Of course, the Inka rarely built multistoried structures, so they emphasized inside-outside contrasts more in the construction of social difference. However, the use of spatial strategies to affirm difference in rank is a key element of palace landscapes.

At least several areas of Vegachayoq Moqo were abandoned relatively early in the history of this building. Portions of the architectural complex were covered with clean, light-colored earth, emphatically proclaiming change.

We can help confirm that Vegachayoq Moqo was a palace by showing that a royal tomb was located very close by. Across the street bordering the south side of Vegachayoq Moqo is the Monjachayoq sector of Huari (Figures 2.8 and 2.9; Pérez 1998b, 1999; Solano and Guerrero 1981). Surface architectural remains are poorly preserved, at least in part because of intensive looting. Near the north edge of the area are several elongated constructions and a sizable D-shaped building with 18 big niches. Toward the south there was a huge building, but only a few walls and a rounded corner have survived. Between these locations are enormous looters' holes exposing three layers of truly spectacular subterranean chambers.

The first subsurface complex consists of four halls, end to end, of well-made rough-stone masonry with massive dressed-stone slabs for roofs. Originally these halls seem to have been about 1.6 m high and about 1.4 m wide. At the south end of the hall complex is an enormous looters' hole that was reexcavated in 1998 by archaeologist Ismael Pérez (1998b, 1999). Pérez discovered a second level of subterranean construction that must originally have been covered by the complex of halls. This second subterranean level, 3 m below the hallway floors, consists of an architectural block containing 21 cells or small chambers (Figure 2.9). It was constructed of rough stonework combined with dressed-stone blocks, and capped by huge ashlars about 50 cm thick. Many of these capping blocks have disappeared. There is also evidence that extracted stones were recut using iron chisels, so apparently large-scale looting was carried out in colonial times.

Four meters below the complex of cells is a third subterranean level—a large megalithic gallery of complex shape, seeming to represent a llama in profile (Figure 2.9). Pérez (1998b, 1999) observed that the entry shaft was at the mouth of this symbolic animal. Finally, at the tip of the llama's tail is a still deeper element that might be considered a fourth subterranean level. It is a cylindrical shaft or cist-tomb, lined with rough stonework, 3.7 to 4 m deep and 1.2 m in diameter, with a flat stone lid that once sealed its opening.

The llama-shaped gallery (Figure 2.9, shaded area) was also looted in Spanish colonial times. Today it contains rocks and earth that must have fallen into the chamber after it was opened. Fragmentary and disturbed human bones lie among this rubble, all of which is in need of careful investigation. However, I am convinced that Monjachayoq represents a royal tomb. This complex of subterranean architecture is reminiscent of royal burial platforms at Chan Chan, which consist of a grand chamber and numerous secondary cells (Conrad 1982). The major difference is that the Huari sepulcher is completely underground—a royal catacomb, with difference in size and depth expressing relative status between the chambers.

It is unlikely that the royal tomb at Monjachayoq was the grave of the king who reigned from the Vegachayoq Moqo palace. A wooden lintel in one of the leg-shaped sections of the llama gallery produced a radiocarbon date in the mid-eighth century, uncalibrated.[7] Although it is possible that this lintel represents a late repair to the Monjachayoq royal tomb, I believe that the chamber belongs to the end of Middle Horizon Epoch 1 or early Epoch 2, about a century after the palace phase at Vegachayoq Moqo. However, a royal grave in the same sector of Huari as Vegachayoq Moqo promotes the argument that this was a sector of royal residences and tombs, even if we do not know where the king who ruled from Vegachayoq Moqo was buried.

A potential tomb site of the Vegachayoq Moqo king is an extremely salient feature in the palace courtyard: a large D-shaped building (Figures 2.5 and 2.6B). This distinctive structure measures about 19.8 m across and has 18 huge niches in its wall.

D-shaped buildings appear to be ceremonial structures peculiar to Ayacucho and the early rise of Wari. Examples are known from Huari (Benavides 1991; Isbell et al. 1991; Meddens and Cook 2001; Pérez 1999) and its Ayacucho neighbors, Conchopata (Isbell 2001b; Ochatoma and Cabrera 1999,

2001; Pozzi-Escot 1991) and Ñawinpukyu (Machaca 1997:Figure 2.7). Outside the Ayacucho Valley, D-shaped buildings have been discovered at Yako in southern Ayacucho (Meddens and Cook 2001), at Cerro Baúl in the southern coastal Moquegua Valley (Williams et al. 2001), and at Honcopampa in the Callejón de Huaylas (Isbell 1989, 1991a). All of these sites were probably Huari provincial installations. Anita Cook (2001) argues that D-shaped buildings relate to the construction of power by emerging kings, providing special contexts for sacrifices to dead royalty. If she is correct, then Vegachayoq Moqo's D-shaped structure would seem to relate to a second phase in the building's history, when it functioned more as a mortuary monument to the deceased king than as his palace.

Unfortunately, the excavation of Vegachayoq Moqo's D-shaped building did not explore the stratigraphy of its foundations, and we have no radiocarbon dates to show when it was constructed relative to the sequence of courtyards and pyramid mounds. However, the D-shaped building breaks the symmetry of the Vegachayoq Moqo palace, and its floor is higher than the rest of the courtyard. I believe that it was added after the courtyard and pyramidal mounds served as Huari's royal palace, in a second architectural phase (Figure 2.6B).

At some time in the architectural history of Vegachayoq Moqo, a number of rooms were built against the base of the first terrace of the long pyramid (Figures 2.5 and 2.7). They are not bonded to the pyramid, so they probably represent late additions to the architecture of Vegachayoq Moqo. Perhaps they were built during the palace phase, but they could have been added during the mortuary monument phase of Vegachayoq Moqo's existence.

Another highly salient architectural feature at Vegachayoq Moqo that breaks the symmetry of the courtyard and pyramid complex is a massive wall bounding the courtyard on the west, at least during the final history of the building complex (Figures 2.5 and 2.6C). Clearly, this wall was a late addition, and I believe that the courtyard originally continued to the west far beyond it. This thick west wall does not align with the other buildings, and the northern mound was cut away to accommodate it. At its northern end, the wall turns west, away from the Vegachayoq Moqo mound. In fact, it might even be considered part of another building complex except for its niches and rooms, which definitely became part of the Vegachayoq Moqo courtyard. Perhaps in this third construction phase at Vegachayoq Moqo the focus of activity had shifted to the west, and away from the U-shaped mound. The palatial facilities may already have been interred, and numerous megalithic ashlars from the top of the terraced pyramid may already have been carried away for use in new constructions within the city.

Facing into the Vegachayoq Moqo courtyard, the west wall has a row of at least 25 large niches (Figure 2.5). They measure about 98 × 98 cm, and one unlooted example contained the bones of four secondary burials with deformed skulls, tied into bundles. Many other burials and human ossuaries were sealed up in this wall. Some of the tombs contain simple pottery that may postdate the Middle Horizon, but at least one burial, discussed above, included diagnostic Middle Horizon pottery, along with fine Huari textiles, proving that some of the burials were made while the city was still a thriving center.

A few of the burials in Vegachayoq Moqo's west wall had attractive artifacts. However, many of the human remains were interred without anything of significance. Consequently, the cemetery function of the west wall included individuals of modest social status, certainly not just elites.

Elongated rooms were constructed against the great western wall, intruding into Vegachayoq Moqo's courtyard. Their masonry is consistently inferior to the rooms on the east side of the court, further implying that they were lower-status additions to the building complex late in its history. Probably, they relate to funeral rituals of the commoners interred in the wall during the third phase of the architectural history of Vegachayoq Moqo, when it was a popular cemetery. I infer that the great west wall represents the end of Vegachayoq Moqo's architectural history. Apparently the building complex had ceased to function as a palace and as the mortuary monument of a great king. It was a cemetery where the bones of individuals of much more modest means were placed—and in at least some cases, it served as a place for secondary burials after the flesh had disappeared.

Evaluating the palace identification, Vegachayoq Moqo shares several features with Pachacamac as well as Inka palaces. Its emphasis on elevation to create spatial difference is more consistent with coastal Pachacamac elite residences. Vegachayoq Moqo was a walled enclosure, where the residential area was further secured by raising it on a platform. It had at least one large court and a long, covered area within a U-shaped architectural complex for ceremonial occasions. A residential area with numerous rooms probably existed on top of the pyramid mound, but there does not seem to have been room for a zoo or garden area beyond. Several parts of the building were retired by interment, and late in the history of the compound it served mortuary functions, initially probably for royal mortuary activities and eventually followed by commoner burials. A great subterranean chamber—so large that it can hardly be anything but a royal tomb—in an adjacent compound across the street strengthens the inference that this part of Huari was occupied by several royal palaces.

A Royal Palace at Conchopata

Conchopata was the second-largest city in the Middle Horizon Ayacucho Valley (Figure 2.2). It may never have exceeded 20 hectares in area, so at its maximum it was no more than 10 to 20 percent of the extent achieved by the city of Huari. Not surprisingly, what I identify as a palace at Conchopata is smaller than Huari's Vegachayoq Moqo. Furthermore, the Conchopata palace is probably about a century later than Vegachayoq Moqo. A burned roof beam from the floor of the inner courtyard produced an uncalibrated radiocarbon date late in the eighth century.[8] If this represents wood cut for the final roofing of the palace, it must already have been occupied for decades, but perhaps no earlier than about A.D. 700, uncalibrated.

With its earthen platform, the Vegachayoq Moqo palace was built to emphasize vertical as well as horizontal differences in space. However, the remains of the building tentatively identified as a palace at Conchopata lack platforms or terraces, appearing to have been as flat as Inka palaces. Of course, multistory construction is indicated for some Middle Horizon architecture of the Huari-Conchopata tradition, so the vertical dimension may have figured in the spatial geometry of Conchopata's palace. But the remains excavated at Conchopata to date do not imply second floors.

The building tentatively identified as a palace at Conchopata seems more consistent with Inka than with Pachacamac canons, providing the opportunity for a systematic comparison of its architectural configurations with the ideal list of diagnostics for Inka palaces.

1. *Careful enclosure of the palace complex by strong walls.* Excavations at Conchopata in 2000 showed that the core of the site appears to have been enclosed by a more or less rectangular perimeter wall (Figure 2.10). Within the great enclosure there seem to have been smaller compounds, some doublewalled, and each perhaps with its own orientation. The exact form of the architectural core is still difficult to determine until more excavation is completed, but it consisted of walled compounds built according to plans, not organic urban landscape where rooms and patios were added cumulatively.

2. *An outer plaza and an inner patio that decline in size as access became more restricted.* An orthogonal cellular building in the northeast portion of Conchopata has a central patio about 13 × 17 m in size. Its entrance probably faced the west but was destroyed by the construction of a modern house. Immediately to the west of the patio is a confusing but apparently open area I have named the North Ambit (Figure 2.11). Two more or less oval ceramic kilns in this area belong to an earlier construction phase and were probably not in use when these courtyards defined the space of a royal palace. Farther west we have identified an area named the Pink Plaza. So, an architectural complex might have included a set of courtyards running from the Pink Plaza to the patio group, with open spaces declining in size as access was increasingly controlled.

3. *Imposing and defensible gateways, portals, or passages controlling access to each courtyard.* No gateways are known at Conchopata that might have been entrances into a palace. However, we do not really know what the plan of a Conchopata-Huari gateway should look like. It is clear that gateways to central-coast palaces were walled and baffled mazes, usually of adobe. On the other hand, Inka gateways were characterized by megalithic masonry capped by a monumental lintel. We must learn more about Middle

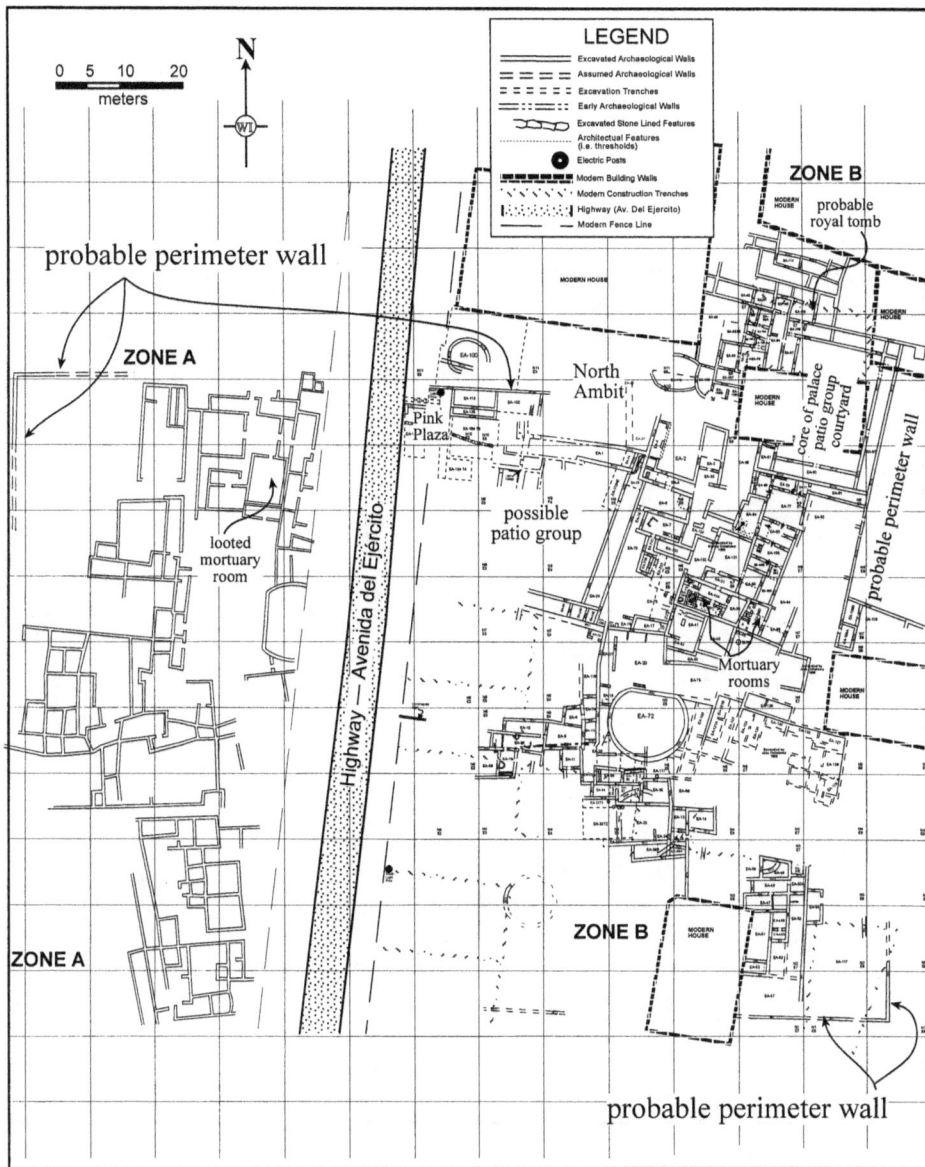

FIGURE 2.10 Conchopata excavation zone, showing probable perimeter wall

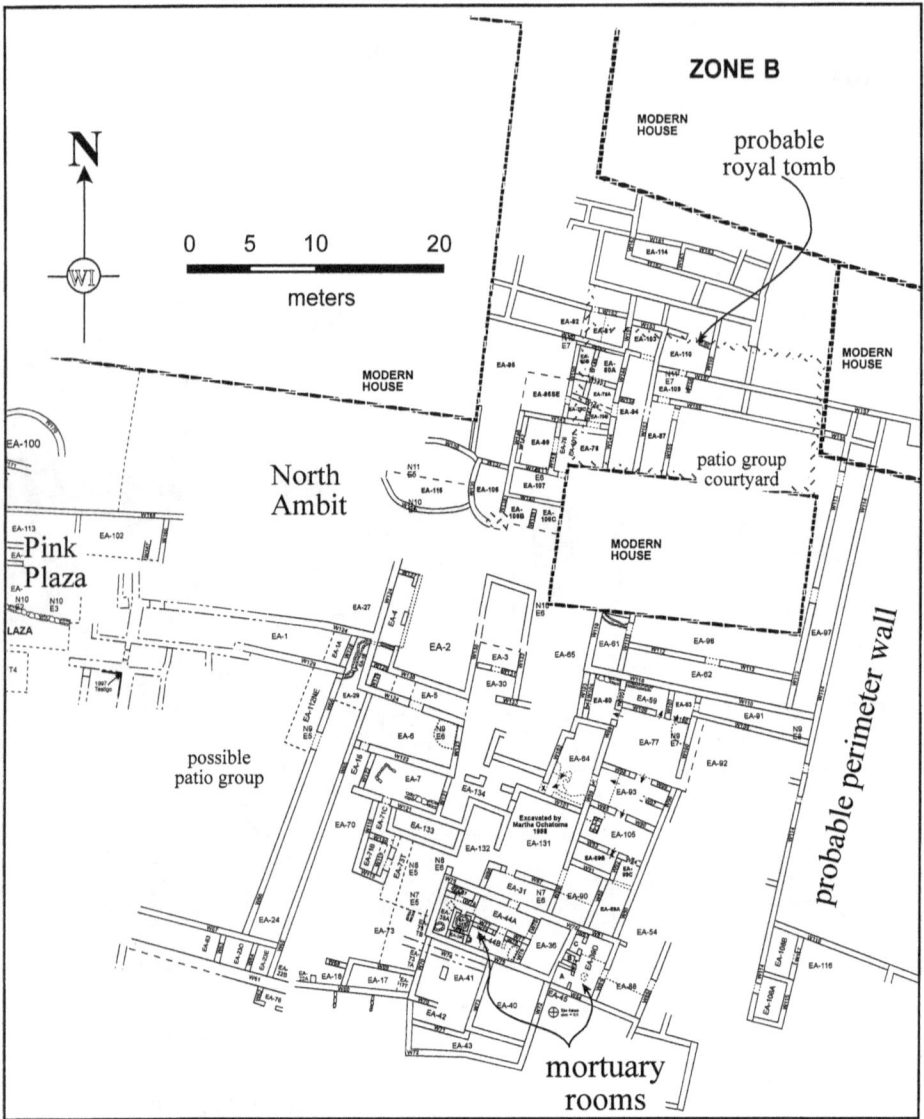

FIGURE 2.11 Conchopata royal palace map

Horizon Ayacucho architecture before the issue of palatial gateways can be evaluated. Of course, in the case of the palace complex at Conchopata, the most probable location for a gateway is covered by a modern house.

4. *Various special-function buildings around the first plaza and the second patio, where noble captains awaited commissions from the king and administrative business could be conducted.* If the North Ambit or the

Pink Plaza constituted the larger plaza, and the patio group enclosed the smaller patio of a palace, it appears that special-function rooms bordered these spaces. Elongated rooms enclose the patio group, and other elongated structures border the Pink Plaza and the North Ambit, at least along the south side, which has been excavated. Much of the north side of this important area is covered by modern construction. More should be learned from future excavation, but it is likely that a Conchopata palace had buildings appropriate for the activities of state bordering its assembly spaces.

5. *A proliferation of elaborate and relatively private residential buildings associated with or beyond the second courtyard, probably including a water source and a bath.* The number and size of private rooms or residential compounds associated with the patio group is one of the things that most supports the inference that this portion of Conchopata functioned as a royal palace, or at least some kind of expanded elite household. Two or more spacious residential complexes are attached to the south side of the patio group. Each consists of interconnected rooms effectively separated from its neighboring residential compound group. Each compound is organized around an open courtyard and includes one or more kitchens, rooms with low benches —probably for sleeping—and other domestic spaces. One patio, EA-2, has a nicely constructed canal entering it. Originally, I assumed that the canal functioned as a drain, but the gradient shows that it brought water into the courtyard, not away from it. Although we did not find the kind of sunken chamber characteristic of most Inka baths, this feature could have furnished bathing water for Conchopata's royal family members.

6. *Large halls in front of, or as part of, the entrance to the palace. These buildings housed the palace guard and also furnished roofed space for public ceremonies during rainy weather (Inka halls of this type are frequently called* kallanka *or* carpawasi*).* Large halls in front of Conchopata's probable palace include both EA-2 and EA-65 (Figure 2.11). Unfortunately, so much of Conchopata has been damaged by Middle Horizon rebuilding, and then by a modern road, house, and other constructions, that we still cannot define the palace's front entrance. But several spacious enclosures are associated with the most probable gateway location.

7. *Superior architecture as well as artifacts, especially among the relatively private residential rooms.* None of the buildings at Conchopata are impressive by cross-cultural standards or even by comparison with the great walled compounds of the contemporary Huari city. But if survival into modern times is any indicator, the structures of Conchopata's architectural core significantly exceeded the quality of buildings beyond the core and at neighboring Huamanga Basin sites such as Ñawinpukyu and Acuchimay. The patio group and residential compounds to its south are well made, sturdy, and spacious. Many, if not all, of the walls were coated with clay and finished with white plaster. Some have traces of red paint. Many floors are of hard white plaster or of red clay. Furthermore, artifacts from these rooms, and

especially from their graves, are of high quality. A definite conclusion is premature until a range of building classes has been defined for the Conchopata-Huari architectural tradition, but it is certainly possible that the buildings excavated at Conchopata do represent superior architecture containing elite artifacts.

8. *Space for a garden and zoo beyond the area of private rooms, probably with its own water supply.* Archaeological excavations at Conchopata have not revealed a space associated with the patio group or its residential compounds that would accommodate gardens and a zoo. Of course, there is much that remains to be excavated, and an unoccupied area appears to have existed immediately east of the patio group that might have accommodated gardens and a zoo. However, gardens and a zoo are characteristics only of the Inka palace. They were not characteristic of Pachacamac palaces and may never have been associated with any but the palaces of the grandest potentates. This issue requires more investigation before meaningful conclusions can be drawn.

9. *Location for the mummified body of a king within the palace structure. After the death of a king his body was mummified and treated more or less as though it were still alive. It was kept within the royal palace, and there is no indication that significant architectural modifications, such as construction of a royal tomb, were required.* Inka ancestor worship dictated that the living should venerate the bodies of their deceased ancestors. Consequently, important cadavers were not buried but were sheltered in dry places where mummification was encouraged. The mummies of ancestral founders, rulers, and high nobles were especially important for their descendants' claims to lands and other resources, as well as their spiritual access to fecundity, health, and well-being. All these depended on fulfilling obligations to founding ancestors (Isbell 1997a). The mummies of Inka kings, and apparently those of their close relatives, were kept in the palaces they built during their life, where their descendants could attend them and enjoy the estate the ancestor had accumulated. Consequently, dead Inka kings occupied the mansions and holdings where they had lived.

The Conchopata palace differs from the Inka palace in that there is no evidence for mummies, royal or other, being venerated within residences of the living. However, the deceased of the Conchopata palace were kept close to home, at least the high-status dead, and it is possible that even though buried, they continued to interact with the living.

Three kinds of tombs have been found within the rooms that appear to constitute Conchopata's palace. The two more prominent types are *bedrock cavity interments* and *mortuary building interments* (Isbell 2001b, 2004a; Isbell and Cook 2002). Bedrock cavity interments consist of deep tombs excavated into the bedrock that underlies the site. All examples discovered were located under the floors of buildings, some probably residential rooms, and contained several individuals. Bedrock cavity tombs have different forms, probably because shape was determined by fissures and cracks that made it easier to cut a sepulcher into the rock. Some examples are similar to shaft tombs, and others are simply amorphous holes with small openings. During the 1999 and 2000 excavations, examples of bedrock cavity interments were discovered below Rooms EA-9, EA-31, EA-64, EA-77, and EA-105.

Mortuary building interments are even more elaborate than bedrock cavity interments. The two mortuary buildings excavated at Conchopata in 1999 and 2000 were both severely disturbed, meaning that information is incomplete and confusing. However, Conchopata's mortuary buildings resemble rooms at Moraduchayuq, Huari, that contained burial cists (Isbell et al. 1991), and they should probably be included in the same class. In other respects, Conchopata's mortuary buildings resemble monumental chamber tombs at Cheqo Wasi, Huari. They consist of groups of more- and less-megalithic chamber tombs that were enclosed by rough-stone walls (Benavides 1984, 1991; Pérez 1999). If all of these constructions are classified as mortuary building interments, we create a class that ranged from simple rooms with several burial cists to truly megalithic mortuary complexes. I believe that this broad class of interment type has much to teach us, but for this discussion I base my description on the two mortuary buildings excavated within Conchopata's palace (Isbell 2001b; Isbell and Cook 2002).

Conchopata's two palace mortuary building interments included numerous individuals placed in several tombs within the same room or complex of rooms. Characteristically, the burials were placed in cylindrical or cubical stone-lined cists that were capped with a heavy rock slab. Generally, this lid had a circular hole or deep notch communicating into the cist, which was probably sealed with a stone plug shaped like a champagne cork and inserted into the hole. It may be that in each mortuary building, one cist was primary and the others were secondary. Some cists contain the remains of more than one individual, but all the cists have been disturbed, so we only know that they contained human remains along with grave furnishings.

Both the capped cists of mortuary rooms and the bedrock cavity tombs seem to have been designed to be opened relatively easily, and it seems from both their form and contents that at least some of the tombs were reopened frequently. We excavated an untouched bedrock cavity interment containing 15 individuals. The final burial, placed near the mouth of the grave, disturbed earlier burials, scattering their bones. The position of the bones suggests that connective tissue was still holding some of the skeletal parts together when they were disturbed, so time intervals between grave openings were probably not terribly long. In addition, some individuals in the tomb were incomplete, showing that skulls and other bones were probably removed after the flesh had disappeared.

Finds of ossuaries containing collections of skulls at both Huari and Pikillacta (Benavides 1991; McEwan 1987) suggest that some defleshed bones were destined for communal ceremonial deposits. It is also possible that some defleshed skeletons were removed more or less completely from reopened tombs. Secondary bundle burials in a large niche at Vegachayoq Moqo, Huari, document another destination for defleshed human bones (Bragayrac 1991). Human long bones and secondary burials placed in the walls of certain buildings (Topic and Topic 1992; Zapata 1997) may represent yet another way of treating the remains of the deceased, although such practices are yet to be documented at Conchopata. However, what is apparent at this early point in the investigation of Conchopata-Huari mortuary behavior is that there is a great deal of evidence for the manipulation of defleshed human bones, and this is a practice that was not described for the Inka.

The unlooted bedrock chamber interment containing 15 individuals that was excavated in Room EA-105 of the palace residential area included 6 adult women (one pregnant), 2 fetuses in jars, 3 infants, part of a child, a juvenile, 1 adult male, and an incomplete skeleton whose sex and age could not be determined (Tung 2003; Tung and Cook 2002). I believe that the grave represents the interment of a high-status male, probably a nobleman, with his wives and infant children. The male skeleton was seated deep in the cavity tomb, with fine offerings. The final burial, a woman near the mouth of the tomb, may have been a wife who outlived her husband by many years. Interestingly, the male skeleton was never disturbed by the removal of bones. Perhaps this is not surprising. If an ancestor's bones were used in rituals that affirmed the status of descendants, in a highly polygynous society, many half siblings would share the same father. Consequently, mothers would determine differences in rank among close kinsmen. We need only remember the importance of mothers in Inka society. There was no question that Huascar was Huayna Capac's son, but to confirm him as heir to the Inka throne, his mother had to become Huayna Capac's primary wife.

All mortuary buildings discovered so far at Conchopata and Huari have been looted, so it is impossible to determine what burials were placed in their cist graves. However, at Conchopata, most of the remains from mortuary rooms represent women. As in the bedrock cavity interment, I believe that mortuary rooms were intended for important men, who occupied the primary cists, and were surrounded by their wives, infant children, and perhaps servants. Presumably, the bedrock cavity interments and mortuary building interments in Conchopata's palace represent high-status nobles.

A third type of tomb at Conchopata is represented by a single example on the north side of the patio group courtyard of the palace. It was more severely damaged than any other tomb. A small copper belt buckle from deep within Room EA-87 suggests that this looting took place in the nineteenth or early twentieth century. The looters emptied a huge chamber below Room EA-110. What remains today is a great cavity cut into the bedrock, about 2 m wide and longer than the room (the cavity continues under the east wall of EA-110, beyond our excavations). Disturbed fill in adjacent rooms, particularly EA-109, EA-104, and EA-94, contained numerous fragments of human bone, pieces of luxury objects, and miniature ceramic vessels—tiny replicas of oversize offering urns.

The bedrock cavity in EA-110 is beyond the magnitude of other graves excavated at Conchopata. If it was a tomb, and if we consider it within the parameters of other mortuary facilities at Conchopata, it is reasonable to infer that we have discovered a supreme sepulcher, probably the grave of a *curaca* or king. Unfortunately, looters of the past century plundered everything of value and destroyed almost everything of interest in their search for wealth. But the large bedrock cavity, the fragmentary human bones, and the occasional luxury objects imply the original function. This huge cavity tomb appears to document a level of wealth and power beyond anything indicated previously. It reveals a paramount or royal ruler.[9]

The probable palace at Conchopata, like Inka palaces, appears to have fulfilled royal mortuary functions, although treatment of the dead was significantly different from Inka mummies. There are, of course, features of the Inka palace that are absent at Conchopata, but this probable palace exhibits enough diagnostics to at least support its interpretative classification as a royal palace of Wari style.

Rural Estates and Hinterland Palaces

Huari and Conchopata both appear to have had one or more palaces in the early centuries of the Middle Horizon. What is more, there are reasons to think that Huari's Vegachayoq Moqo was but one palace within a regal sector of that ancient city. Even the Conchopata palace may not have been the only example in its civic center. The next question is, were other palaces involved in the production of Wari royal power? I believe the answer is yes, for there is evidence of a more extensive regal landscape.

A Wari settlement at Aqo Wayqo (Cabrera 1996; Ochatoma 1988) was destroyed by the expansion of modern Ayacucho during the 1980s and 1990s. It probably represents a rural Wari community. The ruins consisted of a southern sector with small rooms of rough-stone masonry attached to one another that were probably residences and work spaces. A northern sector contained larger, elongated rooms organized around an approximately rectangular space. This larger residential complex also included graves and several kinds of offerings suggesting occupants of moderately high status.

Several of Ayacucho's other hinterland Wari settlements have buildings similar to those of Aqo Wayqo, but they also include a very distinctive kind of architecture that was not found at Aqo Wayqo. The buildings resembling Aqo Wayqo constructions belong to what I call cumulative residential architecture. The buildings unlike those of Aqo Wayqo are of planned orthogonal architecture.

Cumulative residential buildings consist of complexes of small rooms

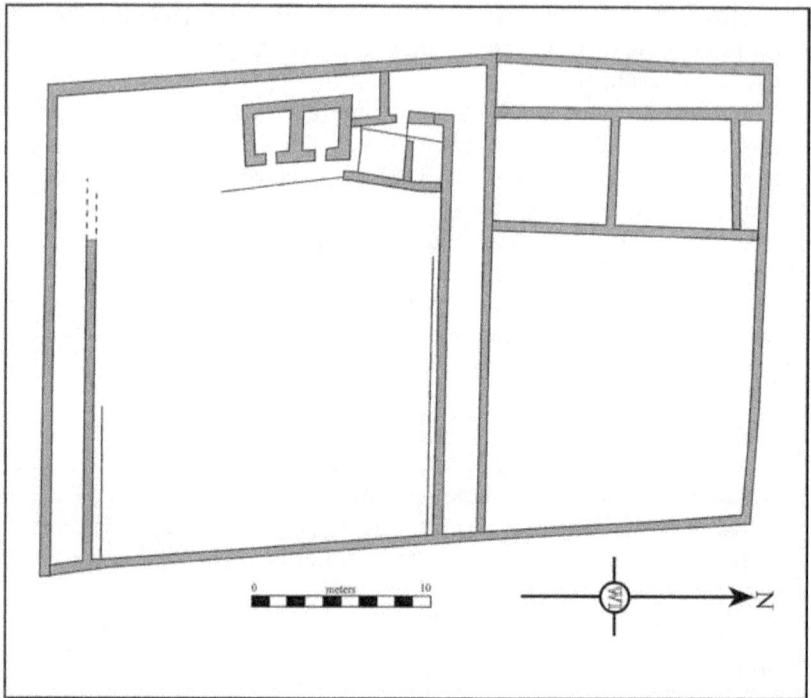

FIGURE 2.12 Jargampata hinterland palace estate, north unit of planned orthogonal architecture. Redrawn from Isbell 1978:FIGURE 6.

constructed one after another. After erecting a small rectangular building, subsequent rooms were constructed by adding two or three walls to one side of the older room. By this means an agglutinated complex of rooms gradually took shape. In many cases, there are several nuclei of cumulative residences a short distance from one another. Cumulative architecture could easily be erected with nothing more than family organization, and its sequence of additions probably expresses the growth of a household social group. Planned orthogonal architecture consists of a rigidly rectangular compound with a large patio or plaza in one sector and orderly room complexes in another. Orthogonal compounds were built in one or two construction phases, probably employing communal labor, for family organizations would find it difficult to mobilize enough workers to collect the construction materials and assemble so much masonry, to say nothing of maintaining the formal plan.

Jargampata was the first and smallest example of planned orthogonal architecture excavated in the Huari hinterland (Figure 2.12). It is actually located in the neighboring San Miguel Valley, across a high mountain pastureland, about 35 km from Huari (Isbell 1977). The walk would have taken no more than two days (Figure 2.2). Just below Jargampata the San Miguel Valley broadens, and irrigation canals originating at that point can water several hundred hectares of fertile land located between 2,200 and 2,500 meters above sea level. This is ideal for the production of semitropical crops, but particularly corn, which was so important for brewing beer for political and ceremonial reunions.

The ruins at Jargampata include two architectural groups, one a planned rectangular enclosure and the other a residential compound of cumulative architecture, placed some 15 m from one another. The planned compound consisted of a square enclosure, about 25 m to a side, to which a smaller rectangle about 14 m wide was subsequently attached (Figure 2.12). Sample excavations showed that elongated lateral rooms were located along the north and south sides of the main enclosure. These rooms had a low, narrow bench running the length of the wall where it joined the patio, which made a good work surface and a good seat during public assemblies. In the northwest part of the enclosure were rooms with residential debris, including an especially well-built pair of rooms. The north rectangle, attached to the initial enclosure, also seems to have contained residential rooms.

The architecture of the rectangular compound was constructed in two building periods, and each was carried out in accord with a formal plan. Ceramics from the planned enclosure included the same range of vessel shapes present in the cumulative residential architecture, but in different frequencies (Isbell 1978, 1984, 1985, 1987, 1988; Isbell and Schreiber 1978). In the residential compound, open vessels most appropriate for serving constitute about 45 percent of the assemblage. Necked vessels more appropriate for cooking and storage constitute another 45 percent, and vessels with special shapes make up the remaining 10 percent. In the planned compound, the open shapes total almost 60 percent, whereas necked vessels are only about 30 percent of the inventory, with the other 10 percent made up of vessels with special shapes. I infer from these relative frequencies that activities in the planned compound emphasized serving food and drink over storage and cooking activities. Consequently, it seems likely that this enclosure and its sizable patio were employed during public eating and drinking events, at least often enough to generate a significant amount of refuse. This probably represents feasting, a principal activity expected of Andean kings and nobles.

The second architectural compound at Jargampata is a domestic room complex constructed in numerous additions (Figure 2.13). Farther away are facilities such as hillside terraces and what may have been a reservoir for storing water.

Years ago I argued that Jargampata represented an administrative compound (Isbell 1977), although I did not attempt to determine the nature of the administrators. Recently, I have become increasingly convinced that Jargampata was the center from which agricultural production on the adjacent

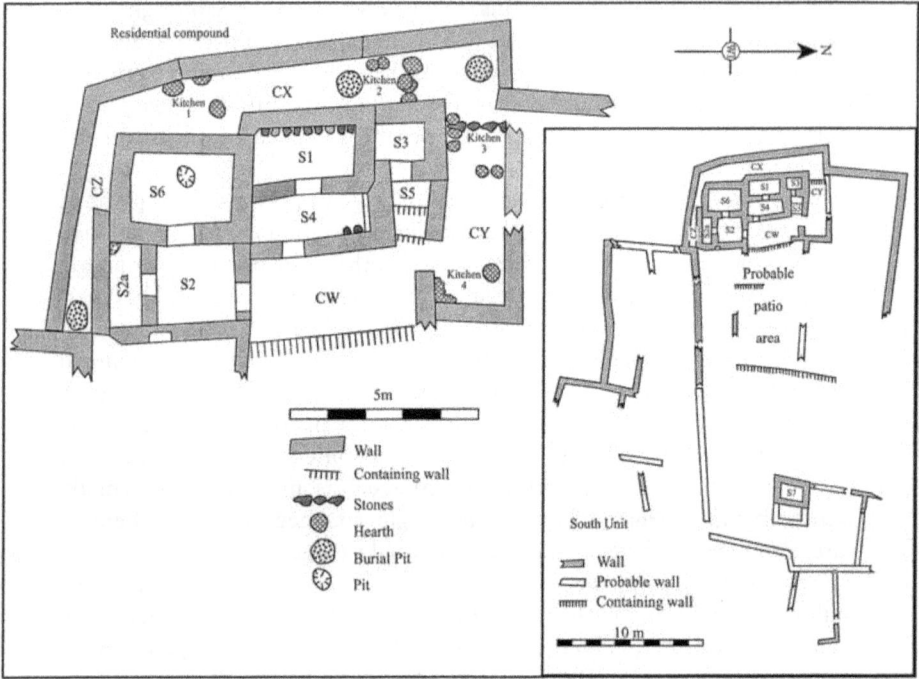

FIGURE 2.13 Jargampata hinterland palace estate, south unit residential house group. Redrawn from Isbell 1977:FIGURE 4.

irrigated bottomlands was managed, and that it was probably the rural estate of a Huari king or nobleman. I suspect that the rectangular enclosure was a work space that doubled as a place of assembly, including festivals at which workers were treated to the generosity of their lord. Initially, the *curaca* or king could have resided in the western rooms when visiting, but the addition of the north rectangle provided a significantly larger space for housing family and guests during country recesses.

Jargampata's cumulative residential architecture was probably the residence of intermediate-status retainers. Though not particularly fancy, this building complex is certainly more sturdy and elaborate than the perishable homes of the modern peasants who occupy the San Miguel Valley. Perhaps the inhabitants were overseers for the proprietor, in charge of workers residing in more modest homes. If so, I infer that these foremen were responsible for organizing farming on surrounding lands for the benefit of the *curaca* or noble.

Radiocarbon dates place the occupation of Jargampata somewhat later than the Vegachayoq Moqo palace, and probably overlapping with the Conchopata palace (Isbell 1977).[10] Ceramics from Jargampata are primarily Middle Horizon Epoch 2 (Knobloch 1991).

If Jargampata included a planned architectural compound that might have been part of a king's hinterland estate, Azángaro is a vastly more impressive complex that may have been a rural royal palace (see Anders 1986, 1991). Azángaro is located in the low Huanta Basin, a little less than 20 km from Huari (Figure 2.2). Like Jargampata, it is in prime bottomland ideal for corn and other irrigated crops. Its planned orthogonal enclosure is huge, measuring 175 × 447 m, and divided into three sections (Figure 2.14). The northern part was subdivided into patio groups with lateral rooms. A royal family and entourage could have resided comfortably in such buildings, although some of this architecture appears unfinished.

The central sector contained 20 rows of small buildings attached to their neighbors. A street runs down the center, and there is a corridor in front of each row of rooms. This probably housed workers, although storage functions are also implied by a row of stone corbels around the little rooms that seem to have supported an upper floor a short distance above flagstones set on the ground.

Azángaro's third sector was a large open courtyard. This was probably an assembly place like the patio of the compound at Jargampata. However, someone built a complex of residences in the middle of this patio that are characterized by the same kind of cumulative architecture that appears in Jargampata's domestic buildings. A second set of cumulatively constructed houses was located in the entranceway into Azángaro's rectangular enclosure. Could overseers have lived in the middle of the communal patio, and in the only apparent entrance to the big compound? Certainly there was still

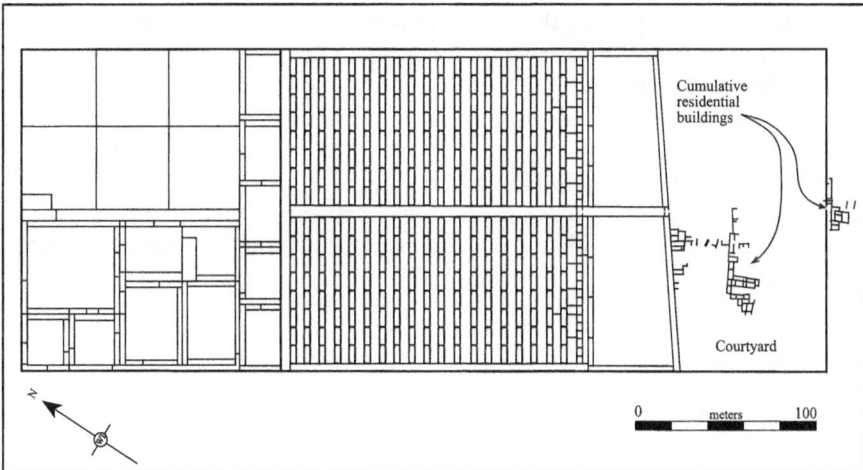

FIGURE 2.14 Azángaro hinterland palace estate with planned orthogonal architecture and cumulative residential architecture. Redrawn from Anders 1986:Figures 3.1–3.4.

ample open space in the plaza, but it may be that activities and functions at Azángaro changed, perhaps in relation to the life and death of the ruler, as I suggested for the Vegachayoq Moqo palace.

Ceramics from Azángaro are in the styles of Middle Horizon Epoch 2 (Knobloch 1991). Radiocarbon dates suggest that its architectural outlines were complete and that the central sector was occupied only a few decades after the principal occupation at Jargampata. But activities continued at Azángaro for more than a century, with the latest occupation in the cumulative residential buildings (Anders 1986:622–624).[11]

Before we pass to provincial capitals, there is another recently excavated Ayacucho Valley building complex that, in my opinion, has not been recognized as the rural Huari palace or mansion that it almost certainly was. Marayniyoq (Valdez et al. 1999) is located only about 5 km northeast of Huari (Figure 2.2), at midvalley elevation rather than on low valley bottomlands. However, a prosperous hacienda was located there until the agrarian reform of the late 1960s, and the majestic old hacienda house is no more than a few hundred meters from the archaeological ruins. Apparently the Marayniyoq area is still attractive to elites, for it has fine agricultural lands watered by canals from the high lakes above the east side of the valley.

To date, archaeological excavation has been conducted in only one small area to reveal Marayniyoq's most impressive relics: parts of a megalithic floor composed of giant, perfectly fitting, dressed-stone slabs (Figure 2.15). In the future, the entire site should be defined and its complex occupational history determined, including an inventory of the massive stone slabs removed for paving in the modern hacienda house[12] and others that were left in place but reused as grinding stones.[13] Actually, the name Marayniyoq means "grinding place," showing that this is almost certainly a modern function for the site. The selective destruction focusing on the most monumental construction materials has left Marayniyoq only a shadow of its original self. Although there are no radiocarbon dates for the site, I am convinced that it was one of several mansions or royal estate palaces ringing the ancient city of Huari during Middle Horizon Epoch 2. An investigation of the Huari suburbs should be undertaken in the future to further our understanding of the urban periphery and to place the Marayniyoq discoveries into better cultural contexts.

Provincial Palaces: Pikillacta and Viracochapampa

Most Andean prehistorians believe that Huari conquered a sizable empire during the Middle Horizon. The material evidence consists of widely distributed Wari artifacts, especially ceramics, textiles, and religious iconography. Also during the Middle Horizon, Wari peoples invented and diffused a new architectural style known as the orthogonal cellular horizon (Isbell 1991b). The buildings are characterized by rigidly orthogonal enclosures, subdivided

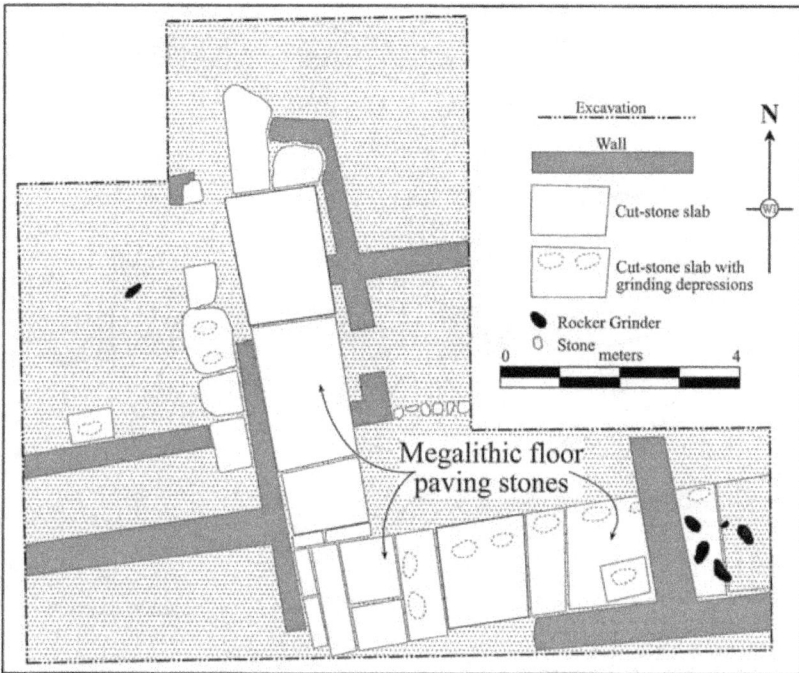

FIGURE 2.15 Marayniyoq hinterland palace estate excavation area. Redrawn from Valdez et al. 1999:FIGURE 2.

into smaller rectangular or square compounds. The internal organization of the smaller compounds follows a limited number of standard patterns, creating a cellular structure of repeating modular units, especially the patio group consisting of a central court surrounded by elongated lateral rooms.

Orthogonal cellular architecture is known at Huari (Isbell 1997b, 2001a; Isbell et al. 1991), at Conchopata (Isbell 2001b; Isbell and Cook 2002), and at many more distant sites. The orthogonal cellular sites far from the Ayacucho Valley were obviously intrusive, and they have been interpreted as provincial administrative centers. Some provincial towns, such as Honcopampa (Figure 2.16; see also Figure 2.1), have only modestly developed orthogonal cellular features, although the basic building form is the Wari patio group (Isbell 1989, 1991a). Other sites possess irregular versions of orthogonal cellular architecture, such as Cerro Baúl (Moseley et al. 1991; Williams et al. 2001; Williams and Nash 2002) and perhaps also Huaro (Glowacki and McEwan 2001). The most rigidly orthogonal cellular of the sites are Jincamocco (Schreiber 1991, 1992), Pikillacta (McEwan 1991, 1996, 1998a), and Viracochapampa (J. Topic 1991). Pikillacta and Viracochapampa are huge sites far from Huari, located in major Andean valleys, very well preserved, and at least partially investigated. They are consummate Wari provincial

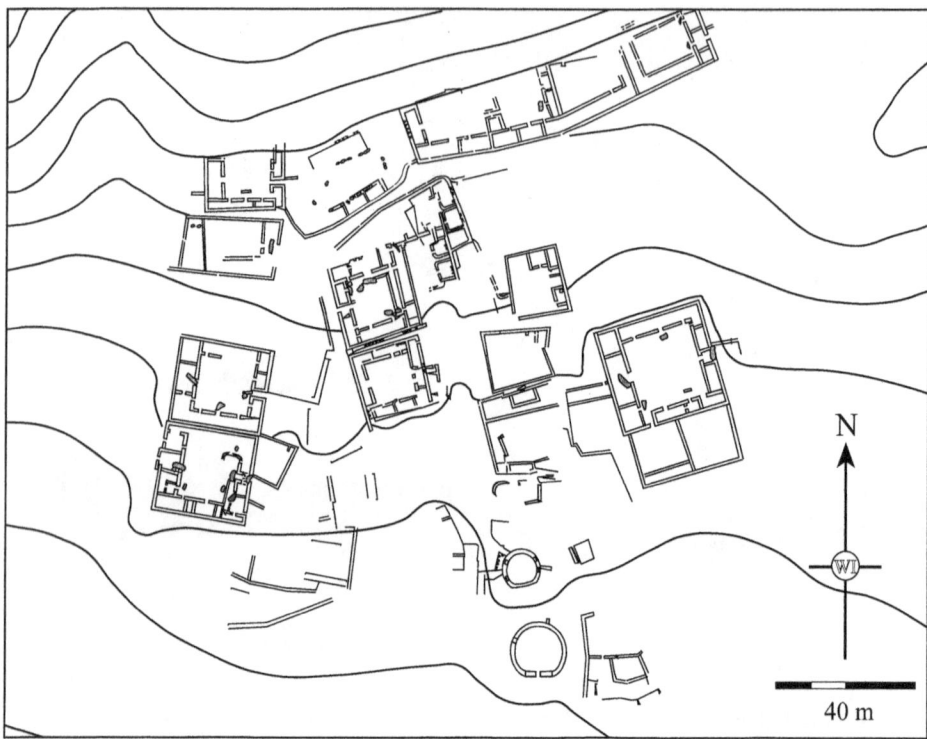

FIGURE 2.16 Honcopampa map of palaces in civic center

administrative capitals, and I believe that they are best understood as vast palace complexes.

Pikillacta (Figure 2.17; see also Figure 2.1) is the best preserved and most thoroughly investigated of all the Wari provincial centers (McEwan 1984, 1985, 1987, 1991, 1996, 1998a, 2005). Its orthogonal cellular construction consists of a few modular architectural forms that were repeated over and over within a rectangular grid of cells. At the exact center of Pikillacta is an unusually large central cell that has a courtyard measuring about 50 × 70 m, surrounded by narrow rooms as well as two great *kallanka*-like buildings. Following John Topic,[14] archaeologist Gordon McEwan (1998b) calls these buildings "niched halls" (Figure 2.17). This courtyard and niched-hall complex may be large enough to be considered Pikillacta's central plaza, even though it was enclosed and separated from the rest of the city by high walls and echelons of narrow rooms.

The center of Pikillacta was densely built up, but there are open spaces along the northwestern and southwestern sides of the great rectangular enclosure. Archaeological excavations show them to be empty or to contain typical architectural forms that were never completed (McEwan 1996, 1998a).

Some archaeologists argue that this means that Huari's administrative centers were abandoned before they were completed, but this perspective fails to recognize the transformational nature of Wari architecture. It looks to me as though the Wari architects designed Pikillacta for a sequence of changes that would take several generations to unfold. Apparently, within the original design, undeveloped land was enclosed for future construction of modular units.

Viracochapampa (Figure 2.18; see also Figure 2.1) is the second-best preserved of Huari's provincial administrative centers (J. Topic 1986, 1991). It is strikingly similar to Pikillacta, except that it has more open areas for future development. Besides its huge perimeter wall and interior orthogonal cellular layout, the greatest similarity is Viracochapampa's large central cell, with a courtyard that measures about 75 × 90 m. It was walled and surrounded by rooms, including two enormous *kallanka*-like niched halls.

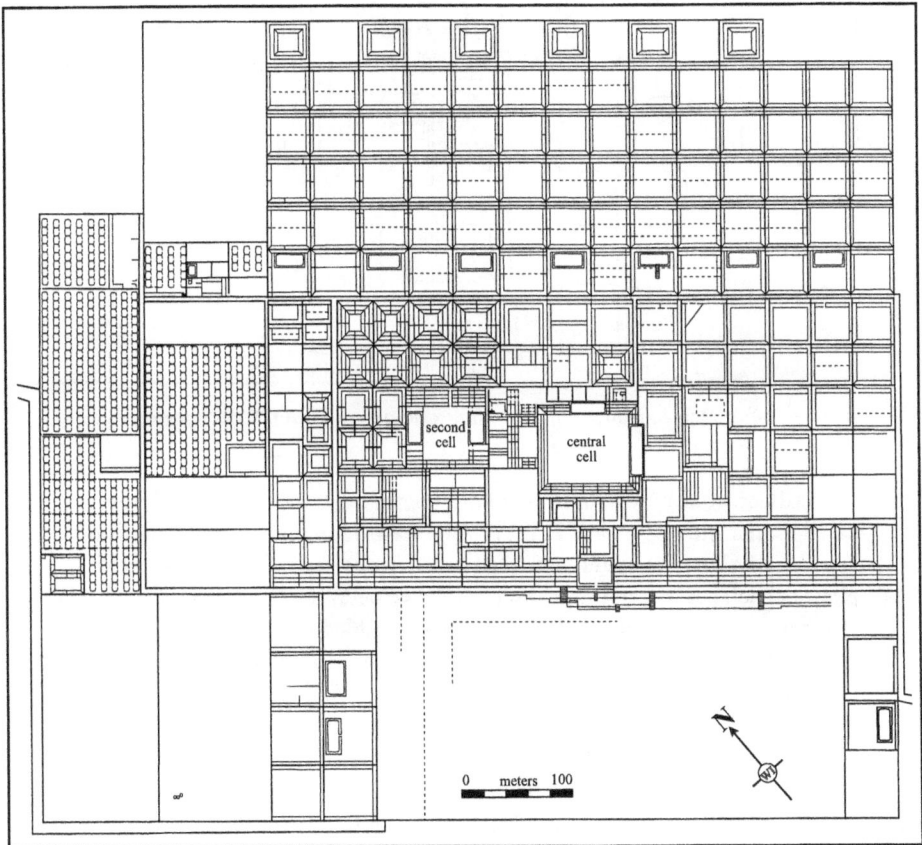

FIGURE 2.17 Pikillacta palace complex. Redrawn from McEwan 2005:Figures 4–7.

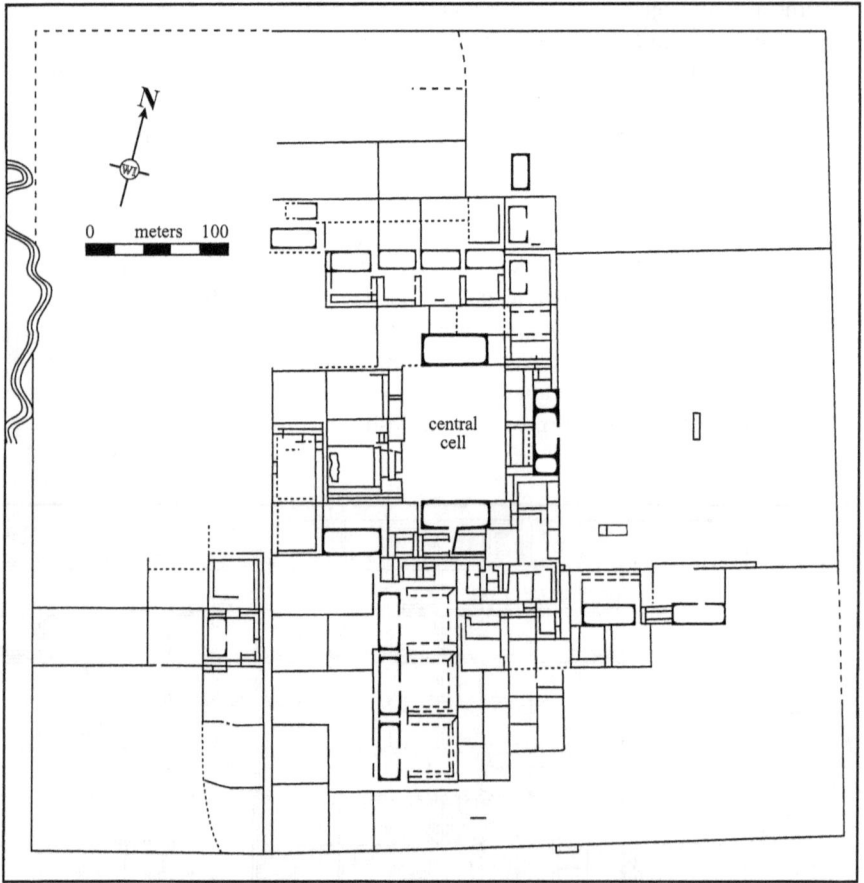

FIGURE 2.18 Viracochapampa palace complex. Redrawn from J. Topic 1991:FIGURE 2.

Pikillacta and Viracochapampa both have a central cell bordered by elongated rooms and two niched halls. If Middle Horizon niched halls functioned like Inka *kallanka*, providing roofed space for palace celebrations, then the plaza of each central cell would seem to have been the courtyard of a palace. Furthermore, if provincial Wari palaces resembled central-coast palaces in the use of elevation to signal social difference, it is likely that the walls forming echelons of narrow rooms around these courtyards were intended to support capacious second-floor halls.[15] Even the entrances into the palace compounds may have been at the level of the second floor, so the floor plans of these Wari provincial centers may be deceiving archaeologists about the original circulation of traffic, to say nothing of room sizes and forms.

Pikillacta and Viracochapampa differ from one another in that much of Pikillacta's architecture not immediately surrounding the central cell appears to be associated with a second cell of larger-than-normal size. It has numerous echelons of narrow rooms about it, as well as two large niched halls (Figure 2.17). Significantly, this second cell seems to duplicate the central cell on a slightly smaller scale, and it is located a modest distance from the center of Pikillacta's great perimetric enclosure.

Because Pikillacta's second large cell so nearly duplicates the form of the central cell, I suggest that it fulfilled the same social and ceremonial functions. Both were palace complexes. As presented above, I suspect that both sites had open space intended for a sequence of transformational additions. The architectural evidence suggests that Pikillacta experienced two of the intended phases. The initial palace complex was replaced by a second palace complex. By contrast, Viracochapampa has only one central cell, and it has a great deal of open space close to the central palace cell. I infer that Viracochapampa contained only one palace complex, although it was designed for a similar sequence of palace additions.

If I am correct, what can we say about Pikillacta and Viracochapampa? First, the central cells at Pikillacta and Viracochapampa were palaces of kings or powerful governors. Second, at the moment of construction, Huari's provincial administrative centers were intended to function as palaces that would undergo a sequence of transformations. One palace complex would be replaced by another within the great rectangular enclosure. By analogy with Inka Cuzco, Chimu's Chan Chan, and arguments about Huari's Vegachayoq Moqo presented above, a palace may have become a mortuary monument in its second phase. However, elite burial at Huari and Conchopata implies the veneration of tombs, and perhaps the removal of defleshed bones from elite tombs, not royal mummies as among the Inka. If Vegachayoq Moqo is an adequate model, former palace mortuary monuments eventually became common cemeteries.

What can we say about the dating of Pikillacta and Viracochapampa? Radiocarbon dates for Pikillacta run from the mid-sixth century to the mid-ninth century A.D. (McEwan 1991:111–112), whereas ceramics belong primarily to Middle Horizon Epoch 1B styles (Knobloch 1991). Though a bit confusing, this seems to indicate that early construction at Pikillacta overlapped with the late occupation of Vegachayoq Moqo but continued long after. Viracochapampa has not been excavated enough to provide dates, but its similarity to Pikillacta suggests that the two palaces were contemporary.

Conclusion

Archaeologists have not emphasized the study of palaces in the Andean past, but it seems that there is a rich and extensive record of regal buildings that participated in the construction of a royal landscape of power. In this chapter I sought to expand knowledge of palaces in the Inka capital into a broader Andean tradition by examining Middle Horizon Huari. The nascent condition of palace research demanded a detour into the issue of how Middle Horizon palaces should be identified. Critical examination of a Tiwanaku building classified as a palace showed that the criteria employed were too idiosyncratic to permit a subsequent comparative study of Andean palaces. A more solid basis of study was required.

My definition of lists of formal characteristics for both Inka and Pacha-camac palaces puts archaeologists on a more rigorous track for identifying royal residences in the Andean past. While many problems remain to be resolved, these criteria helped identify a number of probable Wari palaces. Provisionally identified Wari palaces and royal estates must be investigated more extensively, but if I am broadly correct, this chapter reveals a remark-ably complex web of elite residences, creating nothing less than a royal land-scape for the production and maintenance of regal power. This, in turn, pro-vides us a material record for investigating the nature and development of regal power, for, of course, king and palace are interdependent. *King* refers to a social institution of rule, while *palace* refers to a spatial and architectural machine where power was generated.

Vegachayoq Moqo represents the earliest Middle Horizon royal palace yet identified, and it is the best example from Huari itself. Very important is the hint, implied by a probable royal tomb at Monjachayoq across the street from Vegachayoq Moqo, that it was located within an entire sector of royal palaces at Huari. So perhaps Cuzco, described as a civic center composed of royal palaces, was not at all unique among Andean capital cities. Perhaps palaces were the fundamental building blocks of Andean urbanism.

I suspect that the palace form developed at Vegachayoq Moqo was influ-enced by niched halls from the north highland Huamachuco Valley (Topic 1986). John and Theresa Topic (Topic and Topic 1992) argue against a regal type of government in Huamachuco prehistory, but increased understanding of palaces and other royal facilities may permit us to critically examine this issue. Of course, Wari kings could have employed architectural forms asso-ciated with confederations as they expanded control through militarism and conquest. Furthermore, the history of Wari palace form may be much more complex than we can currently appreciate. By A.D. 600, the Huari capital was surely in contact with many contemporary civilizations, from Tiwa-naku in the south to Pampa Grande in the north (Figure 2.1). Kings and royal architects probably had a wealth of novel architectural ideas with which to experiment.

Huari's Vegachayoq Moqo palace seems to have shared features with both Inka and central-coastal Pachacamac palaces. It is likely that the tradition emerging at Huari was ancestral to both later palace types. But we need a great deal more investigation. At present, we are in danger of confirming our suspicions though circular reasoning.

The most surprising discovery of this study is the transformational nature of Wari palaces. This is particularly clear at Vegachayoq Moqo, Pikillacta, and Viracochapampa, but it could also be true of Conchopata. Was formal and functional transformation of buildings an old peculiarity of Wari culture, coming perhaps from ancient ideas about the cosmos? Or was architectural transformation a new ideology for concentrating power in the hands of monarchs? Whatever the case may be, Wari royal authority was associated with a cosmological vision founded on a concept of change in the human universe. But chaos and mutation were securely under the control of the engine of power, the royal palace. Whether the rhythm of change was generational, dynastic, or something we don't yet understand, enclosed palace space tamed the chaos of change. Of course, palace-based control of cosmic change made the future predictable by assuring continuity in royal power.

We need excavation-based studies of more palaces at Huari and Conchopata, including the buildings associated with the royal tomb at Monjachayoq. Within our current tiny sample, the second-oldest palace is not from Huari but is probably at Pikillacta, a provincial center. Viracochapampa is probably contemporary, although it seems not to have been occupied as long. Next oldest is probably the palace at Conchopata.

The Conchopata palace is later than Vegachayoq Moqo and generally contemporary with at least the later occupation at Pikillacta. By comparison with Pikillacta, the Conchopata palace is small and modest. Even Vegachayoq Moqo is significantly larger than the Conchopata palace. This may mean that the Conchopata palace was a secondary or subsidiary palace, occupied by a ruler subordinate to the king at Huari. This could be tested with comparisons of public space, residential area, and mortuary architecture, but what we know at present is out of balance, since most of our knowledge of the Conchopata mansion comes from residential and mortuary remains, and most of what we know of Vegachayoq Moqo seems to relate to public and ceremonial space.

At Conchopata there are hints of a large, rectangular perimeter wall, or perhaps a series of smaller perimeter walls, around complexes of buildings that maintained similar orientations (Figure 2.10). Could Conchopata have been a Pikillacta-like center in the Ayacucho Valley, certainly less rigidly orthogonal cellular in form, but a planned space that was gradually filled in with a succession of palaces? If a patio group courtyard and an elite mortuary building identify Conchopata palaces, another example may have been located immediately west of the Conchopata palace we have been excavating (Figure 2.10).

Were the palaces at Pikillacta and Viracochapampa regal residences for *curacas* of newly created kingdoms, or the palaces of governors subservient to Huari? Additional study is needed, but we can make an educated guess on the basis of information presented here.

Royal hinterland estates about the capital were surely essential parts of the power wielded by the Huari monarchs or *curacas*. Estate palaces probably document power backed up by force. I suspect that the rural estates provided *curacas* with agricultural wealth that was theirs to use as they chose. Such a resource, cleverly employed, could go far toward freeing a king from consensus with noble kinsmen and leaders of other great houses as a prerequisite for action. Furthermore, overseers, foremen, and workers on royal estates would have depended on the king alone. Since dependence promotes loyalty, the royal estate provided the *curaca* with a body of followers, who were potentially troops who could be counted on unconditionally. While a conscript militia might refuse to take the part of the king, retainers from his hinterland estate could be ordered into action, and the wealth produced could be used to hire mercenaries. Finally, the royal rural estate provided the king a protected place to which he could retreat in case of threat, and where he could entertain other nobles to construct alliances of mutual support. Being entertained at a wealthy rural estate would make it clear that an alliance was with the king himself, not his office or empire.

Rural estates may document growth in royal power within Huari, for they seem to belong only to the second part of the Middle Horizon. Both Jargampata and Azángaro have only hints of Epoch 1B occupation, but most of their ceramics and dates are consistent with Middle Horizon Epoch 2. Such centers deserve a great deal more investigation. But with this in mind, it is significant that I cannot identify anything resembling a Huari rural estate around Pikillacta or Viracochapampa. If Huari kings depended on their rural estates for power, and if new kingdoms were established at Pikillacta and Viracochapampa, these new monarchs would surely have created hinterland estates for themselves. For this reason, I suspect that Pikillacta and Viracochapampa were Huari provincial palaces occupied by governors whose power was limited.[16]

No rural estates have been identified around Conchopata. Of course, many sites have been damaged by the expansion of the modern city of Ayacucho, so we must make more effort to collect whatever information remains. At present, however, it seems likely that the *curaca* residing in the palace at Conchopata had no hinterland estates. Apparently, he did not wield the quantity and quality of power available to his counterpart at Huari. Whatever the relationship, we can probably conclude that Conchopata's king was subservient to the Huari king, at least by Middle Horizon Epoch 2.

I have no doubt that some of the great monuments at Huari's sister city of Tiwanaku supported royal palaces on their apexes. More research is required at Tiwanaku sites, but I can find only one example of what appears to be a provincial palace within Tiwanaku's sphere of influence. Identified as a temple (Goldstein 1993), this palace is located at Omo, in the coastal Moquegua Valley (Figure 2.1). Not only does it seem to be unique in Tiwanaku's provincial domain, but it is tiny by comparison with Huari's Pikillacta and Viracochapampa. Perhaps even more important, I know of no sites around Tiwanaku that have the kind of architectural facilities associated with Huari's royal hinterland estates. Certainly, there are sites with monumental ceremonial masonry and even megalithic sculptures. But we know of no planned facilities that might have served as rural mansions for Tiwanaku kings, and from which they and their servants could have administered agricultural production. Even preliminary information about palaces and royal estates implies a fundamental difference between the quality and quantity of power in the hands of Huari rulers as opposed to Tiwanaku's rulers. If they could not back up their authority with force, Tiwanaku's potentates may indeed have been priestly lords.

The investigation of pre-Inka Andean palaces is only beginning. This preliminary study suggests that Huari had developed a regal landscape dominated by royal palaces of diverse forms and functions. Operating synchronically, the network of Wari palaces promoted powerful kingship. Diachronically, the transformation of Wari palaces ensured continuity of leadership and power. Huari's *curacas* apparently enjoyed many of the prerogatives of later Inka kings. They were strong and effective agents backed by spatial and architectural engines capable of producing the power required to rule.

Notes

1. Huari is spelled in two ways, Huari and Wari. The name refers to the type site and capital of an ancient state/empire and to various regional manifestations throughout the Central Andes. I have proposed that to avoid confusion, "Huari" be employed for the type site and ancient capital, the empire ruled from it, and all archaeological remains from the capital (Isbell 2002, 2004a). By contrast, "Wari" should be used for the broadly dispersed culture, including the archaeological remains from other sites and locations throughout the Central Andes during the Middle Horizon.

2. Hydrological studies (Ortloff 1996:164–165) show that it is impossible for a sacred center to have been defined within the city of Tiwanaku by a moat filled with water. Standing water within the city of Tiwanaku would have waterlogged the entire urban terrain.

3. The Tiwanaku polity must have included subjects numbering in the hundreds of thousands, and perhaps more. But the Palace of the Multicolored Rooms, 8 × 22 m in size (Kolata 1993:Figures 5.36a, 5.36b) is no larger than the home of the Natchez's Great Sun—about 12 × 16 m—who ruled only some 4,000 persons.

4. This model infers that each pyramid with ramp was a religious embassy, explained more or less as follows. The influential deity of a successful shrine like the one at Pachacamac would be an attractive object of veneration for neighboring peoples, who might petition for a representative of the deity in their homeland. If the petition was accepted, an image and a priest (or several) would be sent. In this case, the recipient community would construct a temple facility in their homeland, providing it with economic resources—probably lands and/or herds as well as labor to develop them—for the benefit of the image and cult. Of course, the new image would be associated with the principal deity, probably by kinship (younger brother, son, wife, etc.), so the products of the junior image's lands and herds would belong to the principal deity as well. Many of these products would be passed on to the ceremonial center of the principal shrine, where members of the new community would establish a presence, working for the benefit of the principal image and participating in its rituals.

This would require the new community to construct itself an inn or "embassy" at the shrine center. At this embassy compound, representatives of the community, or its clergy, would receive and store tribute, assist community participation in ritual, house workers involved in sanctioned projects, perhaps conduct economic exchanges, and perform other activities. The model emphasizes the adaptive complementarity of Andean ecology as well as the goods from diverse communities that participated in Pachacamac's (and other shrines') politico-religious spheres (Bueno 1974–1975, 1982, 1983a, 1983b; Burger 1988; Jiménez 1985; Jiménez and Bueno 1970; Patterson 1985; Rostworowski 1972, 1989, 1992; Shimada 1991).

5. The uncalibrated dates are A.D. 640±50 and A.D. 670±50. Calibrated at 2 sigma, these dates are slightly later, A.D. 655–875 and A.D. 645–795.

6. Unfortunately, only the sides of this pyramid group facing the plaza have been excavated, and even those only partially, so the comprehensive form of this architectural complex remains unclear.

7. The date is A.D. 750±80. Two sigma calibration yields A.D. 665–1005.

8. The date is A.D. 780±60. Two sigma calibration yields A.D. 700–1000.

9. Excavations conducted after this chapter was written showed that the tombs in Room EA-110 and adjacent spaces consisted of a collection of cist graves like those of other mortuary building interments. However, gold was found among the severely damaged tombs, confirming that this grave group was very elaborate by Conchopata standards and probably contained the body of a ruler and his wives and closest relatives.

10. Two dates, A.D. 700±110 and A.D. 760±90, are close enough to confirm one another. They were calculated using the Libby half-life, so they should be considered about 30 years older, uncalibrated. A third date, A.D. 1220, may represent a reoccupation or a contaminated charcoal sample (Isbell 1977).

11. Three dates are A.D. 760±75, A.D. 880±50, and A.D. 990±65, uncalibrated. These dates were calculated using the Libby half-life, making them slightly older than indicated.

12. Today, several of the large paving slabs lie in the courtyard of the abandoned hacienda house. Apparently many more were removed in the past, leaving only a shadow of the original grandeur at Marayniyoq.

13. The excavators of Marayniyoq (Valdez et al. 1999) argued that these remains represent a Huari state milling center. I firmly disagree, for the milling function does not account for the exquisite pavement of large rectangular stones (that do serve well as grindstones) alternating with well-fitted, narrow, and elongated stones (that do not serve as grindstones). Furthermore, there is abundant evidence for stone robbing, with reuse of the surviving megaliths for grinding in recent times.

14. The name "niched hall" was coined by John Topic (1986, 1991; see also J. Topic and T. Topic 1982, 1983, 1985; T. Topic and J. Topic 1984) to describe long, spacious buildings with large niches in the walls, which characterize the architecture of the Huamachuco Valley, especially the Middle Horizon sites such as Viracochapampa.

15. John Topic (1986) showed that Huamachuco's niched halls were sometimes two storied. One technique for supporting the second floor of the spacious hall was to divide the lower floor level into narrow rooms with walls that were intended to reach only the base of the second floor to support its beams. Topic calls this support a "septal wall." I suspect that Huari architectural forms, known almost exclusively from first floors that emphasize long, narrow rooms parallel to one another, may also have been septal walls for the support of upper floors. If this is correct, then where we see long, narrow cells in Huari architectural floor plans, second floors may have been sizable halls fit for assembly.

16. It is possible that Huaro, a Middle Horizon center some 20 km south of Pikillacta, was the hinterland estate of a monarch who ruled at Pikillacta. However, Mary Glowacki (1998; Glowacki and McEwan 2001) shows that Huaro was probably larger than Pikillacta, and it may have been settled at an earlier date. These data seem to contradict the inference that the impressive Huari occupation at Huaro could have been the hinterland estate of a king who established an independent, Huari-style state at Pikillacta.

References Cited

Alva, Walter
1988 Discovering the New World's Richest Unlooted Tomb. *National Geographic* 174(4):510–550.
1990 New Tomb of Royal Splendor. *National Geographic* 177(6):2–15.

Alva, Walter, and Christopher B. Donnan
1993 *Royal Tombs of Sipán.* Fowler Museum of Culture History, Los Angeles.

Anders, Martha Biggar
1986 Dual Organization and Calendars from the Planned Site of Azángaro: Wari Administrative Strategies. Ph.D. dissertation, Cornell University.
1991 Structure and Function at the Planned Site of Azángaro: Cautionary Notes for the Model of Huari as a Centralized Secular State. In *Huari Administrative Structure: Prehistoric Monumental Architecture and State Government,* edited by William H. Isbell and Gordon F. McEwan, pp. 165–197. Dumbarton Oaks Research Library and Collection, Washington, DC.

Benavides C., Mario
1984 *Carácter del estado Warí.* Universidad Nacional San Cristóbal de Huamanga, Ayacucho, Peru.
1991 Cheqo Wasi, Huari. In *Huari Administrative Structure: Prehistoric Monumental Architecture and State Government,* edited by William H. Isbell and Gordon F. McEwan, pp. 55–69. Dumbarton Oaks Research Library and Collection, Washington, DC.

Bennett, Wendell C.
1953 *Excavations at Wari, Ayacucho, Peru.* Yale University Publications in Anthropology, No. 49, New Haven.

Bragayrac Dávila, Enrique
1982 *Wari: Excavaciones en el sector Vegachayoq Moqo—Temporada 1982.* Informe al Instituto Nacional de Cultura, Filial Ayacucho, Peru.
1991 Archaeological Excavations in the Vegachayoq Moqo Sector of Huari. In *Huari Administrative Structure: Prehistoric Monumental Architecture and State Government,* edited by William H. Isbell and Gordon F. McEwan, pp. 71–80. Dumbarton Oaks Research Library and Collection, Washington, DC.

Brown, James A.
1990 Archaeology Confronts History at the Natchez Temple. *Southeastern Archaeology* 9(1):1–10.

Bueno Mendoza, Alberto

1974–1975   Cajamarquilla y Pachacamac: Dos ciudades de la costa central del Perú. *Boletín Bibliográfico de Antropología Americana* 37(46):171–211.

1982   El antiguo valle de Pachacamac: Espacio, tiempo y cultura (primera parte). *Boletín de Lima* 4(24):10–29.

1983a   El antiguo valle de Pachacamac: Espacio, tiempo y cultura (segunda parte). *Boletín de Lima* 5(25):5–27.

1983b   El antiguo valle de Pachacamac: Espacio, tiempo y cultura (tercera parte). *Boletín de Lima* 5(26):3–12.

Burger, Richard

1988   Unity and Heterogeneity within the Chavin Horizon. In *Peruvian Prehistory*, edited by Richard W. Keatinge, pp. 99–144. Cambridge University Press, Cambridge.

Burger, Richard L., and Lucy C. Salazar

2004   Lifestyles of the Rich and Famous: Luxury and Daily Life in the Households of Machu Picchu's Elite. In *Palaces of the Ancient New World: Form, Function, and Meaning*, edited by Susan Toby Evans and Joanne Pillsbury, pp. 325–358. Dumbarton Oaks Research Library and Collection, Washington, DC.

Cabrera Romero, Martha

1996   *Unidades habitacionales, iconografía y rituales en un poblado rural de la época Huari.* Tesis para optar el grado de Licenciado en Arqueología, Universidad Nacional San Cristóbal de Huamanga, Ayacucho, Peru.

Chang, Kwang Chih

1980   *The Shang Dynasty.* Yale University Press, New Haven.

1986   *The Archaeology of Ancient China.* 4th ed. Yale University Press, New Haven.

Chávez Ballón, Manuel

1970   Ciudades incas: Cuzco capital del imperio. *Wayka* (Departamento de Antropología, Universidad Nacional del Cuzco) 3:1–14.

Conrad, Geoffrey W.

1982   The Burial Platforms of Chan Chan: Some Social and Political Implications. In *Chan Chan, Andean Desert City*, edited by Michael E. Moseley and Kent C. Day, pp. 87–117. School of American Research and University of New Mexico Press, Albuquerque.

Cook, Anita G.

1992   The Stone Ancestors: Idioms of Imperial Attire and Rank among Huari Figurines. *Latin American Antiquity* 3(4):341–364.

1994   *Wari y Tiwanaku: Entre el estilo y la imagen.* Pontificia Universidad Católica del Perú, Lima.

1996a   Huari. In *Andean Art at Dumbarton Oaks*, Vol. 1, edited by Elizabeth H. Boone, pp. 163–188. Dumbarton Oaks Research Library and Collection, Washington, DC.

1996b   The Emperor's New Clothes: Symbols of Royalty, Hierarchy, and Identity. *Journal of the Steward Anthropological Society* 24(1–2):85–120.

2001 Huari D-Shaped Structures, Sacrificial Offerings, and Divine Ruler-
ship. In *Ritual Sacrifice in Ancient Peru*, edited by Elizabeth P.
Benson and Anita G. Cook, pp. 137–163. University of Texas Press,
Austin.

Donnan, Christopher B.
1988 Unraveling the Mystery of the Warrior-Priest. *National Geographic*
174(4):551–555.

Donnan, Christopher B., and Luis Jaime Castillo
1992 Finding the Tomb of a Moche Priestess. *Archaeology* 45(6):38–42.

Eeckhout, Peter
1997 Pachacamac (côte centrale de Pérou): Aspects de fonctionnement, du
développment et de l'influence du site durant l'Intermédiare récent.
Unpublished doctoral thesis, Université Libre de Bruxelles.

1998a Pirámide con rampa No. 3, Pachacamac: Nuevos datos, nuevas
perspectivas. Unpublished manuscript, submitted to *Boletín del
IFEA*, vol. 27.

1998b Offrandes funéraires à Pachacamac et Pampa de las Flores: Examples des relations entre les côtes nord et central du Pérou à
l'époque pré-Inca. *Bessler-Archiv Neue Folge* (Berlin) 46:1–66.

1999a *Pachacamac durant l'Intermédiaire récent: Étude d'un site monumental préhispanique de la côte centrale du Pérou*. BAR International Series, 747, Hadrian Books, Oxford.

1999b Le temple de Pachacamac sous l'empire Inca. *Journal de la Société
des Américanistes* (Paris) 84:18–50.

2000 The Palaces of the Lords of Ychsma: An Archaeological Reappraisal
of the Function of Pyramids with Ramps at Pachacamac, Central Coast of Peru. *Revista de Arqueología Americana* (Journal of
American Archaeology, Revue d' Archéologie Américaine. Instituto
Panamericano de Geografía e Historia) 17–19(July 1999–December
2000):217–254.

Farrington, Ian S.
1995 The Mummy, Palace, and Estate of Inka Huayna Capac at Quispe-
quanca. *Tawantinsuyu* 1:55–65.

Fitzgerald, Patrick
1978 *Ancient China*. Elsevier-Phaidon, Oxford.

Franco Jordán, Régulo
1993 El centro ceremonial de Pachacamac: Nuevas evidencias en el templo
viejo. *Boletín de Lima* 86:45–62.

1996 Arquitectura monumental en Pachacamac. *Arkinka* 1(11):82–94.

1998 La pirámide con rampa no. 2 de Pachacamac: Excavaciones y nuevas
interpretaciones, Trujillo, Peru.

Galaty, Michael L., and William A. Parkinson
1999a Putting Mycenaean Palaces in Their Place: An Introduction. In *Rethinking Mycenaean Palaces: New Interpretations of an Old Idea*,
edited by Michael L. Galaty and William A. Parkinson, pp. 1–8.
Monograph 41, The Cotsen Institute of Archaeology, University of
California, Los Angeles.

Galaty, Michael L., and William A. Parkinson (editors)
1999b *Rethinking Mycenaean Palaces: New Interpretations of an Old Idea.*

Monograph 41, The Cotsen Institute of Archaeology, University of California, Los Angeles.

Geertz, Clifford
1980 *Negara: The Theatre State in Nineteenth-Century Bali.* Princeton University Press, Princeton.

Glowacki, Mary
1998 The Huaro Archaeological Project, 1997–1998: Report to the Curtiss T. Brennan and Mary G. Brennan Foundation (on file).

Glowacki, Mary, and Gordon F. McEwan
2001 Pikillacta, Huaro y la región del Cuzco. In *Boletín de Arqueología PUCP, No. 5, 2000 Huari y Tiwanaku: Modelos vs. evidencias, segunda parte,* edited by Peter Kaulicke and William H. Isbell, pp. 31–50. Departamento de Humanidades, Especialidad de Arqueología, Pontificia Universidad Católica del Perú, Lima.

Goldstein, Paul S.
1993 Tiwanaku Temples and State Expansion: A Tiwanaku Sunken-Court Temple in Moquegua, Peru. *Latin American Antiquity* 4(1):22–47.

González Carré, Enrique, and Enrique Bragayrac Davila
1986 El Templo Mayor de Wari, Ayacucho. *Boletín de Lima* 8(47):9–20.

González Carré, Enrique, Enrique Bragayrac Davila, Cirilo Vivanco Pomacanchari, Vera Tiesler Blos, and Máximo López Quispe
1996 *El Templo Mayor en la ciudad de Wari.* Laboratorio de Arqueología, Facultad de Ciencias Sociales, Universidad Nacional San Cristóbal de Huamanga, Ayacucho, Peru.

Guaman Poma de Ayala, Felipe
[1615] 1980   *El primer nueva corónica y buen gobierno.* Edited by John V. Murra and Rolena Adorno with translation by Jorge L. Urioste. 3 vols. Siglo XXI, Mexico City.

Guisso, R. W. L., Catherine Pagani, and David Miller
1989 *The First Emperor of China.* Birch Lane Press, New York.

Hemming, John
1970 *The Conquest of the Incas.* Harcourt, Brace, Jovanovich, New York.

Hemming, John, and Edward Ranney
1982 *Monuments of the Incas.* A New York Graphic Society Book. Little, Brown, Boston.

Hiltunen, Juha J.
1999 *Ancient Kings of Peru: The Reliability of the Chronicle of Fernando de Montesinos.* Bibliotheca Historica 45. Suomen Historiallinen Seura, Helsinki.

Isbell, William H.
1968 New Discoveries in the Montaña of Southeastern Peru. *Archaeology* 21(2):108–114.
1971 Un pueblo rural ayacuchano durante el imperio Huari. *Actas y Memorias del 39° Congreso Internacional de Americanistas* 3:89–105.
1977 *The Rural Foundation for Urbanism.* Illinois Studies in Anthropology No. 10. University of Illinois Press, Urbana.
1978 El imperio Huari: ¿Estado o ciudad? *Revista del Museo Nacional* 43:227–241.

1984 Huari Urban Prehistory. In *Current Archaeological Projects in the Central Andes*, edited by Ann Kendall, pp. 95–131. BAR International Series 210. British Archaeological Reports, Oxford.

1985 El origen del estado en el valle de Ayacucho. *Revista Andina* 3(1):57–106.

1987 State Origins in the Ayacucho Valley, Central Highlands Peru. In *The Origins and Development of the Andean State*, edited by Jonathan Haas, Shelia Pozorski, and Thomas Pozorski, pp. 83–90. Cambridge University Press, New York.

1988 City and State in Middle Horizon Huari. In *Peruvian Prehistory*, edited by Richard W. Keatinge, pp. 164–189. Cambridge University Press, Cambridge.

1989 Honcopampa: Was It a Huari Administrative Center? In *The Nature of Wari: A Reappraisal of the Middle Horizon in Peru*, edited by R. Michael Czwarno, Frank M. Meddens, and Alexandra Morgan, pp. 98–115. BAR International Series 525. British Archaeological Reports, Oxford.

1991a Honcopampa: Monumental Ruins in Peru's North Highlands. *Expedition Magazine* 33(3):27–36.

1991b Huari Administration and the Orthogonal Cellular Architecture Horizon. In *Huari Administrative Structure: Prehistoric Monumental Architecture and State Government*, edited by William H. Isbell and Gordon F. McEwan, pp. 293–315. Dumbarton Oaks Research Library and Collection, Washington, DC.

1996 Household and *Ayni* in the Andean Past. In *Structure, Knowledge, and Representation in the Andes: Studies Presented to Reiner Tom Zuidema on the Occasion of His 70th Birthday*, edited by Gary Urton, pp. 247–305. *Journal of the Steward Anthropological Society* 24:1&2, University of Illinois, Urbana.

1997a *Mummies and Mortuary Monuments: A Postprocessual Prehistory of Andean Social Organization*. University of Texas Press, Austin.

1997b Reconstructing Huari: A Cultural Chronology from the Capital City. In *Emergence and Change in Early Urban Societies*, edited by Linda Manzanilla, pp. 181–227. Plenum Press, New York and London.

2001a Huari: Crecimiento y desarrollo de la capital imperial. In *Wari: Arte precolombino peruano*, edited by Luis Millones, pp. 99–172. Fundación El Monte, Sevilla.

2001b Repensando el horizonte medio: El caso de Conchopata, Ayacucho, Perú. In *Boletín de Arqueología PUCP, No. 4, 2000 Huari y Tiwanaku: Modelos vs. evidencias, primera parte*, edited by Peter Kaulicke and William H. Isbell, pp. 9–68. Departamento de Humanidades, Especialidad de Arqueología, Pontificia Universidad Católica del Perú, Lima.

2002 Reflexiones finales. In *Boletín de Arqueología PUCP, No. 5, 2001 Huari y Tiwanaku: Modelos vs. evidencias, primera parte*, edited by Peter Kaulicke and William H. Isbell, pp. 9–68. Departamento de Humanidades, Especialidad de Arqueología, Pontificia Universidad Católica del Perú, Lima.

2004a   Mortuary Preferences: A Wari Case Study from Middle Horizon Peru. *Latin American Antiquity* 15(1):3–32.

2004b   Palaces and Politics in the Andean Middle Horizon. In *Palaces of the Ancient New World: Form, Function, and Meaning*, edited by Susan Toby Evans and Joanne Pillsbury, pp. 191–246. Dumbarton Oaks Research Library and Collection, Washington, DC.

Isbell, William H., Christine Brewster-Wray, and Lynda Spickard

1991   Architecture and Spatial Organization at Huari. In *Huari Administrative Structure: Prehistoric Monumental Architecture and State Government*, edited by William H. Isbell and Gordon F. McEwan, pp. 19–53. Dumbarton Oaks Research Library and Collection, Washington, DC.

Isbell, William H., and JoEllen Burkholder

2002   Iwawi and Tiwanaku. In *Andean Archaeology*, Vol. 1: *Variations in Sociopolitical Organization*, edited by William H. Isbell and Helaine Silverman, pp. 199–241. Kluwer Academic/Plenum Publishers, New York and London.

Isbell, William H., and Anita G. Cook

2002   A New Perspective on Conchopata and the Andean Middle Horizon. In *Andean Archaeology*, Vol. 2: *Art, Landscape, and Society*, edited by Helaine Silverman and William H. Isbell, pp. 249–305. Kluwer Academic/Plenum Publishers, New York and London.

Isbell, William H., and Gordon F. McEwan

1991a   A History of Huari Studies and Introduction to Current Interpretations. In *Huari Administrative Structure: Prehistoric Monumental Architecture and State Government*, edited by William H. Isbell and Gordon F. McEwan, pp. 1–18. Dumbarton Oaks Research Library and Collection, Washington, DC.

Isbell, William H., and Gordon F. McEwan (editors)

1991b   *Huari Administrative Structure: Prehistoric Monumental Architecture and State Government*. Dumbarton Oaks Research Library and Collection, Washington, DC.

Isbell, William H., and Katharina J. Schreiber

1978   Was Huari a State? *American Antiquity* 43(3):372–389.

Jiménez Borja, Arturo

1985   Pachacamac. *Boletín de Lima* 7(38):40–54.

Jiménez Borja, Arturo, and Alberto Bueno Mendoza

1970   Breves notas acerca de Pachacamac. *Arqueología y Sociedad* 4:13–25.

Knobloch, Patricia

1991   Stylistic Date of Ceramics from the Huari Centers. In *Huari Administrative Structure: Prehistoric Monumental Architecture and State Government*, edited by William H. Isbell and Gordon F. McEwan, pp. 247–258. Dumbarton Oaks Research Library and Collection, Washington, DC.

Kolata, Alan L.

1993   *The Tiwanaku: Portrait of an Andean Civilization*. Blackwell, Cambridge, MA, and Oxford, UK.

Lumbreras, Luis G.

1960   La cultura Wari, Ayacucho. *Etnología y Arqueología* 1(1):130–226.

Machaca Calle, Gudelia
1997 Secuencia cultural y nuevas evidencias de formación urbana en Ñawinpuquio. Tesis para optar el Título de Licenciada en Arqueología. Universidad Nacional San Cristóbal de Huamanga, Ayacucho, Peru.

Matos Mendieta, Ramiro
1994 *Pumpu: Centro administrativo inka de la puna de Junín.* Editorial Horizonte, Lima.

McEwan, Gordon F.
1984 The Middle Horizon in the Valley of Cuzco, Peru: The Impact of the Wari Occupation of Pikillacta in the Lucre Basin. Ph.D. dissertation, University of Texas at Austin.
1985 Excavaciones en Pikillacta: Un sitio Wari. *Diálogo Andino* (Departamento de Historia y Geografía, Universidad de Tarapacá) 4:89–136.
1987 *The Middle Horizon in the Valley of Cuzco, Peru: The Impact of the Wari Occupation of Pikillacta in the Lucre Basin.* BAR International Series 372. British Archaeological Reports, Oxford.
1990 Some Formal Correspondences between the Imperial Architecture of the Wari and Chimu Cultures, and Their Implications for the Origin of the Architecture of Chan Chan. *Latin American Antiquity* 1:97–116.
1991 Investigations at the Pikillacta Site: A Provincial Huari Center in the Valley of Cuzco. In *Huari Administrative Structure: Prehistoric Monumental Architecture and State Government,* edited by William H. Isbell and Gordon F. McEwan, pp. 93–120. Dumbarton Oaks Research Library and Collection, Washington, DC.
1996 Archaeological Investigations at Pikillacta, a Wari Site in Peru. *Journal of Field Archaeology* 23(2):169–186.
1998a The Function of Niched Halls in Wari Architecture. *Latin American Antiquity* 9(1):68–86.
1998b The Archaeology of Inca Origins: The Selz Foundation Excavations at Chokepukio. Paper presented at the 17th Annual Meeting of the Northeast Conference on Andean and Amazonian Archaeology and Ethnohistory. Binghamton, New York. October 17–18.
1999 The Selz Foundation Excavations at Chokepukio, Cuzco, Peru: Report of the 1999 Excavations. Unpublished report, Department of Sociology and Anthropology, Wagner College, Staten Island, New York.
2005 *Pikillacta: The Wari Empire in Cuzco.* University of Iowa Press, Iowa City.

McEwan, Gordon F., Arminda Gibaja O., and Melissa Chatfield
1995 Archaeology of the Chokepukio Site: An Investigation of the Origin of the Inca Civilization in the Valley of Cuzco, Peru. A Report on the 1994 Field Season. *Tawantinsuyu* 1:11–17.

Meddens, Frank, and Anita G. Cook
2001 La administración Wari y el culto a los muertos: Yako, los edificios en forma "D" en la sierra sur-central del Perú. In *Wari: Arte precolombino peruano,* edited by Luis Millones, pp. 212–228. Fundación El Monte, Sevilla.

Menzel, Dorothy
1964 Style and Time in the Middle Horizon. *Ñawpa Pacha* 2:1–106.
1968 New Data on Middle Horizon Epoch 2A. *Ñawpa Pacha* 6:47–114.
Morris, Craig
2004 Enclosures of Power: Multiple Spaces of Inka Administrative Palaces. In *Palaces of the Ancient New World: Form, Function, and Meaning*, edited by Susan Toby Evans and Joanne Pillsbury, pp. 299–324. Dumbarton Oaks Research Library and Collection, Washington, DC.
Morris, Craig, and Donald E. Thompson
1985 *Huánuco Pampa: An Inca City and Its Hinterland.* Thames and Hudson, London.
Moseley, Michael, Robert Feldman, Paul Goldstein, and Luis Watanabe
1991 Colonies and Conquest: Tiwanaku and Huari in Moquegua. In *Huari Administrative Structure: Prehistoric Monumental Architecture and State Government*, edited by William H. Isbell and Gordon F. McEwan, pp. 121–140. Dumbarton Oaks Research Library and Collection, Washington, DC.
Neitzel, Robert S.
1965 Archaeology of the Fatherland Site: The Grand Village of the Natchez. *Anthropological Papers of the American Museum of Natural History* (New York) 51(1).
Niles, Susan A.
1987 *Callachaca: Style and Status in an Inca Community.* University of Iowa Press, Iowa City.
1988 Looking for "Lost" Inca Palaces. *Expedition* 30(3):56–64.
1999 *The Shape of Inca History: Narrative and Architecture in an Andean Empire.* University of Iowa Press, Iowa City.
Ochatoma Paravicino, José
1988 *Aqo Wayqo: Poblado rural de la época Wari.* Consejo Nacional de Ciencia y Tecnología, Lima.
1992 Acerca del formativo en Ayacucho. In *Estudios de arqueología peruana*, edited by Duccio Bonavia, pp. 193–214. Fomciencias, Lima.
Ochatoma Paravicino, José, and Martha Cabrera Romero
1997 *El modo de vida en un poblado rural Huari.* Escuela de Formación Profesional de Arqueología e Historia. Universidad Nacional San Cristóbal de Huamanga, Ayacucho, Peru.
1999 Recientes descubrimientos en el sitio Huari de Conchopata—Ayacucho. Paper presented at the 64th Annual Meeting of the Society for American Archaeology (Publicado por la Facultad de Ciencias Sociales, Universidad Nacional San Cristóbal de Huamanga), Chicago.
2001 Arquitectura y áreas de actividad en Conchopata. In *Boletín de Arqueología PUCP, No. 4, 2000 Huari y Tiwanaku: Modelos vs. evidencias, primera parte*, edited by Peter Kaulicke and William H. Isbell, pp. 449–488. Departamento de Humanidades, Especialidad de Arqueología, Pontificia Universidad Católica del Perú, Lima.
2002 Religious Ideology and Military Organization in the Iconography of a D-Shaped Ceremonial Precinct at Conchopata. In *Andean Archaeology*, Vol. 2: *Art, Landscape, and Society*, edited by Helaine Silver-

man and William H. Isbell, pp. 225–247. Kluwer Academic/Plenum Publishing, New York and London.

Ortloff, Charles

1996 Engineering Aspects of Tiwanaku Groundwater Agriculture. In *Tiwanaku and Its Hinterland: Archaeology and Paleoecology of an Andean Civilization,* edited by Alan L. Kolata, pp. 153–168. Smithsonian Institution, Washington, DC, and London.

Paredes Botoni, Ponciano

1984 El Panel (Pachacamac): Nuevo tipo de enteramiento. *Gaceta Arqueológica Andina* 3(10):8–9,15.

1985 La huaca pintada o el templo de Pachacamac. *Boletín de Lima* 7(41):70–77.

1988 Pachacamac—pirámide con rampa no. 2. *Boletín de Lima* 10(55):41–58.

Paredes Botoni, Ponciano, and Régulo Franco

1985 Excavaciones en la huaca pintada o el templo de Pachacamac. *Boletín de Lima* 7(41):78–84.

1987 Pachacamac: Las pirámides con rampa, cronología y función. *Gaceta Arqueológica Andina* 4(13):5–7.

1987/1988 Excavaciones en el templo viejo de Pachacamac. *Willay* 27–28:25–27.

Patterson, Thomas C.

1985 Exploitation and Class Formation in the Inca State. *Culture* 5:35–42.

Pérez Calderón, Ismael

1998a Excavación y definición de un taller de alfareros Huari en Conchopata. *Conchopata: Revista de Arqueología* (Universidad Nacional San Cristóbal de Huamanga, Oficina de Investigación) 1:93–137.

1998b *Informe de los trabajos de arqueología y conservación en el sector de Monqachayoc, Huari.* Informe al Instituto Nacional de Cultura de Perú, Filial Ayacucho.

1999 *Huari: Misteriosa ciudad de piedra.* Facultad de Ciencias Sociales, Universidad Nacional San Cristóbal de Huamanga, Ayacucho, Peru.

Pérez Calderón, I., and José A. Ochatoma Paravicino

1998 Viviendas, talleres y hornos de producción alfarera Huari en Conchopata. *Conchopata: Revista de Arqueología* (Universidad Nacional San Cristóbal de Huamanga, Oficina de Investigación) 1:72–92.

Pillsbury, Joanne, and Banks L. Leonard

2004 Identifying Chimú Palaces: Elite Residential Architecture in the Late Intermediate Period. In *Palaces of the Ancient New World: Form, Function, and Meaning,* edited by Susan Toby Evans and Joanne Pillsbury, pp. 247–298. Dumbarton Oaks Research Library and Collection, Washington, DC.

Pozzi-Escot B., Denise

1991 Conchopata: A Community of Potters. In *Huari Administrative Structure: Prehistoric Monumental Architecture and State Government,* edited by William H. Isbell and Gordon F. McEwan, pp. 81–92. Dumbarton Oaks Research Library and Collection, Washington, DC.

Protzen, Jean-Pierre
1993 *Inca Architecture and Construction at Ollantaytambo.* Oxford University Press, Oxford.

Rostworowski de Diez Canseco, María
1972 Las etnias del valle del Chillón. *Revista del Museo Nacional (Lima)* 38:250–314.
1989 *Etnia y sociedad: Costa peruana prehispánica.* Instituto de Estudios Peruanos, Lima.
1992 *Pachacamac y el Señor de los milagros: Una trayectoria milenaria.* Instituto de Estudios Peruanos, Lima.

Rowe, John H.
1967 What Kind of a Settlement Was Inca Cuzco? *Ñawpa Pacha* 5:59–76.

Sampeck, Kathryn E.
1991 Excavations at Putuni, Tiwanaku, Bolivia. Master's thesis, University of Chicago, Department of Anthropology.

Schreiber, Katharina J.
1991 Jincamocco: A Huari Administrative Center in the South Central Highlands of Peru. In *Huari Administrative Structure: Prehistoric Monumental Architecture and State Government,* edited by William H. Isbell and Gordon F. McEwan, pp. 199–213. Dumbarton Oaks Research Library and Collection, Washington, DC.
1992 *Wari Imperialism in Middle Horizon Peru.* Anthropological Papers of the Museum of Anthropology, No. 87. University of Michigan, Ann Arbor.

Shelmerdine, Cynthia W.
1997 Review of Aegean Prehistory VI: The Palatial Bronze Age of the Southern and Central Greek Mainland. *American Journal of Archaeology* 101:537–585.

Shimada, Izumi
1991 Pachacamac Archaeology: Retrospect and Prospect. In *Pachacamac: A Reprint of the 1903 Edition by Max Uhle,* edited by Izumi Shimada, pp. xv–lxvi. University Museum Monograph 62. The University Museum, Philadelphia.

Solano Ramos, Francisco F., and Venturo P. Guerrero Anaya
1981 *Estudio arqueológico en el sector de Monqachayoq, Wari.* Tesis para optar el grado de Bachiller en Ciencias Sociales: Antropología, Universidad Nacional San Cristóbal de Huamanga, Ayacucho, Peru.

Swanton, John R.
1911 *Indian Tribes of the Lower Mississippi Valley and Adjacent Coast of the Gulf of Mexico.* Bureau of American Ethnology Bulletin 43. Smithsonian Institution, Washington, DC.

Thomas, Carol G., and Craig Conant
1999 *Citadel to City-State: The Transformation of Greece, 1200–700 B.C.E.* Indiana University Press, Bloomington.

Topic, John R.
1986 A Sequence of Monumental Architecture from Huamachuco. In *Perspectives on Andean Prehistory and Protohistory,* edited by Daniel H. Sandweiss and D. Peter Kvietok, pp. 63–83. Latin American Studies Program, Cornell University, Ithaca.

1991 Huari and Huamachuco. In *Huari Administrative Structure: Prehistoric Monumental Architecture and State Government*, edited by William H. Isbell and Gordon F. McEwan, pp. 141–164. Dumbarton Oaks Research Library and Collection, Washington, DC.

Topic, John R., and Theresa Lange Topic

1982 The Huamachuco Archaeological Project: Preliminary Report of the First Season, July–August 1981. Trent University Department of Anthropology, Peterborough, Ontario.

1983 The Huamachuco Archaeological Project: Preliminary Report on the Second Season, June–August 1982. Trent University Department of Anthropology, Peterborough, Ontario.

1985 El horizonte medio en Huamachuco. *Revista del Museo Nacional* (Lima) 47:13–52.

1992 The Rise and Decline of Cerro Amaru: An Andean Shrine during the Early Intermediate Period and Middle Horizon. In *Ancient Images, Ancient Thought: The Archaeology of Ideology*, edited by A. Sean Goldsmith, Sandra Garvie, David Selin, and Jeannette Smith, pp. 167–180. University of Calgary Archaeological Association, Calgary, Canada.

Topic, Theresa

1991 The Middle Horizon in Northern Peru. In *Huari Administrative Structure: Prehistoric Monumental Architecture and State Government*, edited by William H. Isbell and Gordon F. McEwan, pp. 233–246. Dumbarton Oaks Research Library and Collection, Washington, DC.

Topic, Theresa Lange, and John R. Topic

1984 *Huamachuco Archaeological Project: Preliminary Report on the Third Season, June–August 1983*. Trent University Occasional Papers in Anthropology No. 1. Peterborough, Ontario.

Tung, Tiffiny A.

2003 A Bioarchaeological Perspective on Wari Imperialism in the Andes of Peru: A View from Heartland and Hinterland Skeletal Populations. Ph.D. dissertation, Department of Anthropology, University of North Carolina at Chapel Hill.

Tung, Tiffiny A., and Anita Cook

2002 Intermediate Elites and Their Role in Wari Imperialism as Identified through Bioarchaeological Mortuary Analysis. Paper presented at the 67th Annual Meeting of the Society for American Archaeology, Denver.

Uhle, Max

1991 *Pachacamac: A Reprint of the 1903 Edition by Max Uhle, and Pachacamac Archaeology: Retrospect and Prospect*. Introduction by Izumi Shimada. Reprinted. The University Museum of Archaeology and Anthropology of the University of Pennsylvania, Philadelphia. Originally published by the Department of Archaeology, University of Pennsylvania.

Valdez, Lidio M., J. Ernesto Valdez, Katrina J. Bettcher, and Cirilo Vivanco

1999 Excavaciones arqueológicas en el centro Wari de Marayniyoq, Ayacucho. *Boletín del Museo de Arqueología y Antropología* 2(9):16–19.

Wheatley, Paul
1971 *The Pivot of the Four Quarters: A Preliminary Enquiry into the Origins and Character of the Ancient Chinese City.* Aldine, Chicago.

Williams, Patrick Ryan
2001 Cerro Baúl: A Wari Center on the Tiwanaku Frontier. *Latin American Antiquity* 12(1):67–83.

Williams, Patrick Ryan, Johny Isla, and Donna Nash
2001 Cerro Baúl: Un enclave Wari en interacción con Tiwanaku. In *Huari y Tiwanaku: Modelos vs. evidencias, segunda parte. Boletín de Arqueología PUCP, No. 5, 2001,* edited by Peter Kaulicke and William H. Isbell, pp. 69–88. Departamento de Humanidades, Especialidad de Arqueología, Pontificia Universidad Católica del Perú, Lima.

Williams, Patrick Ryan, and Donna Nash
2002 Imperial Interaction in the Andes: Huari and Tiwanaku at Cerro Baúl. In *Andean Archaeology, Vol. 1: Variations in Sociopolitical Organization,* edited by William H. Isbell and Helaine Silverman, pp. 243–265. Kluwer Academic/Plenum Publishing, New York and London.

Wilson, David J.
1999 *Indigenous South Americans of the Past and Present: An Ecological Perspective.* Westview Press, Boulder, CO.

Zapata, Julinho
1997 Arquitectura y contextos funerarios Wari en Batan Urqu, Cusco. In *La muerte en el antiguo Perú. Boletín de Arqueología PUCP, No. 1,* edited by Peter Kaulicke, pp. 165–206. Pontificia Universidad Católica del Perú, Lima.

Zilin, W.
1985 The Museum of Quin Shi Huang. *Museum* 147:140–147.

CHAPTER 3

Lords of the Great House
PUEBLO BONITO AS A PALACE

Stephen H. Lekson

Palaces in the United States? Perhaps for colonial governors or railroad barons or newspaper moguls, but surely not for pre-Columbian natives. That seems odd: native peoples built palaces in Mexico, but not (apparently) in the United States. In this chapter, I argue that the idea of "palace" be allowed to cross that border. Rather than an extended description of elite residences, palaces, and palace life in the pre-Columbian cultures of the present United States, I limit this essay to an examination of U.S. archaeological attitudes toward palaces and their implications, using Southwestern cultures as my primary examples (Figure 3.1).

The idea of pre-Columbian palaces in the lower 48 states seems somehow absurd. Why? There are two obvious reasons and a third one that is less obvious and perhaps more sinister. I address the two evident reasons first and save the third for later in the discussion. Why are we disinclined to use the term *palace* in the continental United States? First, the political implications of the term make us nervous. Palaces imply states. Second, palaces are complicated, multifunctional facilities. We like architecture simple and straight: "house," for example. The third problem faced by palaces is the "glass ceiling" placed by anthropology over Native American societies. I will address the first two objections and return to the third in the conclusions of this chapter.

Palaces imply states. And, indeed, palaces in many parts of the world were accoutrements of state-level polities. In the eastern Mediterranean and the classical lands, palaces are type-fossils of states and empires: Minoan and Aegean civilizations were palatial and palace centered. Only short-lived democracies avoided palatial excrescence. Thus, to call a building a palace is to imply that its occupants ruled a state, but U.S. archaeology doesn't permit pre-Columbian states north of Mexico.

The obvious, best candidate for a pre-Columbian state is the great eleventh- to fourteenth-century site of Cahokia, near modern St. Louis (Pauketat 2004, among others). Cahokia was a cosmopolitan city of tens of thousands of people, with monumental architecture that included an earthen pyramid (Monks Mound) rivaling in mass and scale those of Teotihuacan. But

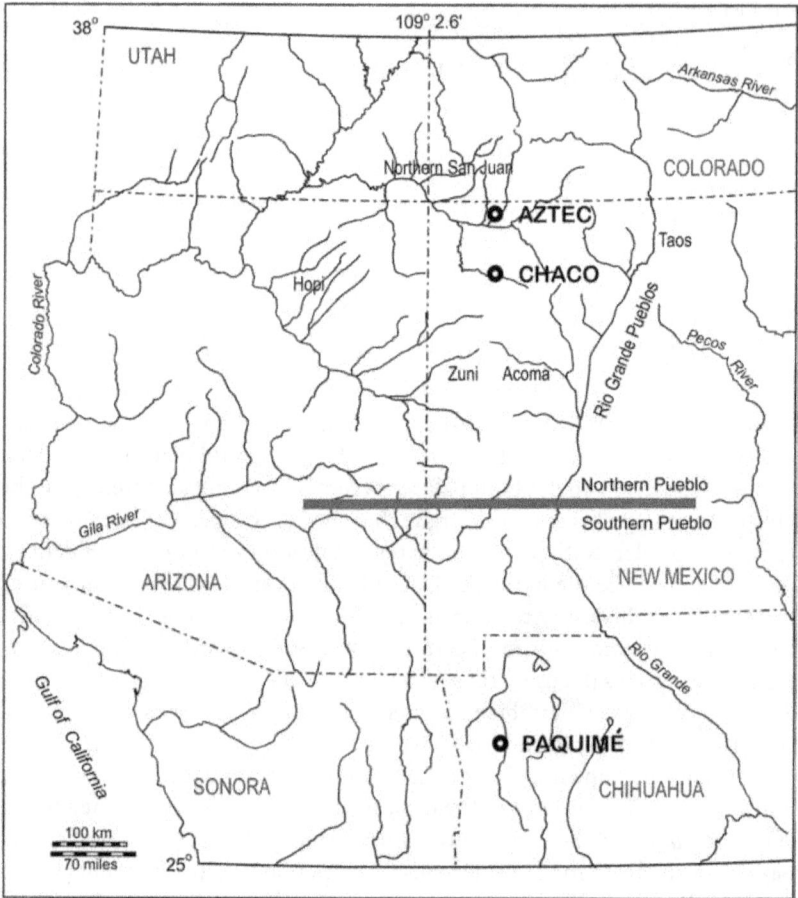

FIGURE 3.1 Map of the Southwest

a Cahokia state has been demoted by an establishment archaeology seemingly intent on leveling the pre-Columbian playing field (most recently, Milner 1998, among others). Our (distantly) second-best candidate, the Chaco-Aztec-Paquimé nexus of the ancient Southwest (Lekson 1999), is similarly discounted by sane and sober archaeologists (Renfrew 2001; Vivian 1990). (We will return to Cahokia, Chaco, Aztec, and Paquimé shortly.) We do not speak of Native palaces in the United States—outside Hawaii—because it is generally accepted that no Native state ever existed in our country. No states, therefore no palaces.

Our second objection to the term *palace* comes from the bundle of functions and activities we expect to see encompassed within such buildings. Minoan (and other) palaces had storerooms and specialist workshops for economic functions; temples and shrines for ritual functions; assembly areas and audience halls for governance; armories for warfare; and—we can only hope—private apartments for the king or queen to curl up with the latest adventures of Gil and Enki and a rhyton of the best. For many archaeologists, it is the architectural attachment of those key functions—economic, ritual, government, military—to a royal or sovereign household that defines palaces.

There was even more to palaces than compartmentalized functions: palaces were capital *A* architecture, built environments that mirrored or projected structures of power. If peasant houses reflect something about domestic worldview (Nabokov and Easton 1989; Rapoport 1969), palaces manifest larger cosmologies and economies in both their incorporated functions and formal design. We can speak of palatial canons: rules of geometry and layout that both structure and monumentalize larger political realities. Monumentality is a clue, but so is formal layout. There were many large buildings— *casas grandes*, or "great houses"—in ancient North America. But size alone is not enough.

Are there rulers' houses with attached economic, ritual, governmental, and military functions in Native societies north of Mexico? The chiefly houses of the Mississippian Natchez and the Northwest Coast Kwakiutl were multifunctional, incorporating assembly, ritual, and residence, but they lacked palace guards, palace craftsmen, palace priests—the anticipated (but perhaps not necessary) appurtenances of kingship. A case can be made, I think, for palacelike architecture in the ancient American Southwest, in the land of the modern Pueblo peoples. The sites of Chaco, Aztec, and Paquimé are my candidates (Figure 3.1), but before discussing these sites, I must digress slightly to set the stage. The claim of palaces in the ancient Southwest seems unlikely, even perverse: Pueblo peoples are famously egalitarian, famously peaceful, famously Apollonian. Ruth Benedict codified this view in 1934 in *Patterns of Culture*. Consider Benedict's description of Zuni Pueblo government, or nongovernment:

Zuni is a theocracy to the last implication. . . . To our sense of what a governing body should be, they [the major priests] are without jurisdiction and without authority. (Benedict 1934:67)

Was it always so? Indeed, was it *ever* so? Zuni origin stories tell of epic battles and warfare (Wright 1988) and of earlier forms of government that seem rather more centralized, rather less Apollonian. Frank Hamilton Cushing, who lived at Zuni a half century before Benedict's book was published, reconstructed a pre-Columbian government that was only faintly echoed at Zuni in his day, and even less so in Benedict's time.

The body which governed . . . was a council composed of the chief "priests" of the six cardinal directions. . . . These august figures were the

"Masters of the Great House"—"house" in this context meaning literally their place of meeting, thought to be located at the exact center of
the world. (Green 1990:373)

The Masters of the Great House did not work; they and their families were
supported by tithing taxes called the "good share." They appointed officers of
the Pueblo who administered Zuni's economic, social, legal, and ritual life—
a protobureaucracy. I have argued (Lekson 1999:26–28) that the Masters of
the Great House at preconquest Zuni were themselves a pale reflection of a
ruling class first apparent, half a millennium earlier, at Chaco Canyon. I like
Cushing's locution, and I have altered his phrase to fit the Chacoan situation:
"Lords of the Great House."

Chaco was a ceremonial city, the center of Pueblo political, economic,
and social life from about A.D. 900 to 1125 (at least according to Lekson
1999; for recent summaries of Chaco research, see Frazier 2005; Mills 2002;
Noble 2004). Its monumental Great Houses—icons of Pueblo architecture
(Figure 3.2)—attracted archaeological attention in the 1880s that continues
undiminished into the present. Great Houses began in the tenth century as
monumentally upscaled versions of regular domestic structures—the tiny
single-family "unit pueblos" ubiquitous across the Southwest—but Great
Houses soon took a canonical turn in form and function that distinguished
them forever from regular residences (Lekson 1984). The scale of the Great
Houses was hugely larger than that of the unit pueblos; an entire unit pueblo
would fit into a single large room at a Chaco Great House. The dozen major
Great Houses at Chaco were placed over a 15 km length of the canyon,
but the largest were concentrated in a "downtown" zone 2 km in diameter
around Pueblo Bonito.

Pueblo Bonito is not so much typical as archetypical: it took almost three
centuries (ca. A.D. 850 to 1125) to complete this huge building (Lekson 1984;
Windes and Ford 1996). The roads of ancient Chaco led viewers to the edge
of Chaco's sheer sandstone cliffs, where the D shape of Pueblo Bonito was
spectacularly evident.

The building began as a huge version of ninth-century unit pueblos, built
three stories tall (whereas a conventional unit pueblo was one short story).
But the ninth-century masonry was not up to the task of supporting multiple stories. When the rear wall failed in the early eleventh century, Chaco
architects preserved the old building by enveloping it in an exterior wall of
superior stonework, buttressing the sagging older structure. In many other
cases, existing sections of Great Houses (including Pueblo Bonito) were razed
to make way for new construction, but Old Bonito remained the heart of the
building throughout its long history. Beginning about A.D. 1020, the architects of Pueblo Bonito began a series of a half dozen major additions, each of
which was enormously larger than anything previously built in the Pueblo
world. The culmination, when building ceased about A.D. 1125, was almost

FIGURE 3.2 Photo of Pueblo Bonito, Chaco Canyon, New Mexico

700 rooms, stacked four and perhaps five stories tall, covering an area of almost 0.8 hectares. The remarkable D shape was maintained throughout the long history of construction and modification, as was the original orientation of the building, to the southeast, until late in its history when a meridian orientation (focused on a north-south line) replaced the older, presumably solar layout. Entering the building from the valley floor, the visitor would walk past two huge platform mounds south of the building, through a single entry in a forbidding plaza-enclosing wall, and into one of two plazas—the D had been bisected by a dividing wall running exactly north–south. In the center of each plaza was a huge subterranean Great Kiva—an assembly chamber for larger groups—and each plaza was edged by a row of round rooms (also conventionally called kivas but more likely residences), behind which were terraced masses of rectangular rooms. Only the outermost of these rooms had sunlight; the other interior rooms—and there were hundreds and hundreds of interior rooms—were dark and had limited access, suited only for storage. We now believe that only a score of families lived in this huge building. They were very important families, and they had control of (or at least access to) enormous numbers of storage rooms.

Pueblo Bonito, like other Great Houses, was expensively built. That is, the labor per unit measure of floor area or roofed volume or total mass was hugely larger than that needed to build unit pueblos. Pueblo Bonito and the other Great Houses were distinguished by their site preparation (leveling and terracing); extensive foundations; massive, artfully coursed masonry walls; overtimbered roofs and ceilings (hundreds of thousands of large beams brought from distant forests); carpentry, which can only be appreciated today from masonry remnants of elaborate wooden stairways, balconies, and porticoes; and features and furniture unique to these remarkable buildings. Among these last were colonnades (an import from Mexico), unique raised platforms (for storage or sleeping?) built within rooms, and the use of large sandstone disks (approximately 1 m in diameter and 30 cm thick), stacked like pancakes beneath major posts (particularly in Great Kivas) as foundations or dedicatory monuments or both. The division of labor, manifested architecturally, was unlike the family economy of unit pueblos: at Great Houses, whole rooms were devoted to batteries of corn-grinding metates fixed in bins, where meal was prepared by gangs of grinders for larger groups; and huge ovens were found in the plazas, where, presumably, cooking for larger groups took place. The few families who actually lived in Pueblo Bonito could not possibly have built that building themselves. It was built by others, and it seems likely that much of the domestic work (grinding corn, cooking, etc.) was done by others as well.

Elite burials—deep, wood-lined crypts with astonishing wealth and scores of retainers—have been found at Pueblo Bonito, the largest and arguably the most important of the Chaco Great Houses. Two middle-aged men were buried in these crypts in the early to middle eleventh century, deep in the rooms of the original late ninth- and early tenth-century construction at Pueblo Bonito, that is, Old Bonito (Aikens and Schelberg 1984). (Other Chaco Great Houses have not produced such burials, but only a few Great Houses have been thoroughly excavated.)

These two men may well have been the Chaco rulers remembered as "our kings" by a traditional Navajo man from a Chaco-area clan (Taft Blackhorse, personal communication, 1999). They may have been principals among those "people at Chaco who gained power over people"—improperly, disastrously in present Pueblo worldview—alluded to by Paul Pino, from the Pueblo of Laguna: "In our history we talk of things that occurred a long time ago [at Chaco], of people who had enormous amounts of power: spiritual power and power over people . . . these people were causing changes that were never meant to occur" (in Sofaer 1999). Other Pueblo accounts similarly describe stern political leaders and their city, which rose and fell in ancient times (summarized in Lekson 1999:143–150). These "people with enormous power over people" were probably the two middle-aged men in the crypts. Found anywhere else in the world, the high-status burials of Pueblo Bonito would suggest political power at Chaco: Lords of the Great House.

The lords may also have been the architects, or that role may have been held by specialists. An elevated role for planners, designers, or architects is suggested by the buildings' remarkable shapes. Formal geometries structure the D shape of Pueblo Bonito and other Great Houses, which (we must assume) were meant to be viewed from the cliffs above. There were canons of Chacoan Great House design: Alignments, ratios in plan, and patterns of massing followed rules that we are only beginning to decode (Sofaer 1997). These rules and ratios were continued and respected in other, lesser Great

Houses. We are, perhaps, behind in this effort because archaeologists *did not expect to find* this sophistication north of the border, but a glance at the much earlier Hopewell geometric earthworks of the Ohio Valley (Morgan 1999) demonstrates that Natives north of modern Mexico were the engineering equals of their southern contemporaries. The architects of Chacoan Great Houses worked within a well-developed continental tradition or school of geometry.

The Great Houses are sited in a complex, planned cityscape that mirrors and manifests the ruling cosmology: the Chacoan world order (Fritz 1978; Sofaer 1997). The great families or clans represented by these several buildings may or may not have been dominated by Pueblo Bonito; but, together, the Chaco Great Houses represented a political center unknown in contemporary or ethnographically described Pueblo life, but remembered in Pueblo traditional histories (a subject to which we will return). Recent reanalysis of Pueblo Bonito supports the conclusion that Pueblo Bonito was an elite residence, among other things (Neitzel 2003). Jill Neitzel concludes that Pueblo Bonito began as an elite residence of a "network" hierarchy (*sensu* Blanton and Feinman [Blanton et al. 1999]), and then shifted in dominant function to a ceremonial center of a "corporate" hierarchy at about A.D. 1050. Elite residence ceased about 1150, but ceremonial structures at Pueblo Bonito continued to be maintained for a century thereafter (Neitzel 2003).

Early excavations established that Chaco was a magnet for exotic prestige items, such as tropical birds and copper artifacts from western Mexico (Mathien 1986), and for more local rarities, most notably turquoise (Mathien 2001; Weigand and Harbottle 1993). Later excavations discovered turquoise workshops in both the Great Houses and their attendant not-so-great peasant residences (Mathien 2001). Turquoise mining and production in the eleventh- and twelfth-century Pueblo world was probably controlled by Chaco.

Still later analyses have linked Chacoan political power to military force: Chaco was not Tenochtitlan, but it was the biggest, nastiest kid on the block (LeBlanc 1999; Turner and Turner 1999). I argue elsewhere that Chacoan power was projected, at least in part, by the socially sanctioned use of force, manifest in the brutal group executions discovered in excavations at scores of sites throughout the Chacoan region (Lekson 2002). Chaco ruled in an era of "unprecedented peace," in the words of Steven LeBlanc (1999), but that "Pax Chaco" came with a price: coercive enforcement.

Almost every statement I have made in the preceding paragraphs would be heatedly challenged by varying fractions (factions?) of my Southwestern colleagues. However, my reconstruction is based on good data and peer-reviewed research (mostly others' research, summarized in Lekson 1999, 2002). That is, my reconstruction is not *unreasonable* in terms of standard archaeological practice. It is only (and merely and importantly) *unthinkable* in view of stereotypes of happy, peaceful Pueblo people, living in harmony with their environment and their neighbors, projected backward a millennium into the deep and different Southwestern past.

Another argument I make, based on others' research but which many of my colleagues would reject, is this: Chaco was followed by two subsequent capitals, each of which legitimized itself by conscious reference back to Chaco, the primate center (Lekson 1999). Chaco ended about A.D. 1125. It was followed, in turn, by Aztec Ruins from 1110 to 1275, and then by Paquimé from 1250 to 1450 (Figure 3.1). I suggest that remarkable similarities in palace architecture at these three sites mark a possible dynastic, historic, or at least symbolic linkage from one capital to the next. We know relatively little about Aztec, but it is emerging archaeologically as a second Chaco, built 80 km due north of the first capital (McKenna and Toll 1992). We know much more about Paquimé, so let us make a great leap forward to the third and final Pueblo capital.

Paquimé is located in northern Chihuahua, Mexico (Di Peso 1974; Figure 3.1). Its beginnings are safely dated to A.D. 1250 (Dean and Ravesloot 1993). Paquimé has also been called Casas Grandes—Great Houses—not to be confused with the smaller Casa Grande (singular) near Phoenix, Arizona —to which we will return later.

Paquimé was a city of poured adobe (Figure 3.3). The massive walls reached four stories high—a perilous undertaking for that material, but apparently the importance of verticality overrode mere technical concerns. Designers specified deep foundations (like those of Chaco and Aztec) and included many-cornered rooms (unlike any at Chaco or Aztec)—some of which, in plan, resemble giant pixilated butterflies. The many corners and short wall segments functioned to buttress (almost to corrugate) the high walls. In any event, the building stood monumentally tall over the floodplain of the Casas Grandes River, creating a fabulous city surrounded by Mesoamerican-style ballcourts, platform mounds, and (small) pyramids.

Paquimé continued canons used in Chaco and Aztec (Figure 3.3), as well Chaco's remarkable penchant for exotic prestige goods. Just as Chaco was the regional epicenter of exotica in its time, Paquimé was an astonishing treasure trove—a warehouse—of exotic shell, copper bells and other objects, and tropical macaws and parrots (Di Peso 1974; see also Lekson 1999:94–101). Indeed, macaws were raised on a commercial scale—one of at least four craft specializations documented at Paquimé (Minnis 1988). As at Chaco, elites at Paquimé were buried in elaborate subfloor tombs with impressive grave offerings and—again, like Chaco—scores of retainers. Paquimé itself was massed rather differently than Chaco: at Chaco, a dozen Great Houses were spread over a 15 km stretch of canyon, whereas Paquimé appears to represent a score of Great House–sized, palacelike structures conjoined in side-by-side proximity. Built of poured adobe rather than the sandstone masonry of Chaco, Paquimé would have looked a bit like modern Taos Pueblo—but Paquimé was not Taos.

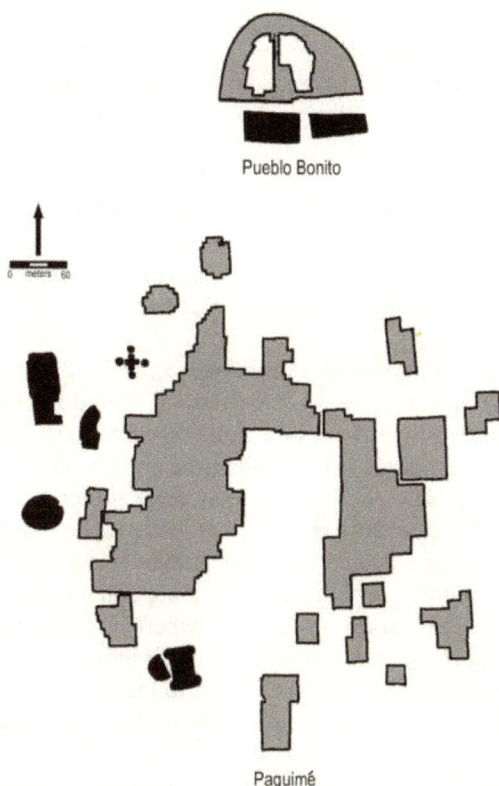

Pueblo Bonito

Paquimé

FIGURE 3.3 Plans of Pueblo Bonito, Chaco Canyon, New Mexico, and Paquimé, Chihuahua, Mexico

At both Chaco and Paquimé—and, by interpolation and (some) evidence, at Aztec—elite groups lived in monumentally constructed buildings. And those monumental buildings were only partly residential; they also incorporated warehouses, craft workshops, public and private ritual structures, and—perhaps—guard rooms or barracks. An argument can be made that palace functionaries and bureaucrats were also housed in or near the Great Houses: at Chaco, for example, a Great House shows evidence of a dozen or more elite households, but only two primary elite burials. That is, not everyone who lived in the Great House, and enjoyed its luxuries, was buried with pomp and circumstance. Many of those living in the Great House may have added to the circumstance—by being buried as retainers alongside their rulers.

Are Great Houses and Casas Grandes palaces? They are monumental architectural complexes that combine elite residence, governance, craft workshops, warehouses, public and private ritual, bureaucracies, and—perhaps—military functions. They are canonical in construction, and those canons

survived from at least A.D. 900 to at least 1450, a five- or six-century run—
not bad by any standards.

Chaco, Aztec, and Paquimé were, in my opinion, palaces. Can we have
palaces without the state? Why not? The 1980s and 1990s saw the deconstruction and demolition of old lockstep political taxonomies. Those old
ordered progressions of band, tribe, chiefdom, state have been confounded
and their constituent elements reassembled in odd iterations of alterative
formulations. Hierarchies devolve into heterarchies. Collectives construct
monuments of Neolithic Europe (and no chiefs need apply). In the stateless,
pre-Columbian, temperate North America, these brave new nonhierarchies
are warmly welcomed.

U.S. archaeology is nothing if not temperate, seeking safety in simplicity.
Cahokia a state? Never! Chaco-Aztec-Paquimé something more than Ruth
Benedict's Zuni? Not in my backyard! Political complexity had a short, swift
time in Southwestern archaeology, riding the crest of a more cosmopolitan
New Archaeology. New Archaeology may have suffered from acute (even
fatal) scientism, but it did at least think globally while it acted too locally.
Cross-cultural contexts and comparative studies were the order of the day,
in the service of middle-range theory. In that hopeful if naïve context, Chaco
looked like starter-kit kingdoms seen elsewhere and at other times in our
world (Schelberg 1984). But that cross-cultural divide could not, in the end, be
crossed. Why? With the postmodern retreat to local scales and local stories,
even otherwise un-deconstructed, science-minded U.S. archaeologists em-
brace the idea of social simplicity and small scales. We cling to the idea of a
stateless Native United States as we do to our hope of heaven. Again, why?

That question brings me to the other Casa Grande—the one near Phoenix, Arizona (Figure 3.4). Contemporary with and (to some degree) related to
the larger Mexican Paquimé, the Arizona Casa Grande is a fine example of
the Great Houses of the Upper Sonoran Desert. Arizona Great Houses are
often considered variants or outgrowths of platform mounds—the ground
floor of Casa Grande was apparently filled to provide an elevated platform.
Platform mounds and Great Houses have been the particular focus of archaeological study in the last decade (see Dean 2000 for a review). One of
the larger recent research programs, a New Archaeology relict, approached
platform mounds as elite residences, visible monuments to social and political hierarchy. The archaeologists *assumed* that platform mounds were elite
residences. That view has been supported and attacked along the same familiar ideological lines that structure debates about Chaco. Recent thinking,
paralleling Old World developments in the deconstruction and demotion of
monuments, seems to be swinging toward interpreting platform mounds not
so much as elite residences—protopalaces—but as communal ritual structures, built collectively, without hierarchy (see papers in Mills 2000).

That view runs counter to many Native traditional histories. Pima people
remember the residents of platform mounds as rulers, and not necessarily

FIGURE 3.4 Casa Grande, Phoenix, Arizona

benign rulers (Bahr et al. 1994; Teague 1993). The Pima, led by a culture-hero, rose up and destroyed those leaders, going from mound to mound to dispatch hierarchical overlords. This was class warfare—an American revolution four centuries before Lexington and Concord. Pima traditional history and archaeology seem congruent and complementary: Arizona Great Houses certainly can be interpreted as elite residences or chiefly houses—indeed, that *was* the ruling interpretation until wind from France blew into American journals and textbooks—and Pima histories confirm that ascription. I am not so much concerned about the truth of Great Houses and platform mounds: they may be elite residences, they may be communal ritual facilities, or (more likely) they may be both. I *am* concerned about our precipitate abandonment of interpretations leaning toward political complexity, in favor of those proposing kindler, gentler forms of collective action: heterarchies, collectives, ritualities. These social formations are simpler, and *therefore they are preferable* to older, more complex formations like chiefdoms and states.

There is a confusion, I think, between the simplicity of Ockham's razor and the simplicity of social forms. What I have come to call the Sin of Ockham is this: misapplication of the razor to the question of interest rather than to the logic of its answer. Life was always more complicated than we would represent by a close reading of the data. Humans do not now live, nor have they ever lived, parsimoniously, else we would still be swinging through trees. To err cautiously in archaeology is to err egregiously.

Competing accounts of *complex* phenomena can vary in their *logical* simplicity, but there is no imperative to understand the phenomena themselves as simple over complex. The complexity of the stock exchange remains, whatever the simplicity of its explanation. We seem to have extended the criterion of logical simplicity to a more generalized application: Reconstructions of an archaeological entity as a simple society seem inherently safer, better, more temperate than reconstructions that propose higher degrees of political complexity. An ancient society may have left archaeological evidence that is ambiguously simple or complex; we set simplicity as the default option. In general, these are *not* arguments of evidence; the evidence is there for either reading, simple or complex, and both readings can survive (but need not necessarily survive) the lottery of peer review, our ultimate criterion for acceptable work.

Then, how are we to judge? In the absence of tools for resolving ambiguity, our rules of evidence are, quite simply, either authority or consensus. Authority is ultimately ad hominem; consensus (an extended form of peer review) too often entails a lowest common denominator. In both, I believe, ascriptions of historical simplicity conflate the safety of Ockham (mistakenly) and personal, professional safety. Scholars who take chances pay the price. The confusion of logical and substantive simplicity is, after all, relatively benign, and professional survival is a Darwinian imperative.

Neither authority nor consensus is, however, inherently evil—just scholarly business as usual. But there is, I fear, the possibility of a real, unexamined evil at the heart of U.S. archaeology's great leveling—our disciplinary discomfort with ancient Native societies *within the United States* playing the same political games we see in societies south of the border or, for that matter, on every other continent. This is our third and final objection to places. *It is simply impossible:* Mississippian and Southwestern societies were *not capable* of political expansion beyond the bubble of chiefdoms, at best. As a discipline, we cannot see or allow a past that exceeds those tight limits.

That limiting view of ancient Native Americans is inherited from earlier days—we are a young discipline, but old enough to have passed through a half dozen academic generations. Oddly enough, our conservatism and temperance may begin with the early nineteenth-century normalization of the mythical Mound Builders—a chapter in U.S. archaeology's history that we view with pride. Phoenicians, Lost Tribes, and other even more imaginative non-Native candidates were dismissed in favor of our own Indians as the architects and builders of Hopewell and Mississippian monuments. That was a good thing, initially. But parsimony and uniformitarian conservatism, working through the years of unilineal evolutionary thinking, produced an archaeological worldview that the U.S. past could be simpler, but never more complex, than ethnographically known Native American social formations. Unexamined, our insistence on a placid, safe, simple past sets a glass ceiling on ancient Native American history. Other peoples have rises and falls, alarms and excursions, winners and losers—but not the Native peoples of the United States.

In conversations and debates with Mississippian and Southwestern archaeologists, there almost always comes a time when those denying Chaco-Aztec-Paquimé or demoting Cahokia say: "They couldn't have done that." At one Southwestern meeting, I was sternly admonished by a senior scholar to "remember the scale of the societies we are dealing with." I find that troublesome: Chaco and Paquimé were the size of a second-tier Mesoamerican city; and Cahokia was much larger, as large as many well-known Mesoamerican capitals. Why is it so impossible to imagine a past that differs from the stereotype model of Zuni or from French accounts of the poor tattered Natchez? Why do we insist that "they couldn't have done it"?

A close analysis of that glass ceiling will not reflect well on the deeper history of archaeology in the United States (for a polemical but sobering analysis, see Kehoe 1998). There is, I fear, at a distant intellectual remove, an almost racist aspect to the limits we set for *what might have been*. American intellectuals who set the tone of anthropological discourse long before anthropology was an accepted discipline—not today's archaeologists—saw the Indian as inferior, not capable of establishing lasting political formations, much less the state. That attitude toward Natives made their dispossession philosophically acceptable and propelled Manifest Destiny (see, for example, Kehoe 1998 and Kennedy 1994). Today's archaeologists do not share the antique racism—our anthropology rejects racism—but we are heirs to the founding intellectual traditions, at whatever remove in time and theory. And this is the third, far-from-obvious but most alarming objection to pre-Columbian palaces in the United States. Ancient societies in temperate zones around the world flirted with statehood; ancient societies around the globe built palaces. Yet we find these possibilities unthinkable for Natives within our national boundaries. But not, I think, for lack of evidence.

References Cited

Aikens, Nancy J., and John D. Schelberg
1984 Evidence for Organizational Complexity as Seen from the Mortuary Practices at Chaco Canyon. In *Recent Research on Chaco Prehistory*, edited by W. James Judge and John D. Schelberg, pp. 89–102. Reports of the Chaco Center 8. National Park Service, Albuquerque.
Bahr, Donald, Juan Smith, William Smith Allison, and Julian Hayden
1994 *The Short Swift Time of Gods on Earth: The Hohokam Chronicles*. University of California Press, Berkeley.
Benedict, Ruth
1934 *Patterns of Culture*. Houghton Mifflin, Boston.
Blanton, Richard E., Gary M. Feinman, Stephen A. Kowalewski, and Peter N. Peregrine
1999 A Dual-Processual Theory for the Evolution of Mesoamerican Civilization. *Current Anthropology* 37(1):1–14.

Dean, Jeffrey S. (editor)
2000 *Salado.* University of New Mexico Press, Albuquerque.

Dean, Jeffrey S., and John C. Ravesloot
1993 The Chronology of Cultural Interaction in the Gran Chichimeca. In *Culture and Contact: Charles C. Di Peso's Gran Chichimeca,* edited by Anne I. Woosley and John C. Ravesloot, pp. 83–103. University of New Mexico Press, Albuquerque.

Di Peso, Charles C.
1974 *Casas Grandes: A Fallen Trading Center of the Gran Chichimeca.* Amerind Foundation, Dragoon, AZ.

Elson, Mark D., Miriam T. Stark, and David A. Gregory (editors)
1995 The Roosevelt Community Development Study: New Perspectives on Tonto Basin Prehistory. Anthropological Papers 15. Center for Desert Archaeology, Tucson.

Frazier, Kendrick
2005 *People of Chaco.* 3rd ed. W. W. Norton, New York.

Fritz, John M.
1978 Paleopsychology Today: Ideational Systems and Human Adaptation in Prehistory. In *Social Archaeology: Beyond Subsistence and Dating,* edited by Charles L. Redman and others, pp. 37–59. Academic Press, New York.

Green, Jesse (editor)
1990 *Cushing at Zuni: The Correspondence and Journals of Frank Hamilton Cushing, 1879–1884.* University of New Mexico Press, Albuquerque.

Kehoe, Alice
1998 *The Land of Prehistory: A Critical History of American Archaeology.* Routledge, New York.

Kennedy, Roger G.
1994 *Hidden Cities: The Discovery and Loss of Ancient North American Civilization.* Free Press, New York.

LeBlanc, Steven A.
1999 *Prehistoric Warfare in the American Southwest.* University of Utah Press, Salt Lake City.

Lekson, Stephen H.
1984 *Great House Architecture of Chaco Canyon.* University of New Mexico Press, Albuquerque.
1999 *The Chaco Meridian: Centers of Political Power in the Ancient Southwest.* Altamira, Walnut Creek, CA.
2002 War in the Southwest, War in the World. *American Antiquity* 67(4):607–624.

Lekson, Stephen H., Thomas C. Windes, John R. Stein, and W. James Judge
1988 The Chaco Canyon Community. *Scientific American* 259(1):100–109.

Mathien, Francis Joan
1986 External Contacts and the Chaco Anasazi. In *Ripples in the Chichimec Sea: New Considerations of Southwestern-Mesoamerican Interactions,* edited by Francis Joan Mathien and Randall H. McGuire, pp. 220–242. Southern Illinois University Press, Carbondale.

2001 The Organization of Turquoise Production and Consumption by the Prehistoric Chacoans. *American Antiquity* 66(1):103–118.

McKenna, Peter J., and H. Wolcott Toll

1992 Regional Patterns of Great House Development among the Totah Anasazi. In *Anasazi Regional Organization and the Chaco System*, edited by David E. Doyel, pp. 133–143. Papers of the Maxwell Museum of Anthropology 5. Maxwell Museum of Anthropology, Albuquerque.

Milner, George R.

1998 *The Cahokia Chiefdom: The Archaeology of a Mississippian Society.* Smithsonian Institution Press, Washington, DC.

Mills, Barbara

2000 *Alternative Leadership Strategies in the Prehispanic Southwest.* University of Arizona Press, Tucson.

2002 Recent Research on Chaco: Changing Views on Economy, Ritual, and Society. *Journal of Archaeological Research* 10(1):65–117.

Minnis, Paul E.

1988 Four Instances of Specialized Production at Casas Grandes, Northwestern Chihuahua. *The Kiva* 53:181–193.

Morgan, William N.

1999 *Precolumbian Architecture in Eastern North America.* University Press of Florida, Gainesville.

Nabokov, Peter, and Robert Easton

1989 *Native American Architecture.* Oxford University Press, New York.

Neitzel, Jill E. (editor)

2003 *Pueblo Bonito: Center of the Chacoan World.* Smithsonian Institution Press, Washington, DC.

Noble, David grant (editor)

2004 *In Search of Chaco.* School of American Research Press, Santa Fe, NM.

Pauketat, Timothy R.

2004 *Ancient Cahokia and the Mississippians.* Cambridge University Press, Cambridge.

Rapoport, Amos

1969 *House Form and Culture.* Prentice-Hall, Englewood Cliffs, NJ.

Renfrew, Colin

2001 Production and Consumption in a Sacred Economy: The Material Correlates of High Devotional Expression at Chaco Canyon. *American Antiquity* 66(1):14–25.

Schelberg, John D.

1984 Analogy, Complexity, and Regionally Based Perspectives. In *Recent Research on Chaco Prehistory*, edited by W. James Judge and John D. Schelberg, pp. 5–21. Reports of the Chaco Center 8. National Park Service, Albuquerque.

Sofaer, Anna

1997 The Primary Architecture of the Chacoan Culture: A Cosmological Expression. In *Anasazi Architecture and American Design*, edited by Baker H. Morrow and V.B. Price, pp. 88–132. University of New Mexico Press, Albuquerque.

Sofaer, Anna (producer)
1999 *The Mystery of Chaco Canyon.* Video. Bullfrog Films, Oley, PA.
Teague, Lynne S.
1993 Prehistory and the Traditions of the O'odham and Hopi. *The Kiva* 58(4):435–454.
Turner, Christy G., II, and Jaquiline A. Turner
1999 *Man Corn: Cannibalism and Violence in the Prehistoric American Southwest.* University of Utah Press, Salt Lake City.
Vivian, R. Gwinn
1990 *The Chacoan Prehistory of the San Juan Basin.* Academic Press, San Diego.
Weigand, Phil C., and Garman Harbottle
1993 The Role of Turquoise in the Ancient Mesoamerican Trade Structure. In *The American Southwest and Mesoamerica: Systems of Prehistoric Exchange,* edited by Jonathon E. Ericson and Timothy G. Baugh, pp. 159–177. Plenum Press, New York.
Windes, Thomas C., and Dabney Ford
1996 The Chaco Wood Project: Chronometric Reappraisal of Pueblo Bonito. *American Antiquity* 61(2):295–310.
Wright, Barton (editor)
1988 *The Mythic World of the Zuni as Written by Frank Hamilton Cushing.* University of New Mexico Press, Albuquerque.
Young, Biloine Whiting, and Melvin L. Fowler
2000 *Cahokia: The Great American Metropolis.* University of Illinois Press, Urbana.

PART 2

*Palaces as Active Stage Sets
of Political Ideology*

CHAPTER 4

Sacred and Profane Mountains of the Pasión
CONTRASTING ARCHITECTURAL PATHS TO POWER

Arthur A. Demarest

Recent debate in Maya archaeology has emphasized the great regional variability of Classic Maya civilization. Controversy has also centered around the *nature* of ancient Maya states, that is, the degree to which they were "centralized" or "decentralized" and the realms of action of Classic-period rulers —economic, political, or ideological (see, for example, Fox et al. 1996). More recently, scholars have begun to accept that both perspectives are in part correct, with the degree of centralization and economic involvement of state authority varying over time and space in Classic Maya history (Demarest 1992, 1996a; Marcus 1993). Evidence suggests that in some regions during the Late Classic there were more centralized states (e.g., Caracol, Tikal, Calakmul) with an active state role in economic infrastructure and local community integration (Aoyama 1996, 1999; Chase and Chase 1996; Folan 1992; Folan et al. 1995). Yet, in general, most Maya centers seem to have had less centralized authority or settlement and a heavy reliance on warfare and/or ritual as sources of royal power to hold together their loose hegemonies of satellite centers and sustaining populations (Ball and Taschek 1991; Demarest 1992; Fox and Cook 1996; Sanders and Webster 1988).

Recent excavations and settlement surveys across the Maya lowlands have recovered even more evidence of regional variability. Classic Maya states appear to have ranged from small, ritual-dominated polities to much larger and more centralized urban centers. Even within a single region, kingdoms experienced both gradual changes and radical shifts in their degree of centralized power; the extent of their hegemonies; and the varying economic, military, and ideological bases of the power of the kings (Demarest 1992, 1996a, 1996b, 1997; Marcus 1993; Martin and Grube 2000).

Realization of this variability and attention to its parameters have increased in the past decade. This attention to regional and local variability responds to the inductive discoveries of archaeology and epigraphy. Yet it also reflects the current theoretical content of American anthropology, which has been struggling to join the postmodern or "postprocessual" discourses (Bourdieu 1977; Foucault 1972; Giddens 1984) of critical theory, hermeneutics, and constructivist theory, even within the subfield of archaeology (Hodder 1985, 1986; Preucel 1991; Shanks and Tilley 1987, 1992).

These new perspectives have led to greater interest in aspects of conscious agency, including individual and class strategies. Fields of strategic action and practice included politics, ritual, and "ideology" broadly defined. Renewed interest in agency and ideology has focused attention in new ways on the constructed settings of such practice, in both public and residential architecture.

As rulers competed in the volatile Classic political landscape, they did so as conscious individual and group agents. They were constantly adjusting their strategies of gaining and maintaining power and authority in response to the resistance of competing elites and other individual and group interests within their society. Long-distance exchange networks, manipulation of dynastic history, lavish religious rituals, and status-reinforcing monuments and architecture were elements employed in their political struggles as individuals and as agents of subgroup or community interest. Palaces, as the principal sites for ritual and political events, were also among the instruments of power utilized by elites in their status rivalry with other rulers and their efforts to generate, consolidate, and legitimate their power and authority over their local and regional populations, courts, and vassals.

For these reasons, palace architecture and geographical settings may reflect the political strategies of the particular Classic city-state, dynasty, or ruler. Palaces were not casually constructed in the Maya world; they were carefully placed, constructed, and ornamented to reflect and reinforce conceptions of sacred authority (Christie 2003; Inomata and Houston 2001). Analyses of these palaces and their relation to cultural geography can help us to understand the varying strategies and bases of Maya royal power. In turn, these insights, together with other archaeological, paleoecological, and historical evidence, may help us to understand the protean nature of the Classic Maya state.

Pasión River Palaces

In this volume we are exploring the role of elite residences as instruments of power, not merely as areas of occupation. Such a perspective has been an active element of research design in the past ten consecutive seasons of Vanderbilt University projects in the western Petén (Figure 4.1), including the Petexbatun project from 1989 to 1994 (Demarest and Houston 1989; Demarest et al. 1992; Demarest et al. 1991; Demarest and Valdés 1995; Valdés et al. 1993), the Punta de Chimino project in 1996 and 1997 (Demarest et al. 1996), and the ongoing Cancuén archaeological project (Demarest and Barrientos 1999, 2000, 2001), which began with reconnaissance in 1998. Each of these projects excavated hundreds of Classic Maya houses, but about a dozen of these were full-blown palaces, that is, elaborately constructed residences

FIGURE 4.1 Map showing western Petén, including Dos Pilas, Aguateca, and Cancuén

of royal families in which a variety of political functions were also carried out. Each of these palaces was distinctive as assessed in terms of: (1) how it was placed in relation to natural surface features deemed significant by the builders, (2) the incorporation of cosmological models into structure orientation and design, (3) orientation to subterranean features, (4) defensive considerations, (5) projections of social distance, and (6) functions carried out within or adjacent to the palace compounds.

The types of activities for which specific areas of Maya palaces were designed included royal residence; feasting and alliance; and rituals witnessed by elite visitors, court members, and local subordinates. Palaces provided a segregated social context for elite ancestor worship, conjuring, visions, and prophecy. Areas for presentation of captives, formal audiences, and witnessing of processions were all incorporated into some Pasión Valley palaces. Yet other palaces served as areas for production of polychrome ceramics and painting and for the work of scribes and other artists. In a few cases, palaces even served to claim access to or control of special resources or activities. Some palaces, or portions of palaces, were more secluded spaces whose political functions included the creation of status-reinforcing social distance for the royal family and court. All of these activities were carried out and were reflected (to greater or lesser degree) in the various palaces of the Pasión region.

The specific set of features found in each palace could be used to interpret the political and historical agendas and stratagems of the ruling elites of that particular center during the period or periods involved. Some contrasting examples of Pasión Valley palaces highlight the active role of palaces as instruments of power and the differing strategies of elites. In each case, architecture and engineered landscapes were used by the royal families to pursue their particular political strategies. Conversely, we can speculatively "read" the details of these Pasión Valley palaces—and those of other Classic states—as clues to the range of forms and functions of the Maya state.

Dos Pilas and the Petexbatun Hegemony

The first three examples of Pasión Valley elite complexes come from the Petexbatun capital center of Dos Pilas and its second capital at Aguateca (Figure 4.1). The political context of the palaces relates to the history of the Petexbatun dynasty, whose first king was enthroned at Dos Pilas early in the seventh century after having escaped the power struggles at Tikal (Fahsen et al. n.d.; Houston and Mathews 1985; Mathews and Willey 1991). From this newly established dynastic seat, the rulers of Dos Pilas sought to become a major power. First, they embarked on wars with Tikal as part of an interregional strategy devised by an alliance of centers led by Calakmul (Fahsen et al. n.d.; Martin and Grube 2000:54–67). Then they focused on regional wars and alliances that gave them control of much of the Pasión River trade route through dominance of Arroyo de Piedra, Tamarandito, Punta de Chimino, Aguateca, and later Seibal (Demarest 1996b, 1997; Demarest and Valdes 1995).

Yet warfare was only one of the tools of Dos Pilas expansionism. Like other K'ul Ajaw (Sacred Lords), the Dos Pilas dynasty drew upon cosmology, ritual, sacred geography, alliance, feasting, patronage networks in exotic goods, and kinship to establish its authority and its claims to royal power, to legitimate that power, and to extend its hegemony. The use of all these tools of dynastic policy may be "read" from (or into) its various royal residences. The late date of Dos Pilas's entry into the power politics of the Maya world and its intrusion into the Petexbatun region perhaps required redoubled efforts in the use of all possible devices. Recall that in the eighth century, status-rivalry between competing rulers and their subordinates had led to an intensification of inter-elite contacts, a proliferation of centers with their own emblem glyph designation, and the creation of a variety of subordinate offices and power-sharing arrangements (Culbert 1991; B. Fash et al. 1992; W. Fash 1991; Stuart 1995:273–277). In the Petexbatun, the palaces described here were constructed on the eve of a period of intensified warfare (A.D. 760–830), manifest in the construction of walled fortifications and moats encircling Dos Pilas, Aguateca, Punta de Chimino, and many other sites (including villages) in the region. Obviously, in such a volatile political landscape, the rulers of Dos Pilas—overlords of the Petexbatun hegemony—would need to utilize devices of every kind, including architecture.

The Murciélagos Palace

One of the principal royal residences of the Dos Pilas dynasty was its Murciélagos Palace (Figure 4.2). The palace was located in the center of the site, directly between its two ritual epicenters, the West Plaza Group and the eastern El Duende Complex. Burials and an inscribed throne identify this group as a royal residence, probably of Rulers 3 and 4 of the Dos Pilas dynasty. The palace was placed in this location late in the site's history, atop a hill with a gushing spring and a cave system beneath it—a most revered location in Mesoamerican concepts of sacred geography. Hills with caves and springs were seen as the womb of the earth from which people, gods, and sacred waters emerged (Brady 1991, 1997; Coe 1988; Heyden 1973, 1975, 1981; MacLeod and Puleston 1979). Perhaps in deference to its sacred location, there had been no occupation at all on this hill prior to the palace construction in the mid-eighth century. The Murciélagos Palace sat astride the east-west axis of the subterranean universe of Dos Pilas, as surveyed and excavated by James Brady and the Petexbatun Caves Survey Subproject (Brady 1997; Brady et al. 1997). The cave system passes beneath the great eastern El Duende Complex, Murciélagos, and the West Plaza Group, with the caves emerging in springs at each key sacred node: in front of El Duende, below Murciélagos, and on the edge of the West Plaza (Figure 4.3). Surface architecture was placed in relation to this subterranean system, especially in the Murciélagos complex, where all the architecture is aligned with the cave system.

The ideologically strategic position of the Murciélagos complex in the geography of Dos Pilas was further enhanced by its position astride the surface east-west processional axis of the site, incorporating a portion of the path between the El Duende Complex and the West Plaza Group and its temples (Figure 4.3). Rites are epigraphically identified as having been repeated in both the east and west complex. The procession path was guided into the Murciélagos royal compound by an impressive entry ramp on the

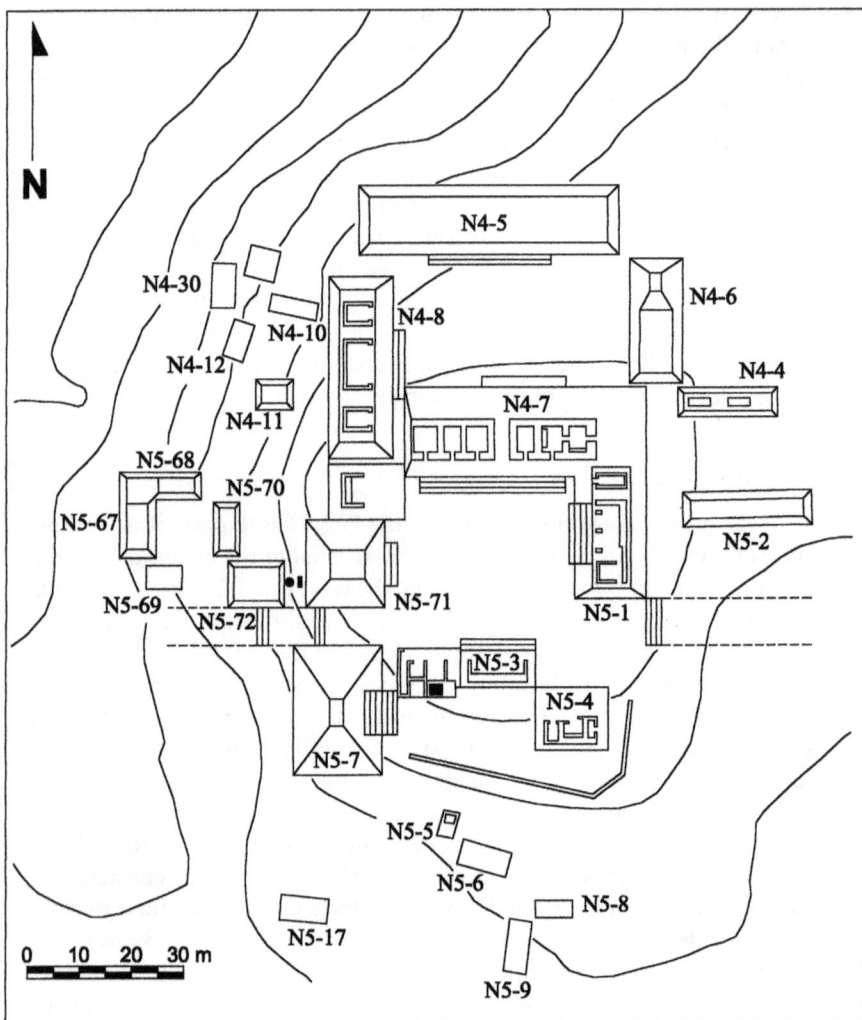

FIGURE 4.2 Map of the Murciélagos Palace at Dos Pilas

western side between two ancestor shrines, then passed presentation palaces and the royal throne room with its inscribed throne (Figure 4.4). The path then left the compound through a formal stair to continue to the east to the terraces, monuments, and plaza before the huge 70 m high El Duende temple.

The use of the Murciélagos Palace as an instrument of ideological legitimation may be seen in the placement and details of each structure in the two nested plaza groups of the compound. As has been detailed elsewhere (Demarest et al. 1995), throne rooms, presentation palaces, shrines, and residences were aligned with the surface and subterranean ritual circuit of Dos Pilas to create a series of well-defined arenas. These theaters were sacralized loci of elite rituals, feasting, and other interactions with visiting elites or local leaders. The positioning of the palace and its features would have allowed many of these events to occur at the time of the public events and processions in and between the more open large arenas of the Dos Pilas Plaza Group and El Duende terraces. The populace would have been aware of elite activities yet excluded from them, reinforcing the social distance of the ruling family and of those permitted to enter its elevated and restricted (literally and physically, as well as symbolically) inner circle.

The northern plaza group of the palace formed a more restricted family compound with residences, kitchens, and associated probable retainer house platforms (Demarest et al. 1995; Wolley and Rodas 1995). Yet a small, higher, narrow structure, N4-6, was set on the east side of the plaza in the typical "Plaza Plan 2" position (Figures 4.2 and 4.4) of an ancestral tomb and

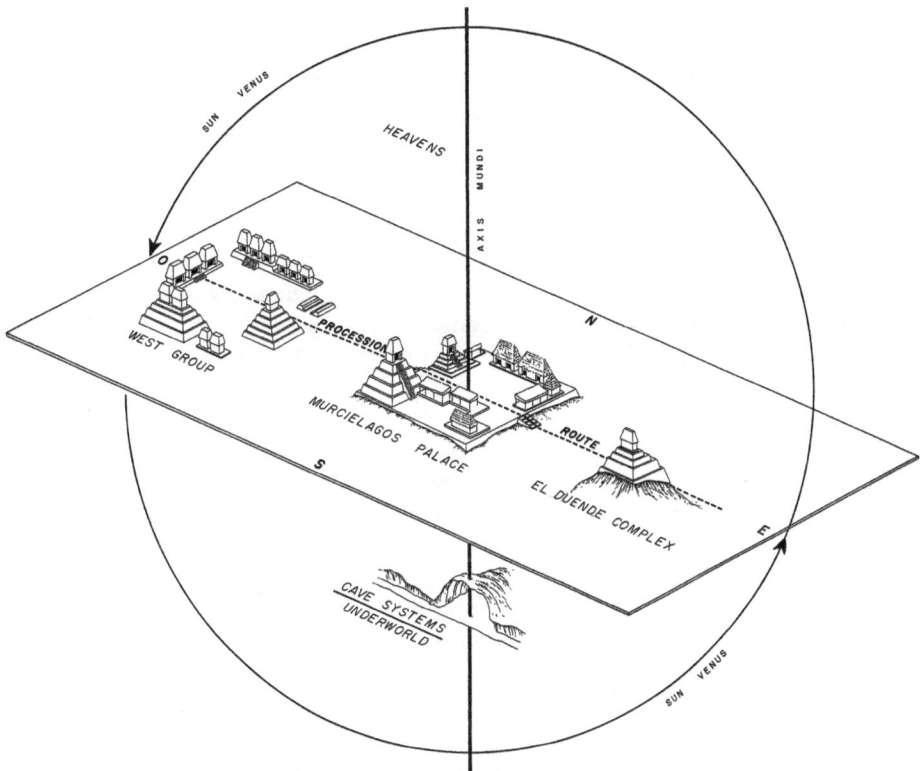

FIGURE 4.3 Position of the Murciélagos Palace in relation to the surface procession route, the subterranean universe, and the sacred cosmogram of Dos Pilas

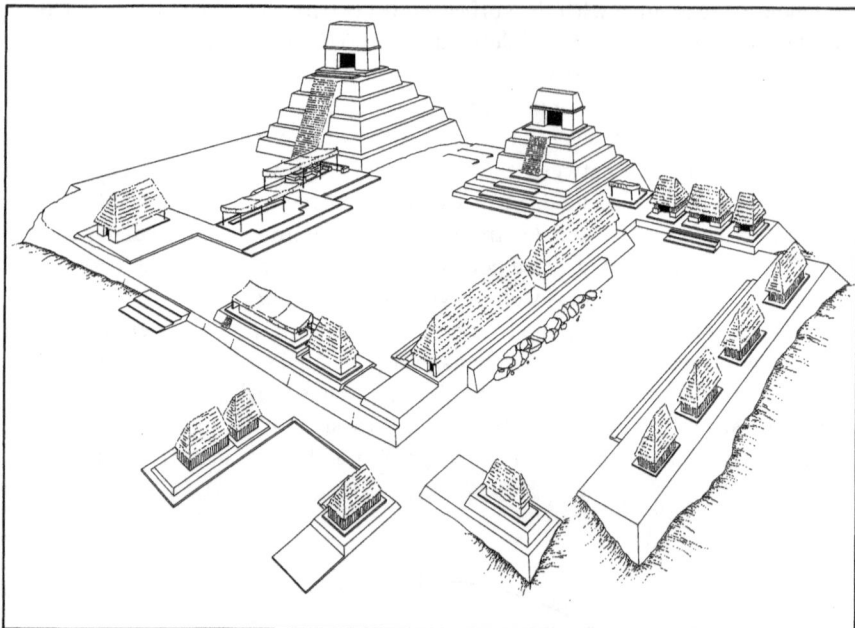

FIGURE 4.4 Reconstruction of the Murciélagos Palace at Dos Pilas

family shrine (Demarest et al. 1995). Such structures or burials were the foci of family identity, daily worship, and the sacralization of residential space throughout the Classic Maya lowlands at all levels of society (McAnany 1995). In elite contexts, such Plaza Plan 2 shrines generally contain a prestigious buried male ancestor. Excavation of N4-6 did discover the typical burial offering of three vessels—a polychrome vase, bowl, and plate (Demarest et al. 1995). But rather than a skeleton alongside these objects, there was a wide crevice in the bedrock blocked with an artificial fill of black earth, stones, and eroded ceramics. Clearing the fill revealed a narrow natural cleft in the bedrock that led down toward the east-west cave system directly below the palace. The shrine in the northern royal family residential compound symbolically entombed the east-west cave system, the path of the Night Sun and Venus through Xibalba (Figure 4.3).

The shrine had completed the association of the royal family with this Maya cosmogram. The ruler and his family then sat upon the sacred mountain, its spring, and its cave, and astride both the east-west path of procession and of movement of the Sun and Venus and the east-west cave system to which the axis mundi was connected by the royal family shrine and cave. Both the solar and subterranean planes had been symbolically and physically captured by the Murciélagos Palace, enhancing the authority of its beleaguered K'ul Ajaw. The palace complex was a brilliant tool of ideological legitimation, drawing on the natural, yet sacred, geography of its placement. The palace also provided a constructed setting where the frequent practice of activities was sacralized by architecturally enhanced sacred associations.

The "Lady of Cancuén" Palace

Another strategy of Maya rulers was alliance formation sealed and marked by royal marriages linking dynasties. This mechanism of maintaining and expanding hegemony was celebrated at another, smaller elite residential complex at Dos Pilas. This palace group, consisting of structures L4-39, 40, 41, 42, 43, and a nearby smaller platform, was located just to the west of Dos Pilas's major West Group epicenter and less than 100 m north of one of its major royal palaces. It has been identified by its carved throne and royal burial as the residence of a principal wife of one of Dos Pilas's great rulers, designated Ruler 3 (Houston and Stuart 1990).

Ruler 3, a king or perhaps a regent of Dos Pilas (Martin and Grube 2000:60–62), had expanded his Petexbatun hegemony by the conquest of Seibal in A.D. 735, an event celebrated in monuments at his capitals at Dos Pilas and Aguateca, as well as at Seibal. Yet, perhaps an equally strategic move by this ruler was his marriage to the Lady of Cancuén, also celebrated in hieroglyphic texts (Martin and Grube 2000:61–62; Palka 1990; Wolley and Wright 1990). With the conquest of Seibal, clear domination of the Petexbatun region, and this alliance with Cancuén, the Dos Pilas dynasty had secured control of the Pasión River Valley trade route, the major trade artery of the western Petén region. At the base of the highlands and the exact beginning of the navigable portion of the Pasión River—technically the "head of navigation"—was the royal center of Cancuén, with its protected portage and enormous royal palace (see below), the latter surrounded by workshops in imported highland and Motagua Valley exotics. The more ancient, prestigious, and wealthy dynasty there (Fahsen and Demarest 2001), and its control of upper Pasión trade routes, made Ruler 3's Cancuén bride a figure of great importance at Dos Pilas.

It is not surprising, then, that this strategic move was commemorated and its effect amplified by architecture and monuments, and by the rituals that presumably accompanied their erection. In the Late Classic Maya lowlands, rulers and their advising inner circles were clearly empowered and conscious agents, manipulating existing symbolic systems in a competitive context. The "Lady of Cancuén" Palace was an instrument of the alliance strategy, making a clear statement to allies, rivals, and supporters, as well as providing an arena for specific events and elite practice related to these dynastic affiliations.

The importance of this particular alliance was reflected in the extraordinary (and anomalous!) architecture of the "Lady of Cancuén" Palace. Most elite architecture at Dos Pilas reflects the rapid and late construction of this

FIGURE 4.5 Panel 19 of Dos Pilas showing Ruler 3 and the Lady of Cancuén witnessing the prince's bloodletting

capital in the late seventh century, with its few rows of finished masonry and very few corbeled vaults, even in its royal palaces. In contrast, this queen's compound had finely crafted masonry, corbeled-vaulted chambers, stuccoed sculpture, and finely crafted monuments. Excavations there (Wolley and Wright 1990) uncovered this fine architecture, the queen's carved death throne, and her burial beneath it. Her rich grave goods included not only vessels but also jade encrustations in her teeth. This was an unusual feature at Dos Pilas but a common one at her parents' kingdom of Cancuén, a major jade-working center.

The political and ritual uses of this queen's residential complex are suggested by a fragmented panel found nearby. Panel 19 (Palka 1990, 1997) makes these uses even more explicit (Figure 4.5). It shows a scene of the type of ritual probably held there, with the Lady of Cancuén and Ruler 3 featured as witnesses to a genital bloodletting by a young boy, possibly the next ruler (Ruler 4, K'awiil Chan K'inich). The scene is overseen, perhaps sponsored, by a lord from Calakmul (Houston and Stuart 1990; Martin and Grube 2000:60–

61). Taken together with the palace death throne, the burial, and the exquisite corbeled-vault architecture, the panel confirms the stratagem of the complex as announcing, celebrating, and utilizing Dos Pilas's alliance with Cancuén. Particularly in the presence of foreign lords, Ruler 3 wished to stress his relationship with that older southern dynastic power—a prestige-enhancing kinship, which also secured control of southern products and status-reinforcing goods. The "Lady of Cancuén" Palace, its features, and its monuments attest to the alliance-building skills of these Late Classic Petexbatun K'ul Ajaw.

The Palace at Aguateca

The same Dos Pilas lords (at least during the reign of Rulers 3 and 4) who had their principal ceremonial seat at the Murciélagos Palace had a secondary palace less than 10 km away at Aguateca. The royal family and elements of the court presumably moved between their residences and administrative seats at Dos Pilas and Aguateca. Such multiple palaces for kings were common elsewhere, including Mesoamerica (Evans 2001). The twin-capital structure has also been observed in the Maya lowlands at Cahal Pech and Buenavista (Ball and Taschek 2001).

What is interesting about the Dos Pilas–Aguateca movement between capitals is that the respective palaces seem to have had different, though overlapping, functions. As discussed above, the Murciélagos Palace sat astride the ceremonial surface circuits of that site and drew its power from cosmology, ritual, and sacred geography. The palace of Aguateca more clearly served a defensive function, reflecting the costs of the Dos Pilas lords' most celebrated political and economic stratagem, that of warfare and conquest. Of course, all functions and strategies (as interpreted from activity areas and architecture) were practiced to varying degrees at all palaces, and after the defeat and destruction of Dos Pilas in A.D. 761, the palace at Aguateca continued as the major royal seat of its somewhat smaller kingdom until about A.D. 800.

During the principal reigns of the Dos Pilas lords, however, some *primary* functions of the Murciélagos and Aguateca residences may have been distinctive, and perhaps complementary. The later lords of Dos Pilas presided over major processions and rituals from their Murciélagos capital seat, but they had a highly secure defensible residence at Aguateca. There the royal residential complex has been extensively explored by Takeshi Inomata, first with the Vanderbilt Petexbatun Projects and later with his continuing research there (Demarest 1997; Inomata 1995, 1997, in press; Inomata et al. 1998).

The security of this royal residence could not have been greater. The royal residences and associated court and elite buildings were constructed on a tongue of escarpment with steep cliffs on one side and a 60–70 m chasm on the other. This epicenter was connected to the rest of the site only by two

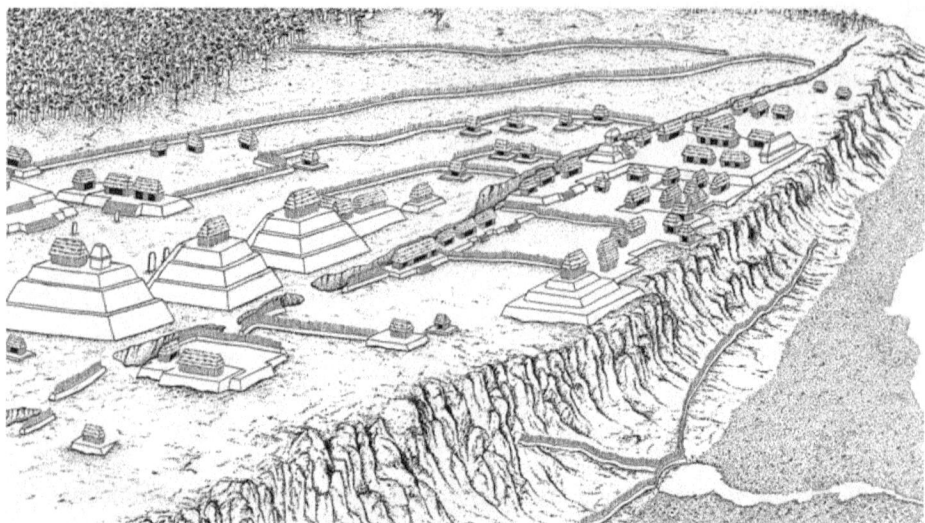

FIGURE 4.6 The citadel and defenses at Aguateca (ca. A.D. 800)

narrow land bridges. As warfare intensified in the region, these natural defenses were augmented by the construction of a series of long stone walls to
sustain palisades, enclosing the royal compound within several nested defensive perimeters (Figure 4.6). For the last kings of Dos Pilas and the later
Aguateca dynasty, the formidable setting of Aguateca's palace provided a
secure site for daily residence, administration, and the crafting of elite high-
status goods.

Excavations of rapidly abandoned and burned structures at Aguateca recovered in situ evidence of elite craft production, which was another major
function of this palace and its associated court residences (Inomata 1995,
2001, in press; Inomata and Stiver 1998; Inomata and Triadan 2000). Inomata
has elucidated the skilled crafting activities carried out near the palace by
artisans who were themselves high elites, possibly even relatives or members of the royal family. The skills and knowledge of these court artisans gave
them a "cultural capital" that allowed them to function as prestigious specialists creating status-reinforcing goods for their own use or exchange as
well as for the patronage networks of the nearby K'ul Ajaw (Inomata 2001).
Such elite craft artisans, sometimes functioning as attached specialists and
sometimes controlling the distribution of their products, were probably associated with and resident near most Classic lowland royal palaces (Hendon
1991; Stuart 1989). In the Petexbatun kingdom, however, the Aguateca Palace
provided the most secure setting for patient completion of the crafting of
such highly valued goods.

Furthermore, by the reign of Ruler 4, the royal family and its court, including artisan elites, might have physically resided more often at Agua-

teca than at Dos Pilas. The Murciélagos Palace may have been the center of elaborate rituals and processions of the kingdom at its cosmologically most sacred residence. Yet by the reign of Ruler 4, it would not have provided a safe residence for the court or its associated elite artisans, given the volatile landscape of increasing status-rivalry, with its attendant dangers of war, usurpation, or assassination. The latter dangers were well demonstrated by the defeat and sacking of Dos Pilas in A.D. 761 and the thorough ritual destruction of the royal throne within the Murciélagos Palace (Wolley 1995), and, a generation later, by the destruction of Aguateca itself (Inomata 1995, in press).

The Royal Palace at Cancuén

I have speculated above on the uses of elite residential architecture at the Murciélagos complex for control of public as well as elite ceremony and for the capture of ideological power. The "Lady of Cancuén" Palace made a clear statement celebrating and cementing alliance. At Aguateca, the palace and its adjoining structures provided a defended area for royal residence and elite craft production (the latter was both an economic and an ideological activity). These Petexbatun centers and their palaces can be contrasted with the site of Cancuén and the far more impressive palace of the affinal relatives of the Petexbatun lords. A single sprawling complex, the palace combined a wide range of functions. Cancuén was a more ancient kingdom than Dos Pilas, and it had survived and flourished since the fourth century on its strategic economic position and its political alliances.

Cancuén is located just north of the last rapids of the upper Pasión (Figure 4.1), that is, at the portage that marks the beginning of the navigable portion of the Pasión River. From this point to Mexico, the Pasión River formed a calm, wide navigable trade artery for the entire western lowlands. Throughout the Classic period, the Cancuén dynasty controlled this gateway between the lowlands and the highlands, providing them with the extraordinary wealth that is reflected in the site's caches, monuments, and oversized palace (Demarest and Barrientos 1999, 2000, 2001). Continuous alliances allowed this very economically oriented center to survive the hegemonic wars of the Classic period, first through association with the Teotihuacan-related dynasty of Tikal, then with the rising hegemony of Calakmul, and subsequently, in the early eighth century, with the Petexbatun kingdom, by forging the famous marriage alliance, discussed above, that was celebrated in monuments and in the "Lady of Cancuén" Palace at Dos Pilas. Finally, in the later eighth and early ninth centuries, the Cancuén kingdom was allied with Machaquila, and together they controlled the upper Pasión region. Monumental inscriptions at Cancuén and other sites confirm each of these associations and alliances (Fahsen and Demarest 2001; Fahsen et al. 2002).

The palace at Cancuén provided a spectacular series of settings for feast-

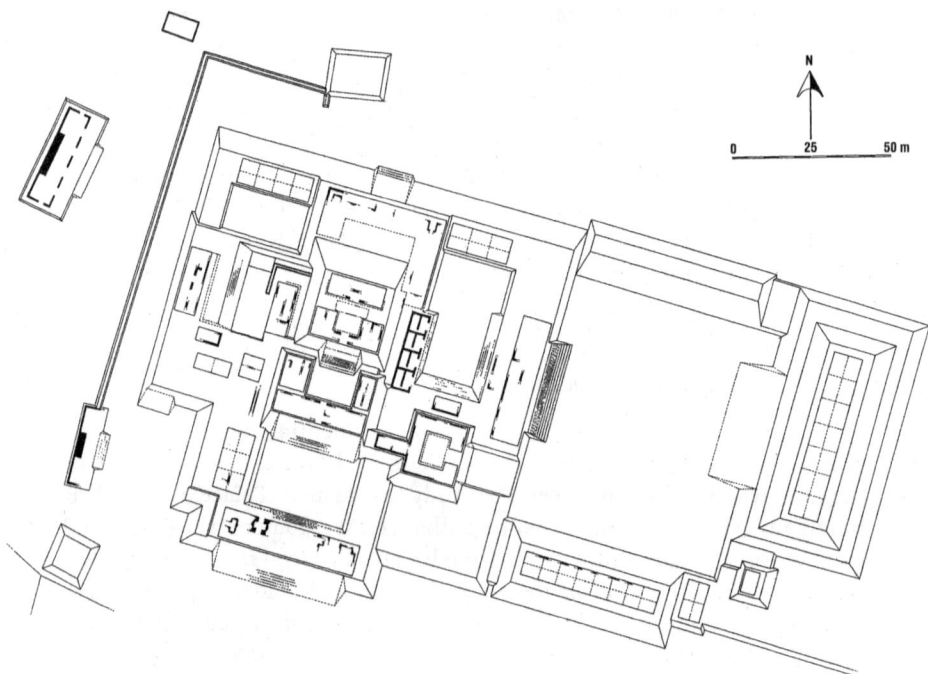

FIGURE 4.7 Preliminary map of the palace at Cancuén

ing and alliance formation, as well as for ceremonies and rituals. It was also a seat of economic power, in contrast to the more ideological orientation of the palaces like Murciélagos. The entire site of Cancuén lacked the type of very large temples and presentation structures found at the West Plaza Group and the El Duende Complex at Dos Pilas. Indeed, there is no clear stage for *public* spectacles such as Katun-ending bloodlettings or other public rites. (This lack of temples may be one explanation for why such a large, important center has received minimal archaeological attention.) One speculative explanation for the minimal religious architecture at Cancuén is that it lies at the interface between the highlands and the lowlands, just a few kilometers from highland steep karst hills filled with caves that were used as sacred shrines (Woodfill et al. 2002). At Cancuén, the Maya shamans and elites may have used the original *uitz*, or "sacred mountains with caves in them," as ritual foci rather than the "artificial imitations" used at most centers. This hypothesis will be confirmed or rejected by coming seasons of cave research and settlement studies in the upper Pasión. It is also possible that the presence of such cave shrines may have moved some ritual activities out of the realm of authority of its K'ul Ajaw.

The Cancuén Palace was very large and finely constructed (Figure 4.7), in contrast to the shoddy Pasión-Usumacinta architecture found to the north. About 200 stone-masonry corbeled-vaulted rooms were arranged around a series of restricted courtyards, beginning with large but closed courts, and moving to successively smaller courtyards connected via stairways (at least one hieroglyphic) flanked by carved panels, stelae, altars, and other monuments (Figure 4.8). Some rooms were built with oversized, pretentious walls of pure masonry more than seven meters high. It was an ideal setting for feasting and for inspiring awe in visiting elites, but its activities were restricted from public view, without any *apparent* ideologically oriented architectural devices or the use of sacred geography, so notable at the Murciélagos Palace at Dos Pilas. The location of the palace has no specific cosmological significance, at least none yet perceived by the excavators (Barrientos et al. 2002; Barrientos and Luin 2002).

The palace was, however, placed just to the south of Cancuén's best-defined and best-protected portages and large, open public plazas. A key role for the Late Classic rulers in the site's economic activities may be reflected in the presence of workshops in chert and obsidian as well as jade and pyrite, many just to the south of the palace (Kovacevich et al. 2001). Jade working was being carried out on a massive scale in which large jade nod-

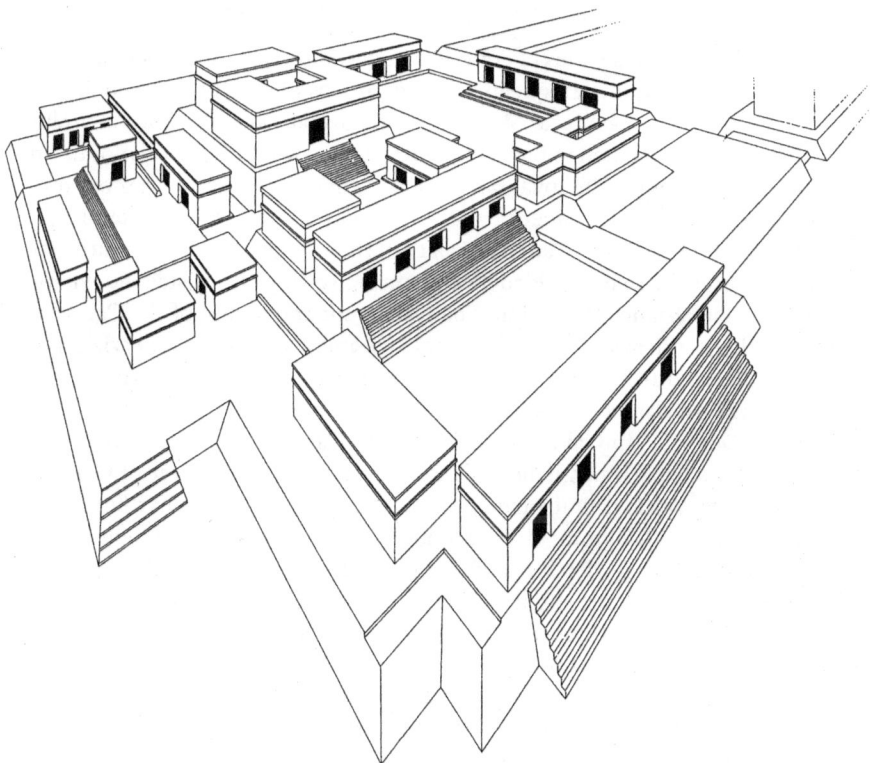

FIGURE 4.8 Reconstruction view of the western courtyards and stairs of the Cancuén Palace

ules (one boulder weighed more than 35 pounds) were sliced into blanks for plaques, and other pieces were broken, pounded, and polished into beads. Over 1,200 fragments of jade, unfinished pieces, and debitage were recovered by preliminary excavation of deposits at one corner of one workshop (Kovacevich and Neff 2002; Kovacevich et al. 2002). These deposits attest to the key economic position of Cancuén in controlling highland and southern-lowland lithics and their processing, transport, and exchange via the Pasión River trade route that begins with the portage located within 100 m of the palace.

In all respects, this oversized palace, with its nine closed courts for elite activities, suggests royal concern with exotics exchange and alliance formation. The paucity of large ritual architecture at the site may also reflect this distinctive political and economic state strategy (Barrientos et al 2002; Fahsen and Demarest 2001). As the many buried portions (more than 100 of its rooms) are unearthed, we will discover whether elite craft loci (as at Aguateca) and other types of activity areas were incorporated into this sprawling complex, the largest of the Pasión Valley palaces.

Discussion: Palaces and Varying Sources of Royal Power

Obviously, we have a series of contrasts between the palace of Cancuén, the Murciélagos and Cancuén queen's palaces at Dos Pilas, and the second Dos Pilas royal seat at Aguateca. Murciélagos Palace at Dos Pilas was an architectural device designed to harness the religious power of a sacred mountain and associate it with the royal family. The Aguateca Palace was a more protected, secure place of residence and craft production for the same family (at least until A.D. 761). The Cancuén Palace of their in-laws far to the south was a larger complex that provided awe-inspiring settings for residence, visits, feasting, and alliance formation. The placement and nature of the Cancuén Palace also confirm that dynasty's probable involvement in supervision of the portage and in the production and exchange of lithics and exotics, the basis of the wealth of the Cancuén polity. The palace of the "Lady of Cancuén" at Dos Pilas linked the Petexbatun and Cancuén royal dynasties.

There has been much debate about the "basis" of the power of Classic-period kings. Agricultural management, market control, redistribution of long-distance trade commodities, production and distribution of high-status artifacts, military leadership and tribute collection, theater-state performance, and shamanistic ritual have all been identified by various scholars as *the* principal basis of royal power. Clearly, all these fields of action were important, but probably to differing degrees in each polity. As with so much in Classic Maya archaeology, we find that variability was the only rule—with elites in different regions and in different circumstances relying to varying degrees on these alternative sources of power and authority.

What we have learned in the past twelve years of Pasión Valley research is that a key to identifying the *specific* activities and sources of power for each particular dynasty may be found in the nature of their elite residential architecture. As active instruments of political agency, the palaces reflect directly the basis of their power or what the elites themselves claimed to be the basis of their authority. The degree to which such claims were successful can be judged by the histories of each kingdom. But the intent of royal stratagems can be ascertained from the nature of the palaces themselves— literally the architectural settings and instruments of political strategy.

Acknowledgments

All figures are by Luis Fernando Luin, courtesy of Vanderbilt University Press, the Vanderbilt Petexbatun Project, and the Vanderbilt Cancuén Project. For advice, help, and critique on this paper, I would like to thank Brigitte Kovacevich, Federico Fahsen, Rudy Larios, Tomás Barrientos, Luis Fernando Luin, Claudia Wolley, Héctor Escobedo, Juan Antonio Valdés, and Ron Bishop. The research described in this chapter was supported by the National Geographic Society, the H. F. Guggenheim Foundation, the Swedish International Development Authority, Alimentos Kern, S.A., and Vanderbilt University.

References Cited

Aoyama, Kazuo
1996 Exchange, Craft Specialization, and Ancient Maya State Formation: A Study of Chipped Stone Artifacts from the Southeast Maya Lowlands. Unpublished Ph.D. dissertation, University of Pittsburgh.
1999 *Ancient Maya State, Urbanism, Exchange, and Craft Specialization: Chipped Stone Evidence from the Copán Valley and the La Entrada Region, Honduras.* University of Pittsburgh Memoirs of Latin American Archaeology No. 12. Department of Anthropology, University of Pittsburgh.
Ball, Joseph W., and Jennifer Taschek
1991 Late Classic Lowland Maya Political Organization and Central Place Analysis: New Insights from the Upper Belize Valley. *Ancient Mesoamerica* 2(2):149–165.
2001 The Buenavista–Cahal Pech Royal Court: Multi-Palace Court Mobility and Usage in a Petty Lowland Maya Kingdom. In *Royal Courts of the Ancient Maya: Case Studies*, Vol. 2, edited by Takeshi Inomata and Stephen Houston. Westview Press, Boulder, CO.
Barrientos, Tomás, Arthur A. Demarest, Ron Bishop, and Federico Fahsen
2001 Redescubriendo Cancuén: Nuevos datos sobre un sitio fronterizo entre las Tierras Bajas y el Altiplano Maya. In *XIV Simposio de Investigaciones Arqueológicas en Guatemala*, edited by Laporte, Suasnavar, and Arroyo, pp. 569–588. Ministerio de Cultura y Deportes, IDAEH, Asociación Tikal, Guatemala City.
Barrientos, Tomás, and Luis Fernando Luin
2002 Excavaciones en el Palacio y Epicentro de Cancuén. In *Proyecto Ar-*

queológico Cancuén: Informe Temporada 2001, edited by Arthur A. Demarest and Tomás Barrientos. Instituto de Antropología e Historia de Guatemala, Guatemala City, and Department of Anthropology, Vanderbilt University, Nashville.

Barrientos, Tomás, Rudy Larios, Arthur A. Demarest, and Luis Fernando Luin

2002 El Palacio Real de Cancuén: Análisis preliminar de sus característi-
cas y planes de investigación. In *XV Simposio de Investigaciones Arqueológicas en Guatemala*, edited by Laporte, Suasnavar, and Arroyo. Ministerio de Cultura y Deportes, IDAEH, Asociación Tikal, Guatemala City.

Bourdieu, Pierre

1977 *Outline of a Theory of Practice.* Cambridge University Press, Cambridge.

Brady, James E.

1990 Investigaciones en la cueva de "El Duende." In *Proyecto Arqueológico Regional Petexbatún: Informe Preliminar #2—Segunda Tem-
porada*, edited by Arthur A. Demarest and Stephen D. Houston, pp. 334–352. Instituto de Antropología e Historia de Guatemala, Guatemala City, and Department of Anthropology, Vanderbilt University, Nashville.

1991 The Petexbatún Regional Cave Survey: Ritual and Regional Cave Survey. Paper presented at the 47th International Congress of Ameri-
canists, Tulane University, New Orleans.

1997 Settlement Configuration and Cosmology: The Role of Caves at Dos Pilas. *American Anthropologist* 99:602–618.

Brady, James E., Ann Scott, Allan Cobb, Irma Rodas, John Fogarty, and Monica Urquizú Sánchez

1997 Glimpses of the Dark Side of the Petexbatun Project: The Petexbatun Regional Cave Survey. *Ancient Mesoamerica* 8:353–364.

Chase, Arlen F., and Diane Z. Chase

1987 *Investigations at the Classic Maya City of Caracol, Belize, 1985–
1987.* PARI Monograph 3. Pre-Columbian Art Research Institute, San Francisco.

1996 More than Kin and King: Centralized Political Organization among the Late Classic Maya. *Current Anthropology* 37(5):803–810.

Christie, Jessica (editor)

2003 *Maya Palaces and Elite Residences.* University of Texas Press, Austin.

Coe, Michael D.

1988 Ideology of the Maya Tomb. In *Maya Iconography*, edited by Elizabeth Benson and Gillett Griffin, pp. 222–235. Princeton University Press, Princeton.

Culbert, T. Patrick (editor)

1991 *Classic Maya Political History: Hieroglyphic and Archaeological Evidence.* Cambridge University Press, Cambridge.

Demarest, Arthur A.

1987 Archaeology and Religion. In *The Encyclopedia of Religion*, edited by Mircea Eliade, 1:373–379. Macmillan, New York.

1989 Ideology and Evolutionism in American Archaeology: Looking beyond the Economic Base. In *Archaeological Thought in the Americas*, edited by C. C. Lamberg-Karlovsky. University of Cambridge Press, Cambridge.

1992 Ideology in Ancient Maya Cultural Evolution: The Dynamics of Galactic Polities. In *Ideology and Pre-Columbian Civilizations*, edited by Arthur A. Demarest and George Conrad, pp. 137–157. University of New Mexico Press, Albuquerque.

1996a The Maya State: Centralized or Segmentary? *Current Anthropology* 37(5):821–824.

1996b War, Peace, and the Collapse of a Native American Civilization. In *A Natural History of Peace*, edited by Thomas Gregor, pp. 215–248. Vanderbilt University Press, Nashville and London.

1997 The Vanderbilt Petexbatun Regional Archaeological Project 1989–1994: Overview, History, and Major Results of a Multi-disciplinary Study of the Classic Maya Collapse. *Ancient Mesoamerica* 8(2):209–227.

Demarest, Arthur A., and Tomás Barrientos (editors)

1999 *Proyecto Arqueológico Regional Cancuén: Informe Preliminar #1—Primera Temporada, 1999*. Instituto de Antropología e Historia de Guatemala, Guatemala City, and Department of Anthropology, Vanderbilt University, Nashville.

2000 *Proyecto Arqueológico Cancuén: Informe Preliminar #2—Temporada 2000*. Instituto de Antropología e Historia de Guatemala, Guatemala City.

2001 *Proyecto Arqueológico Cancuén: Informe Preliminar #3—Temporada 2001*. Instituto de Antropología e Historia de Guatemala, Guatemala City.

Demarest, Arthur A., Héctor Escobedo, and Matt O'Mansky (editors)

1996 *Proyecto Arqueológico Punta de Chimino 1996-97: Informe Preliminar*. Instituto de Antropología e Historia de Guatemala, Guatemala City.

Demarest, Arthur A., and Steve Houston (editors)

1989 *El Proyecto Arqueológico Regional Petexbatún: Informe Preliminar #1*. Instituto de Antropología e Historia de Guatemala, Guatemala City.

1990 *Proyecto Arqueológico Regional Petexbatún: Informe Preliminar #2—Segunda Temporada*. Instituto de Antropología e Historia de Guatemala, Guatemala City, and Department of Anthropology, Vanderbilt University, Nashville.

Demarest, Arthur A., Takeshi Inomata, and Héctor Escobedo (editors)

1992 *Proyecto Arqueológico Regional Petexbatún: Informe Preliminar #4—Cuarta Temporada*. Instituto de Antropología e Historia de Guatemala, Guatemala City.

Demarest, Arthur A., Takeshi Inomata, Héctor Escobedo, and Joel Palka (editors)

1991 *Proyecto Arqueológico Regional Petexbatún: Informe Preliminar #3—Tercera Temporada*. Instituto de Antropología e Historia de Guatemala, Guatemala City.

Demarest, Arthur A., Kim Morgan, Claudia Wolley, and Héctor
Escobedo
2003 The Political Acquisition of Sacred Geography: The Murciélagos
Complex at Dos Pilas. In *Maya Palaces and Elite Residences*, edited
by Jessica Christie. University of Texas Press, Austin.
Demarest, Arthur A., Irma Rodas, and Kim Morgan
1995 Investigación de Estructura N4-6, una estructura oratorio en el
Grupo Murciélagos: Suboperación DP39F. In *Proyecto Arqueológico Regional Petexbatún: Informe Preliminar #6 — Tercera Temporada 1994*, edited by Arthur A. Demarest, Juan Antonio Valdés, and
Héctor Escobedo, pp. 357–361. Instituto de Antropología e Historia
de Guatemala, Guatemala City.
Demarest, Arthur A., and Juan Antonio Valdés, and Héctor Escobedo
(editors)
1995 *Proyecto Arqueológico Regional Petexbatún: Informe Preliminar
#6 — Sexta Temporada, 1994.* Instituto de Antropología e Historia
de Guatemala, Guatemala City, and Department of Anthropology,
Vanderbilt University, Nashville.
Demarest, Arthur A., Claudia Wolley, Kim Morgan, and Irma Rodas
1995 Limpieza y excavación del Palacio de Presentación en el Grupo Murciélagos: Suboperación DP39E. In *Proyecto Arqueológico Regional
Petexbatún: Informe Preliminar #6 — Sexta Temporada, 1994*, edited
by Arthur A. Demarest, Juan Antonio Valdés, and Héctor Escobedo,
pp. 301–306. Instituto de Antropología e Historia de Guatemala,
Guatemala City, and Department of Anthropology, Vanderbilt Uni-
versity, Nashville.
Evans, Susan
2001 Aztec Noble Courts. In *Royal Courts of the Ancient Maya: Case
Studies*, Vol. 2, edited by Takeshi Inomata and Stephen Houston.
Westview Press, Boulder, CO.
Fahsen, Federico, and Arthur A. Demarest
2001 El papel del reino de Cancuén en la historia de las Tierras Bajas
Mayas: Nuevos datos epigráficos. In *XIV Simposio de Investigacio-
nes Arqueológicas en Guatemala*, edited by Laporte, Suasnavar, and
Arroyo. Ministerio de Cultura y Deportes, IDAEH, Asociación Tikal,
Guatemala City.
Fahsen, Federico, Arthur A. Demarest, Jeannette Castellanos, and
Luis Fernando Luin
n.d. New Hieroglyphic Stairways at Dos Pilas, Guatemala, and Their
Implications for Maya Political History. Manuscript submitted for
publication.
Fahsen, Federico, Sarah Jackson, Ian Graham, Arthur A. Demarest, and
Tomás Barrientos
2002 Nuevos datos e interpretaciones sobre la dinastía de Cancuén y otros
reinos del sur de Petén durante el período Clásico. In *XV Simposio
de Investigaciones Arqueológicas en Guatemala*, edited by Laporte,
Suasnavar, and Arroyo. Ministerio de Cultura y Deportes, IDAEH,
Asociación Tikal, Guatemala.

Fash, Barbara, William Fash, Sherrie Lane, Rudy Larios, Linda Schele, Jeffrey Stomper, and David Stuart
1992 Investigations of a Classic Maya Council House at Copán, Honduras. *Journal of Field Archaeology* 19(4):419–442.

Fash, William
1991 *Scribes, Warriors, and Kings: The City of Copan and the Ancient Maya.* Thames and Hudson, London.

Folan, William J.
1992 Calakmul, Campeche: A Centralized Urban Administrative Center in the Northern Petén. *World Archaeology* 24(1):158–168.

Folan, William J., Joyce Marcus, Sophia Pincemin, María del Rosario Domínguez Carrasco, Laraine Fletcher, and Abel Morales López.
1995 Calakmul: New Data from an Ancient Maya Capital in Campeche, Mexico. *Latin American Antiquity* 6(4):310–334.

Foucault, Michel
1972 *The Archaeology of Knowledge.* Pantheon Books, New York.

Fox, John W., and Garret W. Cook
1996 Constructing Maya Communities: Ethnography for Archaeology. *Current Anthropology* 37(5):811–821.

Fox, John W., Garret W. Cook, Arlen F. Chase, and Diane Z. Chase
1996 Questions of Political and Economic Integration: Segmentary versus Centralized States among the Ancient Maya. *Current Anthropology* 37(5):795–801.

Giddens, Anthony
1984 *The Constitution of Society: Outline of a Theory of Structuration.* University of California Press, Berkeley and Los Angeles.

Hendon, Julia A.
1991 Status and Power in Classic Maya Society: An Archaeological Study. *American Anthropologist* 93(4):895–918.

Heyden, Doris
1973 ¿Un Chicomostoc en Teotihuacan? La cueva debajo de la Pirámide del Sol. *Boletín del Instituto Nacional de Antropología e Historia* 6:3–18.
1975 An Interpretation of the Cave underneath the Pyramid of the Sun at Teotihuacan, Mexico. *American Antiquity* 40:131–147.
1981 Caves, Gods, and Myths: World-View and Planning in Teotihuacan. In *Mesoamerican Sites and World-Views,* edited by Elizabeth P. Benson, pp. 1–39. Dumbarton Oaks Research Library and Collection, Washington, DC.

Hodder, Ian
1985 Post-Processual Archaeology. In *Advances in Archaeological Method and Theory,* Vol. 8, edited by Michael B. Schiffer, pp. 1–26. Academic Press, New York.
1986 *Reading the Past: Current Approaches to Interpretation in Archaeology.* Cambridge University Press, Cambridge.

Houston, Stephen D., and Peter Mathews
1985 *The Dynastic Sequence of Dos Pilas.* PARI Monograph 1. Pre-Columbian Art Research Institute, San Francisco.

Houston, Stephen D., and David Stuart
1990 Resultados generales de los estudios epigráficos del Proyecto Petexbatún. In *Proyecto Arqueológico Regional Petexbatún: Informe Preliminar #2—Segunda Temporada*, edited by Arthur A. Demarest and
Stephen D. Houston, pp. 568–577. Instituto de Antropología e Historia de Guatemala, Guatemala City, and Department of Anthropology,
Vanderbilt University, Nashville.
Inomata, Takeshi
1995 Archaeological Investigations at the Fortified Center of Aguateca,
El Peten, Guatemala: Implications for the Study of the Classic Maya
Collapse. Unpublished Ph.D. dissertation, Department of Anthropology, Vanderbilt University, Nashville.
1997 The Last Day at a Fortified Classic Maya Center: Archaeological Investigations at Aguateca, Guatemala. *Ancient Mesoamerica* 8(2):337–
351.
2001 The Power and Ideology of Artistic Creation: Elite Craft Specialists
in Classic Maya Society. *Current Anthropology* 42:3.
In press *Warfare and the Fall of a Fortified Center: Archaeological Investigations at Aguateca, Guatemala.* Vanderbilt Petexbatun Regional Archaeological Monograph Series, Arthur A. Demarest,
general editor. Vanderbilt University Press, Nashville.
Inomata, Takeshi, and Stephen D. Houston (editors)
2001 *Royal Courts of the Ancient Maya*, Vol. 1. Westview Press, Boulder, CO.
Inomata, Takeshi, and Laura Stiver
1998 Floor Assemblages from Burned Structures at Aguateca, Guatemala:
A Study of Classic Maya Households. *Journal of Field Archaeology*
4:431–452.
Inomata, Takeshi, and Daniela Triadan
2000 Craft Production by Classic Maya Elites in Domestic Settings: Data
from Rapidly Abandoned Structures at Aguateca, Guatemala. *Mayab*
11:2–39.
Inomata, Takeshi, Daniela Triadan, Erick Ponciano, Richard E. Terry,
Harriet F. Beaubien, Estela Pinto, and Shannon Coyston
1998 Residencias de la familia real y de la elite en Aguateca, Guatemala.
Mayab 11:23–39.
Kovacevich, Brigitte, Tomás Barrientos, Michael Callaghan, and
Karen Pereira
2002 La economía en el reino Clásico de Cancuén: Evidencia de produc-
ción, especialización e intercambio. In *XV Simposio de Investigacio-
nes Arqueológicas en Guatemala*. Ministerio de Cultura y Deportes,
IDAEH, Asociación Tikal, Guatemala City.
Kovacevich, Brigitte, Tomás Barrientos, Arthur A. Demarest,
Michael Callaghan, Cassandra Bill, Erin Sears, and Lucia Moran
2001 Producción e intercambio en el reinado de Cancuén. In *XIV Simposio
de Investigaciones Arqueológicas en Guatemala*, edited by Laporte,
Suasnavar, and Arroyo. Ministerio de Cultura y Deportes, IDAEH,
Asociación Tikal, Guatemala City.

Kovacevich, Brigitte, and Hector Neff
2002 Preliminary MS-ICP-LA Results from a Jade Workshop at Cancuén, Guatemala. Paper presented at the 65th Annual Meeting of the Society for American Archaeology, Boulder, CO.

MacLeod, Barbara, and Dennis Edward Puleston
1979 Pathways into Darkness: The Search for the Road to Xibalba. In *Tercera Palenque Round Table, 1978, Part 1*, edited by Merle Greene Robertson, pp. 71–79. University of Texas Press, Austin.

Marcus, Joyce
1993 Ancient Maya Political Organization. In *Lowland Maya Civilization in the Eighth Century A.D.*, edited by Jeremy A. Sabloff and John S. Henderson, pp. 111–183. Dumbarton Oaks Research Library and Collection, Washington, DC.

Martin, Simon, and Nikolai Grube
2000 *Chronicle of the Maya Kings and Queens: Deciphering the Dynasties of the Ancient Maya*. Thames and Hudson, London.

Mathews, Peter, and Gordon R. Willey
1991 Prehistoric Politics of the Pasion Region. In *Classic Maya Political History: Hieroglyphic and Archaeological Evidence*, edited by T. Patrick Culbert. Cambridge University Press, Cambridge.

McAnany, Patricia
1995 *Living with the Ancestors: Kinship and Kingship in Ancient Maya Society*. University of Texas Press, Austin.

Palka, Joel
1990 Operación DP15: Excavaciones en el Grupo Residential K4-1. In *Proyecto Arqueológico Regional Petexbatún: Informe Preliminar #2—Segunda Temporada*, edited by Arthur A. Demarest and Stephen D. Houston, pp. 145–165. Instituto de Antropología e Historia de Guatemala, Guatemala City, and Department of Anthropology, Vanderbilt University, Nashville.
1997 Reconstructing Classic Maya Socioeconomic Differentiation and the Collapse at Dos Pilas, Peten, Guatemala. *Ancient Mesoamerica* 8(2):293–306.

Preucel, Robert W. (editor)
1991 *Processual and Postprocessual Archaeologies: Multiple Ways of Knowing the Past*. Center for Archaeological Investigations Occasional Paper No. 10. Southern Illinois University at Carbondale.

Sanders, William, and David Webster
1988 The Mesoamerican Urban Tradition. *American Anthropologist* 90:521–546.

Shanks, Michael, and Christopher Tilley
1987 *Re-Constructing Archaeology: Theory and Practice*. Cambridge University Press, Cambridge.
1992 *Re-Constructing Archaeology: Theory and Practice, Second Edition*. Routledge, London and New York.

Stuart, David
1989 The Maya Artist: An Epigraphic and Iconographic Study. Unpublished B.A. thesis, Princeton University.

1995 A Study of Maya Inscriptions. Unpublished Ph.D. dissertation,
      Vanderbilt University, Nashville.
Valdés, Juan Antonio, Antonia Foias, Takeshi Inomata, Héctor Escobedo,
and Arthur A. Demarest (editors)
1993 *Proyecto Arqueológico Regional Petexbatún: Informe Preliminar
      #5 — Quinta Temporada.* Instituto de Antropología e Historia de
      Guatemala, Guatemala City.
Wolley, Claudia
1995 Investigaciones en la Estructura N5-3A del Grupo Murciélagos.
      In *Proyecto Arqueológico Regional Petexbatún: Informe Prelimi-
      nar #6 — Tercera Temporada, 1994,* edited by Arthur A. Demarest,
      Juan Antonio Valdés, and Héctor Escobedo, pp. 331–341. Instituto de
      Antropología e Historia de Guatemala, Guatemala City, and Depart-
      ment of Anthropology, Vanderbilt University, Nashville.
Wolley, Claudia, and Irma Rodas
1995 Suboperaciones DP39L, DP39M, DP39N, DP39O, and DPO39P. In
      *Proyecto Arqueológico Regional Petexbatún: Informe Preliminar
      #6 — Tercera Temporada, 1994,* edited by Arthur A. Demarest, Juan
      Antonio Valdes, and Héctor Escobedo, pp. 362–366. Instituto de
      Antropología e Historia de Guatemala, Guatemala City, and Depart-
      ment of Anthropology, Vanderbilt University, Nashville.
Wolley, Claudia, and Lori E. Wright
1990 Operación DP7: Investigaciones en el Grupo L4-4. In *Proyecto Ar-
      queológico Regional Petexbatún: Informe Preliminar #2 — Segunda
      Temporada,* edited by Arthur A. Demarest and Stephen D. Houston,
      pp. 44–65. Instituto de Antropología e Historia de Guatemala, Guate-
      mala City, and Department of Anthropology, Vanderbilt University,
      Nashville.
Woodfill, Brent, Matt O' Mansky, and Jon Spenard
2002 Asentamiento y sitios sagrados en la región de Cancuén. In *XV Sim-
      posio de Investigaciones Arqueológicas en Guatemala.* Ministerio de
      Cultura y Deportes, IDAEH, Asociación Tikal, Guatemala City.

CHAPTER 5

Political Dimensions of Monumental Residences on the Northwest Coast of North America

Colin Grier

Large, multifamily households were a central socioeconomic institution in ethnographic and prehistoric Northwest Coast societies. Households were an important arena for the construction of political power, and houses were important vehicles for the expression and broadcast of the power and status of household elite members. Historic-period descriptions of Northwest Coast houses illustrate that their construction, spatial layout, and symbolic embellishment were imbued with messages that served the efforts of house chiefs to solidify leadership and unify potentially divisive household groups.

We know much less about the role that houses played in the construction and reproduction of political power and hierarchical social orders in prehistory. Poor preservation of house architecture in coastal environments prevents prehistoric architecture from being studied directly. However, other types of archaeological data, including house spatial layout and the portable material culture that houses contain, provide clues as to the nature and importance of the household context in reproducing economic, social, and political hierarchies. In this chapter, architectural, spatial, and artifact data from a large Marpole-period (ca. 1500 B.P.) plankhouse residence in coastal southwestern British Columbia, Canada, provide the basis for an examination of the ways in which hierarchical relations of political power and social stratification were promoted and reproduced in the domestic sphere.

Northwest Coast Residences

The Northwest Coast represents an important context for understanding the construction of political power in small-scale societies. For at least the last two millennia, most Northwest Coast societies included a hereditary elite with preferential access to material and symbolic resources (Ames 1994, 1995; Ames and Maschner 1999; Burley 1989; Grier 2001; Suttles 1987a). Ethnographically, Northwest Coast societies were stratified into minimally two and often three distinct social classes that can be generally glossed as elites/

nobles, free commoners, and slaves (Ames 1995; Donald 1997; Suttles 1987c). Social inequality was strongly marked (including visually through cranial deformation and labret use), and differences in status had real implications for access to basic material resources (Ames 1995; Grier 2001; Suttles 1987c). Such stratification and sociopolitical complexity were unusual in that (1) Northwest Coast societies were based on intensive fishing, hunting, and gathering rather than on an agricultural economic base, and (2) the area lacked well-developed, centralized regional polities (Ames 1995; Mitchell and Donald 1988). The last two conditions have been considered critical for the florescence of institutionalized social inequality and class stratification (Donald 1985).

The Northwest Coast also generally lacks the nonresidential temples, palaces, and widespread monumental earthworks and stoneworks visible in the archaeological record of many New World prehistoric agricultural societies. A relatively short-lived prehistoric burial-mound tradition did exist in the years between roughly 1500 B.P. and 1000 B.P. in the Gulf of Georgia region of southern British Columbia (Ames and Maschner 1999; Thom 1995). The temporal and spatial expression of this burial tradition has been more systematically documented in recent years (Lepofsky et al. 2000). Also, remnants of large earthen defensive structures called trench embankments can be found in some areas of the same region and likely date to the last two millennia (Mitchell 1968; Moss and Erlandson 1992). Monumental burials and earthworks were, however, relatively rare in Northwest Coast prehistory, and nonresidential political structures (e.g., palaces, temples) are entirely lacking in the known archaeological record.

The salient constructions that were monumental were the residences — the large and visually impressive wooden post-and-beam plankhouses widely described and pictured in ethnographic and popular literature (Figure 5.1). Large Northwest Coast houses can be thought of as elite residences in that they housed high-status individuals. But they did not house only elites; people of all classes and social ranks were often members of the same co-residential, multifamily household (Drucker 1951; Suttles 1987c). This complex household was a central institution in ethnographic Northwest Coast societies, and archaeological data are increasingly indicating a similar situation obtained for at least the last two millennia (Ames and Maschner 1999:147–148; Grier 2001; Samuels 1991). Plankhouses gave material and spatial form to this social institution and were the stage for many economic, social, and political endeavors that were conducted in public architecture or in exclusively elite contexts in many other New World complex societies (Suttles 1991).

The earliest plankhouse remains on the Northwest Coast date to roughly 4500 B.P., and large plankhouses became common in many areas of the coast by 2000 B.P. (Chatters 1989; Coupland 1996; Grier 2003). From an archaeological perspective, it is unfortunate that the architectural elements of these

FIGURE 5.1 Historic-period Haida plankhouse from Haina village on Haida Gwaii (Queen Charlotte Islands, British Columbia, Canada). Photograph by Richard and Hannah Maynard © 1888. Courtesy of the Field Museum of Natural History, Chicago.

structures were crafted from cedar trees and in most cases are poorly preserved, if at all. It is rare that a house older than two centuries exhibits standing architecture, and even then it is usually limited to a couple of fragile house posts (MacDonald 1983; though see Samuels 1991 for a remarkable exception). As a result, the data available to study ethnographic and prehistoric houses differ markedly (the same can be said of many aspects of Northwest Coast material culture, given its predominantly perishable nature), and study of the materialization of social power in the built environment in prehistory lags behind ethnographic studies. The ethnographic record contains numerous photographs and drawings of standing houses, coupled with rich text descriptions of the many types of activities conducted within them (Barnett 1955; MacDonald 1983; Smith 1947; Suttles 1991). For prehistoric houses, however, we must reconstruct very basic aspects of architectural design from often subtle posthole patterns and the spatial organization of domestic features such as hearths (Grier 2001; Mauger 1991).

In the reconstruction of prehistoric houses and households there unavoidably emerges a reliance on the ethnographic record, a situation evident in much of Northwest Coast archaeology (Burley 1989:43–50; Matson and Coupland 1995). This has at times resulted in only passing consideration of the significance of the scale of changes in demography and cultural practices that took place at and following contact. Even so, to eschew ethnography as a source of information would be to severely limit our potential to understand prehistoric societies on the coast. As always, however, ethnographic analogies must be treated as hypotheses about the past rather than explanations for the archaeological record.

In this chapter, I examine Northwest Coast plankhouses from an architectural and spatial perspective, focusing on how construction and design were used by house elites to promote a social order founded on hierarchical relations of social and political power. I consider both the ethnographic and prehistoric periods, drawing initially on the extensive ethnographic information available to characterize the nature of power, status, and leadership in Northwest Coast societies. I then consider ethnographic houses and their variability, focusing on how different aspects of their construction, design, and symbolic embellishment were employed to send political messages that served to legitimize and entrench household hierarchies. I next look to the prehistoric period and present a case study from my own archaeological work at the Dionisio Point village on coastal southwestern British Columbia, Canada. I examine these data to illuminate the way in which power was constructed in the context of one prehistoric household and to show how these data fit into longer-term models for the development of social stratification on the prehistoric Northwest Coast.

Power on the Northwest Coast

To investigate how houses were used as vehicles to promote and legitimize political power and leadership, it is first useful to consider the nature of political power on the Northwest Coast. The particular combination of social stratification, household-based political power, and a hunting-fishing-gathering economy has fostered many discussions about the unique character of power in both ethnographic and prehistoric Northwest Coast societies (Ames 1995; Donald 1985; Mitchell 1983). Previous discussions, drawing primarily on ethnographic data, have been concerned with identifying what power chiefs of various descriptions enjoyed (Ames [1995] provides a substantial discussion and synthesis of this topic).

Ethnographically, it is clear that the prominent political position, mirroring the importance of the household in society, was that of household chief (Ames 1995; Drucker 1951). House chiefs held title to most household property and resources and represented the household politically in external dealings, but they lacked the power to appropriate goods or labor from others (except from slaves) within their own household. In this sense, the power of house chiefs over free individuals was, as Ken Ames (1995) describes it, power to organize rather than power directly over individuals or an organization. With slaves, the situation was different. Slaves were property owned by elites. They could be handled as property, they could be forced to labor, and their lives apparently could be taken at the whim of their owners (Donald 1997).

There is little evidence that house chiefs exercised significant power beyond their own household. Even wealthy or powerful house chiefs attained no more than the ability to influence other house chiefs and the activities of other households. Occasional references do exist to village chiefs, yet these "offices" only reflected consensual authority either to play a lead role in organizing cooperative, short-term endeavors that involved multiple households (e.g., salmon fishing) or to represent multiple households in political events such as potlatches and feasts (Blackman 1990:251–252).

House chiefs were drawn exclusively from the elite/noble class. Noble status was hereditary and typically ascribed at or near birth (Matson and Coupland 1995). The noble class enjoyed significant privileges unavailable to common free people, including access to ownership titles, ritual knowledge, and leadership positions, which they often acquired through inheritance (Suttles 1987c). Commoners generally did not possess any of these resources, and only under exceptional circumstances could they obtain them, as class divisions effectively limited access to rights, titles, and resources to the upper class (Suttles 1987a, 1987c). All noble class members enjoyed some authority and power by virtue of their ascribed status, but, as with house chiefs, this power was limited primarily to influence rather than direct power over other free individuals (Suttles 1987c).

Two points relevant to households and power are important to take away from the preceding discussion of the ethnographic situation. First, in the case of house chiefs specifically and the noble class generally, each, though enjoying privileges related to their position in the social system, had little direct control over the lives and actions of free individuals (Ames 1995). Second, though class was inherited and ascribed, leadership positions were not. Thus, household chiefs constructed and maintained power rather than assumed unquestioned authority based on an office that they occupied. House chiefs achieved leadership positions and power through their own efforts by making use of the opportunities provided by their preferential access to re-

sources (material and labor), specialized (often ritual) knowledge, and ownership of property (Ames 1995; Suttles 1987c).

Power in the Household Context

In what specific ways were houses and the household context relevant for
the construction of political power? A key element is that elites typically
owned house locations and were in a position to organize and marshal labor
for house construction, allowing them significant control over the built environment (Marshall 1989; Suttles 1991). However, more broadly, power on
the Northwest Coast was solidly rooted in economics, and households were
the productive engines of the Northwest Coast's subsistence and political
economies. Because the household was the main arena in which power and
leadership operated (Ames 1995), the construction of power relied on the
adeptness with which aspiring and existing house chiefs could attract and
retain household labor and orchestrate production, distribution, and consumption of household resources (Ames 1995; Chatters 1989; Drucker 1951).
Households were, however, complex social entities composed of many individuals and groups of different status and interests, and as such, they contained potentially divisive and fractious propensities. In particular, the class
system in Northwest Coast societies worked to both symbolically and materially reinforce social difference between elites and commoners, both of
whom may have resided in the same domestic context (Elmendorf 1971:361–
363). Were households fraught with tension between corporate unity and
obvious social and material difference?

Ethnographic accounts hint that conflicts over status claims, leadership
positions, and access to resources occasionally resulted in fissioning and the
establishment of new households (Marshall 1989; Suttles 1991). Yet clearly
many households were successful and more or less stable over time in that
they existed over periods of at least several generations. Moreover, archaeological data are increasingly showing that prehistoric households may have
existed (spatially and architecturally, at least) for many centuries (Ames et al.
1992; Grier 2005). How, then, were potentially divisive forces within the
household overcome and a stable yet hierarchical social order established
and maintained?

Although ethnographic data do not offer a long-term diachronic view,
they do provide useful detail in terms of the dynamics of intrahousehold
relations relevant to this question. The information presented below is derived and synthesized primarily from ethnographic accounts of the Coast
Salish of the southern British Columbia inner coast, the region for which I
am most familiar with the ethnographic record and where I have conducted
archaeological research since 1996. It is important to note that the Coast
Salish had perhaps the most flexible social system of all major Northwest
Coast groups in terms of kin relations, residence patterns, and household

membership (Suttles 1987a, 1990). In general, social systems were more rigid in northern areas of the coast among groups such as the Tlingit, Tsimshian, and Gitksan. The following discussion therefore pertains most specifically to ethnographic Coast Salish household dynamics. However, such dynamics can be expected to have obtained throughout the entire coast to some degree.

As discussed previously, the power of elite over free people was not direct, as it was for elite or free person over slave. On the Northwest Coast, house chiefs needed to effectively organize and manage large households composed of relatively autonomous people. The system of class stratification that existed may have provided the authority and resources for elite class members to assume leadership positions. But possessing the prerogative to rule and adeptly ruling can be different matters altogether.

Labor was a limiting factor in terms of household productivity, so maximizing household membership was a key factor in household success (Ames 1996). Yet, the general flexibility of Coast Salish social organization (bilateral kinship, bilocal residence patterns [Suttles 1987a, 1987b]) provided individuals and families with numerous residence options (Suttles 1987a). As a result, a critical issue that house leaders had to confront was that free peoples within the household could have shifted residences if unhappy with their current situation or if they had found better prospects elsewhere. Interestingly, the architecture of the Coast Salish shed-roof house consisted of a series of relatively independent compartments that would have accommodated frequent changes of residence, suggesting that house membership was indeed dynamic (Grier 2001; Suttles 1991). This architectural flexibility provided individual (free) families with some autonomy with respect to the household to which they attached themselves. Individual families within households may in fact have owned their own planks and could presumably have added them to any house. Thus families could be strategic about where they contributed their labor, knowing that (1) they had multiple residence options and (2) their labor was a desired commodity.

The other side to the leader-follower dynamic lies in the benefits entailed in being part of a successful household. For untitled free people, the social and economic benefits derived from being members of a successful household would have far exceeded those available elsewhere or by operating independently. However, the corollary of being able to leave a household was that, by making the choice to stay, free people likely had to voluntarily surrender some of their own autonomy and buy into a common household strategy and set of economic and sociopolitical objectives. In short, they must let themselves be ruled.

Although there was clearly a two-sided dynamic, the social bottom line often stemmed from the economic bottom line. With the constant potential to lose members to other households, household leaders had to continually demonstrate through actions and results the reasons for commoners with other options to stay committed to the household. Thus, achieving a high level of economic production was a critical factor in the success of household leadership.

Certainly more could be said on the subject of how household elites specifically mobilized labor and economic resources. But the point I wish to emphasize again is that the power obtained by elites and elite chiefs within households was constructed, promoted, and reproduced through their ability to convince others to commit their energies to the household. Households also acted as political units in many capacities, including hosting feasts and other ritual activities that demonstrated to outsiders the capacity of the household to be a player on the social map. The efficacy of the household in this respect would have rested on its capacity for coherent political as well as economic action, which meant ensuring that its members maintained a commitment to the political as well as economic objectives of the household, and, again, to the hierarchical social order of the household.

The Materialization of Hierarchies: The House as Political Message

Following this ethnographic review of power and leadership in Northwest Coast household groups, it is productive to consider the specific mechanisms through which household elites promoted a household social order that served their agendas, that is, unified a set of relatively autonomous families under a coherent economic and political strategy. Many factors undoubtedly entered into this equation. However, in the remainder of this chapter I consider how aspects of house construction and design served this end, both generally, using ethnographic data, and in a specific case, using archaeological data. Two core questions are addressed: (1) how were the notions of hierarchy and unity encoded in house architecture, and (2) how did elites actively use or manipulate symbolism in house design as part of their efforts to promote, maintain, and reproduce a household hierarchy? In various respects, the built environment can be viewed as a resource used by elites to express their position at the head of the household social hierarchy and also potentially to resolve contradictions between the dual objectives of integration and differentiation of household members.

House Construction

The construction of a plankhouse was itself the expression of the social order in action. The house was designed and its construction was directed by elites (Blackman 1990; Suttles 1987c). An incredible amount of labor, which elites directed, was required for construction. And though a significant amount of unskilled labor would have been required, the process also involved skilled woodworkers, who were typically members of the elite class (Ames 1995; Drucker 1951; Grier 2001). Woodworking specialists had prominent roles in Northwest Coast societies, often as artists and canoe builders. House sites were typically owned by specific elite individuals or families who could reckon their descent to an initial founding village ancestor, reinforcing notions of elite ownership to those who labored in the construction of the house (Blackman 1990:251–252).

Spatial Layout

Many aspects of the architectural design and organization of interior space promoted the ethic of the household as a unified, though strongly hierarchical, grouping (Marshall 1989). Throughout the Northwest Coast, the location where people lived within a house was of political and social significance. Philip Drucker's (1951) ethnographic work with the Nuu-chah-nulth of the outer coast of Vancouver Island indicates that a family's or an individual's ordinal rank within the household hierarchy was signaled by where they resided, with the back corners, farthest from the door, containing elite families of the highest rank (Figure 5.2B). This spatial arrangement was not an expression of kinship relations specifically but rather of political and status relations (Marshall 1989:17). The precise rank of the house chief and of individual elite family heads was also expressed through a strict pattern of seating at ritual events (Figure 5.2A). The spatial distribution of rank may have clearly marked social difference within the plankhouse. But most Nuu-chah-nulth houses also included a large central hearth to act as the focus for communal activities and rituals, providing an integrative element to balance the differentiation expressed in ritual and residence.

For the Coast Salish, less is known about the specific relationship between political or social rank and intrahouse residence patterns. Wayne Suttles (1991) suggests that, in general, the Coast Salish downplayed an overt emphasis on formal rank within the elite class. Therefore, the spatial organization of families within residences according to status may not have been as formalized. Elements of Coast Salish house design are consistent with a less-formalized household spatial order. As mentioned earlier, the main residential dwelling typically used by the Coast Salish along the southern British Columbia coast was a structure typically described as a shed-roof house due to its single-pitch rather than gable roof (Figure 5.3). These dwellings were segmented in their architectural design, having been composed of a number of "compartments" consisting of the space between pairs of rafter support posts. This design contrasts with the gable-roof house typical of the Nuu-chah-nulth and groups on the north coast such as the Haida. Gable-roof houses were essentially one large box whose spatial footprint was defined at the time of initial construction by the four corner posts and the length of the gable beam (compare Figures 5.3 and 5.4; Suttles 1991).

Neither house type was physically partitioned with walls into separate rooms, but, unlike the gable-roof house, the segmented architecture of the

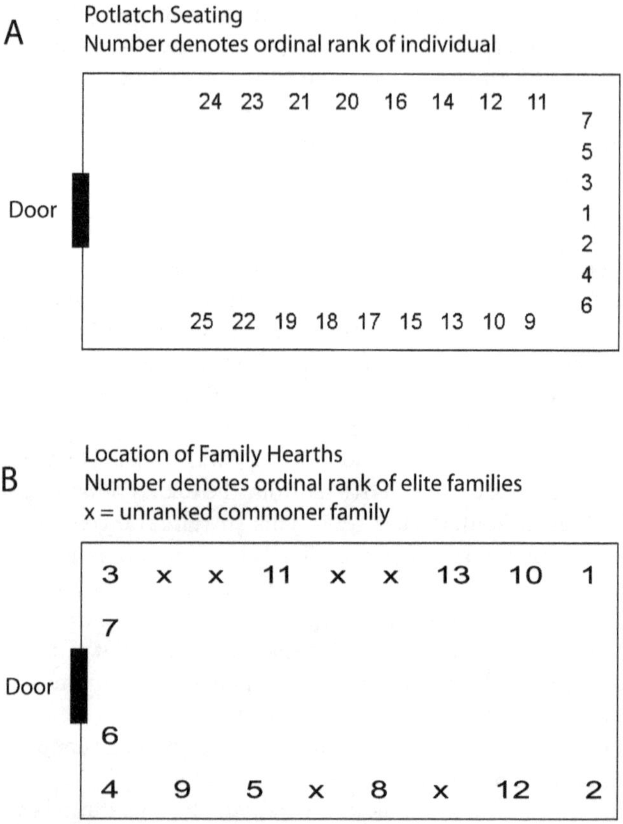

A   Potlatch Seating
    Number denotes ordinal rank of individual

```
         24  23  21  20  16  14  12  11
                                          7
                                          5
                                          3
Door                                      1
                                          2
                                          4
                                          6
         25  22  19  18  17  15  13  10  9
```

B   Location of Family Hearths
    Number denotes ordinal rank of elite families
    x = unranked commoner family

```
  3   x   x   11   x   x   13   10   1

  7


Door

  6

  4   9   5   x   8   x   12   2
```

FIGURE 5.2 Relationship between Nuu-chah-nulth intrahouse spatial and social organization as reflected in (A) the ranking of elite individuals at a ritual event and (B) ranked family residence locations (after Marshall 1989:20)

shed-roof house allowed expansion or contraction of the house structure by the addition or removal of rafter pairs (and thus compartments) to accommodate changes in household size and membership. This segmented aspect to shed-roof houses is also reflected in their internal layout, which was divided into redundant family spaces, each containing a domestic hearth. Gable-roof houses typically had a large central fire pit accompanied by small domestic-use hearths along the perimeter of the house floor. Most ethnographic Coast Salish houses lacked a prominent, large central hearth (Suttles 1991).

The segmented nature of shed-roof houses hints at only a weak level of integration to the household. The lack of a common spatial focus, specifically the large central hearth, has been cited as a material expression of the flexibility and perhaps transience of at least some members of households (Suttles 1991). It does seem as though the architectural design and spatial layout of the shed-roof house does little to promote or impose a clear social hierarchy. Again, ordinal ranking among elites may have been less emphasized among the Coast Salish than in other areas of the coast. Although house design may reflect this situation, this is not to say that the spatial layout of families within the house was not of importance in broadcasting individual or family status in the Coast Salish households. Rather, it may have been more overtly expressed in other areas of material and ideational culture, as discussed below.

Symbolic Representations on Architectural Elements

More superficial aspects of Northwest Coast houses also served to reinforce and reproduce the political organization of the household. In Coast Salish shed-roof houses, the use of symbolic embellishment on interior house posts appears to have been designed to convey messages concerning the house political hierarchy inward to its residents. The common image of Northwest Coast houses is that they were fronted with a totem pole (see Figures 5.1 and 5.4). External poles broadcast messages about household identity quite widely, both to other houses and to village visitors. Yet, large, imposing external poles were primarily a northern-coast phenomenon and not a central-

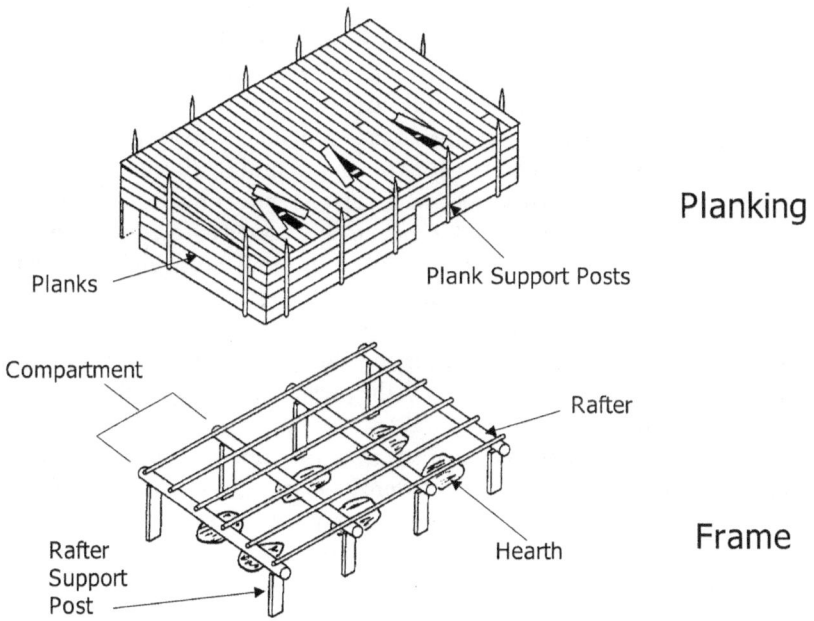

Planking

Planks — Plank Support Posts

Compartment — Rafter

Rafter Support Post — Hearth

Frame

FIGURE 5.3 Typical design and layout of the shed-roof house type built by the central Coast Salish

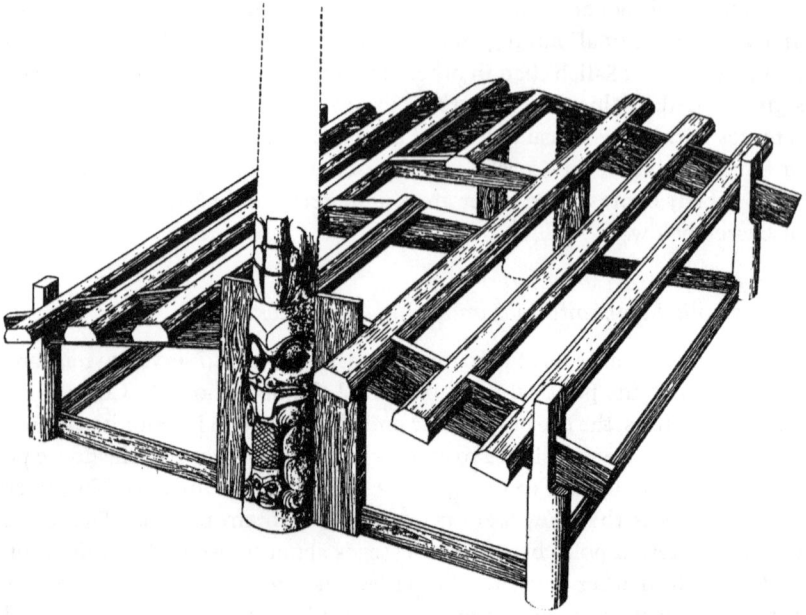

FIGURE 5.4 Northern-style gable-roof house (Haida) with frontal pole (after Mac-Donald 1983:19).

coast tradition in ethnographic Coast Salish societies. Shed-roof houses were rarely decorated externally to any great degree; the vast majority of the decorative aspects of houses were found inside.

The main rafter support posts inside shed-roof houses were typically decorated with symbolic design elements or carved into figures (Figure 5.5). A house post at Lummi was inscribed with a glyph representative of wealth and power (Suttles 1984:79), a post at Musqueam was carved to represent a founding ancestor, and at Nanaimo a post depicts a spiritual-cleansing dancer. Unfortunately, we have no descriptions of where specific house posts may have stood in relation to the residential areas of individuals of various class and rank, and the ethnographic record is too thin (at least in this specific respect) to allow statistical evaluation of the prevalence and spatial patterning of house-post decoration.

Nevertheless, existing evidence suggests that images conveying power and the ancestral legitimacy of elites were primarily incorporated as *interior* design elements in shed-roof houses. Among the Coast Salish, the target audience for images of power added to houses thus appears to have been members of the resident household. In contrast, rituals and events that involved participation by individuals from outside the household or village were often conducted on the roof, out of view of interior house decoration (Suttles 1990:469). The directing of symbolic imagery inward hints at a desire

FIGURE 5.5 Contemporary reproductions of internal rafter support house posts depicting ancestral images. Photograph by Colin Grier. House posts by Susan Point (Musqueam), 1997. Collection of the Museum of Anthropology, Vancouver, Canada.

on the part of elites to constantly be asserting to members of their own household the order of the household hierarchy and the legitimate position of elites at its head.

Investigating Prehistoric Houses: The Dionisio Point Village

A consideration of architectural data indicates that many elements of historic-period house design were imbued with political messages and imagery that played a role in establishing and maintaining a social order. Investigating similar ideas concerning the construction and maintenance of power and social hierarchies within prehistoric households has been one of my objectives within the context of a broader household archaeology program at the prehistoric Dionisio Point village site in the Gulf Islands of southern British Columbia, Canada (Figure 5.6). As mentioned earlier, when looking to the archaeological record to address these issues, we rarely encounter the actual architecture. Instead, we must make adept use of that which has survived, which is typically limited to stone and bone portable material culture and decomposed architectural elements such as postholes and hearths. Such data may seem scant at first, but they do provide important clues into the workings of household social, economic, and political hierarchies, as outlined below.

The Dionisio Point village site dates from roughly 1700 B.P. to 1500 B.P. No standing architecture remains, but the site does contain five prominent house depressions (Figure 5.7). One of these house depressions, House 2 (H2 in figure), was the subject of major excavations in 1998, revealing a relatively clear record of the layout of interior space. Spatial reconstruction and analyses presented elsewhere (Grier 2001) indicate that House 2 was a segmented 20 × 10 m structure largely consistent in design with ethnographically described shed-roof houses. House 2 contains a number of hearths, indicating that four or perhaps five distinct domestic family spaces existed within (Figure 5.8). Posthole distributions suggest the house included three pairs of rafter support posts, forming two large compartments.

Artifacts were also abundant in House 2. In addition to a sizable collection of utilitarian goods that reflect various economic pursuits, house excavations recovered artifacts that shed light on the prehistoric representation of status, consumption of wealth, and use of symbolically laden material culture in household ritual. The spatial location of recovery of these artifacts is critical in that it indicates which domestic spaces (and thus families) such items were associated with, allowing inferences concerning the social status and identity of various household subgroups. Below I consider specific examples of this material culture recovered from House 2 to shed light on the expression of sociopolitical hierarchies in the domestic sphere. These data help clarify hierarchical spatial-social relationships that appear only weakly expressed in shed-roof house architecture itself, as discussed previously.

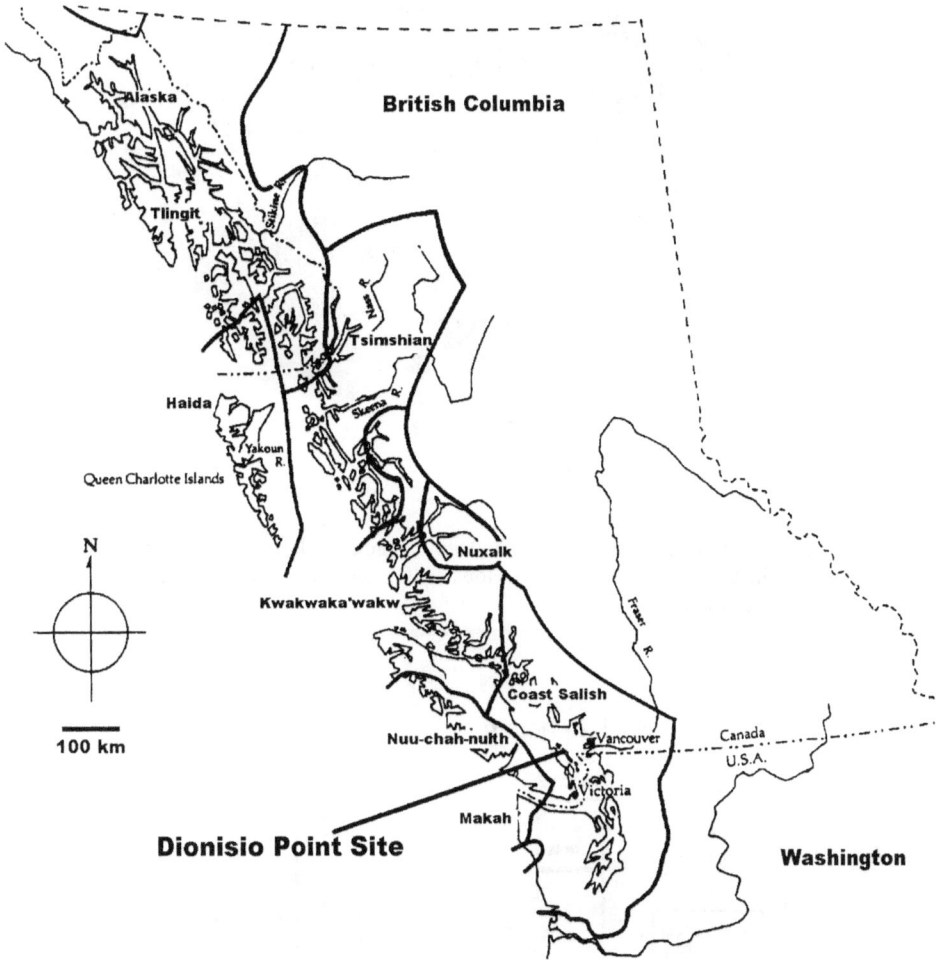

FIGURE 5.6 Location of the Dionisio Point site on the southern British Columbia coast

Two carved stone bowls were recovered from the house. The bowl illustrated in Figure 5.9 was carved in the shape of a human head and was stained on top and inside its depression with ochre, a substance used extensively in ritual on the Northwest Coast. The other bowl was similar in form, though without visible ochre staining. These bowls were part of a regional complex of stylistically coherent sculpture believed to have been of ritual significance (Duff 1956; Grier 2003; Suttles 1984). The recovery of two stone bowls within the household suggests that the system of symbols employed throughout the region was in use within the Dionisio Point household. As ritual performance was (ethnographically, at least) the prerogative of high-status indi-

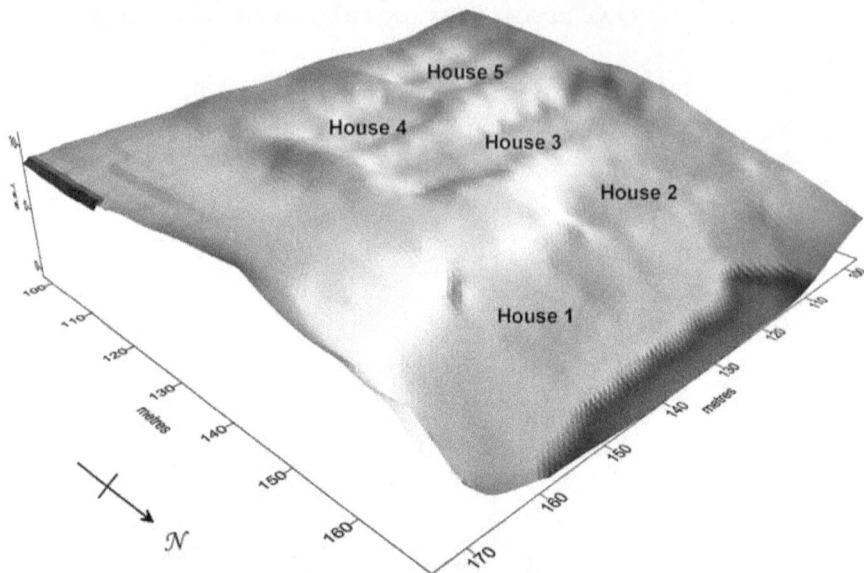

FIGURE 5.7 Surface reconstruction of the Dionisio Point village, showing the five known prehistoric house depressions. House 2 (H2) was the subject of extensive excavations in 1998.

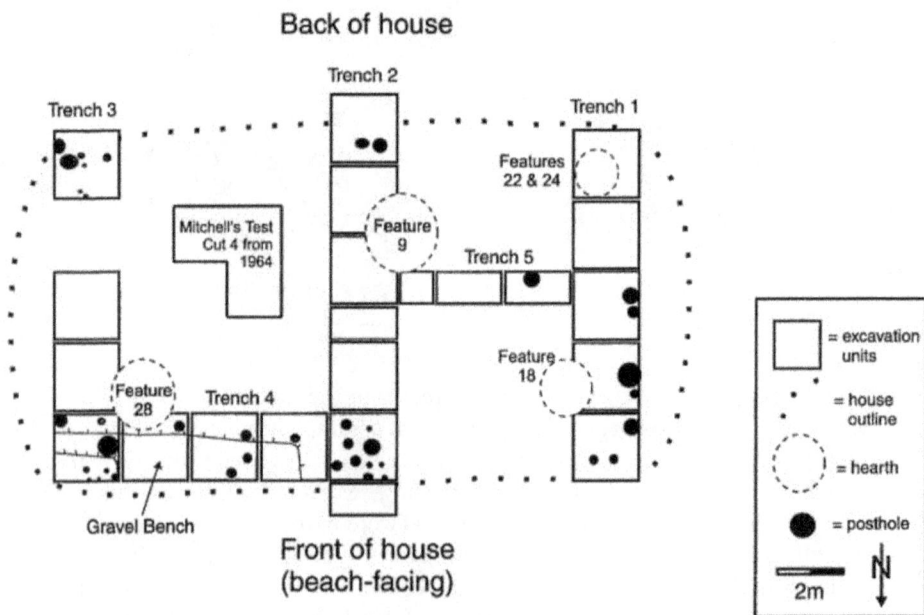

FIGURE 5.8 Schematic view of the interior of House 2, Dionisio Point, showing major hearth locations as focal features of distinct domestic spaces

FIGURE 5.9 Ochre-stained stone bowl from House 2 at Dionisio Point

viduals, the occurrence of the two bowls provides an (albeit indirect) indication that individuals of elite status resided within the house (Grier 2001).

Interestingly, only one domestic space within the house appears to have contained a bowl at any given time. Radiocarbon dating and the occurrence of the bowls in separate strata indicate that they were not in use at the same time. One bowl was recovered in primary context from the southwestern corner of House 2 and was likely deposited at the time of final abandonment of the house. The second bowl was found in the central area of the house (also in primary context) and appears to have been deposited midway through the house occupation. Perhaps only one elite family or individual directed ritual within the house.

Two labrets (lip plugs commonly used as status markers on the Northwest Coast [Keddie 1981]) were also recovered from House 2 (Figure 5.10), one from the center front (spatially associated with one of the stone bowls) and one from the back of the center of the house. Inserted through the lip and visible on the face, labrets were relatively unambiguous and highly visible markers of an individual's status. Ethnographically, high class—though perhaps also high rank within that class—was typically conveyed through wearing these items (Keddie 1981; Matson and Coupland 1995). In addition to labrets, cranial deformation has been used as a marker of status in many areas of the coast over the last two millennia. This technique differs in that it must commence at a young age, when the cranium is plastic, and therefore cranial deformation typically marked hereditary, ascribed status (i.e., class). Labrets can be worn and removed at any time and therefore could have been used more easily to mark achieved status (i.e., rank; see discussions in Ames 1995:163–167 and Matson and Coupland 1995:209–210). Both are, however,

FIGURE 5.10 Labrets recovered from House 2 at Dionisio Point

highly visible means of communicating social differentiation, and the presence of labrets points to the existence of individuals of status who chose to broadcast that status, at least in part, through labret wear.

Another potential realm of differentiation of individuals or groups within the household can be seen in the form of a cache of over 3,000 slate and shale beads (Figure 5.11). These beads were recovered from a single small pit in the center of House 2. An interesting aspect to this cache is that, like the stratigraphically lower bowl, it was deposited midway through the house occupation and was not recovered by subsequent house occupants. These beads are labor-intensive to manufacture and may have been produced by specialists. At a most basic level, the existence of the beads points to the consumption of labor for nonsubsistence tasks, suggesting some level of surplus or affluence within the household. However, the caching event itself perhaps represents the intentional disposal of a great deal of labor value. If the interpretation of this event as an incident of wealth consumption is correct, the act itself may have been an important expression of affluence by specific individuals of status.

This interpretation for the cache, and that of restricted access to ritual symbols, wealth items, and status markers more generally within the household, is suggested by the spatial distribution of bowls, labrets, and beads. All three classes of items are associated almost exclusively with the center of the house (Figure 5.12). In a detailed analysis of House 2 presented elsewhere (Grier 2001), I have argued that the central area represents domestic rather than communal space. The convergence of most sources of wealth and power in one domestic area of the house may be pointing to the existence of a group of household elite who resided in the central area of the house.

This central area also contained a large hearth (Feature 9 in Figure 5.8) that exhibits evidence of more substantial burning than the other hearths identified in House 2. This hearth may have played some ceremonial function in addition to a domestic role. Given its size (2 m in diameter), perhaps the visual aspect of the fire may have been important in communal ritual. Centrally located large fires in gable-roof houses were often ceremonial in function, unlike the smaller, more remotely located domestic hearths at the perimeter of interior floor space (Drucker 1951; Suttles 1991). Although the contrast between the central hearth and other hearths in House 2 at Dionisio Point is not nearly as marked as that seen in most gable-roof houses, the central hearth may have served additional nondomestic functions.

Interpretations of the existence of an elite group within the household are consistent with other classes of data from the area that bear on "eliteness." Marpole-period evidence for class stratification comes from burial remains at the nearby False Narrows village site (Burley 1989). False Narrows is similar to Dionisio Point in that it was a large Marpole village. Although similarly fine-grained house context data are lacking, mortuary data indicate that cranial deformation within the burial population was restricted to a specific set of individuals independent of age and sex. These data point to

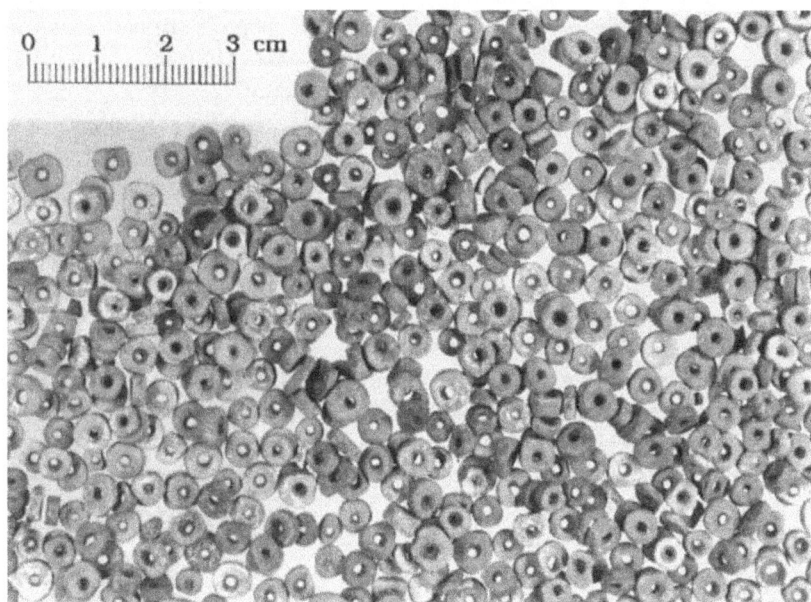

FIGURE 5.11 Ground-stone beads recovered from the cache pit in the center of House 2 at Dionisio Point

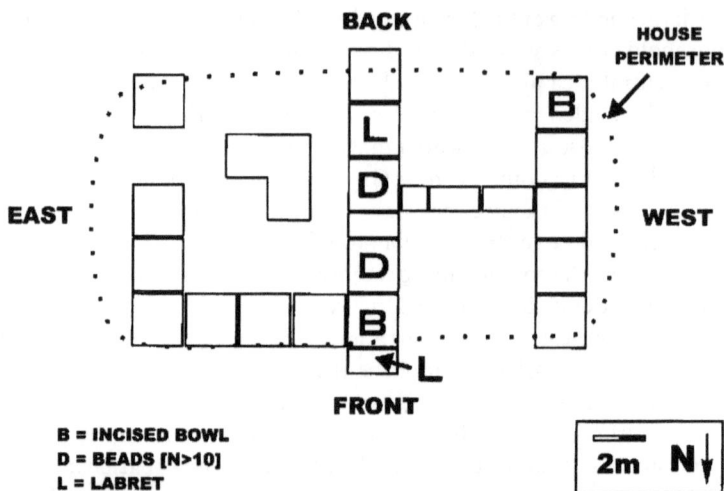

FIGURE 5.12 Occurrence of wealth- and status-related artifacts within House 2 at Dionisio Point

the existence of an ascribed, hereditary status system (Burley 1989; Burley and Knusel 1989; Matson and Coupland 1995). It cannot be securely stated that prehistoric status-ascription systems operated in an identical fashion to those described ethnographically, but the False Narrows burial population does provide the earliest secure evidence for social stratification on the southern British Columbia coast. In light of these data, the inference of intra-household social differentiation appears more secure.

Although the superstructure of House 2 at Dionisio Point itself has long since disappeared, it is important to appreciate that portable material culture was likely but one element used to broadcast messages concerning the social order within the domestic sphere. Certainly more impressive material manifestations of wealth, ritual, and hierarchy are known from other regions of the prehistoric world; however, the data from House 2 at Dionisio Point suggest a convergence of a variety of dimensions of power and trappings of status documented in ethnographic Northwest Coast societies. These elements have been identified as critical resources in the strategies of elite leadership on the coast (Suttles 1987c). Ethnographically, portable objects were used in concert with and against a backdrop of architectural features and symbolic embellishment of the built environment to promote ideologies and agendas. As Suttles (1991) has argued, large houses at times functioned as ritual theaters. The shed-roof house appears to have been less overtly organized in its spatial and architectural layout to convey rank, but the portable material culture recovered from the interior area indicates that there were in fact marked differences in the consumption and use of symbolic resources and wealth.

Conclusions

Consideration of the design of ethnographic Northwest Coast houses and social systems and examination of the prehistoric Dionisio Point archaeological data provide the following conclusions concerning the role of residences in the construction and maintenance of social power on the Northwest Coast.

1. The spatial order within Northwest Coast houses conveyed information about the social order. This information helped communicate the authority of the elite as a distinct and privileged class, as well as the legitimacy and necessity of the household status hierarchy. This information reinforced the effective power of elites within the household context.

2. The control by elites of many classes of symbolically and politically resonant material culture would have conveyed a compelling message about inequality as a natural and legitimate social order. Such messaging would have assisted in drawing diverse members of the household into a single unified hierarchy that could be put in service of elite objectives. This was advantageous, and perhaps even necessary, for the household to elevate its chances for success as an economic, social, and political entity.

3. House spatial organization and the restricted distribution of politically significant symbols likely acted as two ways in which what might be ambiguous or contentious within the household socioeconomic hierarchy was made extremely clear—as Yvonne Marshall (1989) also noted in her discussion of Nuu-chah-nulth houses. Legitimizing differentiation is important in a society dominated by the domestic mode of production in which elites were not divorced from participation in basic productive tasks.

Where do these conclusions lead us more generally in terms of understanding the development of hierarchies, social inequality, and status systems on the prehistoric Northwest Coast? Data from Dionisio Point and False Narrows allow a glimpse into the early workings of institutionalized inequality in Northwest Coast social systems, and they give us some indication of the range of house and household resources that were drawn upon in support of this system. Even though we cannot study how eliteness was specifically conveyed on long-perished architectural components, the portable material culture recovered from House 2 provides another set of data with which to understand the role of the household context in the construction of political hierarchies.

Another interesting observation arising from the prehistoric data is that it appears that house elites were relatively successful in their attempts to create a stable social order within households. House 2 at Dionisio Point, which was inhabited for as much as two centuries with no major reconfiguration of interior house space, was clearly an enduring physical structure. This suggests that the household was also an enduring corporate unit. This degree of stability implies some success at resolving incongruities in the household social order. In many areas of the world, architecture has been intimately involved in the reproduction and legitimization of social orders (Blanton 1995; papers in Kent 1990). In many societies, however, public or elite monumental architecture provides the physical setting for this. In few societies was the domestic context as politically charged as it was on the Northwest Coast. Here, the centrality, size, and complexity of households; the monumental nature of houses; and the sheer productive capacity of large households combined to create a domestic sphere that was a critical locus for the construction of political power. The enduring nature of households and status systems on the Northwest Coast indicates a rather successful strategy of marshaling resources in service of the maintenance of political power and social inequality, with ancient monumental residences having played a prominent role in this process.

References Cited

Ames, Kenneth M.
1994 The Northwest Coast: Complex Hunter-Gatherers, Ecology, and
      Social Evolution. *Annual Review of Anthropology* 23:209–229.
1995 Chiefly Power and Household Production on the Northwest Coast.
      In *Foundations of Social Inequality*, edited by T. Douglas Price and
      Gary M. Feinman, pp. 155–187. Plenum Press, New York.
1996 Life in the Big House: Household Labor and Dwelling Size on the
      Northwest Coast. In *People Who Lived in Big Houses: Archaeological
      Perspectives on Large Domestic Structures*, edited by Gary Coupland
      and E. B. Banning, pp. 131–150. Monographs in World Archaeology
      No. 27. Prehistory Press, Madison, WI.
Ames, Kenneth M., and Herbert D. G. Maschner
1999 *Peoples of the Northwest Coast: Their Archaeology and History.*
      Thames and Hudson, London.
Ames, Kenneth M., Doria Raetz, Stephen Hamilton, and
Christine McAfree
1992 Household Archaeology of a Southern Northwest Coast Plank
      House. *Journal of Field Archaeology* 19:275–290.
Barnett, Homer G.
1955 *The Coast Salish of British Columbia.* University of Oregon Press,
      Eugene.
Blackman, Margaret B.
1990 Haida: Traditional Culture. In *Northwest Coast*, edited by Wayne
      Suttles, pp. 240–260. Handbook of North American Indians, Vol. 7,
      William C. Sturtevant, general editor. Smithsonian Institution, Washington, DC.
Blanton, Richard E.
1995 *Houses and Households: A Comparative Study.* Plenum Press, New
      York.
Burley, David V.
1989 *Senewe'lets: Culture History of the Nanaimo Coast Salish and the*

False Narrows Midden. Royal British Columbia Museum Memoir No. 2. Royal British Columbia Museum, Victoria, BC.

Burley, David V., and Christopher Knusel
1989 Burial Patterns and Archaeological Interpretation: Problems in the Recognition of Ranked Society in the Coast Salish Region. In *Development of Hunting-Fishing-Gathering Maritime Societies along the West Coast of North America*, edited by A. Blukis Onat, unpaginated. Washington State University Press, Pullman.

Chatters, James C.
1989 The Antiquity of Economic Differentiation within Households in the Puget Sound Region, Northwest Coast. In *Households and Communities*, edited by Sean MacEachern, David J. W. Archer, and Richard D. Garvin, pp. 168–178. The University of Calgary Archaeological Association, Calgary, AB.

Coupland, Gary
1996 The Evolution of Multi-Family Households on the Northwest Coast of North America. In *People Who Lived in Big Houses: Archaeological Perspectives on Large Domestic Structures*, edited by Gary Coupland and E. B. Banning, pp. 121–130. Monographs in World Archaeology No. 27. Prehistory Press, Madison, WI.

Donald, Leland
1985 On the Possibility of Social Class in Societies Based on Extractive Subsistence. In *Status, Structure, and Stratification: Current Archaeological Reconstructions*, edited by Marc Thompson, María Teresa García, and François J. Kense, pp. 237–244. University of Calgary Archaeological Association, Calgary, AB.
1997 *Aboriginal Slavery on the Northwest Coast of North America*. University of California Press, Berkeley and Los Angeles.

Drucker, Philip
1951 *The Northern and Central Nootkan Tribes*. Bureau of American Ethnology Bulletin 144. Smithsonian Institution, Washington, DC.

Duff, Wilson
1956 Prehistoric Stone Sculpture of the Fraser River and the Gulf of Georgia. *Anthropology in British Columbia* 5:15–151.

Elmendorf, William W.
1971 Coast Salish Status Ranking and Intergroup Ties. *Southwestern Journal of Anthropology* 27:353–380.

Grier, Colin
2001 The Social Economy of a Prehistoric Northwest Coast Plankhouse. Unpublished Ph.D. dissertation, Department of Anthropology, Arizona State University, Tempe.
2003 Dimensions of Regional Interaction in the Prehistoric Gulf of Georgia. In *Emerging from the Mist: Studies in Northwest Coast Culture History*, edited by R. G. Matson, Quentin Mackie, and Gary Coupland, pp. 170–187. University of British Columbia Press, Vancouver.
2005 Temporality in Northwest Coast Houses. In *Household Production on the Northwest Coast*, edited by Kenneth G. Ames, Elizabeth Sobel, and Ann Trieu. International Monographs in Prehistory. Ann Arbor, MI. In press.

Keddie, Grant R.

1981 The Use and Distribution of Labrets on the North Pacific Rim. *Syesis* 14:60–80.

Kent, Susan (editor)

1990 *Domestic Architecture and the Use of Space: An Interdisciplinary Cross-Cultural Study.* Cambridge University Press, Cambridge.

Lepofsky, Dana, Michael Blake, Douglas Brown, Sandra Morrison, Nicole Oakes, and Natasha Lyons

2000 The Archaeology of the Scowlitz Site, SW British Columbia. *Journal of Field Archaeology* 27:391–416.

MacDonald, George F.

1983 *Haida Monumental Art.* University of British Columbia Press, Vancouver.

Marshall, Yvonne

1989 The House in Northwest Coast, Nuu-Chah-Nulth, Society: The Material Structure of Political Action. In *Households and Communities,* edited by Sean MacEachern, David J. W. Archer, and Richard D. Garvin, pp. 15–21. The University of Calgary Archaeological Association, Calgary, AB.

Matson, R. G., and Gary Coupland

1995 *The Prehistory of the Northwest Coast.* Academic Press, New York.

Mauger, Jeffrey E.

1991 Shed-Roof Houses at Ozette and in a Regional Perspective. In *Ozette Archaeological Project Research Reports,* Vol. 1, *House Structure and Floor Midden,* edited by Stephen R. Samuels, pp. 31–173. Reports of Investigations 63. Department of Anthropology, Washington State University, Pullman.

Mitchell, Donald H.

1968 Excavations at Two Trench Embankments in the Gulf of Georgia Region. *Syesis* 1:29–46.

1983 Sebassa's Men. In *The World Is as Sharp as a Knife,* edited by Don N. Abbott, pp. 79–88. British Columbia Provincial Museum, Victoria, BC.

Mitchell, Donald H., and Leland Donald

1988 Archaeology and the Study of Northwest Coast Economies. In *Prehistoric Economies of the Pacific Northwest Coast,* edited by Barry L. Isaac, pp. 293–351. Research in Economic Anthropology Supplement 3. JAI Press, Greenwich, CT.

Moss, Madonna L., and Jon Erlandson

1992 Forts, Refuge Rocks, and Defensive Sites: The Antiquity of Warfare along the North Pacific Coast of North America. *Arctic Anthropology* 29(2):73–90.

Samuels, Stephen R. (editor)

1991 *Ozette Archaeological Project Research Reports.* Vol. 1, *House Structure and Floor Midden.* Reports of Investigations 63. Department of Anthropology, Washington State University, Pullman.

Smith, Marian W.

1947 House Types of the Middle Fraser River. *American Antiquity* 4:255–267.

Suttles, Wayne

1984   Productivity and Its Constraints: A Coast Salish Case. In *Indian Art Traditions of the Northwest Coast*, edited by Roy L. Carlson, pp. 67–87. Archaeology Press, Simon Fraser University, Burnaby, BC.

1987a   Affinal Ties, Subsistence, and Prestige among the Coast Salish. In *Coast Salish Essays*, edited by Wayne Suttles, pp. 15–25. University of Washington Press, Seattle.

1987b   The Persistence of Intervillage Ties among the Coast Salish. In *Coast Salish Essays*, edited by Wayne Suttles, pp. 209–230. University of Washington Press, Seattle.

1987c   Private Knowledge, Morality, and Social Classes among the Coast Salish. In *Coast Salish Essays*, edited by Wayne Suttles, pp. 3–14. University of Washington Press, Seattle.

1990   Central Coast Salish. In *Northwest Coast*, edited by Wayne Suttles, pp. 453–475. Handbook of North American Indians, Vol. 7, William C. Sturtevant, general editor. Smithsonian Institution, Washington, DC.

1991   The Shed-Roof House. In *A Time of Gathering: Native Heritage in Washington State*, edited by Robin K. Wright, pp. 212–222. University of Washington Press, Seattle.

Thom, Brian D.

1995   The Dead and the Living: Burial Mounds and Cairns and the Development of Social Classes in the Gulf of Georgia Region. Unpublished Master's thesis, Department of Anthropology and Sociology, University of British Columbia, Vancouver.

CHAPTER 6

Rising Above

THE ELITE ACROPOLIS OF EL TAJÍN

Patricia Joan Sarro

El Tajín, on the Mexican Gulf Coast, is a city and culture most often associated with the Mesoamerican ballgame. And with good reason: 17 courts of various sizes and configurations, together with temples, platforms, and multiroom structures, stood at the center of the city and its ritual life (Figure 6.1). Images of the game and its attendant rituals appear in sculpture throughout the site (Figures 6.2 and 6.3).

The term *palace* has rarely been used to describe any of the city's buildings. Of the three major types of elite structures found throughout Mesoamerica, the palace, the temple, and the ballcourt, the palace is the most difficult to identity, and the term is one of the most loosely used. Ballcourts can readily be identified by their parallel walls. These are sometimes vertical, but more commonly they slope above a low, vertical banquette (Figure 6.4). Both forms can be found at El Tajín. Following the "formula" generally accepted by Mesoamericanists, the distinction between temples and palaces has been made on the analysis of form.[1] Relatively small superstructures of one or few rooms, set on high, truncated pyramid platforms are designated temples. Low, relatively small, truncated pyramid platforms are called altars. Multiroom structures set on lower pyramid platforms are generally identified as elite residences, places of governance, or both.

In his urban analysis of El Tajín, archaeologist Jürgen Brüggemann followed this schema throughout the city, both in the lower area and in the acropolis of Tajín Chico above. In doing so, he has identified nearly all the buildings of Tajín Chico, but few of those below, as places of high-status residence and city rule (Brüggemann 1991:100). José García Payón, who oversaw excavations at the site from the 1930s through the early 1960s, also identified Tajín Chico as an area dedicated to elite residence and administration (1965:22).

Some scholars have referred to a number of Tajín Chico's buildings as palaces (Wilkerson 1987). Others have reserved the term for the Building of the Columns (Lira 1995), noting its scale and ornamental imagery, particularly the narrative images on the large columns that give the building its name (Figure 6.3).

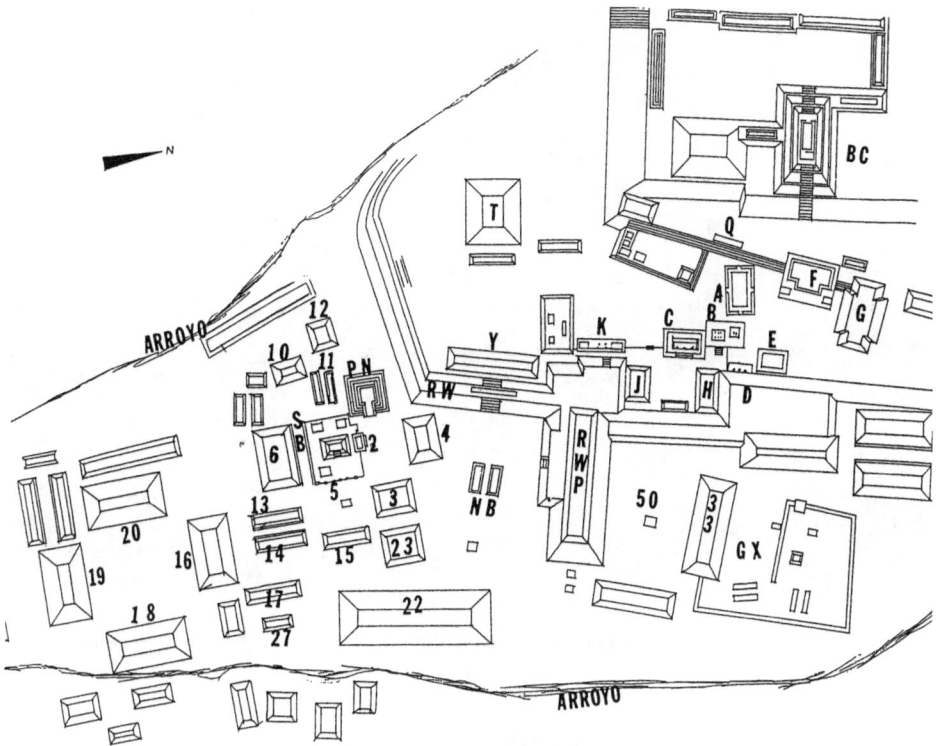

FIGURE 6.1 Plan of El Tajín. Author's drawing after Wilkerson 1987.

Many authors, including myself, have shied away from the term *palace* altogether with regard to the buildings of El Tajín. However, in light of revised analysis, in this chapter I argue that the city's "palace" comprised not only the Building of the Columns but also the plazas and buildings of Tajín Chico, all set above the more public sector of ballcourts and temples. The Building of the Columns is, in this view, only the largest and most restricted element within a larger group forming a complex of the type found in lowland Maya cities such as Tikal.[2] That city's Central Acropolis was the locale of the most elite residence and restricted religious ritual, as well as of the rulership of the city and region. Set apart, in every sense, from the rest of the city's zone of ritual and civic life via restricted access, enclosure, and cosmic imagery, this area was not only the location of power but also its most public statement.

In adopting the palace-complex model, I do not mean in any way to suggest that El Tajín was a Maya or even a "Mayoid" city. Over the years, a number of arguments have been made that El Tajín was culturally dependent on Teotihuacan, the Classic Maya, or both.[3] I have argued elsewhere (Sarro 2004) that although El Tajín's connections with both these areas can be established, it was the cultural colony of neither. The ballgame, for ex-

FIGURE 6.2 Northwest panel of the South Ballcourt, El Tajín. Author's photograph.

FIGURE 6.3 Column fragment, Building of the Columns, Tajín Chico. Author's drawing after Wilkerson 1990:FIGURE 80, with additional information from Wilkerson 1987.

FIGURE 6.4 Ballcourt 13/14, El Tajín. Author's photograph.

ample, is throughout Mesoamerica believed to be a path to deity-human interaction and a vehicle for the continuation of life. But the images at El Tajín do not suggest a reworking of the Maya hero-twin myth of ballgame and resurrection, but rather depict a pantheon and narrative specific to this city and culture.

Similarly, the palace complex of El Tajín exhibits several architectural and iconographic characteristics not found elsewhere. There are few surviving images of the rulers themselves or of their deeds, and certainly none on a scale to be appreciated from below. The strongest formal statement of power is in fact a relatively small structure in Tajín Chico's central plaza: Building A (Figures 6.5 and 6.6). Placed at the juncture of two large courtyards and at the foot of the staircase that leads to the Building of the Columns, Building A is a focal point in the complex. As I argue below, it represents nothing less than the axis mundi, the meeting place of the earth, the underworld, and the celestial realm of the gods. In keeping with the game's importance to the city, it does so by representing the earthly realm as four miniature ballcourts. Thus the game becomes the world, and those who control it, rulers by virtue of that control. Beyond elevation, scale, restricted access, and ruler imagery, the palace complex of El Tajín states the power of those who live and rule there in terms of the earthly ballgame and its cosmic powers.

FIGURE 6.5 Building A, Tajín Chico. Author's photograph.

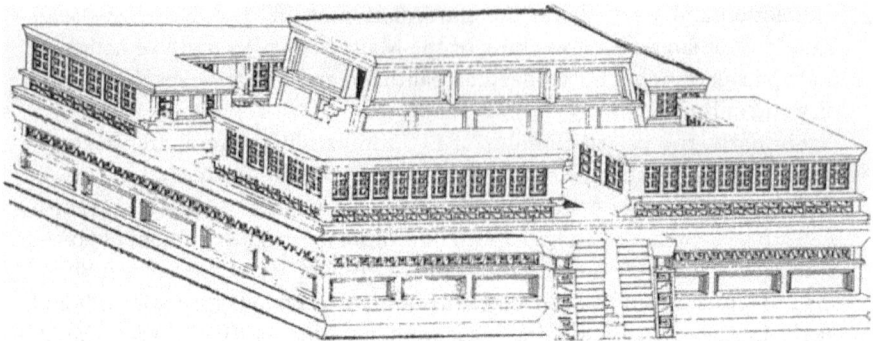

FIGURE 6.6 Building A, Tajín Chico, reconstruction. Wilkerson 1987:49.

The City Below and Above

The center of El Tajín is divided into two major sectors by elevation and the high Retaining Wall (see Figure 6.1:RW). The lower sector contains temples, plazas, altars, and, most significantly for both the life of the city and our image of it, all 17 of its ballcourts.[4] The palace complex of Tajín Chico constitutes the higher sector to the north and west, set apart by elevation and more limited access.

Although framed and separated from the surrounding area by partial walls and two arroyos that form a V at the center's southernmost end, the lower area is the more accessible of the two. The land gently rises from south to north, a rake undesignated by any clear steps or walls. Its many temples, plazas, altars, and ballcourts identify it as a place for large gatherings and publicly accessible rituals. The route from one plaza or structure to another may be, at times, angular or indirect (see, for example, the plazas to the north and to the east of Building 5 in Figure 6.1), but they are also unrestricted, and each area may be entered from a number of points.

The lower city's plan is far more irregular as experienced than as read in the plan provided here. As one passes from the southernmost end where the two arroyos meet, the effect is one of a seemingly endless flow of spaces and structures, the vistas opening up as one passes from one plaza to another. Always, however, there is the acropolis of Tajín Chico above the Retaining Wall visible ahead. Due to the architectural and ornamental similarities of the two sectors, the acropolis reads as both separate from and an extension of the lower sector.

The lower and upper areas come together at the Plaza of the North Ballcourt (Figure 6.1:NB). Here two wide staircases rise to Building Y and the Retaining Wall Platform (Figure 6.1:Y and RWP), visually connecting the two zones. Above them can be seen a number of the buildings of the acropolis's outer rim. Many of these have three-sided rooms or porticoes, open to the lower sector. But, as I discuss below, this connection is more visual than actual. The wide staircases lead to low ridges from which narrow passages and small staircases provide the only access to the plazas and buildings beyond.

There are no ballcourts within Tajín Chico, and only one structure, not yet excavated, may have been a temple (Figure 6.1:T). Most of the buildings contain a number of small rooms, and several have open porticoes from which the residents and others can view the activities in its several plazas and, in turn, be viewed themselves. These buildings are, as Jürgen Brüggemann (1991) has suggested, suitable for elite residence and city government. A number, in fact, have rooms lined with benches, like the central hall of the Building of the Columns. This suggests council halls or places of royal audience. Individually, none of these buildings suggests a discrete palace structure. Together, they form a palace complex.

The Palace in Mesoamerica and Mesoamerican Studies

The term *palace* is one that has been variously applied by scholars working in Mesoamerica. Often it simply designates a relatively large structure set on a low pyramid platform, made up of a number of rooms and constructed of fine materials. The presence of sculptural or painted imagery of high quality or depicting royal or cosmic figures or events has also led to the term's usage. In some cases, only one palace has been named within a given city, implying that it was the seat of highest power. Often, however, several unconnected buildings have been so titled, making the relationship between structure and power less clear.

In the past few years, however, a number of scholars working in Mesoamerica and throughout the pre-Columbian world have turned again to the issue of palaces, emerging with a far more complex image—one that, aside from differing from a European-based model, may differ from region to region as well. In a recently published volume based on a 1998 Dumbarton Oaks conference (Evans and Pillsbury 2004), several authors working throughout Mesoamerica and the Andes presented examples, and in some cases definitions, of palaces in their regions. While these examples are shown to vary greatly from one another, Susan Toby Evans, in her introduction to the volume (p. 2), writes that "patterns have begun to emerge" from our information on palace activities and configurations. These include a place for royal residence, housing for retainers, rooms for storage and ceremony, benched rooms, and courtyards. Both the Maya palace complexes and the Aztec palaces would seem to fulfill these criteria, although in very different configurations.

In her own study of Aztec palaces and their antecedents, Evans (see Chapter 10, this volume) utilizes both archaeological findings and conquest-era texts and drawings to form our clearest image yet of Aztec palaces and palace activities. These sources indicate that, for the Aztec at least, palaces consisted of several types of rooms and spaces, set around courtyards, and dedicated to various activities and purposes. In these halls and chambers, royal and attendant residence was standard, as were rooms for council and audience, entrance halls, and space for the storage of items for warfare and ritual.

The Aztec palace may have faced onto a large public plaza, as in the capital city of Tenochtitlan, but it was, nonetheless, a single and discrete structure. This does not seem to have been the case among the Classic lowland Maya, for whom a similar range of activities often took place in a complex of structures and spaces less unified and seemingly more subject to growth and adaptation than the Aztec version. George Andrews (1975) has named this configuration a "palace group." He defines it as being set apart by restricted access and, in many cases, growing over time, responding as bureaucratic and residential needs changed and expanded. Palace groups seem to have shared many of the same functions as the Aztec palace, including residence, rooms for royal audience marked by benches and thrones, and various spaces for storage and the everyday needs of a dynamic space serving both private and civic functions. Private religious rituals were also practiced within these complexes, as evidenced by the small temple structures incorporated within them, such as Tikal's Building 66 (Harrison 1999:Figure 118).

Andrews's work is based on the archaeological record of a number of Maya cities. Dorie Reents-Budet (1994, 2001) has taken that archaeological record, combined it with translations of Maya inscriptions, and then used the melded information to analyze the palace scenes depicted on Maya polychrome vessels. In doing so, she has greatly refined our knowledge of the activities that took place in these spaces. Palace activities documented in these images include scenes of presentation of tribute and prisoners, state visits, and ritual dances.

What Andrews defines as the "palace group," together with the palace activities suggested by him, Reents-Budet, and other Maya scholars, most closely approximates the image of Tajín Chico as a unified palace complex that I am suggesting here. Such a grouping of structures is marked by restricted access, placement on a platform, interior courtyards, internal/external orientation, and no real hierarchy between the component structures. There are spaces for elite residence, and places of gathering, as evidenced by thrones or benches, and often small temples. The iconography is royal or cosmic or both, implying a divine source for human rulership. Taken as a whole, the acropolis of Tajín Chico, including the Building of the Columns, can easily fit into this model.

El Tajín's Acropolis as a Unified Palace Complex

One characteristic of all elite architecture, regardless of its function, is a setting apart, a physical separation from the ordinary. Power, in part, derives from this separation. This can be achieved through building type, quality of materials and workmanship, imagery, placement, restricted access, or any combination of these. Any or all of these send a clear message of separation—of place from place, persons from persons. There is a distinct sense of insider/outsider, within and without. One need not ever enter the elite space to know this; the message is clearly projected to the outside.

In the case of Tajín Chico, this "otherness" is first announced by the Retaining Wall that rises above the lower sector (Figure 6.7). Elevation is a powerful sign of distinction, one recognized throughout Mesoamerica in the high platforms of so many temple structures. At the same time, the Retaining Wall joins the disparate structures and spaces of the acropolis into a whole and states their unified nature and purpose. The running vertical panel of deep frets topping the sloping wall mimics the *talud/tablero/contratalud* profile common to many of the structures below, compounding the impression of a cohesive whole.[5] This impression holds whether one views

FIGURE 6.7 Plaza of the North Ballcourt of El Tajín, with the Retaining Wall of Tajín Chico behind. Author's photograph.

the acropolis from the plazas to the south or from the plazas and ballcourts of the northernmost points of the lower sector, which skirt the eastern edge of Tajín Chico (Figure 6.1:50 and GX).

There is, however, a mixed message in the elevation of Tajín Chico. As an acropolis rising in stages from the public area below, Tajín Chico is more visible than, say, a Maya royal sector or a palace set on a relatively low base. Tajín's elite area, or at least its outer edges, looms over the rest of the city. This is a powerful statement in itself and an indication of the relationship between the ruler and the ruled. Takeshi Inomata and Stephen Houston (2001:13–14) note that the nature of kingship is inherently contradictory, "at once remote and close, residing both at the center of society and outside it."

The Retaining Wall sends just such a dual, self-conflicting message of restriction and access. Its height alone, physically as well as visually, separates what is above from what is below. Its winding, continuous horizontal lines of wall and capping row of niches are, however, cut vertically by two large staircases on the north and west sides of the Plaza of the North Ballcourt. These steps imply welcoming and a calling forth, a bridge between the public and private, the common and the royal. By implication, stairs are a point of access, and so these steps visually serve to open the acropolis.

This impression of openness is undercut, however, by the reality of the restricted nature of this access. The steps on the north side lead only to an open platform (Figure 6.1:RWP). Those on the west wall are interrupted by a small platform or structure, just below the entrance to Building Y.[6] This may have served simply as a place for ritual display, but it might also have acted as a sentry post, limiting further access. Only by being admitted at this point could one have passed beyond, into the higher and more private courtyards and buildings of the palace complex via a series of small staircases and spaces between buildings.

Only Building Y can be entered directly from its staircase above the Retaining Wall. All the other buildings on the outer rim or visible from below (J, K, and D on Figure 6.1) are entered only from the courtyards hidden behind them.[7] Building K, for example, has one small set of steps and its only true entrance on its west side, away from the Retaining Wall stairs. To enter its rooms or portico, one would have had to pass through the small open space to its east, up the small steps between K and C, and into the courtyard behind K. Visually, however, Buildings J, K, and D all appear, because of their porticoes, to be both open and accessible from below.

The visual message of accessibility in the form and placement of these structures belies their protected nature. In effect, the buildings of the outer rim provide another kind of wall around the acropolis while, at the same time, reinforcing the connection between the elite residents and the ritual and civic life of the lower sector. Buildings J and Y and the Retaining Wall Platform all face onto the Plaza of the North Ballcourt, the largest open space in the city. David Webster (2001:150) has suggested that the out-facing rooms of Tikal's Central Acropolis were utilized to display items of ritual importance or signs of prestige onto the Central Plaza. The porticoes of Tajín Chico may have been settings for the display of the elites themselves. At the same time, they were platforms from which the elite could witness the ballgame and other rituals below, as has been suggested for the hieroglyphic Staircase of Copán (see Fash 1991:Figure 89). These two lines of vision in no way contradict one another. Royal viewing is in itself a form of display, one that connects the royal personage to the ritual while underlining his unique status.

Forms and Functions

David Webster (2001:130), writing on Maya palaces, mentions that despite the wealth of information known about Maya kingship, little can be said concerning the specific locations of court activities. Exactly where in the palace, for example, were crafts produced, audiences held, and the various members of the court housed? Webster is, of course, contrasting the position of the Mayanist, who must depend primarily on archaeological and pictorial evidence, to that of the Aztec scholar, who also has information from conquest-era texts. The information available for El Tajín is more limited still. Stone relief images picture a number of royal and ritual events, but these give little information that would indicate the location of such events in real space. Images of buildings that might be palace structures may represent temples, and they tell us little of the activities that took place within them.

More information, however, is available concerning the ballgame and its attendant rituals, although the game itself is never depicted. Six relief panels from the South Ballcourt (Figure 6.1:SB) illustrate a number of these rituals, but none are shown as taking place within the palace complex. Many of the figures wear the protective kneepads and protective hip yokes of the ball-player, and they are shown as elite by their elaborate headdresses. Two of the scenes, including one of human sacrifice, are shown taking place on the ball-court, as indicated by the parallel sloping walls that frame the central par-ticipants (Figure 6.2). There is no reason to assume, however, that the other four events, though related to the ballgame ritual, took place on the courts themselves. The narratives depicted on two of the other panels of the South Ballcourt take place in what resemble El Tajín temple or palace buildings, seen in profile in "X-ray" images and flooded with water (Kampen 1972:Fig-ures 24 and 25).[8] The activities and most of the participants are not from the earthly realm. Rather than images of the royal court, or even ballgame-related activities, these depictions, most scholars agree, are of events that take place in mythic time or space, most likely after the completion of the game and the sacrifice of the ballplayer (Wilkerson 1987).

Small raised structures are depicted on the Building of the Columns, but the activities taking place in them are undefined, and they do not appear to show any obviously royal events (Kampen 1972:Figure 33b). Other sculptural examples from the city appear to depict mythic, rather than earthly, space, as, for example, the scroll-like stepped platform with a grotesque figure be-low and a gesticulating skeletal creature among those above (Kampen 1972: Figure 5a). The more clearly human and royal activities of the ruler 13 Rab-bit, portrayed on one of the columns, takes place in ambiguous space that may or may not be enclosed by a structure that the artist has chosen not to indicate (Figure 6.3).

At El Tajín, as elsewhere, there is no clear evidence from which to for-mulate an equation of form to function. Also, spaces may often have served several purposes, in palaces as in any residence. The bedrooms of many Euro-pean kings were also council halls and powerful audience chambers where dignitaries were received. The palace of Versailles is the most-often-cited example of this, but the practice is known to have occurred in many Euro-pean castles and palaces for centuries before and after the court of the Sun King. The structures that make up Maya palaces may also have served sev-eral functions, both contemporaneously and over time. There is evidence at Tikal, for example, of changes in both the access and the orientation of build-ings of the Central Acropolis (see, for example, Harrison 1999:186). These

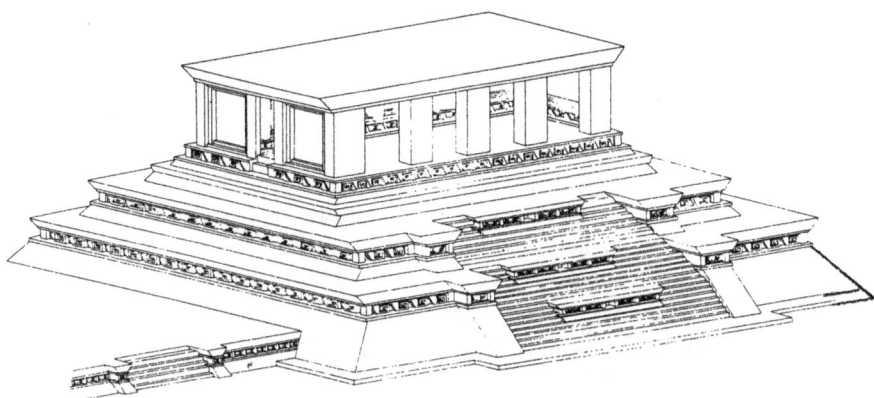

FIGURE 6.8 Building C, Tajín Chico, reconstruction. Wilkerson 1987:39.

would, most likely, have altered both building function and status. The following suggestions of how some of the structures and spaces of El Tajín's palatial acropolis were used are, of necessity, based on interpretation and comparison to the somewhat better understood palaces of the Aztec and the Maya.

The Building of the Columns is certainly the city's most prominent edifice, due to its size and location, and its imagery is directly royal (Figure 6.3). Excavations in the early 1990s revealed a large central room or courtyard lined with benches and surrounded by a number of smaller rooms (Lira 1995). This would make it a suitable place for audiences or gatherings for decision making, two of the activities known to have taken place in Aztec palaces. The surrounding rooms may have been residential, or spaces for the preparation for such gatherings. These are only a few of the possible palace activities, and it does not seem that the Building of the Columns had ample space for others, such as storage of ritual or military objects. If the Building of the Columns served alone as the royal palace, it did so by a very limited definition.

With the probable exception of Building T, the majority of the acropolis buildings contain a small number of rooms gathered in a C formation around or behind an open-sided room or a portico (Figure 6.8). These rooms vary in size, but all are relatively small, making it equally likely that they were used for storage or residence, or even that their purpose changed over time. Due to the poor preservation of many upper walls, it cannot be determined in many cases if these rooms had windows, which would have made for more comfortable sleeping accommodations. Building A does have windows preserved in some of its rooms but not others.

Aspects of at least some of these buildings do give some indication as to their specific uses. Porticoes, as stated, are semipublic spaces, places both to observe and be observed. This is not to say, however, that this more visible area is not purposely housed within the same structure where the royal or elite figures actually lived and slept. Buildings J, K, and C have both porticoes and surrounding rooms suitable for residential use.

Several buildings include spaces that, like the central court of the Building of the Columns, appear to have been constructed for gatherings such as council meetings and royal audiences. George Andrews (1975) used the presence of benches as a way to identify sleeping quarters in lowland Maya palace complexes. But the benches in Tajín Chico's buildings are too narrow for sleeping, and they line the walls of the room, making them more suitable for sitting than for sleeping, which suggests that these were council rooms and audience chambers rather than bedrooms. In addition, in most cases (Buildings J, K, and C, for example) these benches line the walls of the open porticoes. Benches do, however, surround interior rooms in two instances. One is a room on the upper floor of Building B; the central room of the Building of the Columns is the other. Although these rooms are more private than the porticoes of J, K, and C, they, too, are quite clearly meeting rooms rather than sleeping quarters.

Building J contains the only example yet excavated at El Tajín in which the bench deepens at the center of the back wall to form what may be a royal throne like those depicted in Maya art. This throne room, like the halls of Building B and the Building of the Columns, is a more private space, although it is an open portico. Rather than facing out from the acropolis, however, it opens onto a small courtyard formed by Buildings J, C, and the unexcavated Building H. The imagery of its murals depicts otherworldly beings, crouching creatures with long snouts adorned with headdresses on their heads, tails, and backs and gesticulating humanoid figures. These murals were later covered with rows of stucco rattles, and the configuration of the room altered (see Ladrón de Guevara 1991, figures on pp. 110–111). This relatively small and private space may, in both stages, have been reserved for intimate gatherings and rituals of the highest rank.

This number of buildings with similar high-status elements, such as benches and porticoes, might be interpreted as indicating a form of social structure in which power was shared by a number of individuals or families. However, the structures of the acropolis indicate characteristics individual enough to imply different functions. Gatherings of varying sizes and for several purposes could have taken place within these and other palace rooms and courtyards. The restricted nature of the acropolis signals the elite nature of both these events and their participants and audiences. I would suggest that, like the physical and visual relationships between the city's upper and lower sectors, the rituals taking place in each were also both related and distinct. In the following sections I propose that at least some of the rituals of Tajín Chico were dedicated to the completion of the ballgame ritual and related to its intent: contact with the deities and the power of rebirth. Extending these rituals to the royal sector would have restated royal control over them and their power.

FIGURE 6.9 Building A, Tajín Chico, north side. Model in the Museo Nacional de Antropología, Mexico City. Author's photograph.

Palace Ornament and Association

Ornamentation of the buildings of the acropolis may, at first, seem their least palatial aspect. Except for the columns of the uppermost structure, there is none of the fine carving found in the lower sector. Instead, outer and, in some cases, inner walls are decorated with row on row of geometric elements, similar to textile designs (Figure 6.9). These are formed of plaster over stone armature, resulting in a relatively shallow design quite unlike the deep stone mosaic of the niches and frets adorning the buildings of the lower sector (Figure 6.10).

Although the plaster-over-stone technique may be seen as inferior in quality, its use was probably more practical to its purpose. With the application of plaster and paint, the effect would have been similar to that of deep stone mosaic. This technique quickly and relatively cheaply, in both materials and man-hours, achieves a form of ornamentation well suited to the more privatized nature of the palace complex. Within the palace complex, only the frets of Building C are created in stone mosaic (Figure 6.8). Building C, it must be noted, is clearly visible from below above the point where the Retaining Wall turns to enclose the Plaza of the North Ballcourt. With its deep mosaic of frets, it reads from below as a second level to the Retaining Wall

FIGURE 6.10 Pyramid of the Niches, El Tajín, detail. Author's photograph.

itself, reinforcing the view of the acropolis as a whole, set on a templelike platform.

Building C's ornamentation is a continuation of that of the lower sector; the ornamentation of other structures on the acropolis is a reinterpretation.[9] Much of it is, in fact, a series of quotations of forms that appear on the buildings of the lower sector. Building A is one that contains several of these manipulated, miniaturized restatements of architectural and ornamental form, and so it serves as the most complex example of this phenomenon.

The steps leading to Building A (Figures 6.5 and 6.6) are narrow and tunnel-like. A false staircase formed of plaster only 3 cm deep frames these. This "staircase" is designed to look like that of a number of other temple platforms in the lower sector. The plaster step design is in turn bordered on the right and left by plaster "balustrades" of stepfrets topped by niches, mimicking the deep mosaic design of those staircases. A row of equally shallow panels runs along Building A's outer walls. These reference the mosaic stone niches not only of the Pyramid of the Niches but of many lower-sector temples.

Perhaps the most unusual formal quotation on the façade of Building A is the reverse layering of the *talud/contra-talud*. The profile of most of El Tajín's lower-sector buildings consists of an inward-angled *talud* on which rests a vertical *tablero* topped by an outward-angled *contra-talud*. In just a few instances, the profile consists only of the *talud* and *contra-talud*.[10] On the façade of Building A, these are reversed. The *contra-talud* of the lower level is topped by the *talud* of the upper level, a configuration that completely negates the usual supporting function of the *talud*. What is structural in most buildings of El Tajín is here transformed into the purely ornamental.

These formal quotations and manipulations serve the same function as the deep, nichelike frets of Building C and the seemingly open and welcoming forms of the Retaining Wall staircases and the porticoes above. Through them the acropolis is connected with, and yet made distinct from, the lower sector. They signify the relationship between the two sectors and that between the ruler above and the powerful rituals below.

Building A: The Palace as the Place of Cosmic Passage

The courtyards, rooms, and porticoes of Tajín Chico and the Building of the Columns would easily have accommodated the palace functions of royal and elite residence; storage of ritual goods; exterior spaces for larger-scale gatherings; and rooms for governing council, halls of judgment, and royal audience halls. But no space so far described could accommodate the role of ruler/priest, one usually associated with the palace itself as well as with more public temples like the many in lower Tajín. The Aztec palaces of Tenochtitlan were located in close proximity to the city's main temple complex. Classic lowland Maya palace complexes, such as those of Tikal and Copán, included high platformed temples among their many buildings. Building T of the palace complex of El Tajín may have been a temple of traditional form. I have suggested elsewhere that Building A was more than simply a space for royal gatherings and other activities; it was also a major setting for ballgame-related rituals. These rituals, like so many elements of the palace complex, connected the ruler with the ruled, and the palace with the ballcourts and temples below.[11]

Sculpted images imply that much of El Tajín's ritual life revolved around the ballgame. Most of our information concerning the game, played in one form or another throughout Mesoamerica, comes from early colonial texts on the Aztec and from the Quiché Maya *Popol-Vuh*. According to early Spanish writers, there were two ballcourts in the sacred precinct of Tenochtitlan. One of these was considered to be for the use of men, the other for the use of the gods, implying that there were both sacred and secular versions of the game. Multiple courts at some Classic-period sites suggest that similar distinctions were made at these sites, as some scholars suggest (see, for example, Miller and Houston 1987:48). The variety of ballcourt shapes and sizes across Mesoamerica, and even in individual cities such as El Tajín, may also indicate various forms of play, or perhaps the use of different courts by different social groups.

The ballgame itself was, however, only the central event of a number of connected rituals. The six stone relief panels from El Tajín's South Ballcourt depict a number of these, which include preparations for the game and for battle as well as human sacrifice, all overseen by elite figures and supernatural beings (Figure 6.2). Two of the panels appear to transport a human figure, perhaps the ballplayer, to the realm of the gods (see Kampen 1972:Figures 20–25). Although scholars disagree on details of interpretation, all hold that the end result of the ballgame ritual cycle is this meeting of human and divine that results in favor to humankind in the form of life itself.

These South Ballcourt images are, of course, within the public sector where the game itself is played—an area with plazas, temples, and altars where the associated rituals most likely took place. The ballgame cycle is again portrayed in the far more privatized space of the Building of the Columns on the highest terrace of the palace complex. However, rather than depicting multiple, apparently unnamed elites, these sculptures contain the city's only known glyphic inscriptions, many of which identify a single individual named 13 Rabbit. This lordly personage is shown at the center of an image that conflates the several events of the ballgame ritual complex into a single moment (Figure 6.3). A parade of named elite war captives passes before 13 Rabbit. The sacrifice has already been completed, as evidenced by the decapitated body to his left. Its head lies at his feet, together with the rubber ball used in the game. The gods have responded with the reward of vegetation that grows directly from the sacrificial victim's body.

The final step of divine reward requires direct contact between men and gods. On the central panels of the South Ballcourt, this meeting takes place within a templelike structure. The unique form of Building A transports this event to the center of the royal palace. I have already shown that Building A's false staircase mimics that of El Tajín's temples. I suggest further that passing through this false staircase by climbing the true tunnel-like staircase within is to re-create the passage between the earth and the underworld that completes the ballgame cycle.

In the Mesoamerican worldview, the earth is composed of four quarters oriented to the four directions. The three realms of heavens, earth, and underworld form a fifth, vertical line of orientation. The form of Building A replicates this cosmic map. Its lowest level is solid fill, the dense mass of the underworld. The second level, with its four sets of rooms, is the earth inhabited by man. The open space of the aisles between the rooms creates a cross of four equal arms. The plan of the second level of Building A thus fits the pan-Mesoamerican construct of the universe as comprising four quarters associated with the four cardinal directions.[12] At the building's center rises a sloped base, which once supported a room or pair of rooms (García Vega 1936). This templelike form represents the celestial.

The four aisles of the upper level of Building A duplicate the sloped-sided ballcourt type that is the dominant one at El Tajín, although on a far smaller scale (see Figure 6.4). In the second level of Building A, the four quarters of the earth are therefore represented by the ballcourts of El Tajín. The building's tunnel-like entrance is then analogous to the passage between the earth and the underworld, a passage created through the activities of the ballgame cult, as depicted in the relief sculptures of the South Ballcourt and the Building of the Columns. Walter Krickeberg (1966) describes the ballgame in Aztec mythology as a metaphor for the sun's journey across the heavens, into the underworld, and back to the heavens. At El Tajín as well, the ballcourt serves as the link between the earth and the underworld, the royal and the divine. To enter or leave Building A, one literally passes through the floor of one of the ballcourt aisles, descending into the underworld or rising above it (see Sarro 2000:Figure 9.12).

Examples of a cross-shaped cartouche representing the opening to the underworld can be found in Mesoamerican art as early as Preclassic Olmec times (Schele and Freidel 1991:308). This is a liminal space of great power. Depicting a powerful figure in this place states his right to rulership. One early example of this type of illustration is the rock carving known as El Rey at the Olmec site of Chalcatzingo. In it the cross form is shown in profile, framing a powerful, headdressed figure.[13] The result of the ruler's communication between the earth and the underworld is fertility. Phallic raindrops fall to earth, nourishing the plants of the earth. The early ballcourt markers of Copán show humans and underworld deities united in the ballgame within a similar frame (Fash 1991:Figure 69). In Building A, the actual ruler/priest stands within the cross or quatrefoil space, having emerged from the liminal threshold of the tunnel entrance.

Building A may well have been used for residential purposes. Its location at the base of the staircase to the Building of the Columns and between two large plazas indicates that it was central to the palace complex in every sense. I am suggesting that it most likely served several purposes, one of which was as the stage set for a royal ritual of underworld passage and emergence. This ceremony, like the ballgame, directly connected the earthly and the divine realms, with the ruler as the cosmic traveler. This event may be the subject of the enigmatic murals that decorate the benches and throne of the palace complex's Building J.

The possibility of an emergence ritual at Building A is supported by other

Mesoamerican examples. One of the few excavated structures of Morelos Paxil, Veracruz, is a low pyramid platform, that site's Building A (García Payón 1939). Its surface can be reached only by climbing a staircase on the side opposite the plaza. In this it is much like the outer-rim buildings of El Tajín's palace complex. A ritual participant would have to pass through the body of the platform to emerge onto the surface on the plaza side, suddenly appearing to those watching from the plaza.

Two other, earlier examples of platforms with hidden entrances have been found at the Late Preclassic northern Maya site of Yaxuná. David Freidel and Charles Suhler (1999), their discoverers, have concluded that these may have been used as dance platforms. In a Quiché Maya ritual described in the sixteenth century, two dancers, representing the Hero Twins in the underworld, first disappear and then reappear in a cloud of smoke, utilizing a trap door (Coe 1989:161–162).

Building A may have been used similarly in ceremonies connecting the rulers with the power of emergence and rebirth resulting from the ballgame ceremonial complex. It faces onto two large plazas, one to the north and one to the south. There is only one entrance on its south side. However, on the opposite, north side, below one of the four ballcourt-shaped aisles, narrow panels of geometric decoration frame a shallow niche (Figure 6.9). This stucco design can be compared to the formal arrangement of entrance and balustrades typical of El Tajín's many temples. It forms a second "entrance" to the building, a "face" to this plaza. The evidence of Yaxuná's probable dance platforms and Building A of Morelos Paxil suggests that Building A of Tajín Chico may also have been utilized in a ceremony of emergence, one in which the ruler-priest entered on the south side of the building and then emerged onto its ballcourt-like surface above and "appeared" to those in the north plaza below. Such a ceremony, with all its implications of power beyond the human realm, could only have increased the prestige of the palace complex and its residents, the ruler and his court.

The performance of such a rite taking place in Building A also sheds light on the impact of the porticoed buildings along the Retaining Wall. Emerging high above people standing in the Plaza of the North Ballcourt, the ruler and members of his court would appear as if from a mythic realm.

The rulers of El Tajín declared and consolidated their power through the control of the ritual life of the city and, no doubt, the surrounding area. In narrative images, the most elite are shown in acts of warfare and ballgame ritual that lead to the granting of divine favor. The palace complex of Tajín Chico rises above and embraces the city's largest ritual space, the Plaza of the North Ballcourt, declaring royal connection and control. Building A, in its form and in the ceremonies that took place there, claims the full ballgame ritual cycle and its sacred power for the rulers of the city. The narration of the ballgame myth and its significance in this restricted, elite locale declare the rights of kingship to be grounded in the rites of the ballgame.

The acropolis of El Tajín fits well the configuration of a palace complex as found in the great Maya cities. It is, however, the unique product of a local cultural vision of kingship. The form of its buildings, and the dual message of accessibility and restriction that they imply, is a very specific notion and statement of royal power. The emphasis on the ballgame and its rituals, so evident in the numerous ballcourts and sculpted imagery of the lower sector, is transported to the palace itself in the form of Building A, and perhaps in the rituals performed there. Even the throne room of Building J includes the mural depiction of figures performing the underworld passage associated with the game and its attendant rituals. A palace is always a statement of royal power. At El Tajín, that power is clearly imaged as rooted in royal control over the ballgame and its rituals, and the divine favor that is their result.

Notes

1. On the distinction between temples and palaces, see, for example, George Kubler (1973) on Teotihuacan, and George F. Andrews (1975:39–46) on Maya architecture.

2. In my doctoral dissertation (Sarro 1995:48–50), I argued that the Building of the Columns should be considered a structure and a region separate from Tajín Chico, based on its higher elevation. I no longer believe this for several reasons, some of which are discussed herein.

3. As recently as 2000, at a Mesa Redonda held at Teotihuacan on the topic of Tajín/Teotihuacan connections, several scholars argued for more than a trade relationship between the two cities, although none suggested direct political control.

4. Only a small number of the 17 have been fully excavated. There may well, in fact, have been even more, currently mapped as unexcavated mounds. Ballcourt 11/11bis was for years so mapped, until its excavation in the 1990s revealed it to be a small roomed structure and a platform mound that, together, border a ballcourt.

5. The term "Tajín Chico," or "Little Tajín," originally meant only Building C, believed to be the sole structure on the then completely unexcavated ridge (see, for example, Galindo y Villa 1912). At the time, "Tajín" referred only to the building long since titled the Pyramid of the Niches. The identity of the visible section as part of a single structure was, of course, based on the limited information available at the time.

6. As reconstructed by the Proyecto Tajín in the 1990s, this appears as a small panel of stepfrets topped by a *contra-talud*. Such intrusions onto staircases are found on a number of the buildings of El Tajín.

7. The building called J in both the text of this article and in Figure 6.1 is, in many publications, called Building I.

8. Rex Koontz (1994:82–83) and others identify the flooded temple as Tajín's Building 10, which is close to the South Ballcourt, based on the roofline crenellation and construction. There is nothing in the reconstructed Building 10, however, to imply it might have been flooded for ritual events. The event depicted is, in any case, outside the ordinary sphere, and certainly outside the palatial.

9. A detailed discussion of the ornamental motifs and styles of Tajín Chico can be found in Sarro 1995:68–75, 84–89.

10. See Sarro 1995:Figure 30 for examples of both profiles.

11. Much of the following discussion of Building A's cosmic symbolism has been presented in greater detail in a previous publication; see Sarro 2000.

12. The orientation of Building A and the surrounding buildings is actually 40 degrees east of north.

13. See Grove 1984:Figure 5.

References Cited

Andrews, George F.
1975 *Maya Cities, Placemaking and Urbanization*. University of Oklahoma Press, Norman.
Brüggemann, Jürgen K.
1988 Introducción a la Temporada 1988 de Proyecto Tajín. In *Informes Proyecto Tajín*, Vol. 1. Archivo Técnico, Instituto Nacional de Antropología e Historia, Mexico City.
1991 Análisis urbano del sitio arqueológico del Tajín. In *Proyecto Tajín*, Vol. 2, edited by Jürgen K. Brüggemann, pp. 81–126. Instituto Nacional de Antropología e Historia, Mexico City.
Coe, Michael
1989 The Hero Twins: Myth and Image. In *The Maya Vase Book*, Vol. 1, edited by Justin Kerr, pp. 161–184. Kerr Associates, New York.
Evans, Susan Toby, and Joanne Pillsbury (editors)
2004 *Palaces of the Ancient New World: Form, Function, and Meaning*. Dumbarton Oaks Research Library and Collection, Washington, DC.
Fash, William
1991 *Scribes, Warriors, and Kings*. Thames and Hudson, London.
Freidel, David, and Charles Suhler
1999 The Path of Life: Toward a Functional Analysis of Ancient Maya Architecture. In *Mesoamerican Architecture as a Cultural Symbol*, edited by Jeff K. Kowalski, pp. 274–297. Oxford University Press, New York.
Galindo y Villa, Jesús
1912 Las Ruinas de Cempoala y del Templo de Tajín. *Anales del Museo Nacional de Mexico* 3 (May).
García Payón, José
1939 Exploraciones en el Totonacapan Septentrional y Meridional (en el Tajín y Misantla), Temporada de 1939. In *Informes CXXVI, Estado de Veracruz, Tajín*, Vol. 2, *1936–1940*, pp. 944–945. Archivo Técnico, Instituto Nacional de Antropología e Historia, Mexico City.
1965 La ciudad arqueológica del Tajín. *Revista Jaroche* (Veracruz) 34–35:21–25.
García Vega, Agustín
1936 Informe de los trabajos de exploración de las ruinas del Tajín. In *Informes CXXVI, Estado de Veracruz, Tajín*, Vol. 2, *1936–1940*, pp. 941–942. Archivo Técnico, Instituto Nacional de Antropología e Historia, Mexico City.
Grove, David
1984 *Chalcatzingo*. Thames and Hudson, London.
Harrison, Peter D.
1999 *The Lords of Tikal*. Thames and Hudson, London.

Inomata, Takeshi, and Stephen Houston
2001 Opening the Maya Court. In *Royal Courts of the Ancient Maya,* Vol. 1, edited by Takeshi Inomata and Stephen Houston, pp. 3–23. Westview Press, Boulder, CO.

Kampen, Michael
1972 *The Sculptures of El Tajín, Veracruz, Mexico.* University of Florida Press, Gainesville.

Koontz, Rex A.
1994 The Iconography of El Tajín, Veracruz, Mexico. Unpublished Ph.D. dissertation, University of Texas at Austin.

Krickeberg, Walter
1966 El juego de pelota mesoamericano y su simbolismo religioso. In *Traducciones mesoamericanistas,* Vol. 1, edited by Paul Kirchoff, pp. 191–313. Sociedad Mexicana de Antropología, Mexico City.

Kubler, George
1973 Iconographic Aspects of Architectural Profiles at Teotihuacan and in Mesoamerica. In *The Iconography of Middle American Sculpture,* texts by Ignacio Bernal et al., pp. 24–39. The Metropolitan Museum of Art, New York.

Ladrón de Guevara, Sara
1991 Pintura e escultura. In *Tajín,* edited by Jürgen Brüggemann, Sara Ladrón de Guevara, and Juan Sánchez Bonilla, pp. 98–131. Citibank, Mexico City.

Lira López, Yamile
1995 El palacio de Edificio de las Columnas en El Tajín. In *El Tajín, Estudios Monográficos,* with Héctor Cuevas Fernández et al., pp. 85–124. Universidad Veracruzana, Xalapa, Mexico.

Miller, Mary Ellen, and Stephen Houston
1987 Stairways and Ballcourt Glyphs: New Perspectives on the Classic Maya Ballgame. *Res* 14:47–66.

Raesfeld, Lydia
1991 Los juegos de pelota de El Tajín. In *The Mesoamerican Ballgame,* edited by Gerard W. van Bussel, Paul L. F. van Dongen, and Ted J. J. Leyanaar, pp. 181–187. Rijksmuseum voor Volkenkunde, Leiden.

Reents-Budet, Dorie
1994 Pictorial Themes of Classic Maya Pottery. In *Painting the Maya Universe,* edited by Dorie Reents-Budet, pp. 234–289. Duke University Press, Durham, NC.
2001 Classic Maya Concepts of the Royal Court. In *Royal Courts of the Ancient Maya,* Vol. 1, edited by Takeshi Inomata and Stephen D. Houston, pp. 195–233. Westview Press, Boulder, CO.

Sánchez Bonilla, Juan
1992 Similitudes entre las pinturas de las higueras y las obras plásticas del Tajín. In *Tajín,* edited by Jürgen Brüggemann, Sara Ladrón de Guevara, and Juan Sánchez Bonilla, pp. 132–159. Citibank, Mexico City.

Sarro, Patricia Joan
1995 The Architectural Meaning of Tajín Chico, the Acropolis of El Tajín,

Mexico. Unpublished Ph.D. dissertation, Columbia University, New York.

2000 The Form of Power: The Architectural Meaning of Building A of El Tajín. In *Landscape and Power in Mesoamerica*, edited by Rex Koontz, Katheryn Reese-Taylor, and Annabeth Hedrick, pp. 230–256, Westview Press, Boulder, CO.

2004 Investigating the Legacy of Teotihuacan in the Architecture of El Tajín. In *La costa del Golfo en tiempos teotihuacanos: Propuestas y perspectivas, Memorias de la Segunda Mesa Redonda de Teotihuacán*, edited by María Ruíz Gallut and Arturo Pascual Soto, pp. 329–347. Instituto Nacional de Antropología e Historia, Mexico City.

Schele, Linda, and David Freidel

1991 The Courts of Creation, Ballcourts, Ballgames, and Portals to the Maya Otherworld. In *The Mesoamerican Ballgame*, edited by Vernon L. Scarborough and David R. Wilcox, pp. 289–315. University of Arizona Press, Tucson.

Webster, David

2001 Spatial Dimensions of Maya Courtly Life: Problems and Issues. In *Royal Courts of the Ancient Maya*, Vol. 1, edited by Takeshi Inomata and Stephen D. Houston, pp. 130–167. Westview Press, Boulder, CO.

Wilkerson, S. Jeffrey K.

1987 *El Tajín, A Guide for Visitors*. Universidad Veracruzana, Xalapa, Mexico.

1990 El Tajín: Great Center of the Northeast. In *Mexico: Splendors of Thirty Centuries*, pp. 155–181. Metropolitan Museum of Art, New York.

PART 3

Correspondences between Material Aspects of Elite Residences and Social Status

CHAPTER 7

The Residence of Power at Paso de la Amada, Mexico

Michael Blake, Richard G. Lesure, Warren D. Hill,
Luis Barba, and John E. Clark

Introduction

Beginning around 1600 B.C., ancient Mesoamericans started their "Neolithic Revolution." They became increasingly reliant on cultivated plants, settled into permanent villages, began manufacturing pottery and ceramic figurines, and traded over vast areas for a wide range of exotic goods, including obsidian and jade. Archaeologists recognize that there was variation in the exact timing and characteristics of this transition from relatively mobile hunting-fishing-gathering cultures to those of settled villagers. However, by 600 B.C. most of Mesoamerica's peoples were organized into complex social and political units that were the forerunners of all later civilizations (Grove and Joyce 1999; Stark 2000). Unlike their egalitarian ancestors, peoples living in later Mesoamerican urban centers, such as Teotihuacán, Monte Albán, and Tikal, were organized into complex states that controlled regional political hierarchies and possessed rigid social stratification (Blanton et al. 1993). The question of how these early complex societies evolved is a central question in archaeological research today (Arnold 1996; Price and Feinman 1995).

Our recent excavations at sites along the Pacific coast of Chiapas, Mexico, and Guatemala have provided much new evidence for the emergence of social and political complexity between the advent of the first villages (around 1600 B.C.) and the widespread appearance of large regional centers (by 600 B.C.; Clark 1994; Clark and Blake 1994; Clark and Pye 2000; Lesure 1997). This fieldwork, carried out between 1985 and 1995, was aimed at determining the basic characteristics of Early Formative–period village sites in the Mazatán zone of the Soconusco region (Figure 7.1). Building on earlier archaeological research in the region (Ceja 1985; Green and Lowe 1967; Lowe 1975), we retested some sites and discovered many new well-preserved village sites along the coastal plain, particularly in the region between the Cantileña swamp system to the northwest and the Coatán River to the southeast.

One of the largest and most intensively studied sites in this region is Paso de la Amada, an ancient village, the core of which covers over 80 hectares

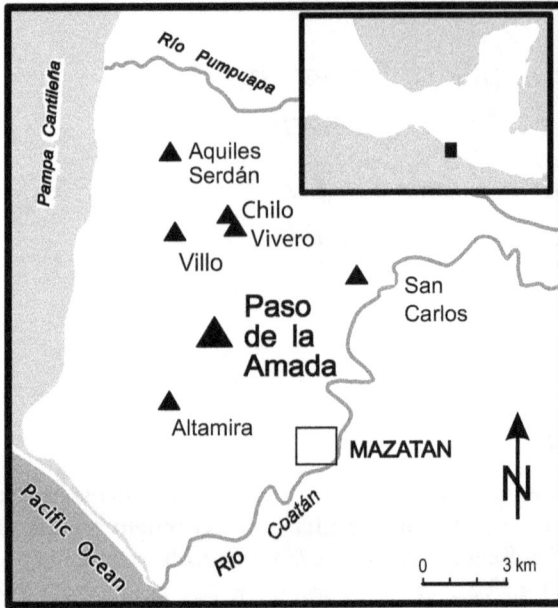

FIGURE 7.1 Soconusco region of southeastern Mexico, showing location of Paso de la Amada

and contains at least 50 visible mounds on the present-day surface. Extensive excavations in 2 of these mounds with well-preserved building sequences (Mounds 6 and 12), as well as tests of many others, have helped us to determine their functions and to demonstrate that hereditary social inequalities had emerged by 1400 B.C.

In this chapter, we present new analyses of the building sequences in Mounds 6 and 12 and argue that the activities that took place there were primarily those of residential groups, or households, much like those found throughout the community. In the analyses that follow, we show that there are significant similarities and differences between the two mounds, leading us to interpret the two structural sequences as belonging to households with different social statuses. Specifically, we analyze construction volumes, structure plans and layout features in and around the floors, distributions of micro-artifacts embedded in the floors, and distributions of chemical traces linked to past activities on the floors. Most of the patterns in these data indicate that Mounds 6 and 12 are more similar than different. On the one hand, the analyses of micro-artifact and chemical distributions in the floors of both mounds lead us to interpret both sets of structures as household residential buildings whose inhabitants were engaged in the same general range of activities. On the other hand, analyses of the architectural features indicate that the residents of Mound 6 invested much more labor in architectural elaboration and display than the householders occupying Mound 12.

Public Buildings and Residences in Transegalitarian Societies

It has long been noted that in egalitarian societies corporate groups may construct large public works, including buildings for meetings, ceremonies, and feasts. Unlike their frequent construction of public buildings, egalitarian societies seldom have residential buildings that are substantially larger or more elaborate than others. It is mostly in chiefly and state-level societies that special residences for the highest-status members of society are permitted. Ethnographic studies in the New World have shown that residential elaboration was the most frequently used means of signaling status in pre-state societies (Feinman and Neitzel 1984). One of the reasons for this could be that the range of activities and the kinds of functions for which chiefs are responsible, some of which may take place in chiefly residences, are much greater than those of non-elite community members. In their sample of 51 societies, Feinman and Neitzel (1984) mention the following as the most common functions of leaders in pre-state societies: ceremonies, feasts, ambassadorial affairs, dispute settlement, hosting visitors, organizing warfare, and organizing subsistence activities, and it is easy to imagine the increased frequency with which some of these might take place in their residences. Many of these same kinds of activities also take place in public meeting places, such as men's houses or plazas, so we do not expect them to be restricted to leaders' residences. In egalitarian societies, there is infrequent correspondence between these activities and individual residences; instead, most public actions take place in public facilities.

In transegalitarian societies—societies moving from egalitarianism to hereditary social inequality over the course of several generations (Blake and Clark 1999:57; Hayden 1995:18)—we might expect to see public buildings and facilities in which such activities and events took place. However, in some cases, we might also see evidence of emerging hereditary leaders, perhaps with elevated social status, investing in elaborate residences. At the same time, they may have coordinated public events, organized the construction of public facilities, and even hosted some public activities in their own residences. There are many additional possibilities for such activities, and they have been discussed in detail elsewhere (Earle 1997:4–14; Hayden 1995:76–77; Marcus and Flannery 1996:76–92; Spencer 1993).

Following the discussion in Lesure and Blake (2002), we restrict our attention in this chapter to a test of the kinds of evidence for transegalitarian processes that one might expect to find within buildings. In particular, we expect the following possibilities for the types of activities represented in (1) public buildings, (2) high-status residences, and (3) low-status residences. In public buildings, there should be evidence of ritual activities that are exclusive to those buildings. The more specialized the public activities in such buildings, the less likely would there be features and artifacts from generalized residential activities. In high-status residences, there should be evidence of at least the same range of household activities as in lower-status residences. Some evidence for public activities hosted by the residents of the household might occur, but decidedly less than would be found in more specialized public buildings. Finally, in lower-status residences, one should find only evidence for the range of domestic activities found in all households, and no evidence of public ritual, although evidence of household-level rituals could be present. Before turning to an analysis of several lines of evidence that can be used to distinguish between the three types of building functions, we will briefly describe the building sequences for Mounds 6 and 12.

Paso de la Amada: Mounds 6 and 12

Paso de la Amada was founded during the Barra phase (ca. 1550–1400 B.C.), grew to its largest size during the Locona phase (1400–1250 B.C.), and continued to be occupied during the Ocós (1250–1100 B.C.) and Cherla phases (1100–1000 B.C.). By the Cuadros (1000–900 B.C.) and Jocotal (900–850 B.C.) phases, population had shifted out of Paso de la Amada, and it was no longer an important settlement in the region (Blake et al. 1995).

Excavations at Paso de la Amada between 1985 and 1995 focused on 10 mounds (of the more than 50 mounds at the site), each of which rises no more than 2 m above the surrounding agricultural fields. Here we discuss the evidence from Mounds 6 and 12, and we occasionally refer to the ballcourt at Mound 7 (Figure 7.2). Mound 6 is one of the largest mounds at the site and has been intensively excavated during four field seasons. The main goals of these excavations were to expose complete floors for each of the construction episodes represented in the mound and recover information about the functions of the buildings. A series of at least nine structures and associated deposits was uncovered, dating to the Locona and Ocós phases. Mound 12, a smaller mound, was excavated in 1993 as part of the project's goal of fully exposing smaller structures that might be compared with the larger ones at Mound 6. The latest and largest platform construction in this mound dated to the Cherla phase, and it capped a series of what are interpreted to have been residential floors dating to the Locona and Ocós phases. Mound 7, by far the largest mound at the site, was excavated in 1995. Excavations revealed that it was a ballcourt rather than a residence; except for earthen construction fill, the deposits were unlike any of those recovered in the other mounds at the site (Hill 1999; Hill et al. 1998). Its construction dates to the early part of the Locona phase, and it was used until the end of the Ocós phase.

We examine five classes of information in order to identify the range of functions for each of the structures in Mounds 6 and 12: (1) mound platform volumes; (2) building structures, shapes, alignments, and superpositioning; (3) features such as floors, hearths, pits, and burials; (4) distributions of microartifacts on the floors, including obsidian, ceramics, charcoal, and bone; and (5) chemical traces on structure floors, including pH levels, phosphates, fatty acids, and albumen.

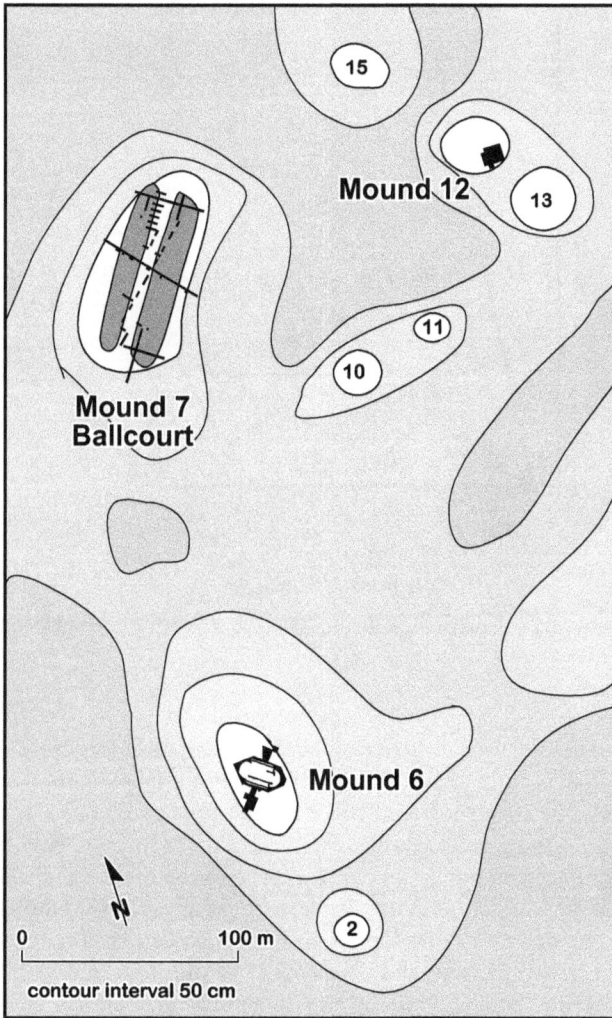

FIGURE 7.2 Map of Paso de la Amada, showing locations of eight major mounds in the site center and excavations referred to in this chapter

Platforms

Mound 6 had been repeatedly plowed since the 1950s, lowering it by one meter and spreading the resulting fill around its base. Even so, it preserves a remarkable sequence of continuous construction, refurbishment, and expansion from the Early Locona phase through the Ocós phase, spanning some 200 to 250 years. We found well-preserved structural remains for the lowermost five Locona-phase structures and platform construction data for

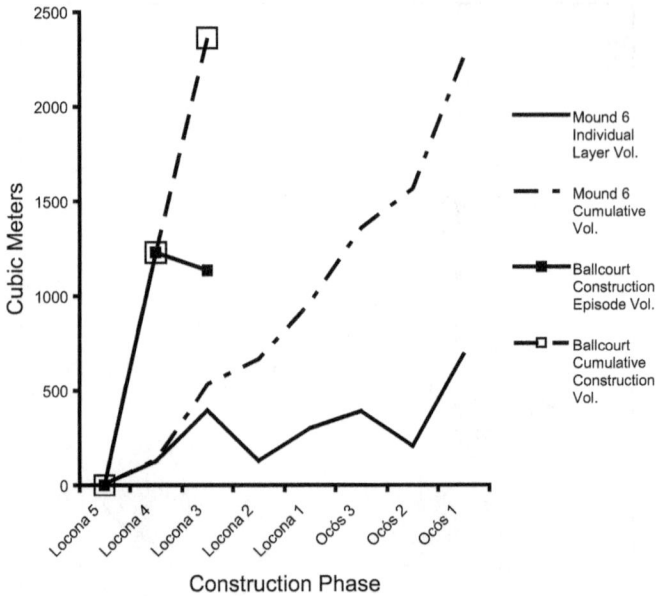

FIGURE 7.3 Mound 6 construction volumes compared with those of Mound 7, the ballcourt

the four uppermost structures (the last Locona-phase structure and three Ocós-phase structures above it). The structures are labeled, from top to bottom, Ocós Structures 1 to 3 and Locona Structures 1 to 6.

A detailed stratigraphic analysis was carried out in 1999, collating information from approximately 25 profiles through the mound and allowing an estimate of the horizontal extent and thickness of each of the superimposed platforms. In almost all cases, prior to the construction of a new building, a layer of earthen fill was laid down over the old floor and features, completely covering them and raising and extending the platform on which the new building would be built.

Figure 7.3 graphs the sequence of estimated construction volumes for Mound 6 (also presented in Table 7.1), showing both the individual construction layer volumes and the cumulative volumes. The additions to Mound 6 after Structure 5 varied between approximately 130 m³ and 688 m³, yielding a cumulative total of 2,256 m³.

At Mound 7, the ballcourt, there was one initial construction of two parallel mounds that Warren Hill (1999:97–98) estimates were 1,229 m³, three times the size of many of the largest expansions of Mound 6 (and almost twice the volume of the last and biggest expansion). Later, approximately contemporary with Locona Structure 3, the ballcourt mounds were rebuilt and expanded with an additional 1,135 m³ of fill, giving them a total of ap-

TABLE 7.1. Volume estimates for structure platforms in Mound 6

Platform	Base Length m	Length Radius m	Base Width m	Width Radius m	Mound Height m	Layer Thickness m	Volume Estimate[a]	
							Layer Volume m³	Cumulative Volume m³
Ocós Str. 1	36.00	18.00	28.50	14.25	4.20[d]	0.60	688.48	2256.29
Ocós Str. 2[b]	34.00	17.00	22.30	11.15	3.60[d]	0.35	208.42[b]	1567.81
Ocós Str. 3	33.50	16.75	25.00	12.50	3.10[d]	0.35	391.78	1359.39
Locona Str. 1	32.00	16.00	21.00	10.50	2.75	0.20	301.41	967.61
Locona Str. 2	29.70	14.85	16.80	8.40	2.55	0.30	131.81	666.20
Locona Str. 3	28.00	14.00	16.20	8.10	2.25	1.45	397.74	534.38
Locona Str. 4	21.70	10.85	10.10	5.05	0.80	0.75	129.10[c]	136.64
Locona Str. 5	19.20	9.60	10.00	5.00	0.05	0.05	7.54[c]	7.54

[a]Unless noted, for the calculation of Ellipsoid Volume Estimate, the mound is considered to be ½ of an ellipsoid, that is, $\pi = 0.5$ (⁴⁄₃π × length radius × width radius × mound height). Each layer's volume estimate is calculated by subtracting the cumulative total from the previous cumulative total.

[b]The value for Ocós Structure 2 uses an Ellipse Area Estimate (π × ½ length × ½ width × layer thickness) because it is not completely contained within the Structure 1 mound above it.

[c]Volume is calculated using Ellipse Area Estimate because walls are vertical, not ellipsoid.

[d]Mound height and layer thickness are estimates only, based on slope of stratigraphic layers in mound skirt.

proximately 2,364 m^3. Since Mound 7 has been plowed during the past 40 years, the mounds were at one time even higher and would have had an even greater total volume than we have estimated. As Figure 7.3 illustrates, even at our minimal estimate of 2,364 m^3, the ballcourt would have had a greater volume than the cumulative volume of Mound 6. In other words, what took about 200 years to accomplish in Mound 6 — in at least nine separate construction episodes — was done in two short episodes for the public ballcourt.

Mound 12 presents a different story. The area under and around the mound was the site of residential occupation contemporary with the occupation of Mound 6 and the ballcourt. We identified a series of poorly preserved floors, one of which (Floor 2) contained a dense concentration of postholes marking the location of a small building. Neither it nor subsequent floors in the mound was associated with significant platform construction. It was not until the Cherla phase that a large platform was built on this spot, and its relationship to the Locona and Ocós structures is not at all clear (Lesure 1997). Cherla-phase builders erected a huge platform containing some 380 m^3 of earthen fill, almost twice as much as any single layer of fill in Mound 6. However, if this Cherla platform was built in two stages, then it would represent approximately the same maximum amount of platform construction labor at any one time as in Mound 6. This suggests that the idea of large-scale mound building continued at the site after Mound 6 was abandoned at the end of the Ocós phase.

Structures

The successive buildings composing Mound 6 provide a remarkable opportunity to study architectural continuity and change. Figure 7.4 shows the structure profiles and plans for each of the Locona-phase buildings in Mound 6 (unfortunately, the last Locona-phase floor and all the Ocós-phase floors were too badly destroyed by plowing to reconstruct and so are not included here). The structures were approximately the same size, and they all maintained the same orientation: the short axis of each building aligns closely with the peak of the Tacaná volcano, 60 km to the east, and nearly parallels the long axis of the ballcourt.

Mound 12 also contained a long series of superimposed structures, but because each was not covered with a thick layer of construction fill, their remains were fragmentary. Each was penetrated by later postholes and pit features. Three of the superimposed floors are well enough preserved to show alignments of postholes, ditch features, and floor surfaces. These remnants, though in no case complete, do provide enough information to reconstruct the alignment of the structures. They show that the long axis of the superimposed buildings appears to be perpendicular to the long axis of Mound 6 and parallel to the long axis of the ballcourt. The ends of the structures are missing, but the buildings would have been a minimum of 10 m long.

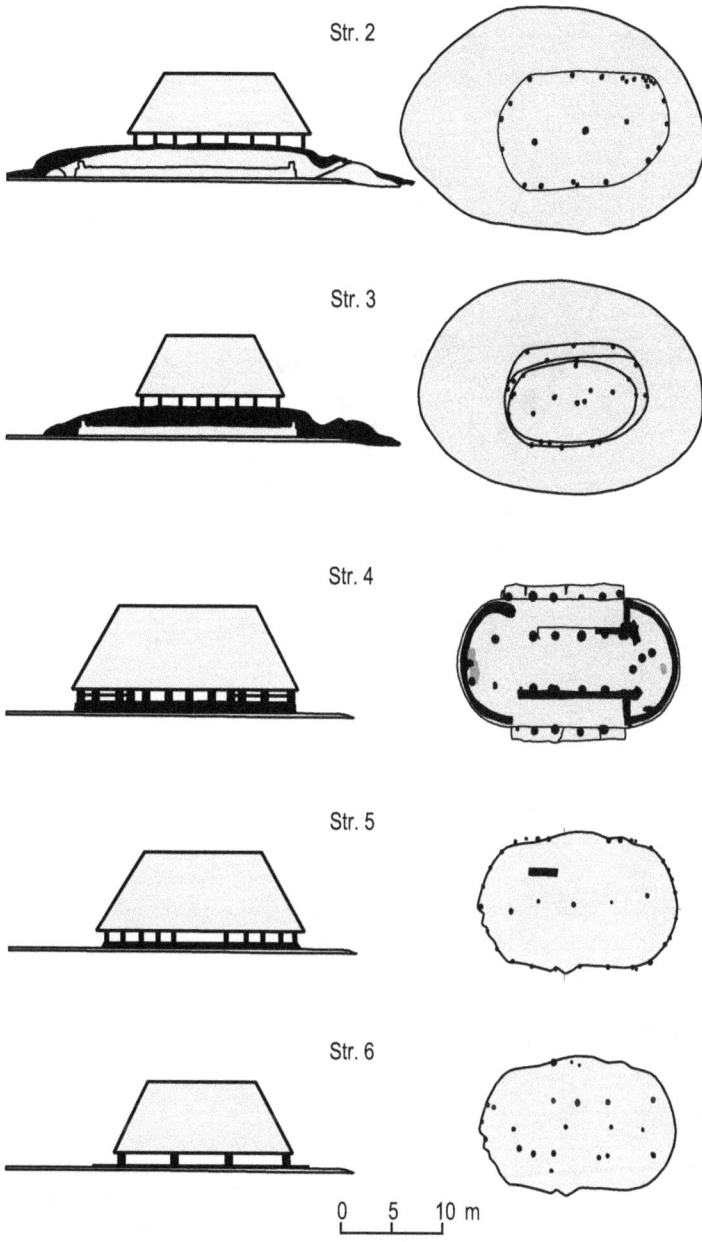

FIGURE 7.4 Plans and profiles of Locona-phase structures in Mound 6. Reconstructed buildings are shown atop mound profiles on left.

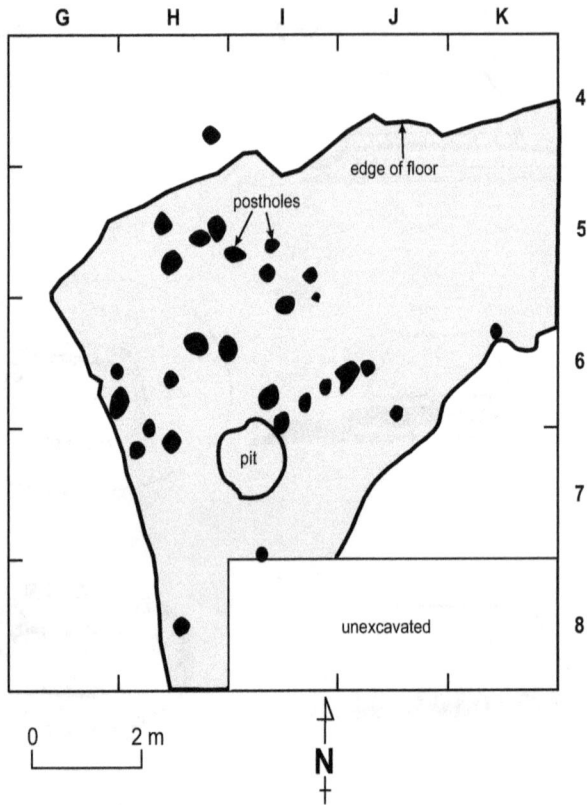

FIGURE 7.5 Plan of Floor 2 in Mound 12

Floor 2, the lowermost of these floors, is the best preserved and is the only one we can compare with Mound 6 (Figure 7.5). We are not certain if Floor 2 was inside or outside the main structure. The many postholes in it suggest that there may have been a small outbuilding on the spot—a similar pattern was found outside the main structures at Mound 6.

Features

The Locona–Ocós phase sequences in Mound 6 and 12 have several features in common, whereas others are unique to each (Table 7.2). At Mound 6, we discovered an Ocós-phase burial pit containing a female and an infant, similar to a burial in Mound 12 containing two adult individuals. In addition, Mounds 6 and 12 each had an infant burial and a dog burial.

Both mounds also have large midden areas and trash-filled pits. Several surfaces in the zone surrounding Mound 6 had dense scatters of artifacts, in some cases filling pits that may have been dug for other purposes. One large

TABLE 7.2. Shared and unique features in Mounds 6 and 12

Shared Features	Unique Features
human burials	interior hearths (M. 6)
dog burial	very large pits (M. 12)
small trash-filled pits	large ceramic-vessel fragments in provisional discard (M. 12)
refuse accumulation on surfaces	earth oven (M. 6)

oven pit was filled with cooking debris and a wide range of other artifacts and materials (Blake 1991). Both the back and front sides of the mound had other refuse pits that contained high densities of many types of artifacts.

Some of the structures in Mound 6 had well-made clay floors (especially Str. 5); however, most did not. Most were built directly on the platform fill that had been raised above the previous floor. Structures 4, 5, and 6 had clearly preserved burned areas on their floors, most of which we interpret to have been hearths. There were two main posthole patterns in the Mound 6 structures. Structures 6 and 4 had two parallel lines of posts running down the center of their floors. Structures 5, 3, and 2 had a single line of central posts and smaller posts surrounding the periphery of the floor, outlining each structure's interior.

The pattern for Floor 2 in Mound 12 is not so clear. Its posthole patterns suggest an apsidal shape, but there is no clear pattern delineating a formal floor. Instead, the floor is marked by hardened sand. The area outside the floor has few postholes or other features, but it does contain denser trash deposits. There were no hearths recorded on Floor 2.

Micro-artifact Distributions

In both Mounds 6 and 12, we collected micro-artifact samples to examine the range of activities and their locations on the structure floors. The distributions of artifacts on the floors of structures are often taken to be reliable indicators of the types and locations of activities that took place within them. However, large broken artifacts on floors are usually the result of post-abandonment activity and not a direct indication of the activities and events that took place inside a building during its life. A much more reliable indicator of the activities that took place on a floor, particularly earthen floors, is the presence and distribution of micro-artifacts—those below the size range that would normally be swept up and carried off during daily or regular floor cleaning. Micro-artifacts consist of material usually between 0.5 and 1.0 mm in size; they were collected by water screening using a 0.5 mm mesh screen. We think that these materials were trampled into the floor and represent primary activity areas and discard locations.

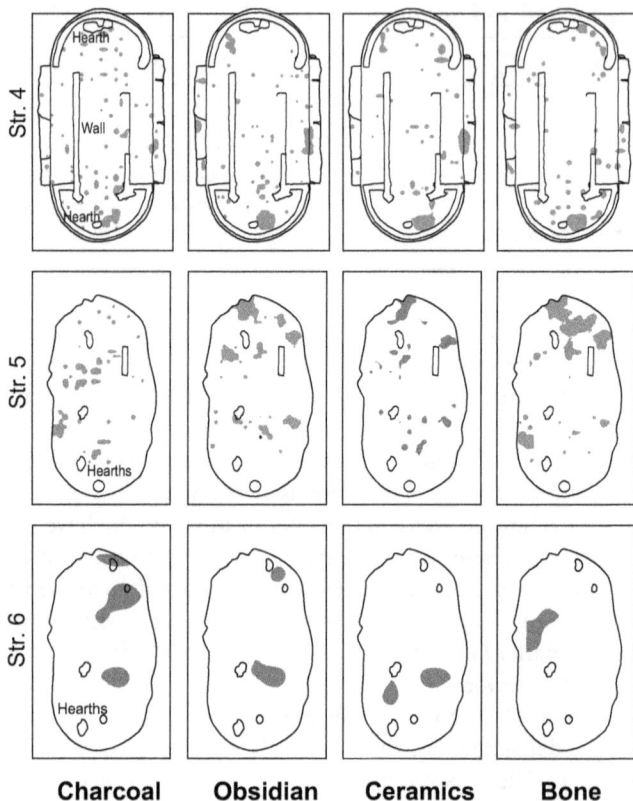

FIGURE 7.6 Micro-artifact distributions on the floors of Structures 4, 5, and 6 in Mound 6. Only concentrations of one standard deviation or more above the mean are plotted as dark gray areas. Unshaded areas represent hearths, pits, or walls.

Obsidian microflakes resulted both from manufacturing obsidian tools and from using them. Ceramic microfragments were produced by pot use and breakage in situ. Bone microfragments incorporated into the floor should represent locations of food consumption and discard, and charcoal distributions probably represent hearth sweeping and the remnants of cooking locations (especially when associated with burned floor patches).

For Mound 6, we have micro-artifact samples from Structures 6, 5, and 4, and for Mound 12, we have samples from Floor 2. The samples were collected by first laying out a 50 × 50 cm grid square over each floor. We then scraped off a 1.0 cm thick layer of floor material over the entire surface of each 50 × 50 cm grid square, filling a one-liter container. The soil was then passed through a 0.5 mm mesh screen. Items were then sorted into categories, including the following: charcoal, obsidian, ceramics, bone, mica, chert, and shell. There were few of the last three types of microtraces on each floor, so the present analysis is confined to charcoal, obsidian, ceramics, and bone. Each class of material was then plotted on a map of the floor surface. Figure 7.6 shows the distributions for Structures 4, 5, and 6 in Mound 6, and Figure 7.7 presents the distributions for Floor 2 in Mound 12. The micro-artifact distribution maps, for each category of material, plot the locations of grid squares containing more than one standard deviation above the mean value for all the squares on the floor. This allows us to see only unusually high concentrations of micro-artifacts—more than might be expected from a background presence in the earth used for construction materials. The patterns suggest that all the structures hosted similar activities, leading to similar depositional patterns. We note also that all the floors show locations where there were relatively few items, indicating areas of low micro-artifact-producing activity. If the three structures examined in Mound 6 were used for specialized activities, such as public ceremonies or specialized craft manufacture, these activities left no traces distinguishable from those observed in Mound 12.

One thing is clear from the distribution patterns on each of the four floors:

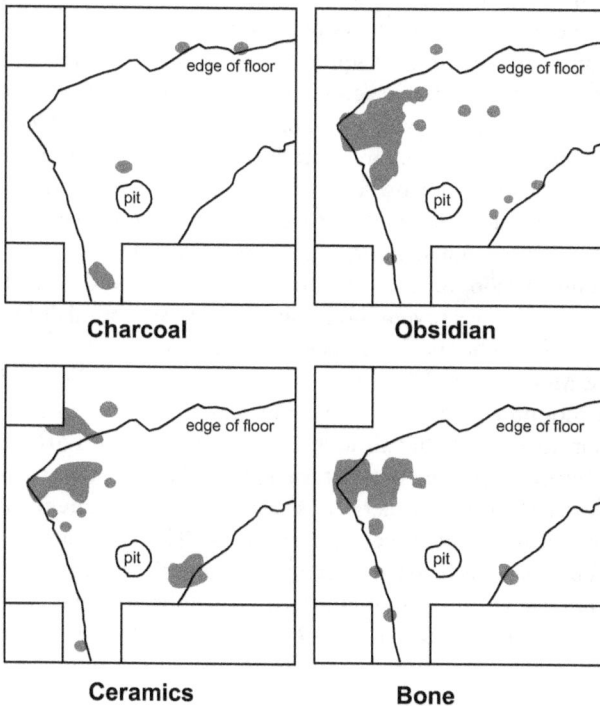

FIGURE 7.7 Micro-artifact distributions on Floor 2, Mound 12. Only concentrations of one standard deviation or more above the mean are plotted as dark gray areas.

most artifact types occur in significant clusters with a good deal of spatial overlap with other types of artifacts. An additional analysis that is being planned is the statistical association of the different classes of micro-artifacts to determine whether there are any differences or similarities from structure to structure. The current analysis suggests that activities resulting in con-centrations of obsidian microflakes, ceramic fragments, charcoal fragments, and bone (usually burned) took place within these structures and most often near the edge of the walls. This probably indicates that the central floor areas were more frequently swept clean and that refuse accumulated around the peripheries and in areas less frequented by heavy traffic. In Structure 4, we clearly see the densest patterns of accumulation around the two hearths, one at each end of the building.

Chemical Distributions

Four types of chemical residues were detected on the structure floors, using methods described previously (Barba and Ortiz 1992; Manzanilla and Barba 1990). They include soil pH, phosphates, fatty acids, and albumen, each re-lating to different organic processes and activities. Chemical constituents of the Mound 6 and Mound 12 floors were determined by Luis Barba and his as-sociates at the National University of Mexico, using soil samples collected from the same 50 × 50 cm grid squares used in the micro-artifact analysis. PH level measures the relative acidity/base characteristics of the soil; phos-phates are left behind by a wide range of organic substances that could have been left in the floor; fatty acids are produced mainly from animal products; and albumen is a substance present in blood and egg white and also in some plants. So far, Paso de la Amada represents the earliest recovery of preserved chemical residues on house floors studied in Mesoamerica.

Initial comparison of the structures within Mound 6 and between Mounds 6 and 12 shows several broad similarities. We found different distri-butions of the four chemical residues on each floor. Figure 7.8 shows these patterns for Mound 6, and Figure 7.9 shows the same for Floor 2 in Mound 12. Within Mound 6, the patterns are not repeated in the same areas from floor to floor, suggesting that although the same sets of activities took place in each structure, they were not patterned in predictable ways through time. In other words, the different activities resulting in these chemical distribu-tions shifted across floors in each building phase. This variation also suggests that the accumulations on each floor are not natural, but result from human activities. Finally, we found that Floor 2 in Mound 12 has levels of these resi-dues that are similar to those levels observed on the Mound 6 floors.

Interpretations

The key difference between the two mounds appears to be architectural. Mound 6 was constructed by periodic incremental expansion of the plat-

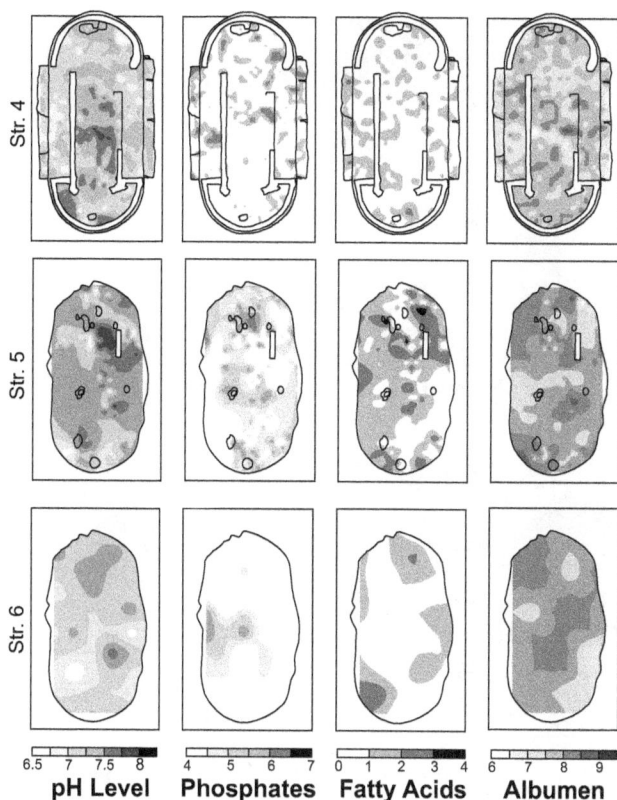

FIGURE 7.8 Chemical distributions on the floors of Structures 4, 5, and 6 in Mound 6

form, increasing both its height and its areal extent. This led to a continuous increase in the size of the platform on which each successive building was perched. However, the associated structures did not always increase in size. Most structures remained about the same size: 18–22 m long and 9–10 m wide. Unexpectedly, the smallest structure (Locona Str. 3) was built on the volumetrically largest platform expansion.

The floor plans of the preserved structures in Mound 6 show a striking consistency in layout and shape, with precise superpositioning through the sequence. It is unfortunate that we could not recover a clear floor plan for the earliest structure, Structure 6, or for the last Locona structure and the later Ocós-phase structures that were removed by plowing.

Unlike the floors of Mound 6, the structures preserved under Mound 12 were not individually covered by layers of platform fill. Because of this, the six or so rebuildings, as suggested by the floor remnants in Mound 12, actually contributed to the disturbance and destruction of earlier floors. This left one of the earliest floors, Floor 2, with a bewildering posthole pattern and several later Ocós-phase pits intruding into the floor. Interestingly, this re-

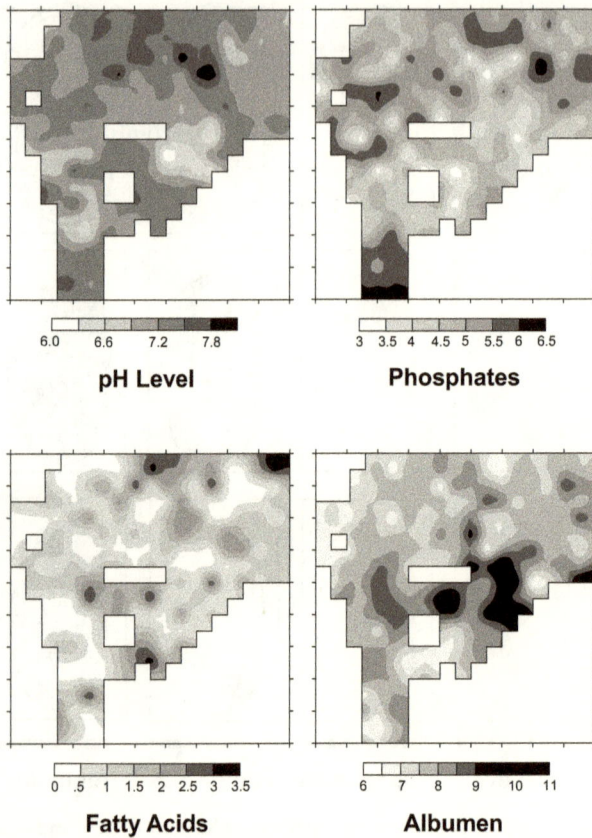

FIGURE 7.9 Chemical distributions on Floor 2, Mound 12

building is similar to what happened to Structure 6 in Mound 6 and also the later Structure 3.

These construction differences between Mound 6 and Mound 12 suggest two interpretations: (1) the social groups occupying and building each set of structures had different access to labor resources, and (2) those occupying Mound 6 had the social status to be able to express this difference by means of a visible and relatively permanent architectural display. This status distinction would have been reinforced by the similarity between Mound 6 and Mound 7, the ballcourt. The grandeur of Mound 6 was only surpassed by the ballcourt—the one public building that dominated the settlement. The ballcourt mounds would have been highly visible within the community and would have required more than twice the labor of the Mound 6 constructions. For the residents of Mound 6, it may have been both possible and desirable to display a greater social status than the other households in the community while at the same time refraining from superceding the entire community's display of status as expressed in the ballcourt.

The household-feature data, micro-artifact distributions, and chemical patterns all suggest different interpretations than do the architecture data. The general similarities from floor to floor in the Mound 6 sequence and between Mound 6 and Mound 12 suggest that there were no significant differences in the activities that left micro-artifactual or chemical traces. On the one hand, this pattern could mean that buildings of different social function and inhabited by different kinds of social groups could have been used for roughly the same kinds of general activities. Thus, based on the architectural evidence alone, the Mound 6 structures could have been public buildings such as men's houses, as suggested by Joyce Marcus and Kent Flannery (1996). In this scenario, the activities that took place in these public buildings were essentially the same as those that took place in smaller, simpler residential buildings such as Mound 12. On the other hand, the indistinguishable range of activities suggested by the artifacts, features, and chemical traces could mean that the groups occupying Mounds 6 and 12 were homologous, both carrying out the same range of domestic activities. In this scenario, the architectural differences between the two sets of structures would have signaled differences in social status, wealth, and/or prestige between these two households.

The second of these alternatives is, to us, the most parsimonious and the one that best fits most of the evidence. It also accords well with previously noted ethnographic evidence that residential elaboration is one of the most common trappings of the higher status of community leaders in pre-state societies in the Americas (Feinman and Neitzel 1984).

Conclusions

Using construction data spanning several generations of continuous occupation in Mound 6, one of the largest structures at Paso de la Amada, which is the largest center in the Mazatán region, we can see clear evidence of rebuilding and expansion of a high-status residence. The buildings in Mound 6 were, collectively, potent and visible symbols of household status at the community level. We suggest that, compared with residents of other less-prominent households at the site, the occupants of Mound 6 possessed the social clout and the political power to express and maintain their high status over several generations.

The present evidence supports the interpretation that the occupants of the Mound 6 buildings were members of a high-ranking household, perhaps the highest-status household in the community. The members of the household represented by the remains in Mound 12 were of a somewhat lower status. Both households carried out the same range of activities in their houses, but the residents of Mound 6 had more elaborate architecture. Paradoxically, the analyses presented here, combined with earlier work, suggest that although architectural differences were significant, there were few notable differences in wealth-related artifacts or trade items between the households at the site in the Locona and Ocós phases (Clark 1994; Lesure 1995; Lesure and Blake 2002). This parallels the finding presented here that the basic patterns of activities, features, and chemical traces were also similar among the houses examined.

We conclude that the occupants of Mound 6, over many generations, were most likely among the highest-ranking households in their community and in the larger region. Their increasingly prominent household architectural display, and the large size of the household, was most likely the main way that their status was exhibited in the community. In most other respects, though, they shared the material culture and engaged in the same household activities of the larger community. This suggests that status differences as stated in residential architecture can be an enduring expression of social power and prestige and were probably one of the first symbols of "eliteness" to be employed by emerging leaders in transegalitarian societies. In this sense, the sequence of residential structures in Mound 6 represents the material symbol of social power carried across several generations.

References Cited

Arnold, Jeanne E. (editor)
1996 Emergent Complexity: The Evolution of Intermediate Societies. International Monographs in Prehistory 9. Ann Arbor, MI.

Barba, Luis, and Agustín Ortiz
1992 Análisis químico de pisos de ocupación: Un caso etnográfico en Tlaxcala, México. Latin American Antiquity 3(1):63–82.

Blake, Michael
1991 An Emerging Early Formative Chiefdom at Paso de la Amada, Chiapas, Mexico. In The Formation of Complex Society in Southeastern Mesoamerica, edited by William R. Fowler, Jr., pp. 26–43. CRC Press, Boca Raton, FL.

Blake, Michael, and John E. Clark
1999 The Emergence of Hereditary Inequality: The Case of Pacific Coastal Chiapas, Mexico. In Pacific Latin America in Prehistory: The Evolution of Archaic and Formative Cultures, edited by Michael Blake, pp. 55–73. Washington State University Press, Pullman.

Blake, Michael, John E. Clark, Barbara Voorhies, George Michaels, Michael Love, Mary E. Pye, Arthur A. Demarest, and Barbara Arroyo
1995 A Revised Chronology for the Archaic and Formative Periods along the Pacific Coast of Southeastern Mesoamerica. Ancient Mesoamerica 6:161–183.

Blanton, Richard E., Stephen A. Kowalewski, Gary M. Feinman, and Laura M. Finsten
1993 Ancient Mesoamerica: A Comparison of Change in Three Regions. 2nd ed. Cambridge University Press, Cambridge.

Ceja Tenorio, Jorge F.
1985 Paso de la Amada: An Early Preclassic Site in the Soconusco,

Chiapas, Mexico. Papers of the New World Archaeological Foundation 49. New World Archaeological Foundation, Provo, Utah.

Clark, John E.
1994 The Development of Early Formative Rank Societies in the Soconusco, Chiapas, Mexico. Unpublished Ph.D. dissertation, Department of Anthropology, University of Michigan, Ann Arbor.

Clark, John E., and Michael Blake
1994 The Power of Prestige: Competitive Generosity and the Emergence of Rank Societies in Lowland Mesoamerica. In *Factional Competition and Political Development in the New World,* edited by Elizabeth M. Brumfiel and John W. Fox, pp. 17–30. Cambridge University Press, Cambridge.

Clark, John E., and Mary E. Pye
2000 The Pacific Coast and the Olmec Question. In *Olmec Art and Archaeology in Mesoamerica,* edited by John E. Clark and Mary E. Pye, pp. 217–251. Studies in the History of Art, Vol. 58, Center for Advanced Study in the Visual Arts, Symposium Papers 35. National Gallery of Art, Washington, DC, and Yale University Press, New Haven.

Earle, Timothy
1997 *How Chiefs Come to Power: The Political Economy in Prehistory.* Stanford University Press, Stanford.

Feinman, Gary, and Jill Neitzel
1984 Too Many Types: An Overview of Sedentary Prestate Societies in the Americas. In *Advances in Archaeological Method and Theory,* Vol. 7, edited by Michael B. Schiffer, pp. 39–102. Academic Press, New York.

Green, Dee, and Gareth W. Lowe
1967 *Altamira and Padre Piedra, Early Preclassic Sites in Chiapas, Mexico.* Papers of the New World Archaeological Foundation 20. New World Archaeological Foundation, Provo, Utah.

Grove, David C., and Rosemary A. Joyce (editors)
1999 *Social Patterns in Pre-Classic Mesoamerica: A Symposium at Dumbarton Oaks.* Dumbarton Oaks Research Library and Collection, Washington, DC.

Hayden, Brian
1995 Pathways to Power: Principles for Creating Socioeconomic Inequalities. In *Foundations of Social Inequality,* edited by T. Douglas Price and Gary M. Feinman, pp. 15–86. Plenum, New York.

Hill, Warren D.
1999 Ballcourts, Competitive Games, and the Emergence of Complex Society. Unpublished Ph.D. dissertation, Department of Anthropology and Sociology, University of British Columbia, Vancouver.

Hill, Warren D., Michael Blake, and John E. Clark
1998 Ball Court Design Dates Back 3,400 Years. *Nature* 392:878–879.

Lesure, Richard G.
1995 Paso de la Amada: Sociopolitical Dynamics in an Early Formative Community. Unpublished Ph.D. dissertation, Department of Anthropology, University of Michigan, Ann Arbor.

1997 Early Formative Platforms at Paso de la Amada, Chiapas, Mexico. *Latin American Antiquity* 8:217–235.

Lesure, Richard G., and Michael Blake
2002 Interpretive Challenges in the Study of Early Complexity: Economy, Ritual, and Architecture at Paso de la Amada, Mexico. In *Journal of Anthropological Archaeology* 21(1):1–24.

Lowe, Gareth W.
1975 *The Early Preclassic Barra Phase of Altamira, Chiapas.* Papers of the New World Archaeological Foundation 38. New World Archaeological Foundation, Provo, Utah.

Manzanilla, Linda, and Luis Barba
1990 The Study of Activities in Classic Households: Two Case Studies from Coba and Teotihuacan. *Ancient Mesoamerica* 1:41–49.

Marcus, Joyce, and Kent V. Flannery
1996 *Zapotec Civilization.* Thames and Hudson, New York.

Price, T. Douglas, and Gary M. Feinman (editors)
1995 *Foundations of Social Inequality.* Plenum, New York.

Spencer, Charles S.
1993 Human Agency, Biased Transmission, and the Cultural Evolution of Chiefly Authority. *Journal of Anthropological Archaeology* 12(1):41–74.

Stark, Barbara L.
2000 Framing the Gulf Olmecs. In *Olmec Art and Archaeology in Mesoamerica,* edited by John E. Clark and Mary E. Pye, pp. 31–53. Studies in the History of Art 58. National Gallery of Art, Washington, DC, and Yale University Press, New Haven.

CHAPTER 8

When Is a House a Palace?

ELITE RESIDENCES IN THE VALLEY OF OAXACA

Sarah B. Barber and Arthur A. Joyce

Introduction

In this chapter we use elite residential architecture in the Valley of Oaxaca to trace shifting conceptualizations of social and political power through time. We frame our discussion by making a heuristic distinction between elite residences and palaces. Although this latter term is often used simply to describe an elite residence, we envision palaces here as multipurpose structures that combine both domestic and public functions. Unlike a residence, a palace provides a physical location for the "pomp and circumstance" surrounding an important individual or individuals (as opposed to deities, deceased persons, or institutions), and may also include civic spaces such as council rooms, storage facilities, and ritual areas (Flannery 1998; Soles 1991; Webster 1998). By implication, the explicit fusion of public and private roles in a palace ties individuals or kin groups to a set of social and governmental activities in a more comprehensive way than does a private residence located in physical proximity to public buildings. Power and social roles are materialized differently in each case, implying different conceptions of power. To track changes in the notion of power in the Valley of Oaxaca, we describe elite residences from the Early Formative (1800–850 B.C.) to the Postclassic (A.D. 800–1521) periods (Table 8.1). We argue that through time a growing number of elites in the Valley of Oaxaca began to build palaces that provided a physical location for the celebration of individual and familial power. We see in these changes a growing expression of power as individualized, exclusive, and materially explicit.

In this chapter, we take a diachronic approach, providing a résumé of the currently available data on pre-Columbian elite residences from the Valley of Oaxaca. A variety of research (Flannery, ed. 1976; Whalen 1981; Winter 1974) has provided an excellent source of information on Formative-period elite and non-elite domiciles. There are also a few well-documented Terminal Classic and Postclassic residences (Bernal and Gamio 1974; Lind 2001; Lind and Urcid 1983; Winter et al. 1997). We have attempted to collate what

TABLE 8.1. Valley of Oaxaca Regional Chronology

Time Period	Regional Phase	Dates
Late Postclassic	Monte Albán V	A.D. 1250–1521
Early Postclassic	Liobaa	A.D. 800–1250
Late Classic	Monte Albán IIIb–IV	A.D. 500–800
Early Classic	Monte Albán IIIa	A.D. 200–500
Terminal Formative	Monte Albán II	100 B.C.–A.D. 200
Late Formative	Monte Albán Ic	300–100 B.C.
	Monte Albán Ia	500–300 B.C.
Middle Formative	Rosario	700–500 B.C.
	Guadalupe	850–700 B.C.
Early Formative	San José	1150–850 B.C.
	Tierras Largas	1400–1150 B.C.
	Espiridión	1800–1400 B.C.
Archaic	NA	8000–1800 B.C.

data are available for all these periods in order to trace changes in the spatial organization, architectural elaboration, and locale of elite residences. We have focused on these aspects of elite residences because this information is available for all time periods. Indeed, despite a lack of detail in much of the published data, we argue that the available evidence demonstrates a clear shift in the way elite residences were shaped and tied into their surroundings. By providing an increased connection between public and private space, elite residences in the Valley of Oaxaca developed from high-status houses into palaces.

The Social Construction of Residential Architecture

We follow a variety of other social scientists in looking at architecture to describe and explain social phenomena (Bachelard 1969; Foucault 1995; Rapoport 1969, 1982). Domestic architecture, in particular, has enjoyed extensive study and is well theorized (Blanton 1994; Kent 1990; Santley and Hirth 1993; Wilk and Ashmore 1988; Wilson 1988). Elite residences, like all built forms, are culturally negotiated and socially meaningful entities that serve to communicate ideas to residents and outside viewers (Blanton 1994; Rapoport 1969, 1982). In Mesoamerica, for instance, the presence of elite residences at early sites has provided researchers with a means of demonstrating the existence of status distinctions (Cliff 1988; Flannery, ed. 1976; Flannery and Marcus, eds. 1983). Variation in the size, elaboration, and labor requirements of elite residences has led other archaeologists to distinguish social classes based on architectural data (Abrams 1994; Flannery 1983a; Willey and Leventhal 1979; Winter 1974). Inscriptions and architectural sculpture on residences at sites like Copán, Honduras, have enabled researchers there to identify specific individuals and their self-proclaimed social status in the archaeological record, as well as to describe the organization of ancient hierarchies (Webster 1989; Webster et al. 1998). Like these researchers and many others, we look to elite residential architecture as a means of studying social phenomena that extend far beyond the front door of the domicile itself.

We rely on three characteristics of residential architecture to demonstrate conceptions of power in the Valley of Oaxaca: spatial organization, architectural elaboration, and locale. Spatial organization, or residential layout, enables architecture to shape space in ways that reflect and often reinforce social action (Blanton 1994; Bourdieu 1977; Rapoport 1969). The residence, as the site of socially defined interactions and relations, shapes where and how such action occurs. The residence provides an organizational framework for a variety of social activities, and its layout will inhibit or encourage some activities over others. Furthermore, as a common metaphor for concepts like the body, the community, or the universe (Gillespie 2000b; Knapp 1999; Oliver 1987; Smith and David 1995; Wilson 1988), the residence serves to reaffirm cultural norms as residents' use of domestic spaces situates them within the universe as they understand it (Bourdieu 1977:89–90). At the same time, spatial organization is nondeterministic. The residence does not simply impose behaviors and social notions on inhabitants; there is instead a creative interaction between people and their built environment (Gutman 1976; Rapoport 1976). As Robert Gutman (1976:45) observed,

> the organization of space in . . . a room can influence our capacity to concentrate on the task of exchanging information, thoughts, and understandings, and it can lead us towards these ends, but it cannot dictate that we will reach them.

The existence of interaction between residences and residents enables people to continually reformulate their surroundings to meet emerging social and environmental situations.

Through architectural elaboration, residences transmit messages regarding social identity (Blanton 1994:10). Architectural elaboration serves its purpose for all viewers: it informs nonresidents of the social positions of those who inhabit a structure while reaffirming that position for residents themselves. As Jeff Kowalski (1999:8) observes, "Architecture provided one of the most monumental, visually impressive, and semiotically potent expressions of the authority and power of Mesoamerican elites." He, like Blanton and many others, emphasizes the power of architecture to convey messages relating to status, power, social positioning, wealth, and access to particular knowledge or resources. Residential architecture, in particular, is vital to any expression of these social categories because a residence is definitively related to particular individuals, groups, or genealogies—"house forms and their resident social groups are mutually constituting" (Birdwell-Pheasant and Lawrence-Zúñiga 1999:4). Domestic architectural elaboration thus provided ancient elites with a means of expressing their social condition to others while at the same time reiterating it to themselves.

Locale is the final element of elite residences that we deem pertinent to a discussion of architecture and notions of power. Drawing on archaeological landscape studies and the concept of sacred geography, we define a residence's locale as its placement on the culturally defined and modified landscape. A variety of researchers have noted that Mesoamerican peoples have a long tradition of mapping cosmological principles onto a horizontal plane (Ashmore 1991, 1992; Sugiyama 1993). Placement of a residence within this materialization of cosmology would have provided a means of situating the inhabitants not only in geographical space but also within an ideological universe (Joyce 2000, 2003).

Domestic architecture orders space, and human action imbues it with meaning. As cultural artifacts, residences themselves reflect the "webs of significance" through which human groups structure their world (Geertz 1973:5). Clifford Geertz (1973:17) argues that "it is through the flow of behavior—or, more precisely, social action—that cultural forms find articulation." Residences arrange, direct, and organize the flow of behavior at the most basic level. They thus provide a central forum for the creation and re-creation of culture (Bourdieu 1977). Residences also provide a physical location for the social entities that inhabit them by ordering space in such a way as to signal who belongs and who does not (Wilson 1988). Ultimately, the physical and social entities that make up a residence are inseparable (Gillespie 2000a). Together, a residence and its residents form a culturally negotiated "unit" expressive of the wider world to which they belong.

House and Palace

Each of the aspects of residential architecture described above plays out in our distinction between an elite residence and a palace. A residence, for our purposes, is a structure built for the purpose of encapsulating domestic activities. This definition is regrettably vague, but it acknowledges that domestic activities, like residences, are culturally defined. All residences, however, share the purpose of providing a physical space for the enactment of daily productive and reproductive tasks without explicit reference to public performance. Residences are first and foremost *inhabited* structures shaping the space around private, small-scale social interactions. The distinction between an elite residence and any other residence is one of scale rather than function. All residences maintain a private, controlled, inward focus that makes them distinct from more open, public venues.

For this chapter, we envision palace architecture as explicitly defining public spaces in addition to private ones. Along with its residential function, a palace is a hub of governmental and ritual activity, often including council rooms, audience halls, state storage rooms, and ritual spaces (Andrews and Fash 1992; Evans and Pillsbury 2004; Flannery 1998; Inomata and Houston 2001; Klingensmith 1993; Miller 1998; Soles 1991; Thurley 1993). Palaces often function as physical celebrations of specific individuals, with open spaces for audiences to observe activities carried out by a palace's residents and an emphasis on organizing space around the display of a ruler or primary resident (Miller 1998). For instance, Klingensmith (1993:5) notes that "as the place where the ruler was 'at home,' the palace was preeminently the seat of ceremonies" for the Bavarian electorate. An important function of a palace, as opposed to an elite residence, is to provide space for the public display of one or several residents. The "public" witnessing such displays could in fact be relatively small, often limited only to other nobles (Klingensmith 1993; Thurley 1993), but was nonetheless distinguishable from the actual inhabitants of the palace. Another characteristic distinguishing a palace from a residence is the incorporation of institutional activities such as the storage of state surplus or the administration of political activity. The palaces of Crete, for instance, incorporated commercial and storage functions along with residential ones (Soles 1991:70). Palaces in early Renaissance England included Chapels Royal for the performance of religious services in addition to their audience and residential rooms (Thurley 1993). The Potala, the residence of the Dalai Lama in Tibet, incorporated residential, religious, and state functions in one massive structure (Iyer 1993). In each of these cases, and in many others worldwide, the domestic function of a palace becomes inextricably tied to larger institutional activities. A palace is home to both the administrators and the administration of power.

Looking at each of these architectural forms from the viewpoint of the characteristics of residential architecture described above, several distinctions appear. The spatial organization of an elite residence and a palace might in fact share many characteristics. As representations of social relations and ideas, both types of structure draw upon a similar lexicon of social concepts. The use of domestic architecture to represent cosmological principles will also occur in a palace, although palace space may be formed to refer to specific residents and their position in the cosmic order. For instance, both Stephen Houston (1998) and Susan D. Gillespie (2000b) note the Classic Maya use of house as a metaphor for container: the house represents "a man-made container for both the living and the deceased" (Gillespie 2000b:146). This is visible in the presence of hieroglyphic benches in Maya palaces at Palenque (Miller 1998) and Copán (Andrews and Fash 1992; Webster 1989; Webster et al. 1998). Inscriptions on the bench in Structure 9N-82 clearly situate the bench's ancient owner within both the celestial and political realms of Copán (Fash 1993). At a more basic level, a palace's layout will facilitate some actions and social relations while discouraging others. Many throne rooms, for instance, place the ruler in an elevated position. This spatial distinction makes material the ideological distinction between a king and a lesser noble, putting the ruler both physically and socially higher in social interactions. The presence of nondomestic spaces within a palace also presents distinctions from a residence. A palace provides a physical space for activities such as public display or governance, formalizing this element of palace function. Most importantly, however, palaces situate particular forms of power in the home of an individual or group, inextricably tying the two together. A palace makes it impossible to separate the power from the residents, since the two "live" together. A palace provides the physical location for an individualized or familial power—a power that is inseparable from its wielders.

We suggest that the type of power demonstrated by palaces did not exist in the Valley of Oaxaca until late in that region's pre-Columbian history. In the following pages, we present an overview of elite residential architecture from the Early Formative through the Late Postclassic periods to propose that concepts of power may have shifted through time from corporate to more restricted, individualized forms.

Early and Middle Formative Residences in the Valley of Oaxaca

The Valley of Oaxaca is a semiarid valley located in the highlands of southern Mexico (Figure 8.1). The valley floor lies at an elevation of 1,500 to 1,700 masl, with surrounding peaks exceeding 3,000 m. It is a Y-shaped valley, with the arms forming three subregions: the Etla arm is to the north, extending east is the Tlacolula arm, and to the south is the Valle Grande. Archaeological and linguistic evidence (Flannery and Marcus, eds. 1983; Winter 1989) suggests that the Zapotec ethnolinguistic group has a deep history in the Valley of Oaxaca, extending back to the Archaic period (ca. 8000–1800 B.C.). This region of Mesoamerica is one of the most intensively studied by archaeologists (Blanton 1978; Caso 1932, 1935, 1938; Caso et al. 1967; Flannery, ed. 1976; Flannery and Marcus, eds. 1983; Joyce 2000; Joyce and Winter 1996; Kowalewski et al. 1989; Winter 1989, 1994). This research has shown that settlement in the Valley of Oaxaca extends back to mobile populations of the Archaic period. It is not until the Early Formative period (1800–850 B.C.), however, that the first sedentary agricultural villages developed, which included the earliest residential structures in Oaxaca (Flannery, ed. 1976). Toward the end of the Early Formative, during the San José phase (1150–850 B.C.), archaeological evidence suggests the first differentiation in size and elaboration of residential architecture occurred, although it is not clear if these differences reflect the development of hereditary social inequality (cf. Blanton et al. 1999; Marcus and Flannery 1996).

Early Formative people in the Valley of Oaxaca lived in small agricultural villages usually about 1 to 2 ha in area (Marcus and Flannery 1996). The site of San José Mogote in the Etla arm, however, was considerably larger than other communities, reaching perhaps 70 ha and a population estimated at 1,000

Mesoamerica

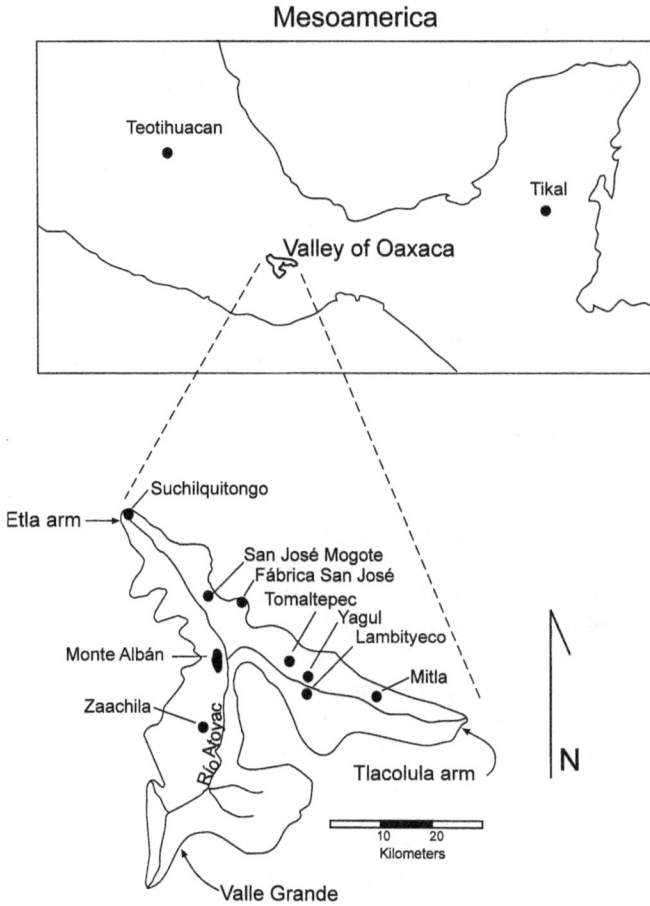

FIGURE 8.1 Mesoamerica and the Valley of Oaxaca

people by the San José phase (Marcus and Flannery 1996:106). Early Formative houses in the Valley of Oaxaca were generally small one-room wattle-
and-daub structures with thatched roofs and floor areas ranging from about
18 to 24 m² (Flannery 1976; Winter 1976, 1986b:332–340). An area of about
300 m² that contained domestic features such as ovens, human burials, and
bell-shaped storage pits surrounded each house.

By the San José (1150–850 B.C.) and Guadalupe (850–700 B.C.) phases, residences began to exhibit differences in architectural elaboration and associated evidence for wealth inequality. Most residences continued the earlier
pattern of small single-room wattle-and-daub structures (Drennan 1976;
Flannery and Marcus 1983a; Whalen 1981; Winter 1972, 1986b). More elaborate residences included House 2 and the House 16-17 complex from San José
Mogote, Tomaltepec Unit ESJ-1, and Fábrica San José Households LG-1 and

LG-6. These residences were architecturally similar to lower-status houses, although some of them included walls with whitewash over the daub, larger posts, drains, and stone foundations (Flannery and Marcus 1983a:55; Whalen 1981:34–38). San José Mogote House 16-17 included a residential building (House 17) and a roofed work area (House 16) where occupants apparently manufactured chert bifaces.[1] These "higher-status" houses exhibited greater evidence for participation in craft activities such as the manufacture of chert tools, baskets, shell ornaments, and pottery, as well as woodworking and sewing (Blanton et al. 1999; Flannery and Marcus 1994:333; Whalen 1981:58–59). Members of these households also had greater access to deer meat and exotic items like marine shell, jade, imported pottery, ceramic masks, stingray spines, fish spines, and drum otoliths (Flannery and Marcus 1994:333; Marcus and Flannery 1996:104).

During the San José phase, most adults were interred in communal cemeteries (Flannery and Marcus 1983a; Whalen 1981). Kent Flannery and Joyce Marcus (1994) argue for the presence of several residential wards at San José Mogote, which may suggest affiliations with restricted social groupings such as lineages or moieties (also see Blanton et al. 1999:39–42). It has been argued that these possible social divisions were symbolized in were-jaguar and fire-serpent motifs on decorated pottery (Blanton et al. 1999; Marcus and Flannery 1996; Pyne 1976), although other scholars disagree with this interpretation (Clark 2001; Winter 1989:28–29). By the Guadalupe phase, some people were buried near their houses, often in multiple burials with an adult male and female and sometimes children, although communal cemeteries continued to be present (Drennan 1976; Winter 1972). This change in mortuary patterns may reflect an increasing identification with the residential group. Burial data also suggest rising inequality during the Guadalupe phase, although it is unclear whether status differences were hereditary.

In the San José and Guadalupe phases, the differences between residences and associated artifacts indicate a continuum from lower- to relatively higher-status households (Flannery and Marcus 1983a:55). Based on a variety of factors, Marcus and Flannery (1996:93–110) argue that hereditary social inequality had developed in the Valley of Oaxaca by the San José phase. Richard Blanton and his colleagues (1999:36–42) disagree, arguing instead that the evidence for social inequality does not demonstrate ascribed status differences. Although hereditary social inequality remains a possible explanation for San José–phase social organization, the available data seem more consistent with fairly modest differences in social status at this time. Domestic spatial organization was open, such that craft production and other activities in patios would have been visible to passersby. Architectural elaboration was limited, with whitewashed walls possibly communicating higher status. There does not appear to be locational data suggesting distinct differences in social status such as associations between high-status residences and public buildings. Overall, the residential data from the Early Formative and the beginning of the Middle Formative reflect a continuum in status distinctions rather than fundamental differences between elite and commoner residences that might symbolize hereditary and especially class differences. Although hereditary inequality could have existed without being reflected in residential patterning (Marcus and Flannery 1996), it is also possible that these distinctions did not arise until the latter part of the Middle Formative (700–500 B.C.; see Blanton et al. 1999:42–47).

Ideology and the Origins of Elite Residences at San José Mogote

The Rosario phase (700–500 B.C.) in the Valley of Oaxaca was a time of interpolity conflict and innovations in politico-religious ideas and practices that contributed to increasing social inequality, including hereditary status distinctions (Blanton et al. 1999:42–47; Joyce 2000; Joyce and Winter 1996; Marcus and Flannery 1996:121–138). These social transformations resulted in the founding of Monte Albán at 500 B.C., which would become the Valley of Oaxaca's first urban center and capital of a state polity. The social changes of the Rosario phase are reflected in transformations in architecture and the spatial setting of high-status residences. For the first time in the Valley of Oaxaca sequence, status distinctions were being communicated via fundamental differences in the spatial layout, architectural elaboration, and location of high-status residences. These developments in residential patterning can be related to ideological changes that would contribute to the creation and legitimation of a Zapotec noble class (Joyce 2000).

Rosario-phase residences at lower-order sites such as Fábrica San José in the Etla arm and Tomaltepec in the Tlacolula arm generally reflect a continuum of status distinctions much as in earlier periods. Observable status differences are based on relative concentrations of exotic items like shell, obsidian, and greenstone, as well as associated burials with greater quantities of offerings (Drennan 1976:111, 133; Whalen 1981:64–74). Household Unit R-1 at Tomaltepec, however, exhibited a number of architectural features that appear to have differentiated it from simpler houses. The household unit consisted of two residential structures surrounding a patio rather than a single structure, as was typical of most residences. In addition, each house had a well-laid stone and adobe mortar foundation about 0.6 m wide. The size of these foundations suggests that they supported substantial adobe, rather than wattle-and-daub, walls (Whalen 1981:67). The presence of a large oven or roasting pit and a relatively high bowl-to-jar ratio suggests the occupants might have sponsored communal feasts (Whalen 1981:67–70). Feasting could have been a means by which social obligations, identities, and authority were extended within and between communities (Clark and Blake 1994; Dietler and Hayden 2001). Household Unit R-1 is also located only about 15 m north of Structure 12, a public building, which could be indicative of the emergence of an elite-ceremonial precinct consisting of a high-status residence and public buildings where communal rituals were performed. These data suggest that elite residences were being located in areas where public ceremonies were also carried out, although there is no evidence suggesting that the residential buildings were designed to house administrative activities.

Evidence for the development of architectural and spatial patterns that indicate high-status residences is even more clearly demonstrated at the first-order center of San José Mogote. During the late Rosario phase, a series of high-status residences were built on Mound 1, a natural hill architecturally modified into a huge platform (Flannery and Marcus 1983a). The best-preserved of these residences consisted of three structures (Structures 25, 26, and 30) surrounding an interior patio. The rooms had stone foundations that supported adobe walls similar to those of Household Unit R-1 at Tomaltepec. Structure 26 included a storage room (Room 1) with its floor more than 1 m below the patio. The storeroom contained several large serving bowls, a cooking pot, and an anthropomorphic incense brazier—objects that could have been used in feasting (Marcus and Flannery 1996:131). Associated with these elite residences were two tombs, the first formal stonemasonry tombs known in the Valley of Oaxaca. The most elaborate was Tomb 10, which was found beneath the patio floor and consisted of a chamber and an antechamber with a coating of mud plaster on its interior (Marcus and Flannery 1996:133). Most of the contents of the tomb were removed in antiquity, but an offering of 11 small obsidian projectile points buried in a deposit of red ochre remained.

The location of elite residences on Mound 1 suggests an increasing separation between elites and commoners. Mound 1 was the largest structure at San José Mogote, and prior to the late Rosario phase, it supported only public buildings (Marcus and Flannery 1996). The construction of the elite residences adjacent to the temples on Mound 1, therefore, created an elite-ceremonial precinct that was spatially segregated from the rest of the community. Not only were the temples and high-status residences in close proximity to one another, but the 15 m elevation of Mound 1 would have restricted physical access to the area as well as people's ability to observe the activities of its residents. The increasingly enclosed patio spaces of high-status residences would also have restricted access to elite residential activities, indirectly communicating the increasing social separation of elites and commoners.

The Rosario-phase data from Tomaltepec and San José Mogote indicate the presence of hereditary elites in the Valley of Oaxaca. This social group was living in larger and more elaborate residences that were increasingly associated with public ceremonial spaces and buildings, creating distinct elite-ceremonial precincts. These changes in high-status residences were occurring at a time of social and political upheaval in the region, including major transformations in the politico-religious ideas and practices that created and legitimated elite power (Flannery and Marcus 1976; Joyce 2000; Marcus and Flannery 1996). By considering the broader social context of the Rosario phase, it is possible to show that changes in the size, form, and locale of elite residences were directly related to the communication and negotiation of ideological principles and practices that were altering power relations in the Valley of Oaxaca.

Regional data suggest that the Rosario phase was a period of political crisis at San José Mogote (Joyce 2000). Increasing interpolity conflict within the valley is indicated by a high frequency of structures destroyed by fire and a sparsely occupied buffer zone separating the Etla arm of the valley from the two other arms, each of which were occupied by competing polities (Kowalewski et al. 1989:70–75). At approximately 600 B.C., just prior to the construction of the elite residences at San José Mogote, a temple on Mound 1 was burned to the ground, perhaps as a result of raiding (Marcus and Flannery 1996:129). The destruction of the temple suggests that a raiding party penetrated the most restricted and ritually important part of the site. At the same time, survey data indicate that San José Mogote was losing population, with the area of the site decreasing from 70 ha during the Guadalupe phase to 34 ha by the Rosario phase. These data suggest that elites were unable to maintain their coalition of supporters and that commoners were "voting with their feet" and leaving San José Mogote.

The creation of an elite-ceremonial precinct on Mound 1, coupled with evidence for changes in sacrificial practices, suggests a transformation in structural principles involving people and the sacred. In response to the political crisis of the Rosario phase, elites may have tried to develop more potent means of contacting the sacred on their own behalf and that of their followers, through changes in sacrificial practices and rituals involving ancestors (see Joyce 2000). In pre-Columbian Mesoamerican creation myths, sacrifice was shown to be a fundamental condition of human existence based on the formation of a sacred covenant between people and the gods (Monaghan 2000). In the sacred covenant, humans agreed to offer sacrifices to the gods, with death representing the ultimate sacrifice, and in return, the gods allowed people to practice agriculture and achieve fertility and prosperity. Mesoamerican elites occupied a special place in relation to the sacred covenant and the acts of sacrifice it required. Human and autosacrifice performed by and on the bodies of nobles were the most potent forms of sacrifice (Boone 1984; King 1988; Schele and Miller 1986). Sacrifice therefore operated as a kind of social contract between commoners, elites, and supernaturals (Monaghan 1994:23), with nobles acting as intermediaries between people and the sacred. Sacrifice and ancestor veneration were key idioms through which power relations were constructed and negotiated.

Evidence from Mound 1 at San José Mogote indicates major changes in sacrificial ideas and practices during the Rosario phase, suggesting that people were struggling to develop new and more potent ways to contact the sacred. The first evidence for the practice of human sacrifice in the Valley of Oaxaca is found on Mound 1 in the form of a possible sacrificial victim buried beneath Structure 26 and on a carved stone (Monument 3) depicting a victim of heart sacrifice. By offering a new, more dramatic form of sacrifice — human sacrifice — to the deities, nobles at San José Mogote were struggling to respond to the political crisis as well as demonstrating their ritual potency and generosity to followers. The elites living on Mound 1 were also carrying out more traditional autosacrificial bloodletting rituals, as shown by the recovery of an obsidian bloodletter (Marcus and Flannery 1996:133).

The evidence for the increasing religious significance of noble ancestors, especially their interment in formal masonry tombs seen for the first time with the Mound 1 residences, further suggests that elites were expanding the ways in which they communicated with the sacred. Based on the principles of the sacred covenant, the interment of elites in formal masonry tombs can be interpreted in sacrificial terms. Nobles interred in tombs were not sacrificing their bodies at death in the same way as commoners, since their bones remained in the tombs and were not assimilated by the earth in the same way as those of other people. As a result, nobles could directly consult their ancestors by reopening the tomb and performing appropriate rituals (Miller 1995). The separate and accessible resting place of elites in tombs may have helped deify noble ancestors. The anthropomorphic incense brazier recovered in Structure 26 also suggests an increasing concern with elite ancestors, since it represents one of the earliest examples of a type of incense burner used in later periods to communicate with deceased nobles (Flannery and Marcus 1994:61).

These changes in religious ideas, institutions, and practices were communicated in the architecture and spatial setting of high-status residences. The increasingly enclosed and private setting of elite households, their increasing size and architectural elaboration, the interment of elites in tombs, and the close association of elite residences and public buildings were means by which the identity of nobles came to be marked as fundamentally separate from that of commoners (Joyce and Winter 1996; Marcus 1992). In particular, the presence of subpatio tombs in elite residences, a pattern that would continue through the remainder of the pre-Columbian period, communicated principles of sacrifice and ancestor veneration that legitimated the power of nobles. During the Rosario phase, some commoners continued to be buried in communal cemeteries (Drennan 1976:129; Drennan and Flannery 1983:70), but by Monte Albán I (500–100 B.C.) commoners were also interred beneath their households. Although this meant that the living resided in the midst of the dead, these tombs facilitated reentry rituals that enabled direct consultation with the dead. It is uncertain whether the innovation of tombs in elite residences on Mound 1 at San José Mogote marks the beginning of the deification of noble ancestors, but it clearly implies a greater religious significance of those ancestors.

Despite the political and ideological changes of the late Rosario phase at San José Mogote, by 500 B.C. monumental construction on Mound 1 ceased and the site may have continued to decline in size (Kowalewski et al. 1989:89–90; Marcus and Flannery 1996:139). At approximately 500 B.C., a group of Etla Valley nobles and commoners founded the hilltop site of Monte Albán that would soon grow into the Valley of Oaxaca's first urban center (Marcus and Flannery 1996; Winter and Joyce 1994). The changes in ideology and ritual that were creating and legitimating elite power would continue to be communicated in the sacred geography of Monte Albán, including in the architecture and spatial symbolism of high-status residences.

Late/Terminal Formative Noble Residences and the Symbolics of Power at Monte Albán

Monte Albán was founded about 500 B.C. on a previously unoccupied series of hills in the center of the Valley of Oaxaca. By the end of the Monte Albán Ia phase (500–300 B.C.), Monte Albán far exceeded any other site in the Valley of Oaxaca in size, population, and scale of monumental architecture (Blanton 1978; Kowalewski et al. 1989; Winter and Joyce 1994). The civic-ceremonial center of the site was the Main Plaza, a huge public plaza measuring roughly 300 m north–south by 150 m east–west. In its final form, the Main Plaza was bounded on its north and south ends by high platforms supporting numerous public buildings. The eastern and western sides of the Main Plaza were defined by rows of monumental buildings; a third row of structures ran north to south through the center of the plaza. As Figure 8.2 shows, the Late Formative or Monte Albán I (500–100 B.C.) version of the Main Plaza consisted of only the plaza itself, along with the western row of buildings and much of the eastern half of the North Platform (Winter and Joyce 1994). The central and eastern rows of buildings and probably the South Platform do not appear to have been built until the Terminal Formative or Monte Albán II (100 B.C.–A.D. 200; see Figure 8.3; Acosta 1959; Winter 2000). Monte Albán grew rapidly, covering 320 ha by the end of the Monte Albán Ia phase (500–300 B.C.) and 442 ha during Monte Albán Ic (300–100 B.C.). A reason for the dramatic growth in population at Monte Albán may have been the popularity of the religious principles and practices that were a central motivating factor for the early inhabitants of the site. An important way in which these principles were symbolically communicated was through sacred geography, involving the symbolism of the spatial arrangement of architecture and iconography in and around the Main Plaza. Elite residences were an important component of Monte Albán's sacred geography throughout its history of occupation.

Evidence from Monte Albán suggests that a goal of the earliest inhabitants was to construct a ceremonial center that symbolized the version of the sacred covenant developed at San José Mogote during the previous cen-

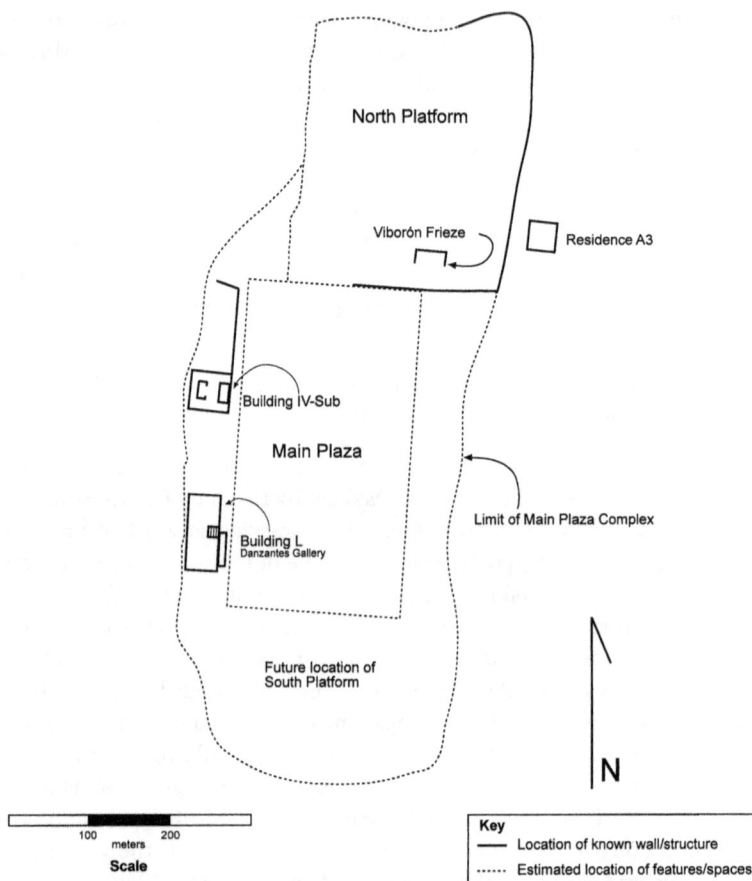

FIGURE 8.2 Main Plaza, Monte Albán I (500–100 B.C.)

tury (Joyce 2000, 2003). From Monte Albán's earliest years, its sacred geography resembled that of other Mesoamerican cities where the cosmos was rotated onto the surface of the site's ceremonial center such that north represented the celestial realm and south the earth or underworld (Ashmore 1991; Sugiyama 1993:123). The southern end of the Main Plaza contained iconographic references to earth, sacrifice, and warfare. These references included over 300 carved stones representing sacrificial victims that were erected in Monte Albán I (the Danzantes of Building L); the conquest slabs of Monte Albán II, with their depictions of conquered places and decapitated rulers; and the South Platform program of bound captives from Monte Albán III (A.D. 200–800). The North Platform included iconographic references to sky, rain, and lightning in the form of the Monte Albán Ic Viborón Frieze, with its depiction of a skyband with clouds, rain, and possibly Cocijo, the Zapo-

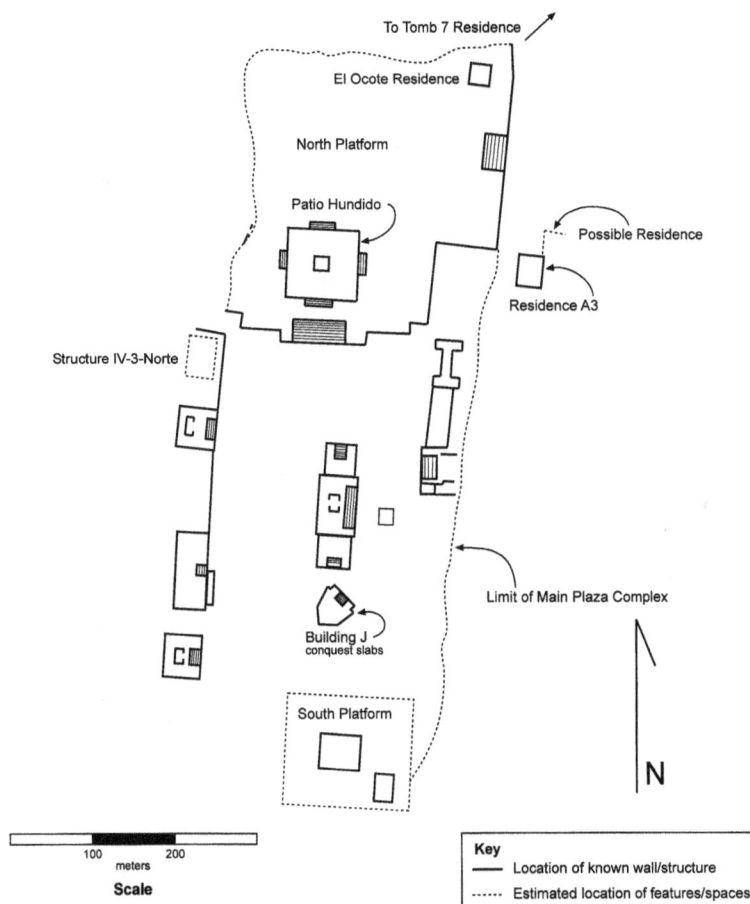

FIGURE 8.3 Main Plaza, Monte Albán II (100 B.C.–A.D. 200)

tec lightning (sky) deity. During Monte Albán III, the North Platform was marked by numerous depictions of the "jaws of the sky" motif on carved stones. Also known as the *fauces del cielo*, this motif referred to noble descent (Marcus 1983b:139) and the divine home of elite ancestors (Miller 1995). The sacred geography of the Main Plaza was a symbol of the Zapotec vision of the cosmos, and it invoked the creation myth in which sacrifice led to the creation and continual renewal of the world (Joyce 2000). The Main Plaza was also a public arena where people were engaged in state rituals, including sacrifice, that communicated ideological principles and bound people to rulers and other state symbols.

The location of high-status residences at Monte Albán was part of the sacred geography of the site and communicated aspects of the dominant ideology. Although the configuration of early buildings is not completely understood, due to later construction activities, from Monte Albán I until Monte Albán IIIa (A.D. 200–500) the vast majority of elite residences and tombs were concentrated in areas around the North Platform (Joyce 2003; Martínez et al. 1995; Miller 1995:54; Winter 1995; Winter and Joyce 1994). The placement of elite residences around the northern end of the Main Plaza indicates an association between the celestial realm, nobles, and noble ancestors. Tombs in these residences often contained effigy vessels depicting Cocijo. These data suggest not only an increasing association of nobles with the celestial realm but also the deification of noble ancestors (Marcus and Flannery 1996:159). An increasing association between elite residences and religious symbols and artifacts beginning in Monte Albán I further indicates that nobles were gaining greater control of politico-religious rituals (Joyce and Winter 1996:36).

The earliest high-status residence known from Monte Albán, Residence A3 (see Figure 8.3), was excavated during the Proyecto Especial Monte Albán 1992–1994 (PEMA) directed by Marcus Winter (Winter 1994, 2000; Winter and Joyce 1994). Residence A3 was built on the hillslope east of the North Platform in an area of huge terraces constructed over bedrock. The terraces supported several platforms that were probably high-status residences dating from Monte Albán Ia to Monte Albán II. Residence A3 was built on a low platform on one of the terraces. The platform supported the walls of an elite residence with a stuccoed patio, a red-painted east wall, and a large subpatio tomb (Tomb 204). The tomb had a chamber and antechamber, and although these were largely cleaned out in antiquity, fifteen Monte Albán Ic vessels remained. Residence A3 was expanded in size in Monte Albán Ic and again in Monte Albán II. Another probable Monte Albán I residence was associated with a high-status burial (Burial VI-12) located about 400 m northeast of Residence A3.

Though neither Residence A3 nor the high-status residences on Mound 1 at San José Mogote were completely excavated, based on available data, they appear to have been similar architecturally. Both residences were larger and more elaborate architecturally than low-status households. Commoner households continued to be typified by small single houses, although by Monte Albán I they usually had adobe walls on stone foundations and occasionally had areas with flagstone pavements (Winter 1974:982). The high-status residences at Monte Albán and San José Mogote both had multiple rooms partially or entirely enclosing a patio, had subpatio tombs, and were located in relatively restricted locations.

Excavation data from the PEMA suggest that an early version of the Patio Hundido, or Sunken Patio, in the North Platform was also built during Monte Albán I. Several researchers have argued that the Patio Hundido was the ruler's palace at Monte Albán, especially by Monte Albán III (Blanton 1978:61–63; 1993:93; Flannery 1983a:133–134). We disagree with this interpretation, since there is little evidence for domestic activities and, architecturally, the Patio Hundido conforms more closely to a temple-patio-altar complex (Winter 1986a) than a residence (also see Flannery 1998:34; Miller 1995:56–57). Instead, we agree with Flannery's (1998:34) more recent interpretation that the Patio Hundido was a nonresidential governmental building.

The only other Monte Albán I high-status residences that have been excavated in the Valley of Oaxaca come from the sites of Tomaltepec in the Tlacolula arm and El Palenque in the Valle Grande.[2] By Monte Albán I, Tomaltepec was a small administrative center of 5 to 8 ha (Whalen 1981, 1988). During Monte Albán Ia, the occupation of the higher-status Rosario-phase residence continued and included a pavement of adobe bricks, which made it more elaborate than other Monte Albán Ia houses at the site. The residents of this household (Unit Ia-1) had greater access to deer meat, obsidian, fine chert, mica, and shell than other residences, although these differences were relatively modest. By Monte Albán Ic, however, a significantly more elaborate residence (Unit Ic-1) was constructed in this area, consisting of at least two platforms with cut-stone foundations, adobe walls, and plaster floors that probably surrounded a patio. Built into the center of the northernmost of the two platforms was a slab-covered, adobe-walled tomb containing burials of two adults and a child, along with offerings of jade and 37 ceramic vessels. The high-status residence is located to the north of a plaza, flanked by probable public buildings on its east (Structure 13) and west (Mound 2) sides. Its location indicates the continuation from the Rosario phase of the elite-ceremonial precinct and perhaps a sacred geography similar to Monte Albán's that associated nobles with the northern/celestial realm. Though the Monte Albán Ic residence at Tomaltepec was more elaborate than other houses, both its structural and tomb architecture were not as fancy as those of Residence A3 from Monte Albán. The residents of Unit Ic-1 may have been a family of lesser nobles who were administering this small center (Whalen 1988). By the Monte Albán II phase Tomaltepec was in decline, and by Monte Albán IIIa it was abandoned.

El Palenque was a Monte Albán Ic regional center for the Valle Grande, located near the modern town of San Martín Tilcajete, and appears to have been independent of and in conflict with Monte Albán at this time (Elson 2001; Redmond 2000; Spencer 1999; Spencer and Redmond 2001). The excavations at El Palenque exposed Structure 7, a high-status residence measuring 16 × 16 m and located on the north side of the site's main plaza, which was bounded on the east by temples (Spencer and Redmond 2001). Structure 7 was built on a masonry platform 80 cm high and consisted of eight rooms surrounding a central patio. Excavations at El Palenque suggest that the site was under siege and may have been conquered by Monte Albán, leading to the subsequent establishment of the Monte Albán II hilltop center at Loma de los Mogotes, which by then was incorporated into the Monte Albán state (Elson 2001; Spencer and Redmond 2001).[3]

During the Monte Albán II phase at Monte Albán, large, architecturally elaborate residences continued to be concentrated in the northern end of the Main Plaza (Figure 8.3; Winter 1994, 2000). Definite Monte Albán II residences at Monte Albán included Residence A3 and probably others in the same area, a large residential complex known as El Ocote on the northeastern corner of the North Platform, Structure IV-3-Norte located on the northwestern corner of the Main Plaza (see Figure 8.3), and the Tomb 7 Residence. Though none of the Monte Albán II elite residences have been totally cleared, they follow the floor plan of earlier high-status residences in having multiple rooms enclosing a central patio. The El Ocote complex probably had a larger number of rooms and a more complex layout than the other high-status residences of this period. El Ocote is the first elite residence at Monte Albán that does not appear to have had a tomb. Structure IV-3-Norte is the first elite residence directly facing the Main Plaza, which might suggest that this residence was more "public" than others, although the entrance to the structure was to the north rather than to the east onto the Main Plaza. The Tomb 7 Residence was located northeast of the North Platform. Excavations of this residence uncovered fragments of three stucco floors, a formal stairway, and a subpatio tomb (Tomb 7 bis; Martínez 2002).

Monte Albán II high-status residences are also found in some of Monte Albán's barrios beyond the Main Plaza. By the Monte Albán IIIb–IV phase the site appears to have included 15 barrios, many of which had a resident elite family and public buildings (Blanton 1978:66–93). In Monte Albán I all of the known high-status residences were located around the Main Plaza. By Monte Albán II, however, there was apparently an elite residence at the El Pitayo barrio that included two tombs (Tombs 77 and 96). Possible elite households were also present at Paragüito, Atzompa, and El Gallo. The presence of high-status residences at lower-order sites like El Palenque and Tomaltepec by Monte Albán Ic, as well as at Oaxaca's barrios by Monte Albán II, suggests an expansion of the nobility and probably the emergence of a state bureaucracy.

Outside of Monte Albán, high-status residences have been investigated at the subregional centers of San José Mogote and Loma de los Mogotes. Excavations in Mound 9 at the northern end of the Main Plaza at San José Mogote exposed a possible high-status residential complex consisting of multiple patios surrounded by three or four rooms (Marcus and Flannery 1996:180). At Loma de los Mogotes, Christina Elson (2001, 2003; also see Redmond 2000) excavated a high-status residence built on a stonemasonry platform measuring 12 × 12 × 1.6 m and with remains of a stuccoed exterior surface. The residence consisted of six to eight rooms surrounding a central patio. As at its predecessor, El Palenque, the elite residence at Loma de los Mogotes was located on the north end of a plaza with a temple to the east. A second probable residence was excavated on a terrace to the east and downslope from the plaza.

The increasing number of high-status residences during the Monte Albán I and II phases at Monte Albán and other sites in the valley indicates further institutionalization of changes in ideology and political relations that legitimated noble status. By the Late/Terminal Formative (500 B.C.–A.D. 200), a separate noble identity, with an accompanying set of practices, was increasingly evident in the Valley of Oaxaca (Joyce 2000; Joyce and Winter 1996; Marcus 1992). Noble identities were symbolized by the increasing size and elaboration of elite residences, the close association of elite residences and public buildings, interment in masonry tombs, performance of special rituals like human sacrifice, as well as the control of exotic artifacts such as urns and incense burners and of knowledge such as hieroglyphic writing and calendrics. These ideas and practices marked nobles as fundamentally different from commoners and contributed to the legitimation of politicoreligious power in the Valley of Oaxaca. There are also some indications of the beginnings of differentiation in the size and elaboration of elite residences that might suggest variation in social roles, status, wealth, and power within the nobility. For example, by Monte Albán II there were high-status residences both with and without tombs. This variation could be the consequence of the growth of the nobility, resulting in a group of lesser nobles in addition to rulers. Another possible explanation is the differentiation of religious and secular authorities. Additional research is needed to better document the variation in Late/Terminal Formative elite residences and to investigate what this might mean in terms of social organization.

The Formalization of Elite Power: Monte Albán IIIa

Elite residences during the Monte Albán IIIa phase present a formalization of trends that began during Monte Albán I and II. Elite residences were essentially larger standardized versions of the same floor plan found in residences at all status levels: groups of rooms around a square patio. Commoner residences (Winter's "Type 1" [1974]) generally consisted of earthen patios outlined by a single course of faced stones. Measuring between 3.5 and 4 m a side, these patios were not always enclosed by rooms on all four sides. The rooms themselves were ephemeral and often lacked the stone foundation walls found in more elaborate buildings. Like all other residences in the Valley of Oaxaca at this time, commoner residences contained subfloor interments, usually slab-lined burials. Elite residences had enclosed flagstone patios surrounded by rooms with stone foundation walls (Winter's "Type 2" and "Type 3" residences). The variation seen in Monte Albán II residences became more formal by Monte Albán IIIa, with patios in elaborate residences ranging from 4 to 13 m per side (Winter 1974:983). This diversity probably reflects the existence of a more formalized social hierarchy with a number of noble status positions by the Classic period.

We use Residence W1-A, a Type 2 residence recently excavated as part of the PEMA, to exemplify the characteristics of Classic-period elite residences at Monte Albán (see Figure 8.7, a similar residence; Morales et al. 1999). Residence W1-A consisted of approximately eight rooms surrounding a central patio. The flagstone patio measured 10.2 m per side, the edges of which were marked by low steps leading up into the various rooms of the residence. A stone-slab drain ran from the southeast corner of the patio, beneath the structure's southeast room, to the outside. Of the structure's eight rooms, four were large and rectangular and four others filled the corner space between each of the main rooms. The south room was the best preserved and showed greater elaboration than any of the other four main rooms. It measured 6.22 m × 2.95 m. The south room's access stairway was set between sloping basal walls that flanked the patio. Beneath the west room lay a tomb containing a secondary burial and some Monte Albán IIIa ceramics. The residence's entrance was probably to the east. Although not preserved in this instance, other elite residences had an L-shaped passage that served to screen the patio from outside view as well as to channel the movement of anyone entering or exiting the residence. Beneath the patio, excavators encountered an offering of 10 whole and partial vessels accompanied by a burned rock—a possible dedicatory cache. No floor features related to domestic activities, such as hearths or ovens, were uncovered, although domestic middens have been found outside of residence walls (Winter et al. 1997). Storage facilities, such as the bell-shaped pits of earlier periods (Winter 1974, 1986b), were not present within the confines of this structure.

Architectural elaboration of residential space occurred through monumentality and tomb ornamentation. Known elite residences from Monte Albán IIIa, like the El Ocote complex on the North Platform or the Tomb 7 Residence, were often quite large. Elaborately decorated residential tombs also serve to distinguish elite residences from those of non-elites, which have only simple burials. A number of transitional IIIa to IIIb–IV tombs have been excavated that provide insight into elite behavior and the organization of power in the Early Classic period. Most notable are Tombs 103, 104, 105, and 112, all of which contained painted murals, providing a unique source of information on elite art and ideology (Caso 1938; Miller 1995).

The most famous of these, Tomb 104, lay underneath an elite residence measuring 20 m on a side, with a patio measuring 9.2 × 10 m (Winter 1974). The tomb itself was cut into the bedrock beneath the large western room of the structure (Miller 1995). The tomb façade includes an effigy urn that may represent a human wearing a Cocijo mask (Marcus 1983b:148; Masson 2001). A single male skeleton, along with a variety of offerings, including several anthropomorphic effigy urns, was interred within (Caso 1938; Miller 1995). A capstone bearing glyphic inscriptions covered the doorway to the tomb. The walls of the tomb's main chamber are covered with elaborate polychrome murals that appear to depict either contemporary relatives or ancestors of the tomb's occupant (Marcus 1983b:140; Miller 1995:126). Arthur G. Miller

(1995:126) further elaborates: "The subject matter concerns the family lineage of the residents inhabiting the house above the tomb . . . this funerary subject matter concerns the 'ascent' or 'return' to the 'fauces celestiales' (the ancestral abode)." The tomb's iconography describes the journey of the deceased into the celestial realm (Marcus 1983b:137; Miller 1995:129). The residence's locale on the north side of the North Platform provides a spatial reiteration of these ideas. The differences in style between the various elements of the tomb led Miller (1995) to suggest that Tomb 104, like many other tombs in the Valley of Oaxaca, was reopened and reused several times. Few other tombs in the region are as well preserved, but Tombs 103, 105, and 112 all had mural paintings dating to the late Monte Albán IIIa phase. These painstakingly ornamented residential spaces were remarkable in their variance from the daily-use spaces above. The tombs of Monte Albán IIIa — and indeed of all later periods as well — were brilliantly decorated and highly communicative of elite power and status. They were, however, invisible to all but the select few who participated in tomb rituals.

The locale of Monte Albán IIIa elite residences largely followed the pattern that developed during Monte Albán I and II. The vast majority of elite residences were located close to, or north of, the North Platform (Figure 8.4). The occupation of several Monte Albán II residences continued into Monte Albán IIIa, notably the El Ocote complex, Structure IV-3-Norte, and the Tomb 7 Residence. Another large residence, perhaps measuring as much as 20 m per side, was built north of the North Platform. This residence, like the El Ocote structure, does not appear to have contained a tomb. Two additional large residential groups were built around the North Platform in Monte Albán IIIa (Winter 1994, 2000). The first sits at the edge of a slope just off the southwest corner of the North Platform (PNLP-1). The PNLP-1 consisted of at least one, and perhaps several, enclosed-patio residences (Peeler 1994; Winter 2000; Winter and Joyce 1994). The only tomb associated with the PNLP-1 dates to Monte Albán IIIa, with reuse evident in Monte Albán V (Marcus Winter, personal communication, 2001). A second residential grouping lies on the southeast corner of the North Platform (PSA) and includes three residences separated by narrow passageways. The largest structure, with a patio measuring approximately 8 × 8 m, did not contain a tomb (Peeler 1994).

The Monte Albán IIIa residential data demonstrate a continuation of trends begun during earlier periods at Monte Albán, and several elements of elite residential architecture and tombs also foreshadow later patterns. The standard enclosed-patio residence that had fully developed by Monte Albán IIIa was to remain the defining floor plan of elite residences in the Valley of Oaxaca until after the Spanish Conquest. These enclosed and highly restricted domestic spaces served to limit access to elites and maintain an elevated level of privacy. Non-elite residences mirrored this organization of space. The only architectural space unique to elite residences was the tomb.

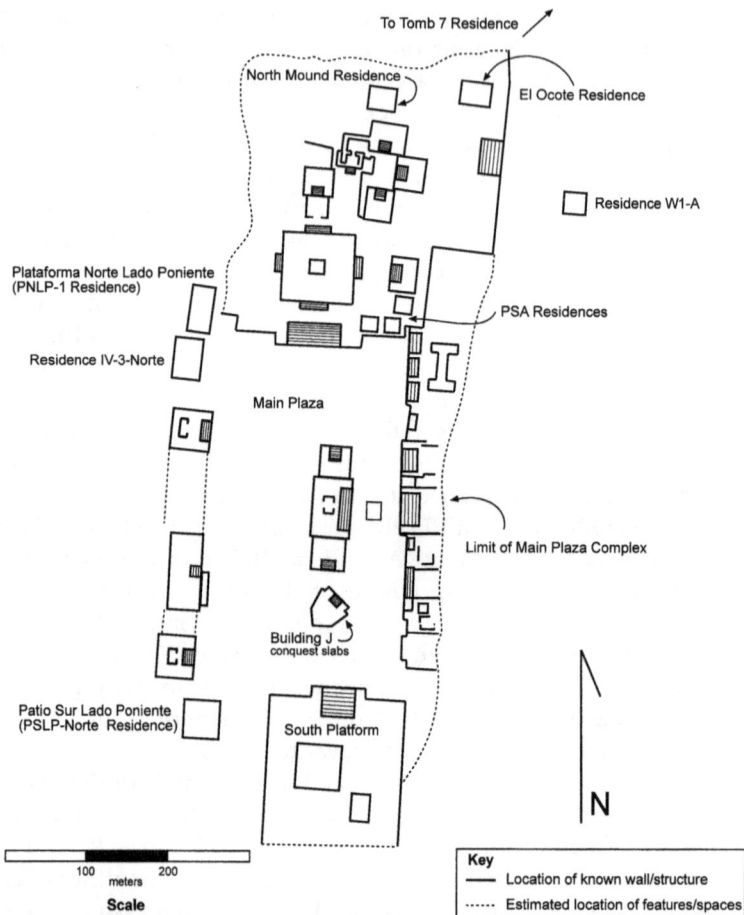

FIGURE 8.4 Main Plaza, Monte Albán IIIa (A.D. 200–500)

The most elaborate Monte Albán IIIa tombs were considerably more ornate than those of earlier periods but nonetheless present a continuation of burial patterns that began in the Rosario phase. Tombs provided elites with a space within which they could connect with their distinguished ancestors and retain their special relationship to the sacred. Noble ancestors were kept in close proximity to the living, thus tying a residence's inhabitants more closely to one of their major sources of power. Tombs also provided a private but explicit architectural expression of elite power. Nobles did not make use of external architectural elements such as fretwork or sculpture to express their superior status. Structure size and the labor input such structures required were the only outward manifestations of elite status provided through architectural elaboration. Locale also served to demonstrate status, since elite residences during this time continued to cluster around the North Platform. The sacred geography established during Monte Albán I still retained social significance in Monte Albán IIIa.

Overall, noble status and power appear to have been communicated through rather subtle means at this time. The "audience" viewing such signals as tomb ornamentation would have been quite small. The inward-focused layout of elite residences discouraged the public display of individual or familial dignity, a fact emphasized by the lack of architectural elaboration beyond monumentality. Although elite power remained tied to ancestry, and residences were home to both the living and the dead, residential architecture did not supply a public forum for the expression of power during Monte Albán IIIa.

Elite Residences and the Changing Face of Power at Monte Albán: Monte Albán IIIb–IV

The Monte Albán IIIb–IV phase (A.D. 500–800)[4] encompasses the florescence of Monte Albán (Blanton 1978; Kowalewski et al. 1989; Lind and Urcid 1983; Martínez et al. 2000). Elite residential architecture during this 300-year span demonstrates what we believe to be a qualitative shift from preceding eras, stemming from changing conceptions of power. These changes are visible in the spatial organization of a few elite residences in which ritual spaces tied to ancestry were architecturally formalized. Changes in architectural elaboration included increased embellishment of tombs and expressions of ancestry in more visible aboveground settings. New patterns in the locale of residences further demonstrated an emerging reconceptualization of power and its representation (Joyce 2003).

While the spatial organization of most Monte Albán IIIb–IV elite residences at Monte Albán and surrounding sites followed the Monte Albán IIIa pattern, three notable exceptions stand out. The first is the Tomb 7 Residence (Martínez 2002). At some point during Monte Albán IIIb–IV, a two-room temple with columns in each doorway was constructed on the west side of the patio above the residence's large tomb. Two-room temples, such as that constructed at the Tomb 7 Residence, had been built in public contexts in the Valley of Oaxaca since Monte Albán II. The Tomb 7 temple, however, was the first and only such building to be constructed within a residence at Monte Albán. The size of the audience that could have witnessed and participated in events at the Tomb 7 temple was considerably smaller than audiences for events occurring in two-room temples located on Monte Albán's Main Plaza. The residence retained its enclosed layout, and the interior patio was only 10 × 6 m. Yet the melding of a traditionally public architectural form with a domicile in Monte Albán IIIb–IV demonstrates a clear shift in the organization of elite domestic space from previous periods.

Residences on Mounds 190 and 195 at the site of Lambityeco on the valley floor reiterate this shift. Both structures have been described in detail elsewhere (see Lind 2001; Lind and Urcid 1983, 1990), but several aspects of these residences merit discussion here. The Mound 190 residence (Structure 190-4) consisted of two connected patios enclosed by rooms (Lind and Urcid 1990). The entry patio on the west lacked a subpatio tomb. The more secluded eastern patio, however, had a small temple on its western side and a tomb on its eastern side. The façade of the temple was renovated at least once, and in its best-preserved iteration (dating to A.D. 650–700), it consisted of stucco sculptures depicting Cocijo holding symbols of lightning and rain. The spatial organization of the Mound 190 residence, like that of the Tomb 7 Residence, encompassed formal ritual space of a type that was found only in public contexts prior to Monte Albán IIIb–IV. The Mound 195 residence was considerably more elaborate and consisted of six superimposed residences spanning the years A.D. 600–750 (Lind 2001; Lind and Urcid 1983). In its earliest phases, the Mound 195 residence followed the standard Classic-period pattern of rooms enclosing a patio, with a tomb beneath the room opposite the entrance (Lind 2001). The third incarnation of the Mound 195 residence (Structure 195-4, A.D. 640 ± 100), however, broke from this pattern with the construction of a second, connected enclosed patio immediately to the north (Lind 2001). In addition, a raised bench or altar was built above the tomb in the east room of the original patio (Lind 2001:119).

The fourth version of Structure 195 (195-3, A.D. 690 ± 100; Figure 8.5) further developed the link between the east room of the south patio and the individuals interred in the tomb (Lind 2001). A large area of the south patio was remodeled to create a large "altar complex" along the eastern portion of the patio: several rooms were filled in, and a tripartite altar was placed just at the eastern edge of the patio (Lind 2001). The altar and the wall behind it were adorned with stucco panels depicting the faces and names of at least six individuals (Lind 2001; Lind and Urcid 1983; Miller 1995). The men were all depicted holding a human femur in their right hand, a symbol of rulership (Lind and Urcid 1983). The two-chambered tomb beneath this "altar" contained the remains of six individuals, both male and female (Lind and Urcid 1983:81). Javier Urcid (personal communication, 2001) suggests that the area had several uses, including as a throne, as an altar or table for offerings, and as a mausoleum with a genealogical record. The south patio of the Mound 195 residence had become a formal location for practices reiterating the ancestry, sacredness, and power of individuals from a particular domestic group. Whether these practices were public or semipublic is unclear, given the small size of the residential patio. By the final phase of occupation, however, public activities tied to the residence's inhabitants were certainly under way. Mound 195-1 (A.D. 730 ± 100) was attached to a civic-ceremonial building on the east side of a large public plaza. The inhabitants of the final residence on Mound 195 were living in a public building: a residential structure that incorporated highly public ceremonial space.

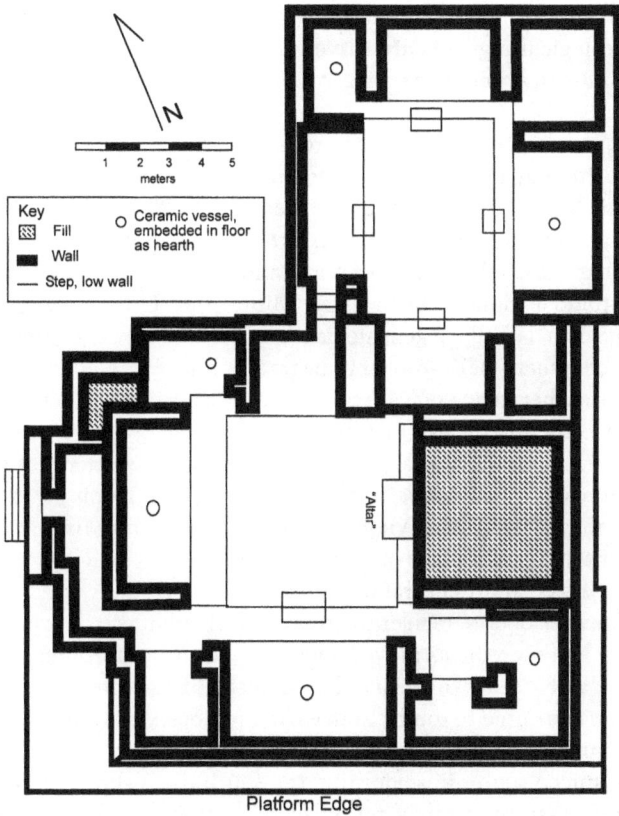

FIGURE 8.5 Structure 195-3, Lambityeco. Redrawn from Lind 2001.

Elite residences also became increasingly elaborate during the Monte Albán IIIb–IV phase. Much of this elaboration occurred underground, where elites built numerous large and ornate tombs. Across Monte Albán, tombs proliferated: 88 of the site's 214 tombs (41%) have been securely dated to Monte Albán IIIb–IV. Other tombs, such as Tombs 7, 104, and 105, were built earlier but experienced continued use into this period (Miller 1995). Indeed, tombs from this time period at Monte Albán and other sites in the valley demonstrate ongoing use—with later burials, reentry, and repainting clearly in evidence (Miller 1995). Funerary iconography from tombs at Monte Albán and other valley sites also provided a fuller expression of the genealogy-ancestry theme first articulated in late Monte Albán IIIa tombs like 103 and 104 (Marcus 1983b). The murals of Tomb 105, which were repainted at least once and probably more, depicted the ancestors related to the interred individual (Marcus 1983b). Marcus (1983b:191) sees these murals as a precursor to the "genealogical registers" found in Monte Albán IIIb–IV tomb art at other sites in the Valley of Oaxaca, such as Tomb 5 at Suchilquitongo in the Etla arm. Genealogical registers are carved monuments found in Monte Albán IIIb–IV tombs that detail the ancestry of one or more individuals (Marcus 1992:283–284).

Suchilquitongo Tomb 5 was extraordinarily ornate, with iconographic elements that included 10 bas-relief doorjambs, two modeled-stucco lintels, 17 murals, one carved stela (the "genealogical register"), and several other incised and painted glyphs (Miller 1995; Urcid 1992a). A cruciform antechamber mirrored the enclosed patio floor plan of elite residences and literally made the tomb a "house" for the dead (Miller 1995; Urcid 1992a). The doorjambs appear to describe a genealogical sequence, whereas the stela—set in the tomb chamber itself—probably bears the image of a conjugal pair and is similar to other genealogical registers (Marcus 1983a; Miller 1995; Urcid 1992a). Ancestry and the association between genealogy and domesticity are emphasized in both the spatial plan and the decorative elements of Tomb 5 to a degree previously unknown in the Valley of Oaxaca. Tomb 5 was an elaborate home for the dead, glorifying the power of a particular lineage and tying that power to a certain place on the landscape.

In most cases, architectural ornamentation remained within the highly restricted spaces of elite residential tombs. At Lambityeco, however, images of ancestry and sacredness moved aboveground to adorn rooms at both the Mound 190 and Mound 195 residences. In residential contexts, depictions of Cocijo were restricted to tombs from earlier periods. At Mound 190, this traditional tomb imagery was materialized aboveground. In the case of Mound 195-3, the stucco sculptures adorning the south patio altar presented genealogical information strongly reminiscent of that found in Monte Albán IIIb–IV tombs across the valley (Lind and Urcid 1983). In this instance, however, ancestral power became publicly materialized in a space that would have been accessible to groups beyond the household itself. Although still restricted, these images of ancestors and supernaturals were far more public and explicit than tomb art. The architectural sculptures of both residences would have served as a frame of reference for the activities of certain individuals in a household, placing them within specific genealogical and supernatural contexts.

The locale of elite residences presented a further change from previous eras. At Monte Albán, several new residences were constructed on or near the southern end of the Main Plaza, violating the sacred geography of earlier eras (Figure 8.6; Joyce 2003). Excavations by the PEMA uncovered 11 Monte Albán IIIb–IV residences near the southwest corner of the South Platform (Winter et al. 1997). Only three of these residences were occupied at any one time. A large residence was also constructed on the southeastern side of the Main Plaza, just north of the South Platform. Known as the Palacio, Plataforma Este, or Building S, this residence is set on a high substructural platform and lacks a tomb (Figure 8.7). Two smaller residences flank

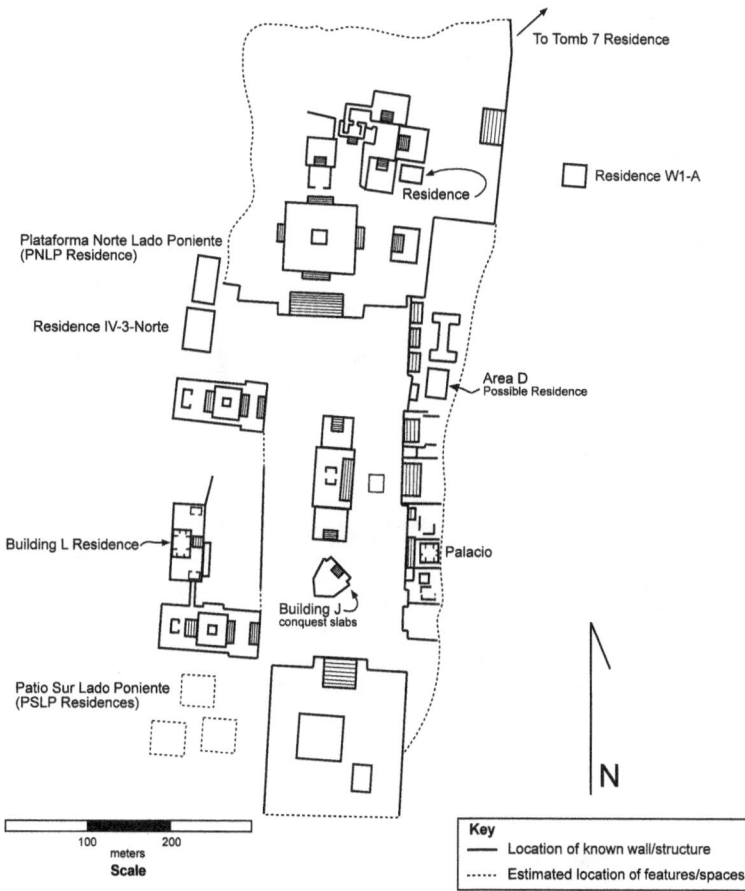

FIGURE 8.6 Main Plaza, Monte Albán IIIb–IV (A.D. 500–800)

the Palacio on its north and south sides, creating a multipatio residential group. The Palacio's patio measures nearly 10 m on a side, and the external walls measure 26 (N–S) × 22 m (E–W; Winter 1974). Another large residence was set on the substructural platform of Building L directly across the Main Plaza from the Palacio (Peeler 1994). Its patio measures approximately 5 to 7 m per side, and its external walls are approximately 17 to 18 m per side (Peeler 1994:N16E26). Building L was built in Monte Albán I as a public building and was adorned with images of sacrificial victims, better known as the Danzantes Gallery. It retained its public use through various renovations in Monte Albán II and IIIa. Both the Palacio and the Building L residence are in very public locations: they open onto the Main Plaza itself, they are set on elevated platforms, and one (Building L) is located above a structure that was previously public and ceremonial in use.

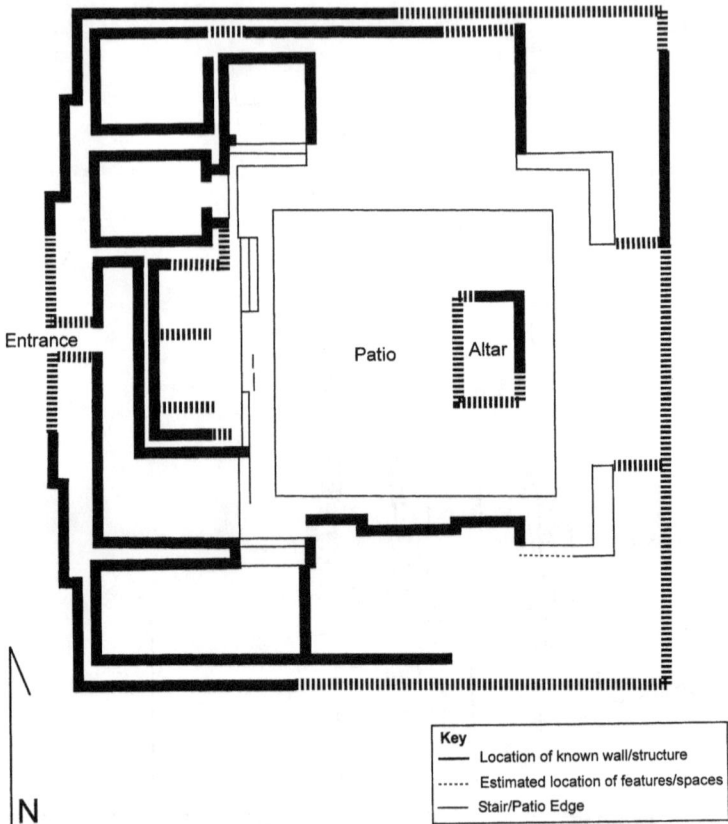

FIGURE 8.7 Plan view, the Palacio, Monte Albán IIIb–IV. Redrawn from Caso, Bernal, and Acosta 1967.

Monte Albán IIIb–IV elite residences reveal an emerging conceptualization of power as more individualized, exclusive, and explicit. The spatial organization of the Tomb 7 Residence and the two Lambityeco residences suggests a conflation of public social roles with particular kin groups. In a sense, corporate practices tied to the state were being domesticated—brought under the control of certain lineages. A budding connection between some state activities and particular kin groups would also have served to make those activities more exclusive. Both the participants in, and the witnesses to, activities in domestic ceremonial contexts were necessarily smaller than those in public ceremonial spaces. The increasing importance of ancestry as a source of power was emphasized in the proliferation of tombs and in elites' heavy investment in elaborate tomb art depicting genealogy. Elites also began to materialize their powerful ancestry more explicitly with embellishments such as the Mound 190 Cocijo sculptures and the Mound

195-3 residential altar. In both cases, powerful imagery that—in residential contexts—had once been limited to the highly restricted spaces of tombs began to appear aboveground. Elites were more openly signaling the sources of their power, a power that was exclusive and individualized because it was due to a specific genealogy. A break with earlier periods was also manifested by the increased number of residences on the southern end of Monte Albán's South Platform. The sacred geography that originally shaped Monte Albán's spatial layout may have been altered at this time (Joyce 2003). Overall, some elite residences of Monte Albán IIIb–IV began to resemble palaces: the Tomb 7 Residence incorporated a temple type previously associated with public facilities; the Mound 190 residence also contained a specialized and elaborate ritual space; and the Mound 195-3 residence had a throne/altar surrounded by symbols of nobility and ancestry. By the middle of the eighth century, the Mound 195 residence was a palace—a domestic public structure.

The Public Display of Exclusive Power: Monte Albán V

Elite residential architecture from the Valley of Oaxaca's Late Postclassic period (A.D. 1250–1521) demonstrates an entrenchment and elaboration of the individualized and exclusive power first manifested in Monte Albán IIIb–IV. The enclosed-patio residence remained the basic form for elite residential architecture even into this late period. Many elite residences—such as those at Yagul (Bernal and Gamio 1974) and Mitla (Miller 1995; Robles 1986)—were built along the lines of Lambityeco Structure 195, with patio groups connected by narrow passageways. The Palace of the Six Patios at Yagul (Bernal and Gamio 1974) represents an extreme form of this architectural plan.

By Monte Albán V, the distinctions between public and domestic space had become blurred at several elite residences. Monumental architecture at Yagul and Mitla explicitly combined residential and public functions into one structure. The Palace of the Six Patios at Yagul, a monumental residence consisting of five intricately connected residential patios and a sixth public patio, provides a clear example. Just below the Palace, to the south, are Yagul's ballcourt and a ceremonial precinct (Bernal and Gamio 1974:Plano 1). Four long, narrow rooms surrounded each patio. The corner spaces were sealed off and unused. Rooms were elevated above the patio surface and were distinguished by a triple entryway created by dividing each doorway with two pillars (Bernal and Gamio 1974). Many interior walls were stuccoed and painted red. Patios B and E, the middle pair, had low columns surrounding the patio outside the residential rooms (Bernal and Gamio 1974:87). Patio F is of particular interest due to the fact that its south room opened out toward the site's ballcourt (Figure 8.8). Anyone using this room would have been visible from the public ceremonial spaces of the site. A low bench runs along the length of the room's back (north) wall (Bernal and Gamio 1974:56).

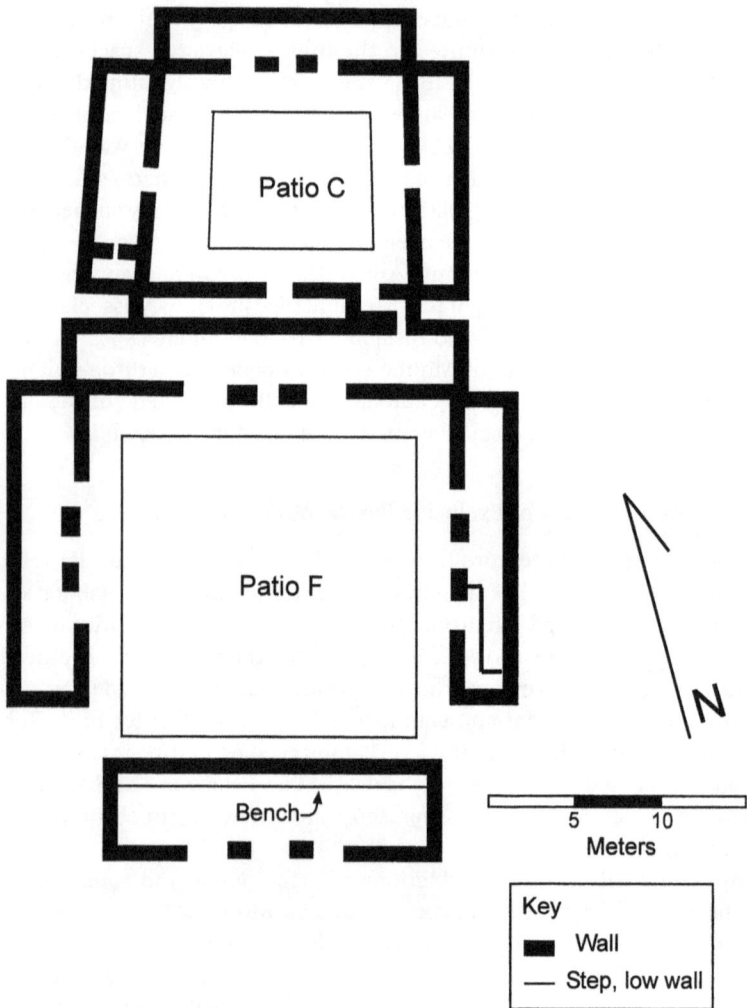

FIGURE 8.8 Plan view of Patios C and F of the Palace of the Six Patios, Yagul. Redrawn from Bernal and Gamio 1974.

Patio F's south room was not connected to the other three rooms of the residence; it was instead constructed slightly farther south than expected for a standard square patio. Its outward orientation and location on a high platform above the ballcourt made it a visible public space closely associated not only with residential architecture but also with ceremonial buildings. The terminal occupation at Yagul was probably during early to middle Monte Albán V, given radiocarbon dates in the thirteenth and fourteenth centuries (Bernal and Gamio 1974:93–94).

At the later site of Mitla, a major Zapotec center into the Colonial period, the tie between residential and public ceremonial space became even more explicit. Although Mitla was occupied as early as the Tierras Largas phase, only its late Monte Albán V architecture has been well documented (Flannery and Marcus 1983b; Miller 1995). Several large, multipatio residential groups similar to Patios C and F at Yagul have been preserved at Mitla since pre-Columbian times. Two Mitla patio groups, the Arroyo Group and the Church Group, consist of three patios surrounded by three or four narrow triple-entry rooms. Both structures have murals painted on the lintels above room entrances (Miller 1995:217; Pohl 1999). John Pohl argues that the murals present historical and mythological narratives that describe the relations of particular lineages with both earthly and divine locations. "Ancestor worship thereby became not only a primary religious concern but also a means of determining class, rank, paramountcy, and titles to elite domains" (Pohl 1999:16). The mural paintings of Mitla's residences, like the earlier stucco sculptures of Lambityeco, provided viewers with a framework for interpreting the social and ideological placement of the individuals who used particular domestic spaces.

The nearby Group of the Columns was a combined residential and public area near the center of the ancient town of Mitla. The group consists of two plazas (approximately 40 m on a side), or large patios, aligned north–south and surrounded by four buildings set on high substructural platforms (Pohl 1999; Robles 1986). Both exterior and interior walls are extensively decorated with the stone mosaics for which Mitla is famous. The southern patio contains two large cruciform tombs, but the northern patio has none. The Hall of the Columns, on the north side of the north patio, is a narrow room with six columns set in a line along its east-west axis (Flannery and Marcus 1983b; Robles 1986). This room provided access, through a narrow passageway, to a domestic patio surrounded by four rooms that is highly reminiscent of Classic-period elite residences. Flannery and Marcus (1983b:296–297), citing the 1580 *Relación de Tlacolula y Mitla* by Juan de Canseco, state that the south patio was the location of government activity and the small patio north of the Hall of the Columns was the residence of a high priest. The Hall of the Columns is a palace: it was a public space fronting a very private residential structure. At least one religious leader at Mitla lived within the bounds of the temple, with access to the residence only possible by passing through the temple itself.

Although detailed information on elite residences in Monte Albán V is fairly limited, the spatial organization, elaboration, and locale of those structures that have been documented demonstrate a crystallization of the processes begun in Monte Albán IIIb–IV. The spatial organization of these residences created and reiterated a permanent connection between residents and particular offices or social roles. The Palace of the Six Patios at Yagul was designed to include a "public" domestic space. The Group of the Columns at Mitla, which was both a temple and a domestic space, formalized the connection between specific people and specific public offices. Beyond monumentality, architectural elaboration at Yagul was limited. Architectural features such as columns were present, as was the use of stucco and red paint, although columns occurred only on interior patios away from the casual viewer. At Mitla, architectural elaboration took multiple forms. The intricate masonry mosaics at the Group of the Columns represented the first preserved outward residential elaboration in the Valley of Oaxaca beyond monumentality. The murals of several Mitla residences contained images explaining and justifying certain domestic groups' privileged position in relation to the sacred, based on ancestry. Finally, elite residences in Monte Albán V are located in very public places. The south room of Patio F at Yagul overlooks the site's ballcourt. Both the Palace of the Six Patios at Yagul and the Group of the Columns at Mitla fall under our definition of a palace. In each case, residential architecture incorporated public or ceremonial space, creating a permanent link between the residents and their public positions. In these cases, power "lived" with its wielders.

Discussion

Diachronic changes in the spatial organization, architectural elaboration, and location of elite residences over time in the Valley of Oaxaca demonstrate shifting representations of power despite an underlying conservatism regarding its sources. We follow Joyce (2000, 2003) in arguing that elite power in the Valley of Oaxaca stemmed in part from the ability of nobles to contact the supernatural world and invoke the sacred covenant between humans and deities. Noble ancestors served as important intermediaries between the living and the supernatural world, providing living elites with more potent means of connecting to the supernatural than commoners. Based on evidence from elite residences, this fundamental understanding regarding sources of power did not change for millennia. Beginning in Monte Albán IIIb–IV, however, elites began to reframe expressions of power to make them more individualized, exclusive, and materially explicit.

The spatial organization of elite residences followed a basic pattern from early in the valley's history. Beginning in the Guadalupe phase, higher-status domestic groups lived in multiple-room residences facing onto a patio. Through time, this pattern became increasingly formalized such that Monte Albán III elite residences were standardized across Monte Albán and the valley in general. Elite residences also revealed a growing emphasis on closed, private spaces (Winter 1974, 1986b). The patios of many Formative-period high-status residences appear to have been open on one or more sides, making the daily activities of elites to some extent visible. This was certainly not the case for most late Monte Albán II and Monte Albán IIIa elite residences, where domestic spaces were very private and inward-focused.

Elite residential patios, though considerably larger than non-elite versions, nonetheless organized space in a similar manner. The same set of residential characteristics found in non-elite residences—subfloor inhumation, enclosed patios, and lack of storage structures or other floor features—were present in elite residences as well. Unlike palaces, elite residences in the Valley of Oaxaca were not designed to hold large audiences. The patio of the Palacio at Monte Albán, for instance, measured only 9.85 m per side, and the entire structure itself was only 25.6 × 21.85 m (Winter 1974:Table 1). Compare that to the contemporary Great Palace at Palenque, which filled a substructural platform of 100 × 80 m (Sharer 1994), or the patio of Court 2 at the Central Acropolis at Tikal, which measured 40 × 25 m (Coe 1980). Zapotec elite residences did not organize space in a way that allowed for the large-scale public expression of individual, lineage-specific power prior to late Monte Albán IIIb–IV.

By the end of the Classic period, however, residential architecture had come to include spaces designed to create a frame of reference for the activities of particular individuals. The south patio of the Structure 195-3 residence at Lambityeco contained an elevated area that may have served as a throne (Lind and Urcid 1983:Figure 3). This patio, though still enclosed and lacking a large open area for public viewing, provided residential space within which an individual or individuals could be situated within a specific genealogical context. By early Monte Albán V, elite residential space had been architecturally "reopened." At Yagul's Palace of the Six Patios, Patio D had only three surrounding structures (Bernal and Gamio 1974). Neither of the southern corners of Patio F was closed off, and the south room of the patio faced outward. With its internal bench, the south room of Patio F provided yet another formal frame within which individuals associated with the residence could be viewed. Unlike Structure 195-3's viewing space, however, the south room of Patio F at Yagul was open and unrestricted. It was set on a high platform above the public ritual space created by the site's ballcourt. Occupants of this room would have been easily visible to a large audience. At Lambityeco's Structure 195-1 and Mitla's Group of the Columns, the residence is fronted by a public building. These residences not only provided a "public" domestic area but also merged the public and the residential into a single structure. Furthermore, the size of the public space at the Group of the Columns is considerably larger than that of earlier residences. Both patios at the Group of the Columns were over 40 m per side, providing ample space for the presence of large groups of people, probably numbering in the hundreds (Bernal 1965).

The growth of more individualized and explicit power was also expressed through architectural elaboration. Through Monte Albán IIIa, monumentality and labor-intensive building techniques provided the primary means of communicating status through architecture. Socially expressive architectural ornamentation—such as carved-stone monuments or murals—was rarely used in residences to express elite power. Only in the secluded context of elite residential tombs did elaborate murals, plasterwork, and stone carving make an appearance. By Monte Albán IIIb–IV this pattern shifts. Although the ornamental plasterwork of Lambityeco Mounds 190 and 195 was still relatively private, it did, nonetheless, appear aboveground. The plaster friezes surrounding the Mound 195-3 south patio altar would have provided important contextual meaning to anyone viewing an individual sitting in that area. The images of named ancestors, coupled with the presence of their bones in the tomb immediately beneath the dais, would have clearly communicated the genealogy—and thus the cosmic connections—of a ruler seated in that place (Javier Urcid, personal communication, 2001). The ruler would literally have been sitting among his ancestors, propped up by their bones.

Mitla's Monte Albán V residential murals and mosaics would also have made explicit the power of elites. Mural paintings remained relatively private, although both the Arroyo and Church Group murals faced onto patios and would have been visible to outsiders entering the more secluded areas of the residence. The theme of these murals remained consistent with that of previous eras: ancestry and its relation to the social and ideological realms. Richly crafted stone mosaics were more public. The mosaics appear on both public and residential structures at Mitla during Monte Albán V, perhaps indicating a breakdown in the distinction between the two types of architectural space. The interior walls of the Hall of the Columns also bear extensive mosaic designs. Thus, these geometric images had associations with both ritual and elite domestic space.

Zapotec elites also relied on locale to advertise their distinguished position. As early as the Middle Formative Rosario phase, elite residences in the Valley of Oaxaca were constructed on or near public ritual spaces. With the founding of Monte Albán in the Late Formative, the spatial tie between elites and sacred space became more formalized. Joyce (2000, 2003) argues that the plan of Monte Albán's ceremonial core represented an expression of the sacred covenant made material through the organization of space. The concentration of elite residences on and around the North Platform helped to create the sacred geography of Monte Albán by connecting elites and their ancestors to the north. The celestial and genealogical themes of elite residential tomb art contrasted with the militaristic images from the South Platform and southern portion of the Main Plaza (Joyce 2000, 2003; Marcus 1983b; Urcid 1992b). The southern monuments depicted bound captives, elite individuals holding weapons, sacrificial victims, and military victories. Sacrifice and militarism were publicly displayed, whereas elite ancestry and the power it provided were only expressed in secluded, private contexts. The placement of elite residences in and around the North Platform also served to emphasize seclusion and privacy. The large North Platform residences from Monte Albán II and IIIa, especially El Ocote and the North Mound complexes, were separated from the Main Plaza by a number of monumental constructions.

Again, this pattern broke down during Monte Albán IIIb–IV (Joyce 2003). At Monte Albán, a number of elite residences were constructed south of the North Platform. Most notably, the very large residences of the Palacio and Building L were constructed directly on the Main Plaza, on elevated substructural platforms along the southern end of the Main Plaza. These buildings were set in public locations, a fact emphasized by their elevation above the level of the Main Plaza itself. Situated toward the south end of the Main Plaza, they are discordant with the sacred geography created in previous eras. The same sacred geography of Monte Albán does not appear to have existed at later sites, either. Neither Yagul nor Mitla has a formal ceremonial space similar in form or size to Monte Albán's Main Plaza. The organizing principle of Monte Albán's sacred geography may have been transformed toward the end of the site's occupation. And it certainly was not present in the same way in later times.

Conclusions

In concluding, we return to our original distinction between a house and a palace. We argue that for most of the Valley of Oaxaca's history, elites did not construct palaces in our sense of the word. Elite residences prior to Monte Albán IIIb–IV lacked public or semipublic audience rooms. Zapotec elite residences never included the massive storage areas found in the palaces of Crete (Flannery 1998; Soles 1991) and at Chan Chan, Peru (Moseley and Day 1982). Architectural elaboration was never employed by Zapotec elites the way it was in other parts of Mesoamerica. The ornate stone carvings found on the exteriors of Classic-period Maya palaces at Palenque and Copán, for instance, have no parallel in the Valley of Oaxaca. The exclusionary connection between individuals and social or political power so evident in the multipurpose palace does not appear until late Monte Albán IIIb–IV with Structure 195-1 at Lambityeco. Truly multipurpose palaces were only fully present in Monte Albán V, at Yagul and Mitla.

The architectural data indicate a major shift during Monte Albán IIIb–IV in the way elites chose to express and emphasize their social position. Prior to that time, elite residential architecture demonstrated elite power and status through characteristics such as locale, structure size, and highly restricted spaces. Zapotec elites did not undertake the blatant public advertisement of individual and familial status so common in the elite residences of other early states. Instead, spatial organization followed the format used by the rest of the population; depictions of elite power were restricted to subterranean contexts; and elite separateness was communicated through privacy, seclusion, and location. Beginning in Monte Albán IIIb–IV, however, the communication of elite status through architecture became more explicit. Residential floor plans began to include spaces for the public presentation of an individual. The "altar complex" at Lambityeco and the south room of Patio F at Yagul both provided a frame for the carefully staged presentation of noble individuals. Architectural ornamentation in residential patios also began to depict the exclusive genealogical ties that would have provided such individuals with their power. These depictions, though still somewhat private, were present on the walls of rooms facing domestic patios. Residential location also made explicit the connection between ceremonial spaces and particular kin groups. The construction of two large residences directly on the Main Plaza of Monte Albán, for instance, placed specific domestic groups in close and public association with civic space. This configuration continued through Monte Albán V at Yagul and Mitla, where residential space was clearly visible or connected to public space.

The foundation of elite power, namely elites' special connection to the sacred and to noble ancestors, did not change in its fundamentals for nearly 2,000 years. Over time, however, the way in which elites represented their power shifted from the communal to the individual or familial. This was reflected in the construction of palaces by the end of Monte Albán IIIb–IV. At this time, elites' expressions of power became more explicitly connected to specific ancestry. Elites began to publicize their differences from the mass of the population through changes in the spatial organization, architectural elaboration, and location of their residences. By the Late Postclassic period, the connection between elite individuals and the public functioning of the polity had become architecturally formalized through the presence of palaces that demonstrated qualitative differences from non-elite residences.

Acknowledgments

We would like to thank the editors, Jessica Christie and Patricia Sarro, for asking us to participate in this volume. We are also indebted to Marc Levine and Christine Ward for their assistance in preparing the figures. Many thanks to Marcus Winter and Cira Martínez López for reading this manuscript and for sharing their knowledge of archaeological research in the Valley of Oaxaca.

Notes

1. Two structures originally believed to have been high-status residences, Structure 16 from San José Mogote and Structure 11 from Tomaltepec, are now viewed as "special-purpose" buildings (Flannery and Marcus 1994:362–363).

2. Six Monte Albán I adobe tombs were excavated from residential terraces at Yagul, although there is no information on the associated residences, which presumably were high-status (Chadwick 1966). A burial from Abasolo with jade and 21 ceramic vessels as offerings is also presumably from a high-status residence (Marcus and Flannery 1996:170).

3. Since this chapter went to press, Charles Spencer and Elsa Redmond (2004) have published a more detailed description of Structure 7 and associated features. They refer to the entire complex as the "Area I Palace." Although Spencer and Redmond distinguish between residences and palaces, they focus on different criteria than we do here. Their findings indicate that some of the architectural features we define here as palatial have much earlier antecedents than previously suspected.

4. Although these phase names were originally designed to represent two archaeological time periods—the Late Classic (IIIb) and Postclassic (IV)—most archaeologists working in the Valley of Oaxaca have combined these two phases together due to a lack of distinguishing characteristics for the Early Postclassic ceramic assemblage in the region (Martínez et al. 2000:2–5). The material remains of the Early Postclassic period, what is today called the Liobaa phase (Muzgo 2000), are still poorly defined. For this reason, we follow our discussion of residences from Monte Albán IIIb–IV with a discussion of Late Postclassic Monte Albán V residences without specific reference to the Early Postclassic period.

References Cited

Abrams, Elliot M.
1994 *How the Maya Built Their World: Energetics and Ancient Architecture.* University of Texas Press, Austin.
Acosta, Jorge R.
1959 Exploraciones arqueológicas en Monte Albán, XVIIIa Temporada (1958). *Revista Mexicana de Estudios Antropológicos* 15:7–50.
Andrews, E. Wyllys, and Barbara W. Fash
1992 Continuity and Change in a Royal Maya Residential Complex at Copán. *Ancient Mesoamerica* 3:63–88.
Ashmore, Wendy
1991 Site-Planning Principles and Concepts of Directionality among the Ancient Maya. *Latin American Antiquity* 2:199–226.
1992 Deciphering Maya Architectural Plans. In *New Theories on the Ancient Maya*, edited by Elin C. Danien and Robert J. Sharer, pp. 173–184. University Museum Symposium Series, Vol. 3. University Museum of the University of Pennsylvania, Philadelphia.
Bachelard, Gaston
1969 *The Poetics of Space.* Beacon Press, Boston.
Bernal, Ignacio
1965 Architecture in Oaxaca after the End of Monte Albán. In *Handbook of Middle American Indians*, Vol. 3, *Archaeology of Southern Mesoamerica*, Part 2, edited by Robert Wauchope and Gordon R. Willey, pp. 837–848. University of Texas Press, Austin.
Bernal, Ignacio, and Lorenzo Gamio
1974 *Yagul: El Palacio de los Seis Patios.* Universidad Nacional Autónoma de México, Mexico City.
Birdwell-Pheasant, Donna, and Denise Lawrence-Zúñiga
1999 Introduction: Houses and Families in Europe. In *House Life: Space, Place and Family in Europe*, edited by Donna Birdwell-Pheasant and Denise Lawrence-Zúñiga, pp. 1–35. Berg, Oxford.

Blanton, Richard E.
1978 *Monte Albán: Settlement Patterns at the Ancient Zapotec Capital.*
      Academic Press, New York.
1993 *Ancient Mesoamerica: A Comparison of Change in Three Regions.*
      2nd ed. Cambridge University Press, Cambridge.
1994 *Houses and Households: A Comparative Study.* Plenum Press, New
      York.
Blanton, Richard E., Gary M. Feinman, Stephen A. Kowalewski, and
Linda M. Nicholas
1999 *Ancient Oaxaca.* Cambridge University Press, Cambridge.
Boone, Elizabeth H. (editor)
1984 *Ritual Human Sacrifice in Mesoamerica.* Dumbarton Oaks Research
      Library and Collection, Washington, DC.
Bourdieu, Pierre
1977 *Outline of a Theory of Practice.* Cambridge Studies in Social Anthro-
      pology 16. Cambridge University Press, Cambridge.
Caso, Alfonso
1932 *Las exploraciones en Monte Albán, Temporada 1931-1932.* Publica-
      ción No. 7. Instituto Panamericano de Geografía e Historia, Mexico
      City.
1935 *Las exploraciones en Monte Albán, Temporada 1934-1935.* Publica-
      ción No. 18. Instituto Panamericano de Geografía e Historia, Mexico
      City.
1938 *Exploraciones en Oaxaca, quinta y sexta temporadas, 1936-1937.*
      Publicación No. 34. Instituto Panamericano de Geografía e Historia,
      Mexico City.
Caso, Alfonso, Ignacio Bernal, and Jorge R. Acosta
1967 *La cerámica de Monte Albán.* Memorias del Instituto Nacional de
      Antropología e Historia, Vol. 13. Instituto Nacional de Antropología
      e Historia, Mexico City.
Chadwick, Robert
1966 The Tombs of Monte Albán I Style at Yagul. In *Ancient Oaxaca:
      Discoveries in Mexican Archaeology and History,* edited by John
      Paddock, pp. 245-255. Stanford University Press, Stanford.
Clark, John E.
2001 Olmec Supernaturals and Scholarly Muddles: Gods, Totems, Cults, or
      Clans? Paper presented at the 66th Annual Meeting of the Society for
      American Archaeology, New Orleans.
Clark, John E., and Michael Blake
1994 The Power of Prestige: Competitive Generosity and the Emergence of
      Rank in Lowland Mesoamerica. In *Factional Competition and Politi-
      cal Development in the New World,* edited by Elizabeth Brumfiel and
      John Fox, pp. 17-30. Cambridge University Press, Cambridge.
Cliff, Maynard B.
1988 Domestic Architecture and Origins of Complex Society at Cerros.
      In *Household and Community in the Mesoamerican Past,* edited
      by Richard R. Wilk and Wendy Ashmore, pp. 199-226. University of
      New Mexico Press, Albuquerque.

Coe, William R.
1980 *Tikal: A Handbook of the Ancient Maya Ruins*. Piedra Santa, Guatemala City.
Dietler, Michael, and Brian Hayden (editors)
2001 *Feasts: Archaeological and Ethnographic Perspectives on Food, Politics, and Power*. Smithsonian Institution Press, Washington, DC.
Drennan, Robert D.
1976 Fábrica San José and Middle Formative Society in the Valley of Oaxaca. In *Prehistory and Human Ecology of the Valley of Oaxaca*. Memoirs of the Museum of Anthropology, Vol. 4. University of Michigan, Ann Arbor.
Drennan, Robert D., and Kent V. Flannery
1983 The Growth of Site Hierarchies in the Valley of Oaxaca: Part II. In *The Cloud People: Divergent Evolution of the Zapotec and Mixtec Civilizations*, edited by Kent V. Flannery and Joyce Marcus, pp. 65–71. Academic Press, New York.
Elson, Christina M.
2001 *Excavations at Los Mogotes, San Martín Tilcajete, Oaxaca: A Terminal Formative Subregional Center in the Valley of Oaxaca*. Grant report submitted to the Foundation for Mesoamerican Studies. http://www.famsi.org/reports/99055/index.html.
2003 Elites at Cerro Tilcajete: A Secondary Center in the Valley of Oaxaca, Mexico. Unpublished Ph.D. dissertation, University of Michigan, Ann Arbor.
Evans, Susan, and J. Pillsbury (editors)
2004 *Palaces of the Ancient New World*. Dumbarton Oaks Research Library and Collection, Washington, DC.
Fash, William L.
1993 *Scribes, Warriors, and Kings*. Thames and Hudson, London.
Flannery, Kent V.
1976 The Early Mesoamerican House. In *The Early Mesoamerican Village*, edited by Kent V. Flannery, pp. 16–24. Academic Press, New York.
1983a The Legacy of the Early Urban Period: An Ethnohistoric Approach to Monte Albán's Temples, Residences, and Royal Tombs. In *The Cloud People: Divergent Evolution of the Zapotec and Mixtec Civilizations*, edited by Kent V. Flannery and Joyce Marcus, pp. 132–136. Academic Press, New York.
1983b Major Monte Albán V Sites: Zaachila, Xoxocotlán, Cuilapan, Yagul, and Abasolo. In *The Cloud People: Divergent Evolution of the Zapotec and Mixtec Civilizations*, edited by Kent V. Flannery and Joyce Marcus, pp. 290–295. Academic Press, New York.
1998 The Ground Plans of Archaic States. In *Archaic States*, edited by Gary M. Feinman and Joyce Marcus, pp. 15–57. School of American Research Press, Santa Fe, NM.
Flannery, Kent V. (editor)
1976 *The Early Mesoamerican Village*. Academic Press, New York.
Flannery, Kent V., and Joyce Marcus
1976 Formative Oaxaca and the Zapotec Cosmos. *American Scientist* 64:374–383.

1983a The Growth of Site Hierarchies in the Valley of Oaxaca: Part I. In *The Cloud People: Divergent Evolution of the Zapotec and Mixtec Civilizations*, edited by Kent V. Flannery and Joyce Marcus, pp. 53–64. Academic Press, New York.

1983b Urban Mitla and Its Rural Hinterland. In *The Cloud People: Divergent Evolution of the Zapotec and Mixtec Civilizations*, edited by Kent V. Flannery and Joyce Marcus, pp. 295–300. Academic Press, New York.

1994 Early Formative Pottery of the Valley of Oaxaca, Mexico. In *Prehistory and Human Ecology of the Valley of Oaxaca*. Memoirs of the Museum of Anthropology, Vol. 10. University of Michigan, Ann Arbor.

Flannery, Kent V., and Joyce Marcus (editors)

1983 *The Cloud People: Divergent Evolution of the Zapotec and Mixtec Civilizations*. Academic Press, New York.

Foucault, Michel

1995 *Discipline and Punish: The Birth of the Prison.* 2nd ed. Vintage Books, New York.

Geertz, Clifford

1973 *The Interpretation of Cultures.* Basic Books, New York.

Gillespie, Susan D.

2000a Beyond Kinship: An Introduction. In *Beyond Kinship: Social and Material Reproduction in House Societies*, edited by Rosemary Joyce and Susan D. Gillespie, pp. 1–21. University of Pennsylvania Press, Philadelphia.

2000b Maya "Nested Houses." In *Beyond Kinship: Social and Material Reproduction in House Societies*, edited by Rosemary Joyce and Susan D. Gillespie, pp. 135–160. University of Pennsylvania Press, Philadelphia.

Gutman, Robert

1976 The Social Function of the Built Environment. In *The Mutual Interaction of People and Their Built Environment: A Cross-Cultural Perspective*, edited by Amos Rapoport, pp. 37–50. Mouton Publishers, The Hague.

Houston, Stephen D.

1998 Classic Maya Depictions of the Built Environment. In *Function and Meaning in Classic Maya Architecture*, edited by Stephen D. Houston, pp. 333–372. Dumbarton Oaks Research Library and Collection, Washington, DC.

Inomata, Takeshi, and Stephen Houston (editors)

2001 *Royal Courts of the Ancient Maya.* Westview Press, Boulder, CO.

Iyer, Pico

1993 The Potala, Tibet. In *Living in a Dream: Great Residences of the World*, edited by Janet Gleeson, Fiona Keating, and Allison Macfarlane, pp. 134–161. Simon and Schuster, New York.

Joyce, Arthur A.

2000 The Founding of Monte Albán: Sacred Propositions and Social Practices. In *Agency in Archaeology*, edited by Marcia-Ann Dobres and John Robb, pp. 71–91. Routledge, London.

2003 Sacred Space and Social Relations in the Valley of Oaxaca. In *Mesoamerican Archaeology*, edited by Julia A. Hendon and Rosemary Joyce, pp. 192–216. Blackwell, Oxford.

Joyce, Arthur A., and Marcus Winter
1996 Ideology, Power, and Urban Society in Pre-Hispanic Oaxaca. *Current Anthropology* 37:33–86.

Kent, Susan (editor)
1990 *Domestic Architecture and the Use of Space.* Cambridge University Press, New York.

King, Mark B.
1988 Mixtec Political Ideology: Historical Metaphors and the Poetics of Political Symbolism. Unpublished Ph.D. dissertation, University of Michigan, Ann Arbor.

Klingensmith, Samuel John
1993 *The Utility of Splendor: Ceremony, Social Life, and Architecture at the Court of Bavaria, 1600–1800.* Edited by Christian F. Otto and Mark Ashton. University of Chicago Press, Chicago.

Knapp, Ronald G.
1999 *China's Living Houses: Folk Beliefs, Symbols, and Household Ornamentation.* University of Hawaii Press, Honolulu.

Kowalewski, Stephen A., Gary M. Feinman, Laura Finsten, Richard E. Blanton, and Linda M. Nicholas
1989 *Monte Albán's Hinterland, Part II: Prehispanic Settlement Patterns in Tlacolula, Etla, and Ocotlán, the Valley of Oaxaca, Mexico.* Memoirs of the Museum of Anthropology, Vol. 23. University of Michigan, Ann Arbor.

Kowalski, Jeff Karl
1999 *Mesoamerican Architecture as a Cultural Symbol.* Oxford University Press, New York.

Lind, Michael D.
2001 Lambityeco and the Xoo Phase (ca. A.D. 600–800): The Elite Residences of Mound 195. In *Memoria de la Primera Mesa Redonda de Monte Albán: Procesos de cambio y conceptualización del tiempo*, edited by Nelly M. Robles García, pp. 113–128. Instituto Nacional de Antropología e Historia, Mexico City.

Lind, Michael D., and Javier Urcid Serrano
1983 The Lords of Lambityeco and Their Nearest Neighbors. *Notas Mesoamericanas* 9:78–111.
1990 La zona arqueológica de Lambityeco. In *Lecturas históricas del Estado de Oaxaca*, edited by Marcus Winter, pp. 287–307. Época prehispánica, Vol. 1. Instituto Nacional de Antropología e Historia, Oaxaca City.

Marcus, Joyce
1983a Changing Patterns of Stone Monuments after the Fall of Monte Albán, A.D. 600–900. In *The Cloud People: Divergent Evolution of the Zapotec and Mixtec Civilizations*, edited by Kent V. Flannery and Joyce Marcus, pp. 191–197. Academic Press, New York.
1983b Stone Monuments and Tomb Murals of Monte Albán IIIa. In *The Cloud People: Divergent Evolution of the Zapotec and Mixtec Civili-*

zations, edited by Kent V. Flannery and Joyce Marcus, pp. 137–143. Academic Press, New York.

1992 *Mesoamerican Writing Systems: Propaganda, Myth, and History in Four Ancient Civilizations*. Princeton University Press, Princeton.

Marcus, Joyce, and Kent V. Flannery

1996 *Zapotec Civilization: How Urban Society Evolved in Mexico's Oaxaca Valley*. Thames and Hudson, New York.

Martínez López, Cira

2002 La residencia de la tumba 7 y su templo: Elementos arquitectónico-religiosos en Monte Albán. In *La religión de los Binnigulasa*, edited by V. de la Cruz and Marcus Winter, pp. 219–272. IEEPO-IOC, Oaxaca City.

Martínez López, Cira, Robert Markens, Marcus Winter, and Michael D. Lind

2000 *Cerámica de la Fase Xoo (Época Monte Albán IIIB–IV) del Valle de Oaxaca*. Contribución No. 8 del Proyecto Especial Monte Albán 1992–1994. Centro INAH Oaxaca, Oaxaca City.

Martínez López, Cira, Marcus Winter, and Pedro Antonio Juárez

1995 Entierros humanos del Proyecto Especial Monte Albán 1992–1994. In *Entierros humanos de Monte Albán: Dos estudios*, edited by Marcus Winter, pp. 2–10. Contribución No. 7 del Proyecto Especial Monte Albán 1992–1994. Centro INAH Oaxaca, Oaxaca City.

Masson, Marilyn A.

2001 El sobrenatural Cocijo y poder de linaje en la antigua sociedad zapoteca. *Mesoamérica* 40:1–30.

Miller, Arthur G.

1995 *The Painted Tombs of Oaxaca, Mexico: Living with the Dead*. Cambridge University Press, Cambridge.

Miller, Mary

1998 A Design for Meaning in Maya Architecture. In *Function and Meaning in Classic Maya Architecture*, edited by Stephen D. Houston, pp. 187–222. Dumbarton Oaks Research Library and Collection, Washington, DC.

Monaghan, John

1994 Sacrifice and Power in Mixtec Kingdoms. Paper presented at the 59th Annual Meeting of the Society for American Archaeology, Anaheim, CA.

2000 Theology and History in the Study of Mesoamerican Religions. In *Supplement to the Handbook of Middle American Indians*, Vol. 6, *Ethnology*, edited by Victoria Reifler Bricker and John D. Monaghan. University of Texas Press, Austin.

Morales, Claudia, Cira Martínez López, and Marcus Winter

1999 Area W residencias. In *Exploraciones en el Area W al este de la Plataforma Norte*, edited by Marcus Winter. Contribución No. 9 del Proyecto Especial Monte Albán 1992–1994. Centro INAH Oaxaca, Oaxaca City.

Moseley, Michael E., and Kent C. Day

1982 *Chan Chan, Andean Desert City*. School of American Research Advanced Seminar Series. School of American Research, Santa Fe, NM.

Muzgo Torres, Alicia Herrera
2000 Apéndice G: Algunas categorías cerámicas de la Fase Liobaa. In *Cerámica de la Fase Xoo (Época Monte Albán IIIB–IV) del Valle de Oaxaca*, edited by Cira Martínez López, Robert Markens, Marcus Winter, and Michael D. Lind, pp. 299–312. Contribución No. 8 del Proyecto Especial Monte Albán 1992–1994. Centro INAH Oaxaca, Oaxaca.

Oliver, Paul
1987 *Dwellings: The House across the World*. University of Texas Press, Austin.

Peeler, Damon E.
1994 *Mapa de Monte Albán*. Contribución No. 6 del Proyecto Especial Monte Albán 1992–1994. Centro INAH Oaxaca, Oaxaca City.

Pohl, John
1999 The Lintel Paintings of Mitla. In *Mesoamerican Architecture as a Cultural Symbol*, edited by Jeff Karl Kowalski. Oxford University Press, New York.

Pyne, Nanette M.
1976 The Fire-Serpent and Were-Jaguar in Formative Oaxaca: A Contingency Table Analysis. In *The Early Mesoamerican Village*, edited by Kent V. Flannery, pp. 272–279. Academic Press, New York.

Rapoport, Amos
1969 *House Form and Culture*. Foundations of Cultural Geography. Prentice-Hall, Englewood Cliffs, NJ.
1982 *The Meaning of the Built Environment*. Sage, London.

Rapoport, Amos (editor)
1976 *The Mutual Interaction of People and Their Built Environment: A Cross-Cultural Perspective*. Mouton Publishers, The Hague.

Redmond, Elsa M.
2000 *Excavations at El Palenque, San Martín Tilcajete: A Late Formative Subregional Center in the Oaxaca Valley, Mexico*. Grant report submitted to the Foundation for Mesoamerican Studies. Crystal River, FL.

Robles García, Nelly M.
1986 Problemática urbana de la Zona de Monumentos de Mitla. *Cuadernos de Arquitectura Mesoamericana* 7:17–26.

Santley, Robert, and Kenneth G. Hirth (editors)
1993 *Prehispanic Domestic Units in Western Mesoamerica: Studies of the Household, Compound, and Residence*. CRC Press, Boca Raton, FL.

Schele, Linda, and Mary Ellen Miller
1986 *Blood of Kings: Dynasty and Ritual in Maya Art*. George Braziller and Kimbell Art Museum, New York and Fort Worth.

Sharer, Robert J.
1994 *The Ancient Maya*. 5th ed. Stanford University Press, Palo Alto, CA.

Smith, Adam, and Nicholas David
1995 The Production of Space and the House of Xidi Sukur. *Current Anthropology* 36:441–471.

Soles, Jeffrey S.
1991 The Gournia Palace. *American Journal of Archaeology* 95:17–78.

Spencer, Charles S.
1999 Palatial Digs. *Natural History* 108:94–95.
Spencer, Charles S., and Elsa M. Redmond
2001 Multilevel Selection and Political Evolution in the Valley of Oaxaca, 500–100 B.C. *Journal of Anthropological Archaeology* 20:195–229.
Sugiyama, S.
1993 Worldview Materialized in Teotihuacan, Mexico. *Latin American Antiquity* 4:103–129.
Thurley, Simon
1993 *The Royal Palaces of Tudor England: Architecture and Court Life, 1460–1547.* Yale University Press, New Haven.
Urcid, Javier
1992a La tumba 5 de Cerro de la Campana, Suchilquitongo, Oaxaca, México: Un análisis epigráfico. *Arqueología* 8:73–112.
1992b *Zapotec Hieroglyphic Writing.* Ph.D. dissertation, Department of Anthropology, Yale University, New Haven, CT.
Webster, David
1998 Classic Maya Architecture: Implications and Comparisons. In *Function and Meaning in Classic Maya Architecture*, edited by Stephen D. Houston, pp. 5–48. Dumbarton Oaks Research Library and Collection, Washington, DC.
Webster, David, Barbara Fash, Randolph Widmer, and Scott Zelznik
1998 The Skyband Group: Investigation of a Classic Maya Elite Residential Complex at Copán, Honduras. *Journal of Field Archaeology* 25:319–343.
Webster, David L. (editor)
1989 *The House of the Bacabs, Copán, Honduras.* Studies in Precolumbian Art and Archaeology, Vol. 29. Dumbarton Oaks Research Library and Collection, Washington, DC.
Whalen, Michael E.
1981 *Excavations at Santo Domingo Tomaltepec: Evolution of a Formative Community in the Valley of Oaxaca, Mexico.* Prehistory and Human Ecology of the Valley of Oaxaca, Memoirs of the Museum of Anthropology, Vol. 12. University of Michigan, Ann Arbor.
1988 House and Household in Formative Oaxaca. In *Household and Community in the Mesoamerican Past*, edited by Richard R. Wilk and Wendy Ashmore, pp. 249–272. University of New Mexico Press, Albuquerque.
Wilk, Richard R., and Wendy Ashmore (editors)
1988 *Household and Community in the Mesoamerican Past.* University of New Mexico Press, Albuquerque.
Willey, Gordon R., and Richard M. Leventhal
1979 A Preliminary Report on the Prehistoric Settlement at Copán. In *Maya Archaeology and Ethnohistory*, edited by Norman Hammond and Gordon R. Willey, pp. 75–102. University of Texas Press, Austin.
Wilson, Peter J.
1988 *The Domestication of the Human Species.* Yale University Press, New Haven, CT.

Winter, Marcus

1972 Tierras Largas: A Formative Community in the Valley of Oaxaca, Mexico. Unpublished Ph.D. dissertation, University of Arizona, Tucson.

1974 Residential Patterns at Monte Albán, Oaxaca, Mexico. *Science* 186:981–987.

1976 The Archaeological Household Cluster in the Valley of Oaxaca. In *The Early Mesoamerican Village*, edited by Kent V. Flannery, pp. 25–31. Academic Press, New York.

1986a Templo-Patio-Adoratorio: Un conjunto arquitectónico no-residencial en el Oaxaca prehispánico. *Cuadernos de Arquitectura Mesoamericana* 7:51–59.

1986b Unidades habitacionales prehispánicas en Oaxaca. In *Unidades habitacionales mesoamericanas y sus áreas de actividad*, edited by Linda Manzanilla, pp. 325–374. Universidad Nacional Autónoma de México, Mexico City.

1989 *Oaxaca: The Archaeological Record.* Minutiae Mexicana, Mexico City.

1994 El Proyecto Especial Monte Albán 1992–1994: Antecedentes, intervenciones y perspectivas. In *Monte Albán: Estudios recientes*, edited by Marcus Winter, pp. 1–24. Contribución No. 2 del Proyecto Especial Monte Albán 1992–1994. Centro INAH Oaxaca, Oaxaca City.

1995 Introducción. In *Entierros humanos de Monte Albán*, edited by Marcus Winter, pp. 2–10. Contribución No. 7 del Proyecto Especial Monte Albán 1992–1994. Centro INAH Oaxaca, Oaxaca City.

2000 Palacios, templos y 1,300 años de vida urbana en Monte Albán. Paper presented at La Ciudad Antigua: Espacios, Conjuntos e Integración Sociocultural en la Civilization Maya, Valladolid, Spain.

Winter, Marcus, and Arthur A. Joyce

1994 Early Political Development at Monte Albán: Evidence from Recent Excavations. Paper presented at the 93rd Annual Meeting of the American Anthropological Association, Atlanta.

Winter, Marcus, Virginia Zanabria, Cira Martínez López, and Claudia Morales

1997 *Exploraciones en el Area PSLP-S (Plataforma Sur Lado Poniente-Sur).* Proyecto Especial Monte Albán 1992–1994. Informe Final. Centro INAH Oaxaca, Oaxaca City.

CHAPTER 9

Rulership and Palaces at Teotihuacan

William T. Sanders and Susan Toby Evans

Introduction

Of all the Classic-period capitals in Mesoamerica, Teotihuacan was unique in terms of its size, the scale of its public architecture, its large population, and the indications that it managed an expansive domain of political relations. In consequence, Teotihuacan's palace architecture should be conspicuous—on a larger scale and more luxurious than the city's other residences and than the palaces of other Classic sites. Unfortunately, identifying the residence—or residences—of Teotihuacan's rulers has been an archaeological challenge, a problem almost as difficult as understanding the nature of Teotihuacan's rulership.

In this chapter, we examine evidence for Teotihuacan's main palaces. We hypothesize that the most important of these was the Street of the Dead Complex, but that other elite administrative compounds may have been established in the northeastern sector of the city and at the Ciudadela. Furthermore, we explore the relationship among these structures, Teotihuacan's rulership and the extent of its domain and influence, and the cult of the Feathered Serpent, suggesting that the mythical departure of the Feathered Serpent from the Central Highlands of Mexico reflects events in culture history that may have occurred not once, but repeatedly. Evidence from Matacapan, along the Gulf Coast, and Maya Tikal reveals that Teotihuacan's incursions into foreign lands created the opportunity for the development of the city's large middle class and, in turn, were underwritten by this affluent group, whose wealth is evidenced in its palatial housing compounds.

Teotihuacan and Its Residential Architecture

For a Mesoamerican society, Teotihuacan had a highly unusual type of residential architecture and household structure. As Mesoamerica's first large city, Teotihuacan had its demographic peak in the Early Classic period, at which time a significantly high proportion of the city's estimated 125,000 residents were organized into over 2,200 large multifamily households (Millon 1973, 1981, 1993; Millon et al. 1973). Each of these walled compounds formed a unit on the city grid extending over 20 km² and separated from other, similar units only by narrow alleys. This urban grid and its large residential compounds stand in sharp contrast to the housing and household patterns of other Mesoamerican communities.

Although Teotihuacan's compounds varied considerably in size, layout, and quality of finishing, they were generally square, the modal size being about 60 m on a side. Each compound's exterior walls ensured privacy, and access to the interior was highly restricted, with one exterior entrance leading, via passageways, to a central courtyard of modest size. This central courtyard is found in virtually all the compounds that have been extensively excavated. Commonly, this kind of courtyard featured a small central platform, identified by most archaeologists as an altar (adoratorio). The central courtyard was typically surrounded by platformed rooms that archaeologists originally identified as "temples," although subsequent research has confirmed the domestic nature of the compounds, and common sense would dictate that such "temple" structures could serve several purposes beyond strictly ritual ones.

The balance of the space within a compound was occupied by a series of apartments, and regardless of the status, formality of overall planning, or size of the household, this fundamental residential nodule of Teotihuacan consisted of a small patio surrounded by two or more structures, each usually comprising an enclosed back room and an open but roofed portico. Associated artifacts demonstrate conclusively that these are residences of the fundamental social unit of Teotihuacan society: the nuclear family or a small extended family.

It should be noted that as more compounds are excavated, the diverse range of floor plans becomes apparent, and this points to three major problems with respect to the representativeness of the excavated sample of compounds. First, the excavated sample is extremely small. Second, within this sample of excavated compounds, only a few have been completely excavated. A third problem is that fewer than half the excavated compounds were investigated within the research context of modern household archaeology; the rest were excavated primarily to recover public architecture or to search for mural paintings. In spite of these problems, the sample of compounds covers a substantial range of sizes and layouts.

This heterogeneity among the households is the most distinctive feature of any complex society. Such heterogeneity refers, in part, to variation in the amount of power, prestige, and wealth controlled by the households or, more specifically, by household heads. Teotihuacan's residential architecture indicates that there was a large middle class, but what was the basis of its apparent wealth or power? The answer may lie, in part, in the city's unique combination of resources (a concentrated area of highly productive agricultural land and locally available obsidian for toolmaking) and its peculiar demographic history. The growth of the city from 20,000 people to minimally 125,000 over a period of a few centuries was due to intrinsic growth and several kinds of immigration: an influx of former residents of Cuicuilco, fleeing from the volcanic eruptions that threatened their city, plus rural people attracted to urban life or even compelled by some coercive action of the Teotihuacan state.

The city's peak population was considerably larger than could be supported by the prime agricultural land of the Lower and Middle Teotihuacan Valley, that is, the irrigated alluvial plains. Furthermore, considering that there were at least 20,000 people living in rural communities in the Teotihuacan Valley, the population total exceeded the productive capacity of the valley as a whole—a situation that must have produced intense competition over land resources. We suggest that the status of the middle class was partially due to their control of substantial amounts of land in the prime areas of the valley, perhaps because the middle class represented the original inhabitants of the city. These lands, in many cases, would have been cultivated by tenant farmers, who were probably, in part, the migrants from Cuicuilco and from rural areas.

Excavations in these middle-class house compounds have not revealed evidence of craft activities. This may have been an oversight, resulting from biases in the goals of the excavators, but if such a lack reflects the actual material culture record, then it suggests that the higher status of the residents and their greater wealth and access to labor was based on some nonproduction role in Teotihuacan society. Besides landholding, other sources of wealth and status for Teotihuacan's middle class may have derived from their special political, religious, and economic roles. Based on an analogy with Aztec-period Tenochtitlan, some were probably bureaucrats and administrators; others were wealthy merchants (and, in fact, excavations in the merchants' barrio have located some of their residences [Rattray 1987] and possibly storage buildings). Some of them were probably elite artisans producing the fine craft products restricted in use to the middle and upper class, and others were probably professional warriors (their barrio may have been northeast of the Pyramid of the Moon [Millon 1993]). Some elite residences have been hypothesized to have been priestly quarters: the Palace of Quetzalpapalotl, associated with the Moon Plaza, and the palace on the basal platform of the Pyramid of the Sun. At the very top of the Teotihuacan social pyramid were the rulers, and they may have resided, at various times in the city's history, in several different compounds.

Teotihuacan Rulership and Rulers' Palaces

Considering the city's growth and development, three main stages and their associated patterns of rulership are identified here. First, the city achieved

TABLE 9.1. Teotihuacan Chronology (Rattray 1997:15, with bracketed additions)

Phase	Dates
[Mazapan]	[900–1100]
[Coyotlatelco]	[700–800/900]
Metepec	650–750 [traits may persist to 900]
Late Xolalpan	A.D. 550–650
Early Xolalpan	A.D. 400–550
Late Tlamimilolpa	A.D. 300–400
Early Tlamimilolpa	A.D. 200–300
Miccaotli	A.D. 150–200
Late Tzacualli	A.D. 50–150
Early Tzacualli	A.D. 1–50
Patlachique	150 B.C.–A.D. 1

dominance in the Basin of Mexico around the beginning of the first millennium A.D., when the magnificent Pyramid of the Sun was built and construction began at the site of the Pyramid of the Moon. The large population of recent immigrants was apparently housed in unprepossessing quarters, quickly built. The ruling elite may have lived in the northeast sector, near the pyramids. Xalla (or Xala [Millon et al. 1973]), the largest compound in this area, may have been a rulers' palace at some time. Next, in the third century A.D. (the Tlamimilolpa phase; see Table 9.1),[1] the last of the city's great pyramids was built within the confines of the Ciudadela, a huge square enclosure: this was the Temple-Pyramid of the Feathered Serpent, and it was flanked by residential structures. Recent research indicates that the Ciudadela was the focus of rulership, but that this episode seems to have ended with a change in government. This period ended with the desecration of the Temple-Pyramid by the addition of the Adosado in front of it, and with a revolutionary new construction program as Teotihuacan laid out a citywide grid of residential compounds, including the greatest compound of all, the Street of the Dead Complex, a massive palatial compound in the very center of the city and possibly the seat of rulership in the last era of Teotihuacan's greatness.

Turn of the Millennium: The Zone of the Great Pyramids

The city's first great period of monumental construction focused on the northern sector, with the Pyramids of the Sun and the Moon. The large compound identified as Xalla (Figure 9.1) was thought to date from the Patlachique and Tzacualli phases, based on sherd concentrations identified in the course of the Teotihuacan Mapping Project (Cowgill 1974:385). Recent radio-

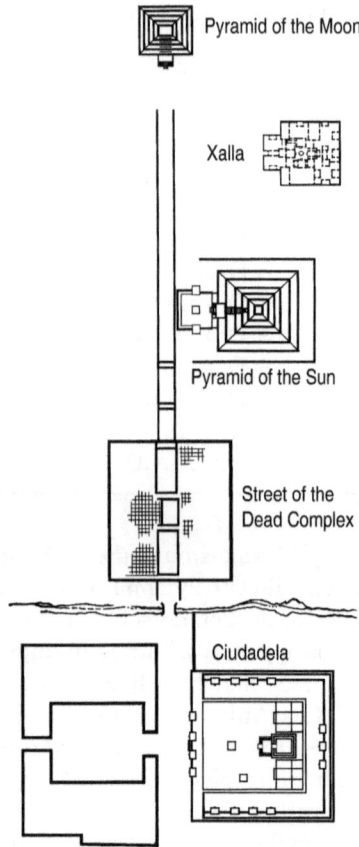

FIGURE 9.1 Major monumental architecture along the Street of the Dead at Teoti-huacan (Mexico). The distance from the north side of the Pyramid of the Moon, at top, to the south side of the Great Compound (left) and Ciudadela (right) is about 2.2 km (ca. 1.4 mi.). The Xalla compound is at upper right, with architecture as hypothesized from survey (Millon et al. 1973). The Pyramid of the Sun is at right center, and just south of it, the Street of the Dead Complex straddles the great north–south avenue. The east-to-west-running Río de San Juan separates the Street of the Dead Complex from the Great Compound and Ciudadela as the Street of the Dead continues south. Map by Evans based on Millon et al. 1973.

carbon dates set some construction at the compound at A.D. 200–250 and A.D. 350–550 (Manzanilla and López 2001:6), indicating that Xalla was in use throughout the active period of Teotihuacan's monumental core.

Xalla has only recently begun to be explored,[2] and the surface architecture that was perceptible to Millon's Mapping Project may represent later rebuilding (Millon et al. 1973:31). The compound was roughly square, measuring 174 m north to south and 213 m east to west, occupying about 35,554 m², and having eight large patios (Manzanilla and López 2001:5). Thus, Xalla covered 10 times as much space as would the average compound (about 60 m on a side). Xalla's central patio (about 30 m across),

> was the scene of the principal ceremonies of the presumed palace . . . In a surprising way, this space departs completely from the Teotihuacan norm. In contrast to the typical patio with three temples, the Plaza Central of Xalla has four temples in the cardinal directions, and a fifth— slightly smaller—in the center. . . . Among the most significant finds in the Plaza Central . . . [were] two sculptures of a plumed feline.[3] (López and Manzanilla 2001:15)

The plumed feline sculptures and other motifs at Xalla closely resemble materials found at the foot of the Pyramid of the Sun, and this may indicate close ties between the two monumental constructions (ibid.)

In fact, looking at Figure 9.1, we see that Xalla is located so as to have a startlingly balanced spatial relationship between the two great pyramids: the Xalla compound and the front projection of the Pyramid of the Moon seem to face onto the midpoints of the eastern and northern sides of a huge square, roughly 500 m on a side, whose southern limit is defined, in part, by the northern edge of the Pyramid of the Sun's platform. This square space was dotted with three-temple groups, and these are thought to be quite early (Millon 1993:29). Until more is known about the chronology of Xalla and the development of the Pyramid of the Moon and the three-temple groups at its base, it is difficult to ascertain the nature of this great square at the time that Xalla may have served as an important elite compound. It is possible, therefore, that this square space was the early city's great plaza, when Xalla was its palace. It should be noted that at this early date, the Pyramid of the Moon may have only consisted of a complex of small platforms, later covered by the Adosado; the massive body of the pyramid seems to be much later, dating from perhaps the fourth century A.D. (Cabrera and Sugiyama 2001).

Third Century: The Ciudadela Compound

Construction of the Ciudadela in the late second century A.D. (Miccaotli phase) may represent a new stage of rulership.

> What is striking about the Ciudadela is that it was not built earlier, along with the pyramids, but later; . . . a new center was created for the city that made the pyramids peripheral. From many places inside the Ciudadela enclosure the pyramids are either not visible or only partly visible. The Ciudadela seems to be the architectural representation of a major change in the social and political structure of Teotihuacan. . . . A powerful leader may have literally redesigned the city, putting the palace—and thus rulership—at its center. (Pasztory 1997:115)

The vast complex known as the Ciudadela is clearly one of the primary public spaces of Teotihuacan, and from the beginning of research at the site it has been identified as a major religious precinct. This identification was based on its massive size, very large central court,[4] the formal array of small temples on top of the four great platforms defining the compound, the monumental access stairway into the complex, and the Temple-Pyramid of the Feathered Serpent that dominates its interior space, clearly the ritual shrine of a cult that may have been led by the ruling lineage of that time. In strong support of this reconstruction is the evidence that the Temple-Pyramid was a funerary monument, probably dedicated to a ruler from that lineage whose looted tomb lies at its center, and it was sanctified with human sacrifices on a scale not known from earlier periods at Teotihuacan (Sugiyama 1992). The Temple-Pyramid's façade is dominated by sculpted images of the Feathered Serpent, but also of the Fire Serpent, which in Aztec times was associated with warfare, and this militaristic interpretation has also been made convincingly for Teotihuacan (Sugiyama 1992, 2000; Taube 1992, 2000).

Stratigraphic work at the Ciudadela confirms that it had the same basic form throughout the history of the complex (Cabrera 1982; Cabrera et al. 1982, 1991). In the area now occupied by the "palaces," test pitting revealed earlier levels, but, unfortunately, these excavations were small in scale and thus, though we know that at least two phases of residential building occupied the same site during earlier times, we have no idea as to the floor plans of these structures. Of further interest is a less-formal residential complex within the Great Courtyard of the Ciudadela and built up against the staircases of North Palace, in the northeast corner of the courtyard. It dates from an earlier period, during which the great platform that underlies the North and South Palaces was lower in height and smaller in area, indicating that the noted complex within the plaza was integrated with one of these earlier structures. There is a distinct possibility (and we emphasize that, given the dearth of data, this is only a possibility) that during earlier periods, a significant portion of the interior plaza of the Ciudadela may have been occupied by roofed-over residential space like the excavated complex in the northeast. Excavations within the peripheral platform also show that the plaza was surrounded by earlier versions of the platforms. They probably link in some way with the earlier versions of palace construction.

Some time during the Tlamimilolpa phase (late third century or early fourth century [Cowgill 1997:152]), the flamboyant Temple-Pyramid of the Feathered Serpent was shrouded by the severe outer garment of its Adosado, indicating that the powerful cult associated with the establishment of the Ciudadela and its accompanying features may have been overthrown or suppressed (see Sugiyama 1998). Most Teotihuacan scholars would now agree that a reaction against the power holders set in, and a new regime was installed that directed the city's last massive construction project: the gridded layout and the residential compounds. "Perhaps the rulers' residence shifted to the Avenue of the Dead Complex during the political changes that may have occurred somewhere between 250 and 350 CE" (Cowgill 1997:152).

We will discuss the Street of the Dead Complex below, but we wish to emphasize the importance of this transition in the city's history and to propose architectural markers for it. The Ciudadela as we now know it, including the North and South "palaces," represents a posttransition architectural monument. On lower platforms to the north and south of the Temple-Pyramid were rooms and patios whose layout suggests residential functions. Pedro Armillas (1964) considered the Ciudadela to be the residence of the royal family of Teotihuacan as well as a major religious precinct, an interpretation that was echoed by many later researchers interested in the nature of Teotihuacan society. Recent excavations of these room complexes have again given rise to the speculation that the Ciudadela functioned partly as a royal palace complex.

Although the enclosure-like character of the Ciudadela as a whole, in its final phase, presents a superficial resemblance to the typical residential compound, most of the features noted above contrast very sharply with those of the typical residential compound. Most important is the central court's vast size, in absolute and relative terms, and its lack of residential architecture on three sides, indicating a more public function than merely a royal palace. Although preindustrial states often integrated political and religious symbols, and leaders often played dual political and religious roles, the relatively small area dedicated to residential space seems decidedly odd.

We suggest that in the course of renovations within the Ciudadela's Great Courtyard, the existing (and now stratigraphically buried) room complexes were leveled, and plaster floors were constructed over these areas to bring them to their present size. The two "palaces" were then rebuilt, in the form seen today. These Ciudadela room compounds are nearly identical squares, each less than 100 m on a side, that frame the Temple-Pyramid of the Feathered Serpent (see Figure 9.1).[5] Each consists of five almost identical room groups, each with rooms facing onto an interior patio the same size as the rooms (Cabrera 1982:12). The five groups surround an interior patio equal to the size of one of the groups (Figure 9.2).

All this symmetry has a ritual or even military feel to it, not a domestic one. Establishments in which real ruling families live and from which complex states are governed must accommodate considerable bureaucratic and domestic paraphernalia, multiplied by such effects as polygyny, the presence of servants and retainers, and the necessity for adequate space for governmental functions. The layout of the Ciudadela "palaces" reveals none of the architectural apparatus for actual living by such households. These structures, though probably involved in rulership, were not residential palaces, but they may have served otherwise to uphold the apparatus of state administration.

An alternative possibility is that there were two separate, almost identical

CIUDADELA NORTH COMPLEX OR PALACE

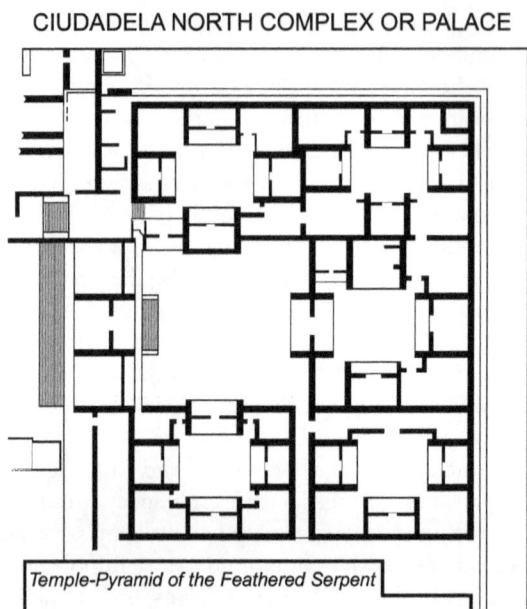

Temple-Pyramid of the Feathered Serpent

FIGURE 9.2 The Ciudadela's northern room complex, basically a mirror image of the southern room complex, measures about 80 m (ca. 260 ft.) on a side. Drawing by Evans, based on Cabrera 1982 and Cabrera et al. 1982, 1991.

"palace" buildings even during the early phases, suggesting the institution of some kind of dual rulership at the time of the renovations of the Ciudadela. The administrative and residential establishments of two lineages may have been located within the Street of the Dead Complex, whereas the Ciudadela "palaces" may have served ritual functions associated with the two ruling lineage cults, such as quarters for priests and schools for educating upper-class youth, like the Aztec calmecac.

A Palace for a Renovated City: The Street of the Dead Complex

The Street of the Dead Complex (Figure 9.3), at the very center of the city, was, in its final phase, the city's most extensive residential compound, "straddling the Avenue and . . . incorporating the old three-temple com-plexes" (Pasztory 1997:116–117). This huge square compound, about 350 m on a side, may have been the city's administrative-residential capitol for the rest of its history as a great civic and ceremonial center—until all the build-ings along the Street of the Dead were abandoned several hundred years later (Morelos 1993).

The Street of the Dead Complex may have been built around A.D. 300, possibly when the construction of apartment compounds became the city's

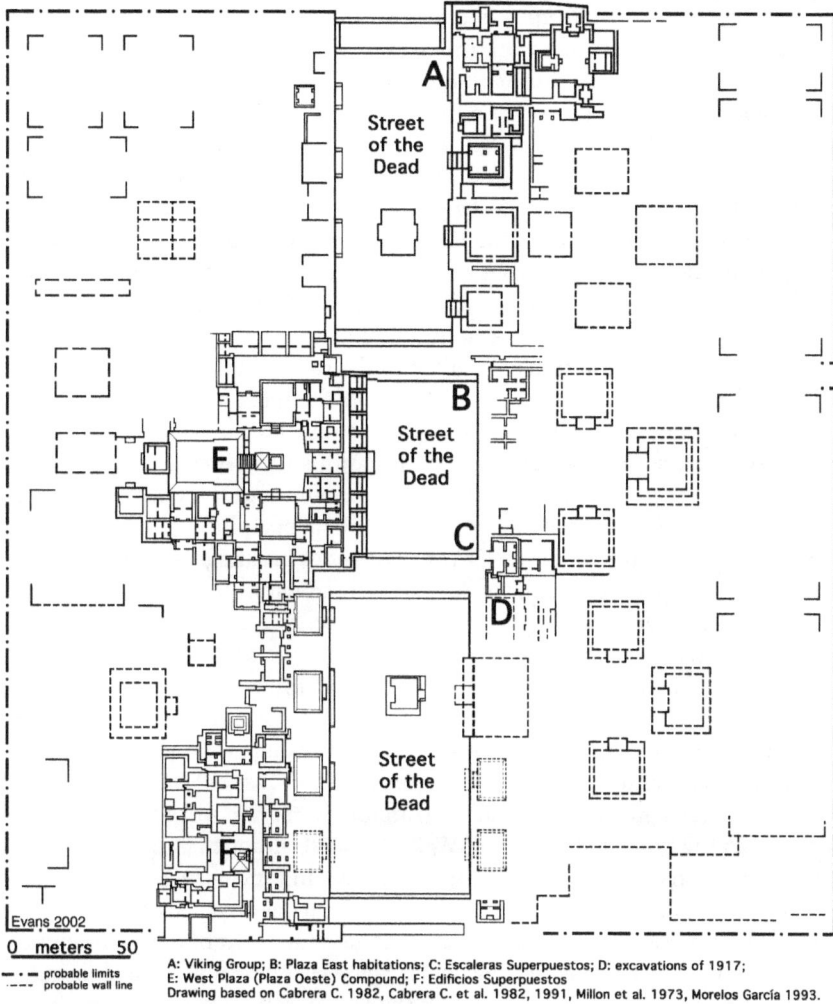

STREET OF THE DEAD COMPLEX
(Teotihuacan, Mexico)

A: Viking Group; B: Plaza East habitations; C: Escaleras Superpuestos; D: excavations of 1917;
E: West Plaza (Plaza Oeste) Compound; F: Edificios Superpuestos
Drawing based on Cabrera C. 1982, Cabrera C. et al. 1982, 1991, Millon et al. 1973, Morelos García 1993.

FIGURE 9.3 The Street of the Dead Complex at Teotihuacan measures about 330 m (ca. 1,080 ft.) on a side. Only about one-fourth of its architecture has been excavated, and dashed lines and corner brackets indicate the larger complexes located in survey (Millon 1973). "A" is the Viking Group, "B" is the Plaza Oeste (West Plaza) Compound, and "C" is the East Plaza Compound. Drawing by Evans, based on Cabrera 1982; Cabrera et al. 1982, 1991; Millon et al. 1973; and Morelos 1993.

greatest public-works project. The gridded plan of the city; the apartment compounds, each different yet conforming to a broadly similar pattern; the central compound as a *primus inter pares* — these and other iconographic features suggest that Teotihuacan turned away from an emphasis on sanctified dynasts, such as the one presumably entombed in the Temple-Pyramid of the Feathered Serpent, and toward a hierarchy of relatively depersonalized bureaucrats. This does not mean that the highest-ranking bureaucrats were not members of ruling dynasties, or that rulership was not held by one or several related lineages (see discussion below), but that the rulers' identity as individual power holders was masked, as expressed in the depictions of humans in plastic and graphic art forms — figurines, "theater censers" (so-called because of their elaborate display of many small elements), and murals — for which Classic-period Teotihuacan is famous.

In terms of the evolution of architectural forms as a reflection of changing ways of government, the Street of the Dead Complex marks a most interesting transformation. From its size and layout, the complex clearly could have served functions pertaining to both administration of the state and residences for the rulers, their extended households, and their retainers. It is a compound of courtyards and symmetrical rooms, plus all the backstage areas necessary for daily life. Yet this vast set of buildings is perfectly congruent with what seems to have been the self-effacing ethos prevalent in the city after the demotion of the Feathered Serpent cult. In stark contrast to the city's great pyramids and the distinctive three-temple groups around the Pyramid of the Moon, the Street of the Dead Complex would have been invisible as a monument (Pasztory 1997). It would not have loomed over the other apartment compounds. Looking at the city map, we find that it would also have been almost invisible to the celestial gods, as well (see Figure 9.1) — it was not recognized or defined as an architectural unit until the Teotihuacan Mapping Project identified it (Wallrath 1967), although parts of the complex had been excavated as separate structures in previous years.

However, once recognized, it is striking in its central location, massive size, and symmetrical placement within the framework of the monuments built during earlier eras of Teotihuacan power. Not only did it dominate the heart of the city, it also broke up the Street of the Dead, restricting access between the Ciudadela and the Pyramids of the Sun and the Moon. Anyone who has walked up the Street of the Dead from the Great Compound and the Ciudadela toward the Pyramids of the Sun and the Moon finds that this part taxes the pedestrian with its "barricades" — they form an internal division of space that represents the central portion of the complex. The Street of the Dead was obviously a ritual setting for processionals (of rulers? warriors? merchants? citizenry?). The Street of the Dead Complex would have "captured" such processions, architectonically forcing their participants to present themselves within its walls. It is also possible that ballgames took place in one or more of these sunken courtyards — ballgame imagery is known from Teotihuacan, but no formal ballcourt has ever been identified.

The Street of the Dead Complex is defined by a massive outer wall, more like the outer walls of other Teotihuacan compounds than the Ciudadela's rampart, with its arrangement of great platforms surrounding a large central court. In further contrast to the Ciudadela, in which the courtyard accounts for one-third of the area, only 15 percent of the Street of the Dead Complex's interior space is occupied by central open spaces. Furthermore, the open area represented by the three courts of the Street of the Dead itself makes up only one-fifth the area of the Ciudadela's courtyard. In the Street of the Dead Complex, approximately one-half the interior is occupied by roofed-over space, and the balance, by open spaces and small temples.

Excavation of the Street of the Dead Complex has taken place largely in the western half and in perhaps one-fourth of the eastern side. Areas defined as roofed-over space show considerable variation within a larger pattern of bilateral symmetry of east to west. In some areas, small adjacent rooms, lacking porches and mutual access, each with a separate doorway, are lined up along what may be either roofed halls or more probably open alleys. They contrast very sharply with the typical Teotihuacan residences and may have had administrative functions. Other units consist of very large walled spaces that may have had storage functions.

Other room complexes are arranged in much the same way as those in the typical residential compound, with patios, porches, and back rooms. Interior courtyards have central altars, making them into shrines like those in other Teotihuacan residential compounds, wherein veneration of the compound's ancestors was a central concern. Of the room complexes, the Viking Group (Figure 9.3:A) is outstanding in that it is more spacious than other Teotihuacan residences. A single apartment in the Viking Group measures 2,000 m^2 in area. It has the largest rooms, porches, and patios of any of the residences excavated at Teotihuacan and may have been the residence of someone of very high status, possibly even the head(s) of the compound and of the Teotihuacan state. Other excavated residences of the Street of the Dead Complex have the same basic plan but are much smaller in size, possibly indicating these are the homes of clients or lower-ranking members of the royal lineage residing within the royal compound.

The overall east-west architectural symmetry of the layout of the Street of the Dead Complex strongly suggests that dual leadership either continued or was initiated here. The West Plaza Compound has three "temples" defining the edges of a plaza in the center of the complex, which is otherwise surrounded by typical residential architecture. Its twin on the east side of the street has an even larger "temple," a bit of asymmetry that may indicate an imbalance in the parallel relationship between two ruling groups. The sculpted heads on the balustrade of the main "temple" in the West Plaza Compound include serpents and felines, and it would be very interesting to find out what adorns the balustrade of the East Plaza Compound "temple," but the East Plaza Compound has not been extensively excavated, so generalizations about its layout must be based on extrapolation from existing excavations and from the excavated areas of the West Plaza Compound. Each of these temple complexes is bordered by additional residential space and three-temple complexes, along with rows of individual temples facing onto the main street.

Accepting our reconstruction of possible dual leadership at Teotihuacan during this phase, then which buildings were the residences of the two kings? Here we run into a fundamental disagreement with traditional interpretations of structure function at Teotihuacan. There is a regrettable tendency to identify as "temples" all buildings that are placed on high terrace platforms and adorned with sculptures, forgetting that in early states, religious ideology and political practice were combined, and they were often embodied in the ruler. We suggest that the so-called main temple in the West Plaza Group was actually the residence of a king, and, based on the sculpture on the façade, he may have held the title of Quetzalcoatl. He would have been the only occupant of the "temple" building, which would have been his reception room and sleeping quarters. The rest of his household, that is, his wives, children, and retainers, would have occupied the nearby residential complexes. This is a striking parallel with our interpretation, above, of the function of the Teotihuacan central courtyard in other apartment compounds.

Unfortunately, it will be difficult to prove the function of these "temples" through archaeological evidence, because rarely does domestic refuse remain associated with important rooms in high-ranking residences. The same problem arose at Copán in the excavation of the House of the Bacabs, a residential compound of a nobleman (Webster 1989). In that compound, Structure 9N-82 Center was the actual house of the noble head of a large, complex household residing in this multipatio compound. Like the central "temple" of the Street of the Dead's West Plaza Compound, this building occupied the compound's most important place and was on a high platform. It had a sculptured throne in the interior, and its façade was adorned with sculpture that combined religious and political themes. At each side of this central structure were masonry buildings divided into apartments, probably the residences of the compound head's wives. Virtually no refuse was associated with the buildings, although middens with typical household refuse were found behind the substructure.

Along with the Street of the Dead Complex's residential areas and special-purpose room groups are six ceremonial plazas, three located on each side of the street. Three have the typical Teotihuacan three-temple layouts, with their open sides facing the Street of the Dead; two others may have the same plan. Another consists of four temples arranged around a court. Besides these religious precincts, there are approximately fifteen isolated temple-platforms lined up along both sides of the street, and they communicate directly with the street.

The Street of the Dead Complex clearly had sacred functions as well as residential and administrative ones, based on the abundance of religious themes expressed in its art and architecture. Several of Teotihuacan's signature artifacts—carved stone masks and ceramic theater censers—are known to have been associated with ancestor veneration, and thus with the mediation of the relationship between the living and the spirit world of the dead. The masks have seldom been found in context, but at least one was unearthed near the Street of the Dead Complex (Cabrera 1993:186), and various lines of evidence suggest that they were part of oracle bundles (Headrick 1999). Teotihuacan theater censers have ceramic masks of a design similar to the ones made of stone, and many have a butterfly-shaped element that hides the mouth. "The Aztecs saw butterflies and moths as the souls of dead warriors and sacrificial victims" (Pasztory 1997:167), and this may have been true of Teotihuacanos, as well. Possibly, the mask's butterfly mouthpiece represented an oracular function, a true agent for the transmission of ancestral advice. Teotihuacan's new leaders may have depended on such means to maintain societal cohesion, turning away from the mass sacrifices that underwrote the Temple-Pyramid of the Feathered Serpent.

In fact, private courtyard rituals may have been coordinated, in apartment compounds all over the city. Given the height and centrality of the Pyramid of the Sun, the view from its summit would have allowed its priests to monitor such activities as they took place in all the city's residential compounds, including that of the Street of the Dead Complex. One can imagine conch-shell trumpets sounding through the air or the heavy rumble of drums signaling the hours when residents of the compounds would turn to their altars to honor lineage progenitors, and the wisps of incense smoke rising from thousands of courtyards would bear their homage to the sky and serve as public testimony to their piety.

The Street of the Dead Complex can be interpreted as the administrative and political center of the city during the Classic period. Because of the unfortunately insufficient stratigraphic data on the history of the growth of the compound, its development as the capitol cannot be confirmed. The precise meaning of the spatial arrangements of structures within the Street of the Dead Complex is at present obscure, in part because much of the complex remains unexcavated, and in part because of the lack of published associations of artifacts and features, contexts that might assist in the identification of activity areas.

Nevertheless, we can make some preliminary observations. If the complex had the variety of functions we are suggesting, then the six-, three-, and four-temple complexes might relate to major divisions of the city, like the four great wards of Aztec Tenochtitlan. The 15 smaller temples lined up along the Street of the Dead could relate to smaller spatial divisions of the city, somewhat comparable to the Aztec *calpullec*, or "wards." Some of the temples seem to be associated with the specialized room structures we have suggested as having administrative functions. Fray Bernardino de Sahagún's informants described *calpulli* temples within the Templo Mayor enclosure, where each *calpulli*'s patron deities were worshiped (Sahagún 1981 [1569]). This analogy would suggest that there might have been approximately 15 *calpulli*-like divisions at Teotihuacan and recalls the 15 small temple-platforms on the great platforms that define the Ciudadela. These units were clearly much larger in size than the 80–100 at Tenochtitlan. Though it is difficult to ascertain because of the large unexcavated area, most of the residential portions of the complex seem not to be directly related to particular temples or temple/complexes.

Royal Palaces and Teotihuacan's Larger Realm

Clearly, the three compounds that we hypothesize as being the seats of rulership for three different periods suggest changes in type of administration, judging merely from their respective sizes and layouts. Xalla and the Ciudadela seem suited for the internally oriented developments of Teotihuacan in its earlier phases, but the Street of the Dead Complex displays the size and complexity of layout that would be well suited to administration of the city plus long-distance enterprises undertaken in pursuit of military and commercial interests. To contextualize the Street of the Dead Complex during this period of several centuries (late third century A.D. to mid-sixth century A.D.), let us now review the extent of Teotihuacan's influence on other regions of Mesoamerica, with particular focus on Maya Tikal.

Teotihuacan's Influence Abroad

The nature of Teotihuacan as an "imperial" power has long been a matter of debate. For several decades there has been convincing archaeological evidence of Teotihuacan's wide impact on outlying areas—for example, at Cholula (Puebla), at Monte Albán (Oaxaca), at many sites in the state of Guerrero, at Matacapan (Veracruz), at Kaminaljuyú in highland Guatemala, and at Tikal and other Classic Maya sites in the southern part of the Yucatán Peninsula. The question remained: Were these contacts political and ideological, or were they primarily related to international trade?

Teotihuacan's imperial power seems to have been evidenced most clearly at Matacapan (Santley 1994), where the Teotihuacan presence was at a much larger scale than has been suggested for other sites such as Kaminaljuyú.[6] Excavations at Kaminaljuyú suggested that there were probably commercial contacts between the two places and that a small resident colony of Teotihuacan merchants, perhaps married to local Maya noblewomen, resided at Kaminaljuyú (Sanders and Michels 1977).[7]

Teotihuacan and Tikal

There is convincing epigraphic evidence that Teotihuacan directly intervened in the political affairs of the Maya area, especially at Tikal, the largest of the Maya centers (Coggins 1993; Proskouriakoff 1993; Stuart 2000).[8] Teotihuacan presence at Tikal was first identified from archaeological evidence such as the funerary offerings associated with burials in the North Acropolis (the royal cemetery at Tikal; Coe 1990), which are comparable to those found at Mounds A and B at Kaminaljuyú. Additionally, several stelae showed Teotihuacan personages carrying military equipment such as shields and spear-throwers and darts.[9]

The recent revolution in epigraphic decipherment, engendered by research by Tatiana Proskouriakoff and others, has provided the historical data that may corroborate the archaeological evidence of this "arrival of strangers" (Proskouriakoff 1993; Stuart 2000). Epigraphers now interpret Tikal's Stela 31 as showing Tikal's ruler Stormy Sky (aka Siyaj Chan K'awiil II, reigned 411–456) flanked by depictions of the ruler's father and predecessor, Curl Snout (aka Yax Nuun Ayiin I, reigned 379–404), who was a son of the Teotihuacano Spear-Thrower Owl (Stuart 2000).[10]

The events are reconstructed as follows: in January A.D. 378, a man named Siyah K'ak' (aka Smoking Frog), the emissary of Spear-Thrower Owl, arrived at Tikal, and immediately after, Tikal's ruler Chak Tok Ich'aak (Jaguar Paw) died. Siyah K'ak' had first visited El Perú and Uaxactun, and then moved on to Tikal itself. Within a year, he had sponsored the rulership, at Tikal, of Yax Nuun Ayiin I. Siyah K'ak' continued to visit Maya sites (Río Azul in 393, for example) and to introduce Teotihuacan themes of rulership—and in several recorded cases, new rulers (Martin and Grube 2000:30). The marriages of Spear-Thrower Owl's descendants or representatives to Maya noblewomen over several successive generations of rulers further legitimized the outsiders' claims of kingship.

Spear-Thrower Owl seems to have instigated the incursion that Siyah K'ak' directed, but no evidence suggests that Spear-Thrower Owl was ever actually in the Maya region. His titles indicate that he was not just a king but a great overlord, ruling from A.D. 374 to his death in A.D. 439. His capital is not known, but possibly it was Teotihuacan itself (Stuart 2000). "The idea that the 'rulership' concerned was that of Teotihuacan is tempting indeed and, if correct, would constitute one of the first real insights into the government of this mighty but mysterious city" (Martin and Grube 2000:31). At Teotihuacan itself, there is little evidence of rulers' lives and nothing like the inscriptions and portraits on the personal monuments publicly displayed by Classic Maya rulers.[11] In fact, Teotihuacan is often contrasted in this regard with the Maya, whose rulers commonly made highly personalized public statements. However, if this reconstruction of Spear-Thrower Owl's identity is correct, then he was very likely residing in the Street of the Dead Complex.

Some clarification about the role of Spear-Thrower Owl can be derived from Teotihuacan iconography, from which we learn that both the spear-thrower and the owl are associated with militarism. The other important component of ideology that Teotihuacan was exporting was related to calendrics. Teotihuacan's Pyramid of the Sun was legendary for being "the place where time began," and its orientation was toward sunset on about 12 or 13 August, the date when time began in the Maya Long Count calendar, in 3114 B.C. (Coggins 1993:142). This concordance of calendric-origin indicators points toward a Mesoamerica-wide belief, but additionally, the widespread iconographic references at Teotihuacan to the 260-day Sacred Round calendar amount to something of a state religion, according to Clemency Coggins. Calendrical reckoning may have been an important export, along with militarism and green obsidian (Aveni 2000; Coggins 1980).

Dramatic confirmation of the Teotihuacan presence at Tikal is exhibited in several forms besides Stela 31. Tikal's Mundo Perdido Complex shows the effects of the change in government brought about by Spear-Thrower Owl's contingent. The complex is located approximately 300 m southwest of the North Acropolis. This was an E-group, a set of buildings that apparently functioned as a horizon calendar throughout the Middle and Late Formative periods, continuing until approximately A.D. 250. The complex was repeatedly rebuilt, and in the Manik 2 phase (A.D. 300–378), the complex was an important ritual locus where rulers were buried, and its pyramid, at 31 m, was Tikal's tallest structure (Laporte and Fialco 1990:37). It was during this phase that *talud*-and-*tablero* elements were added to some of its structures, and this practice continued and was expanded into Manik 3, which began in A.D. 378. The North Acropolis continued to be used as a political center, but it was not used for elite burials between A.D. 250 and 400. Sometime after A.D. 400, and after the establishment of the Teotihuacan-inspired dynasty, the North Acropolis again became the royal cemetery.

Equally intriguing is the residential compound Group 6C XVI, 300 m south of the Mundo Perdido Complex. Here a residential compound very similar in plan and construction to "Early Classic residential groups . . . such as at Teotihuacan and Monte Alban" was built with *talud*-and-*tablero* façades (Laporte and Fialco 1990:46). Group 6C XVI was used by some members of the Teotihuacan-established Tikal lineage, possibly as a residence that may also have functioned as a ritual place associated with the ballgame. In the center of one of the patios was an altar, a pattern common in Teotihuacan. In a cache in the altar was found a ballcourt marker very similar to that found at Teotihuacan; the marker had probably graced the top of the altar prior to being ritually interred. Inscriptions on it reveal the events of the Teotihuacan takeover at Tikal, including the death of the old ruler and the installation of Spear-Thrower Owl's son. The data suggest a synthesis of ballgame and political iconography.

For the century after A.D. 379, Tikal became the major player in Classic Maya politics and conducted successful military campaigns against a number of neighboring Maya sites, including its major rival, Calakmul. It is tempting to associate these successes with the military presence of Teotihuacan in the area, and possibly to the professional warriors carrying spearthrowers, although these weapons were never widely adopted in the Maya lowlands (Hassig 1992). In fact, Teotihuacan's actual influence upon the Maya seems to have been relatively limited: it provided certain catalysts for local alliances and conflicts, and it also contributed some lasting, prestige-laden symbols of rulership.

Meanwhile, back in the highlands, Teotihuacan was enjoying a last period of well-being before its reversals began around A.D. 500. Ancient cities in general were stressful places to live, and to maintain their size they depended on a constant influx of rural migrants. Teotihuacan had drawn virtually the whole population of the Basin of Mexico into itself at around the turn of the millennium, and when the inevitable problems of inadequate sanitation and insufficient food bore heavily upon the health of the population, there were few potential replacements available (Storey 1992).

Another stress may have pushed the city from preeminence to backwater: global climate indicators suggest that between A.D. 530 and 590 there was a cold period, possibly precipitated by a proto-Krakatoa eruption in about A.D. 535 (Gill 2000:293). As projected for a potential "nuclear winter," the main effects of such an event would be associated with drought, and in the already semiarid Teotihuacan Valley, a disruption of the rains and the disappearance of the sun would not only be ruinous to productivity, it would seriously undercut the faith of the populace in the effectiveness of the rulers as mediators with the spirit world (Evans 2004a:280). And it was around A.D. 500 that burning occurred along the Street of the Dead (Fash et al. 2004; Wolfman 1990), in what has long been interpreted as an internal uprising (though readers should note that many scholars still use more traditional chronologies that put these events as late as the eighth century). In any event, Teotihuacan remained a large city, relative to the vast majority of communities in Mesoamerica. Its Late Classic size amounted to several tens of thousands of people distributed in a ring around the once-vital Street of the Dead and its civic and ceremonial architecture—living communities encircling the great pilgrimage center, a pattern that persists to this day. Even the perspective of abandonment of the civic-ceremonial core of the city may be overdramatized; in their enthusiasm to find evidence of Teotihuacan's heyday, past investigators have been known to fail to report evidence of occupation during the very Late Classic and Early Postclassic Coyotlatelco and Mazapan phases, because these were thought to have been of no cultural consequence.

Tikal's era of success ended in A.D. 562. Invasion by Calakmul resulted in an inactive period lasting until A.D. 692 (130 years), which is sometimes known as the Classic Maya Hiatus, during which no sculptured monuments in honor of kings were erected at Tikal. It is tempting to relate this "hiatus" to Teotihuacan's decline, which would be another line of evidence substantiating the close relationship between the two centers. In A.D. 692 a new ruler assumed Tikal's throne, claiming descent from the earlier, Teotihuacan-derived dynasty, and the eighth century saw Tikal once again become the major player in Classic Maya affairs.

Late Classic Maya references to Teotihuacan seem to reflect respect for a revered but dead ancestral power, rather than honoring a living force (Stuart 2000). In contrast, Early Classic Maya inscriptions suggest that Teotihuacan was an imperial power that intervened in foreign political affairs, even in the distant Maya lowlands. As we have seen, Teotihuacan's large middle class could have functioned in various productive and bureaucratic capacities to facilitate this expansion of external influence and power. Whether or not these political features operated on the scale of Tenochtitlan, the much-better-known Aztec capital, is debatable, and in fact we authors of this article have debated it between ourselves and have come to no agreement. On the one hand, Teotihuacan lacked the crowded hinterland of tribute- and service-paying farmer-artisans so useful to the Aztecs as the material and personnel basis for their far-flung ventures. On the other hand, some features of Teotihuacan's foreign involvements have the earmarks of true coercive power. A thorough exploration of Teotihuacan's potential external influence, compared to that of Tenochtitlan, is beyond the scope of this paper.

The Teotihuacan State and Society

The variety in Teotihuacan households demonstrates that its society was considerably different from other Classic-period Mesoamerican societies. Especially distinctive, perhaps even unique, is the implication that the uppermost strata at Teotihuacan wielded an exceptional degree of power. Underwriting this statement are the public architecture and orderly ground plan of the city. These features are unparalleled in other Classic sites— in fact, in all of Mesoamerica—and are dramatic material evidence of that power. The massive size of the city, compared to second-level communities within its political domain, and its wide-ranging geographic interests and contacts with other Mesoamerican societies are further incontrovertible manifestations of power.

If the present interpretation of the Street of the Dead Complex is confirmed, it would indicate that the structure of the Teotihuacan state was similar to that of the Aztec state, that is, that the two states differed only in scale, in the size of the demographic base of the heartland, and in the external territory controlled. In terms of governing structure, dual rulership, possibly sustained at Teotihuacan, may have been manifested at Tenochtitlan in the shared authority between the two highest offices, *tlatoani* and *cihuacoatl*. The balance between these two would have been upset in the last half century of the Aztec Empire, when a dynamic buildup of wealth flowed to the *tlatoani*. At Teotihuacan, dual leadership may have been sustained by far more limited economic input.

In terms of its sphere of strong influence, the Teotihuacan state may have covered 20,000 km² and had a population of half a million (Sanders et al. 1979). If, however, one includes Teotihuacan administrative and residential colonies, such as at Matacapan, these estimates may need to be revised upward. Nevertheless, the estimates will still indicate a polity significantly smaller than the Aztec Empire.

If we were able to excavate Mexico City on a large scale, we might find that Tenochtitlan's architectural layout was quite similar to that of Teotihuacan. The Templo Mayor and its great enclosed precinct represent the architectural remains of the Aztec religious institution, and they compare to the Ciudadela in scale. In fact, the Aztec enclosure has many more buildings, and the Templo Mayor itself is considerably larger than the Temple-Pyramid of the Feathered Serpent. Next to the Templo Mayor precinct were the massive palaces of the Aztec kings, including that of Moctezuma Xocoyotzin, with its outlying and physically separate appendages, and together these would be comparable in size and nature to the Street of the Dead Complex. Finally, at Tenochtitlan, as at Teotihuacan, we would find a very large number of middle-status residences representing the households of a landed aristocracy and of a large middle class of merchants, professional warriors, priests, administrators, and elite artisans.

In Summary: Teotihuacan Palaces, Rulers, and Mesoamerican Culture History

Changes over time in Teotihuacan's palaces may reflect two major changes in political organization. The first involved the ascendance of the Feathered Serpent cult and the establishment of the Ciudadela. The second involved a change in the locus of rulership from the Ciudadela to the Street of the Dead Complex and may have been a repudiation or limitation of the influence of the Feathered Serpent cult, or perhaps a reaction against the sacrifices associated with the Temple-Pyramid and its militaristic iconography. This reaction, related to the construction of the Adosado during the Early Tlamimilolpa phase, may also have been expressed in the reconfiguration of the Ciudadela's residential architecture.

It is very tempting to relate these events to those described for Tikal and the "arrival of the strangers" from the West (Proskouriakoff 1993; Stuart 2000). Following this scenario, the king of Teotihuacan—or his emissary—exerted strong influence over Tikal, installing his son as Tikal's ruler. Given what we know of the situation in Teotihuacan in the late fourth century, what might this represent? A dynasty in exile? The more militaristic of two ruling Teotihuacan dynasties sent south to expend its bellicose energies on disruption of the Maya? Or a dynasty on a proselytizing mission to teach the Maya deeper truths about calendrics and spear-throwers? Given the international flavor of Teotihuacan's population, Maya living there may have inspired this expeditionary force. In any event, the Early Classic period witnessed the demotion of the Feathered Serpent cult at Teotihuacan at roughly the same time that Teotihuacan's political maneuvering in the Maya region began.[12]

The more dramatic scenario, of dynasts in exile, has a strong resemblance to the storied events of the Early Postclassic: the flight of Quetzalcoatl from Tula in the tenth century. Quetzalcoatl, or the Feathered Serpent, was said to have been exiled and to have become a major power player in Maya affairs in northern Yucatán. There are several parallels in the history of northern Yucatán in the Postclassic. Paintings at Chichén Itzá show Mexican invaders carrying spear-throwers and darts facing Maya warriors holding long, thrusting spears. The ruler of Mayapan, to expand his power over neighboring kingdoms, imported professional Nahua warriors from the Chontalpa area (Roys 1962). As noted above, the Maya apparently never adopted the spear-thrower, and this unfamiliarity might have disadvantaged them at least twice in the history of the Maya region.

The departure of the Feathered Serpent from a Central Highlands homeland called Tollán is told in sixteenth-century accounts that seem to have some genuine historical basis—with reservations. The accounts refer to a people called the Toltec, the people of Tula or Tollán.[13] In view of this, it is interesting to consider that the glyph for Teotihuacan that has been identified at Tikal is translated as Tollán, "the place of reeds." Although the Tollán concept has been recognized as having a much more general Mesoamerican application than simply to Tula de Hidalgo, this identification of Teotihuacan as one of the Tolláns marks it as a very early use of the concept in association with an actual place. In connection with these events, there is a widespread distribution of the Fire Serpent and Feathered Serpent symbolism in Middle and Late Classic Maya ideology and in its material expression in sculpture and painting. Finally, to complete this remarkable parallel of ethnohistory and archaeology, we find that at Tula, material evidence of a kind of religious and political revolution, as described by ethnohistorical sources, was discovered in excavations atop Structure B, where the temple was razed and the sculptures were buried in the fill of a rebuilt version of the same temple, according to Jorge Acosta's research (cited in Mastache et al. 2002). Also, at both Teotihuacan and Tula the cult of Quetzalcoatl continued to play a major role in the political history of the two towns.

Whether any of the "Tollán" history refers to Teotihuacan is clearly questionable. What is not questionable, however, is that Teotihuacan was the first major urban center and the first center of an imperial state in Central Mexico and that it created a complex religious and political ideology that validated that status. This ideology was used by succeeding generations of rulers in Central Mexico and beyond[14] to validate their claims to the right to rule and to hold this same status. Duality of power, repeating cycles of time, and the sanctity of militarism are among the strongest forces that have motivated Mesoamerican culture history. Teotihuacan is surely a place where these were forged as instruments of the expansionist state, in a series of palaces that represent different patterns of rulership.

Acknowledgments

This chapter evolved out of ideas first presented in the symposium "New World Residences: The Context of Political Power" organized by Patricia Joan Sarro and Jessica Christie for the 2000 Annual Meeting of the Society for American Archaeology in Philadelphia. We appreciate their encouragement and suggestions and also appreciate comments on these ideas that have been shared by Tony Aveni, Dorie Reents-Budet, and David Webster. Given the difficulty of establishing solid dates for Teotihuacan's history, we anticipate the possibility that some of our hypotheses will turn out to be wrong, and of course we accept this responsibility as fully our own.

Notes

1. Teotihuacan's chronology is somewhat problematic because of early researchers' assumptions that the city declined at the end of the Classic period, ca. A.D. 900. Evidence has mounted that the burning along the Street of the Dead occurred in the sixth century, which requires a revision of the established chronology. Thus the literature on Teotihuacan comprises a wide range of chronological schemes.

2. Xalla compound has recently been under investigation in projects led by Leonardo López Luján, Linda Manzanilla, and William Fash (Fash et al. 2004; López and Manzanilla 2001; Manzanilla 2001; Manzanilla and López 2001), and this research promises to contribute significantly to our knowledge of the architecture and rulership of early Teotihuacan.

3. Author's translation of "fue el escenario de las principales ceremonias del presunto palacio . . . De manera sorprendente, este espacio sale completamente de la norma teotihuacana. A diferencia de la típica plaza de tres templos, la Plaza Central de Xalla cuenta con cuatro templos que ocupan los extremos cardinales y un quinto—ligeramente menor—en el centro. . . . Entre los hallazgos más signficativos realizados en la Plaza Central . . . [fueron] dos esculturas de felino emplumado" (López and Manzanilla 2001:15).

4. The enclosure of the Ciudadela (external dimension, about 400 m on a side) would be the "main courtyard," and, as George Cowgill has calculated, could serve to convene all Teotihuacanos (1983:322).

5. Cowgill (1983:151–152) analyzed the so-called palaces of the Ciudadela as seats of rulership, setting up a dichotomy between societies in which rulers had restricted control over resources and used one residence in succession (e.g., the White House in the United States), and societies in which each ruler built a new palace, demonstrating unrestricted control over resources. He cited the Aztecs as a case in point for the latter pattern, but unfortunately this generalization does not hold. There were eight known Mexica rulers of Tenochtitlan and only two, or perhaps three, known palaces, the newest having been built a few years before the Spaniards arrived (Evans 2004b).

6. Matacapan's urban area of 4–5 square kilometers exhibits the presence of a large resident population from Teotihuacan, as indicated by their household ritual artifacts such as *candelero*-style incense burners, which are related to household ritual life at Teotihuacan and are a powerful indicator of actual residence in the town by families from Teotihuacan. Matacapan may be compared to the Postclassic-period town of Tochtepec, which is nearby. Tochtepec was a provincial capital, commercial center, and garrison peopled by colonists from the Basin of Mexico.

7. When archaeologists first perceived the strength of Teotihuacan's presence at Kaminaljuyú, it seemed to suggest a Teotihuacan "empire" comparable to that of the Aztecs. But the Late Postclassic–period Basin of Mexico's population was over one million (Sanders et al. 1979), whereas the base population of the Classic-period Teotihuacan core state and the Basin of Mexico as a whole was relatively small, perhaps several hundred thousand people. This situation favored a commercial explanation for Teotihuacan traits at Kaminaljuyú: Following this line of reasoning, the base population would have been too small to have exercised military control over such a large area in the manner of the Aztec tribute empire.

8. Tikal had a population of no more than 10–20,000 during the period of Teotihuacan influence. The landscape of the southern Maya lowlands was politically fragmented, and many Maya polities probably had populations of 5,000 people or fewer.

9. Central Mexicans, even in Classic times, may have practiced a more professional type of warfare than did the Maya, gaining a certain advantage in military confrontations because of the large number of full-time professional warriors well trained in military tactics (Hassig 1992).

10. An interesting blackware ceramic vessel found at Tikal seems to portray a specific historical event, possibly pertaining to the arrival of Teotihuacanos at Tikal in A.D. 378 (Martin and Grube 2000:29). The vessel, a Teotihuacan-style cylindrical tripod, shows a file of Teotihuacan warriors marching from a structure with a typical *talud*-and-*tablero* façade and approaching a seated Maya king.

11. Ironically, it is the Mayanists themselves who have argued that Maya kings had little significant economic or political power or functions, and that their "powers" were essentially derived from their prestige as leaders with privileged access to special calendrical or shamanic knowledge, and most particularly from their role as directors of public ceremonies (see Fash 1991 and Schele and Miller 1986). These ceremonies and the erection of public monuments that accompanied them were apparently necessary to reinforce constantly what was essentially a rather weak dynastic structure. Accepting this evaluation of Maya political organization, why would we expect the Teotihuacan dynasts to behave in a similar fashion? In fact, the self-aggrandizement of Maya rulers is extreme for Mesoamerica: at no other Mesoamerican Classic or Postclassic sites, *including Aztec Tenochtitlan*, do we find such a high level of public display of individual power as that found in Classic Maya sites. With their emphasis on their preferential access to privileged knowledge, it is logical that the Maya rulers would accentuate Spear-Thrower Owl's exalted position.

12. We must emphasize that our hypotheses depend on a chronology of building episodes at Teotihuacan that is subject to revision, particularly with regard to the crucial Early and Late Tlamimilolpa phases.

13. The most detailed accounts are found in the *Annals of Cuauhtitlan* (1945) and the *Historia Tolteca-Chichimeca* (1947). Each source provides a migration legend explaining the origin of the Toltec, a dynastic list with dates, a brief outline of significant events in the history of the expansion of the Toltec state, and an account of the destruction of Tula. The lists of kings show some redundancy in names (but reuse of names was common) and overlap chronologically only with the reign of Topiltzin. The

TABLE 9.2. Lists of Toltec Rulers

Ixtlilxochitl List	Annals of Cuauhtitlan
Huemac, migrant priest leader	
Chalchiuhtlanetzin, A.D. 510–562	
Ixtlilcuechahauac, A.D. 562–614	
Huetzin, A.D. 614–666	
Totepeuh, A.D. 666–718	
Nacoxoc, A.D. 718–770	
Mitl Tlacomihua, A.D. 770–829	
Xihuiquenitzin (Queen), A.D. 829–833	
	Mixcoamazatzin, migrant military leader Huetzin, A.D. 869–?
Iztaccaltzin, 883–885	
	Totepeuh, A.D.?–887
	Ihuitimal, A.D. 887–923
Topiltzin, 885–959	Topiltzin, A.D. 923–947
	Matlacxochitl, A.D. 947–983
	Nauhyotzin I, A.D. 983–997
	Matlaccoatzin, A.D. 997–1025
	Tlilcoatzin, A.D. 1025–1046
	Huemac, A.D. 1047–1122

Source: *Adapted from Vaillant 1948:67, Table V.*

two dynastic lists are shown in Table 9.2, with dates and ruler names as presented in Vaillant (1948). It would be possible to argue that the two dynastic lists are separate accounts of two different Tolláns, and that the account of the *Historia*, with its earlier dates, might conceivably refer to Teotihuacan. The dates, however, are still too late, and given the fact that the earliest rulers each reigned for exactly 52 years, this conformance to the Calendar Round makes the chronology highly suspect. Sanders posits that if it does, in fact, refer to Teotihuacan, it may be that the list refers to the early dynasty of the city prior to the establishment of dual leadership.

14. This ideology was expressed in areas at considerable distances from Central Mexico. For example, the leader of the Quiché dynasty in highland Guatemala claimed that his ancestors were foreigners who spoke the Nahuatl language, originating in this case from southern Veracruz. Eight Deer, the ruler of a small kingdom of the Mixteca, visited a Tollán to be crowned—again, as a means to validate his right to rule.

References Cited

Annals of Cuauhtitlan
1945 *Anales de Cuauhtitlan.* In *Códice Chimalpopoca,* translated by Primo F. Velázquez, pp. 3–68. Universidad Nacional Autónoma de Mexico, Instituto de Historia, Primera Serie Prehispánica, No. 1. Imprenta Universitaria, Mexico City.

Armillas, Pedro
1964 Northern Mesoamerica. In *Prehistoric Man in the New World*, edited by Jesse D. Jennings and Edward Norbeck, pp. 291–329. University of Chicago Press, Chicago.

Aveni, Anthony F.
2000 Out of Teotihuacan. In *Mesoamerica's Classic Heritage: From Teotihuacan to the Aztecs*, edited by Davíd Carrasco, Lindsay Jones, and Scott Sessions, pp. 253–268. University Press of Colorado, Boulder.

Cabrera Castro, Rubén
1993 Mask with Shell Teeth. In *Teotihuacan: Art from the City of the Gods*, edited by Kathleen Berrin and Esther Pasztory, p. 186. Fine Arts Museum of San Francisco and Thames and Hudson, London and New York.

Cabrera Castro, Rubén (coordinador)
1982 *Teotihuacan 80–82. Primeros resultados*. Proyecto Arqueológico Teotihuacan, Instituto Nacional de Antropología e Historia, Mexico City.

Cabrera Castro, Rubén, Ignacio Rodríguez G., and Noel Morelos G. (coordinadores)
1982 *Memoria del Proyecto Arqueológico Teotihuacan 80–82*. Colección Científica 132, Vol. 1, Serie Arqueología. Instituto Nacional de Antropología e Historia, Mexico City.
1991 *Teotihuacan 1980–1982, nuevas interpretaciones*. Colección Científica, Serie Arqueología. Instituto Nacional de Antropología e Historia, Mexico City.

Cabrera Castro, Rubén, and Saburo Sugiyama
2001 The Moon Pyramid Project in Teotihuacan, Mexico. Paper presented in the symposium "State Polity and Ideology Materialized at the Moon Pyramid in Teotihuacan, Mexico" at the 66th Annual Meeting of the Society for American Archaeology, New Orleans.

Coe, William R.
1990 *Excavations in the Great Plaza, North Terrace, and North Acropolis of Tikal*. 5 vols. Tikal Reports 14. University Museum, University of Pennsylvania.

Coggins, Clemency Chase
1980 The Shape of Time: Some Political Implications of a Four-Part Figure. *American Antiquity* 45:727–739.
1993 The Age of Teotihuacan and Its Mission Abroad. In *Teotihuacan: Art from the City of the Gods*, edited by Kathleen Berrin and Esther Pasztory, pp. 140–155. Fine Arts Museum of San Francisco and Thames and Hudson, London and New York.

Cowgill, George L.
1974 Quantitative Studies of Urbanization at Teotihuacan. In *Mesoamerican Archaeology: New Approaches*, edited by Norman Hammond, pp. 363–396. University of Texas Press, Austin.
1983 Rulership and the Ciudadela: Political Inferences from Teotihuacan Architecture. In *Civilization in the Ancient Americas: Essays in Honor of Gordon R. Willey*, edited by Richard M. Leventhal and Alan L. Kolata, pp. 313–343. University of New Mexico Press, Albu-

querque; and Peabody Museum of Archaeology and Ethnology, Harvard University, Cambridge.

1997 State and Society at Teotihuacan, Mexico. *Annual Review of Anthropology* 26:129–161.

Evans, Susan Toby
2004a *Ancient Mexico and Central America: Archaeology and Culture History*. Thames and Hudson, London and New York.
2004b Aztec Palaces. In *Palaces of the Ancient New World*, edited by Susan Toby Evans and Joanne Pillsbury, pp. 7–58. Dumbarton Oaks Research Library and Collection, Washington, DC.

Fash, Barbara W., Leonardo López Lujan, William L. Fash, Laura Filloy Nadal, and Pilar Hernández
2004 The Power of Images: Destruction and Desecration of Ritual Space in the Xalla Compound at Teotihuacan. Paper presented in the symposium "The Construction and Consecration of Ritual Space in Mesoamerica," organized by Cameron McNeil and Jorge Ramos, at the 69th Annual Meeting of the Society for American Archaeology, Montreal.

Fash, William
1991 *Scribes, Warriors, and Kings: The City of Copán and the Ancient Maya*. Thames and Hudson, London and New York.

Gill, Richardson Benedict
2000 *The Great Maya Droughts: Water, Life, and Death*. University of New Mexico Press, Albuquerque.

Hassig, Ross
1992 *War and Society in Ancient Mesoamerica*. University of California Press, Berkeley.

Headrick, Annabeth
1999 The Street of the Dead . . . It Really Was: Mortuary Bundles at Teotihuacan. *Ancient Mesoamerica* 10:69–85.

Historia Tolteca-Chichimeca
1947 *Historia Tolteca-Chichimeca*. Translated by H. Berlin and S. Rendon. Fuentes para la Historia de México, No. 1. Antigua Librería Robredo, Mexico City.

Laporte, Juan Pedro, and Vilma Fialco C.
1990 New Perspectives on Old Problems: Dynastic References for the Early Classic at Tikal. In *Vision and Revision in Maya Studies*, edited by Flora S. Clancy and Peter D. Harrison, pp. 33–66. University of New Mexico Press, Albuquerque.

López Luján, Leonardo, and Linda Manzanilla
2001 Excavaciones en un palacio de Teotihuacan: Proyecto Xalla. *Arqueología Mexicana* 9(50):14–15.

Manzanilla, Linda
2001 Agrupamientos sociales y gobierno en Teotihuacan, Centro de Mexico. In *Reconstruyendo la ciudad maya: El urbanismo en las sociedades antiguas*, edited by Andrés Ciudad Ruíz, María Josefa Iglesias Ponce de León, and María del Carmen Martínez Martínez, pp. 461–482. Sociedad Española de Estudios Mayas, Madrid.

Manzanilla, Linda, and Leonardo López Luján
2001 Exploraciones en un posible palacio de Teotihuacan: El Proyecto
Xalla (2000–2001). *Tezontle, Boletín del Centro de Estudios Teoti-
huacanos* (Conaculta-Instituto Nacional de Antropología e Historia,
Mexico City) 5:4–6.
Martin, Simon, and Nikolai Grube
2000 *Chronicle of the Maya Kings and Queens: Deciphering the Dynasties
of the Ancient Maya.* Thames and Hudson, London and New York.
Mastache, Alba Guadalupe, Robert H. Cobean, and Dan M. Healan
2002 *Ancient Tollán: Tula and the Toltec Heartland.* University Press of
Colorado, Niwot.
Millon, René
1973 *Text,* Part One of *Urbanization at Teotihuacan, Mexico,* edited by
René Millon. Vol. 1, *The Teotihuacan Map.* University of Texas Press,
Austin.
1981 Teotihuacan: City, State, and Civilization. In *Supplement to the
Handbook of Middle American Indians,* Vol. 1, edited by Jeremy
Sabloff, pp. 198–243. University of Texas Press, Austin.
1993 The Place Where Time Began. In *Teotihuacan: Art from the City
of the Gods,* edited by Kathleen Berrin and Esther Pasztory, pp. 17–
43. Fine Arts Museum of San Francisco and Thames and Hudson,
London and New York.
Millon, René, Bruce Drewitt, and George Cowgill
1973 *Maps,* Part Two of *Urbanization at Teotihuacan, Mexico,* edited by
René Millon. Vol. 1, *The Teotihuacan Map.* University of Texas Press,
Austin.
Morelos García, Noel
1993 *Proceso de producción de espacios y estructuras en Teotihuacan.*
Colección Científica, Serie Arqueología. Instituto Nacional de Antro-
pología e Historia, Mexico City.
Pasztory, Esther
1997 *Teotihuacan: An Experiment in Living.* University of Oklahoma
Press, Norman.
Proskouriakoff, Tatiana
1993 *Maya History.* Edited by Rosemary A. Joyce. University of Texas
Press, Austin.
Rattray, Evelyn Childs
1987 Los barrios foráneos de Teotihuacan. In *Teotihuacan: Nuevos datos,
nuevas síntesis y nuevos problemas,* edited by Emily McClung de
Tapia and Evelyn Childs Rattray, pp. 243–274. Universidad Nacional
Autónoma de México, Mexico City.
1997 *Entierros y ofrendas en Teotihuacan: Excavaciones, inventario, pa-
trones mortuorios.* Instituto de Investigaciones Antropológicas,
Universidad Nacional Autónoma de México, Mexico City.
Roys, Ralph L.
1962 Literary Sources for the History of Mayapan. In *Mayapán, Yuca-
tán, Mexico,* edited by H. E. D. Pollock, Ralph L. Roys, Tatiana
Proskouriakoff, and A. L. Smith, pp. 25–86. Publication No. 619.
Carnegie Institution of Washington.

Sahagún, Fray Bernardino de
1981 [1569] *The Ceremonies.* Book 2 of the Florentine Codex. Translated and with notes by Arthur J. O. Anderson and Charles E. Dibble. School of American Research, Santa Fe, and University of Utah, Salt Lake City.

Sanders, William T., and Joseph Michels (editors)
1977 *Teotihuacan and Kaminaljuyú: A Study in Prehistoric Culture Contact.* Pennsylvania State University Press, University Park, PA.

Sanders, William T., Jeffrey R. Parsons, and Robert Santley
1979 *The Basin of Mexico: The Cultural Ecology of a Civilization.* Academic Press, New York.

Santley, Robert S.
1994 The Economy of Ancient Matacapan. *Ancient Mesoamerica* 5:243–266.

Schele, Linda, and Mary E. Miller
1986 *The Blood of Kings: Dynasty and Ritual in Maya Art.* Kimbell Art Museum, Fort Worth, TX.

Storey, Rebecca
1992 *Life and Death in the Ancient City of Teotihuacan: A Paleodemographic Synthesis.* University of Alabama Press, Tuscaloosa.

Stuart, David
2000 "The Arrival of Strangers": Teotihuacan and Tollán in Classic Maya History. In *Mesoamerica's Classic Heritage: From Teotihuacan to the Aztecs,* edited by Davíd Carrasco, Lindsay Jones, and Scott Sessions, pp. 465–513. University Press of Colorado, Boulder.

Sugiyama, Saburo
1992 Rulership, Warfare, and Human Sacrifice at the Ciudadela: An Iconographic Study of Feathered Serpent Representations. In *Art, Ideology, and the City of Teotihuacan,* edited by Janet Catherine Berlo, pp. 205–230. Dumbarton Oaks Research Library and Collection, Washington, DC.

1998 Termination Programs and Prehispanic Looting at the Feathered Serpent Pyramid in Teotihuacan, Mexico. In *The Sowing and the Dawning: Termination, Dedication, and Transformation in the Archaeological and Ethnographic Record of Mesoamerica,* edited by Shirley B. Mock, pp. 147–164. University of New Mexico Press, Albuquerque.

2000 Teotihuacan as an Origin for Postclassic Feathered Serpent Symbolism. In *Mesoamerica's Classic Heritage: From Teotihuacan to the Aztecs,* edited by Davíd Carrasco, Lindsay Jones, and Scott Sessions, pp. 117–143. University Press of Colorado, Boulder.

Taube, Karl A.
1992 The Iconography of Mirrors at Teotihuacan. In *Art, Ideology, and the City of Teotihuacan,* edited by Janet Catherine Berlo, pp. 169–204. Dumbarton Oaks Research Library and Collection, Washington, DC.

2000 The Turquoise Hearth: Fire, Self-Sacrifice, and the Central Mexican Cult of War. In *Mesoamerica's Classic Heritage: From Teotihuacan to the Aztecs,* edited by Davíd Carrasco, Lindsay Jones, and Scott Sessions, pp. 269–340. University Press of Colorado, Niwot.

Vaillant, George C.
1948 *Aztecs of Mexico.* Doubleday, Garden City, NY.
Wallrath, M.
1967 The Calle de los Muertos Complex: A Possible Macro-complex of
      Structures near the Centre of Teotihuacan. In Teotihuacan, *XI Mesa
      Redonda*, 1:11–122. Sociedad Mexicana de Antropología, Mexico
      City.
Webster, David L. (editor)
1989 *The House of the Bacabs, Copán, Honduras.* Studies in Pre-Colum-
      bian Art and Archaeology No. 29. Dumbarton Oaks Research Library
      and Collection[?], Washington, DC.
Wolfman, Dan
1990 Mesoamerican Chronology and Archaeomagnetic Dating, A.D.
      1–1200. In *Archaeomagnetic Dating*, edited by J. L. Eighmy and
      R. S. Sternberg, pp. 261–308. University of Arizona Press, Tucson.

CHAPTER 10

Antecedents of the Aztec Palace
PALACES AND POLITICAL POWER IN CLASSIC AND POSTCLASSIC MEXICO

Susan Toby Evans

From Classic-period Teotihuacan to Tenochtitlán in A.D. 1521, the cities of the Basin of Mexico and adjacent Tula region centered on civic and ceremonial architecture, the focus of secular and spiritual power (Figure 10.1). Archaeologically, the architectural obtrusiveness of the temple-pyramid ensured its greater survivability after the demise or transformation of the city. In contrast, the palace, generally a one-story building on a relatively low platform, was less likely to leave a recognizable form beyond that of a large, low mound with artifacts pertaining to domestic functions and possibly of more luxurious forms than those of the average house mound. However, excavations at such structures clarify their size, and the number and layout of their rooms, and such features can help us establish a diagnostic architectural signature for the ruler's official residence and administration building. This chapter uses the Aztec palace, a clear example of the congruence of form and function, to hypothesize about how Teotihuacan's and Tula's palaces looked and operated—and, by extension, how these states were administered.

The *Tecpan*-Palace as Aztec Political Capitol

The great Aztec *tecpan*-palaces of the Late Postclassic period are known to us from many descriptions by eyewitnesses, such as the informants of Juan Bautista de Pomar, Fray Bernardino do Sahagún, Diego Durán, and Fernando de Alva Ixtlilxochitl, and from several excavations of palace remains. The synthesis of these sources reveals a readily recognizable form: a large squarish building facing onto the community's main plaza, with a capacious entry courtyard overlooked by a dais room across from the main entrance (Figure 10.2). These three elements—dais room, courtyard, and plaza—are in a sense analogous to the gradations of Aztec society and political administration in that the ruler, from his vantage point, directed the conduct of state business as negotiated and carried out by the nobles, who in turn organized the common people to fulfill their tribute commitments in goods and labor.

Administration of the polity was one of the foremost functions that these

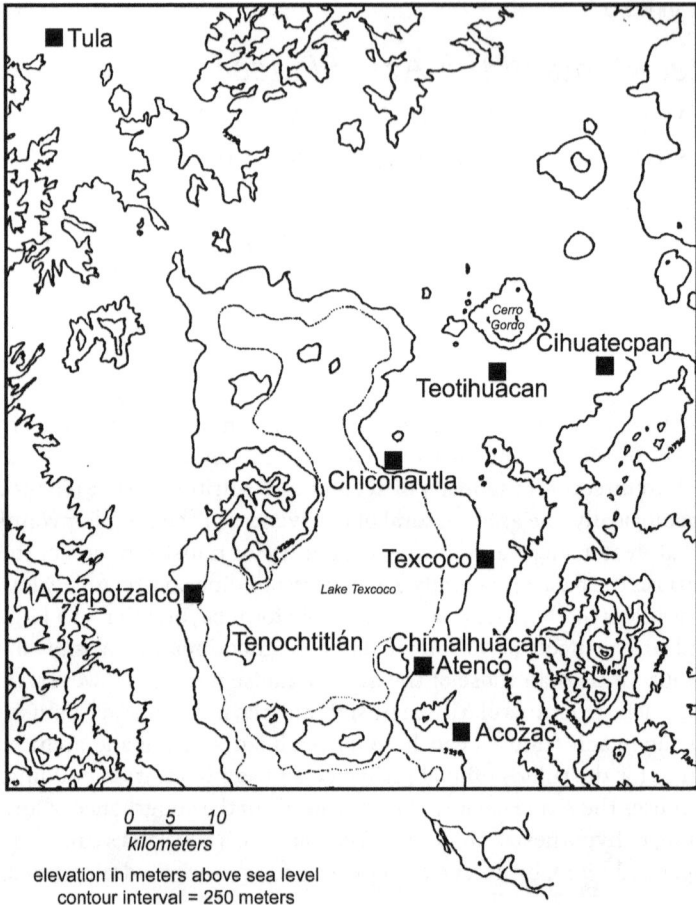

FIGURE 10.1 Central Mexico map, showing the locations of Tenochtitlán, Teotihuacan, Tula, Acozac, Azcapotzalco, Texcoco, Chimalhuacan Atenco, Chiconautla, and Cihuatecpan

palaces served; another was as the residence of the ruler and his family. A ruler's "private" life is virtually nonexistent, of course, because his domestic arrangements and daily occupations bear heavily on the state of the body politic, particularly in an archaic agrarian state where the ruler was assumed to be the living embodiment of sacred forces. However, rulers are but human in many domestic ways and need private space to sleep, share intimate moments with their close companions, meditate, bathe, defecate, and so on. These everyday activities of the ruler must be supported by the ministrations of wives and retainers, who themselves need space to sleep, to take care of their daily needs, and to do the work of the palace. In the case of the Aztecs, the palace women, assisted by servants, produced important commodities such as heirs, feasts, and textiles. Therefore, the architectural signature of an Aztec administrative-residential palace included the messy backstage spaces where all manner of prep work was performed to ensure and subsidize the success of the ongoing political drama of the dais room and main courtyard.

Thus the layout of the *tecpan*—main courtyard, dais room, suites of consultation, storage rooms, and habitation rooms—is a signature of Late Postclassic Central Mexican political administration, and all known cases, archaeological and ethnohistorical, conform to a similar pattern of plaza-courtyard–dais room (Evans 2004). To understand the roots of Aztec political organization, we look to the palace architecture of the Aztecs' predecessors in Central Mexico. Tula's palace architecture expresses some of these key features. Reaching back to Teotihuacan, this form is far less readily recognizable. The distinctions between these palace layouts suggest a transformation

FIGURE 10.2 Nezahualcoyotl's palace at Texcoco, as depicted in the Mapa Quinatzin (1959 [ca. 1542])

in the nature of rulership from Classic-period Teotihuacan to the Postclassic, wherein the *tecpan*-palace provided the appropriate forum for the chief speaker, the *tlatoani*.

The Aztec *Tecpan* as Political Forum

After the Spanish Conquest of Mexico, the job of winning the hearts and minds of the native people fell to the Spanish clergy. Pedro de Gante was among the most effective of the early proselytizers, because he used native contexts to preach the new message. He supported the continuation of certain native customs, such as using costume and dance to enliven rituals, and he perceived the importance of the form of the Aztec palace as a place where social power was displayed and where indoctrination took place. For de Gante's first three years in Mexico, in the early 1520s, he had lived in Nezahualcoyotl's palace complex in Texcoco and had observed how the main courtyard of the palace served as a public forum and an arena for political and theatrical performance (see Figure 10.2).

De Gante correctly perceived the close association of architectural form and societal function, and he used the standardized layout of the Aztec palace as an intellectual transition point, a bridge between two worlds. When, under de Gante's direction, the convent school of St. Francis was built in Mexico City on the ruins of Motecuzoma's aviary and zoo, it was laid out so that the courtyard was the main locus of instruction for the young Aztec nobles being indoctrinated into the new world order (Maza 1972).[1] De Gante's observations of how the decision-making processes of the Aztecs were carried out within a particular architectural layout ring true to what we know of Aztec administrative-residential palaces in general.

In the Aztec world, the ruling lord defined the palace: *tecpan calli* means "lord-place house," conferring the strong sense of the palace as a *place* that depended upon the presence of the *lord* for its status. *Tecpan* was applied to pleasure palaces as well as to the main administrative residential palaces in cities, but it was not a word that was used indiscriminately. There were strict rules governing the establishment of *tecpans*—the Texcocan king Nezahual-pilli had one of his only legitimate sons executed for establishing a palace without his father's permission (Karttunen and Lockhart 1987:157). Because of the courtly/governmental functions taking place in the *tecpan* courtyard, the presence of another *tecpan* in Texcoco may have constituted a rival court.

After the conquest, with the establishment of native governors, *tecpan*'s meaning was simplified to "community house"—a town hall, the place where civic business was conducted (Evans 2001:240; Haskett 1991:32). This emphasizes the old Aztec political forum as a strongly secular place, particularly one where economic matters were dealt with. At the Aztec *tecpan*, the tribute flow of goods and services was coordinated—taking in and accounting for the crops from the lands owned by the palace as an institution; the tributes of goods both quotidian and exotic; the labor of construction workers, sweepers, chocolate makers, musicians, and courtesans—and some of these goods and services were distributed back to the community and the polity. Of course, amid this counting-house atmosphere, the central courtyard was the arena for rituals, entertainments, and courtly displays of rhetoric (Evans 1998a:176–177; 2001:245–246). Many of the words echoing through the tecpan's walls would have had a strong spiritual flavor—the metaphorical nature of the Nahuatl language ensured that every word carried with it a baggage train of associations: related concepts, homonyms and puns thereupon, well-known prayers, adages and poems (Karttunen and Lockhart 1986, 1987; Pomar 1941:39–41; Sahagún 1969, 1979).

However, the Aztec state was based on the flow of materials and labor, and the Aztec political system functioned as a structure for channeling goods and services from the farmer-artisan societal foundation through tecpans at local and regional central places, up to the imperial tecpans in the capitals (Berdan and Smith 1996; Carrasco 1982; Smith and Hodge 1994). The tecpan courtyard functioned as a sort of nexus at each hierarchical level of Aztec society and of the political economy, displaying the power of the related dynastic families who became the most powerful lineages in all of Mesoamerican culture history.

Archaeological evidence of tecpans is scarce, considering their abundance in Aztec times, when there were probably about 500 administrative palaces in the Basin of Mexico (Evans 2004:10). They served nearly a million people and ranged from the great establishments of Tenochca and Texcocan kings, to the administrative residences of city-state tlatoque (sing. tlatoani), to the roomy but unpretentious country villas of local lords overseeing clusters of farming villages.[2] In the Basin of Mexico, significant remains of only four tecpans have been investigated, none of them an imperial palace: three partial examples of city-state palaces, one each at Acozac (Ixtapaluca Viejo), Chimalhuacan Atenco, and Chiconautla, and one complete village tecpan at Cihuatecpan. Investigation of the tecpans at Chimalhuacan Atenco (García et al. 1998) and at Chiconautla (Elson 1999; Vaillant and Sanders 2000) has been limited to peripheral areas of these buildings, not the main courtyard and dais rooms, thus information about them is insufficient to provide a sense of the important features of public political life. At Acozac, survey and excavation operations recovered what seem to have been the main courtyard and the dais room (Blanton 1972; Brüggemann 1983; Contreras 1976).

In fortunate contrast, ethnohistorical sources describing the Aztec period and its aftermath provide reams of description—and a few actual plans—that document palace forms and functions. The courtyard was the focus of the community's secular life, the place where the movers and shakers spent their time, partaking in political events or, more often, waiting for such events to happen while gossiping and feasting (Evans 1991, 2001).

The combination of archaeological and ethnohistoric sources provides a modest range of pertinent examples, with the imperial tecpan represented

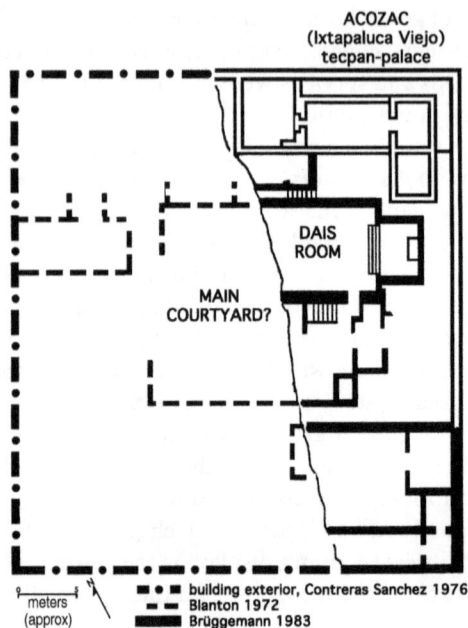

FIGURE 10.3 The city-state *tecpan*-palace at Acozac. This very hypothetical reconstruction of the plan is based on several sources: Jürgen Brüggemann's (1983) plan of the structure as excavated by Eduardo Contreras (1976) in 1973–1974, made after the northwest side of the building was destroyed, and Richard Blanton's (1972) plan of the surface features visible before excavation and before partial destruction.

by the plan of Nezahualcoyotl's palace at Texcoco (see Figure 10.2); the city-state *tecpan*, by the remains at Acozac (Figure 10.3); and the village *tecpan*, by Structure 6 at Cihuatecpan (Figure 10.4). All were situated adjacent to large open spaces—formal or informal plazas. A casual glance at these plans shows striking similarities—the building's square shape and the presence of the main courtyard and dais rooms as dominant features—but in the interest of careful observation, it should be noted that the Acozac plan is fragmentary, even though it shows part of a probable dais room and courtyard. Furthermore, while the Texcoco plan is an abstraction, it clearly shows the courtyard activity crucial to the political economy of the Late Postclassic Basin of Mexico: the convocation of city-state lords, presided over by the paramount lord—in this case, the *huetlahtoani* of Texcoco.

Ancestry of the Tecpan

Given the assumption that the Aztec *tecpan*'s architecture served the state's political and economic functions, it seems logical to assume that examination of Central Mexican elite residences in earlier periods might throw light upon the operation of the political economy administered from them. Moreover, such palaces might reveal something about the *tecpan's* genesis and ancestry. Does the principal palace at Teotihuacan or Tula provide an antecedent form that displays the key architectural elements of the Aztec *tecpan?* Is it adjacent to a plaza? Does it have a large main courtyard, readily accessible from the building's exterior, with a dais room to serve as a stage for political performance in front of the courtyard audience? If these conditions—or some of them—are met, what does it tell us about the forms of government found at Teotihuacan and Tula? Is the dynastic tribute empire a sui generis construct of Late Postclassic Central Mexico, or is its development foreshadowed in the palaces of its cultural forebears?

The answers are far from clear. The archaeological and culture-historical

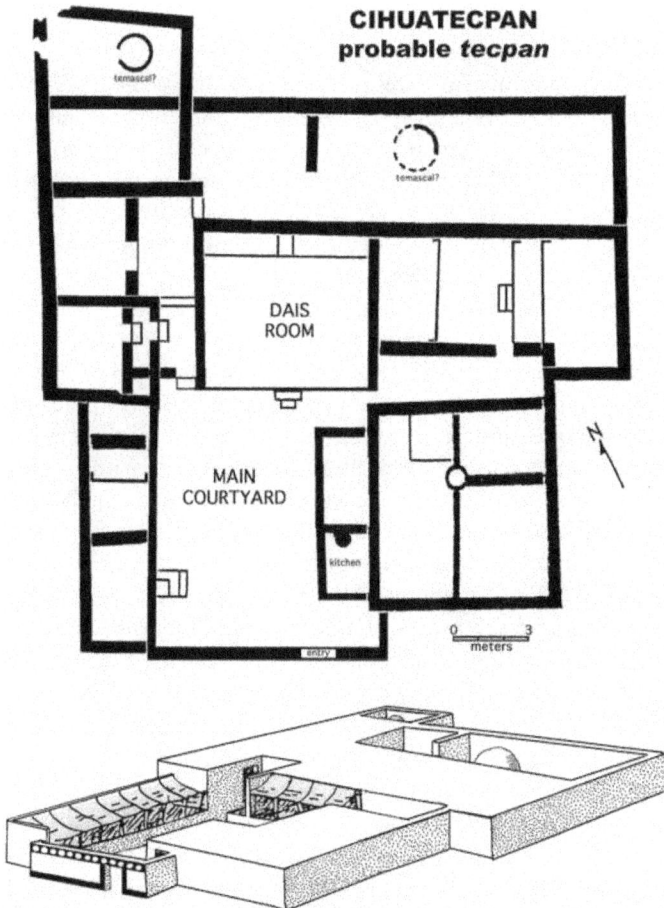

FIGURE 10.4 The village *tecpan* at Cihuatecpan

records are so riddled with lacunae that the fragments of material culture and operational patterns barely form recognizable entities. However, comparison of elite residential architecture at Teotihuacan and Tula with that of the Basin of Mexico in the Late Postclassic period reveals a modest degree of continuity of features, with stronger resemblance between Toltec palaces and Aztec *tecpans* than between Teotihuacan's presumed ruling compounds and those of the Aztecs. Moreover, the key features are not united architecturally in the buildings identified as palaces at Teotihuacan, but they seem to be at Tula. Thus, there seem to be actual disjunctions in form and function among the three cultures, in addition to those created by an inadequate sample of administrative-residential palaces. If such perceptions are genuine, and not merely the product of overenthusiastic reconstruction of a limited database, then they may reflect the different political regimes of the three cultures.

Teotihuacan

Classic-period Teotihuacan's status as an ancestral society to that of the Postclassic Aztecs is logical in spatial and temporal terms, because both cultures matured in and dominated the Basin of Mexico. However, attribution of cultural ancestry is beset by problems of documentation and interpretation.[3] These arise in part from our lack of understanding about *how* power was held in Teotihuacan, much less *who* the power holders were, or *where* they lived and administered their domain.

Elsewhere in this volume (Chapter 9), William T. Sanders and I discuss Teotihuacan's apartment compounds, with emphasis on the different compounds that have been posited as seats of rulership; here I will summarize the cogent points pertaining to the form of Teotihuacan's probable rulers' palaces as an expression of the functions the power holders served, insofar as scholars can reconstruct them. Past and present research (summarized in Chapter 9, this volume) seems to indicate a sequence of palaces adjacent to the Street of the Dead, from the turn of the millennium to the time of the abandonment of the civic-ceremonial core of the city. Possibly, the first palace was the Xalla Compound in the northeastern sector, near the Pyramids of the Sun and the Moon, after which rulership may have moved to the palace complexes of the Ciudadela, and, finally, Teotihuacan's rulers may have occupied the Street of the Dead Complex in the center of the city (Figure 10.5).

Looking at the plans of these compounds (Figures 10.5, 10.6, and 10.7), we see obvious differences as well as strong continuities. One of the strongest continuities is the arrangement of rooms (traditionally called "temples") around interior courtyards. This pattern is typical of apartment compounds throughout the city, regardless of the social status of their inhabitants. Furthermore, there is no clear "dais room," although in the Street of the Dead Complex, the excavated room complex centrally located along the west side

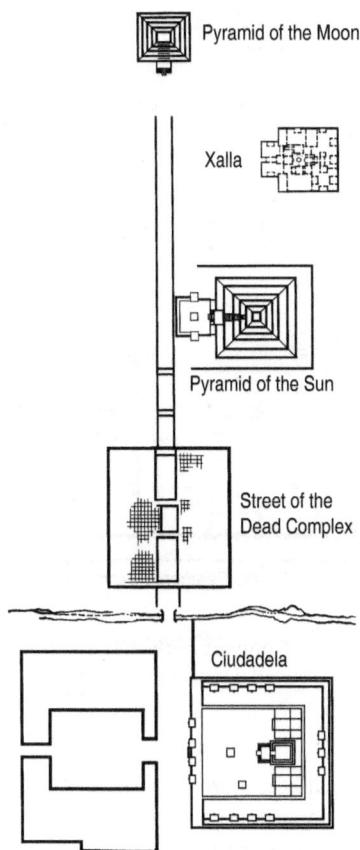

FIGURE 10.5 Major monumental architecture along the Street of the Dead in Teoti-huacan (Mexico). The Xalla Compound is at the upper right; its plan as shown here is based on the surveys of the Teotihuacan Mapping Project (Millon et al. 1973). This map shows its relation to the Pyramid of the Moon and the Pyramid of the Sun. Note how the compound faces onto a large square area, which, after the Terminal Formative period, was covered by the northern extent of the Street of the Dead and a number of three-temple complexes in *talud*-and-*tablero* style. Although the use of this space during the Terminal Formative period is not known, the symmetry of Xalla's relationship to the two large pyramids suggests that they may have shared a large, open ceremonial space, possibly an early civic plaza. Map by Evans based on Millon et al. 1973.

of the Street of the Dead would serve this purpose, and it may be mirrored by another similar complex on the east side.

A major difference among the three possible palaces is their relation to a plaza or main courtyard. The Xalla Compound was first located during the Teotihuacan Mapping Project (Millon et al. 1973:31 [N4E1]). Recent excavations at Xalla have uncovered a central patio, about 30 m across, that "was

CIUDADELA NORTH COMPLEX OR PALACE

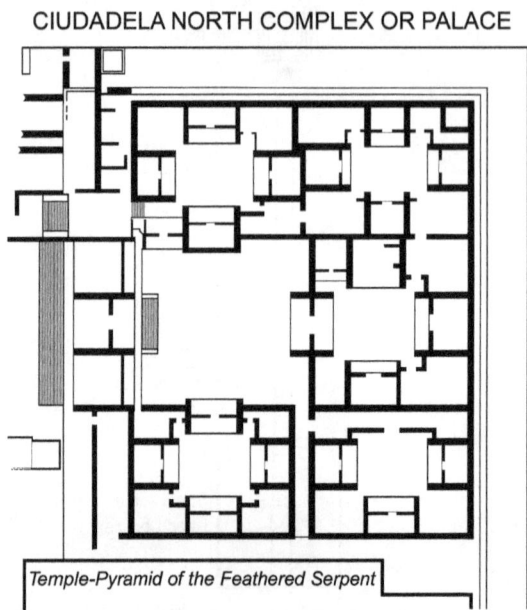

FIGURE 10.6 Plan of the North Complex of the Ciudadela, Teotihuacan (Mexico; the South Complex is nearly identical). Drawing by Evans, based on Cabrera 1982 and Cabrera et al. 1982, 1991.

the scene of the principal ceremonies of the presumed palace . . . In a surprising way, this space departs completely from the Teotihuacan norm. In contrast to the typical patio with three temples, the Plaza Central of Xalla has four temples in the cardinal directions, and a fifth—slightly smaller—in the center" (López and Manzanilla 2001:15).

But the central plaza—one of eight large patios within Xalla—does conform to the Teotihuacan norm, in that it is an interior space, entirely surrounded by suites of rooms. Taking a longer view, Xalla's "main courtyard," in terms of the rituals and convocations presided over by its residents, may have been the huge square space bounded by its western façade on the east, and by the Pyramid of the Moon on the north and Pyramid of the Sun on the southeast (Figure 10.5).

In sharp contrast, the Ciudadela is dominated by its massive interior courtyard, and the whole structure is dramatically enclosed. The courtyard is so large that "up to 100,000 persons could fit into this plaza without much crowding. In other words, at least the entire active adult population of the city" (Cowgill 1983:322). In terms of the plaza-courtyard-dais pattern of the Aztec *tecpan*, the Ciudadela seems to concatenate the plaza into the courtyard, and place the Temple-Pyramid of the Feathered Serpent, a dais fit for a god, in the stage location where the ruler would oversee the drama of statecraft.

The Street of the Dead Complex (Figure 10.7) actually combines the typical Aztec elements best, although in a different configuration, with the Street of the Dead itself forming an entry courtyard, overlooked by the West Plaza Compound ("conjunto plaza oeste" in Morelos 1993, Plan E.4.2 and elsewhere) and perhaps also by its east-side counterpart. As a courtyard, the sections of the Street of the Dead that are enclosed within the compound extend outward into the more public sphere of the other sections of the Street

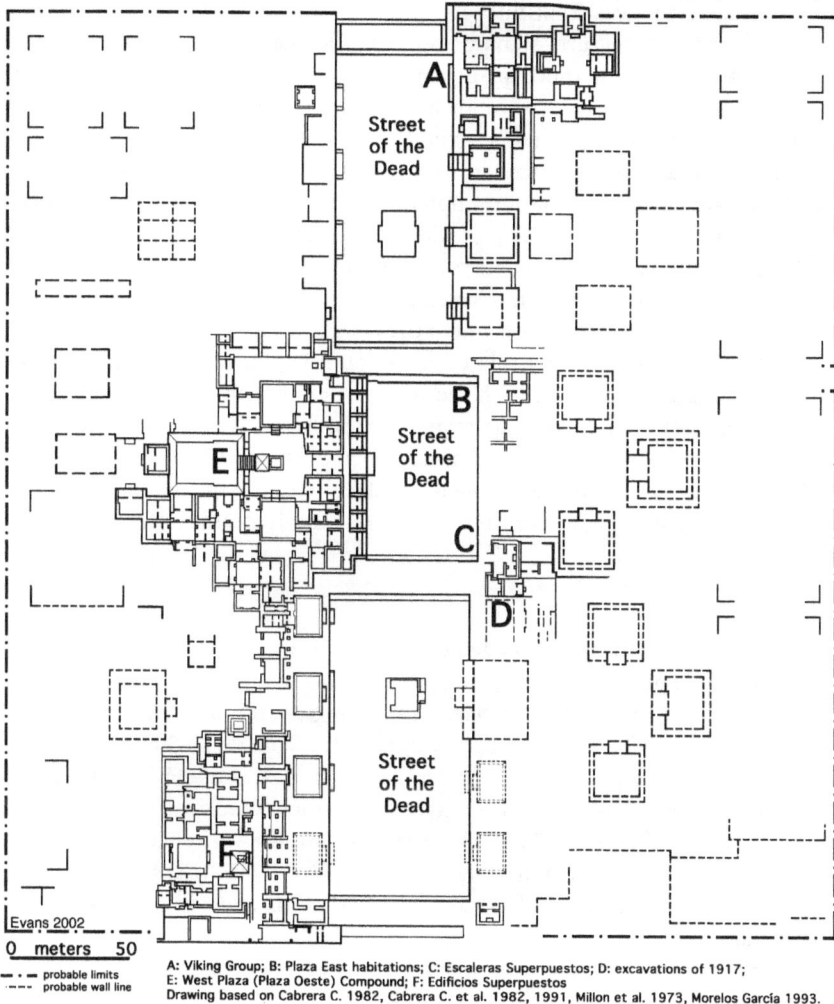

STREET OF THE DEAD COMPLEX
(Teotihuacan, Mexico)

A: Viking Group; B: Plaza East habitations; C: Escaleras Superpuestos; D: excavations of 1917;
E: West Plaza (Plaza Oeste) Compound; F: Edificios Superpuestos
Drawing based on Cabrera C. 1982, Cabrera C. et al. 1982, 1991, Millon et al. 1973, Morelos García 1993.

FIGURE 10.7 Plan of the Street of the Dead Complex, Teotihuacan (Mexico). Drawing by Evans, based on Cabrera 1982; Cabrera et al. 1982, 1991; Millon et al. 1973; Morelos 1993.

of the Dead. The Street of the Dead Complex does not, however, deliver the package of plaza-courtyard-dais as it would function in the context of Aztec political administration.

Teotihuacan's Political Sphere

We know that Teotihuacan's influence was widespread, from northwestern Mesoamerica down to the Guatemalan highlands and beyond, but the nature of this influence is poorly understood. Trade in green obsidian from the Pachuca sources was far-reaching, and Thin Orange, though manufactured in Puebla, evidences Teotihuacan contact. How these items, and iconographic and architectural signatures of Teotihuacan, were transported is a matter of speculation: perhaps by long-distance *pochteca*-style traders, by down-the-line trade, by armies, or more peaceably by colonists seeking to establish their own domains far from Central Mexico.

Although Teotihuacan's range of influence was impressive and its huge concentrated urban population unprecedented, its local hinterland population was very small. The Basin of Mexico's Terminal Formative– and Early Classic–period settlement patterns (Sanders et al. 1979) reveal that Teotihuacan was a primate city with few secondary centers until well into the Classic period. Thus, Teotihuacan was not at the head of a vast Aztec-style dendritic network of towns ruled by related noble families, in a countryside full of villages of farmer-artisans, with the whole system channeling tribute up to the paramount ruler. If we understand that the Aztec *tecpan* courtyard functioned as a place to negotiate administration of the political economy, it is clear that Teotihuacan did not need a palace with a large main courtyard, and Teotihuacan's administrative-residential architecture reflects this.

Tula

In its prime, Teotihuacan needed quantities of limestone, which it sought from the Tula region. The town of Chingú seems to have been established in order to secure this resource (Díaz 1980). Chingú's architecture and some of its artifacts echo Teotihuacan's. However, as the Tula region became a focus of political power in its own right, in the Late Classic and Early Postclassic periods, its culture was forged as a hybrid, of which Teotihuacan's influence was only one of several. Tula, like Teotihuacan, drew strength from militarism and from long-distance trade. Unlike Teotihuacan, Tula's surrounding region was thickly settled with farming towns and villages (Mastache et al. 2002).

In the Early Postclassic Tollán phase (A.D. 900 to 1150 or 1200), Tula was the most powerful city in the Central Mexican region, which encompassed the Basin of Mexico and adjacent areas to the north and west. Tula seems to have been the primary power in a triumvirate that also included the Basin of

Mexico towns Culhuacan and "Otumba."[4] Even after Tula declined, its fame lived on in the popular imagination as a legendary paradise lost, where the streets were paved with gold; chocolate grew on trees; and palaces were made of jade, silver, and shell (Torquemada 1975–1983 [1615] Lib. VI, Cap. XXIV, pp. 81–82).

To date, no construction materials on this order have been identified at Tula; however, many buildings there have been called palaces by archaeologists working at the site for over a century. The insouciance of the use of the term *palace* makes Tula's buildings challenging to interpret: a palace seems to have been any large mound near the site center that was not clearly a temple platform, a ballcourt, or other functionally distinctive structure.

This tendency perhaps derives from Tula's distinctive colonnaded architecture, impressive roofed-over buildings sharing the sacred space of the ceremonial precinct with the two main pyramids. It should be noted that the colonnaded architecture so strongly developed at Tula and her sister city, Chichén Itzá, is not as imposing a feature at Aztec palaces, according to architectural remains or illustrations. Teotihuacan's buildings also featured a more modest expression of multiple colonnades than those at Tula.

This trait is, however, well known from several sites in western and northwestern Mexico: at La Quemada and Alta Vista (both in Zacatecas), colonnaded halls were important features, and both of these sites were flourishing in the period between A.D. 500 and 900 (Kelley and Kelley 2001; Nelson 2001). It was during the end of Tula's pre-Tollán Prado phase (A.D. 700–850) that Tula's civic-ceremonial focus was established, and the Tula region showed an influx of Coyotlatelco peoples, whose culture became widespread, extending from the Bajío and Zacatecas in the northwest to the Basin of Mexico and Puebla (Cobean and Mastache 2001:189).

Coyotlatelco "influence" has intrigued archaeologists for years (Acosta 1945, cited in Cobean and Mastache 2001) but is still poorly understood. In terms of the problems at issue here, the most important question would be: Is the form of the colonnaded hall congruent with a governmental function? Is it a meeting hall? At Tula, examples like the Burned Palace and the Palace of Quetzalcoatl (discussed below) have square rooms with the colonnades surrounding a square central courtyard. The central courtyards here do not seem to have had altars, as would have been the case at Teotihuacan; instead, built-in hearths, called *tlequiles* by the Aztecs, are found among the columned circumference of the courtyard. These are common at Tula's residential complexes (such as El Canal; Healan 1974), as they were at Teotihuacan.

Tula's "Palaces"

Ever since Désiré Charnay's time (1887), large buildings near Tula's pyramids have been called palaces, particularly the Burned Palace and the Palace of

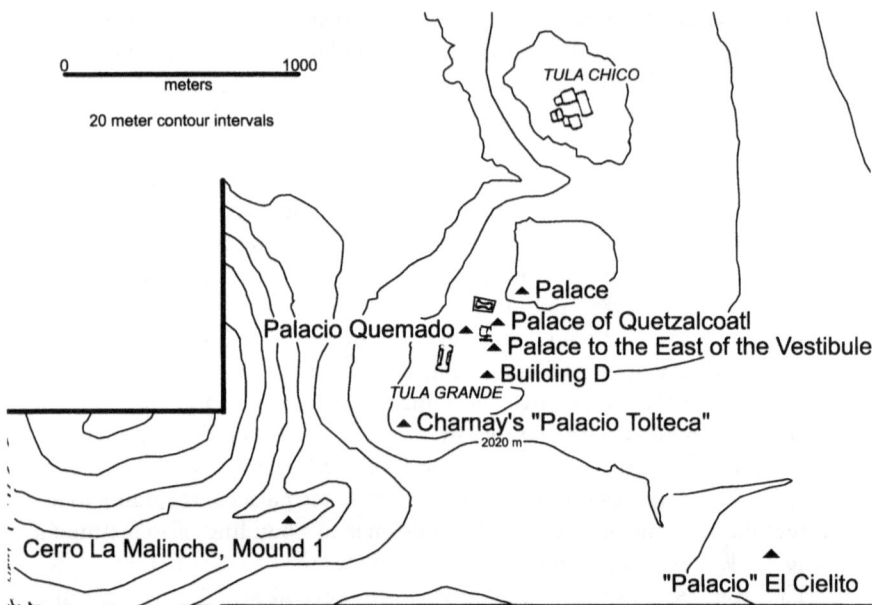

FIGURE 10.8 Tula and surrounding environs, with plan showing location of "palaces."
After Paredes 1990:Plan 2.

Quetzalcoatl. It is useful to consider those buildings named as "palaces" of
Tula to clarify which structures actually were elite administrative residences
(Figure 10.8).

Building 1, the Palace of Quetzalcoatl, is a relatively small, square building, about 20 m on a side, consisting of a single colonnaded room with an
interior square patio. This building, by itself, is probably not an elite administrative residence.

Building 4, the Palace to the East of the Vestibule, extends east of the
colonnaded L-shaped vestibule at the base of Pyramid B and is at the base of
the north side of Tula's largest pyramid, Pyramid C. Recent excavations here
(Cobean et al. 2005) indicate a layout similar to that of Aztec palaces, with
a reception area backed by residential rooms.

Building 2, Palace, consists of fragmentary remains of sets of rooms about
100 m northeast of Ballcourt 1. Some ceramics date from the Tollán phase,
but the bulk of the material remains are from the later Postclassic, with
ceramics of Aztec III and IV types (Paredes 1990:118). This was possibly an
elite residence during the Tollán phase, but evidence is insufficient.

*Building 3, Palacio Quemado ("Burned Palace" or "Palace of the Col-
umns"),* runs for about 80 m along the northern side of Tula's main plaza,
just west of the Pyramid of Tlahuizcalpantecuhtli (Pyramid B). Dominated
by three large, squarish colonnaded rooms, each with an interior patio, this

building seems an ideal setting for certain kinds of ceremonies and for meetings associated with the administration of a sophisticated state.

> Acosta coined the name Palacio Quemado because he thought it was a palace which was burned to the ground when Tula was abandoned. . . . It seems unlikely to have been a residential palace because the layout does not resemble other Toltec houses, no kitchens have been identified, and there are not nearly enough rooms for a palace. Furthermore, Acosta found caches of tobacco pipes and other ceremonial objects which suggest a non-residential function. I suspect the building served as a council hall where priests or rulers met, deliberated, and staged rituals like those shown in the friezes [which adorn its banquettes]. The same was undoubtedly true of the Palacio de Quetzalcoatl. (Diehl 1983:65)

Building D (Annex C) is a large, high platform just south of Pyramid C and may have been the base of ritual or residential buildings.

Cerro la Malinche, Mound 1 ("Un Palacio Tolteca" [Rodríguez 1995]) is an isolated hilltop residence about 1 km southwest of the main plaza of Tula. The remains of many rooms at different levels cover an area at least 20 × 20 m, and the structure is an important Coyotlatelco building, quite possibly an elite residence, but not an administrative-residential palace (Guadalupe Mastache, personal communication, 2000).

Palacio El Cielito is a hilltop complex about 1.5 km southeast of Tula's main plaza. This was the Early Colonial–period home of the local native ruler, one of Motecuzoma Xocoyotzin's sons (Diehl 1981).

Palacio Tolteca. Ironically, the building that Charnay excavated in the late nineteenth century and called the Toltec Palace (Figure 10.9) is one of the most likely candidates for the city's main residential palace. Unfortunately, little functional analysis was done of its layout or other material remains, even in terms of comparison with other Tula residences as to size and plan.

The Palacio Tolteca lies at the southwest corner of Tula's main plaza. If Ignacio Marquina (1951:151) is correct in assuming that the building's central patio is 25 m on a side, then the building measures at least 50 × 50 m, according to the unscaled plan in Charnay (1887:107). In fact, Charnay describes finding "an inner courtyard, a garden, and numerous apartments on different levels, ranged from the ground floor to 8 ft. high . . . the whole covering a surface of 2,500 square yards" (ibid., 108). The building may have been even larger; if it was symmetrical in design, and the "Reception Room" (#4) was centrally located, the front façade of the building may have extended 80 m, making the area it covered roughly 4,000 m².

Although diagnosis of this structure's Tollán-phase layout and size must await further investigation, the plan recovered by Charnay bears much in common with later Aztec palaces, and it seems to fulfill the three *tecpan*

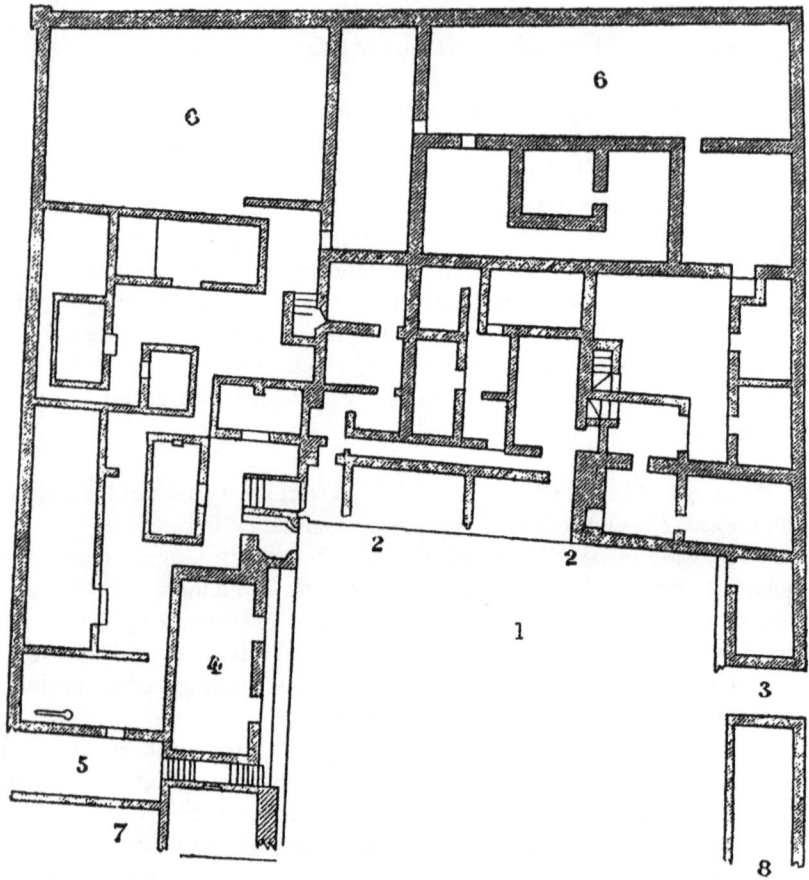

FIGURE 10.9 Plan of Palacio Tolteca, Tula, as reprinted from Charnay 1887:107. Désiré Charnay describes the plan as follows: "No. 1 . . . is the inner courtyard, which
we take as our level; No. 3 to the right, paved with large pebbles, is the main entrance. Facing this to the left, No. 7 is a small room about 4 ft. high, which was
entered by a flight of seven low steps; it is a Belvedere, from which a view of the
whole valley could be obtained. Next comes No. 4, perhaps a reception-room, 32 ft.
long, having two openings towards the court. On the other side, to the north, is a
smaller, narrower Belvedere, from which an ante-room, on a slightly lower level,
furnished with benches, was reached. The main body of the palace consists of ten
apartments of different size, with stuccoed walls and floors. The façade, No. 2, 8 ft.
high, opens on the courtyard; whilst two winding stone staircases to the right, and
an equal number to the left, led to the apartments on the first storey. . . . No. 6,
No. 6, are a kind of yards, without any trace of roof, and if we are to judge from
Aztec dwellings, they were probably enclosures for domestic and wild animals. . . .
Here and there [were] closed-up passages, walls rebuilt . . ." (ibid., 108–110).

criteria: (1) it is next to, and seems to open out on, the city's main plaza; (2) it has a huge main courtyard entered from the outside (in contrast to the much smaller and more private Teotihuacan interior patios); and (3) the entryway faces a raised-dais room (what Charnay calls the "reception-room"; see Figure 10.9). It is also adjacent to other major civic-ceremonial structures, including one of the ballcourts, a propinquity of palace and ballcourt found throughout Mesoamerica from Early Formative Paso de la Amada to contact-era Acozac—and Tenochtitlán.

The central interior patio known to us from Teotihuacan's apartment compounds seems, at Tula's Palacio Tolteca, to have assumed a much greater importance, to have become a substantial courtyard. Courtyards in Tula's residential buildings in general are relatively larger in size and more directly accessible than those at Teotihuacan. An important continuity, from Teotihuacan to Tula, is the central altar, the shrine of ancestor veneration (Richard A. Diehl and Dan M. Healan, personal communications, 1999), although in some cases this feature has been transformed into a rectangular cut-stone hearth, a *tlequil* (see Healan 1977:145 for a discussion of these hearths in Tula's houses). Such hearths would have served several practical and ideological purposes: sources of heat in the thin, chilly air and loci of incense burning to venerate deities, possibly ancestral spirits. Aztec architecture incorporated the *tlequil*—at Cihuatecpan's *tecpan* a *tlequil* is an important feature of the lord's dais room—but both the Toltecs and Aztecs also used huge braziers, which had the advantage of some portability if the different functions of the room required it and also brought the heat closer to the individuals standing around them.[5]

Palace and Society at Tula

Tula represents the dawn of the historical age of Central Mexican culture, in the sense that some events that occurred in the Tollán phase, and even earlier, were recorded in histories that survived into the Colonial period. Scholarly interpretation of the Toltec sphere of influence has posited that Tula held sway over a large area extending up into the Bajío, southwest through Toluca and southeast through the Basin of Mexico, and down into Morelos.[6] The two major activities that might have secured this region into some kind of coherent political unity are trade and militarism. Aztec policies nicely combined these aspects of expansionism in the *pochteca*, but there is no strong evidence of an organized merchant guild at Tula. Nor is there evidence contradicting it. As for a dendritically organized system of tributary towns and villages, linked by the related nobles who ruled over them, we can assume that in most archaic states with a hierarchy of settlement types (in contrast to the Basin of Mexico in Teotihuacan times), such systems were in place, and the historical closeness of the Toltecs to the Aztecs would argue for the continuation of rule by noble houses back into the Early Postclassic past.

The paucity of evidence about Tula's political and economic organization makes it difficult to generalize about how the palace might have functioned in these regards, but the Palacio Tolteca's large courtyard and the dais room overlooking it would argue for convocations of individuals in the presence of the ruler. Possibly, the Burned Palace and Palace of Quetzalcoatl served functions similar to the elite warrior meeting halls adjacent to the Templo Mayor in Tenochtitlán. In fact, a decisive piece of supporting evidence is Tenochtitlán's Red Temple, whose frieze-adorned banquettes were either looted from Tula or copied from Toltec originals. In contrast to meeting halls of elite warriors, the main courtyard of the Palacio Tolteca may have been for meetings of a different kind, conferences of lords ruling towns in the Tula region and beyond (much like the meeting depicted in the Mapa Quinatzin), perhaps to discuss tribute requirements and possible military action, while the rituals of solidarity unifying the cadres of elite soldiers took place elsewhere.

Tula to Tenochtitlán

The architectural transition from Tula to Aztec sites is largely undocumented, but the cultural heritage that the Aztecs drew from the Toltecs of Tula is much better understood than the relationship between Teotihuacan and the Aztecs. The Mexica Aztecs secured their ambitions by copying and appropriating Toltec sources of spiritual power, taking the rootstock of the Tenochtitlán dynasty from that of Culhuacan, Tula's direct descendants in the Basin of Mexico, and taking the core of their tribute empire from the Tepanecs of Azcapotzalco, a newer community founded by migrants into the Basin in the last centuries of Tula's apogee.

We have noted that Basin of Mexico native history emphasizes that Tula shared power with Culhuacan and Xaltocan. Unfortunately, we have no revealing information on administrative-residential architecture at these sites,[7] and ethnohistoric accounts describing this period date from much later, the sixteenth century or after. Culhuacan was Tenochtitlán's spiritual parent, the city that provided the important connection back to Tula and its power and prestige, but in terms of economic power, the Tepanec capital, Azcapotzalco, was Tenochtitlán's mentor. Unfortunately, we have no material evidence of Azcapotzalco's palace, the excavations at Santiago Ahuitzotla having uncovered a large residential building of Classic to Late Postclassic age but uncertain particular function (Tozzer 1921), and excavations at nearby Pueblo Perdido uncovered an Early Postclassic palace (Rattray 1972:203–208). The Codex Xolotl does, however, depict "palace" enclosures, with large courtyards providing entry onto dais rooms (Figure 10.10). Whether this is a projection of later styles back to the earlier part of the Postclassic period or an actual expression of the architecture of the times cannot be resolved without archaeological documentation.

FIGURE 10.10 Maxtla, the Tepanec ruler, receives Nezahualcoyotl of Texcoco in this scene from the Codex Xolotl. Maxtla's palace is abstracted down to three elements: the plaza (lower room); the courtyard (to the right), where Nezahualcoyotl waits; and the dais room (at left), where Maxtla and his wife rather rudely ignore Nezahualcoyotl.

Tenochtitlán and Texcoco took over Azcapotzalco's tribute realm and then made it into something much greater, a tribute empire demanding complex administration. By the time their authority extended to both coasts of ancient Mexico, the Basin of Mexico was thickly settled and its peoples were well integrated into a very regularized system of elite-administered tributes in goods and services. At every level of administration, at *tecpans* large and small, persons responsible for organizing the tribute payments met with the local lords to confer, debate, and negotiate. Feasts and rituals were also very much a part of *tecpan* courtyard life, but it was the business of Aztec political economy and the indoctrination of new generations into Aztec political practices that were the crucial activities taking place there.

Classic Culture, Postclassic Culture, and the *Tecpan*

Mesoamericanist scholars traditionally have emphasized the secular nature of the Postclassic period in contrast to the religious focus of the Classic period. This oversimplification justifiably lost popularity as the actual social complexities of these eras became clearer with closer study. Nevertheless, it must be admitted of the Aztec tribute empire that in no previous era was the administration of the flow of wealth over such a vast area and from such a large tributary population so important. This was a secular transformation of several orders of magnitude, and we would expect that administrative architecture would reflect this essential function.

In spite of problems with the extent of archaeological data and documentary sources covering cultures antedating the Aztec, existing elite residences from Teotihuacan and Tula seem to confirm the trend toward the palace's role in administering an extensive secular domain, which seems to be irrelevant at Teotihuacan, to gain strength at Tula, and to be most strongly expressed among the Aztecs. At the same time, all three cultures drew great economic strength from long-distance trade and from the well-organized militarism that protected it. The return to the capital of armies and cadres of traders and porters provided occasions for dramatic demonstration of the power of the state. Tenochtitlán's long, plastered causeways and central Zócalo; Tula's great plaza and extensive colonnaded halls; and Teotihuacan's Street of the Dead all provided splendid venues for these events.

Even so, Tenochtitlán's array of different kinds of settings for the many administrative and ceremonial events involved in statecraft at such a large scale is of a magnitude and complexity that far transcended earlier Mesoamerican states. Hernán Cortés became part of a great Aztec processional when he was met by Motecuzoma on the causeway from Ixtapalapa. Later, he was impressed by the hundreds of men in daily attendance at Motecuzoma's palace, and he saw the main courtyard activity as characteristic of courtly political and economic life as he knew it from the courts of Spain. Power came from the dais room, was received in the main courtyard, and from there was disseminated out into the public world. The Aztec *tecpan*, to a greater extent than any other Mesoamerican lordly dwelling, was the stage of global power.

Acknowledgments

This chapter was first presented in the symposium "New World Residences: The Context of Political Power" organized by Patricia Joan Sarro and Jessica Christie for the 2000 meetings of the Society for American Archaeology in Philadelphia. I appreciate the help of Bob Cobean, Dick Diehl, Dan Healan, and Guadalupe Mastache in providing suggestions about the interpretation of Tula's architecture, Bill Sanders for insights into Teotihuacan's palaces, and Mike Smith for general suggestions. This study is part of a series of investigations into the Aztec palace stemming from field research at the Aztec site of Cihuatecpan in the Teotihuacan Valley (sponsored by the National Science Foundation and the Instituto Nacional de Antropología e Historia) and documentary research about Aztec palaces (sponsored by the Pre-Columbian Studies program at Dumbarton Oaks, Washington, DC). For other aspects of this research project, see Evans 1991, 1993, 1998a, 1998b,

2000, 2001, and 2004 and Evans and Abrams 1988:118–181. Responsibility for the ideas—and possible misinterpretations—presented herein is mine.

Notes

1. The open-air chapel of sixteenth-century Mexico is also an offshoot of the palace courtyard, as well as an architectural descendant of the temple complex courtyard, as John McAndrew has argued (1965); see also Mendiola 1985:21–24.

2. For a discussion of the rural *tecpan* at Cuexcomate (Morelos), see Smith 1992; the probable rural *tecpan* at Cihuatecpan is described in Evans 1991 and Evans and Abrams 1988:118–181.

3. The Aztecs drew heavily on Teotihuacan's architecture and sculpture for aesthetic and iconographic inspiration, but "[i]n this way, the Mexicas were rescuing a past that was never their own" but were merely adopting its attributes to legitimize themselves (Matos and López 1993:164–165).

4. According to Chimalpahin (Schroeder 1991:168); it should be noted that in the Early Postclassic, Otumba, the "place of the Otomí," was Xaltocan, not the Otumba that became a significant Late Postclassic city-state in the Teotihuacan Valley.

5. " 'They leave fires [lit] in their courtyards, which in this land are very large and elegant; for the people, being too many for the churches, have their chapels in the courtyards so that all may hear Mass on Sundays and feast days while the churches are sufficient for week days' " (Motolinía 1971:91–92).

6. Tula's relationship with northern Yucatán, particularly Chichén Itzá, is a matter of much debate and is outside the scope of this paper.

7. Excavation at Xaltocan may have located a corner of the platform of a public building (Elizabeth Brumfiel, personal communication, 1999).

References Cited

Acosta, Jorge
1945 La cuarta y quinta temporada de excavaciones en Tula, Hgo., 1943–
1944. *Revista Mexicana de Estudios Antropológicos* 7:23–64.
Berdan, Frances F., and Michael E. Smith
1996 Imperial Strategies and Core-Periphery Relations. In *Aztec Imperial Strategies*, by Frances F. Berdan, Richard E. Blanton, Elizabeth Hill Boone, Mary G. Hodge, Michael E. Smith, and Emily Umberger, pp. 209–217. Dumbarton Oaks Research Library and Collection, Washington, DC.
Blanton, Richard E.
1972 *Prehispanic Settlement Patterns of the Ixtapalapa Peninsula Region, Mexico.* Department of Anthropology, Pennsylvania State University, University Park, PA.
Brüggemann, Jürgen K.
1983 Acozac. *Beiträge zur Allgemeinen und Vergleichenden Archäologie* 5:323–334.
Cabrera Castro, Rubén
1982 Presentación. In *Memoria del Proyecto Arqueológico Teotihuacan 80-82*, coordinated by Rubén Cabrera Castro, Ignacio Rodríguez

García, and Noel Morelos García, pp. 9–12. Colección Científica 132, Vol. 1. Instituto Nacional de Antropología e Historia, Mexico City.

Cabrera Castro, Rubén, Ignacio Rodríguez García, and
Noel Morelos García (coordinadores)
1982 Memoria del Proyecto Arqueológico Teotihuacan 80–82. Colección Científica 132, Vol. 1. Instituto Nacional de Antropología e Historia, Mexico City.

Cabrera Castro, Rubén, Ignacio Rodríguez García, and
Noel Morelos García (coordinadores)
1991 Teotihuacan 1980–1982, nuevas interpretaciones. Colección Científica, Serie Arqueología. Instituto Nacional de Antropología e Historia, Mexico City.

Carrasco, Pedro
1982 The Political Economy of the Aztec and Inca States. In The Inca and Aztec States 1400–1800, edited by George A. Collier, Renato I. Rosaldo, and John D. Wirth, pp. 23–40. Academic Press, New York.

Charnay, Désiré
1887 The Ancient Cities of the New World: Being Voyages and Explorations in Mexico and Central America from 1857 to 1882. Harper and Brothers, New York.

Cobean, Robert H., and Alba Guadalupe Mastache Flores
2001 Coyotlatelco. In Archaeology of Ancient Mexico and Central America: An Encyclopedia, edited by Susan Toby Evans and David L. Webster, pp. 187–189. Garland Publishing, New York.

Cobean, Robert H., Alba Guadalupe Mastache, María Suárez Cortés,
Javier Figueroa Silva, Blanca Estela Martínez, Clemente Salazar, and
Fernando Báez Urincho
2005 Proyecto Tula: 2004 Informe. Archivo Técnico, Coordinación Nacional de Arqueología, Instituto Nacional de Antropología e Historia, Mexico City.

Codex Xolotl
1980 [1553–1569]   Códice Xolotl. Edited by Charles E. Dibble. Instituto de Investigaciones Históricas, Serie Amoxtli 1. Universidad Nacional Autónoma de México, Mexico City.

Contreras Sánchez, Eduardo
1976 La zona arqueológica de Acozac, México; temporada 1973–1974. Boletín 16 (n.s.):19–26. Instituto Nacional de Antropología e Historia, Mexico City.

Cowgill, George L.
1983 Rulership and the Ciudadela: Political Inferences from Teotihuacan Architecture. In Civilization in the Ancient Americas: Essays in Honor of Gordon R. Willey, edited by Richard M. Leventhal and Alan L. Kolata, pp. 313–343. University of New Mexico Press, Albuquerque; and Peabody Museum of Archaeology and Ethnology, Harvard University, Cambridge.
1997 State and Society at Teotihuacan, Mexico. Annual Review of Anthropology 26:129–161.

Díaz Oyarzábal, Clara Luz
1980 Chingú: Un sitio clásico del area de Tula, Hgo. Colección Cientí-

fica, Serie Arqueología, no. 90. Instituto Nacional de Antropología e Historia, Mexico City.

Diehl, Richard A.
1981 Tula. In *Supplement to the Handbook of Middle American Indians*, Vol. 1, edited by Jeremy A. Sabloff, pp. 277–295. University of Texas Press, Austin.
1983 *Tula: The Toltec Capital of Ancient Mexico*. Thames and Hudson, London.

Elson, Christina M.
1999 An Aztec Palace at Chiconautla, Mexico. *Latin American Antiquity* 10:151–167.

Evans, Susan Toby
1991 Architecture and Authority in an Aztec Village: Form and Function of the Tecpan. In *Land and Politics in the Valley of Mexico*, edited by Herbert Harvey, pp. 63–92. University of New Mexico Press, Albuquerque.
1993 Aztec Household Organization and Village Administration. In *Prehispanic Domestic Units in Western Mesoamerica*, edited by Robert Santley and Kenneth Hirth, pp. 173–189. CRC Press, Boca Raton, FL.
1998a Sexual Politics in the Aztec Palace: Public, Private, and Profane. *RES* 33:165–183.
1998b Toltec Invaders and Spanish Conquistadors: Culture Contact in the Postclassic Teotihuacán Valley, Mexico. In *Studies in Culture Contact*, edited by James G. Cusick, pp. 335–357. Occasional Paper 25. Center for Archaeological Investigations, Southern Illinois University.
2000 Aztec Royal Pleasure Parks: Conspicuous Consumption and Elite Status Rivalry. *Studies in the History of Gardens and Designed Landscapes* 20:206–228.
2001 Aztec Noble Courts. In *Royal Courts of the Ancient Maya*, edited by Takeshi Inomata and Stephen Houston, 1:237–273. Westview Press, Boulder, CO.
2004 Aztec Palaces. In *Palaces of the Ancient New World*, edited by Susan Toby Evans and Joanne Pillsbury, pp. 7–58. Dumbarton Oaks Research Library and Collection, Washington, DC.

Evans, Susan Toby, and Elliot M. Abrams
1988 Archaeology at the Aztec Period Village of Cihuatecpan, Mexico: Methods and Results of the 1984 Field Season. In *Excavations at Cihuatecpan*, edited by Susan Toby Evans, pp. 50–234. Vanderbilt University Publications in Anthropology 36, Nashville, TN.

García, Raúl, Felipe Ramírez, Lorena Gámez, and Luis Córdoba
1998 *Chimalhuacan: Rescate de una historia*. Municipio de Chimalhuacan and Instituto Nacional de Antropología e Historia, Toluca, Mexico.

Haskett, Robert
1991 *Indigenous Rulers: An Ethnohistory of Town Government in Colonial Cuernavaca*. University of New Mexico Press, Albuquerque.

Healan, Dan M.
1974 Residential Architecture at Tula. In *Studies of Ancient Tollán*, edited

by Richard Diehl, pp. 16–24. University of Missouri Monographs in Anthropology No. 1. Columbia.

1977   Architectural Implications of Daily Life in Ancient Tollán, Hidalgo, Mexico. *World Archaeology* 9:140–156.

Karttunen, Frances, and James Lockhart

1986   The Huehuehtlahtolli Bancroft Manuscript: The Missing Pages. *Estudios de Cultural Nahuatl* 18:171–179.

Karttunen, Frances, and James Lockhart (editors)

1987   *The Art of Nahuatl Speech: The Bancroft Dialogues.* UCLA Latin American Center Publications, University of California, Los Angeles.

Kelley, J. Charles, and Ellen Abbott Kelley

2001   Alta Vista de Chalchihuites. In *Archaeology of Ancient Mexico and Central America: An Encyclopedia*, edited by Susan Toby Evans and David L. Webster, pp. 16–17. Garland Publishing, New York.

López Luján, Leonardo, and Linda Manzanilla

2001   Excavaciones en un palacio de Teotihuacan: Proyecto Xalla. *Arqueología Mexicana* 9(50):14–15.

Mapa Quinatzin

1959 [ca. 1542]   Mapa Quinatzin. In *Mexican Manuscript Painting of the Early Colonial Period*, by Donald Robertson, Plates 13, 46–47, pp. 135–140. Yale University Press, New Haven.

Marquina, Ignacio

1951   *Arquitectura prehispánica.* Memorias del Instituto Nacional de Antropología e Historia, No. 1. SEP/Instituto Nacional de Antropología e Historia, Mexico City.

Mastache, Alba Guadalupe, Robert H. Cobean, and Dan M. Healan

2002   *Ancient Tollán: Tula and the Toltec Heartland.* University Press of Colorado, Niwot.

Matos Moctezuma, Eduardo, and Leonardo López Luján

1993   Teotihuacan and Its Mexica Legacy. In *Teotihuacan, Art from the City of the Gods*, edited by Kathleen Berrin and Esther Pasztory, pp. 156–165. Fine Arts Museum of San Francisco and Thames and Hudson, London and New York.

Maza, Francisco de la

1972   Fray Pedro de Gante y la capilla abierta de San José de los Naturales. *Artes de México* 150:33–38.

McAndrew, John

1965   *The Open-Air Churches of Sixteenth-Century Mexico.* Harvard University Press, Cambridge.

Mendiola Quezada, Vicente

1985   *Arquitectura del Estado de México en los Siglos XVI, XVII, XVIII y XIX.* Ediciones del Gobierno del Estado de México, Toluca, Mexico.

Millon, René, Bruce Drewitt, and George Cowgill

1973   *Maps*, Part Two of *Urbanization at Teotihuacan, Mexico*, edited by René Millon. Vol. 1, *The Teotihuacan Map.* University of Texas Press, Austin.

Morelos García, Noel

1993   *Proceso de producción de espacios y estructuras en Teotihuacan.*

Colección Científica. Instituto Nacional de Antropología e Historia, Mexico City.

Motolinía, (Fray Toribio de Benavente)

1971 [ca. 1540]   *Memoriales, o Libro de las cosas de la Nueva España y de los naturales de ella.* Universidad Nacional Autónoma de México, Mexico City.

Nelson, Ben A.

2001 Northwestern Frontier. In *Archaeology of Ancient Mexico and Central America: An Encyclopedia*, edited by Susan Toby Evans and David L. Webster, pp. 528–535. Garland Publishing, New York.

Paredes, Blanca

1990 *Unidades habitacionales en Tula, Hidalgo.* Colección Científica. Instituto Nacional de Antropología e Historia, Mexico City.

Pomar, Juan Bautista

1941 [1582]   Relación de Tezcoco. In *Relaciones de Tezcoco y de la Nueva España*, by Pomar-Zurita, pp. 1–64. Editorial Salvador Chávez Hayhoe, Mexico City.

Rattray, Evelyn

1972 El complejo cultural Coyotlatelco. In *XI Mesa Redonda: Teotihuacan*, 2:201–210. Sociedad Mexicana de Antropología, Mexico City.

Rodríguez, María J.

1995 Sistema constructivo en un palacio tolteca. In *Arqueología del norte y del occidente de México: Homenaje al Doctor J. Charles Kelley*, edited by Barbro Dahlgren and María Soto de Arechavaleta, pp. 131–145. Universidad Nacional Autónoma de México, Mexico City.

Sahagún, Fray Bernardino de

1969 [1569]   *Rhetoric and Moral Philosophy.* Book 6 of the Florentine Codex. Translated and edited by Charles E. Dibble and Arthur J. O. Anderson. School of American Research, Santa Fe, and University of Utah, Salt Lake City.

1979 [1569]   *Kings and Lords.* Book 8 of the Florentine Codex. Translated and with notes by Arthur J. O. Anderson and Charles E. Dibble. School of American Research, Santa Fe, and University of Utah, Salt Lake City.

Sanders, William T., Jeffrey R. Parsons, and Robert Santley

1979 *The Basin of Mexico: The Cultural Ecology of a Civilization.* Academic Press, New York.

Schroeder, Susan

1991 *Chimalpahin and the Kingdoms of Chalco.* University of Arizona Press, Tucson.

Smith, Michael E.

1992 *Archaeological Research at Aztec-Period Rural Sites in Morelos, Mexico.* University of Pittsburgh Memoirs in Latin American Archaeology 4. Pittsburgh, PA.

Smith, Michael E., and Mary G. Hodge

1994 An Introduction to Late Postclassic Economies and Polities. In *Economies and Polities in the Aztec Realm*, edited by Mary G. Hodge and Michael E. Smith, pp. 1–42. Studies in Culture and Society 6. Institute for Mesoamerican Studies, SUNY Albany, and University of Texas Press, Austin.

Torquemada, Juan de

1975–1983 [1615]   *Monarquía indiana.* 6 vols. Instituto de Investigaciones Históricas. Universidad Nacional Autónoma de México, Mexico City.

Tozzer, Alfred M.

1921 Excavation of a Site at Santiago Ahuitzotla, D.F. Mexico. *Smithsonian Institution Bureau of American Ethnology Bulletin 74.*

Vaillant, George C., and William T. Sanders

2000 Excavations at Chiconautla. In *The Teotihuacan Valley Project Final Report,* Vol. 5, *The Aztec Period Occupation of the Valley,* Part 2, *Excavations at T.A. 40 and Related Projects,* edited by William T. Sanders and Susan Toby Evans, pp. 757–787. Occasional Papers in Anthropology 26. Department of Anthropology, Pennsylvania State University, University Park, PA.

PART 4

Comparison of Palaces across Cultures

CHAPTER 11

Elite Residences at Farfán

A COMPARISON OF THE CHIMÚ
AND INKA OCCUPATIONS

Carol Mackey

Introduction

In seventeenth-century France, the turrets and high walls of a lord's country estate echoed the estate's past function as a fortress, even though military activities had ceased (Girouard 1999). These impressive structures could be seen from far away, and because of their size, they made a lasting imprint upon the landscape. The scale of these estates and their aura of power apply equally to the monumental structures built by the provincial lords who ruled Peru's north coast in the centuries prior to the Spaniards' arrival. The sheer height of the adobe walls and the space they surrounded dominated the coastal desert horizon. Many of these structures served as more than elite residences, especially when the elite were government officials. In these instances, as Morris states, ". . . [the] building is often transformed into a seat of government, becoming literally and symbolically the seat of the state" (Morris 2004).

The Kingdom of Chimor, or Chimú, occupied over 1,000 km of Peru's north coast. The origins of the Chimú polity (A.D. 900–1000) have been traced back to their capital, Chan Chan. Prior to the Inka Conquest around A.D. 1460–1470, Chimor was the largest coastal power in South America. During their expansion, the Chimú established outlying provincial centers that housed government officials who supervised the administration of conquered lands. The Inkas, however, created the largest and most powerful Andean empire. They began their expansion in the fifteenth century from their highland capital, Cuzco. At the apex of their power, they controlled territories that encompassed at least five modern South American countries.

This chapter focuses on the archaeological site of Farfán, located in the Jequetepeque Valley on Peru's north coast (Figure 11.1), which was a major provincial administrative center during the occupation of two empires—the Chimú and the Inka. Like the seventeenth-century French country residences, Farfán retained elements of its past under Chimú rule while the Inkas added or emphasized new activities. Recent excavations at Farfán have

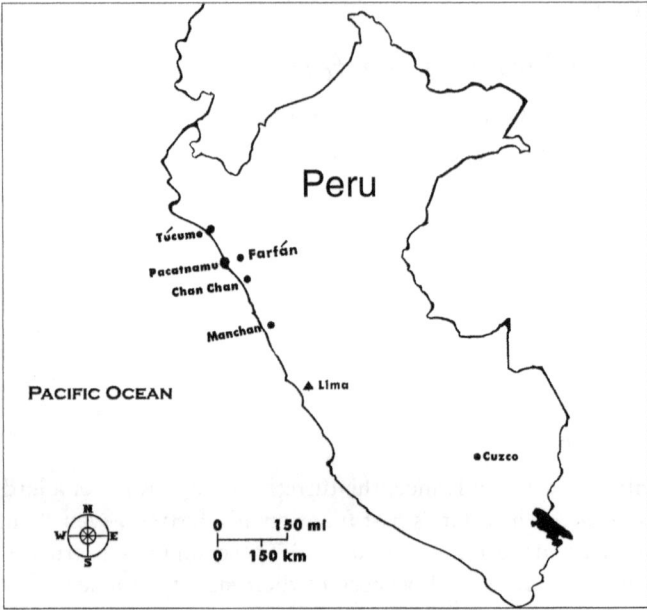

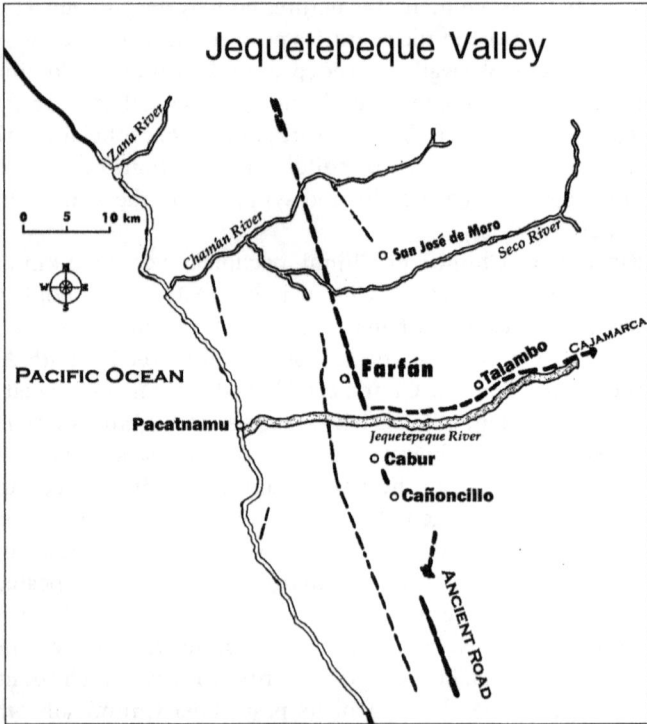

FIGURE II.I Map of Peru and of the Jequetepeque Valley

highlighted the differences in residential patterns during the two occupations, providing a clearer understanding of the ranks of the supervising officials and their duties. By focusing on the numbers, sizes, construction materials and locations of the administrators' residences, as well as the other
activities at the center, it is evident that both empires had different policies
regarding the role and duties of the administrators and the function of the
provincial center. At Farfán, the Chimú ruled through a few high-ranking
officials. These Chimú nobles, it appears, left most of the mundane bureaucratic work to lower-level Chimú officials and local lords who managed various portions of the valley. The Inka, on the other hand, added administrative positions at Farfán and used these functionaries as well as local elites to
manage the valley. Farfán offers an excellent opportunity to study changes in
Chimú and Inka elite residential patterns and administration because of the
site's lengthy occupation—at least 250 years—longer than any other known
Andean administrative center.

Architectural Analysis

In preindustrial societies, the structures that housed the elite show great
variability, especially in rural areas. Since the term *elite* is synonymous
with the "rich, powerful, and privileged in any society" (Chase and Chase
1992), the buildings inhabited by the elite reflect their position within society. Structures communicate power by their size, height, and construction materials. These characteristics reflect the power of the elites in acquir-
ing and controlling natural and human resources. By their very nature, elite
structures evoke some kind of emotion, whether it is awe, a sense of identity based on political or kin relations, security, or ideology. Elites control
the institutions on which society is based, and they shape the policies that
define the political, economic, and ideological aspects of society (cf. Mann
1986). The results of their actions and the policies of the states they represent are manifested in the architecture and layout of their multifunctional
residential-administrative centers.

The analysis of architectural remains is key to understanding behavior
in complex societies. These remains are permanent and, like other artifacts,
can be classified according to type, form, function, construction techniques,
and chronological placement (Moore 1992). Adherence to canons of state architectural style has been used to measure the degree of political dominance
of a conquering society. When the architecture in a subjugated area mimics
that of the dominant society, it either emulates the style of the conquerors
or reflects the coercive power of the dominant society (Covey 2000; Mackey
and Klymyshyn 1990; Menzel 1959).

In addition, architectural analysis can determine social class or rank by
noting the presence or absence of certain architectural elements, such as
types of construction materials and associated artifacts (cf. Klymyshyn 1982;

Topic 1982). Since the Chimú constructed most of Farfán, the Chimú capital, Chan Chan, has provided a baseline for Chimú architectural elements (Keatinge and Conrad 1983). When the Inkas occupied Farfán, they remodeled some structures and constructed new ones. Their building program was more innovative and did not completely adhere to either coastal or highland traditions. Before turning to Farfán, however, we will review state architectural elements of Chan Chan and of Cuzco, the Inka highland capital.

Residences of the Nobility at the Chimú and Inka Capitals

The Chimú Rulers at Chan Chan: The Chimú nobility occupied ten palaces at Chan Chan (Figure 11.2). These rectangular adobe palaces, called *ciudadelas,* resemble fortresses with surrounding walls three stories high (9 m). The city and the palaces that make up its core were built sequentially over 500 years, beginning in approximately A.D. 900–1000. The city core covered an area of 6 km² occupied by some 30,000 inhabitants (Kolata 1990; Moseley 2001; Topic and Moseley 1983).

The highly stratified nature of Chimú society is reflected in the city's built environment. Two social classes resided at Chan Chan: the nobility and the attached craft specialists. The distinct architecture of these groups, which were internally ranked, was defined by construction materials, the size of the structures, and internal architectural elements. Each *ciudadela,* or palace, was a self-contained city, designed to protect the rulers from cradle to grave. During a ruler's lifetime, each palace served as the seat of political, economic, and religious power and, on the ruler's death, as his burial place. Nonroyal nobles lived in smaller structures within the core city, close to the palaces in residences called elite compounds (Klymyshyn 1982). Craft specialists, on the other hand, resided in perishable, cane-walled structures located within and around the city. Although the artisans were not members of the nobility, they did not form part of the lowest class, since their work put them in contact with the nobility. These artisans produced high-status metal, textile, feather, and wood objects encoded with Chimú religious iconography. The goods legitimized the status of the resident nobles and were offered as gifts to ensure the cooperation of conquered elites.

The adobe structures' architectural features are the main criteria used in differentiating the activities and ranks of the noble class. The emblem of noble status and state authority was a room called an *audiencia,* identified by its U shape and niched walls (Figure 11.3). The number of *audiencias* within a given palace averaged 15, and they functioned as residences/working areas for royalty and possibly their families. Although small, these *audiencias* generally had an adjoining patio and were the only rooms consistently roofed. Although roofing was an added architectural detail, it was probably a necessity, since these spaces were used during the day as well as at night (Andrews 1974; Day 1982). Although some of the U-shaped structures are located near the storerooms, it is not clear whether all the noble bureaucrats controlled

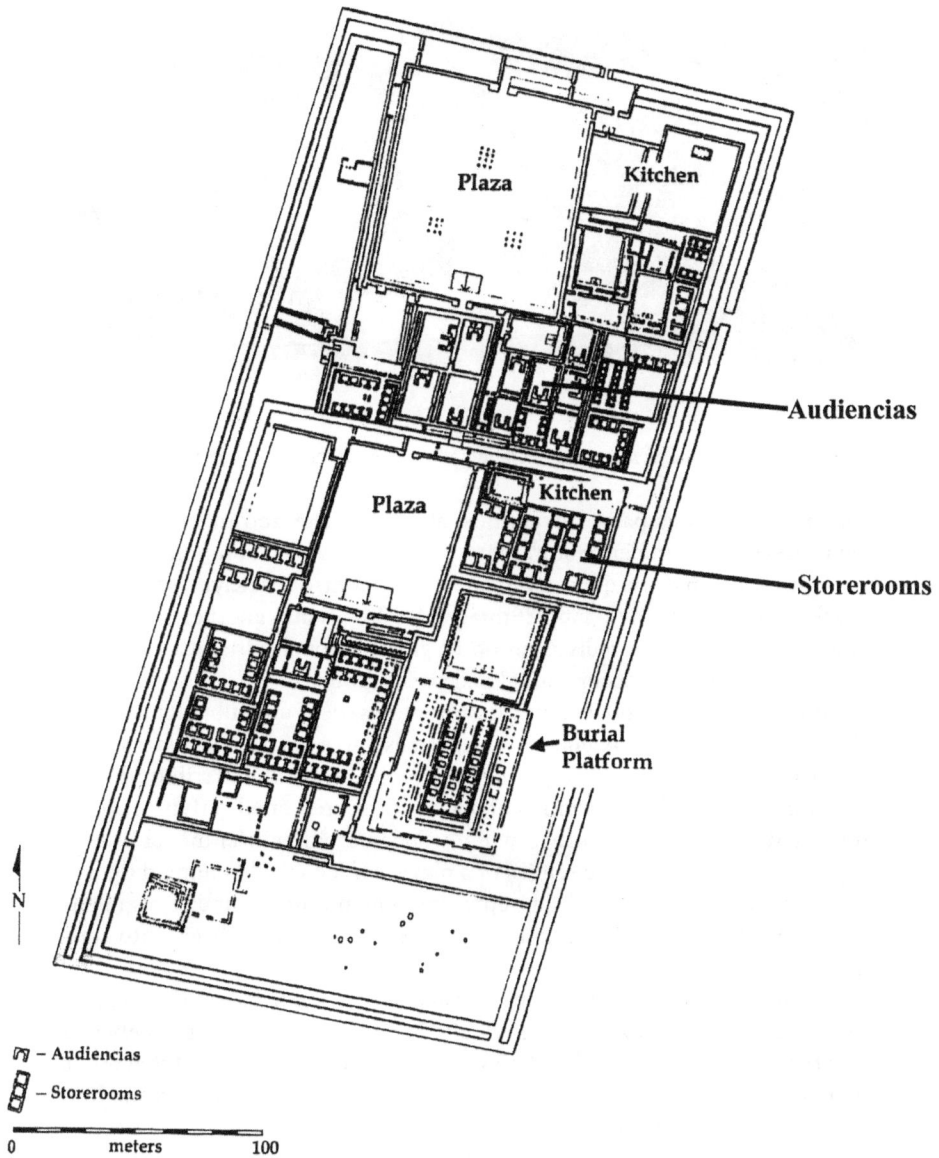

FIGURE 11.2 Plan of Ciudadela Rivero, Chan Chan. After Moseley and Mackey 1974.

storage (see Moore 1996). Given the number of *audiencias* per palace, it is probable that they had functions other than residential (Moseley 2001).

In addition to the *audiencias*, each palace contained other architectural elements such as storerooms, plazas, and a burial platform (Day 1982; Moseley 1975; Pillsbury and Leonard 2004; see Figure 11.2). Warehousing goods was a main function of each palace. Rooms devoted to storage are among

FIGURE 11.3 Example of a late six-niched U-shaped *audiencia* at Chan Chan

the most numerous palace structures, averaging over 200 in each (Klymy-shyn 1987). The number of storerooms underscores the economic power of the ruling elite and the quantity of goods they controlled (Klymyshyn 1987; Mackey and Klymyshyn 1990). Storage also highlights another important Chimú principle—the redistribution of goods through gifts, feasting, and provisioning of other occupational and status groups.

Some of the goods housed in the storerooms were undoubtedly used for the ceremonies that took place in the palaces' large plazas. The plazas symbolize political integration, since the ruling elite redistributed tribute during feasts and rituals. The association of plazas with ceremonial activities is corroborated by the recent discovery of a wooden architectural model (Uceda 1997). Inside the miniature replica of a plaza, carved wooden human figures appear to be honoring the dead, represented by mummy bundles, as musicians play and others pour liquid, most likely *chicha* (maize beer), into cups (Figure 11.4).

Burial platforms also symbolized royal power in the palaces. Although all the burial platforms have been severely damaged by looting, it is believed that the central portion of the tomb was reserved for the king, and that other individuals, mainly females, were sacrificed and buried in the surrounding cells (Conrad 1982; Pozorski 1979).

A group of retainers or servants tended to the needs of the palaces' royal residents. They lived in housing that was generally in the palace interior but segregated from the nobility. The distinction between the two areas is very clear, since the retainers lived in small, perishable cane-walled buildings. Whereas areas devoted to royal or noble residence were swept clean of debris, remains of hearths, cooking vessels, and rubbish point to domestic life in retainer areas (McGrath 1973).

Outside the palaces and scattered among them are the remains of the smaller residences of the lesser nobility. Although these smaller structures share many of the palaces' architectural features, the lack of some features points to important differences in activities and ranks. On-site cooking facilities indicate that these residences and work areas were self-contained. The residences have low exterior walls, little storage space, and no burial platforms (Klymyshyn 1982). Storage areas may have contained commodities, tools, or raw materials used by artisans rather than long-term storage goods. This signals that the lower-level nobility may have supervised labor and the distribution of goods to craft specialists (Klymyshyn 1982; Topic 1990). These elite compounds also lack large plazas, indicating that the lower-level nobles were probably guests in the palaces rather than hosts of their own ceremonies.

This brief review of the palaces at the Chimú capital draws attention to several features, some of which are found in the provinces (Mackey 1987).

FIGURE 11.4 Wooden architectural model showing activities within a Chan Chan plaza. Photograph by Santiago Uceda.

The most notable is the self-contained nature of the compounds. During the Chimú reign, each palace was the focus of the Chimú Empire's political and religious power and represented a variety of state institutions. On the king's death, it became his final resting place. The nobility lived in and among the areas devoted to storage, and scholars have long considered this association as more than just symbolic. It does appear that the palaces, besides serving as royal residences, were actively engaged in accumulating and distributing the empire's wealth. This included foodstuffs, raw materials, and luxury items that depicted elements of Chimú cosmology. Chan Chan's palaces recall Max Weber's (Kolata 1983) term *oikos*, or the princely household, where all the activities and all the other players—the lesser nobility, artisans, and servants—revolved around the palace. Several architectural forms functioned as important identifiers of rank: the burial platform reserved for royalty and the *audiencia* used by all ranks of the nobility (see Figure 11.2). The plaza, an important space for feasting and ceremonies, provided the venue for the nobility to interact with their subjects and to display and distribute the goods they had accumulated.

Residences of the Inka Nobility at Cuzco

The architecture and layout of Cuzco, the Inka capital located in the southern Peruvian Andes, contrasts with the coastal Chimú capital (Figure 11.1). It is impossible to compare the noble residences of the two capitals, since Cuzco, unlike Chan Chan, is a thriving modern city. It was partially destroyed during the Inka rebellion of 1536 and has seen considerable remodeling (Niles 1999; Rostworowski and Morris 1999). Like Chan Chan, Cuzco revolved around the nobility. Inka nobility was also ranked, and the king, who was perceived as a living god, sat at the apex.

Whereas a Chimú ruler focused on his palace, Cuzco's kings focused on the city. Ethnohistoric descriptions indicate that Inka Cuzco showed greater architectural and functional complexity than the *ciudadelas* of Chan Chan. The city's structures included royal palaces, residences of the lower nobility, several plazas—including an imposing central square—as well as a principal temple (Gasparini and Margolies 1980; Hyslop 1990; Kendall 1985; Niles 1999). Like Chan Chan's *ciudadelas*, *kanchas* were walled compounds with one entrance and several buildings in the interior. Despite the similarities between the two capitals, there were differences. In Cuzco, the king's palace was not as self-contained as those of the Chimú monarchs. While the Chimú king could attend to most state business within his palace, the Inka ruler moved around the capital to other state buildings such as the main temple (Qorikancha). Although we cannot pinpoint the location of residences devoted to Cuzco's lesser nobles, we assume that some lived within the city (Niles 1999). Inka bureaucratic hierarchy was much more complex than that of the Chimú, with many more positions to fill as the empire expanded. Nonroyal nobility, called Inkas-by-privilege, were accorded the hereditary status of nobility (Rostworowski and Morris 1999).

The *ushnu* platform, a multitiered stone platform associated with liquid offerings, was an important architectural symbol of the Inka state and served as the political banner of the Inkas in the provinces. It was usually situated in the plaza, the center of Inka public rituals and ceremonies. The immense size of some Inka plazas indicated that, unlike Chimor, more individuals could be included in ceremonies and in the redistribution of tribute. As Jerry D. Moore (1996) points out, one basic difference between the Chimú and the Inkas is the dichotomy between public and private space—the large, generally open plazas of the Inkas contrast with the smaller, enclosed plazas of the Chimú. This same dichotomy is also seen in the placement of warehouses. Chimú storage was restricted to the interiors of Chimú palaces, whereas the Inkas, especially at major highland provincial centers, placed storehouses away from the central administrative core and in open view.

Farfán: A Chimú Regional Center

At the peak of its occupation, Farfán consisted of several adobe compounds (Figure 11.5) that served as the multifunctional residences of elite administrators and symbolized the Chimú state presence in the Jequetepeque Valley. The compounds' exterior walls are not as monumental as those at Chan Chan, but they nevertheless must have been a formidable presence on the landscape. The center was constructed in the shadow of a coastal mountain, Cerro Faclo, and is strategically located at the intersection of the main north–south coastal road and one of the main east–west roads leading to the highlands and the polity of Cajamarca. Recent research has shown that the site was almost 4 km in length, but it did not exceed more than a kilometer in width (Mackey and Zavaleta 2000).

Prior to the Chimú Conquest in the late thirteenth century, Pacatnamu, one of the Lambayeque culture's principal ceremonial-administrative centers, had controlled the Jequetepeque Valley (Donnan and Cock 1997). This impressive site, situated at the mouth of the Jequetepeque River, was one of the independent centers that made up the Lambayeque confederation, whose heartland was located in the valleys to the north. Pacatnamu established a well-developed social-political organization in the valley, and evidence of the Lambayeque presence has been found at San José de Moro (Nelson et al. 2000) and Cabur (Sapp 2002). Architectural and artifactual evidence demonstrates that the Lambayeque polity built and occupied Compound III at Farfán before the Chimú conquered the area. Following the Chimú Conquest, Pacatnamu and Compound III at Farfán were abandoned. Cabur, however, is a Lambayeque lord's residence that continued to be occupied through the Chimú and Inka occupations. North of the Jequetepeque, from the Zaña to the Motupe valleys, the Lambayeque centers continued to function as politi-

Farfán

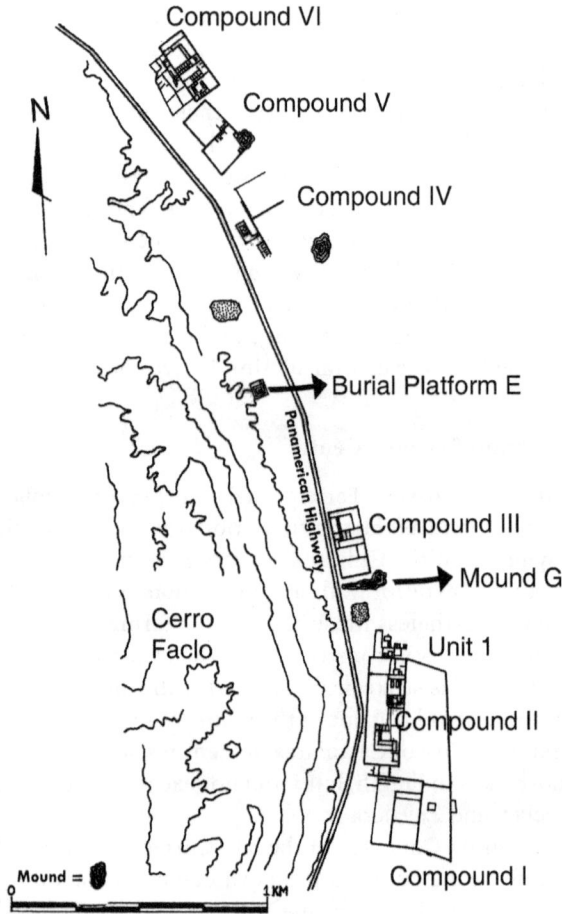

Compound VI

Compound V

N

Compound IV

Burial Platform E

Panamerican Highway

Compound III

Mound G

Cerro Faclo

Unit 1

Compound II

Mound =

0   1 KM

Compound I

FIGURE 11.5 Plan of Farfán. From Mackey and Jáuregui 2003.

cal entities for more than 100 years, until they, too, were conquered by the Chimú (Conlee et al. 2004). In the early years of Chimú expansion, therefore, Farfán and the Jequetepeque Valley exerted great political power, since Farfán represented the northern frontier of the Chimú Empire.

The current chronology for Farfán uses Compound II (Keatinge and Conrad 1983) and Compound VI (Mackey and Jáuregui 2001–2003) to frame the duration of the site's Chimú occupation. These compounds also contain the best-preserved interior architecture and are used throughout this chapter for baseline comparisons. Compound II, excavated by Richard Keatinge and

Geoffrey Conrad in 1978 (1983), produced the earliest date for the site, A.D. 1200, marking the beginning of Chimú presence in the Jequetepeque Valley. A recent radiocarbon date (2004) of A.D. 1310 places the construction of Compound II closer to Keatinge and Conrad's second C¹⁴ assay of A.D. 1325 (Mackey n.d.). Keatinge and Conrad also suggest, based on Spanish documents and architectural features observed in the Chan Chan palaces, that Compound II was the home of General Pacatnamu, the conqueror of the valley (ibid. 1983). In contrast, C¹⁴ dates obtained by the author indicate that Compound VI was constructed some 200 years later. It was the last Chimú compound constructed at Farfán and is located some 3 km north of Compound II.

Compound II

Compound II was one of the first compounds constructed at Farfán, and as such, the compound's architecture and spatial patterning serve as a yardstick to judge the others. Unlike the later compounds, which were divided into three sectors, Compound II contains only two. The evidence indicates that this compound served as the residence of high-ranking individuals who governed the center.

Compound II was the largest of the compounds, measuring 360 m in length and 125 m in width (Figure 11.6). Its floor plan exhibits architectural traits that relate it stylistically to Chan Chan's compounds (Keatinge and Conrad 1983). Keatinge and Conrad (1983) excavated Audiencia 1, suggesting the presence of a single, high-ranking individual who governed the center (Figure 11.7). Our 2003 excavations, however, revealed Audiencia 2 to the northeast, adding to the number of resident noble administrators (Mackey and Jáuregui 2001–2003). Stylistically, the two *audiencias* resemble those found in the earlier Chan Chan palaces. Audiencia 1 was roofed and had niches at the rear and deep bins arranged along the two parallel sides, whereas Audiencia 2 had only niches (Andrews 1974; Keatinge and Conrad 1983; Kolata 1990). Farfán's *audiencias* were located close to the storerooms, recalling those at Chan Chan (Figure 11.6).

A long raised causeway provided access to the second sector, which is distinguished by three features: a burial platform with an attached entry court, storerooms, and a *wachaque,* or walk-in well. The burial platform's size, ramp construction, and remnants of a geometric frieze on the north face conform to the architectural canons of the capital city and point to the royal status of the occupant. Among the looted remains, Keatinge and Conrad (1983) reported finding fragments of high-status artifacts such as textiles and ceramics. The rear portion of the platform contained two storage areas. The contents may have been earmarked for funerary rites or other ceremonies (Mackey 1987). Possibly, the compound's most valuable goods were stored here, since these storerooms were located the farthest distance

Compound II

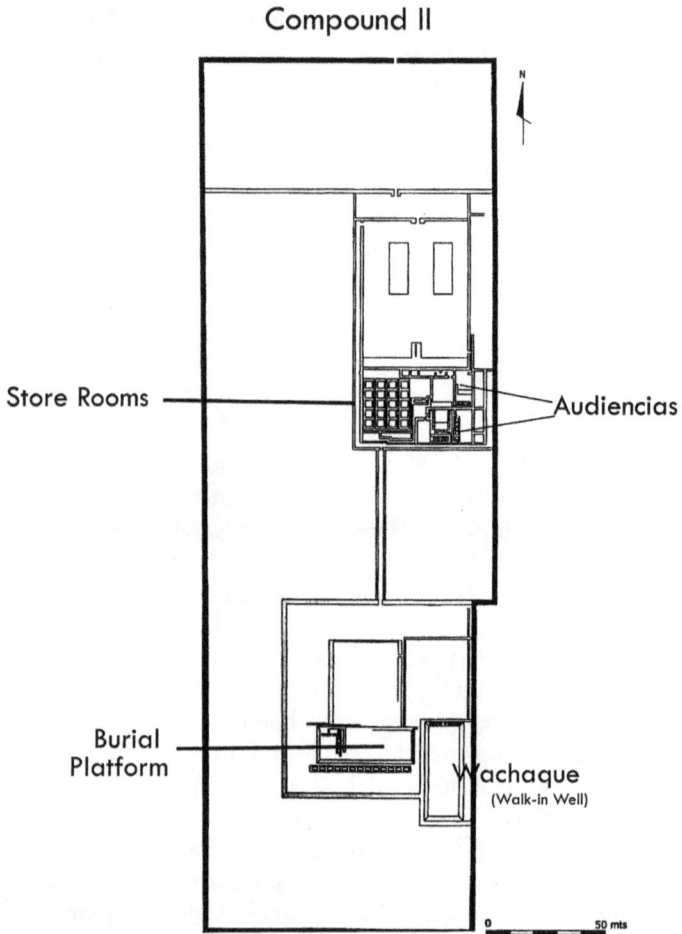

Store Rooms ——————

——————Audiencias

Burial
Platform ——————

Wachaque
(Walk-in Well)

0   50 mts

FIGURE 11.6 Plan of Compound II at Farfán. After Keatinge and Conrad 1983.

from the main entry. The *wachaque* was also protected by its location at the rear of the compound.

Compound VI

The last residential compound to be constructed, Compound VI was 100 m shorter in length than Compound II. Although the architectural features are similar to those of Compound II, its division into three sectors is typical of late Chimú compounds (Figure 11.8).

As in Compound II, the foundations of the *audiencias* in Compound VI suggest that at least two administrators lived here. This area is in poor preservation due to the modern agricultural canal that runs through the eastern edge of Compound VI (Figure 11.8). As in Compound II, the *audiencia* area is directly associated with storerooms. Storerooms are also associated with the burial platform, located in the southern sector. One of the storerooms contained a sunken wide-mouth storage vessel, or *tinaja* (Figure 11.9).

The focus of the southern sector was the burial platform, which reached a height of between 5 and 6 m and had a ramp on its south side (Figure 11.8). We assume that the platform, like its counterpart in Compound II, was the burial chamber of the royal administrator. Unlike the burial platform in Compound II, this platform in Compound VI is well preserved; nonetheless, its small interior chamber is empty and contains only an unworked stone, 52 cm high. Three possible scenarios provide explanations for this empty tomb. First, the body of the deceased noble may have been sent back to Chan Chan, where he was buried and cared for by members of his lineage. A second explanation may be found at Túcume, in the La Leche Valley, where archaeologists also discovered an empty Chimú burial platform. They suggest that the Inkas may have taken the body of the deceased Chimú provincial

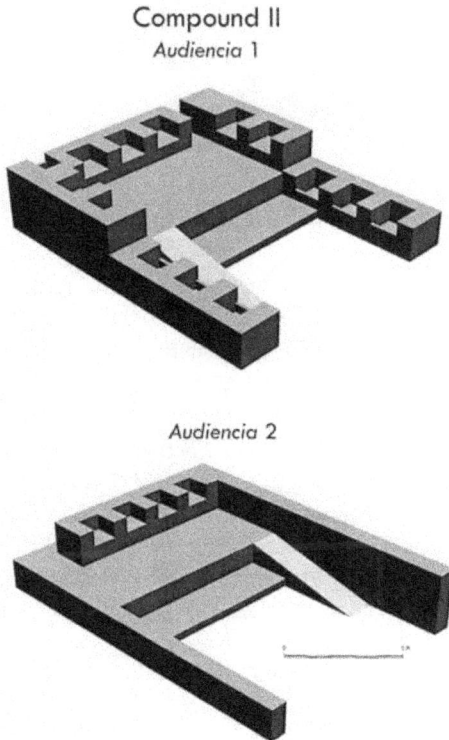

Compound II
Audiencia 1

Audiencia 2

FIGURE 11.7 Three-dimensional reconstruction of Audiencia 1 in Compound II at Farfán. Example of an early *audiencia* with bins below and niches above. After Keatinge and Conrad 1983.

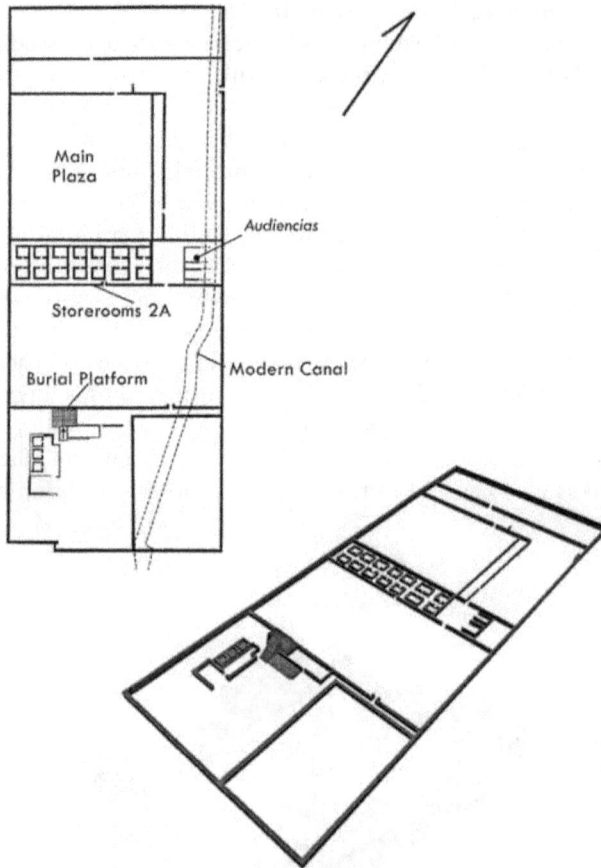

FIGURE 11.8 Plan of Compound VI at Farfán during Chimú occupation. From Mackey and Zavaleta 2000.

ruler to Cuzco, where it was held as a hostage *huaca* (sacred place, person, or object; Heyerdahl et al. 1995; Moseley 1992). Third, the Inka Conquest of the region may have disrupted Chimú rule at Túcume and Farfán, and thus the intended burial platforms were never used. The stone found in Farfán's empty tomb is analogous to what the Spanish cleric Antonio de la Calancha (1977–1979 [1638]) referred to as an Alecpong, which he equated with a deity turned to stone.

The main plaza lies in the northernmost sector (Figure 11.8). This plaza was almost twice the size of the one in Compound II, suggesting that a greater number of individuals could partake in ceremonies. The main entry was located in the northeast wall, close to the plaza.

We have not located the residences of the service personnel or retainer population who supported and cared for the resident nobles. Reconnaissance outside the compounds, especially at the foot of Cerro Faclo, located the remains of perishable structures, generally associated with lower-class populations (Tom Dillehay, personal communication, 1999). Aside from the vestiges of cane walls and some ceramic and organic remains, however, little can be said about this population. We did not encounter evidence for craft production associated with the Chimú occupation, indicating that this important activity was not part of the center's function.

Discussion

Chimú provincial residences share spatial organization and many architectural features with the royal palaces at Chan Chan. The persistence over several hundred years of these architectural traits at Farfán demonstrates the conservative nature of the architectural style. These two compounds also illustrate the practice of installing only a few noble bureaucrats to govern in the name of the Chimú state. Although the form of the *audiencia* changed, it continued to function as the seat of government authority, whereas the burial platform remained a symbol of royalty. The activities of the royal bureaucrats, however, differed markedly from those of their counterparts at the capital. Farfán's elite did not control large amounts of warehoused goods, nor did they oversee craft production or a retainer population. What, then, were the activities of Farfán's administrators and the functions of this pro-

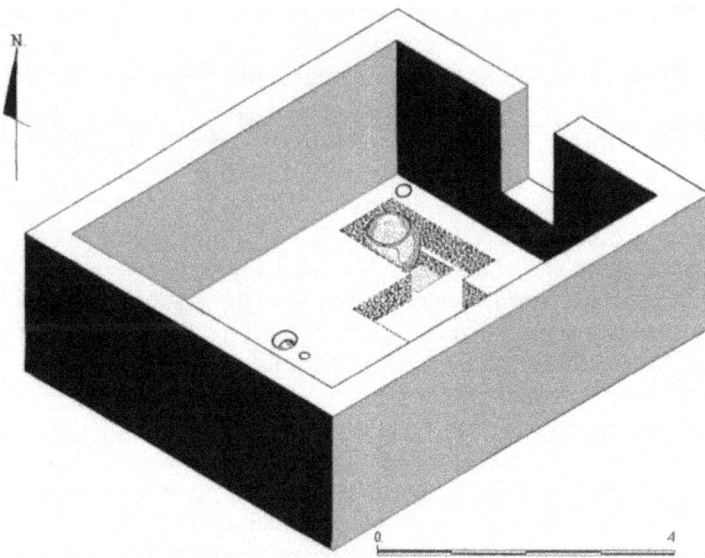

FIGURE 11.9 Three-dimensional reconstruction of a Chimú storeroom in Compound VI at Farfán

vincial center? Before turning to that question, let us explore the strategy and political motives for Chimú expansion into the Jequetepeque Valley.

Chimú Strategy

Based on the number of settlements, their size, and the labor involved in their construction, it is evident that the Jequetepeque Valley was fundamental to Chimú expansion. The use of imperial symbols in architecture and other artifacts indicates that the Chimú imposed their might, probably through warfare, on the Pacatnamu polity. Pacatnamu was part of the noncentralized Lambayeque confederation, and the valley was politically organized into at least two hierarchical administrative levels below Pacatnamu. The Chimú constructed their new provincial capital at Farfán, which had been the site of the former Lambayeque administrative center. The Chimú did not co-opt preexisting structures, but they built around and over them (Mackey 2006; Mackey and Jáuregui 2001–2003). At the same time, the Chimú instituted direct rule in the valley by bringing in their own nobles as administrators at Farfán and at subordinate sites within the valley.

As important as the political conquest was, I argue that Chimú expansion policies were driven by economic gains (Conlee et al. 2004). The Jequetepeque Valley is a large and agriculturally rich valley, and Farfán is strategically placed within the valley. It is one of the richest valleys on the north coast, and this may have provided the impetus for conquest (von Hagen and Morris 1998). The direct control of land and water fell to subordinate centers, such as Talambo (Keatinge and Conrad 1983) and Algarrobal de Moro (Castillo et al. 1997), which were staffed by lower-level Chimú nobles and built in the Chimú architectural style. Though ranked lowest in the settlement hierarchy, sites such as Cabur, the seat of local Lambayeque lords, continued to control land and enjoyed considerable autonomy under Chimú rule (Sapp 2002). The valley's agricultural output was essential for the functioning of the newly formed bureaucratic structure in the valley and also served for exchange and shipment beyond the valley. Transport was facilitated by Farfán's strategic location at the junction of the coast and highland roads. This center may have functioned as a hub for the transport of goods to other Chimú locations (Keatinge and Conrad 1983) and to supply the highlands, especially their new ally, Cajamarca, with goods from the coast (Hayashida 1999; Ramírez 1996; Rowe 1948).

It is probable, however, that the goods Chimor received in exchange for agricultural products acted as the driving force behind its conquest of the Lambayeque polity of Pacatnamu (Mackey 2001). The highland polity of Cajamarca controlled some of the richest gold mines in northern Peru (Shimada 1995). The burgeoning Chimú nobility, dependent on luxury items to legitimize their position to their subjects and within the Chimú hierarchy, created a demand for high-quality metal items.

Activities of Farfán's Chimú Lords

Given the requisites of the empire, the resident Chimú lords had their tasks defined for them. The nobles' main role was to oversee the valley's lower-ranking centers and act as chief negotiators in the exchange of luxury goods. Since daily control of the valley was left to lower-ranking administrators, the noble administrators' main goal was to supervise and relay decisions from the upper to the lower echelons (Keatinge and Conrad 1983; Wright and Johnson 1975). Although storage space was greatly reduced at Chimú provincial centers (Mackey 1987; Mackey and Klymyshyn 1990), Farfán's storage space was sufficient to receive products and to ready them for transport.

The role of entrepôt for raw materials was essential for the manufacture of the prestige goods at Chan Chan, and it undoubtedly increased the status of Farfán's nobles. In addition to precious metals, other raw materials such as *Spondylus* shell, used to manufacture high-status items and as a vital part of religious ritual (Pillsbury 1996), were obtained from Lambayeque intermediaries to the north who controlled the trade of this mollusk from Ecuador (Shimada 1995). Perhaps only high-ranking Chimú officials could negotiate for metals and *Spondylus* because of their precious nature, symbolism, and association with the nobility. In addition, nobles at provincial centers acted as hosts or ambassadors in newly conquered areas. As Craig Morris and Donald Thompson (1985) argue, one of the chief roles of Inka nobles was to serve as hosts at feasts and ceremonies, establishing a state presence and gaining the favor of the local population.

In the provinces, the Chimú nobles had different obligations and perhaps more responsibility than they did at Chan Chan. In spite of the fact that they enjoyed more power and independence, they were still tethered to the capital and were especially dependent on luxury items that were only manufactured at Chan Chan (Kolata 1983; Mackey and Klymyshyn 1990).

The Inka Occupation of Farfán

When the Inkas conquered the Jequetepeque Valley around A.D. 1460–1470, they claimed Farfán as their own. During their rule, they changed the face of this administrative center through an ambitious remodeling and construction program that took place throughout the site, both within and outside the compounds (Figure 11.10). The buildings constructed during the Inka phase share few architectural elements with their traditional style, though the Inkas did use building materials or distinctly sized bricks that serve as markers of this late occupation. They depended on local labor and materials and did not incorporate any stone constructions or trapezoidal niches, typical of their highland architectural style. Even though they did not build in their own style, neither did they imitate the architectural style of the previous coastal cultures. Instead they invented a new regional style, in-

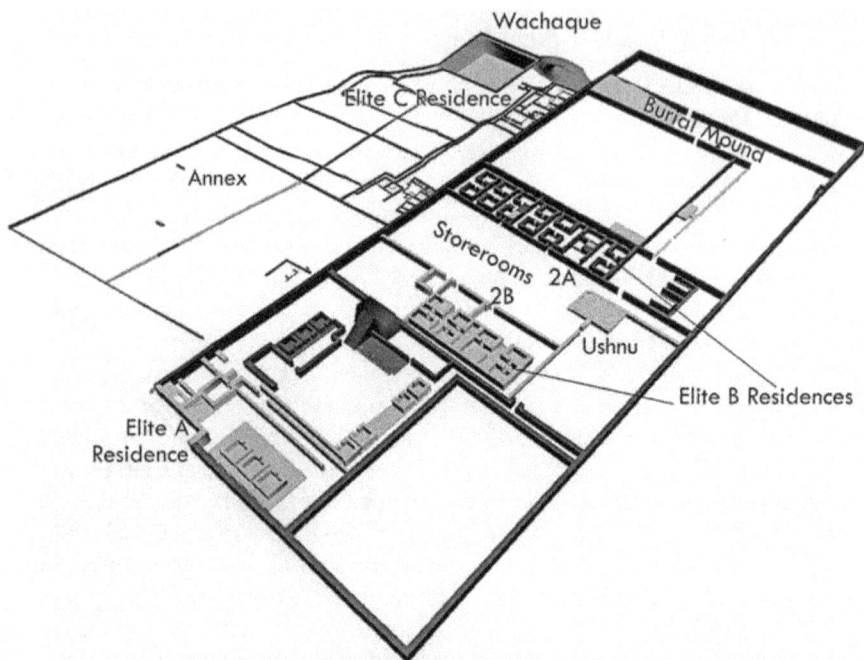

FIGURE 11.10 Plan of Compound VI at Farfán during Inka occupation

corporating some of the older concepts and adding new ones, which I have called conciliatory or diplomatic architecture. Perhaps they did not impose their own architectural symbols on this newly conquered area to thwart any future discontent or rebellion, since the Chimú had resisted the Inka Conquest of their capital (Neatherly 1977).

Changes in Residence Patterns under the Inkas

Inka dominance brought about marked changes in the previous Chimú social organization—changes that were especially evident in the new bureaucratic order instituted by the Inkas and in the residences they constructed for the new administrators. Whereas the Chimú brought in only royal officials who lived and worked in U-shaped *audiencias*, the Inkas introduced a variety of individuals of differing ranks and activities. These administrators will be discussed primarily by their ranks and secondarily by the areas where they resided.

Three ranks of elite Inka officials were identified: Elite A, B, and C. The first set of criteria used to determine the ranks includes residence size, architectural form, and room function. These variables comprise the overall size of the residence, such as the number of rooms and their spatial organization, as well as the diversity of functions within a set of rooms. Proximity to long- or short-term storage facilities is an important aspect of function.

The second variable used to separate the ranks was the security or protection offered by the residence. Higher-ranking individuals—Elites A and B, for instance—lived within the confines of a compound set behind high perimeter walls, but mid-level officials (Elites C) resided in annexes attached to either the northern or western sides of the compounds. Elite A and B residents slept under protective roofs, a feature that is absent in Elite C housing. Roofs are important because of heavy fog caused by the cloud cover over Cerro Faclo.

A third set of variables considered construction techniques and materials. The construction materials, for example, varied among the residences; some lower-rank housing is built of *tapia* (rammed earth), or *tapia* and adobe brick, whereas higher-status residences are constructed only of adobe brick. The height and width of the walls and the absence or presence of plaster were also noted.

Elite A Residences

The largest elite residence, composed of five rooms and a kitchen, measured 9 × 10 m and was located in the southwest corner of Compound VI (Figure 11.11). It was the most secluded of all the residences and was reached through a series of tortuous passageways. The structure was built during a single building episode, as evidenced by the similarity of the construction techniques and the abutment of the walls; however, four separate doorways led to distinct activity areas. Room 1, in the northeast corner, was entered through a narrow pilastered entryway that contained a series of subfloor offerings on both the east and west sides of the passageway. These subfloor holes, measuring 18 cm in diameter, contained similarly placed offerings of shell, animal bone, plant remains, and fragments of pottery (Figure 11.12). Near the south wall of Room 1 we uncovered more offerings, including guinea pig and a whole *Spondylus* shell. Room 1's maintenance and construction were of the highest quality. Its plastered floor, for example, consisted of fine silt, 8 cm thick.

Directly to the south is Room 2, whose open eastern side could only be reached from the adjacent storeroom patio. The main features include a low, narrow bench and a rectangular fire pit, some 70 cm deep. This fire pit was apparently not used for food preparation, as the kitchen, with several hearths and cooking vessels, was located in Room 5 to the northwest. The space could have provided an adjacent sitting room either for the occupants of the residence or for a guard. Room 2 faces three storerooms to the east and may have been associated with these facilities. Room 3, which has a roofed sleeping area built into the corner of the room, opens onto Room 4 and an enclosed patio.

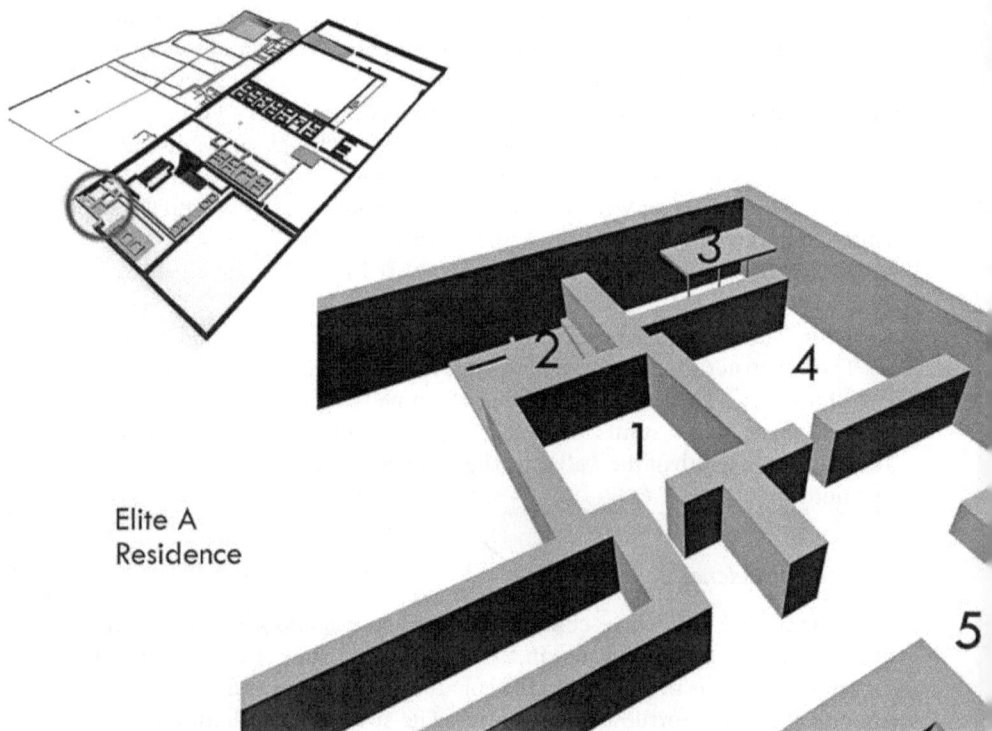

FIGURE 11.11 Plan of an Elite A residence in Compound VI at Farfán during Inka occupation

Elite B Residences

Multiple activities took place in the four Elite B residences in Compound VI. Two of the four residences (Rooms 1 and 2 and Rooms 3 and 4) consist of two joined rooms, whereas rooms 5 and 6 are separate rooms. The Elite B residences are directly associated with long-term storage and are located within the storeroom complexes. The Inkas either remodeled preexisting Chimú storerooms (2A; Figure 11.13), converting them into residences, or they built a new storage complex (2B) that contained Elite B residences. These four residences are not standardized but instead show variations that probably reflect the occupation or activity of the resident. Similar to the Elite A residences, they are well constructed, with a roofed sleeping area, and show typical Inka-style construction techniques.

Rooms 1 and 2: One of the most interesting and intriguing of the Elite B residences is the residential unit consisting of Rooms 1 and 2 (Figure 11.14). In remodeling the storerooms to create the residence, the Inkas removed the south wall. This open room enabled the resident official to monitor goods and people entering or leaving the storeroom complex. Subfloor offerings, like those found in the Elite A residence, were placed within Room 1. These contained various species of shell, such as *Prisogaster niger* and *Polinices uber*. The offerings were placed in prepared subfloor holes aligned in an X shape within the room, along a north–south and east–west axis. The Inkas widened the corridor between Rooms 1 and 2, sealed the east end of the corridor, and created a long, narrow roofed room that probably served as the sleeping area.

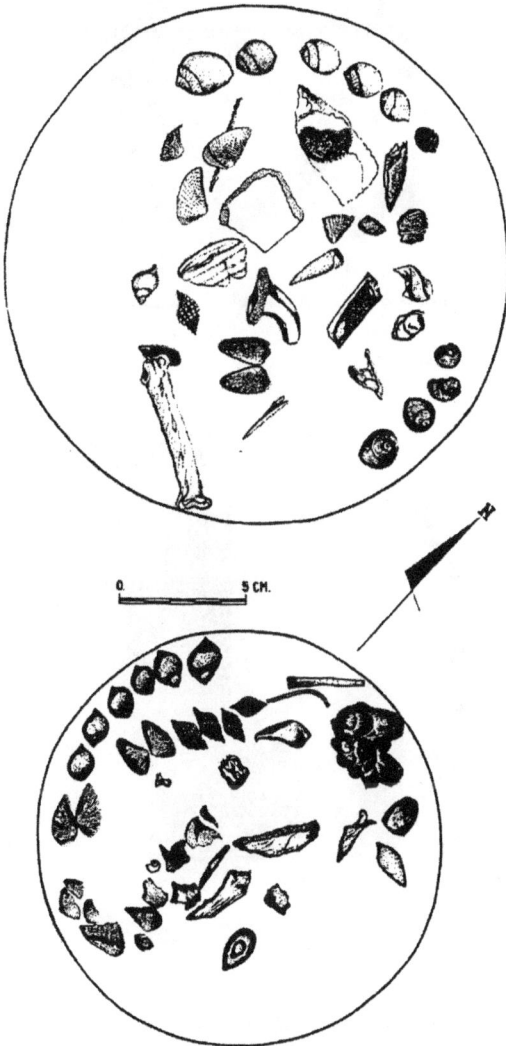

FIGURE 11.12 Examples of offerings found in Elite A and B residences at Farfán

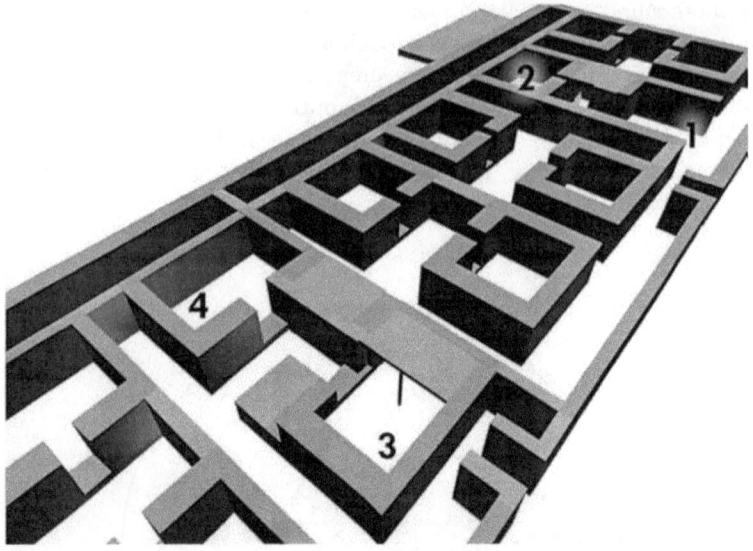

FIGURE 11.13 Three-dimensional reconstruction of two Elite B residences (1–2 and 3–4) in Storerooms Complex 2A, Compound VI, Farfán

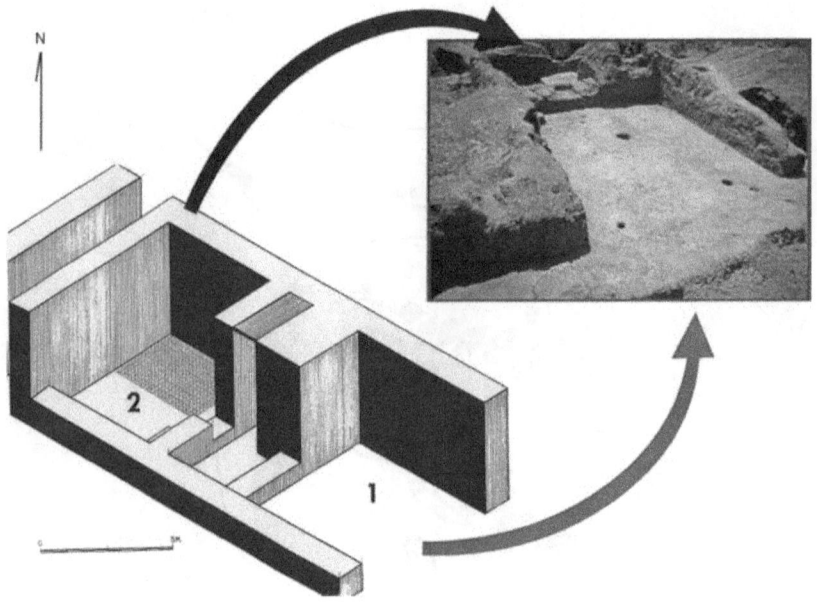

FIGURE 11.14 Three-dimensional reconstruction of an Elite B residence (Rooms 1–2), Compound VI, Farfán

In the ancient Andes, the bureaucratic infrastructure often provided tools for record keeping (Schreiber 1992). In Room 2 we found a unique feature that closely resembles an Inka *yupana,* an aid used in counting large numbers of items (Mackey et al. 1990). Small squares had been incised into the plaster floor on the east side of the room (Figure 11.14). These squares are arranged in a pattern of 17 rows and 23 columns for a total of 391 squares. In the center of each square was a round depression that could have held a small object such as a stone or a kernel of maize, which was counted to obtain the total number of items. This total was knotted onto a *khipu,* or knotted-string device, to record the total number of a given object (Locke 1923; Mackey 1970). The presence of the *yupana,* along with the compound's large storage capacity, may indicate that a *khipukamayuq,* an Inka official in charge of record keeping, resided here. The association between *yupana* and *khipukamayuq* is illustrated by the Spanish chronicler Felipe Guaman Poma de Ayala (1956 [1613]; Figure 11.15).

Rooms 3 and 4: Like Rooms 1 and 2, these rooms are converted Chimú storerooms joined to form one residential unit (Figure 11.16). Room 3 to the south served as the sleeping area and included a roofed section along its east side. The roof was supported by the east wall of the storeroom on one side and by two substantial wooden poles on the west side. Room 4, to the north, did not contain a counting device, but it did have subfloor offerings. We unearthed two offering pits in the northwest corner of the room. These contained guinea pig (*Cavia porcellus*) bones and a shell offering near the door. The official occupying these rooms did not control as many storerooms as the administrator in Rooms 1 and 2, nor was he interested in controlling traffic, perhaps indicating different activities for which he was responsible.

Rooms 5 and 6: These rooms are located in the 2B storeroom complex (Figure 11.10), are separate rooms, and thus are variants of Elite B residences. They are included with this type, however, since they share many characteristics with the other elite residences, such as subfloor offerings and roofing along the eastern wall. They combine a ritual/offering area and a sleeping area in one room, separate features in the other residences. Located in the 2B storeroom complex built by the Inkas, these rooms have the same function as the other B residences: to control or monitor storage areas. It appears that four functionaries controlled storage in the middle sector of Compound VI. Although they shared the same rank, the objects guarded or stored may have differed.

Elite C Residences

Mid-level Elite C officials resided in annexes attached to the north or west sides of Compounds VI and II. Several aspects suggest that the individuals housed in these annexes appear to be of a lower rank: (1) the residential area was located outside the compound and therefore was unprotected by the

FIGURE 11.15 Drawing of a *khipukamayuq* by Felipe Guaman Poma de Ayala (1956 [1613])

compound walls; (2) the interior walls of the residences are lower and narrower and were constructed of *tapia*, or *tapia* and adobe brick; (3) the sleeping areas are unroofed; (4) the residential quarters are communal; and (5) the occupations of the residents differ from those of officials in the compound's interior. These Elite C officials were associated with the collection of goods or the supervision of craft production.

The Annex of Compound VI: The northernmost annex is found on the west side of Compound VI and is the largest in area of all the annexes (Figure 11.10). Only a small portion of it, however, was devoted to residential space. The residential area was divided into two separate functional spaces: the northern group consisted of unroofed rooms with sleeping platforms, and the southern group was composed of a communal kitchen that contained storage, hearths, and a *batán*, or grinding stone. This large kitchen served the communal residence and probably the Elite B residences in the interior (Figure 11.17).

The Annex of Compound II: Another example of an Elite C residence is found in the annex attached to the north end of Compound II (Figure 11.18). This residence is not as well preserved as Annex VI because a modern road destroyed part of the structure. Nonetheless, we excavated and mapped four rooms in a freestanding structure constructed of both *tapia* and adobe brick. One of the rooms contained the remains of a small platform that resembled the sleeping platforms in Annex VI. Associated with the sleeping rooms are a series of small bins, generally three in a row, that measure less than 1 m² and are enclosed by a wall the width of two adobe bricks in height (24 cm). The items found in the bins indicate that they were destined for short-term storage. The bins in Annex II, for instance, included tools related to ceramic production, such as polishing and anvil stones of different sizes.

Summary

The architecture, construction techniques, and social complexity of the Inka residences at Farfán contrast with those of the prior Chimú occupation. There were two elite classes housed within the compounds, Elite A and B, and these residences had multiple rooms and functions. These residences'

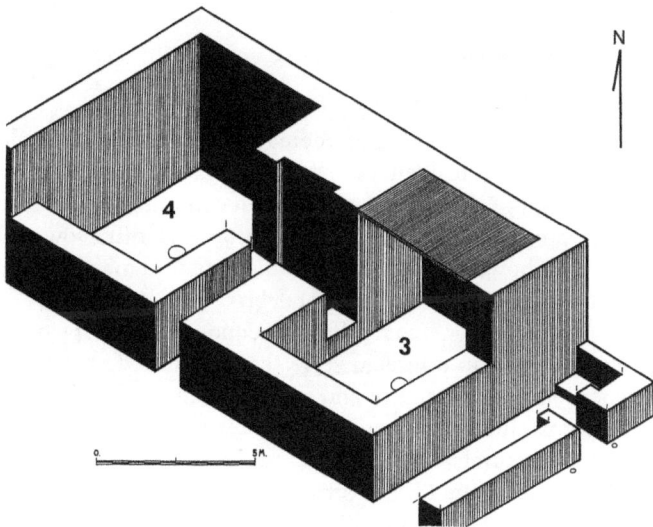

FIGURE 11.16   Three-dimensional reconstruction of an Elite B residence (Rooms 3–4), Compound VI, Farfán

Rooms with sleeping platforms

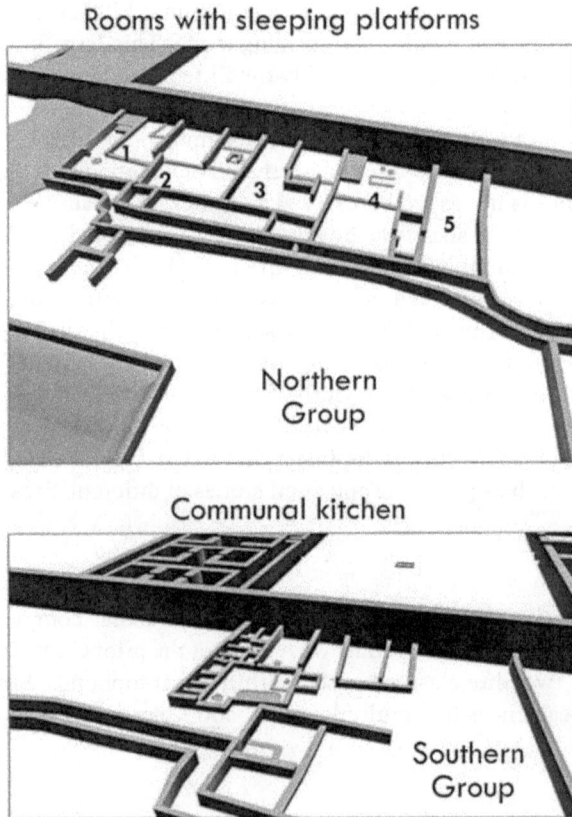

Northern
Group

Communal kitchen

Southern
Group

FIGURE 11.17 Elite C residence in the annex to Compound VI, Farfán

high perimeter walls and roofing protected inhabitants from the elements. All of the Elite A and B residences had rooms that included subfloor offerings. By comparison, Elite C residents lived in communal quarters consisting only of sleeping rooms and an adjoining kitchen. Unlike lower-class domestic structures, however, the Elite C rooms were well maintained and had plastered walls and floors swept clean of debris.

As Katharina Schreiber (1992:32) notes, conquering groups often introduced structures built in a foreign style that contrasted with local architectural canons. The architecture and spatial organization of Farfán's elite rooms fit this description, as they are unique and reflect neither Inka nor north-coast architectural traditions. Separate doorways to each activity area, such as those found in the Elite A structure, for instance, are a distinctive architectural feature. The majority of the site's architecture, whether remodeled or built by the Inkas, is in a new style that I call conciliatory or diplomatic architecture. Farfán's residential architecture and artifacts point to increased political complexity, as demonstrated by the diversity of residents' ranks and occupational specialties. Similar changes have been documented at other Inka installations (Earle et al. 1987; Morris and Thompson 1985). At Farfán, the changes to the social structure were engineered and maintained by Inka officials—perhaps not Inkas by birth, but mid-level Inka administrators.

Further Changes in the Social Structure during the Inka Occupation

The Inka introduced other major changes to Farfán's social structure, manifested throughout the center by new structures and activity areas. These changes emphasized both the economic and the ideological aspects of the system.

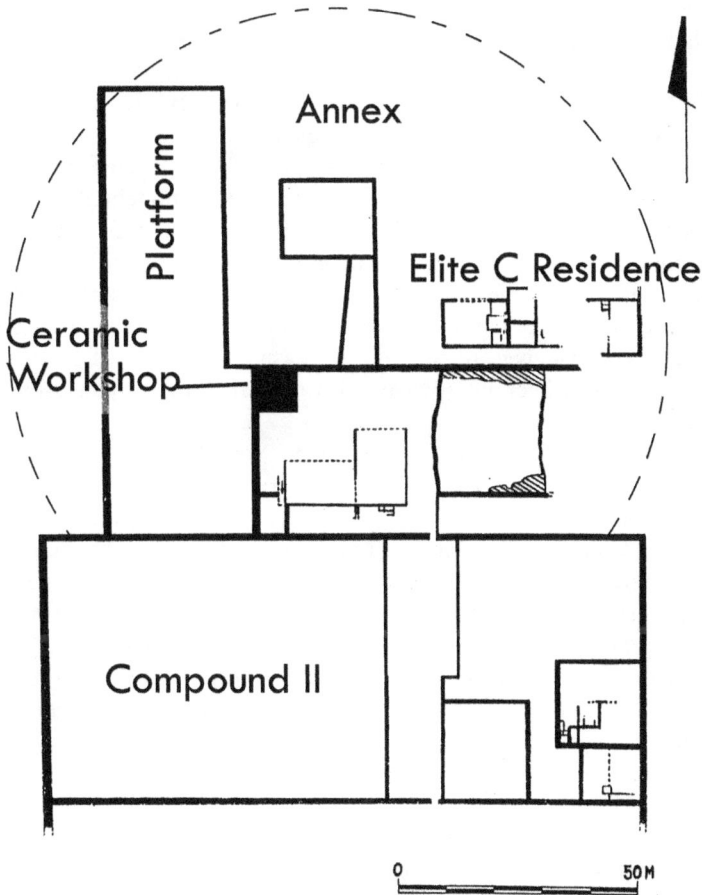

FIGURE 11.18 Plan of the annex to Compound II, Farfán

Changes in the Economy

The Inka instituted major changes in Farfán's economy by increasing the area devoted to storage and by introducing textile and ceramic production.

Storage. An important aspect of Inka provincial policy was the accumulation and storage of goods. Farfán witnessed a new emphasis on storage under the Inkas. The number and capacity of storerooms in Compound VI doubled from the Chimú to the Inka period. Although we do not have data from each compound, I suggest that the Inkas used Farfán as one large storage depot. This hypothesis is reinforced by Pedro Cieza de León (1959 [ca. 1553]:322), who stated that the Inka gathered tribute in the Jequetepeque Valley (referred to in the chronicles as the Pacasmayo Valley) and from there dispatched it to the provincial capital. The most likely and the closest Inka regional center was Cajamarca (Hayashida 1999; Ramírez 1996).

Not only did the Inkas boost the number of storage facilities at Farfán, but they also improved security around the warehoused goods by changing access patterns leading to the storage areas. Although the Chimú are known for the tortuous passageways leading to storerooms and the limited access to storage (Day 1982; Moore 1996), it appears that the Inkas, when remodeling and constructing new storehouses and Elite B residences, increased the security leading to these areas. In storage area 2A, remodeling by the Inkas changed previous Chimú access patterns, creating even more restrictions to the number of storerooms that could be accessed at one time. Although it appears that they were protecting the stored goods, they may also have been protecting the Elite B administrators, whose residences flanked the storage areas. The priority given to security is an aspect of Inka rule on the north coast that has not been noted before. It may reflect Inka concern over possible Chimú rebellion.

Textile Production. There is no evidence for textile or ceramic manufacture at Farfán during the Chimú occupation, but the Inkas introduced production of both. We found evidence for textile production in two of the annexes to Compounds IV and II. The annex to the west of Compound IV contained state-built rooms with bins. These small bins, measuring 1 × 1.5 m and with a short rim around the top, held spinning and weaving implements such as spindles, whorls, and copper needles. These bins could also have served as receptacles for completed textiles. Ethnohistorical sources corroborate the Farfán evidence by stating that Inka administrators provided the implements required for various production tasks (Neatherly 1977).

Ceramic Production. We excavated a ceramic workshop in the annex connected to the northern end of Compound II (Figure 11.18). This workshop produced only one type of pottery vessel—large *tinajas*, some with openings of 50 cm or more—used mainly as vessels for *chicha* or for storing dry goods. The workers were clearly skilled, as these large vessels are constructed of coils and finished by the paddle-and-anvil technique (Banks 1989).

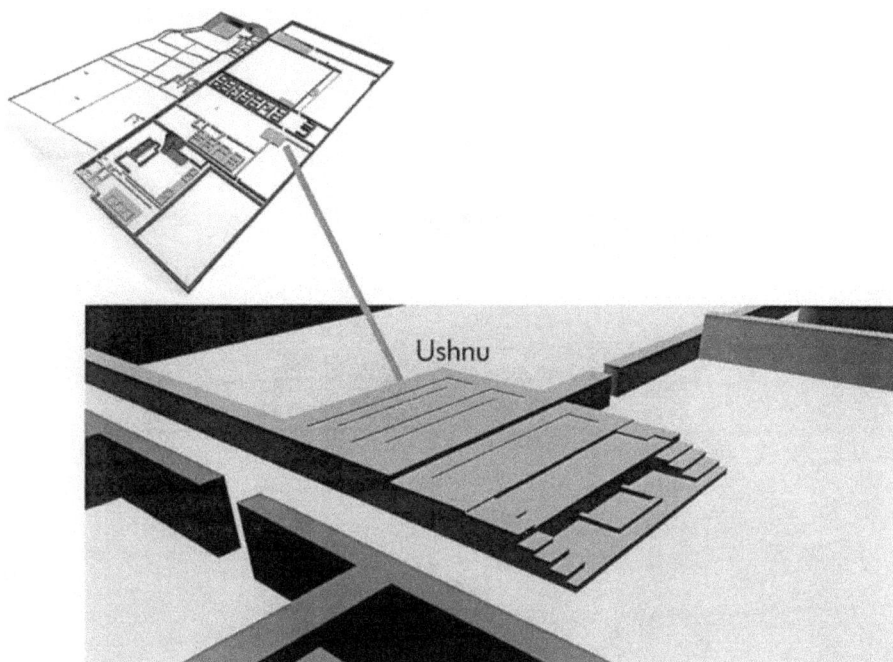

FIGURE 11.19 Plan of Compound VI, Farfán, showing location of the *ushnu* platform

Several features identified this area as a workshop. We found a meter-high pile of *tinaja* rims near the production site as well as in the firing area, which was located nearby in a large area measuring 8 × 6 m. The annex was home to Elite C officials who undoubtedly supervised the production of these vessels, since this residence housed bins that held various implements such as the large flat stones used as anvils for forming and smoothing (Litto 1976). The *tinajas* manufactured at Farfán display a distinctive circle design on their rims. Excavations throughout the site have shown that the *tinajas* were used and distributed within the site in areas dedicated to feasting.

Changes in the Ideological Realm

In addition to the changes in social organization, Inka rule at Farfán also emphasized civil and religious ceremonies. This focus was manifested in three areas, both inside and outside the compounds, and included an *ushnu* for smaller ritual gatherings, "food preparation mounds" outside the compounds to serve large crowds of people, and five areas dedicated to funerary activities and other rituals.

Ushnu. Although the Inkas shied away from using their own imperial architecture, they did construct an *ushnu* at Farfán (Figure 11.19). The *ushnu*

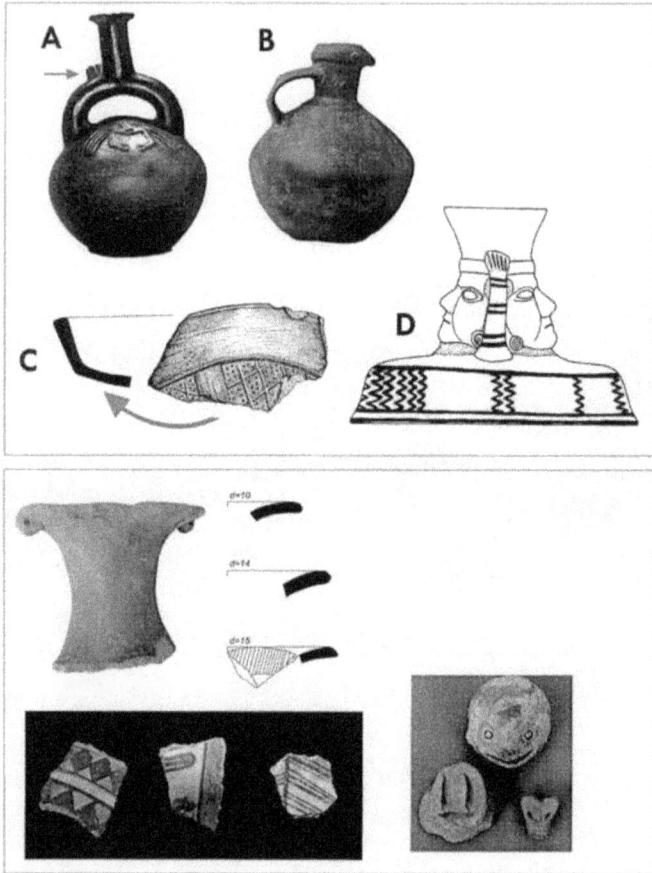

FIGURE 11.20 Chimú-Inka ceramics and Provincial Inka ceramics

figured prominently in Inka civil and religious ceremonies and is generally found at most important Inka installations (Hyslop 1990). Farfán's *ushnu* is a large low adobe platform measuring 17 × 15 m wide and 2 m in height. It faces west toward Cerro Faclo. Its closest analogy in form and construction is the *ushnu* at Tambo Colorado on the south coast. *Ushnus* are generally associated with liquid offerings. Depressions or small canals in the rear portion of Farfán's platform could have been used to receive water or *chicha*. The *ushnu*'s location, in the patio close to the Elite B residences, is revealing because the Inkas intentionally did not place it in the main plaza, but opted instead to locate it close to their own personnel in a more restricted area. Excavations within the *ushnu* platform revealed an undisturbed cache of broken Provincial Inka and Chimú-Inka ceramics (Figure 11.20).

Mounds Associated with Feasting. The large *tinajas* produced in the annex of Compound II and described above were found associated with other food-preparation paraphernalia, such as hearths, guinea-pig pens, and broken bowls and ollas (Figure 11.21). Three of these areas are in specially prepared mounds, and the others are associated with funerary activities. Located on the east side of the three northern compounds (IV, V, and VI), these mounds did not serve as burial platforms, but may have had civil and ritual functions (Mackey and Jáuregui 2001–2003). The long, oval mounds vary in length from 50 to 60 m and stood 2 to 3 m high. Although these mounds may have functioned only as serving areas for large gatherings, they could also have been used by administrators to carry out their ceremonial duties.

Mortuary Practices. The mortuary practices identified at Inka Farfán reflect the site's social and occupational diversity. We excavated five mortuary facilities, located both within and outside the compounds. Four of the cemeteries share similar burial patterns: seated individuals, both adult males and females, and single interments placed in unprepared pits. The graves contained an average of four vessels in the Chimú-Inka style, and aside from an occasional piece of copper or rings, the tombs contained few metal artifacts.

The fifth mortuary facility, located in the center of the site on its western edge, stands apart from the large monumental compounds and is an artificially constructed stepped platform or *huaca* that contained multiple interments in both prepared and unprepared tombs. The *huaca* included

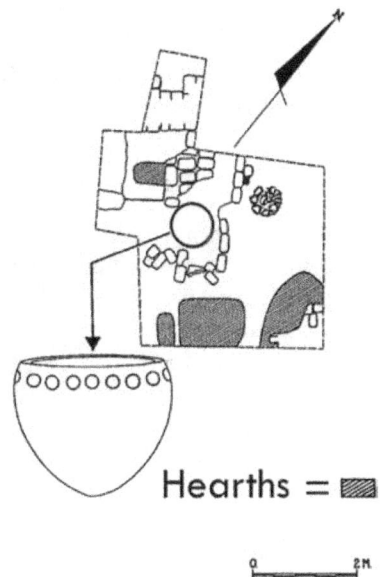

Hearths = ▨

FIGURE 11.21 Food-preparation area, Mound C, Farfán

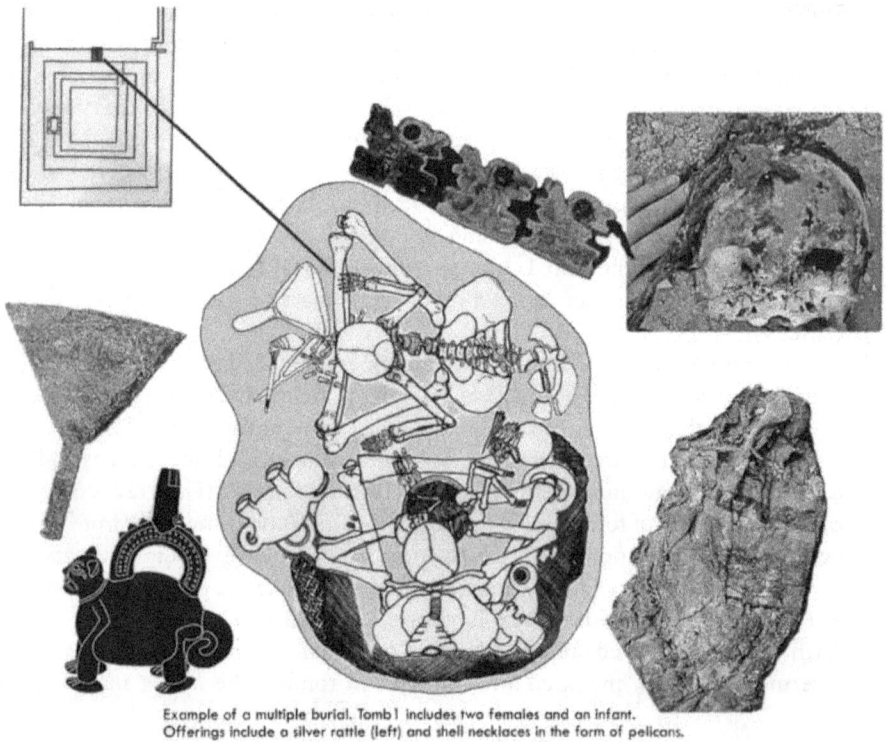

Example of a multiple burial. Tomb 1 includes two females and an infant.
Offerings include a silver rattle (left) and shell necklaces in the form of pelicans.

FIGURE 11.22 Tomb 1, *huaca* burial platform, Farfán

high-status burials, the majority of which are females, although the partial skeleton of one high-status male was also found in a specially prepared burial chamber. The females, who ranged in age from 6 to 45 years, were either secondary burials or had been sacrificed and buried directly in the platform (Figure 11.22). The females were associated with large amounts of ceramics, all in the hybrid Chimú-Inka style, and textile offerings. Many were buried with weaving implements such as raw cotton, spindles, and weaving shuttles as well as sewing baskets. The women buried in Farfán's platform recall the groups of sacrificed women found at Túcume (Heyerdahl et al. 1995) and Pachacamac (Uhle 1991 [1903]). The abundance of textile-production paraphernalia and similar burial contexts suggest that the women buried at these sites were *aqlla* (so-called chosen women, whose duties included weaving) that served the Inka administration.

Summary

One of the major differences between Chimú and Inka provincial rule is that the Chimú allotted limited space to storage away from their capital, whereas the Inkas distributed stored goods in vast warehouse complexes at their principal regional centers (Morris 1967). Even though Farfán's storage facilities do not approximate the storage capacity of some of the highland Inka centers, Farfán appears to be the largest Inka storage depot on the north coast. In addition, the Inkas also introduced textile and ceramic production, key elements in their redistributive system that served as the lynchpin of Inka integration policies. Textiles were offered as gifts to local lords (Murra 1962), and the women who supported this industry were accorded rich burials for their service and were often sacrificed for the state. The redistributive system was supported by ceremonies and rituals. Large-scale feasting played a major role in the incorporation of new territories (Bray 2003; Morris and Thompson 1985).

Discussion

Inka Strategy

As recent research at Farfán has revealed, the Jequetepeque Valley was indeed crucial to Inka expansion. Although the Inkas used the original footprint of the Chimú center, they expended considerable labor in rebuilding the compounds and creating new structures. Certainly, Farfán's strategic location near the main road to Cajamarca and its rich agricultural potential motivated the Inka occupation of the center.

The political strategy used by the Inkas was yet another variation on what Schreiber (1992) has described as their "mosaic of control." Chimor is an example of a state-level society with a typical four-tiered hierarchical organization that viewed Chan Chan as its primary center. After the fall of Chan Chan, Farfán still served as a second-level center with at least two subordinate administrative levels below it. Current research suggests that at Farfán the Inkas eliminated one level of Chimú royal bureaucrats, replacing them with three ranks of elite Inka administrators. The Inkas co-opted many of the lower-level administrative centers within the Jequetepeque Valley built by the Chimú, although it is not clear whether all were managed by Inka personnel.

The evidence points to a more vital, active center under the Inkas than under Chimú rule. Economic factors served as one of the main motivators for strong Inka influence because the valley offered great agricultural potential and the Inkas set up production facilities at Farfán. Economic endeavors were consistent with Inka ideological concerns. Geoffrey Conrad and Arthur A. Demarest (1984) theorize that this concern was a primary impetus of Inka expansion. This is borne out at Farfán, where almost all economic activities were geared to the Inka redistribution and ceremonial system. This ideological aspect was especially active in newly conquered territories to help win the "hearts and minds" of subject peoples.

Activities of Farfán's Inka Elites

The numbers, ranks, sleeping quarters, and duties of Chimú and Inka administrators exhibit striking differences. The Inkas established a larger administrative staff, at least doubling the number of Chimú officials. The Inka officials were low-ranking individuals who may have been Inkas-by-privilege rather than by birth. However, the individual who occupied the Elite A apartment in Compound VI must have been the highest-ranking individual, possibly a noble. The space allotted to him and the architectural details of the residence support this notion, as do his activities and the number of individuals that he oversaw. He controlled not only Farfán's personnel but also lower-level administrators at centers throughout the valley. Though a full settlement-pattern study has yet to be carried out, we know from survey and excavation that the Inkas co-opted several centers in the valley, such as Algarrobal de Moro (Castillo et al. 1997) and Cañoncillo (Donnan 1997). Local Lambayeque lords continued to live in the valley under the Inkas, as demonstrated by excavations at Cabur (Sapp 2002).

All of Farfán's elite residences during the Inka period are associated with the collection, storage, or production of goods. The elites residing in the interiors of the compounds were associated with long-term storage. Some Elite B individuals may have been in charge of counting the goods warehoused in interior storerooms, as suggested by the *yupana*-like device found in Room 1. The people who resided in the exterior annexes, on the other hand, controlled the collection of goods, craft production, and the short-term storage of tools used in craft production.

Conclusion

Comparing the residences of Chimú and Inka administrators at Farfán proved valuable in eliciting the differences between the administrators and between Inka and Chimú governing strategies. As mirrored by their residences, the ranks and duties of the administrators differed. This is also reflected in the priorities of their respective state governments and in the power bestowed upon them. Each empire installed administrators to supervise Farfán and the officials in lower-ranking settlements. Whatever differences they may have had in rank, ultimately both Chimú and Inka administrators gained their power because in this valley they were at the top of the hierarchical order.

Acknowledgments

Our work at Farfán would have not been possible without the collaboration of many people. My thanks to our workforce who commuted every day from the pueblo of San José de Moro, and also to our crew of students from the Universidad Nacional de Trujillo (UNT) and from the Pontificia Universidad Católica del Perú (PUCP) as well as the many universities in the United States, such as Stanford, Michigan, and UCLA. I would also like to express my thanks to the project's two codirectors, Enrique Zavaleta (2000) and César Jáuregui (2001–2004). None of the project would have been possible without financial support, and I would like to thank the individuals, especially Baerbel Struthers and William and Marcia Herrman, and the institutions who supported us. I wish to thank: The Brennan Foundation, The John B. Heinz Charitable Trust, National Geographic Society, and California State University, Northridge. A number of colleagues have made valuable comments and suggestions, and I am grateful for the time they took to read the many versions of this manuscript. Thanks to Christopher Donnan, Daniel Fernández, María Jesús Jiménez, William Sapp, Melissa Vogel, and Adriana von Hagen. A special thanks to César Jáuregui for many of the drawings that appear in this chapter.

References Cited

Andrews, Anthony P.
1974 The U-shaped Structures at Chan Chan, Peru. *Journal of Field Archaeology* 1(3):242–264.
Banks, George
1989 *Peruvian Pottery*. Shire Publications, Aylesbury, UK.
Bray, Tamara L.
2003 Inka Pottery as Culinary Equipment: Food, Feasting, and Gender in Imperial State. *Latin American Antiquity* 14(1):3–28.
Calancha, Antonio de la
1977–1979 [1638] Corónica moraliza del Orden de San Agustín en el Perú. Ignacio Prado Pastor, Lima.
Castillo, Luis Jaime, Carol J. Mackey, and Andrew Nelson
1997 Informe sobre investigaciones de Proyecto Complejo Arqueológico de Moro. Instituto Nacional de Cultura, Lima.
Chase, Diane Z., and Arlen F. Chase (editors)
1992 *Mesoamerican Elites: An Archaeological Assessment*. University of Oklahoma Press, Norman.
Cieza de León, Pedro
1959 [ca. 1553] *The Incas of Pedro Cieza de León*. University of Oklahoma Press, Norman.
Conlee, Christina, Jalh Dulanto, Carol J. Mackey, and Charles Stanish
2004 Late Prehispanic Sociopolitical Complexity. In *Andean Archaeology*, edited by Helaine Silverman, pp. 209–236. Blackwell, Cambridge.
Conrad, Geoffrey
1982 Burial Platforms and Related Structures on the North Coast of Peru: Some Social and Political Implications. Unpublished Ph.D. dissertation, Department of Anthropology, Harvard University, Cambridge.
1990 Farfán, General Pacatnamu, and the Dynastic History of Chimor. In

The Northern Dynasties: Kingship and Statecraft in Chimor, edited by Michael E. Moseley and Alana Cordy-Collins. Dumbarton Oaks Research Library and Collection, Washington, DC.

Conrad, Geoffrey, and Arthur A. Demarest
1984 *Religion and Empire: The Dynamics of Aztec and Inca Expansionism.* Cambridge University Press, Cambridge.

Covey, R. Alan
2000 Inka Administration of the Far South Coast of Peru. *Latin American Antiquity* 11(2):119–138.

Day, Kent C.
1982 Ciudadelas: Their Form and Function. In *Chan Chan: Andean Desert City*, edited by Michael E. Moseley and Kent C. Day, pp. 55–66. School of American Research Advanced Seminar Series. University of New Mexico Press, Albuquerque.

Donnan, Christopher B.
1997 A Chimú-Inka Ceramic-Manufacturing Center from the North Coast of Peru. *Latin American Antiquity* 8(1):30–54.

Donnan, Christopher B., and Guillermo A. Cock (editors)
1997 *Pacatnamu Papers*, Vol. 2. Fowler Museum of Cultural History, University of California Press, Los Angeles.

Earle, Timothy K., Terence N. D'Altroy, Christine Hastorf, Catherine Scott, Cathy L. Costin, Glenn S. Russell, and Elsie Sandefur
1987 *Archaeological Field Research in the Upper Mantaro, Peru, 1982–1983: Investigations of Inka Expansion and Exchange.* Monograph 28. Institute of Archaeology, University of California, Los Angeles.

Gasparini, Graziano, and Luise Margolies
1980 *Inca Architecture.* Translated by Patricia J. Lyon. Indiana University Press, Bloomington.

Girouard, Mark
1999 *Life in the French Country House.* Knopf, New York.

Guaman Poma de Ayala, Felipe
1956 [1613]   *La nueva corónica y buen gobierno.* 3 vols. Editorial Cultura, Lima.

Hayashida, Frances M.
1995 State Pottery Production in the Inka Provinces. Unpublished Ph.D. dissertation, University of Michigan, Ann Arbor.
1999 Style, Technology, and State Production: Inka Pottery Manufacture in the Leche Valley, Peru. *Latin American Antiquity* 10(4):337–352.

Hecker, Wolfgang, and Giesela Hecker
1990 Ruinas, caminos y sistemas de irrigación prehispánicos en la provincia de Pacasmayo, Perú. Instituto Nacional de Cultura, Trujillo, Peru.

Heyerdahl, Thor, Daniel H. Sandweiss, and Alfredo Narváez
1995 *Pyramids of Tucume: The Quest for Peru's Forgotten City.* Thames and Hudson, London.

Hyslop, John
1990 *Inka Settlement Planning.* University of Texas Press, Austin.

Keatinge, Richard W., and Geoffrey Conrad
1983 Imperialist Expansion in Peruvian Prehistory: Chimú Administration of a Conquered Territory. *Journal of Field Archaeology* 10:255–383.

Kendall, Ann
1985 *Aspects of Inca Architecture: Description, Function and Chronology.* 2 vols. BAR International Series 242. British Archaeological Reports, Oxford.

Klymyshyn, Ulana A.
1982 Elite Compounds at Chan Chan. In *Chan Chan: Andean Desert City,* edited by Michael E. Moseley and Kent C. Day, pp. 119–143. School of American Research Advanced Seminar Series. University of New Mexico Press, Albuquerque.
1987 Development of Chimú Administration in Chan Chan. In *The Origins and Development of the Andean State,* edited by Jonathan Haas, Shelia Pozorski, and Thomas Pozorski. Cambridge University Press, Cambridge.

Kolata, Alan L.
1983 Chan Chan and Cuzco: On the Nature of the Ancient Andean City. In *Civilization in the Ancient Americas: Essays in Honor of Gordon R. Willey,* edited by Richard M. Leventhal and Alan L. Kolata. University of New Mexico Press, Albuquerque; and Peabody Museum of Archaeology and Ethnology, Harvard University, Cambridge.
1990 The Urban Concept of Chan Chan. In *The Northern Dynasties: Kingship and Statecraft in Chimor,* edited by Michael E. Moseley and Alana Cordy-Collins, 107–144. Dumbarton Oaks Research Library and Collection, Washington, DC.

Kosok, Paul
1965 *Life, Land, and Water in Ancient Peru.* Long Island University Press, New York.

Litto, Gertrude
1976 *South American Folk Pottery.* Watson Guptil, New York.

Locke, Leland
1923 *The Ancient Quipu, or Peruvian Knot Record.* American Museum of Natural History, New York.

Mackey, Carol
1970 Knot Records in Ancient and Modern Peru. Unpublished Ph.D. dissertation. University of California, Berkeley.
1987 Chimú Administration in the Provinces. In *The Origins and Development of the Andean State,* edited by Jonathan Haas, Shelia Pozorski, and Thomas Pozorski, pp. 121–129. Cambridge: Cambridge University Press.
2001 Los dioses que perdieron los colmillos. In *Los dioses del Antiguo Perú,* Vol. 2. Banco de Crédito del Perú, Lima.
n.d. Chimú Statecraft in the Provinces. In *Foundations of Andean Civilization: Papers in Honor of Michael E. Moseley,* edited by Joyce Marcus, Charles Stanish, and Ryan Williams. Cotsen Institute of Archaeology, UCLA, Los Angeles. In press.

Mackey, Carol, Hugo Pereyra, Carlos Radicati, Humberto Rodríguez, and Óscar Valverde (editors)
1990 *Quipu y yupana: Colección de escritos.* Consejo Nacional de Ciencia y Tecnología, Ministerio de la Presidencia, Lima.

Mackey, Carol, and César Jáuregui
2001–2003   Informes preliminares del Proyecto Arqueológico Farfán. Instituto Nacional de Cultura, Lima.

Mackey, Carol, and A. M. Ulana Klymyshyn
1990 The Southern Frontier of the Chimú Empire. In *The Northern Dynasties: Kingship and Statecraft in Chimor*, edited by Michael E. Moseley and Alana Cordy-Collins, 195–226. Dumbarton Oaks Research Library and Collection, Washington, DC.

Mackey, Carol, and Enrique Zavaleta
2000 Informe preliminar del Proyecto Arqueológico Farfán. Instituto Nacional de Cultura, Lima.

Mann, Michael
1986 *The Sources of Social Power*. Vol. 1, *A History of Power from the Beginning to A.D. 1760*. Cambridge University Press, Cambridge.

McGrath, James E.
1973 The Canchones of Chan Chan, Peru: Evidence for a Retainer Class in a Preindustrial Urban Center. Master's thesis, Department of Anthropology, Harvard University, Cambridge, MA.

Menzel, Dorothy
1959 The Inka Occupation of the South Coast of Peru. *Southwest Journal of Anthropology* 15(2):217–234.

Moore, Jerry D.
1992 Pattern and Meaning in Prehistoric Peruvian Architecture: The Architecture of Social Control in the Chimú State. *Latin American Antiquity* 3(2):95–113.
1996 *Architecture and Power in the Ancient Andes: The Archaeology of Public Buildings*. Cambridge University Press, Cambridge.

Morris, Craig
1967 Storage in Tawantinsuyu. Unpublished Ph.D. dissertation, University of Chicago.
2004 Enclosures of Power. In *Palaces of the Ancient New World*, edited by Susan Toby Evans and Joanne Pillsbury, 299–323. Dumbarton Oaks Research Library and Collection, Washington, DC.

Morris, Craig, and Donald E. Thompson
1985 *Huánuco Pampa: An Inca City and Its Hinterland*. Thames and Hudson, London.

Moseley, Michael E.
1975 Chan Chan: Andean Alternative of the Preindustrial City. *Science* 187:219–225.
1992 *The Incas and Their Ancestors*. Thames and Hudson, London.
2001 *The Incas and Their Ancestors*. Rev. ed. Thames and Hudson, London.

Moseley, Michael E., and Carol J. Mackey
1974 *Twenty-four Architectural Plans of Chan Chan, Peru*. Peabody Museum Press, Harvard University, Cambridge, MA.

Murra, John
1962 Cloth and Its Functions in the Inca State. *American Antiquity* 64(4):710–728.

Neatherly, Patricia
1977 Local Level Lords on the North Coast of Peru. Unpublished Ph.D. dissertation, Cornell University, Ithaca, NY.
Nelson, Andrew, Christine Nelson, Luis Jaime Castillo, and Carol Mackey
2000 The Woman behind the Mask. *Íconos* 4(2):30–43.
Niles, Susan
1999 *The Shape of Inca History.* University of Iowa Press, Iowa City.
Pillsbury, Joanne
1996 The Thorny Oyster and the Origins of Empire: Implications of Recently Uncovered *Spondylus* Imagery from Chan Chan, Peru. *Latin American Antiquity* 7(4):313–340.
Pillsbury, Joanne, and Banks L. Leonard
2004 Identifying Chimú Palaces: Elite Residential Architecture in the Late Intermediate Period. In *Palaces of the Ancient New World,* edited by Susan Toby Evans and Joanne Pillsbury, pp. 247–298. Dumbarton Oaks Research Library and Collection, Washington, DC.
Pozorski, Thomas
1979 The Las Avispas Burial Platform at Chan Chan, Peru. *Annals of the Carnegie Museum* 48:119–137.
Ramírez, Susan E.
1996 *The World Upside Down: Cross-Cultural Contact and Conflict in Sixteenth-Century Peru.* Stanford University Press, Stanford.
Rostworowski de Diez Canseco, María, and Craig Morris
1999 The Fourfold Domain: Inka Power and Its Social Foundations. In *The Cambridge History of the Native Peoples of the Americas,* Vol. 3, Part 1, edited by Frank Salomon and Stuart B. Schwartz. Cambridge University Press, Cambridge and New York.
Rowe, John H.
1948 The Kingdom of Chimor. *Acta Americana* 6(1–2):26–59.
Sapp, William
2002 The Impact of Imperial Conquest at the Palace of a Local Lord in the Jequetepeque Valley, Northern Peru. Unpublished Ph.D. dissertation, University of California, Los Angeles.
Schreiber, Katharina J.
1992 *Wari Imperialism in Middle Horizon Peru.* Museum of Anthropology, University of Michigan, Ann Arbor.
Shimada, Izumi
1995 *Cultura Sicán; dios de riqueza y poder en la costa norte del Peru.* Fundación del Banco Continental para el Fomento de la Educación y la Cultura, Lima.
1997 Organizational Significance of Marked Bricks and Associated Construction Features on the North Peruvian Coast. In *Archaeologica Peruana,* Vol. 2, edited by Elisabeth Bonnier and Henning Bishchof. Reiss Museum, Mannheim.
Topic, John R.
1982 Lower-Class Social and Economic Organization at Chan Chan. In *Chan Chan: Andean Desert City,* edited by Michael E. Moseley and Kent C. Day, 145–175. School of American Research Advanced Seminar Series. University of New Mexico Press, Albuquerque.

1990 Craft Production in the Kingdom of Chimor. In *The Northern Dynasties: Kingship and Statecraft in Chimor*, edited by Michael E. Moseley and Alana Cordy-Collins, pp. 145–176. Dumbarton Oaks Research Library and Collection, Washington, DC.

Topic, John R., and Michael E. Moseley

1983 Chan Chan: A Case Study of Urban Change in Peru. *Ñawpa Pacha* 21:153–182.

Uceda, Santiago

1997 Esculturas en miniatura y una maqueta en madera. In *Investigaciones en la Huaca de la Luna 1995 (Proyecto Arqueológico Huacas del Sol y de la Luna)*, edited by Santiago Uceda, Elias Mujica, and Ricardo Morales. Facultad de Ciencias Sociales, Universidad Nacional de la Libertad, Trujillo, Peru.

Uhle, Max

1991 [1903] *Pachacamac: A Reprint of the 1903 Edition*, published with Izumi Shimada, *Pachacamac Archaeology: Retrospect and Prospect*. University Monograph 62. University of Pennsylvania, Philadelphia.

von Hagen, Adriana, and Craig Morris

1998 *Cities of the Ancient Andes*. Thames and Hudson, London.

Wright, Henry, and G. Johnson

1975 Population, Exchange, and Early State Formation in Southwestern Iran. *American Anthropologist* 77:267–289.

CHAPTER 12

Houses of Political Power among the Ancient Maya and Inka

Jessica Joyce Christie

The purpose of this study is to compare and contrast palaces and elite residences and their political functions in Maya and Inka societies. At first glance, such an undertaking may seem meaningless because the Maya and Inka people were so different in almost any aspect of culture. But it is precisely because of that otherness that a comparison, or rather contrast, of high-status residential architecture will help illuminate political organization and lead to a more general theoretical discussion of how the two political systems are reflected in the architectural and archaeological record. These issues will be illuminated by the engagement of a model developed by Olivier de Montmollin, who emphasizes that differences should be measured in degrees rather than with predetermined typologies.

The Maya have occupied southern Mexico, Belize, Guatemala, and western Honduras from before 600 B.C. to the present. Most of the ancient cities were built in the Classic period between A.D. 250 and 900 and abandoned around A.D. 900, though some cities in the Yucatán continued to thrive into the Postclassic and up to the Spanish Conquest. The Maya were organized in independent city-states, with one ruler in charge of the affairs of each one. These city-states formed alliances with or against each other and warred for sacrificial victims as well as political and territorial expansion. Epigraphic and ethnographic evidence indicates that the ruler did not make political decisions alone but was counseled by a bureaucracy formed by an elite class (see, for example, Sharer 1997:135). Such organization would be reflected in the architectural record: there must have been houses in which the ruler and the elite lived and the same or perhaps other structures in which meetings were held, visitors received, and political decisions made. This chapter will explore to what extent it is possible to reconstruct the political aspects of Maya residential architecture.

In contrast, the Inka appeared much later. They made Cusco their capital in the early fifteenth century and from then on embarked on an aggressive strategy of conquest. By 1500 B.C., they ruled the South American Pacific coast from southern Ecuador in the north to northern Chile in the south, and from the Pacific coastline in the west to some of the jungle areas in the east. The Inka state government remained centralized in Cusco. Again, this kind of political and superb administrative organization should be reflected in the architectural record, especially since in any preindustrial society, architecture is one of the media through which permanent public statements could be made. This study discusses an architectural style that may have made a reference to the Inka state in Cusco as well as in the conquered territories.

The first section addresses formal aspects and functional interpretations based on form, and the second section explores issues of political descent reflected through residential architecture. Finally, the question of ranking is raised, along with the issue of how we can differentiate between palaces and elite residences. The arguments focus on what can be learned about social and political organization by the way palaces and houses were built, located, and used within the overall layout of a city. This discussion is of a more general theoretical nature. I would like to clarify that the term *palace*, as used in this chapter, means a residence of the ruling family and/or a location where the business of governing was conducted. Elite residences are understood as the dwelling places of nobles and priests.

Formal Comparison and Interpretations of Function

A formal comparison between known Maya and Inka palaces reveals significant similarities as well as differences. Maya archaeologists have documented and unearthed a large number of palace structures. Every Maya city had buildings that fall into the general category of palaces. Therefore, this study can draw examples from a significant sample. The problem is that the exact definition of a "palace" is still very vague. The first scholarly visitors to Maya cities in the late nineteenth and early twentieth centuries observed two formally very different building groups that they named in European terminology. All tall structures they called temples. Temples consisted of a pyramidal platform with at least one stairway leading up to the top where the actual temple building sat. These temple buildings were typically small one- or two-room structures.

On the other hand, Maya palaces consisted of a series of courtyards surrounded by buildings of varying sizes. These buildings sat on low platforms, and they were long, gallery-like range structures, that is, they were divided longitudinally into small single rooms. In some cases, these rooms opened to both sides, and in other examples, only to one. Very large palaces could have two longitudinal galleries separated by a central wall. The walls were usually made of stonemasonry, and the majority of the structures exhibited stone corbeled vaults, allowing for only small and narrow interior spaces. Palaces were in use through generations, growing over time, and therefore the layout of individual courtyards was not necessarily symmetrical (Figure 12.1).

Early scholars assumed that Maya palaces were primarily residential in function. In his report on Tikal, Alfred Tozzer (1911) discussed buildings of

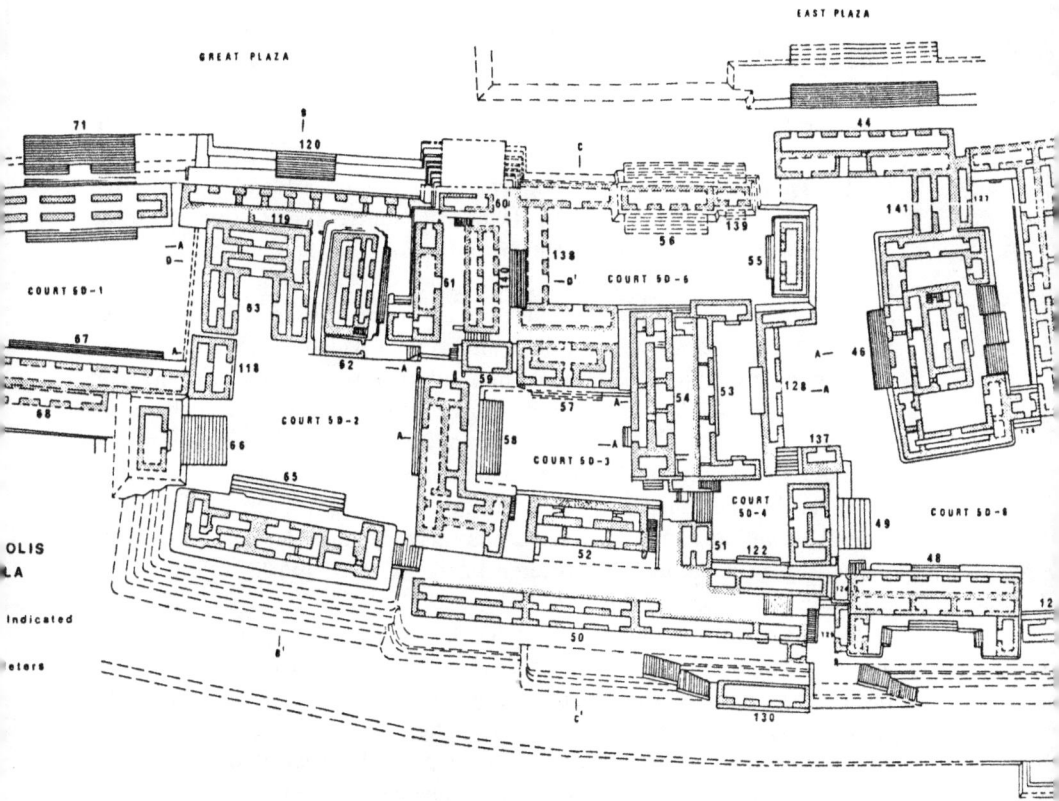

GREAT PLAZA

EAST PLAZA

COURT 5D-1

COURT 5D-6

COURT 5D-2

COURT 5D-3

COURT 5D-4

COURT 5D-5

OLIS
LA

Indicated

eters

of the Central Acropolis, Tikal. Courtesy of Peter Harrison.

what he called the "residential type." He outlined several characteristics of "residential" structures: they contain large numbers of rooms and may be two stories high, they often exhibit two rows of parallel longitudinal rooms and one or two transverse rooms at either end, and they are frequently arranged around courts (Tozzer 1911:96–98). Based on such formal elements alone, Tozzer concluded that these structures had the function of residence.

At the same time, Tozzer noted a close physical connection between residential and religious structures. He suggested that many residences "were probably the homes of the priests" and that they may form a court together with temples (Tozzer 1911:98).

Herbert Spinden's understanding of palaces was quite similar to that of Tozzer. He defined as palaces large buildings, on low terraces, with multiple rooms, and usually arranged around courts. Like Tozzer, he deduced a residential function from the above formal and material aspects (Spinden 1913:98).

His vision was forward reaching when he considered the numerous small mounds seen near temples and palaces at the large sites of Yucatán to be dwellings of the "common people" (Spinden 1913:99). Spinden also realized that palaces could have experienced changes in plan and grown over time and that function could have changed in this course. All of these are issues for which archaeology, at some sites, has now provided material evidence.

Ledyard Smith (1950) reiterated Spinden's (1913) position in his report on Uaxactun. He used formal categories for what constituted a palace that were similar to Tozzer's and Spinden's and made a clear point that the material form of an archaeological "palace" determined the function of "residence." However, he cautioned that some buildings may have been used for residential as well as ritual purposes or may have changed from a temple into a dwelling. Like Spinden, he differentiated "palaces" and "dwellings of the common people" (Smith 1950:71–72).

By 1962, in his report on the Postclassic city of Mayapan, Smith was more aware of the ambiguities associated with the term *palace*. He avoided the term altogether and instead established categories of building types under which he discussed excavated structures. These types of buildings are "dwellings of the poor or unimportant," "dwellings of the wealthy or important," kitchens, oratories, group altars, group shrines, as well as miscellaneous other structures. The main criterion he used to distinguish the dwellings of the poor from those of the wealthy was size. He further noted that the dwellings of the wealthy are almost always arranged in a group and located in the vicinity of the ceremonial center (Smith 1962:217–218). He listed the number of large and really elaborate residences as "probably not more than 50" (Smith 1962:218), but he did not explore what this number might reflect about social structure and political organization at Mayapan. Altogether, Smith's work was important because he advocated more complex building functions that were not limited to religious/ritual or residential.

Linton Satterthwaite was the first scholar to propose a new and more ob-jective archaeological approach to reconstructing function of Maya palaces. In the 1930s, he excavated the palaces on the Acropolis of Piedras Negras. Based on formal elements, he distinguished two plan-types among palace buildings. He defined the term *palace* by these plan-types but was very care-ful not to assign any functional significance (Satterthwaite 1935).

He observed that form alone was insufficient to deduce domestic use of a building and that this kind of conclusion would have to be backed up by material remains of such domestic activities as eating and sleeping (Satterth-waite 1933, 1935). Satterthwaite himself found insufficient evidence for eat-ing and sleeping in the Acropolis palaces. He also described the discomforts associated with living in these palaces: their narrow interior spaces, dark-ness, and humidity, as well as the difficulty of moving daily supplies, and par-ticularly water, up the steep hill of the Acropolis. In Satterthwaite's opinion, the Acropolis palaces were nonresidential, and rooms containing benches with backscreens might have been used for formal audiences and receptions (Satterthwaite 1933).

John Eric Thompson expressed his belief that Maya royalty and priest-hood must have lived in thatch-roofed houses at the periphery of the an-cient cities (1963:48–49). Like Satterthwaite, he stated that stone buildings were unsuited for permanent habitation: ". . . they had no chimneys and no windows, although some rooms had small vents in the walls. More-over, they were damp and ill lit" (Thompson 1959:57–58). He suggested that stone buildings could only have been used for secret rites and for storage of paraphernalia.[1]

In summary, Satterthwaite and Thompson present the view that the pri-mary function of palaces was public in nature and not residential. In their opinion, palaces may have provided spaces for formal audiences, political receptions, religious ceremonies, and storage of precious items.

The most recent research continues to challenge the solely residential interpretation, and data have been accumulated that support a more public-official character of Maya palaces. Two volumes critically reevaluate the ar-chaeological material and interpretations with regard to use and function of Maya palaces. One was edited by me (2003) and grew out of a symposium on Maya palaces and elite residences held at the Society for American Ar-chaeology conference in 1998; the other was edited by Takeshi Inomata and Stephen Houston (2001) and published the papers presented at their confer-ence on royal Maya courts held at Yale University in November 1998.

It is very important to note that the rooms and courtyards in Maya palaces where official business was conducted and public rituals were held were commonly decorated with wall paintings, stucco reliefs, and/or carved stone panels that illustrated and recorded such events for posterity. Paint-ing, sculpture, and inscriptions documented critical events and accomplish-ments in the lives of Maya rulers as they themselves understood such events

FIGURE 12.2 Oval Palace Tablet and Throne in House E, Palace, Palenque. Courtesy of Merle Greene Robertson.

or interpreted and sometimes manipulated them. Imagery and texts were displayed in public space as political propaganda statements. Some of the most eloquent examples come from the Palace at Palenque. In House E, the Oval Palace Tablet depicts K'inich Janaab' Pakal I seated on a jaguar throne and receiving the regalia of office from his mother (Figure 12.2). The text documents his accession, and originally a stone throne stood below the Tablet, surrounded by complex stucco decoration. There is little doubt that this was the historic spot where Pacal became ruler of Palenque.

Present knowledge about Inka palaces is much more limited, and there is no extensive history of research as exists in Maya studies. Few archaeological data are available, and specific studies on Inka palaces have not existed until very recently. For example, there is no separate section on palaces in Graziano Gasparini and Luise Margolies's authoritative book entitled *Inca Architecture* (1980). They address palaces as a type of *kancha* (a courtyard with one-room structures enclosing it) in the chapter "Domestic Architecture" and then again in the following chapter, "The Architecture of Power." In this manner, they avoid the question of what exactly an Inka palace was. Recent discussions of Inka palaces by Craig Morris (2004) and Richard Burger and Lucy Salazar (2004; Burger and Salazar, eds. 2004) have brought into focus palace structures at Huánuco Pampa, La Centinela, Tambo Colorado, and Machu Picchu. William Isbell offers a list of nine diagnostic architectural features of Inka palaces (see Chapter 2, this volume).

Most of the information we do have comes from the Spanish chronicles. The reader is told that the palaces of the Inka emperors were constructed around the main plaza of Cusco. Since colonial buildings have taken their places, few remnants of Inka walls remain visible, and researchers depend on critically evaluating the descriptions left by the Spanish writers.

Felipe Guaman Poma de Ayala presents a comprehensive overview of what an Inka palace was, and other sources focus on more specific details. Guaman Poma de Ayala will be quoted first because of his direct knowledge of Inka culture[2] and because he has also provided a fairly concise description of the various rooms and structures that formed an Inka palace.[3] He says that

> the Royal Courts, palaces, houses or dwellings which belonged to the Inca, as residence and for the functions and proper activities of his government, were the following: *Cuyosmango*, royal palace; *Quinco Uasi*, reserved rooms; *Muyouaci*, circular house; *Carpauaci*, house of three walls, like a corridor; *Suntoruaci*, circular house, room of the Inca; *Uaruya Condo Uaci*, room to receive visitors; *Marca Uaci*, house with only two rooms; *Punona Uaci*, dormitory; *Churacunauaci*, storehouse/depository; *Acauaci*, house for *chicha* preparation; *Masana Uaci*, house for looking after things; *Camachicona Uaci*, house of the servants or lower officials; and *Uaccha Uaci*, house of the poor or subsidiary kin.
>
> Similar houses containing the same or similar structures belonged to the lords *Capac Apoconas*, *Apoconas*, *Curacaconas*, and *Allicacconas*. Their houses varied according to the status and seniority of their owners. The houses did not have names or characteristics different from the Royal Courts and only differed in their dimensions and splendor. (paraphrased from Guaman Poma de Ayala 1987:332 [1615:329–330])

This description is followed by a drawing entitled "Royal Palaces," which depicts and labels some of the building types listed above (Figure 12.3). If one accepts Guaman Poma de Ayala as a reliable source, it could be concluded that the structures forming the *kancha* (see below) contained reserved or

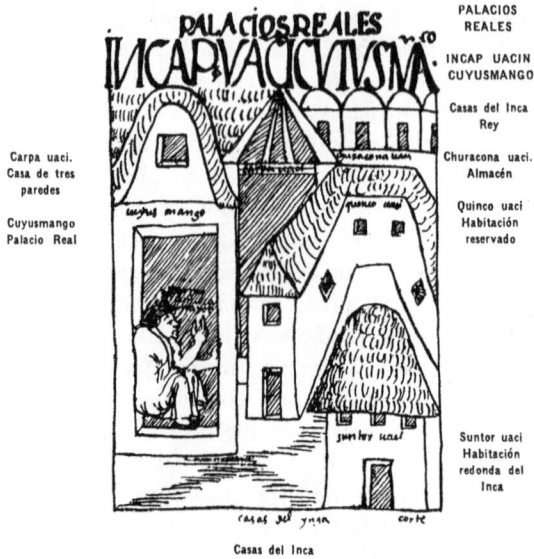

PALACIOS REALES

INCAP UACIN CUYUSMANGO

Casas del Inca Rey

Carpa uaci.
Casa de tres paredes

Cuyusmango
Palacio Real

Churacona uaci.
Almacén

Quinco uaci
Habitación reservado

Suntor uaci
Habitación redonda del Inca

Casas del Inca

FIGURE 12.3 Casas del Inca. Drawing by Guaman Poma de Ayala.

private rooms (Quinco Uasi) and that a circular house nearby held private quarters of the Inka (Suntoruaci). Public official business may have been conducted in a separate building named Cuyosmango.

Guaman Poma de Ayala's account is so important because, first of all, he makes it clear that Inka palaces consisted of many buildings and quarters with many different functions and that members of the nobility resided in similar complexes sized according to their status. Any scholar of Maya palaces faces the very same issues.

Other writers recorded more specific aspects of Inka palaces. Father Bernabé Cobo describes that

> the Palaces and Royal Houses were surrounded by a large enclosure
> (as if fortified) of four walls, and inside this many rooms and lodgings
> were constructed. . . . The roof (was made of) beams tied with ropes and
> thatched with ichu. . . . All the interest of these structures is in their
> walls. (Cobo IV, 14:xii, cited in Kendall 1985:239)

Unlike the Maya examples, Inka palaces were enclosed compounds, but the layout of the buildings inside the walls was probably similar to that in Maya palaces. They were arranged in *kanchas*, which are courtyards surrounded by single-room structures intended for a single function (Figure 12.4). Many Inka walls of high-status buildings were constructed in a very precise masonry style. The individual stone blocks were fitted together exactly so that no mortar was required (Figure 12.5). This stoneworking technique is thought to have been introduced during the reign of Pachacuti Inka Yupanqui.[4] It became a marker of official Inka architecture commissioned by the state government (see below).

Roofs, on the other hand, were always thatched over a wooden framework, as Cobo mentions. The Inka generally did not use stone vaults in residential architecture.[5]

Palaces were without question large *kanchas* that included many additional buildings, as listed above by Guaman Poma de Ayala, and in some royal *kanchas*, one side was formed by a *kallanka* facing the plaza. *Kallankas* were great halls with an open façade designed to house visitors or stage official and religious functions in rainy weather. In Cusco, there were two such halls lined up on one side of the main plaza, Haucaypata: the Cassana and the Coracora (Garcilaso de la Vega, cited in Gasparini and Margolies 1980:197–199). I suggest that Guaman Poma de Ayala's drawing of "Royal Palaces" should not be understood literally; for example, he makes no mention of *kallankas*. He was never trained as an artist and therefore must have been technically overwhelmed by the task of fitting all the different rooms and structures he talks about into one drawing. It is entirely possible that some of the buildings he draws outside the *kancha* were actually within and all others were located nearby.

No material evidence of decoration of Inka palaces has survived. However, some of the Spanish sources describe them as sparkling in gold:

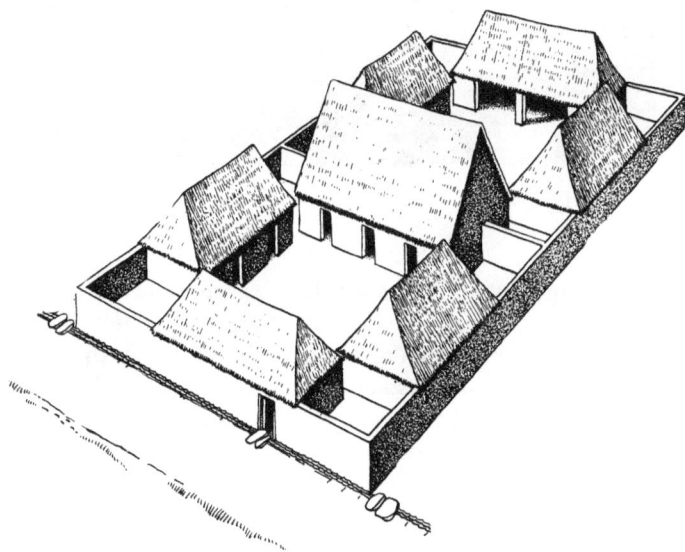

FIGURE 12.4 Hypothetical reconstruction of a double *kancha* enclosure at Ollantaytambo. Adapted from Gasparini and Margolies 1980:190:FIGURE 179.

FIGURE 12.5 Imperial masonry style, Coricancha, Cusco. Photograph by author.

. . . The royal apartments, wherever they existed, were lined with plates of gold, and many gold and silver figures copied from life . . . placed round the walls in spaces and niches which were left for that purpose as the work proceeded. (Garcilaso de la Vega, cited in Kendall 1985:56)

All the royal palaces had gardens and orchards for the Inca's recreation. They were planted with all sorts of gay and beautiful trees, beds of flowers, . . . They also made gold and silver models of many trees and lesser plants . . . and animals . . . (Garcilaso de la Vega, cited in Kendall 1985:56)

. . . the walls were carved with works, and rich and adorned with much gold and embossings (engravings) of the figures and exploits of (the Inca's) predecessors, and other precious stones, . . . (Morúa, cited in Kendall 1985:59)

Such descriptions emphasize that the palaces of the Inka emperors were ornately and lavishly decorated with the most precious materials. In addition, Morúa's account raises the possibility that some of the figure sculpture documented historical events and made political statements. If this were indeed so, narrative art and its perception of history would constitute fruitful points of comparison with Maya art. However, to my knowledge, no physical examples of Inka palace decoration have survived, and due to the absence of a complex writing system, the Inka could not record or illustrate history as clearly as the Maya did.

Issues of Political Descent and Legitimization of Power

While the Maya made their primary political statements of succession through iconography and texts that celebrate individual rulers and oftentimes visualize and record the events that took place in specific palace rooms, the physical volume of the Inka palace itself was a symbol of absolute political authority. It was an Inka custom that

as soon as the royal owner of a palace died, the apartment in which he used to sleep was shut . . . And they at once built new sleeping quarters for the Inca who succeeded him. (Garcilaso de la Vega, cited in Kendall 1985:58)
. . . for each built his own palace, leaving that of his predecessor adorned and standing as he left it. (Zárate, cited in Kendall 1985:58)

In the Inka system of succession, the eldest son inherited the position of Inka emperor at the death of an Inka ruler. One of his immediate responsibilities was to erect his own palace at the main plaza of Cusco. The other male descendants of the dead Inka formed a royal descent group called a *panaca* that was dedicated to supporting the cult, lands, and prestige of their father (Bauer 1998:39). One of the responsibilities of the *panaca* was to attend to the mummy of the dead Inka. The royal mummy continued to "reside" in its palace and was waited on by servants. It was carried to major ceremonies and displayed in public, thus emphasizing the timeless presence and influence of an Inka emperor.

The new emperor was expected to earn his own prestige and eventually to form his own *panaca*. Although all Inka rulers certainly claimed descent from Manco Capac, the legendary founder of Inka power, each one had to individually affirm and legitimize his authority by means of military successes, administrative accomplishments, and building programs.

The chroniclers imply that the successive palaces lined the plaza of

Cusco. However, little can be confirmed archaeologically because the palace remains lie underneath the downtown area of Cusco. On the other hand, though the principal palaces were certainly erected in Cusco, secondary palaces and palacelike complexes were constructed in the Urubamba Valley as well as in farther-outlying territories because the royal court traveled and the Inka was accustomed to visiting the provinces of his empire. One category of palacelike complexes was the royal estate, examples of which have been identified all along the Urubamba Valley (Gyarmati and Varga 1999; MacLean 1986; Niles 1987, 1999; Protzen 1993). Important future research issues are the identification of patterns of any kind that might define royal estates, how they compared with palaces, and how royal estates reflected the political power of their owners and patrons.

In the Maya system of succession, political power was legitimized primarily through descent from a lineage founder. This connection is repeated in the inscriptions and emphasized in the design of palaces. A successor usually continued to live and rule in the palace of his father and added on new buildings. The layout of the Central Acropolis at Tikal shows that the palace of the Early Classic ruler Chak Tok Ich'aak I, Structure 5D-46 in Court 6 (D), remained an important reference point for his Late Classic successors. Structure 5D-46 was identified as the house of Chak Tok Ich'aak I in a carved inscription surrounding the lid of a cache vessel buried beneath the western stair (Harrison 1999:76–78). Even though Chak Tok Ich'aak I was not the lineage founder, his successors continued to occupy his house and they made some additions. The Late Classic rulers Jasaw Chan K'awiil I and Yax Nuun Ayiin II added new palaces to the west, forming an east–west axis of palaces that may well mirror the historical descent line of the Tikal dynasty (Figure 12.6).

In other Maya cities, such as Copan, the connection to the lineage founder or an important earlier ruler was not expressed spatially in the building program but stratigraphically. Loa Traxler's work at Copan has demonstrated that a closed residential group built of adobe and associated with the founder K'inich Yax K'uk' Mo' was the first palace compound beneath the Acropolis. Later rulers enclosed this palace and rebuilt it as masonry courtyard groups. Over time, these palace structures expanded horizontally as well as vertically, so that Traxler (2003) was able to identify levels associated with different rulers. It appears that the Acropolis was a time-honored place and that it was very important to Copan rulers to erect their palaces over the residence of Yax K'uk' Mo', the founder of their dynasty. The stratigraphy of the palaces beneath the Acropolis is the physical manifestation of this line of descent.

One could argue that the design and arrangement of palaces reflect different systems of political succession in Maya and Inka societies. In both societies, palaces sent political messages aimed at helping to legitimize the authority of the ruler or emperor.

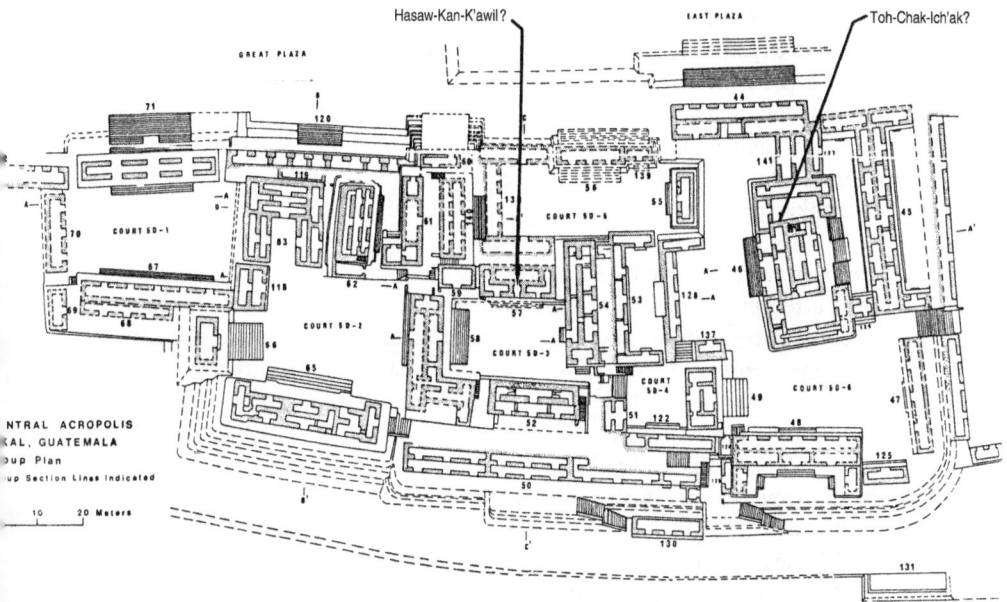

FIGURE 12.6 Plan of the Central Acropolis, Tikal, with possible houses of Chak Tok Ich'aak I and Jasaw Chan K'awiil I. Courtesy of Peter Harrison.

Ranking of Residential Architecture: Palaces versus Elite Residences and Aspects of Political Organization

So far, I have exclusively talked about palaces that occupy the highest order or rank in pre-Columbian residential architecture. I will now discuss houses of lower rank. Such an approach follows a developmental progression in Maya archaeology. The earliest major excavation projects concentrated on the palaces located in the core areas of cities; for example, Roberto García Moll and others worked in the Palace of Palenque from 1926 to 1945 (García 1985), and Peter Harrison conducted extensive excavations in the Central Acropolis at Tikal in the 1960s, sponsored by the University Museum of the University of Pennsylvania (Harrison 1971). The University Museum supported the Tikal Project for 13 years, from 1956 to 1969; therefore, the scope of the work could be broadened and archaeological explorations extended well beyond the core area of the Great Plaza. William A. Haviland (1985) and Marshall J. Becker (1999) supervised excavations in residential areas away from the ceremonial center, and Dennis E. Puleston (1983) worked on the Tikal settlement survey. Another large-scale survey was the Copan Valley Settlement Pattern Project of Harvard University, which was carried out from 1975 to 1977 under the direction of Gordon Willey. The principal goal of the project was to establish the extent of occupation and to begin an analysis of site size and layout (Willey et al. 1978).

The projects listed above demonstrate that the focus of Maya archaeology has expanded from the core to the peripheral areas of cities. It is obvious that the central ceremonial centers continue to receive detailed attention, but the surrounding, in-between, and outlying areas are being explored as well, which is documented in the large number of settlement surveys (for example, Ford 1986). What has come to light is a perplexing number of palacelike structures that were located not only within known ceremonial centers but also outside them. The challenges researchers face are how to categorize and classify Maya residential architecture according to rank, to make attempts at reconstructing which residences were used exclusively for domestic purposes, and to determine which social classes the inhabitants represented. Of course, such analyses cannot be limited to architectural form and must include associated artifacts, burials, and other middens. Discussions of this nature lead to general and broader issues of how Maya society was socially and politically organized, and the amount of literature on this topic is vast (for example, Chase and Chase, eds. 1992; de Montmollin 1995).

In Andean Studies, very few material examples can convincingly be identified as palaces. Two candidates are Wiraqocha Inka's palace at Juchuy Qosqo (see Kendall et al. 1992) and Quispiguanca, Wayna Qhapaq's palace at Urubamba (Niles 1999), both belonging to royal estates. But there are many extant *kanchas*; for example, the still-inhabited *kanchas* that form the grid system of today's village of Ollantaytambo (Gasparini and Margolies 1980:187–191). How did they relate to the high-status architecture of the archaeological site on the other side of the Patacancha River? Or the *kanchas* at Raqchi, which were designed with careful symmetry and utmost precision—what was their relation to the Temple of Wiraqocha located immediately to the north? Machu Picchu is another case in point. This site contains a few temples, but most of the structures were residences of some sort. Many are laid out in *kancha* formations. Recent studies have analyzed the artifacts found in the houses of Machu Picchu, and the consensus now is that it was designed and built as one of Pachacuti Inka Yupanqui's royal estates (see Burger and Salazar 2004; Burger and Salazar, eds. 2004; MacLean 1986).

Given the great complexity of residential architecture in both Maya and Inka societies, the question this chapter poses is: In what ways and to what degree can residences be ranked, and can such ranking provide insights into the ways political power was distributed? It is hoped that this comparison of very different cultures will help clarify political power structures through contrast.

For the Maya area, the database is very large. A vast corpus of literature exists, documenting, discussing, and interpreting excavations of palaces, palacelike structures, and houses in general. The more recent papers and publications have been careful not to advance any interpretations of architecture without addressing burials and artifacts found within or associated with the structures under consideration (for example, Andrews et al. 1998; Chase and Chase 1998; Christie 2003; Guderjan 1998; Hendon 1987; Triadan and Inomata 1998).

Maya residential architecture has been ranked into palaces, elite residences, and houses of commoners. As mentioned above, palaces are defined as long range- and gallery-like structures organized around courtyards. The individual buildings sit on low platforms and contain multiple rooms. Palaces are always large in size and comprise several courtyards. Walls were constructed of dressed-stone masonry and roofs were corbel vaulted. Palaces may display stucco decoration and contain interior furnishings such as benches. Burials have been excavated from palace substructures, and artifacts from palace contexts typically establish evidence for ritual and some domestic activities. Palaces are always located at the site center.

Elite residences are similar in form, but they are smaller in size and found farther away from the site center. In certain cases, their walls were constructed of roughly shaped blocks of stone, and their roofs could be stone vaulted but more often were made of beam and mortar or thatch. Elite residences of high status may exhibit some stucco decoration and contain a few ritual vessels besides evidence of food preparation, eating, and sleeping.

Houses of commoners are the smallest and simplest structures in the hierarchy of residential architecture. They consist of one large room, and the walls were typically made out of poles to which clay was applied in a process known as wattle and daub. Roofs were thatched. These perishable houses often stood on top of low platforms. In general, they are found at the periphery of Maya cities and throughout outlying areas close to fields.

There have been efforts to group and classify Maya residential architecture according to a status hierarchy from simple mounds found in settlement surveys to ceremonial centers. Much of Gair Tourtellot's (1983) work focused on households at Tikal and Seibal that occupy the lower end of this hierarchy. He differentiates between "dwellings," which are oval or rectangular structures placed on low platforms; domestic "units," which consist of one or more dwellings and ancillaries arranged around small, open spaces; and "households," which comprise structures in units, patio spaces, house lots, and their contents (Tourtellot 1983). Gordon Willey created a model of Maya houses that he expanded into a typology of mounds and mound groupings that attempts to cover the full range of hierarchy in Maya residential architecture. His model was applied to Barton Ramie and Copan, among other sites (Leventhal 1979; Leventhal 1983:67–68; Willey and Leventhal 1979).

Richard Leventhal (1979:42–44) and Willey and Leventhal (1979) specified the following types for the Copan Valley:

• Small, low, and isolated platforms occur in more remote areas away from the ceremonial center. They appear similar to Tourtellot's "dwellings."

• Small platform clusters are made up of informal conjunctions of several mounds. They are found in outlying areas and may correspond to
Tourtellot's domestic "units."

• Type I is the first category of a plazuela type of arrangement. Type I
groups have a small courtyard surrounded by two to five mounds,
ranging in height from 0.30 to 1.5 m. Cobbles were commonly used
in platforms and foundations; roofs were thatched.

• Type II sites have one or two plazas and six to nine mounds with a
maximum height of 2.5 to 3.0 m. In the platform and wall construction, more quarried and shaped stones were used. Both Types I and II
fit Tourtellot's definition of a "household."

• Type III sites are very similar to Type II with regard to the number
of plazas and number of mounds. Higher rank is manifested in an increase of maximum height to 4.75 m and a more widespread use of
dressed stone.

• Type IV sites are characterized by multiple plazas, mounds up to 10 m
high, and a more diverse and complex layout. Most structures are
built of ashlar masonry. They may have vaulted roofs and may display
sculpture. Types III and IV are also classified as "minor ceremonial
centers."

• Major centers or civic-ceremonial centers constitute the highest category in the rank system of Maya architecture. They combine residential and temple architecture and act as focal points of a region. (from
Hendon 1987:51–54)

A more recent attempt to rank Maya architecture and sites was undertaken by Olivier de Montmollin. He established five categories of Political
Hierarchies (PH), which he defines as follows: PH1 is a polity capital that
must contain multipyramid plazas and two ballcourts; PH2 is a section capital with at least one multipyramid plaza and one ballcourt; PH3 is a pocket
capital with one ballcourt but no multipyramid plazas; PH4 is a local center without multipyramid plazas or ballcourts; and PH5 is a basal community without any civic-ceremonial buildings (de Montmollin 1989:78–82).
De Montmollin emphasizes that in Maya society, religious activities were
always one aspect of the political system, and he therefore draws little distinction between temples and palaces with regard to their political function—they are both civic-ceremonial buildings.

Based on how differently ranked categories of Maya houses were distributed, arguments have been presented that aim to explain how Maya society
was politically organized. One of the issues that has been debated heavily
is whether the Maya political system resembled a segmentary or a unitary
state. The concept of the segmentary state was formulated by Aidan Southall
(1956) for the Alur of eastern Africa. According to Southall's definition, a
"segmentary state" is based on lineage or kinship arrangements within a
pyramidal social structure in which the "powers exercised . . . are virtually

of the same type at the several different levels"; in contrast, a fully developed "unitary state" exhibits a "hierarchical power structure" because "such powers are delegated from the top of the structure," and "similar powers are not repeated at all levels" (1956:251). Other aspects of Southall's segmentary state are that it exhibits neither a strong central authority nor a bureaucracy and is largely incapable of maintaining control over distant territories. As a direct result of this lack of political control outside a core area, boundaries of a segmentary state are flexible and changing (Southall, cited in Chase and Chase 1992:308). Whereas a segmentary state or polity has a loose aggregation of districts that are replications of one another in their political structure, a unitary polity has a more tightly integrated set of districts, which are often differentiated in their political structure. Segmentary polities are characterized by low degrees of centralization, differentiation, and integration, but unitary polities have high degrees of the same variables: centralization, differentiation, and integration (de Montmollin 1989:19–21).

Closely related to the segmentary and unitary divisions are the categories of mechanical versus organic solidarity. These categories have been derived from Émile Durkheim's studies concerning the division of labor in society, and "solidarity" in this context is understood as economic integration. Mechanical arrangements with economically autarchic districts, limited exchange, and independence of districts are less solidary and cohesive than organic arrangements with a great deal of economic specialization among districts, extensive exchange, and interdependence of districts. Mechanical economies are associated with segmentary polities, and organic economies, with unitary polities (de Montmollin 1989:25). The basic assumption is that economic specialization promotes exchange, which promotes interdependence. However, de Montmollin points out that this very idea that exchange promotes social solidarity has been challenged by economic anthropology (1989:25).

Southall implied that the concept of segmentary versus unitary political units would find widespread application in various areas and cultures, even though he formulated his definition from examples in eastern Africa (1956). This assumption has been questioned by some scholars, such as Diane and Arlen Chase, who "hesitate" to use Southall's bipolar categories in the context of the Maya (1992:308). In general, they feel that "it is very inappropriate to apply Old World analogies for complex organization in the New World without substantial rationale" (Chase and Chase 1992:307). I would disagree and suggest that such methodology is defendable as long as caution is taken to account for cultural differences of any kind that could distort the comparison. I hope the following discussion will clarify this issue.

John Fox, D. T. Wallace, and K. L. Brown argue that the social organization of the Quiché Maya was and is segmentary: "The rise of the Quiché elite is traced from fairly egalitarian alliances of small segmentary lineages, as early as the late A.D. 800s, to their formative segmentary state in post–A.D. 1100" (Fox et al. 1992:187). Their primary evidence comes from the way the architecture was laid out in Quiché civic-ceremonial centers. They describe and illustrate the evolution of Quiché society, beginning with the Early Post-classic center Jacawitz, where the two major lineages, the Ajaw and Cawek, built two adjoining civic plazas in a north–south direction. Lineage houses were undifferentiated in size, and each was about 30 m long. In the 1100s, the Quiché relocated from Jacawitz to Utatlan, where the Ajaw were again situated at the southern side of the main plaza. However, two more lineages were added. As a result, the Cawek were now associated with the west and their temple faced east, whereas the new major lineage, the Nujaib, occupied the eastern side of the plaza and their temple faced west. The second new lineage, the Sakic, was small and was located on the north side. In the site plan, each lineage is associated with a compound of residential structures, and those of the three major lineages were fronted by a dominant temple occupying their side of the plaza. Thus the layout of Utatlan strongly suggests a segmentary organization based on lineages (Fox et al. 1992:169–173). Mural fragments in the Southwest Palace may offer additional insights into lineage ranking and function of the Ajaw (Fox et al. 1992:174–178).

Fox, Wallace, and Brown also looked at economic factors: "Segmentary states are characterized economically by kinship groups that produce their own food and acquire both utilitarian and prestige goods mainly through kinship networks" (1992:182). Brown's excavations at Utatlan sampled three of the major palace complexes. These compounds were compared with seven similar but smaller compounds excavated in the residential area outside the elite center proper. Artifact frequencies from the outlying compounds for individual principal lineages were remarkably similar to those in the elite center area, and eight distinctive zones of craft specialization were identified, each coinciding with a different patrilineage (Fox et al. 1992:182–187). It thus appears that architecture, site layout, iconography, and craft production confirm a segmentary political system, at least for the Quiché.

The Cakchiquel capital Iximche constitutes another example. Iximche is laid out in four main courtyards surrounded by residences, temples, and ballcourts. Although the courtyards are similar, two are larger in size and associated with more complex architecture. Not all the structures lining the eastern courtyard, Plaza E, have been excavated. These courtyards have been related to the four most powerful Cakchiquel lineages and are seen as the most clearly defined architectural expression of a segmentary state (Schele and Mathews 1998:299–311).

Similar arguments have been advanced for Copan. Based on a comparison of the data from the Main Group and the Las Sepulturas zone, David Webster and William Sanders believe

> that the mature Copan polity was characterized by a high degree of segmentation. By this we mean that, although the system was politically centralized around a group of preeminent titled elites (the royal lineage), kinship was still the dominant mechanism in overall social,

political, and economic organization. . . . Our argument is that there were multiple, effective political interest groups in the polity, which we conceive of as maximal lineages with their own internal ranking structures and, most importantly, their own corporate identities and resources. . . . Leaders of such corporate groups (inheriting their positions through some sort of intralineage structure) would be occupants of such impressive Type 3 and 4 groups as 9N-8 (Las Sepulturas), and their supporters/kin would consist not only of other occupants of the elite households, but of segments of the rural populations as well. These second-level elites at Copan, at least some of whom seem to have enjoyed the possession of court titles and ranks, were stewards of large corporate, kin-based land holdings. (Webster 1992:153–154)

I suggest that one would have to test Webster's assessment against the most recent excavation data from the 1990s to measure whether it still holds true for the now expanded database and newly excavated compounds in the Copan Valley.

Chase and Chase express a very different opinion. They postulate that Tikal and Caracol had "centralized bureaucracies" that would better approximate a "unitary state," following Southall's terminology (Chase and Chase 1992:308–309). As mentioned above, they emphasize their uneasiness about using either one of the bipolar categories of a "segmentary state" or a "unitary state."

A new and different approach to analyzing political structure in settlements has been proposed and practiced by Olivier de Montmollin (1989, 1995). He addresses the shortcomings of the traditional way of analysis, which is based on societal typologies: such types require polar thinking, and the categories constructed are so idealized and simplistic that much variability has to be suppressed; societal typologies tend to reify society rather than treat it as a collection of persons and groups (de Montmollin 1989:11–14). Instead, de Montmollin offers an alternative that he refers to as "bundled continua of variation." By this term he means the breaking down of multivariate societal types into their constituent variables and viewing these as continua of variation. He continues to use binary divisions such as segmentary versus unitary structure, pyramidal versus hierarchical regime, group versus individual stratification, mechanical versus organic solidarity, and segmenting versus nonsegmenting organization. The difference is that he does not see them as absolute groupings into which Maya polities have to fit but rather as attempts to investigate to what degree they apply. In this manner, the binary divisions are used as a number of continua bracketed by polar extremes (de Montmollin 1989:16–19). "The argument was not against classification as such, but rather against too simple dichotomous classifications based on presence/absence of traits and against rigid classifications masking interesting variability" (de Montmollin 1989:17).

How would one measure degrees of segmentary and unitary structure?

De Montmollin does this by establishing and comparing several indexes: the Tribute Drawing Index (TDI) measures degrees of tribute-drawing centralization. The number of domestic dwellings is an indicator of local tribute providers, and civic-ceremonial architectural mass is a relative indicator of the tribute received there. The cubic meters of civic-ceremonial architectural mass at a center divided by the number of dwellings at the associated site gives the TDI (de Montmollin 1989:104). The Tribute Load Index is calculated by dividing civic-ceremonial architectural mass at a center (or centers) by the number of dependent dwelling buildings to get a per capita (or per dwelling) measure of tribute load (de Montmollin 1989:107). The close similarities between both indexes and the problems of defining "the number of dwellings at the associated site" versus "the number of dependent dwelling buildings" illuminate some of the dangers and pitfalls in de Montmollin's methodology. The Structure Diversity Index (SDI) is based on the notion that there will be somewhat differing political activities associated with civic-ceremonial buildings of substantially different sizes. It is computed by assigning one point for every civic-ceremonial building type at a given center. The higher the SDI value is, the greater is the range of political functions (de Montmollin 1989:147). Again, I see a problem in the lack of consensus among scholars as to how to exactly define all civic-ceremonial building types.

What can be the outcome of an investigation following de Montmollin's methodology? As expected, his conclusions are that the Rosario polity (which is the subject of his study) shows a tendency toward unitary structure with regard to certain archaeological parameters, while there is a "slight tendency toward more segmentary structure" with reference to other parameters. Obviously, such conclusions are not very meaningful unless they are compared with data from other polities analyzed in the same fashion. De Montmollin is fully aware of this shortcoming and stresses the importance of comparisons; he adds a qualitative and quantitative analysis of data from Rosario itself compared to data from smaller district-scale units within the valley (1989:219–234). To my knowledge, no other researchers have applied de Montmollin's methodology to other Maya sites, and therefore no further comparative results are available. I believe de Montmollin's concept of bundled continua of variation is a very fruitful avenue to pursue and should be tested on other sites and polities.

For the time being, it is also of use in my present study. Looking at Maya and Inka palaces not as exclusive opposites but as clusters at different ends of a continuum will make the comparison more effective and will highlight differing aspects of social organization in Maya and Inka societies.

In Inka architecture, there are very few archaeological data about residences (Morris 2004; Morris and Thompson 1985; Niles 1987, 1999). Many early reports that describe architecture only include quantitative, but little qualitative, artifactual analyses and remain vague about proveniences (Bingham 1986, 1997); only recently have attempts been made to trace the origin of the artifacts from Machu Picchu and place them into architectural context (Burger and Salazar 2004; Burger and Salazar, eds. 2004). Again, the richest sources about Inka palaces and elite residences are the Spanish writers, but their historical correctness has to be constantly tested.

Notwithstanding all these odds, efforts have been undertaken to rank Inka residential architecture based on a style that is anchored in an aesthetic of geometry (see Kendall 1985; Pasztory 1997).[6] I believe this is a fruitful approach, and I will pursue it further in this study and evaluate its application. It will be shown that Inka urban design, the *kancha* complex, imperial masonry, and, to some extent, rock art followed geometric principles that may reflect aspects of political power. Recently, Jean-Pierre Protzen has expressed a differing view. He warned against overemphasizing standardization and repetition in Inka architecture because such an approach would keep the viewer from observing the range of variations and the subtle differences between buildings, which, in his view, constitute the richness of Inka architecture. He concluded that there was not enough empirical evidence to identify general town-planning rules (Protzen 2000:204–211, 216–217).

I would like to clarify that the "geometric principles" I will be investigating are approximations, and most are not exact nor mathematically measured in terms of modern scientific standards. There were many local variations as to how such principles were applied, and topography played a very important role. As Protzen noticed, *kanchas* could be deformed to adjust to an available building site. However, to explore creative and ingenious local adaptations of the official style to specific site conditions would require case studies that clearly go beyond the scope of the present chapter. Therefore, I caution that I cannot uncover a pure geometric system of aesthetics defining Inka architecture, but I think I can show that the "geometric principles," as discussed here, define elements of a general order that was imposed by the state.

It is well known that Cusco had an upper and lower section and that it was divided into four quarters. The origins of these layouts are less clear. The chroniclers inform us that the village of Acamama was located on the future site of Cusco between the two rivers of that valley before the arrival of the Inka. María Rostworowski suggests that Acamama already contained the bipartite division into an upper (*hanan*) and lower (*hurin*) section. Her reasoning is based on the observation that the *hanan* and *hurin* principles were pan-Andean opposites and that *ayllus*, towns, and valleys were all partitioned in this manner. In her understanding, such principles are also related to sociopolitical and economic complementarity. Because each ecological zone had different resources, people developed economic interaction mechanisms that may have found a physical and social reflection in the *hanan/hurin* concept (Rostworowski 1999:6–7). After the arrival of the Inka, the dual division began to take on increased social as well as political connotations. One of the Inka origin myths tells of the Ayar siblings emerging from a cave called Pacariqtambo. There were four brothers, whose names were Ayar Ucho, Ayar Cachi, Ayar Mango, and Ayar Auca, and their four sisters. These legendary brothers and sisters wandered through the mountains, searching for an appropriate place to settle. When they finally found the site of Cusco, only two brothers were left. Ayar Mango, who was now called Manco Capac, and his *ayllus* inhabited lower, or Hurin, Cusco, and the followers of Ayar Auca occupied upper, or Hanan, Cusco (Rostworowski 1999:12–15).

Rostworowski thinks that, in addition, *hanan* and *hurin* in Cusco had a connotation of gender. Garcilaso de la Vega says that the older brothers populated Hanan Cusco and the younger brothers, who were followers of the "queen," settled Hurin Cusco. She interprets this statement to mean that the men of *hanan* were masculine/masculine and those of *hurin* were masculine/feminine (Rostworowski 1999:15). I think that in this context she may be stretching the gender issue too much.

The quadripartite division was also already present at Acamama. Pedro Sarmiento de Gamboa writes that the village of Acamama comprised four sections: Quinti Cancha, or the District of the Hummingbird; Chumbi Cancha, or the District of the Weavers; Sairi Cancha, or the District of Tobacco; and the fourth district, Yarambuy Cancha, which was probably inhabited by Aymara and Quechua speakers (cited in Rostworowski 1999:7). After Manco Capac and his siblings had settled, and after he consolidated his authority, he organized the growing town into the four *señoríos* of Manco Capac, Tocay Capac, Pinahua Capac, and Colla Capac (Rostworowski 1999:50). After the Inka victory over the Chanka and during the reconstruction of the capital city under Pachacuti Inka Yupanqui, Cusco was finally divided into the four well-known *suyus*, or quarters: Chinchaysuyu, Antisuyu, Collasuyu, and Cuntisuyu. The *suyu* division originated in the main plaza, Haucaypata, in Cusco, from where four roads departed in the directions of the *suyus*. It should be noted that these roads did not lead straight north, south, east, and west, but one road went northwest where Chinchaysuyu was located, another departed to the northeast to Antisuyu, the third road went southwest to Cuntisuyu, and the fourth went southeast to Collasuyu. In this manner, the four roads only originated in the center of Cusco, where they determined the urban design of the city. But even more importantly, they led much farther, eventually crossing the entire Inka Empire and forming what became known as Tahuantinsuyu, the state of the four quarters. The political implication is nothing less than that Pachacuti Inka Yupanqui envisioned conquering the four quadrants of the entire world from Cusco.

A second, and perhaps equally important, political implication is that neither the bipartite nor the quadripartite divisions of Cusco were inventions of the Inka. As outlined above, such concepts of organizing space and society were common throughout the Andes and had been in use long before the Inka ever appeared. What the Inka did, however—and I think this was a very intelligent strategic move—was to adopt these principles that were very familiar to their subjects and turn them into instruments of political power.

Similar elements of urban planning have been observed in outlying areas of the empire. Huánuco Pampa, located 150 km by road from the present city of Huánuco, northeast of Lima, was an Inka administrative center. The site was partially excavated and the region surveyed by Craig Morris and Donald E. Thompson in the 1960s and 1970s. Based on the data they recovered and their published studies, more insights have been gained about Huánuco Pampa than for most other Inka cities. As they began with their fieldwork, Morris and Thompson (1985:57–58) quickly noticed that Huánuco Pampa imitates the architecture and ceramic styles of Cusco. Resemblances are most explicit in the plan. Morris argues for the presence of a bi-, tri-, and quadripartition in the design of Huánuco Pampa (Hyslop 1990:215–218; Morris and Thompson 1985:72–73). The center of Huánuco Pampa constitutes a large rectangular plaza, which is laid out almost exactly in a north-south, east-west direction with an inaccuracy of two degrees. The focal point is a large *ushnu* platform in the middle, and the buildings are arranged along the four sides of the plaza (Figure 12.7). Following Tom Zuidema (1964), Morris proposes two possible interpretations of the city's layout. In the first interpretation, the architectural groups on each side of the rectangular plaza are seen as local representations of the four quarters, or *suyus*, of the Inka Empire. The dual division is the result of the main Inka road, which cuts across the plaza in a southeast–northwest direction. In this manner, the northern and eastern sides become *hanan* and the southern and western parts become *hurin* (Morris, cited in Hyslop 1990:215–216). In addition, the buildings in each quarter are divided into three sectors by corridors or walls, which may be a conceptual parallel to the grouping of *ceque* (shrine) lines into clusters of three in each of the *ceque* system's *suyus* in Cusco. The nature of the *ceque* system and its complex ritual, social, and economic connotations have been discussed by John Hyslop (1990) and the many sources he cites, in particular numerous publications by Tom Zuidema (1964; Hyslop 1990:363–364; see also Bauer 1998). I believe a more detailed description of the *ceque* system would lead the present study onto a tangent, and the interested reader may consult the works cited. Suffice it to say that a tripartite division derived from the *ceque* system in Cusco was another possible geometric design element that reflected state planning.

In the second interpretation, the site is divided by an east-west axis formed by a street on the west, the *ushnu* platform, and a set of gateways on the east. Under this scenario, the northern half would be *hanan* and the southern half would be *hurin*. The tripartite classification is eliminated, and four main divisions, formed by the widest streets in the city, are recognized in each half (Morris, cited in Hyslop 1990:216–217). This is not the place or time to debate the validity of each interpretation, but I think the evidence

HUANUCO PAMPA

0 20 50 100 200

METROS

FIGURE 12.7 Plan of Huánuco Pampa. Courtesy of Craig Morris.

presented supports the conclusion that geometric principles of urban planning copied from the capital city of Cusco were exported and applied to administrative centers in the empire, such as Huánuco Pampa, to manifest the
presence of the Inka state.

Hyslop discusses similar concepts of radial planning and bi-, tri-, and
quadripartitioning at the sites of Inkawasi, Pumpu, Chilecito, Chucuito, and
Maucallacta (1990:218-221). In my opinion, his observations at Inkawasi,
Chucuito, and Maucallacta are the most significant. These settlements, or
important sectors within them, are laid out in the form of an arc, with streets
and blocks forming radial divisions. Hyslop proposes that they may be architectural representations of quadrants of the Cusco *ceque* system (1990:218-
220). His interpretation lends support to the view that cities other than
Cusco had a type of *ceque* system—a view that has been debated in the literature (see, for example, Bauer 1998:143-154). The main point in the context
of the present study is that geometric planning principles have been documented at various Inka sites.

Hyslop eloquently sums up the preceding discussion in his section "Other
Cuzcos" (1990:303-306). Some of the early Spanish writers, such as Felipe
Guaman Poma de Ayala, Pedro Cieza de León, and Pablo Joseph de Arriaga,
mention "other" or "new" Cuscos. It has been shown above that multiple
planning concepts employed in Cusco can also be found in many other
settlements. They are not, however, precise physical replications of Cusco,
but they isolated and copied certain design elements that suited local topography and functions. There is consensus that "Inca social, religious, and political concepts developed in Cusco were spread to diverse parts of the state
via the design and specific features of the larger state settlements—which
recreated the 'mythical space' (Rostworowski) of Cusco" (Hyslop 1990:305).

The final—and in my judgment the most impressive—attempt to build
another Cusco occurred at Vilcabamba the Old in the sixteenth century.
Manco Inka abandoned the fortress of Ollantaytambo in July of 1537 after
realizing that the Spanish forces prepared to fight against him were over-
whelming. He retreated to the remote wilderness of Vilcabamba, where a
new capital was taking form, probably under Manco Inka's patronage and
commission. Very little archaeological work has been conducted at this extremely important site, and it is largely covered by jungle. But after exploring
it with Vincent Lee's map and reconstruction in my hand, I am fairly confi-
dent in saying that Vilcabamba the Old was laid out according to the same
principles employed at Cusco (Figure 12.8a). The center of Vilcabamba is a
large plaza, which is surrounded by symmetrically designed *kanchas* on the
southwest and northeast sides and by a *kallanka*, or hall structure, in the
northwest. The arrangement of the house compounds and the remnants of
Inka streets establish evidence that originally four roads converged in this
plaza: from the northeast, southeast, southwest, and northwest. The physical aspects are somewhat confusing because some of the existing trails co-

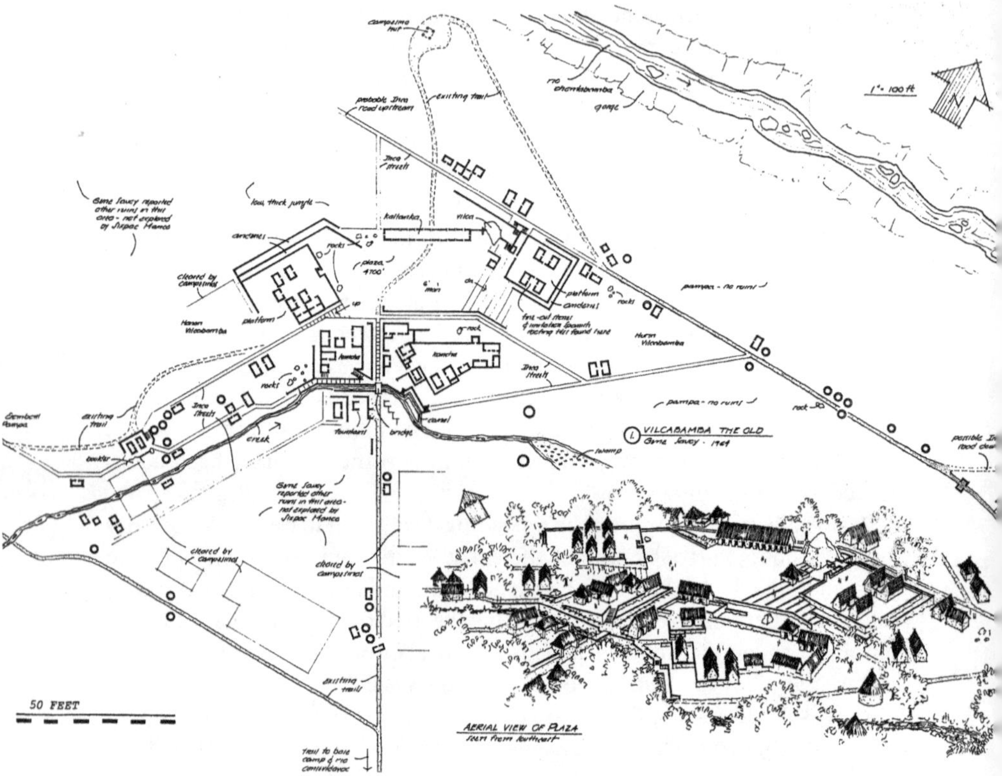

FIGURE 12.8A Plan of Vilcabamba the Old with Inka streets. From Lee 1986:97:
FIGURE 50. Courtesy of Vincent Lee, © 1986.

incide with Inka streets and some do not; for example, one existing trail cuts
through the middle of the *kallanka*. On the other hand, the southeastern
road is clearly of Inka origin, and the structures framing the plaza leave open
spaces in the southwest, northwest, and northeast, which were possibly road
entrances. If this is so, the layout of the central sector of Vilcabamba the
Old replicates that of Cusco. Additional elements copied from Cusco are
the *kallanka* facing the plaza on the northwestern side and the large boulder adjacent to it. Stones and rock outcrops were natural features charged
with supernatural powers in the Inka belief system. They were ubiquitous in
the highland area of Cusco but largely absent in the jungle environment of
Vilcabamba. I cannot say whether the Vilcabamba boulder was a rare natural
occurrence or whether the Inka moved it there, but it was without question
a significant element in the design of the plaza.

Vincent Lee identifies a *hanan-hurin* division between the Upper Groups,
which he numbers 4 to 11 on his plan, and the Lower Groups, corresponding
to his numbers 19 and 20 (1989:97–100; Figure 12.8b). I think that the *hanan*
sector could have been concentrated in Group 16, which is a symmetrical

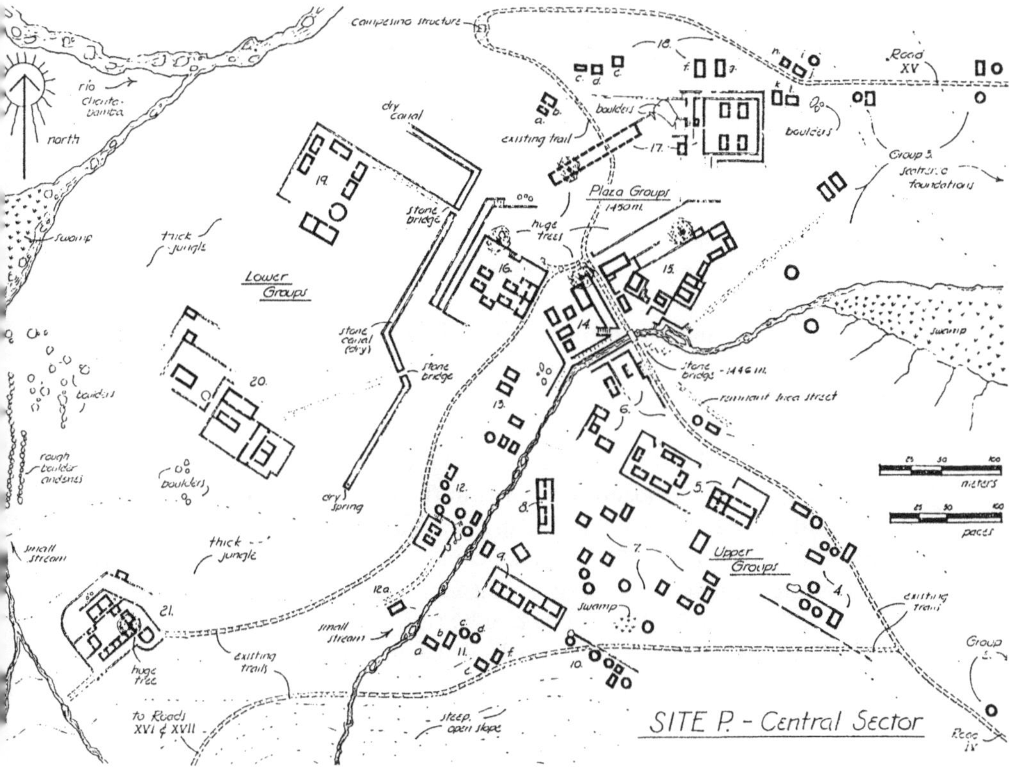

FIGURE 12.8B Plan of Vilcabamba the Old with Group Numbers. From Lee 1986:97:FIGURE 50. Courtesy of Vincent Lee, © 1986.

kancha bordering the plaza on the southwest side. The *hurin* sector would then be represented by Group 17, which is another symmetrical *kancha* on the northeast side of the plaza to which several terraces descend.

Even though so little is known about Vilcabamba, the few elements that have been identified in the plan establish that geometric planning principles were used and that Vilcabamba the Old was likely designed to be the new Cusco. It cannot be stressed enough that Vilcabamba is located in the jungle, an environment unfamiliar to the Inka and lacking the resources the Inka were accustomed to. Nevertheless, they found a way of building another Cusco, which demonstrates the political potency the geometric urban design had accumulated for the Inka state government.

I understand the *kancha* (discussed above) as a smaller version of the quadripartite layout. Gasparini and Margolies (1980:181) suggest that the *kancha* may have been derived from Chimú architecture on the north coast. The adobe *ciudadelas* at Chan Chan were laid out as huge walled rectangular units that contained a great variety of spaces and structures, such as dwellings for the ruling family, storerooms, U-shaped *audiencias* for offices,

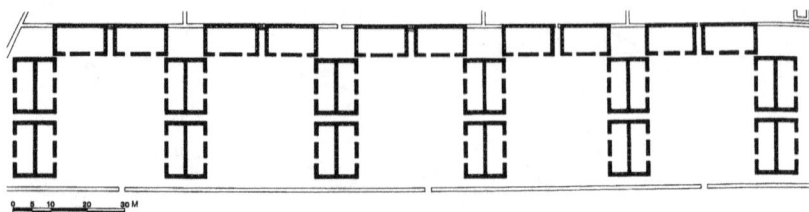

FIGURE 12.9 Plan of *kanchas* to the south of the Temple of Wiraqocha, Raqchi.
Adapted from Gasparini and Margolies 1980:236.

plazas, and a burial platform. If *kanchas* were indeed modeled after the
ciudadelas, they constitute much smaller variants made of stone. A possible closer source is the Wari administrative center Pikillacta, located in
the lower Cusco Valley. The Middle Horizon site of Pikillacta is laid out following a regular plan, with straight streets meeting at right angles, and surrounded by a high enclosure wall. Within the grid units, houses line small
courtyards that are formally and spatially similar to the later Inka *kanchas*.
However, most walls at Pikillacta are constructed of fieldstone laid in clay
and conspicuously lack Cusco-style masonry techniques (see below). The architectural style at Pikillacta and other Wari sites has been named "orthogonal cellular horizon" by William Isbell (see Chapter 2, this volume, and 1991;
see also Isbell and McEwan 1991). Isbell emphasizes that the internal organization of the patio groups creates a cellular structure of repeating modular units.

The central sector of Inka Cusco had a type of orthogonal plan consisting
of rectangular units formed by longitudinal and transverse streets (see, for
example, the hypothetical reconstruction of central Cusco in Gasparini and
Margolies 1980:55:Figure 44). These units may have corresponded to *kanchas*. At the same time, Guaman Poma de Ayala's description (see above)
suggests that the royal palaces that lined the central plaza were larger than
a single *kancha* and included additional buildings.

In general, it is assumed that many *kanchas* forming high-status Inka
residences were symmetrical and precise in the rectangularity of the plan
wherever the topography allowed it. Since very few solid data survive in
Cusco, examples from the Urubamba Valley and farther-outlying areas have
to be cited.

At the site of Raqchi, a series of six perfectly aligned *kanchas* abut the famous Temple of Wiraqocha to the southeast (Figures 12.9 and 12.10). These
kanchas are surrounded by structures on three sides. On the east and west
sides, two houses, each with a central dividing wall, are placed between
one courtyard and the next, so that each half of a house opens onto a different courtyard. On the south side, two single-room structures, each with
two entrances, face each courtyard. In the words of Gasparini and Margolies
(1980:238), the precision of the plan "suggests a complete mastery of units of

measurement to achieve perfectly duplicated contours and to form 90 degree angles."

Interpretation of the function of the Raqchi *kanchas* is largely speculative. Gasparini and Margolies (1980:238) offer suggestions that they were priests' residences or temporary dormitories for pilgrims; or else, the use of the *kanchas* could somehow have been related to the service of the temple or to the storehouses located immediately to the south. Thus the definite functions of these houses remain ambiguous, but they were likely used for residential as well as administrative purposes. Their location at the site core next to the temple and the storehouses leaves no doubt that they were high-status architecture.

FIGURE 12.10 *Kanchas*, Raqchi. Photograph by author.

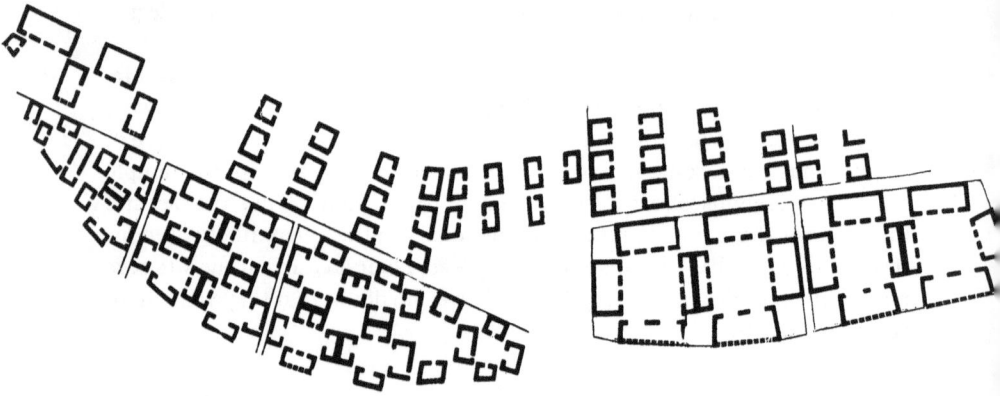

FIGURE 12.11 Plan of Patallacta. From Gasparini and Margolies 1980.

The second eloquent example is the layout of the small town of Patallacta, located near the confluence of the Cusichaca and Urubamba Rivers. The core area of Patallacta sits on a hillside on a large, artificially leveled platform and consists of four residential sectors laid out around two plazas (Figures 12.11 and 12.12). In all four sectors, buildings are arranged in *kancha* formations, but they differ in size, regularity, and quality of construction, suggesting a difference in rank among the occupants. Based on these variations, Ann Kendall (1985) has assigned a hierarchical order to three of the groups.

The "Two-Plaza units" in the southwest of the site were the residence of a senior regional administrator responsible to the imperial government. The "Two-Plaza units" are two *kanchas* made up of two courtyards surrounded by single-room structures on three sides and facing the road that passes through Patallacta on the fourth side. Kendall thinks that this high administrator lived in the compound with a recessed entrance and that the service and servants' facilities were attached in the second unit (1985:194).

The "Large Plaza area" in the northeast might have been inhabited by Quechua-speaking Inkas-by-privilege who helped administer the province. The "Large Plaza area" includes four *kanchas*, each consisting of a quadrangular courtyard formed by four buildings with rooms opening onto it with multiple doorways.

The "Small Plaza area" in the southeast was occupied by an active and permanent residential population of agriculturalists. The "Small Plaza area" contains a large number of small and often irregular courts surrounded by U-shaped structures (Kendall 1985:193–196).

There is a fourth sector in the northwest of the site in which rows of small houses face each other across a courtyard-like open space. Perhaps these were dwellings for the families of the officials who conducted government business in the "Large Plaza area," or else they may have been used for storage (see Kendall 1985:196–200).

Although Kendall's interpretation may be too specific, I believe one can conclude that size as well as symmetry and regularity in residential architecture signaled the presence of the Inka state. Or, to put it differently, ranking was linked to the degree of geometry. The geometric principles, in turn, defined an aesthetic system that was imposed and freely manipulated by the state government to respond to local conditions. As shown above, some elements of style and design were adopted from different regions or earlier peoples, but Inka rulers reinterpreted them and thus turned them into the aesthetic signature of their state. Some scholars now think that Patallacta was part of Pachacuti Inka Yupanqui's landholdings in the wider surroundings of Machu Picchu (Christie 2003, in preparation). I have shown how Pachacuti, in particular, cultivated the dialogue between nature and man-imposed order in his commissions of architecture, sculpted rocks, water works, and agricultural terraces.

I consider the geometric stone blocks fitted in Cusco-style masonry the smallest architectural variants of the quadripartite structure under debate. Cusco-style masonry is defined as the result of quarrying and cutting large stone blocks and fitting them together in a manner that is so exact and precise that no mortar is needed. Here it has to be emphasized that though most blocks are four-sided, others are famous for their irregularity and their 12 and 13 corners. I see such examples not as contradictions but as variations on the theme because they were still subjected to the overall order, precision, and regularity of the masonry wall. This style was introduced by Pachacuti

FIGURE 12.12 "Large Plaza area," Patallacta. Photograph by author.

Inka Yupanqui about A.D. 1450, when he began rebuilding the city of Cusco after the victory over the Chanka. Before the middle of the fifteenth century, Cusco was most likely a small town made up of houses built entirely of adobe, thatch, and other perishable materials. It thus appears that Cusco-style masonry is closely connected with the redefinition of Cusco as the Inka capital, center, and seat of power.

It is also clear that Inka builders did not newly invent this technique but that there were antecedents. The most frequently discussed source of inspiration is Tiwanaku. The east wall of the Akapana at Tiwanaku displays cut and perfectly fitted cubelike stone blocks with smooth faces very similar to those that were used in Cusco at least several centuries later (Figure 12.13). However, one marked difference is that the Akapana wall is flat, whereas Inka blocks are convex and project out to varying degrees (see Figure 12.5). Pachacuti conquered the Lake Titicaca region, including Tiwanaku, around A.D. 1450 and probably saw and was impressed by the Tiwanaku monuments. Bernabé Cobo reports that Pachacuti "ordered his companions to study that perfect technique, unknown to the Inkas, with the idea of applying it in the Cusco region" (cited in Gasparini and Margolies 1980:7).

At the same time, Gasparini and Margolies demonstrate convincingly that Aymara-speaking Lupaqa stoneworkers from Qollasuyu were in great demand in Cusco and that in all likelihood they actively participated in the construction program as their fulfillment of the obligatory labor tribute, *mit'a*. The authors analyzed government inspection reports from the sixteenth century documenting which kinds of tribute different towns and regions delivered to the Inka. They found that one of the *mit'a* services most frequently required from the Lupaqa was the sending of stonemasons to build houses in Cusco, whereas other regions mostly rendered other services (Gasparini and Margolies 1980:11). Nevertheless, the continuity of stonemasonry techniques could be questioned by the fact that several centuries without buildings of cut stone lie between the Tiwanaku monuments and the Inka constructions, so the Lupaqa *mit'a* workers must have had to relearn stone-cutting techniques. Still, the Inka probably preferred them over laborers from other areas because the Lupaqa had the Tiwanaku models in plain sight. It follows that regardless of whether the builders of the new Cusco were Lupaqa or Inka, the source of Cusco-style masonry was without much doubt Tiwanaku.

Again, as could be shown for the *kancha* above, the Inka selected an earlier model, copied it freely, and integrated it into their own developing architectural vocabulary to articulate the ideology of the central state government. Tiwanaku, however, was not like any earlier model. Maarten Van de Guchte (1990) points out that Tiwanaku assumes a prominent role as a place of origin in several Inka myths. It was supposedly at Tiwanaku that Wiraqocha modeled people out of clay, annihilated them after an act of disobedience, and re-created them a second time in stone (Van de Guchte 1990:49).

FIGURE 12.13 East wall, Akapana, Tiwanaku, using Cusco-style masonry. Photograph by author.

Since the Inka were newcomers to the Valley of Cusco, they were in need of respectable ancestors. Claiming to have descended from the people of Tiwanaku and visualizing such a link in state-sponsored architecture was a very intelligent political move apparently devised by Pachacuti Inka Yupanqui. By establishing the connection with Tiwanaku, he gave the Inka a history, and not only a factual history but one that was long and divine and linked them to the supernatural beginnings of mankind.

In general, it can be stated that Cusco-style masonry identified high-status structures that were likely government commissions in Cusco as well as in the Urubamba Valley and farther-outlying centers. Examples are the

Intiwatana sector and the entrance to the upper residential area at Pisaq; parts of the northern sector of Maucallacta, which has two fine masonry gates; and some of the buildings in the eastern sector of Huánuco Pampa. Referring to Huánuco Pampa, Morris and Thompson (1985:58) state that "it is evident that dressed-stone masonry was used to define areas of the city set aside for special activities. Essentially, it was reserved for those precincts devoted to the ceremonies and rituals associated with the state."

In a broader context, I think that the geometric quadripartite structure can also be identified in Inka rock art and textiles. In the characteristic geometric style of the former, vertical and horizontal cuts were made, meeting at 90-degree angles and forming steps, platforms, and niches (Christie 1999; Figure 12.14). In textile arts, the *tocapu* designs (woven squares with different fillers) on the royal tunics announce a very similar structural aesthetic.

Conclusions

The foregoing discussion attempted to show that the Inka developed an aesthetic system that expressed the power and control of the Inka state. This system included formal principles of a bi- and quadripartite division that alluded to the social organization of *hanan* and *hurin*, to the four quarters of the empire, and to the quadrants of the world on a symbolic level. These divisions were not new. The Inka adopted them from the local population in the Cusco Valley, from Tiwanaku, from the Wari, and from the Chimú. But the Inka reformulated these principles and divisions into an aesthetic based on geometry, which they then applied to urban planning, residential architecture, masonry, rock art, and textile designs. This aesthetic became something like a visual language freely articulating symmetry, 90-degree angles, and rectangularity, all of which may have been understood as an abstract rationalization of the order and control enforced by the Inka state. At times, its formal elements were imposed on nature and its political components on subject populations in Cusco, in the surrounding territories, and in the entire empire. At the same time, it has to be made clear that the Inka, and most notably Pachacuti, always maintained a balance between imposing geometry and order on the one hand, and feeling awe and respect for nature as well as granting certain liberties to subjected peoples on the other hand.

In contrast, the Maya never developed or used anything that could be defined as a "city or state architectural style." As demonstrated above, many elements of residential architecture were shared throughout the Maya area, but it would be difficult to identify a specific style that originated in one city and was exported to subjected territories to signal political presence. One might think of the Terminal Classic Puuc style in the Yucatán, but it is my understanding that its origin cannot really be tied to one specific city and that it was a more regional occurrence. However, there is one example

FIGURE 12.14 Carved rock nicknamed "Throne of the Inka," Sacsahuaman, Cusco. Photograph by author.

in which Dos Pilas rulers apparently tried to copy the technically superior masonry techniques from Tikal to show political connections and legitimize descent. Arthur Demarest (2003) argues that Temple N5-7 in the Murciélagos Palace complex exhibits the steep form and fine masonry reminiscent of Tikal temples, possibly to reflect the Tikal origins of the Dos Pilas dynasty. This may well be so, but it is only a case in which a hierarchically lower unit imitates the style of a superior power to improve legitimacy. The higher power—here Tikal—does not export it. Furthermore, Christopher Jones (2001) emphasized in a recent talk that the Maya could probably build their houses around the ceremonial core of Tikal wherever they wished.

The Tikal map shows high irregularity in the layout of residential zones and organic growth evidencing lack of government control.

This leads the discussion back to issues of political organization and how they might be evident in residential architecture. I think one can conclude that Maya society had a more segmentary structure and that Inka society certainly was more unitary. Again, it is helpful to follow de Montmollin's (1989:16–29) approach of bundled continua of variation, that is, to compare and contrast in degrees rather than treating the Maya and Inka as exemplifying all aspects of a segmentary or unitary structure. De Montmollin lists decentralization, replication, loose integration, ascriptive relations, and upward delegation as mechanisms identifying a segmentary structure. Decentralization, replication, and loose integration are implied by the increasing number of residential compounds that are being discovered in the Maya area. One may cite the residential groups at the peripheries of the ceremonial centers of Tikal or Palenque, the Type II–IV units at Copan, or the small residential complexes in western Belize, such as Xunantunich, Kahal Pech, or Buenavista. All of them repeat the arrangement of courtyards formed by range-type structures with evidence of domestic functions. As was discussed above, this layout is the same as that of palaces, with the differences that palaces are located at the core of a city, use higher-quality construction materials and techniques, and are decorated with sculpture and inscriptions. In a general sense, this replication of architectural form may reflect replication of political structure, though with different degrees of authority. The elites may have used similar forms of public display and enjoyed similar trappings and symbols of power but with social and spatial limitations. A fine example is the relation between Las Sepulturas and the Main Group at Copan, as evidenced by the architectural, sculptural, and artifactual records (Grube and Schele 1987; Schele 1987). It is known from the inscriptions that political relations between the ruler and the elites were largely based on ascription or kinship, which is another identifier of a segmentary structure (de Montmollin 1989:17).

In addition, de Montmollin (1989:17) lists a pyramidal regime, group stratification, mechanical solidarity, and a segmenting organization as elements of a segmentary structure. In a pyramidal regime, a set of similar political offices is repeated at each hierarchical level, which could be materialized by the large number of elite residential compounds and small, mid-level sites that dotted the Maya landscape and are now being recorded. One political aspect of stratification is that ascribed groups or groups formed by kinship ties and linked to political offices have the potential to become self-contained units and to compete with a polity's central focus. From an economic perspective, segmentary units develop a form of mechanical solidarity, which is defined as having economically independent districts and limited exchange. Again in rather general terms, it is known that the Maya provided food supplies on a local basis and that trade focused on exotic and luxury items. They did not need extensive storehouses such as those erected by the Inka. Given the relative political and economic independence of ascriptive groups, they have a tendency to fission and sever ties with the central power, a process that further underscores the segmenting organization in general. One could argue that form and settlement patterns of Maya residential architecture suggest and confirm a segmentary social organization. Of course, such a conclusion has to be corroborated by analyses of artifacts, iconography, and texts—if present.

According to de Montmollin's model, one should find centralization, differentiation, tight integration, contractual relations, and downward delegation for the Inka if, indeed, they had a unitary organization. Centralization, tight integration, and downward delegation were all practiced in Cusco as the capital and "navel" of the Inka world, as one translation of the name implies. It is known from the chronicles that the Inka were organized following a strict hierarchical regime. At the lowest level, families were grouped in fives and multiples of five, and they elected a *curaca* who acted as an imperial governor. The *curaca* reported to a *kamayoq*, who supervised a larger multiple of five families. The *kamayoq*, in turn, was subordinate to one of the four *suyuyuq apu*, or Lord of the Suyu. The positions just listed were repeated and replicated in each of the *suyus*. The highest and absolute authority rested in the Inka, or emperor, assisted by a supreme council (Rowe 1963:183–330). This regime is highly hierarchical in that political offices are clearly differentiated according to the level at which they occur, with a wider range of functions at higher levels, with strict downward delegation. The lower political offices were elected positions, but the higher officials were appointed by the state. Thus, political relations were clearly contractual rather than ascriptive or kin based. The Inka economy could best be characterized as an organic arrangement with a great deal of economic specialization among districts and regions, extensive exchange, and regional interdependence. The architectural expression of this kind of economic system is the large number of storehouses that were dispersed throughout the empire and connected by roads. The social and economic aspects outlined above reinforce the nonsegmenting organization of the Inka, which was largely successful until the arrival of the Spaniards.[7]

The one element that does not seem to fit de Montmollin's model of a unitary structure is *differentiation*. If understood in an economic context— and I think this is how de Montmollin understands it—then it is applicable in the sense of the different crops and products each region grew and provided based on their natural and climatic resources. However, with regard to formal aspects, replication rather than differentiation identified the Inka state. As discussed above, the Inka imposed on their cities, architecture, and nature a style derived from geometry that symbolized the control the Inka state exerted and marked Inka presence. I would say it was used as a symbolic tool that helped to enforce tight integration, contractual relations, downward delegation, the hierarchical regime in general, and a nonsegment-ing social organization.

At the same time, one must caution against perceiving the Inka govern-ment as a completely and perfectly centralized, tightly integrated, hierarchi-cal, unitary construction. Morris and Thompson emphasize that although Huánuco Pampa was formally conceived as another Cusco (see above), they did not find much archaeological evidence of a state bureaucracy. Instead the evidence points to feasting and ceremonies centered around the residence of the Inka or his representative (Morris and Thompson 1985:165). Undoubt-edly such ceremonies served to legitimize Inka rule, but they also brought the rulers and the ruled together and formed social ties. Over time, some social ties may have grown into kin-based political relations. This is what de Montmollin (1989:20) calls the "spatial drop in the effectiveness of cen-tralized authority." He points to the existence of peripheral zones with an intermediately segmentary-unitary structure indicated by indirect rule of the central authority. This may well describe the social and political organi-zation of Huánuco Pampa.

To conclude, I think it is possible to reconstruct social and political as-pects of ancient societies by analyzing the form, layout, and settlement pat-terns of residential architecture. It is helpful to limit interpretations to de-grees of similarities and differences, or in de Montmollin's terminology, "bundled continua of variation," rather than to impose stifling typologies on ancient cultures that were once alive and often in a continuous process of change.

Notes

1. Peter Harrison (1970:220) rejects Thompson's argument because he feels it is "based upon ethnocentrism, which must be inadequate for a functional analysis." I would counter that smoke, darkness, and humidity are universal uncomfortable ex-periences that are felt by any individual no matter to which time period or culture the person belongs. That the Yucatec Maya in the 1930s shared such feelings is reported by Robert Wauchope. He observed that when a family had achieved a certain amount of wealth and prestige, they sometimes desired to build a masonry house of the Spanish type. Wauchope visited five of these masonry structures in the village of Chan Kom and "in each case found the house almost devoid of furniture, the entire family living in a bush house (generally called a kitchen) in the back yard. The front house was a display; its owners found themselves more comfortable in the old-style hut to which they were more accustomed" (Wauchope 1938:141).

While the more recent archaeological data have demonstrated that Maya cities were not empty ceremonial centers, as Thompson had claimed, I nevertheless think it is quite possible that royal and noble families maintained secondary dwellings in the form of thatch-roofed houses at the outskirts of their cities to which they retreated be-tween official events and in which some members of the extended family, especially small children, may have permanently lived.

2. Felipe Guaman Poma de Ayala lived from approximately 1534 to 1617. His

father belonged to the dynasty Yarovilca Allauca Huanuco, and his mother was Inka. He spent his entire life in Peru and thus experienced the early Colonial period firsthand.

3. It must be emphasized that Felipe Guaman Poma de Ayala's writings constitute one of the most reliable sources. First of all, he was of noble Inka descent; his mother was the daughter of Emperor Tupac Inka Yupanqui. Secondly, his chronicles were written very early after the Spanish Conquest, sometime between 1567 and 1615. And finally, his accounts are illustrated by drawings, one of which renders an Inka palace.

4. Pachacuti's interest in stonecutting techniques and masonry styles was referenced by Bernabé Cobo (1956:191–192 [1653]), among others, who says that Pachacuti profoundly admired the excellent buildings at Tiwanaku and that he ordered his builders to study this construction technique well because he wanted the structures they erected in Cusco to be of a similar style. However, close observation shows that Tiwanaku walls, such as the east wall of the Akapana, are entirely flat, whereas most of the Inka walls in Cusco show a slight variation in the height of the stone blocks and also have sunken joints. Most, if not all, of the Cusco buildings that still display this masonry style appear to date to the reorganization of Cusco under Pachacuti or later.

5. Some examples of stone corbeled vaults were found in the Lake Titicaca region, such as in the first floor of the Pilco Kayma on the Island of the Sun, which may have been a "palace" built by Aymara *mit'a* labor. The corbeled vault was also used in the building category of *chullpas*, or funerary edifices (see Gasparini and Margolies 1980:147–158).

6. In her discussion of Andean aesthetics, Esther Pasztory has observed a general "preoccupation with spatial relations, mental patterns, and . . . lack of interest in visibility." She mentions that this "habit of thinking in networks and invisible lines" might have developed from the textile arts because designs on textiles must be planned before the weaver begins to move the yarns (Pasztory 1997:63).

7. However, the integrating, nonsegmenting organization of the state did not always extend to the selection of an heir to the highest office. Rostworowski (1953) shows how royal succession was contested, at least from the reign of Inka Roq'a on. The Inka government system broke up in a brutal civil war just before the Spaniards arrived, as Washkar and Atawallpa, two royal sons by different mothers, both claimed to be the rightful successor of Wayna Qhapaq.

References Cited

Andrews, E. Wyllys, W. F. Doonan, G. E. Everson, J. L. Johnson, and K. E. Sampeck
1998 Structure 10L-41, a Maya Building in the Late Classic Royal Residence at Copan, Honduras. Paper presented at the 63rd Annual Meeting of the Society for American Archaeology, Seattle.
Bauer, Brian S.
1998 *The Sacred Landscape of the Inca: The Cusco Ceque System.* University of Texas Press, Austin.
Becker, Marshall J.
1999 *Excavations in Residential Areas of Tikal: Groups with Shrines.* Tikal Report No. 21, University Museum Monograph 104. The University Museum, University of Pennsylvania, Philadelphia.

Bingham, Hiram
1986 *Lost City of the Incas.* Atheneum, New York.
1997 *Lost City of the Incas.* Special Book Services, Lima.
Burger, Richard L., and Lucy C. Salazar
2004 Lifestyles of the Rich and Famous: Luxury and Daily Life in the Households of Machu Picchu's Elite. In *Palaces of the Ancient New World: Form, Function, and Meaning,* edited by Susan Toby Evans and Joanne Pillsbury, 325–357. Dumbarton Oaks Research Library and Collection, Washington, DC.
Burger, Richard L., and Lucy C. Salazar (editors)
2004 *Machu Picchu: Unveiling the Mystery of the Incas.* Yale University Press, New Haven and London.
Chase, Diane Z., and Arlen F. Chase
1992 An Archaeological Assessment of Mesoamerican Elites. In *Mesoamerican Elites: An Archaeological Assessment,* edited by Diane Z. Chase and Arlen F. Chase, pp. 303–317. University of Oklahoma Press, Norman and London.
1998 A Consideration of Classic Maya "Palaces" at Caracol, Belize. Paper presented at the 63rd Annual Meeting of the Society for American Archaeology, Seattle.
Chase, Diane Z., and Arlen F. Chase (editors)
1992 *Mesoamerican Elites: An Archaeological Assessment.* University of Oklahoma Press, Norman and London.
Christie, Jessica Joyce
1999 Inca Rock Sculpture and the Sacred Landscape I. Paper presented at the Annual Meeting of the Society for American Archaeology, Chicago.
2003 The Sculpted Rocks of Machu Picchu. Paper presented at the Rock Art 2003 Conference, Museum of Man, San Diego.
In preparation   The Sculpted Outcrops of the Inka. Manuscript.
Christie, Jessica J. (editor)
2003 *Maya Palaces and Elite Residences: An Interdisciplinary Approach.* University of Texas Press, Austin.
Cobo, Bernabé
1956 [1653]   *Historia del Nuevo Mundo,* edited by Luis Pardo. Vol. 3 (Chapter 12). Cusco, Peru.
Coe, William R., and William A. Haviland
1982 *Introduction to the Archaeology of Tikal, Guatemala.* Tikal Report No. 12, University Museum Monograph 46. The University Museum, University of Pennsylvania, Philadelphia.
Demarest, Arthur A., Kim Morgan, and Claudia Wolley
2003 The Political Acquisition of Sacred Geography: The Murciélagos Complex at Dos Pilas. In *Maya Palaces and Elite Residences: An Interdisciplinary Approach,* edited by Jessica J. Christie. University of Texas Press, Austin.
de Montmollin, Olivier
1989 *The Archaeology of Political Structure.* Cambridge University Press, Cambridge.

1995 *Settlement and Politics in Three Classic Maya Polities.* Monographs in World Archaeology No. 24. Prehistory Press, Madison, WI.
Ford, Anabel
1986 *Population Growth and Social Complexity: An Examination of Settlement and Environment in the Central Maya Lowlands.* Anthropological Research Paper No. 35. Arizona State University, Tempe.
Fox, John W., D. T. Wallace, and K. L. Brown
1992 The Emergence of the Quiché Elite: The Putun-Palenque Connection. In *Mesoamerican Elites: An Archaeological Assessment,* edited by Diane Z. Chase and Arlen F. Chase, pp. 169–190. University of Oklahoma Press, Norman and London.
Frost, Peter
1989 *Exploring Cusco.* Nuevas Imágenes, Lima.
García Moll, Roberto
1985 *Palenque 1926–1945.* Instituto Nacional de Antropología e Historia, Mexico City.
Gasparini, Graziano, and Luise Margolies
1980 *Inca Architecture.* Translated by Patricia J. Lyon. Indiana University Press, Bloomington.
Grube, Nicolai, and Linda Schele
1987 The Date on the Bench from Structure 9N-82, Sepulturas, Copan, Honduras. In *Copan Mosaics Project,* Copan Note 23. Austin: Kinkos.
Guaman Poma de Ayala, Felipe
1987 [1615] *Nueva crónica y buen gobierno.* Vols. A, B, C. Edited by John Murra, Rolena Adorno, and Jorge Urioste. Historia 16, Madrid.
Guderjan, Tom H.
1998 Elite Residences at Blue Creek, Belize. Paper presented at the 63rd Annual Meeting of the Society for American Archaeology, Seattle.
Gyarmati, J., and A. Varga
1999 *The Chacaras of War.* Museum of Ethnography, Budapest.
Harrison, Peter
1971 *The Central Acropolis, Tikal, Guatemala: A Preliminary Study of the Functions of Its Structural Components during the Late Classic Period.* Ph.D. dissertation, University of Pennsylvania. University Microfilms, Ann Arbor.
1999 *The Lords of Tikal.* Thames and Hudson, London.
Haviland, William A.
1985 *Excavations in Small Residential Groups of Tikal, Groups 4F-1 and 4F-2.* Tikal Report No. 19, University Museum Monograph 58. The University Museum, University of Pennsylvania, Philadelphia.
Hendon, Julia A.
1987 The Uses of Maya Structures: A Study of Architecture and Artifact Distribution at Sepulturas, Copan, Honduras. Unpublished Ph.D. dissertation, Department of Anthropology, Harvard University, Cambridge.
Hyslop, John
1990 *Inka Settlement Planning.* University of Texas Press, Austin.

Inomata, Takeshi, and Stephen Houston (editors)
2001 *Royal Courts of the Ancient Maya.* 2 vols. Westview Press, Boulder, CO.

Isbell, William H.
1991 Huari Administration and the Orthogonal Cellular Architecture Horizon. In *Huari Administrative Structure: Prehistoric Monumental Architecture and State Government,* edited by William H. Isbell and Gordon F. McEwan, pp. 293–315. Dumbarton Oaks Research Library and Collection, Washington, DC.

Isbell, William H., and Gordon F. McEwan (editors)
1991 *Huari Administrative Structure: Prehistoric Monumental Architecture and State Government.* Dumbarton Oaks Research Library and Collection, Washington, DC.

Jones, Christopher
2001 Tikal. Paper presented at the 19th Annual Maya Weekend, University of Pennsylvania Museum of Archaeology and Anthropology, Philadelphia.

Kendall, Ann
1985 *Aspects of Inca Architecture: Description, Function, and Chronology.* 2 vols. BAR International Series 242. British Archaeological Records, Oxford.

Kendall, Ann, Rob Early, and Bill Sillar
1992 Report on Archaeological Field Season Investigating Early Inca Architecture at Juchuy Coscco (Q'aqya Qhawana) and Warq'ana, Province of Calca, Dept. of Cuzco, Peru. In *Ancient America: Contributions to New World Archaeology,* edited by Nicholas Saunders, pp. 189–255. Oxbow Monograph 24. Oxbow Books, Oxford, UK.

Lee, Vincent R.
1985 *Sixpac Manco: Travels among the Incas.* Vincent Lee, Wilson, WY.
1986 *Forgotten Vilcabamba: Final Stronghold of the Incas.* Sixpac Manco Publications, 2000, Box 174, Cortez, CO 81321.
1989 *Chanasuyu: The Ruins of Inca Vilcabamba.* Vincent Lee, Wilson, WY.

Leventhal, Richard M.
1979 Settlement Patterns at Copan, Honduras. Unpublished Ph.D. dissertation, Department of Anthropology, Harvard University, Cambridge.
1983 Household Groups and Classic Maya Religion. In *Prehistoric Settlement Patterns,* edited by Evon Z. Vogt and Richard M. Leventhal, pp. 55–76. University of New Mexico Press, Albuquerque.

MacLean, Margaret G.
1986 Sacred Land, Sacred Water: Inca Landscape Planning in the Cuzco Area. Unpublished Ph.D. dissertation, Department of Anthropology, University of California, Berkeley.

Martin, Simon, and Nikolai Grube
2001 *Chronicle of the Maya Kings and Queens.* Thames and Hudson, London.

Morris, Craig
2004 Enclosures of Power: Multiple Spaces of Inka Administrative Palaces. In *Palaces of the Ancient New World: Form, Function, and Meaning,*

edited by Susan Toby Evans and Joanne Pillsbury, 299–323. Dumbarton Oaks Research Library and Collection, Washington, DC.

Morris, Craig, and Donald E. Thompson
1985 *Huánuco Pampa: An Inca City and Its Hinterland.* Thames and Hudson, London.

Niles, Susan A.
1987 *Callachaca: Style and Status in an Inca Community.* University of Iowa Press, Iowa City.
1999 *The Shape of Inca History.* University of Iowa Press, Iowa City.

Pasztory, Esther
1997 Andean Aesthetics. In *The Spirit of Ancient Peru,* edited by K. Berrin, pp. 61–69. Thames and Hudson, New York.

Protzen, Jean-Pierre
1993 *Inca Architecture and Construction at Ollantaytambo.* Oxford University Press, New York.
2000 *Inca Architecture in The Inca World,* edited by Laura Laurencich Minelli, pp. 193–217. University of Oklahoma Press, Norman.

Puleston, Dennis E.
1983 *The Settlement Survey of Tikal.* Tikal Report No. 13, University Museum Monograph 48. The University Museum, University of Pennsylvania, Philadelphia.

Rostworowski de Diez Canseco, María
1953 *Pachacutec Inca Yupanqui.* N.p., Lima.
1999 *History of the Inca Realm.* Cambridge University Press, Cambridge.

Rowe, John H.
1963 Inca Culture at the Time of the Spanish Conquest. In *Handbook of South American Indians,* Vol. 2, edited by J. H. Steward, pp. 183–330. Bureau of American Ethnology Bulletin 143. Smithsonian Institution, Washington, DC.

Satterthwaite, Linton
1933 *Description of the Site with Short Notes on the Excavations of 1931–32.* Piedras Negras Preliminary Papers No. 1. The University Museum, University of Pennsylvania, Philadelphia.
1935 *Palace Structures J-2 and J-6.* Piedras Negras Preliminary Papers No. 3. The University Museum, University of Pennsylvania, Philadelphia.

Schele, Linda
1987 The Figures on the Legs of the Scribe's Bench. In *Copan Mosaics Project,* Copan Note 24. Austin: Kinkos.

Schele, Linda, and Peter Mathews
1998 *The Code of Kings.* Scribner, New York.

Sharer, Robert J.
1997 *Daily Life in Maya Civilization.* Greenwood Press, Westport, CT.

Smith, A. Ledyard
1950 *Uaxactun, Guatemala, Excavations of 1931–1937.* Publication 588. Carnegie Institution of Washington, Washington, DC.
1962 *Residential and Associated Structures of Mayapan.* Publication 619. Carnegie Institution of Washington, Washington DC.

Southall, A.
1956 *Alur Society: A Study in Processes and Types of Domination.* Heffer
      Press, Cambridge.
Spinden, Herbert J.
1913 *A Study of Maya Art, Its Subject Matter and Historical Develop-
      ment.* Memoirs of the Peabody Museum of American Archaeology
      and Ethnology Vol. 6. Harvard University, Cambridge.
Thompson, John Eric
1959 *The Rise and Fall of Maya Civilization.* University of Oklahoma
      Press, Norman.
1963 *Maya Archaeologist.* University of Oklahoma Press, Norman.
Tourtellot, Gair
1983 An Assessment of Classic Maya Household Composition. In *Prehis-
      toric Settlement Patterns,* edited by E. Z. Vogt and R. M. Leventhal,
      pp. 35–54, University of New Mexico Press, Albuquerque.
Tozzer, Alfred M.
1911 *A Preliminary Study of the Prehistoric Ruins of Tikal Guatemala.*
      Memoirs of the Peabody Museum of American Archaeology and
      Ethnology Vol. 5, No. 2. Harvard University, Cambridge.
Traxler, Loa
2003 At Court in Copan: Palace Groups of the Early Classic. In *Maya
      Palaces and Elite Residences: An Interdisciplinary Approach,* edited
      by Jessica Christie, 46–68. University of Texas Press, Austin.
Triadan, D., and Takeshi Inomata
1998 Elite Residential Structures at Aguateca. Paper presented at the 63rd
      Annual Meeting of the Society for American Archaeology, Seattle.
Van de Guchte, Maarten
1990 "Carving the World": Inca Monumental Sculpture and Landscape.
      Unpublished Ph.D. dissertation, Department of Anthropology, Uni-
      versity of Illinois at Urbana-Champaign.
Webster, David
1992 Maya Elites: the Perspective from Copan. In *Mesoamerican Elites:
      An Archaeological Assessment,* edited by Diane Z. Chase and
      Arlen F. Chase, pp. 135–156. University of Oklahoma Press, Norman
      and London.
Willey, Gordon R., and Richard M. Leventhal
1979 Settlement at Copan. In *Maya Archaeology and Ethnohistory,* edited
      by Norman Hammond and Gordon R. Willey, pp. 75–102. University
      of Texas Press, Austin.
Willey, Gordon R., Richard M. Leventhal, and William Fash
1978 Maya Settlement in the Copan Valley. *Archaeology* 31:32–43.
Zuidema, R. Tom
1964 *The Ceque System of Cuzco: The Social Organization of the Capital
      of the Inca.* Translated by E. M. Hooykaas. International Archives of
      Ethnography, supplement to Vol. 50. E. J. Brill, Leiden.

Conclusions

William T. Sanders

In 1987, Arlen and Diane Chase organized a symposium at the Society for American Archaeology annual meeting—a session I also participated in— on the theme of the Mesoamerican elites. Many of the ideas and themes and some of the data presented at that meeting were paralleled and amplified in the 2000 session, "Palaces and Power," on which the present volume is based. The "Mesoamerican Elites" session was published by the University of Oklahoma Press in 1992 (Chase and Chase 1992). This earlier session focused on the archaeological and ethnohistorical evidence for a differentiated sector of Mesoamerican societies that enjoyed measurably more prestige, power, and wealth than the great majority of members of those societies.

The 2000 session differed from the 1987 one in two fundamental ways. First, it focused more on the very top of the social pyramid and the residences of that element in the social system, and second, it covered a much wider geographic range. Two papers in that session describe societies north of Mesoamerica, one on the Pacific Northwest Coast and one in the American Southwest; three were dedicated to sites and societies in the Central Andes, and five focused on Mesoamerica. One paper, by one of the editors of this volume (Jessica Christie), compared Maya and Inka palaces. The sample of societies covered a range in size, degree of socioeconomic heterogeneity, and political power exercised by their leaders: from the small Northwest Coast lineages to the Aztec and Inka Empires—the two largest political entities in the history of the New World.

One of the major contributions of both volumes is the attention devoted by the authors to a clarification of terminology used in categorizing human social behavior. Many social scientists have criticized their colleagues for an overly pedantic focus on typological categories like chiefdoms, states, ranking, and stratification, but, in my opinion, we cannot have a mutual discourse, understanding, and exchange of ideas without them. One of their criticisms has been that it detracts attention from the more important aspects of social life, that is, the study of processes. I disagree with this position and insist that scholars who use these categories, and carefully define them, have also conceptually included process in their discussion. We have always understood that definitions are not an end in themselves, but they do provide models for discussion of cultural process. Indeed, we cannot have any kind of even ordinary conversation without using typological categories—virtually every noun in a language is a typological category; for example, words like *house, family, mother, tree, table,* and *desk* all encompass variety in meaning and are generalizing terms. In fact, the papers in this volume focus very heavily on social, political, and economic processes, though the authors do, as I stated previously, clearly define the terms they use.

A major question raised in all the papers, with the exception of the one about the Northwest Coast, is: What is the archaeological identification of a palace—the residence of the highest-ranking member of the polity in question? An obvious problem in this endeavor is the great variety of architecture from region to region, with respect to materials used, techniques of construction, and some aspects of planning and use of space. The contrast between Pueblo Bonito in Chaco Canyon, at one end of the continuum, and the features and functions of the palaces of the Aztec and Inka rulers, at the other, is considerable, and this volume includes the entire range of intermediary societies as well in terms of size and degree of wealth and power exercised by the supreme leaders of those societies. An equally important question is: What are the commonalities, that is, the shared characteristics of all these building complexes, that enable archaeologists to include them in the typological category of palace?

An important point made by all the contributors is that palaces, in preindustrial polities, are not just the residences of the rulers, that is, they not only include residential quarters for the ruler and his immediate family (and in those cases where polygyny is practiced, this population may be of considerable size), but often have residential space for service personnel and serve as seats of government where political actions and administration take place. In the more complex polities, they may even have residential space for administrators as well (for example, in medieval Edo in Japan). Because of the close integration of political and religious ideology in most preindustrial states, rulers also play major roles in the conduct of religion, and palaces often contain temples, shrines, and altars—structures with primarily religious functions. Because the ruler is often the highest-ranking religious official as well as the political leader, the palace is a shrine and an office building. In the very large states, the palace also plays the role of host to numerous visitors—in the Aztec case, several thousand daily. These visitors were provided with food from the royal kitchens, and high-ranking guests were usually the recipients of gifts. In such polities, palaces need extensive storage facilities, requiring an additional spatial function, and this inserts another dimension to palace architecture. Often added to these spaces are residential quarters and workshop space for the craftsmen who produce the fine objects that are given as gifts. Finally, in both the Inka and Aztec cases, rulers enjoyed private facilities for their own pleasure, such as flower gardens, zoos, and aviaries.

All these functions except the last are found in the palaces of smaller-scale societies. They differ in scale, however, and these differences have an enormous feedback impact on the nature of the political system and the amount of power exerted by these rulers.

Interestingly, some of these functions are found even in the lineage compound of a Northwest Coast chief, where many of the residents are relatives of the chiefs, but the residential population often includes nonkin of inferior rank. The lineage compound is also a place for political meetings, for the conduct of ritual, for entertaining visitors, and for the storage of goods necessary to conduct these activities. In contrast to Moctezuma, who ruled an empire of 5,000–6,000,000 people, the Northwest Coast Indian chiefs led populations of fewer than 100 people, and even in cases where the entire village consisted of a single polity of differently ranked chiefs and compounds, the polity had fewer than 1,000 people.

The focus of this book is on the palaces of rulers, but because of the great architectural variety in the sample, many of the authors broaden their discussions to include elite residences in general, comparable to the discussions in the Chase and Chase (1992) volume. When I read the foregoing chapters, I was struck by two obvious methodological facts. First, it is clear that archaeologists who focus on residential architecture can reconstruct, in surprising detail, ancient social structures. Second, it is also abundantly clear, however, that our sample in all cases where this approach is used is woefully inadequate. To illustrate this point, I will summarize the discussion Susan Toby Evans and I presented in our chapter on Teotihuacan (Chapter 9).

Teotihuacan is virtually a unique case of an unusually large archaeological site, covering some 20 km², with an estimated population of over 100,000 at its peak, that is available (at least until very recently) for studies of residential architecture on a large scale. Most ancient cities of this size are covered by twentieth-century cities of considerable size, such as Athens, Rome, Cuzco, Tenochtitlan—the list is depressingly endless.

Because of these conditions, René Millon (1973), in what I believe is the most ambitious and methodologically most sophisticated study of an ancient city ever undertaken, was able to map and define the locations of over 2,000 structures—the vast majority of them residences—and was able to surface sample all of them. As a result, we have a complete map of an unusually large ancient city, a map that reveals an extraordinary level of urban planning, and we have at least some evidence as to the economic and social heterogeneity of the community. Nonetheless, it is abundantly clear that extensive excavations are needed, on a large scale, of residences that cover the range of social, political, and economic status revealed by the surface sample—and our sample is pitifully small.

The problem of inadequate large-scale excavations applies to the royal palace of Teotihuacan as well. Evans and I identified the Street of the Dead Complex as the royal palace during Teotihuacan's apogee. The excavated architecture revealed a variety of forms that suggest an equally great range of functions, but, unfortunately, less than one-quarter of the entire palace compound has been excavated, so our conclusions are highly speculative.

The same statement could be made of Huari and Moche; they were large communities that served as the centers of polities with extensive domains. I visited both sites in 1964 and was impressed with their extensive residential remains (at that time, Moche was characterized as a ceremonial center similar to Classic Maya centers). It seemed to me then that the Huaca de la Luna was probably the more public portion of a royal palace—not a temple— a position taken by Claude Chapdelaine in his chapter (Chapter 1). He suggests that the excavated residences immediately west of the restored Luna complex may have served as the residential quarters of the complex. I would make an even stronger statement that this residential area extended over even more space in the nearby unexcavated areas. I would make the same suggestion about Huari. Isbell's identified palace is probably only the more public part of a more extensive architectural complex. I assume this because of Huari's very large political domain.

Recent research on the Classic Maya, with respect to the urban status and the nature and focus of leadership in Maya polities, has resulted in a revolution in our thinking about the structure of Classic Maya society, and the chapters in this volume reflect those dramatic changes. Two research methods—the decipherment of the Maya script and surface surveys around the centers—have caused those changes. Instead of a peaceful theocratic society ruled by astronomer priests, we now have a picture of hereditary rulers obsessed with power and fighting incessantly over territory. Buildings once referred to as so-called palaces or just "palaces" are now described without hesitation as residences of kings.

A suggestion that I have made elsewhere (Sanders 1989), and repeat here, is that the entire architectural complex that served as the center of the Maya polity, such as that at Tikal, including the Great Plaza, the North Acropolis, Temples 1 and 2, and the Central Acropolis—an obvious residential complex—should be conceived of as the royal palace, particularly considering the fact that all the other structures are parts of a royal cemetery.

I would make the same suggestion to Sarah Barber and Arthur Joyce in their chapter on Monte Albán (Chapter 8) and to Susan Toby Evans in her discussion of Tula (Chapter 10) with respect to the great plaza complexes at both sites. The associated temples and ballcourts should be conceived of as portions of a very large royal palace that includes a number of residential sectors on the perimeter. In this interpretation, the North Platform at Monte Albán and the colonnaded structures found west of the main temple at Tula (Structure B) should be considered as the administrative portions of the palace complex.

Finally, I found the discussions on the pre–Monte Albán phases in the Valley of Oaxaca (Chapter 8 by Barber and Joyce) and on Paso de la Amada by Blake et al. (Chapter 7) very interesting in terms of a point that Robert Santley and I made many years ago (Sanders and Santley 1989) about the architectural differences in the centers of chiefdoms versus states. Only in the latter case do we have extensive labor committed to the construction of the residences of the leaders, and the houses of the chiefs are usually relatively unimpressive compared to those of rulers, of even relatively small states. Much more effort is expended in structures of a more public nature, such as temples and tombs. With respect to this, I would argue that Pueblo Bonito should not be characterized as a royal palace, as Stephen Lekson seems to be implying in his chapter (Chapter 3). I agree that the recent evaluation of this site and of the entire settlement system of the Chaco Canyon indicates a much more complex society than that of the eighteenth- and nineteenth-century Pueblo. I think we need much more information on the function of the various portions of this complex, however, to more adequately determine the function of the whole and to better understand its role as the center of a political system.

In summary, this volume and the earlier one on the Mesoamerican elite (Chase and Chase 1992) are, I believe, major contributions to our understanding of complex preindustrial societies in the New World and demonstrate the contribution that archaeology can make to the reconstruction and evolution of these societies.

References Cited

Chase, Diane, and Arlen Chase
1992 *Mesoamerican Elites: An Archaeological Assessment.* University of Oklahoma Press, Norman.
Millon, René
1973 *The Teotihuacan Map: Urbanization at Teotihuacan, Mexico.* Vol. 1. University of Texas Press, Austin.
Sanders, William T.
1989 Household, Lineage and State in Eighth-Century Copan. In *The House of the Bacabs, Copan, Honduras,* edited by David L. Webster, 89–105. Dumbarton Oaks Research Library and Collection, Washington, DC.
Sanders, William T., and Robert S. Santley
1989 A Tale of Three Cities: Energetics and Urbanization in Prehistoric Central Mexico. In *Prehistoric Settlement Patterns,* edited by Evon Z. Vogt and Richard M. Leventhal, 243–291. University of New Mexico Press, Albuquerque.

Luis Barba (PhD National Autonomous University of Mexico, 1995) is director of the Geophysical Survey Laboratory at the Institute of Anthropological Investigations at the National Autonomous University of Mexico (UNAM). His research investigations include geophysical survey, archaeochemistry, archaeometry, and remote sensing, all of which contribute to our understanding of past human activities on ancient landscapes.

Sarah B. Barber is a PhD candidate specializing in the archaeology of Mesoamerica at the University of Colorado at Boulder. She has been conducting research on social identity, community, and the household in the Lower Rio Valley of Oaxaca.

Michael Blake (PhD University of Michigan, 1985) is associate professor of anthropology at the University of British Columbia and director of UBC's Laboratory of Archaeology. He has conducted extensive archaeological fieldwork in Chiapas, Mexico, and in the Fraser Valley of British Columbia. His research focuses on emerging social and political complexity, with an emphasis on household and settlement archaeology.

Claude Chapdelaine (PhD Université de Montréal, 1988) is professor of archaeology at the Université de Montréal and has been conducting field research on the North Coast of Peru since 1994. He first worked at the Huacas of Moche Site, documenting the urban zone; in 2000 he moved to the Santa Valley to study the expansionist character of the southern Moche State.

Jessica Joyce Christie (PhD University of Texas, 1995) is assistant professor in the School of Art and Design at East Carolina University. She edited the volume *Maya Palaces and Elite Residences: An Interdisciplinary Approach*. Her research interests include classic and contemporary Maya Year Renewal Ceremonies and palace architecture. She is currently working on a book about the sculpted outcrops of the Inka.

John E. Clark (PhD University of Michigan, 1994) is professor of anthropology at Brigham Young University and director of its New World Archaeological Foundation. His research focuses on the origins of rank society in lowland Mesoamerica, as well as cultural theory, ethnoarchaeology, ancient technology, and craft specialization.

Arthur A. Demarest (PhD Harvard, 1981) is professor of anthropology at Vanderbilt University and director of the Vanderbilt Cancuen Archaeological and Community Development projects. His research interests include the origins, declines, and "collapses" of civilization; ideology; and indigenous rights and development.

Susan Toby Evans (PhD Pennsylvania State University, 1980) is a professor in the Anthropology Department at Pennsylvania State University. Her archaeological and ethnohistorical research focuses on the Aztecs of Mexico. Her recent books include *Palaces of the Ancient New World*, coedited with Joanne Pillsbury, and *Ancient Mexico and Central America: Archaeology and Culture History*, which won the 2005 Society for American Archaeology award.

Colin Grier (PhD Arizona State University, 2001) is a research associate in the Department of Anthropology and Sociology at the University of British Columbia. His archaeological research has focused on complex hunter-gatherers and the origins of social inequality in the context of fieldwork on prehistoric Arctic whaling societies, Paleolithic Europe, and, most recently, the Gulf of Georgia region of Canada's Northwest Coast.

Warren D. Hill (PhD University of British Columbia, 1999) is a senior research analyst with the British Columbia Centre for Disease Control and executive director of the Canadian Viral Hepatitis Network. His research interests center on the evolution of human societies and infectious diseases and include the use of geographic information systems for molecular epidemiology.

William H. Isbell (PhD University of Illinois, 1973) is professor of anthropology at Binghamton University. He is the author of several articles on the Central Andes, particularly Huari. His current research focuses on space, place, and the built environment in the interpretation of the past; he is presently investigating Huari's iconographic relative, Tiwanaku.

Arthur A. Joyce (PhD Rutgers, 1991) is associate professor of anthropology at the University of Colorado at Boulder. His research focuses on the pre-Columbian states of Mesoamerica using poststructuralist social theories of practice and power. He has conducted interdisciplinary archaeological and paleoenvironmental research in Oaxaca since 1986.

Stephen H. Lekson (PhD University of New Mexico, 1988) is curator and associate professor of anthropology at the University of Colorado at Boulder. His research interests are in the origins of government, regional patterning, and architecture in the North American Southwest.

Richard G. Lesure (PhD University of Michigan, 1995) is associate professor of anthropology at the University of California, Los Angeles. He has carried out archaeological fieldwork in both Chiapas and Central Mexico, investigating the role that ideologies of inequality plays in emerging cultural complexity.

Carol Mackey (PhD University of California, Berkeley, 1970) is professor emerita in the Anthropology Department at California State University, Northridge. Her main interest has been the development and political strategies of ancient Andean state societies, focusing on Peru's North Coast and the development and expansion of the Chimu Empire. Most recently, along with Cesar Jauregui, she has co-directed investigations of the Chimú site of Farfán in the Jequetepeque Valley.

William T. Sanders (PhD Harvard University, 1957) has received the AV Kidder Award and is a member of the National Academy of Sciences. He has conducted major research projects in the Basin of Mexico, at Kaminaljuyu (Guatemala), and at Copan (Honduras). His current research is on urbanism in Mesoamerica, with particular emphasis on Tenochtitlan.

Patricia Joan Sarro (PhD Columbia University, 1995) is an associate professor of art history at Youngstown State University. Her studies at El Tajín and Teotihuacan, Mexico, explore the relationship between architectural ornamentation and social structure.

Page numbers in bold refer to figures and tables.

www.ingramcontent.com/pod-product-compliance
Lightning Source LLC
Chambersburg PA
CBHW030634270326
41929CB00007B/69